Evaluating Pupil Growth

principles of tests and measurements

4th edition

Evaluating
Pupil Growth

Principles of Tests and Measurements

J. STANLEY AHMANN

Colorado State University

MARVIN D. GLOCK

Cornell University

Allyn and Bacon, Inc.
Boston

To June and Ruth

Library of Congress Catalog Card Number:
73–135157

Contents

4475

Preface

A person who has worked hard for a goal wants to find out to what degree that goal is realized. So it is with teachers, regardless of subject matter or grade level. Clearly, evaluation of the degree to which educational goals have been achieved is a basic part of teaching and concerns everyone associated with the school.

It follows, therefore, that teachers, counselors, supervisors, administrators, and other educational specialists need the following:

1. Appreciation of the usefulness of measuring instruments in education.
2. Knowledge of the characteristics of a satisfactory measuring instrument.
3. Ability to construct measuring instruments capable of showing to what degree pupils have attained pertinent educational objectives.
4. Knowledge of common achievement and aptitude tests and also personal-social adjustment inventories, which are often included in a schoolwide program of evaluation.
5. Ability to select appropriate measuring instruments for use in a continuous evaluation program.
6. Ability to interpret properly the data yielded by measuring instruments, to use them in diagnosing and remedying pupil deficiencies, and to report them efficiently and accurately to the pupils, their parents, and possibly the entire community.

The fourth edition of *Evaluating Pupil Growth* is written for a one-term college course, whether at the undergraduate or "fifth-year" graduate level, that is designed on the basis of developing attainments such as these. Each of its five parts contributes directly to one or more of the six needs and indirectly to several others. These relationships are often self-evident. In Part One, "Evaluation in Education," the role of pupil evaluation in education is defined, the use of educational objectives as a basis of evaluating is established, and a number of measurement procedures are introduced. Part Two, "Measuring Achievement in the Classroom," contains discussions of teacher-built objective and essay tests, methods by which such tests can be evaluated, and teacher-built instruments recording pupil performance. Part Three, "Characteristics of a Good Measuring Instrument," is devoted to validity, reliability, and means of reporting a pupil's relative test performance. In Part Four, "Standardized Tests, Scales, and Inventories," careful attention is given to commercially available tests and batteries of achievement, aptitude, and personal-social adjustment. In the concluding section of the book, Part Five, "Using Evaluation to Improve Learning," the use of measurement data in diagnosis and remediation is explained, and methods of determining and reporting pupil growth are discussed. Finally, characteristics of a comprehensive schoolwide program of evaluation are listed.

Underlying this book are three significant and, indeed, axiomatic principles. In the first place, the measuring procedures of elementary and secondary school teachers are very similar. Moreover, in those instances in which the procedures differ, the secondary school teacher can profit from knowledge of the unique measuring problems and procedures of the elementary school teacher, and vice versa. This book is designed to serve both groups. Secondly, to be competent in educational measurement, a teacher must have a speaking knowledge of common statistical techniques such as the arithmetic mean, the standard deviation, and the correlation coefficient. He does not need to be skilled in the theoretical aspects of statistics, helpful as that would be. To fill the need for a limited command of statistical procedures, descriptions of statistical techniques are included in the appendices. Each step to be followed when solving for one of these values is shown. The computations are so planned that no prior training in mathematics beyond fundamental arithmetic is needed in order to follow them with ease. Thirdly, before a teacher can successfully build his own measuring instruments or select appropriate commercial instruments for classroom use, he must be thoroughly familiar with basic principles of measurement and evaluation. For this reason an entire chapter is devoted to the topic of validity and another to the topic of reliability. Understand, however, that these chapters, as well as all of the others, are not written for the theorist. The treatment is such that the teacher can make practical use of it in his classroom.

Most of the chapters in this book are interrelated. It is recommended that Part One and Part Two be studied first and in that order. At this point the instructor may vary his choice as he wishes. If possible, the chapters in Part Three (that is, Chapters 8, 9, and 10), which deal with norms, validity, and reliability, should be kept together as a group. The same is true of Part Four (that is, Chapters 11, 12, and 13), which deals with standardized tests and inventories.

Scattered within each chapter are discussion questions, usually more than fifteen in number. They are designed to challenge the student in that no readily determined answers are available. Often the question requires the student to apply what he is learning. Supporting references to educational and psychological literature are regularly given.

At the end of each chapter is a list of suggested readings that, in the opinion of the authors, provide suitable extensions of the material included in the chapter and are written at an appropriate level. These references will provide a more complete view of many of the important topics. In addition, a list of free and inexpensive materials concerning educational measurement and evaluation is given in Appendix F.

Like all such books, this is the product of the efforts of many people. The authors are indebted to the many students at Colorado State University and at Cornell University, and to the school personnel in Colorado and New York and other states who directly or indirectly provided ideas and illustrative material for this book. In addition, the authors are grateful to Professor Helen L. Wardeberg of Cornell University, who provided numerous suggestions for the improvement of the first edition of this book, and to the stenographers who typed various parts of the manuscript, particularly to Miss Grace Roetker of Colorado State University. Finally, many publishers have granted permission to reproduce parts of their publications in this volume. These are acknowledged as they occur.

J. Stanley Ahmann
Marvin D. Glock

Evaluating Pupil Growth

principles of tests and measurements

PART ONE

Evaluation in Education

Many years ago, so it is reported, Speaker Joe Cannon was asked by an anxious freshman congressman to evaluate his maiden speech. His response was a masterpiece of honest diplomacy:

"Well, son," he said, "much of what you said was good, and some of what you said was new. But what was good was not new, and what was new was not good."

This is a clear-cut example of the evaluation that is an integral part of our everyday activities. The merchant periodically inventories his stock to see whether he has realized a profit or a loss on his transactions and to evaluate the merits of his present merchandising practices. The golfer carefully tabulates the strokes needed to play eighteen holes of golf, then checks the results against the listed par or perhaps his total of last Saturday, and on this basis he appraises the quality of his game. The surgeon examines his patient for postoperative developments so that he may better assess the success of the operation he performed and hence the well-being of his patient. The financier regularly reviews his portfolio of stocks and bonds, and checks their values and earnings, and thus draws conclusions on the soundness of his present investment program.

Notice that in each of these illustrations a goal has been identified. For the merchant it is a successful merchandising policy; for the golfer, an improved skill; for the surgeon, a more healthy patient; for the financier, a productive portfolio of stocks and bonds. Notice also that, to evaluate the effectiveness of the endeavor, information is necessary on which a value judgment may be made. In the illustrations cited, a variety of information is needed. The merchant computes the amount of his sales and his expenses; the golfer counts strokes; the surgeon examines temperature charts, blood pressure readings, blood counts, and laboratory reports; the financier, like the merchant, is interested in dollars and cents as well as the trends of the stock market. After weighing the information with respect to a known goal, the individuals judge the current situation as successful, with little or no change necessary, or unsuccessful, with recommended changes to be made in the hope of improvement in the future.

Education has a direct parallel. Goals are established on the basis of pupils' needs. Educational programs are established so that pupils can reach these goals and do so in a reasonably efficient manner. Finally, after the program has begun, information such as test scores and reports of observation of pupil behavior is periodically gathered. The success of the pupil in reaching the goal, and hence the success of the educational program, is evaluated in terms of the objectives. This is the core of educational evaluation.

In Part One we have described in limited detail the nature of the purposes and procedures of educational evaluation. Chapter 1, "The Role of Evaluation in Education," discusses the scope of educational evaluation, particularly pupil evaluation, its purposes, the principal types of testing procedures, the heterogeneous nature of these procedures, and problems resulting from lack of accuracy of the information produced by these instruments. Chapter 2, "Educational Objectives in Pupil Evaluation," is concerned with the nature of pupil needs, translation of these needs into educational objectives, and the role of educational objectives in development of instruments used in evaluating pupil growth.

These two chapters survey the entire field of pupil evaluation by identifying its perimeter and its principal parts, and also offer a basic vocabulary for this complex field. Part One can be compared to the large piece of heavy cardboard on which a child is to assemble the various pieces of an inlay jigsaw puzzle. On it the outline of the puzzle and of each piece is traced so that the child can speedily recognize the relationship of one piece to all the others. As a result, he can assemble the pieces much more rapidly than would otherwise be possible. These chapters provide similar outlines, so that detailed descriptions in later chapters of some of the topics mentioned can be easily grasped and their position in the total outline of pupil evaluation quickly recognized.

CHAPTER 1

Role of Evaluation in Education

A trip to a crowded beach in the summer is a revealing experience. Anyone but the most indifferent observer is impressed by this fascinating view of more or less undraped humanity. Some try to capture the sight on canvas or film; few forget it. Summer reminds us how unique each human body is.

We can easily identify the most obvious characteristics that contribute to individuality. Differences in height and weight, and the sometimes phenomenal distribution of that weight, are prominent. Hair or lack of it, size of feet and hands, and posture are equally noticeable. So are characteristics of the various parts of the head—ears, eyes, chin, and mouth. Other aspects of the physiological entity called man, which remain unseen but are none the less important, are visual and auditory acuity, breathing patterns, strength of grip, and sense of smell.

Most of the bathers are not acquainted with each other. If they were, an entirely new constellation of individual differences would reveal itself. These differences are psychological in nature. Variations in interests, attitudes, motives, and values certainly exist, and so do differences in aptitude, be they scholastic, mechanical, musical, artistic, or clerical. In terms of achievements there are literally thousands of additional dimensions that are sources of individuality. Achievement in the common subject matter areas is just one part of the picture. To it must be added achievement in the multitude of additional everyday activities ranging from skill in driving an automobile to the art of making and keeping friends.

The picture is staggering. Small wonder that psychologists have spent lifetimes identifying sources of individuality and developing means of measuring the amount of a given characteristic a person might have at a given moment. These efforts have clearly established the principle that each person possesses a profile of traits, both physiological and psychological, that are the result of

3

the unique heredity (except for identical twins) and environment of each individual.

Teachers are seldom surprised when the factors of individuality are listed. Each succeeding class brings many new pupils before the teacher; no pupil is exactly like any other in this class or any pupil in one of the preceding classes. The appearance of new and refreshing changes in the educational "raw material" each year is one of the joys of teaching. It is also the source of one of the most perplexing problems of teaching—learning to know your pupils so that educational experiences can be planned to capitalize on the individual differences.

In view of this pupil heterogeneity, how can we succinctly describe the teacher's role in expediting the formal educational process? Actually, this role can be conveniently reduced to four points (Tyler, 1969, p. 1).[1] In the first place, the teacher must identify the educational objectives sought. He must know the nature of the pupil behavior that will be displayed when the educational objectives have been achieved. Secondly, he must determine what educational experiences the pupils must have to achieve the objectives. Thirdly, he must know his pupils so well that he can design and order the educational experiences according to their varied interests, aptitudes, and prior experiences. Lastly, he must evaluate the degree to which the desired changes in pupil behavior have taken place, the degree to which the educational objectives have been achieved. By means of the last step, the effectiveness of the various educational experiences can be inferred. Within the last two steps lie the purposes of pupil evaluation.

USES OF EDUCATIONAL EVALUATION

Educational evaluation is the systematic process of determining the effectiveness of educational endeavors in the light of evidence. As you can see from the breadth of this definition, the uses of educational evaluation are broad and diverse. Four subgroups have been identified (Tyler, 1966):

1. Appraisal of academic achievement of individual pupils.
2. Diagnosis of learning difficulties of an individual pupil or an entire class.
3. Appraisal of the educational effectiveness of a curriculum, instructional materials and procedures, and organizational arrangements.
4. Assessment of the educational progress of large populations so as to help understand educational problems and develop sound public policy in education.

The first two uses constitute pupil evaluation that is based on the rationale of individual differences mentioned in the foregoing paragraphs. It focuses

[1] The references are listed alphabetically at the end of each chapter.

primarily on the pupil as an individual. Judgments about his educational growth are based on pertinent data, which may then be compared with similar data about him obtained at an earlier date, or with similar data from his peer group obtained concurrently. This is the type of evaluation of greatest concern to us, and is described in detail later (see page 8). On the other hand, considerable attention is being given to the third use, that is, evaluation of programs and products, and to the last, that is, assessment of educational progress on a national scale. An examination of them, however brief, is in order.

Evaluation of Programs and Products

Just as there are pronounced individual differences among pupils, so there are differences of similar magnitudes among curricula, teaching methods, administrative organizations, flexible class scheduling plans, textbooks, school physical plants, teacher's guides, films, and even projectors, tape recorders, and encyclopedias. "Over-the-coffee-cup" opinions about these and other aspects of the educational scene are usually easy to obtain. But can a systematic determination of their worth be made? Most certainly yes.

Scriven (1967), Stake (1967), and Stufflebeam (1968) have described in detail how this can be done. The models presented are not concerned with pupils as individuals. Only group response is needed, and sometimes not even that.

One useful model is that designed by Stake (1967). As an initial step in evaluation of an educational program, perhaps a new curriculum, a rationale is first established. This designates the purpose of the evaluation, in other words, the decisions about which you need data. Should the curriculum be adopted permanently or not? Should it be modified in certain respects? Is it an improvement over others designed for largely the same purposes? With questions like these in mind, the evaluator completes a data matrix as in Figure 1 (Stake, 1967, p. 529), with one axis having three subdivisions (antecedents, transactions, and outcomes) and the other four (intents, observations, standards, and judgments).

Briefly, these are defined as follows:

1. Antecedents: Any conditions existing prior to the beginning of the program that may influence the outcomes of the program, for instance, the qualifications of the teachers and pupils as well as the quality of the facilities and equipment.
2. Transactions: The countless encounters between pupils and staff, that is, discussions, lectures, demonstrations, etc.
3. Outcomes: The impact of the program on pupils, teachers, and others, for example, the pupil changes in abilities, achievements, and attitudes resulting from the educational experiences.

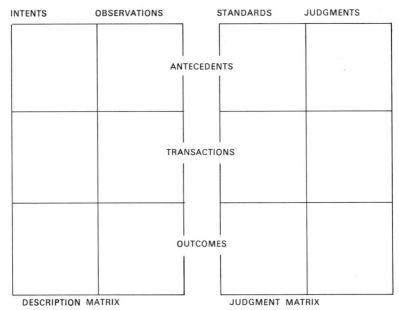

FIGURE 1.   Data Matrices for Statements and Data Collected by
the Evaluator of an Educational Program.

From Stake, 1967, p. 529; reproduced by permission of the Teachers College Record.

4. Intents: The planned-for end product such as the planned-for demonstrations, environmental conditions, and coverage of subject matter.
5. Observations: Descriptions of the situation as it is found, for example, results yielded by data-gathering devices such as tests, inventories, diaries, interviews, etc.
6. Standards: Acceptable and meritorious levels of antecedents, transactions, and outcomes, often arbitrarily established.
7. Judgments: The decision as to what is good, bad, and indifferent in each situation, that is, a degree of importance of any discrepancies found between features of the actual programs and the standards listed for them.

The model shown schematically in Figure 1 may give you two impressions: (1) the broad scope of the plan, and (2) the degree of subjectivity incorporated. This kind of program evaluation leads to systematic evaluation, and hence to decision making based on pertinent data.

National Assessment of Educational Progress

Rather than being concerned with the educational achievement of individual pupils or even groups of pupils, schools, or school systems, the National Assessment of Educational Progress (NAEP) is directed toward determining the educational attainments of large groups of people, for example, nine-year-old girls of higher socioeconomic status from middle-sized cities in western United States. Specifically, its national goals are:

1. To obtain census-like data on the educational attainment of major portions of our national population.
2. To measure the growth or decline in educational attainment that takes place over time in key learning areas.

Serious efforts to achieve these goals began in 1963. As a project of the Education Commission of the States, NAEP has attacked its task systematically. Initially, it identified the subject areas to be used, including at the onset citizenship, science, writing, mathematics, music, literature, social studies, art, reading, and career and occupational development, and later adding consumer education, listening and speaking, and health and physical education. Committees of scholars and school personnel, with the assistance of lay citizens, designed the general and specific objectives for each area. Often still another subdivision is provided; these are suggestions at four different age levels of the kinds of behavior that indicate that the specific objectives are being attained.

The test items vary considerably, some short-answer in nature, others of the essay type. Other exercises include interviews, observations of pupil behavior, questionnaires, performance tasks, and appraisal of work products. For example, in the citizenship education assessment, standardized group situations are used that offer opportunity for direct observation of behavior and the reporting of it by means of checklists and other nontesting techniques (Campbell and Nichols, 1968). Data gathering started in 1969, involving a national sample of over 120,000 individuals. Revision and replacement of objectives and test exercises continually occurs, a new testing cycle taking place about every third year.

For reporting purposes, a number of subdivisions of the national sample are used such as:

1. Four age levels (9, 13, 17, 26–35).
2. Four geographic regions (Northeast, Southeast, Central, and West).
3. Four sizes of communities (large cities, urban fringe, middle-size cities, and smaller places).
4. The two sexes.

Reporting of results is not in the form of test scores for individuals in a particular area of learning. Instead, it takes the following form (Finley, 1969):

For a sample of seventeen-year-old boys from middle-size cities of the Northeast region, it was found that:

1. Ninety percent know the name of the governor of their state, but only 20 percent know the name of their representative to Congress.
2. Eighty-five percent understand the basic concept involved in transplanting vital organs from one human being to another.

This style of reporting prevents comparisons among individuals, schools, or school districts. Nevertheless, supporters of the NAEP program believe that the information gathered is specific enough to tell us what the younger segment of the population is learning and to provide solid data on the basis of which to take intelligent action to improve the educational system. Some critics disagree on these points. For instance, Katzman and Rosen (1970, p. 584) believe that the NAEP program "can be criticized on several grounds: (1) measuring questionable educational outcomes with questionable techniques; (2) classifying student subpopulations on largely irrelevant dimensions and/or insufficient detail; and (3) neglecting to collect any information on school characteristics which would identify policy-performance relationships." Other critics fear that the findings of the NAEP program will ultimately lead to a highly centralized and nationalized educational system (Hand, 1965; Saylor, 1970).

PURPOSES OF PUPIL EVALUATION

Our focus on educational evaluation is restricted to pupil evaluation that concentrates on the pupil as an individual and as a member of a classroom unit. Such evaluation has two purposes: (1) to help the teacher determine the degree to which educational objectives have been achieved, and (2) to help the teacher know his pupils as individuals. The first purpose is basic; changes in pupil behavior are always evaluated in terms of the goals of education. The second purpose is subsidiary to the first, since, naturally, if the teacher is intimately familiar with his pupils, he will be better able to plan educational experiences for them and determine the degree to which educational objectives have been achieved. It is important to realize this fundamental relation between the two purposes. In practice, information on the degree of achievement of educational objectives is always augmented by additional information on the pupil's earlier interests, values, aptitudes, and achievements. Thus, the second purpose supports the first.

Classroom teachers are quick to recognize these two purposes and their relationship to each other. On the other hand, they are sometimes slow to take planned and vigorous action to realize them. This reluctance seriously weakens the effectiveness of the teaching art.

Determining the Achievement of Educational Objectives

The task of the classroom teacher is to assist his pupils in reaching the general and specific goals of education. These educational objectives guide every step of the teaching process. The professional activities of a teacher have meaning insofar as they are oriented toward the educational objectives of his class. In short, educational objectives serve the teacher as road maps serve the traveler; with these aids, the efforts of both are organized and the end of the journey draws steadily closer; without them, they walk in circles.

Educational objectives stem from the needs of youth as they are guided and molded by the democratic society in which they live. Suggestions for educational objectives commonly come from three sources: study of the pupil, study of the democratic society in which he lives, and judgment of the informed educational specialist. Certainly the knowledges and skills a pupil already has, as well as his interests and goals, should influence the educational objectives of the class he is attending. Hence, objectives should be based on pupil needs. By the same token, the democratic society in which the pupil lives has needs; it must be improved and perpetuated. Finally, the informed specialist in a subject matter area can, after intensive study, identify important trends and interrelations that, when translated into new objectives or allowed to influence old ones, may ultimately improve the breadth and direction of the educational program as a whole.

Stating Educational Objectives.   The modern way of expressing educational objectives is in terms of desired pupil behavior, that is, in terms of the behavior that the pupil should exhibit if he has achieved certain objectives. Often cited are specific behavioral patterns related to the pupil's knowledges, understandings, attitudes, appreciations, abilities, and skills in a specified subject matter area. The following shows the type of statement used in expressing specific objectives (Fors, 1969, p. 26):

Curriculum area: Elementary science
Grade levels: 1–3
   The pupil should be able to demonstrate conclusively with a ball or globe and a source of light why only half of the earth has daylight at any given time.
Grade levels: 3–5
   The pupil should be able to construct a system of pulleys by means of which approximately 100 grams could lift 300 grams.
Grade levels: 5–6
   The pupil distinguishes between kinetic energy and potential energy by using an original example.

From the point of view of pupil evaluation, objectives stated in terms of outwardly observable behavior are most suitable. Determining the degree to which objectives have been met is finding out how the pupil is observably different after the educational experiences from what he was before them. Stating the objectives of education in these terms is deceptively difficult. The illustration shows considerable success in this matter.

Identifying Changes in Behavior.   There are many ways to discover what changes, if any, in pupil behavior have occurred as a result of educational experiences. By means of a few liberal interpretations, the multitude of methods can be classified into two groups: testing procedures and nontesting procedures. The testing procedures can be the common paper-and-pencil tests, oral tests, or performance tests. Nontesting procedures include teacher-pupil interviews, anecdotal records, sociometric techniques, general information questionnaires, and ranking and rating methods that summarize the results of observing samples of pupil behavior or products of that behavior. Properly or otherwise, the most commonly used is the paper-and-pencil achievement test.

No matter which of the suggested methods is used to identify changes in pupil behavior, the teacher needs considerable information in addition to knowledge of the technique. That information is a thorough grasp of the typical and atypical behavioral patterns of pupils he is teaching. Standardized testing devices attempt to provide these reference points by means of norms, that is, lists of typical scores made by a sample of pupils thought to be representative of a larger population of pupils for whom the test is designed. Nontesting procedures customarily require a full knowledge of what pupils in a given class or age group are like. The more complete this knowledge, the more adequate will be the evaluation of changes in pupil behavior.

Two notable obstacles prevent a comprehensive evaluation of the degree to which educational objectives have been achieved. First of all, certain educational goals, such as those pertaining to attitudes and interests, are difficult to translate into observable pupil behavior, and changes can be identified only crudely, if at all. Consequently it has not been possible to construct evaluation instruments that can adequately measure the degree to which the pupil has achieved all of the many and varied educational objectives. Secondly, in some instances the total desired change in pupil behavior may not be observable until months or years following the educational experience. Of course, the teacher may not be on the scene at this auspicious moment. However, he may be able to observe changes in pupil behavior indicating partial achievement of an educational objective. For example, one of the broad educational objectives often mentioned is that the pupil will prepare himself adequately for a suitable vocation. The complete achievement of this objective may not be observable for some time. Yet the classroom teacher may observe partial achievement as the pupil masters, for example, verbal and mathematical skills.

Helping a Teacher to Know His Pupils

Every teacher subscribes to the obvious truth that, to be successful, he must know his pupils. He can begin by inquiring about their names, addresses, previous academic experiences, parents, and the occupations of their parents. By observation he may be able to appraise crudely the socioeconomic level from which the pupil comes, his physical vigor, his social training, and even his enthusiasm concerning the anticipated educational experiences.

But what lies beneath the surface? A teacher is more than curious about the pupil's aptitudes, the complete story of his previous academic achievements, and the degree of his personal-social adjustment. These aspects of a pupil cannot be assessed without relying on some of the many techniques here classified as a part of pupil evaluation. Considered guesses based on informal observations are not sufficient. Appraisals need to be based on objective data and organized in a systematic pattern.

Consider for a moment a given pupil about whom a teacher is questioned. Let's call him Mike. According to the teacher, Mike is a "fair" pupil who is "moderately bright" and who seems to be "rather well-liked" by most of his classmates. In general, Mike is not very highly motivated, but appears to be content and causes little trouble. You may have often heard such a description. Undeniably it is a helpful thumbnail sketch. Yet it could be infinitely more helpful if it were more specific and less subjective. One might ask how "fair" is "fair" and how "bright" is "moderately bright"? Test scores from achievement tests and a scholastic aptitude test could underpin this description to a sizable degree. Furthermore, according to the teacher's remarks, Mike seems to be an underachiever. Why? Test scores and teacher ratings of earlier academic achievements may shed light on this question, as may various aptitude test scores. Home conditions should not be ignored even though they can only be casually evaluated. Lastly, how "well-liked" is "rather well-liked"? What kind of trouble is "little trouble"? Sociometric devices and anecdotal records may jointly illuminate these questions.

The list of suggested evaluation techniques could be continued, but the point has been made. The picture of Mike can be brought into focus only by better evaluation techniques. These techniques will never paint a complete profile of a pupil, but they will reveal enough of that profile to justify the time and money their use demands.

Knowing a child is a prolonged, complex process. Ideally it combines the skill of the teacher as an impersonal, astute observer, the skill of the test technician who constructs and validates the standardized measuring instruments, and the skill of a clinician, who carefully amalgamates all the above information and ferrets out likely causes and effects. Although not confronted by the ideal situation, the average classroom teacher can, through extensive effort, attain useful though typically imperfect results.

The rewards for such effort are rich. The teacher can select and time educational experiences for his pupils much more effectively. He can also interpret more realistically the results of his attempts to find out how well his pupils achieved educational objectives.

Problems

1. Using for illustrative purposes a class level and subject matter familiar to you, cite the chief arguments supporting the contention that pupil evaluation is most successful when based on limited, well-defined educational objectives.

2. It is argued that an effective teacher is one who in a minimum amount of instructional time can help the pupil reach pertinent educational objectives commensurate with his abilities. In the light of this statement, to what degree should there be interaction between pupil evaluation and the evaluation of teacher effectiveness? Why?

3. Some critics of the National Assessment of Education Progress believe that this program will result in centralized control over the curriculum of public schools (Hand, 1965; Saylor, 1970). Evaluate this claim in terms of the procedures used in the assessment (Merwin and Womer, 1969, pp. 305–334).

4. Does homogenous grouping of pupils on the basis of test scores yielded by a common group test of mental ability, significantly reduce the importance of the second purpose of pupil evaluation (a) insofar as a secondary school mathematics teachers is concerned, and (b) insofar as an elementary school teacher of the intermediate grade levels is concerned?

DIFFERENCES BETWEEN MEASUREMENT AND EVALUATION

Differentiating between the terms "measurement" and "evaluation" is sometimes difficult. The two terms are related, yet decidely different. Evaluation is a more inclusive term than measurement. Measurement is only a part, although a very substantial one, of evaluation, providing information on which an evaluation can be based.

Characteristics of Measurement

Educational measurement is the process that attempts to obtain a quantified representation of the degree to which a pupil reflects a trait. The use of a paper-and-pencil test to discover the scholastic aptitude or achievement of a pupil is an illustration of educational measurement. In the case of scholastic aptitude, for example, one can easily visualize it as a continuum, that is, as a trait that logically varies from much to some to none and that is theoretically capable of being divided into an infinite number of degrees. Each pupil has a specific position on the continuum. Educational measurement tries to represent that position by means of a numerical value, a scholastic aptitude test score, and to do so in as objective a manner as possible.

The measurement process is fundamentally descriptive of the degree to which a trait is possessed by a pupil and uses numbers rather than words. A teacher can characterize a fourth-grade pupil as "tall," "gifted," or "underweight." These are word descriptions of traits that are continuous. Measuring instruments can change "tall" to "61.5 inches," "gifted" to "Stanford-Binet IQ of 132," and "underweight" to "85 pounds." The advantage of reporting numbers rather than adjectives is obvious. The meaning of any adjective varies from teacher to teacher. Carefully executed measurement data do not change. They are notably less ambiguous than verbal descriptions.

Educational measurement tends to concentrate on a narrow, specific, and well-defined trait or characteristic, and then strives to determine with precision the degree to which that trait is possessed by an individual pupil. This is in many ways comparable to the methods of a photographer who, in trying to capture the individuality of a physique, photographs each part separately, first the hand, then the foot, perhaps then the nose, and so forth. Such a photographer would hope that the result of his work would be a series of revealing photographs, each displaying clearly the status of the physique with regard to the particular part. If totally successful, he could assemble all photographs and recreate a picture of the total physique.

A teacher acts like a photographer when he examines specific pupil traits, such as reading comprehension, vocabularly, and scholastic aptitude, with a series of measuring instruments. Each test measures a certain pupil trait, just as each photograph pictures a part of the physique. Unfortunately, the teacher's task is not so simple as the photographer's. Whereas it is possible that some of the photographer's pictures might be blurred because his camera was out of focus or might have poor black and white contrast because they are underexposed, such lapses are unlikely, especially if he is a professional photographer. In contrast, the teacher using even the best measurement devices may have nothing but somewhat blurred and underexposed "photographs." Worse than that, some traits of the pupil cannot be "photographed" at all since no measuring instruments are available. Hence the total picture of a pupil yielded by combining the results of many measurements of various pupil traits is often somewhat unclear, due to the failure of the instruments to yield precise, unequivocal results, and is invariably incomplete, due to the scarcity of suitable measuring instruments, particularly in the area of personal-social adjustment.

The statement that a measuring instrument fails to yield precise, unequivocal results means that the instrument does not adequately serve the purposes for which it is intended, and that it does not measure with perfect consistency. The failure of an instrument to serve the purposes for which it is intended is known as lack of validity; the failure of an instrument to measure consistently is known as lack of reliability. The concepts of validity and reliability are described and illustrated in Chapters 9 and 10 respectively.

Characteristics of Evaluation

Pupil evaluation is a process in which a teacher commonly uses information derived from many sources to arrive at a value judgment. The information might be obtained by using measuring instruments as well as other techniques that do not necessarily yield quantitative results, such as general information questionnaires, direct observation, and teacher-pupil interviews. An evaluation may or may not be based on measurement data, though appropriate measurements are customarily used if they are available. Thus, evaluation includes not only measuring or in some way identifying the degree to which a pupil possesses a trait or to which his behavior may have been modified as a result of an educational experience, but also judging the desirability and adequacy of these findings. Data from good measuring instruments can provide a sound basis for good evaluation.

The differences between measurement and evaluation can be easily illustrated. Suppose that you are about to buy a new four-door automobile and have decided to restrict your choice to three makes in the low-priced field. Now you face the happy problem of determining which of the three automobiles to buy. Your investigation of the three probably starts with measurement: the cost, the horsepower of the engine, the length of wheelbase, the gasoline consumption at various speeds, and the weight are useful measurement values. Perhaps then, you test-drive a demonstration car, forming judgments on riding ease, maneuverability, rapidity of acceleration, and interior and exterior beauty. Finally, you choose one of the three automobiles. The choice results from a careful consideration of quantitative evidence, qualitative evidence, and highly subjective impressions, and is the end result of an evaluation process.

Within the field of education an excellent example of the differences between measurement and evaluation can be found in the practice of assigning final marks to pupils at the end of a unit of work. Measurements of a pupil's prior achievement and aptitude may have been made before the unit began, and measurements of the changes in pupil behavior follow the termination of the unit. To these pieces of information the teacher frequently adds his reactions to the pupil's attitudes, cooperativeness, motivation, and possibly even his punctuality. The final result is generally a single letter or numerical mark that supposedly indicates the relative success of the pupil as he experienced the unit of work. As in the case of the choice of automobile, an evaluation process has taken place; a value judgment has been made.

Problems

5. In his criticism of the importance placed on final marks, Milton (1968) quotes St. Augustine who wrote:

> "For so it is, O Lord, my God, I measure it;
> But what it is that I measure I do not know."

Explain Milton's point of view of with this question in mind: Should final marks be considered measurements?

6.   Identify the probable significant aspects of measurement and evaluation in the case of a débutante attempting an intensive weight-reduction program with a controlled diet, or a candidate for the varsity football team attempting a strength-development program with isometric exercises.

EDUCATIONAL TESTING

Educational measurement is usually considered to include educational testing. Whether this is true or not depends, of course, on the manner in which educational testing is defined. "Test" is, paradoxically, a simple and widely used term and yet one of somewhat vague meaning. It can be defined in such a broad manner as to include some of the evaluation procedures known as tests, which yield only verbal descriptions of pupil traits. For instance, it can be defined as any systematic procedure for observing a person's behavior and describing it by means of a numerical scale or a category system (Cronbach, 1970, p. 26). Some of these procedures cannot be included within the definition of educational measurement. On the other hand, educational testing can be defined in a more restricted manner so that, practically speaking, all tests can be called measuring instruments.

It is convenient for the purpose of this book to define the word "test" in the more restricted manner. In the first place, a test is nothing more than a group of questions or tasks to which a pupil is to respond. The questions might require the pupil to give the correct meaning of a word, solve an arithmetic problem, or identify missing parts in a picture of an animal. Tasks might require the pupil to thread beads on a string, assemble a small piece of apparatus, or arrange blocks in a prescribed design. These questions and tasks might be presented to the pupil orally or in writing; some are even presented by means of pantomime under certain circumstances. The questions and tasks are known as test items. They are intended to be a representative sample of all possible questions and tasks related to the trait measured by the test that are of suitable difficulty. A pupil's responses to the test items are scored in such a way that, ideally, the results indicate the degree to which he possesses the specified trait. The principal purpose of a test is to produce a quantitative representation of the pupil trait that it is designed to measure. Certainly educational testing is included within educational measurement when this restricted definition of a test is used.

Types of Tests

Tests can differ from each other in many ways. Some contain items of nearly constant difficulty, whereas others contain items of varying difficulty. Some require that rigid time limits be maintained; others do not. Some demand that the pupils to whom the test is to be administered have a complete command of the English language; others do not. Some can be administered to large groups of pupils simultaneously; others to only one pupil at a time. These and other variations have been used to subdivide tests into a relatively restricted list of seventeen types.[1]

In the following discussion, two and sometimes three types of tests are grouped together, as in the case of oral, essay, and objective tests. This grouping is made because the types are more or less contrasting. Sometimes the relative merits of each are vigorously debated by both teachers and testing specialists. In any event, it is a useful way of remembering the types and their general characteristics.

Notice also that a given existing test can simultaneously be classified as more than one type. For example, one popular achievement test used in schools today is a group, verbal, objective, standardized, power test. Such a multiple classification of a test is actually a highly informative thumbnail description. Mastery of such terminology is a necessary prerequisite to an understanding of this part of educational evaluation.

Individual and Group Tests.   Individual tests are tests that can be administered to only one pupil at a time. The examiner has an opportunity to establish rapport with the pupil and to gain insight into the pupil and his reaction to the testing situation. He can even ascertain possible reasons for many of the pupil's answers. Furthermore, the examiner practically always has the responsibility of making a written record of the pupil's answers. A common illustration of an individual test is the *Stanford-Binet Scale, Form L-M.*

Group tests can be administered to more than one pupil at a time. The number of pupils can range into the hundreds if sufficient test proctors are available. In elementary and secondary school situations, however, pupils are often tested as a class. Because of its simplicity and low cost, this type of test is far more popular than the individual test.

You have no doubt experienced the impersonal atmosphere in which group tests are typically given. As the group of pupils becomes larger, this problem increases. Certainly, a number of the desirable aspects of the individual test are found only to a reduced degree in group tests, since they have been sacrificed for economy of time and money.

Classroom and Standardized Tests.   Classroom tests are sometimes called teacher-made tests or "informal" tests. They are tests constructed by a classroom teacher for use in his particular classes under conditions of his choosing. In practically all instances these tests are group tests and measure pupil

[1] Brief descriptions of these and other types of tests can be found in the third edition of Good's *Dictionary of Education* (New York: McGraw-Hill, 1971).

achievement. More of these tests are administered than any other kind. Unfortunately, they often are carelessly constructed and interpreted.

The value of classroom achievement tests stems from one primary consideration—the individual nature of every class. This individuality can be traced primarily to the kind of educational objectives involved in the class and also to the relative emphasis each received. It also can be traced to the quality of the pupils who compose the class. The teacher certainly knows better than anyone else the exact nature of these characteristics of his class. Since the appropriateness of any achievement test item is determined by the educational objectives of the class, the teacher is in an excellent position to build test items that measure suitable areas of the pupils' achievements and that are of suitable difficulty. Thus classroom achievement tests, if properly prepared, are tailor-made for a certain class of pupils taught in a certain manner. On the other hand, standardized achievement tests are designed for many classes of a certain type; these tests attempt to cover those achievement areas thought to be common to all classes for which they are designed.

Standardized tests are constructed almost invariably by teams of individuals rather than by a single person. In the case of standardized achievement tests, teachers qualified in the area tested work with measurement specialists by helping to identifying the scope of an achievement test and its appropriateness. Often they contribute possible test items. In the case of standardized aptitude tests, the role of the teacher is considerably reduced, if not nonexistent.

Characteristically, standardized tests are carefully designed. They are pretested in order to determine the level of difficulty of the test items, the amount of testing time required, the sizes of typical scores made by various types of pupils, and so forth. The manuals accompanying the test contain information concerning the method of developing the test, its purposes, directions for its proper administration, directions for scoring, techniques for interpreting the scores, and reports of research in which the test was involved. In order that any standardized test be used properly, it must be administered only to those pupils for whom it is designed and strictly in accordance with the manual's directions. Furthermore, the scoring of the instrument and the interpretation of those scores must be performed in the manner prescribed for that test.

Oral, Essay, and Objective Tests.   Although common in the early history of achievement testing, oral tests are not popular today. Their use as a means of testing the knowledges and understandings of a candidate for an advanced degree is no doubt their principal single function now. Even in this situation they often are not used alone but in conjunction with paper-and-pencil tests.

The disadvantages of oral testing are not difficult to identify. First of all, it tends to be somewhat unplanned in total. The first questions asked by the teacher can be selected with care; after that, however, the nature of the responses of the pupils often influence the nature of later questions. Soon the sampling of the pupil's knowledges and understandings becomes quite narrow. Consciously or unconsciously, the teacher may be grossly unfair to the pupil. Secondly, pupils, like actors, are affected by their audience. The tension created by a face-to-face contact with an examiner has caused many a pupil, even though he actually knows the correct answer, to blurt out the most unusual conglomeration of words, complete with fractured syntax. Thirdly, oral tests generally require too much time from both teacher and pupil. Fourthly, there is no written record of the pupil's responses.

A principal advantage of oral testing is that it can be diagnostic. Probing questions can reveal the causes of a pupil's error. Such information, needless to say, is extremely useful to a teacher. Oral testing has a further advantage in that it reveals how well a pupil can apply his knowledge to novel situations, though this can be tested by paper-and-pencil tests as well. To this end, specialists in medicine have designed standardized role-playing situations for the purpose of assessing certain complex skills of gathering data and making judgments as demonstrated by candidates for certification (Levine and McGuire, 1968). Simulated diagnostic interviews, proposed treatment interviews, and patient management conferences have been used successfully. In the first two instances, the candidate plays the role of a physician and an examiner plays the role of a patient, while a second examiner uses standard rating scales to record his impressions of the interview. In the third situation, five candidates play the role of physician and their conference is rated by examiners.

Since many of the difficulties associated with oral tests disappear when paper-and-pencil tests are used, essay testing has replaced oral testing in part. Instead of asking the pupil to answer a question orally, he is asked to write his answer. This simple change affects the testing situation drastically. Now many pupils can be tested simultaneously. Each can answer the same questions, except for an optional question or two which some teachers offer. Since only one set of questions is to be used for many pupils, extensive efforts to obtain a cross-sectional sampling of the subject matter in those questions are certainly justified. Moreover, each pupil has an opportunity to compose himself as he attacks each question. Tension is noticeably reduced.

Objective tests are tests that can be scored in such a manner that subjective judgment is eliminated when determining the correctness of a pupil's answers. True-false tests, matching tests, and multiple-choice tests are objective tests in the true sense of the definition. Supply tests (for example, completion tests) are sometimes considered to be objective tests even though the subjective judgment is not entirely eliminated. Occasionally, they are called "semiobjective" test items.

Objective tests are very common. Classroom as well as standardized achievement tests are so constructed. Paper-and-pencil aptitude tests are almost invariably of this type. Clearly, objective scoring is in keeping with the whole purpose of using a standardized test. After all, a standardized test tries to be a universal "yardstick" to measure a specified pupil trait. To prevent the "yardstick" from changing its units such precautions as uniform testing conditions are required. Uniform scoring procedures are equally vital. The test results obtained by a pupil should never be affected positively or negatively by the person who happens to score his paper.

Speed, Power, and Mastery Tests.   A speed test is one in which a pupil must, in a limited amount of time, answer a series of questions or perform a series of tasks of a uniformly low level of difficulty. The near-constant level of difficulty of the questions or tasks is such that, if the pupil had unlimited time, he could easily answer each question or perform each task successfully. The average pupils finds that he does not have sufficient time to attempt all test items. The intent of a speed test is to measure primarily the rapidity with which a pupil can do what is asked of him rather than whether he can do it at all.

Excellent illustrations of speed tests can be found in the case of some clerical aptitude tests. One such test requires the pupil to determine whether two numbers or two names are the same or different. In another the pupil must match combinations of two letters, a letter and a number, or two numbers. Rigid time limits that allow too little time for completion of the test are enforced. If this were not the case, any alert person would certainly have a perfect score.

Speed tests in the pure sense are not common in educational measurement. Usually, not only are comfortable (though controlled) time limits allowed, but also the level of difficulty of the test items is not uniformly low. However, in achievement testing, some instruments tend to be speeded because of poorly chosen time limits. So little time is allowed the pupils that the number of unattempted test items becomes excessive. On the other hand, tests designed to measure speed of reading are closely timed and properly so. The very nature of the characteristic to be measured demands rigid time limits.

In aptitude testing, time limits of an instrument often are quite significant. For example, in group scholastic aptitude tests, time limits typically prevent most pupils from attempting every item. Yet, these instruments are not, strictly speaking, speed tests. The level of difficulty of test items changes; the test items generally become more difficult as the test progresses.

In contrast to a pure speed test is a power test. The items of a power test have different levels of difficulty usually arranged in the order of increasing difficulty. Power tests are sometimes called scaled tests.

Technically, time limits for a power test do not exist. In reality, they frequently do exist. Little is to be gained by giving a pupil unrestricted time for writing a test. There seems to be a point in time after which further contemplation of the test items yields practically no profit for him. Builders of standardized instruments generally agree that a power test should be so timed that a very large percentage of the pupils for whom it is designed will have ample time to attempt all of the items. Although estimates vary as to the proper size of this percentage, 90 percent seems to be an acceptable minimum. Hence, the test is slightly speeded.

Power tests are widely given, particularly when testing achievement. Teachers and pupils alike feel that minimizing the speed factors in a testing situation is desirable. This feeling no doubt stems from the conviction that knowing one's level of maximum achievement as indicated by a power test is more useful than knowing the rapidity with which one can perform simple tasks as indicated by a speed test.

A mastery test resembles both a speed and a power test. The level of difficulty of its items is uniformly low, and in this restricted sense it reminds us of a speed test. On the other hand, it typically has the liberal time limits of a power test. These are two principal characteristics of a mastery test.

A mastery test performs a specific function. It is designed to measure the knowledges and skills that every pupil of the class should have acquired. Hence it is expected that virtually all of the pupils will perform perfectly on the test. No attempt is made to discover how much a pupil may have acquired over and above the minimum everyone should have reached. If you wish, in long tests allowance can be made for an error or two due to chance.

Mastery tests are customarily teacher-constructed. A spelling list, a vocabulary list, or a series of arithmetic computations may constitute such a test. Teachers have used them as quizzes with considerable effectiveness. However, when used alone as an end-of-unit or end-of-term achievement test, their usefulness is less than that of power tests, particularly at the secondary school level.

Sometimes we underestimate the usefulness of mastery tests. For instance, they can serve as end-of-unit achievement tests when used in conjunction with an appropriately designed classroom power test (Trow, 1968). By means of the mastery test, the teacher could determine pupil command of the essentials of the subject matter. Then the power test would be used to sample that material that remains.

Furthermore, emphasis by teachers on learning for mastery (Bloom, 1968) means testing accordingly. Also, the National Assessment of Educational Progress uses various levels of test items, one of which samples knowledges and skills that practically all examinees know. The same point of view is used with criterion-referenced tests (see page 22) when the reporting of test results is "on-off" in nature, for instance, either a 90 percent minimum level of proficiency has been achieved by the pupil or it has not. Finally, mastery tests are used for units of programmed instruction in order to find out whether a pupil should proceed to new material, repeat the material completed, or study remedial material.

Verbal, Nonverbal, and Performance Tests.   A verbal test is a test in which the responding pupil utilizes written or spoken language. This use of language can occur in the directions needed by the pupil, or in his responses to the test items, or in both cases. The widespread use of paper-and-pencil achievement tests in the typical classroom situation clearly illustrates the popularity of verbal tests.

Not all persons can be given a verbal test, however. Illiterates, mentally deficient children, and very young children are incapable of understanding written directions and sometimes even oral directions. Some tests are so constructed that the instructions are orally given and the persons tested respond without use of language. These have been called nonverbal tests, although strictly speaking a nonverbal test does not require the use of language by either the examiner or the person taking the test. Pantomime is used as a means of giving directions. The person may only point to indicate his answer. Geometric drawings and three-dimensional materials have been used in this type of test.

In a discussion of performance tests, it is necessary to differentiate between aptitude performance tests and achievement performance tests. In aptitude testing, performance tests are often nothing more than nonverbal tests. They are designed to measure the aptitudes of those persons unfamiliar with the English language. For example, the manipulation of blocks and the tracing of a maze have been used to assess general mental ability. In achievement testing, performance tests are not devoted primarily to the illiterate. Performance tests attempt to appraise the degree to which a skill has been achieved. For example, a typing speed test is a performance test. The pupil's performance during a specific period of time is scored in terms of quantity and accuracy of the material typed. Athletic events, musical performances, food preparation, and machine operations can serve as performance tests.

Readiness and Diagnostic Tests.   Readiness tests are designed to determine the ability of a pupil to undertake a certain type of learning. They resemble aptitude tests in that they try to forecast the achievement that would occur if appropriate training were given. They differ from aptitude tests in that they deal with a highly specific kind of achievement, such as reading.

Readiness tests are designed to discover whether a pupil is sufficiently advanced to profit from formal instruction in a subject area. To accomplish this purpose, reading readiness tests may use tests of visual discrimination, auditory discrimination, vocabulary, and sometimes motor coordination. Tests of pupil readiness in mathematics and language are also given in secondary school; these are called aptitude or prognostic tests for a given subject matter area.

Whereas readiness tests are administered to pupils before formal instruction is given, diagnostic tests are administered after formal instruction has taken place. The purpose of a diagnostic test is to reveal specific deficiencies in a pupil's background. This information could also point to specific deficiencies in the instruction given. The alert classroom teacher tests in this manner continually, often using tests of his own design.

One outstanding characteristic of diagnostic tests is that any total test scores they might give are of practically no value. The desired information comes from part scores based on a few related test items or from an item-by-item analysis of the pupil's responses. Each individual item or small group of items tests the pupils with regard to a particular part of the materials taught. Thus a pupil's answers are studied on that basis.

Norm-Referenced and Criterion-Referenced Tests.   Test norms are representations of average or common performance based on the results of testing a typical group of pupils for whom the instrument is designed (see pages 252–269). Thus a pupil's score can be compared with tables of norms such as those for percentile ranks; his relative performance can be determined in terms of his rank in a standard group of 100 pupils, for example, 73rd from the bottom of the group or 29th from the bottom.

A norm-referenced test, then, finds a pupil's performance level in relation to levels of others on the same test. This is the usual approach taken in educational testing. Almost all standardized achievement and aptitude tests are norm-referenced instruments.

In contrast, criterion-referenced tests are those used to ascertain a pupil's status with respect to some criterion, for instance, an established performance standard. We want to know what the pupil can do, rather than how he compares with others. An example of this type of test is the Red Cross Senior Lifesaving Test, in which an individual must demonstrate certain swimming skills in order to pass. How well others perform is not important. Individual mastery is the primary issue (Popham and Husek, 1969).

On the basis of its appearance, you will not be able to differentiate between a norm-referenced test and a criterion-referenced test in a subject matter area such as mathematics. Yet the test items in a norm-referenced test are selected in order to produce variability among the test scores, whereas those for a criterion-referenced test are designed to be an accurate reflection of a given criterion behavior. Thus these two types of tests differ in terms of purpose.

They also differ in the manner in which the test items are selected and the kind of information produced by pupil responses. Note that test items in a criterion-referenced achievement test must be a representative sample of the tasks identified by the specific educational objectives of the instruction given. This is most easily accomplished if the objectives are stated in terms of the explicit performance to be demonstrated by the pupil. There needs to be an analysis of the structure of the task (say, ability to add integers accurately) so that components of it and criteria of performance with respect to them are described carefully. The scoring of pupil responses to test items is such that it provides detailed information about which tasks a pupil can perform (Glaser and Nitko, 1970). The desired end product is generally a descriptive statement of the pupil's behavior, like "Frank's performance on the test was such that we believe he can accurately add 80 percent of a universe of pairs of positive integers, none of which has more than three digits."

A well-designed criterion-referenced test, in short, provides a great deal of information about the behavior repertoire of a pupil. We discover what he can and cannot do, that is, whether or not he achieved some of the immediate outcomes of a learning situation. His performance as measured by one or more test items is compared with an external standard representing a specific education objective (Gagné, 1970, pp. 340–343). This type of testing is highly compatible with a teacher emphasis on mastery learning, and can provide information helpful in both pupil evaluation and program evaluation (Cronbach, 1963).

Problems

7. According to the definition of a test used in this chapter, can the following standardized instruments be called tests?
    a. *Mooney Problem Check List*
    b. *Kuder Preference Record*
    c. *Fundamental Achievement Series*
    d. *Thorndike Dimensions of Personality*
    e. *Musical Aptitude Profile*
For each of the foregoing considered to be a test, identify its classification according to the seventeen types of tests described.

8. "Some test items are more objective than others." Is this a meaningful statement? Why?

9. The claim is made that no so-called standardized test is truly a standardized test unless it is administered and its scores interpreted in the light of the specifications included in its test manual. Give illustrations of testing situation that support this statement.

INDIRECT NATURE OF MEASUREMENT PROCEDURES

When a carpenter builds a house, he engages in direct measurement. When he measures the length of a board or the size of the angles at which it is to be cut, he does not need to infer the characteristic being measured. It is clearly and obviously present and measurable. By contrast, the teacher must frequently engage in indirect rather than direct measurement. For example, a pupil's general mental ability is inferred by measuring, by means of a test, what are considered to be the *effects* of general mental ability and not by measuring general mental ability as such. Let us examine this situation more closely.

The expression "general mental ability" (or its near synonym "general intelligence") is widely used today. But exactly what does it mean? One writer defines intelligence as a summation of learning experiences (Wesman, 1968, p. 267). Another says that this term "characteristically designates that combination of abilities required for survival or advancement within a particular culture or subculture" (Anastasi, 1968, p. 293). Still another believes that, along with the strictly cognitive aspects of general mental ability, one must consider heavily "two additional factors; namely, (1) creativity and (2) resistance to emotional or other forces that distort the process of reasoning" (Stoddard, 1966).

These are but three of the multitude of definitions that have been proposed. The fact that they differ at least slightly among themselves and that other definitions differ to some degree from them does not now concern us. The important factor is their similarity. No matter which definition one may choose as most suitable, general mental ability is clearly a less obvious human trait than others such as height and weight. In short, it is a trait that cannot be seen, touched, or handled in a direct manner.

To appreciate the relatively obscure nature of general mental ability, we need only recall how most individuals estimate informally, without the use of instruments, the general mental ability of their acquaintances. Rare is the person who has not identified a number of his acquaintances as having less mental ability than himself. Possibly (and with less certainty, perhaps) this same person also has classified a few of his acquaintances as having more mental ability than himself. How does he arrive at these decisions? Obviously he examines each acquaintance in terms of those aspects and products of his behavior that seemingly reflect the amount of general mental ability present. In other words, the behavior patterns and their products are assumed to be some of the effects of general mental ability.

Ordinarily informal estimates of general mental ability are based on such information as the academic or financial accomplishments of the person, his facility for quickly and correctly identifying the salient point of a humorous story, or perhaps his ability to carry on an interesting conversation. In addition, there may be numerous known instances in which he did or did not seem to "catch on" very rapidly. Although these pieces of information may not be representative of a person's behavior nor directly and completely related to variations in general mental ability, judgment is nevertheless rendered.

Formal attempts to measure general mental ability resemble these informal attempts in one respect. They too evaluate general mental ability in terms of its effects. Observable behavior thought to be directly related to general mental ability is identified, and the trait is measured indirectly by evaluating the observable behavior in some way.

A few of the common types of behavior sometimes used in this measurement are the ability to solve arithmetic problems, to identify the meanings of English words, spatial ability,[1] and the ability to solve number series problems.[2] If a pupil is "gifted," he should be able to answer correctly difficult questions concerning areas such as those mentioned. If he is "average," he should be able to answer correctly many of the pertinent questions in these areas but not the very difficult ones. If he is "dull," he should be able to answer correctly only the very easy questions and may find even these troublesome. Hence, by measuring a pupil's abilities to answer questions in suitable areas, the teacher can infer his general mental ability.

Observe that in this approach an important assumption is made. It is assumed that there is a direct and unchanging relationship between the general mental ability of a pupil and his ability to answer questions in the areas mentioned. If this assumption is not true, the indirect measurement procedure is worthless. Moreover, if the ability to answer these questions is an effect of only certain aspects of general mental ability, then any measurement of general mental ability based only on the type of questions mentioned is incomplete.

Indirect measurement procedures are common. Temperatures are ordinarily measured indirectly by means of a mercury thermometer. When temperatures rise, the column of mercury expands; when they fall, the column of mercury contracts. Traffic congestion and dangerous highway conditions are measured indirectly by means of automobile speed limits. When congestion is serious or when highway conditions are dangerous, speed limits are lowered; when the reverse is true, speed limits are raised. Aspects of a pupil's personal-social adjustment are inferred from his written answers to questions about himself. For example, he may be asked to respond with a "Yes," "Uncertain," or "No" to a question such as: "Are you frequently afraid of adults?" If he answers affirmatively it is assumed that his personal-social adjustment is probably less satisfactory than if he had answered negatively. Attempts have even been made to determine how well a pupil can apply what he has learned by asking him to recite what he has learned. Presumably, the more information he can recall, the better he can apply it. Changes in a pupil's

---

[1] Spatial ability can be evaluated by determining whether a pupil can visualize how a geometric figure will look after it has been rotated or how it will look after it has been divided and the parts reassembled in different positions.

[2] A typical number series problem is the following:
The numbers in the following series proceed according to some rule. Select the next number from among the five possibilities listed.

Series	Next number
6 7 10 11 14 15 18	17 18 19 20 21

attitudes and appreciations have been estimated by rating changes in the pupil's overt behavior in the classroom or on the playground. Changes there have been interpreted to represent deep-seated, perhaps permanent changes, which will be manifested in the home or, in later years, in a vocation.

The commonness of indirect measurement procedures does not mean that they are necessarily desirable. Indirect procedures should be used only when direct procedures cannot be applied. The repeated use of indirect measurement procedures in education stems from the fact that direct ones are often impossible or at least impractical. Psychological traits must be inferred on the basis of specified observable phenomena. Measurement of such characteristics of a pupil as general mental ability, interests, attitudes, and many aspects of achievement is therefore complicated.

Problem

10.   Which of the following can be best classified as direct measurement and which as indirect measurement?
   a. Determining by means of an odometer the distance an automobile travels.
   b. Determining the speed of a sprinter by using a stopwatch to measure the time needed to run 100 yards.
   c. Determining the quality of a university library by counting the number of volumes it contains.
   d. Determining the adequacy of a pupil's vision with a letter chart.
   e. Determining the teaching effectiveness of an instructor with a paper-and-pencil opinionnaire administered to his pupils.
   f. Determining a pupil's ability to subtract two whole numbers (with a minuend less than ten) by means of a criterion-referenced test (Hively and others, 1968).

ACCURACY OF MEASUREMENT PROCEDURES

A carpenter building a new house continually varies the accuracy of his measurement according to the need, and chooses his measuring instruments on that basis. For instance, as he assembles rough scaffoldings to assist in the construction, he probably cuts the board needed at points found by estimating the desired lengths. The angles of the cuts are not drawn but are also estimated. When cutting the joists, however, he uses a steel rule to measure lengths, and no greater than one-eighth of an inch error is allowed. Also, the right angles at the ends of the joists are not the result of estimation, but are drawn by a carpenter's square. Finally, when cutting the interior trim, he now uses the most precise of steel rules to measure length, allowing no more than one-sixteenth of an inch error.

Typically, the classroom teacher also varies the degree of accuracy of his measurement procedures as his purposes change. The measurement of general mental ability again offers a convenient illustration. In the first place, a teacher certainly wants to know whether each pupil in his class has a certain minimum amount of this trait so he can profit from the learning experiences offered. This need be only rough measurement for most pupils. Later the teacher may want to know whether each pupil is achieving in proportion to his capacity to learn. Such a classification of each pupil as an underachiever, normal achiever, or overachiever requires considerably greater accuracy of measurement of general mental ability as well as academic achievement. Determination of amount of overachievement or underachievement demands still greater accuracy.

Finally, certain pupils may be in competition for a highly specialized and technical training program to be started after completion of secondary school. Assume that the majority of pupils who are not qualified or interested are initially eliminated, and that only a few of the remaining pupils are to be chosen. Under these conditions, selecting those pupils who, because of their talents and earlier successes, have the greatest chance of success in such a program will demand even more sensitive measurements of general mental ability, prior achievement, and probably other factors.

The carpenter has an important advantage over the teacher in the matter of accuracy of measurement. The accuracy of his measurement by modern tools comfortably surpasses the minimal accuracy required. He could determine the length of a joist to one-sixteenth or one thirty-second of an inch if it were necessary. The teacher is confronted with a relatively low ceiling above which his accuracy of measurement has not, as yet, reached. For example, when measuring general mental ability, a teacher must be satisfied with identifying a pupil's mental ability test score, which probably does not differ from his true mental ability score by more than five or six points. We simply do not possess instruments that can measure psychological traits with refined accuracy.

Level of Measurement Accuracy

What then, you may ask, is the level of accuracy teachers typically encounter in their measurement attempts? In the first place, the accuracy of measurement procedures varies with pupil traits being investigated. Secondly, although the accuracy available to teachers is considerably less than ideal, it is often sufficient to account the procedure highly useful. These facts are herewith elaborated.

Accuracy Varies with Traits.   That the level of accuracy should vary with the pupil trait being investigated is certainly understandable. Some traits are reasonably well-defined. Perhaps they have been studied more intensively than others, or perhaps they lend themselves more readily to measurement. Accordingly, mental ability is repeatedly mentioned as an area in which the accuracy of measurement procedures is relatively high, though far from perfect. Somewhat the same is said of the procedures used for measuring academic achievement, especially the measuring of a pupil's ability to recall information. After all, it is not difficult to determine a pupil's ability to recall the year in which the Battle of Hastings was fought, to spell properly the word "parallel," or to find the product of 7 and 8.

The accuracy of the measurement procedures used in such relatively simple instances as those above is superior. Furthermore, well-developed standardized tests permit assessment in quantitative units that are of equal or near-equal size. In other words, a difference of one unit between two amounts is the same or essentially the same as a difference of one unit between any other two amounts, just as a difference of one pound between two given weights is the same as a difference of one pound between any other two given weights. Measuring instruments yielding scores that have equal units are classified as interval scales (Selltiz and others, 1959, pp. 186–198).

In contrast, consider efforts to measure aspects of a pupil's personal-social adjustment or the degree to which educational objectives pertaining to changes in attitudes and appreciations have been achieved. Now the pupil traits are subtle, almost nebulous. Such irrelevant factors as "lip service" and tendency to conform to majority opinion on the part of the pupil cloud the measurement attempts. Accuracy here is appreciably less than in measurement of general mental ability. To determine the amounts of some of these traits possessed by a pupil is often impossible. Our measuring procedures may yield information of such a crude nature that ranking the pupils within a group is the most accurate representation of the individual differences that is justified. For instance, Sammy's ability to cooperate willingly with his peers in completing various projects of mutual interest may be observably superior to Sandra's; her ability in this respect may be judged to surpass Jimmy's. Hence Sammy is ranked first, Sandra second, and Jimmy third. Unfortunately, we are not at all certain that Sammy surpasses Sandra to the same degree that she surpasses Jimmy. The intervals between successive ranks are not necessarily equal; thus ranking (that is, the ordinal scale of measurement) is clearly a less precise representation of individual differences than determination of amounts.

All too frequently, crudeness of the information produced by measuring procedures prevents us from even ranking pupils. Instead we must be content with a somewhat general verbal description. For example, instead of ranking Sammy first with respect to his ability to cooperate willingly with his peers our measuring procedures may be so imprecise that the teacher can say only that he "cooperates frequently," or "usually displays little reluctance when the opportunity to cooperate is presented." Verbal descriptions of this type obviously are less precise representations of individual differences than the ranking of members of a group. Classifying pupils in terms of categories that have no apparent sense of order is known as the nominal scale of measurement.

Usefulness of Available Accuracy.   So many negative statements can be written about accuracy of educational measurements that you may well wonder whether the measurement movement has actually "moved" at all. Certainly lack of absolute accuracy is disturbing. Yet sufficient accuracy may exist to justify the statement that measuring procedures are some of the most useful tools a teacher has. To obtain a realistic picture of accuracy of educational measuring instruments and utility of these instruments for classroom teachers, let us examine a comparable situation in meteorology.

In many respects, the teacher views his measurement results as the farmer views the weather forecasts. The success of both parties depends in part on accurate and timely evaluation results. Both recognize that their information is not totally accurate nor even timely in all instances. Both can supplement the reports with their own judgments and speculations, according to their experience.

The farmer generally follows the weather forecasts closely. They help him select dates for planting, cultivating, and harvesting his crop. He is quite aware of their inaccuracies, particularly in the case of the thirty-day forecasts, which predict the temperature and precipitation for the following month. They are couched in general terms. But they represent a bold attempt. Short-term forecasts of one or two days are doubtful enough and, in the case of measurable precipitation, are often stated in terms of probabilities. And the thirty-day forecasts are considerably less accurate despite the fact that they claim to predict only general trends. Even knowing this, the farmer rarely ignores either the long-range or the short-range weather forecasts for they represent a sizable improvement over his own forecasts made without the help of the meteorologist. Their utility is unquestioned.

The informed classroom teacher is in much the same position as the farmer, and recognizes the inaccuracies of the results produced by educational measurement procedures. But he must ask himself the question: "Can the information yielded by these procedures, inaccurate though it is, tell me more about the pupil than I can discover by any other means?" Frequently the answer is in the affirmative. Many instruments can reveal consistently more accurate information than the most popular alternative method, namely, informal judgments by the teacher. Teacher judgments of pupils, like the farmer's own weather predictions, can be exceedingly accurate in a given instance and should be continually made, but they should be used in conjunction with, rather than independently of, evaluation procedures. As a teacher searches for information about his pupils he should use every means at his disposal, such as standardized tests, interviews, and rating scales, and he should be keenly aware of the accuracy of the information that each furnishes.

Problems

11. Classify each of the following in terms of the level of measurement (that is, nominal, ordinal, or interval) that they represent.
    a. Temperature in terms of the Celsius scale
    b. Scores from a well-developed achievement test
    c. Zip code numbers
    d. Dog show results
    e. Social security numbers
    f. Hardness of metals as determined by the Mohs scale of hardness, that is, the ability of minerals to scratch one another.

12. There is a fourth level of measurement known as the ratio level. In addition to having equal intervals, like the interval level, it is characterized by an absolute zero (Selltiz and others, 1959, pp. 194–195). A zero reading means that zero amount exists of the characteristic being measured. Cite illustrations of this level of measurement within the realm of educational measurement.

13. If a measuring instrument has a low degree of validity, it habitually overestimates or underestimates the amount of the characteristic being measured (see page 305). Does it follow that a low level of validity is nothing more than a low level of accuracy?

PUPIL EVALUATION TODAY

Pupil evaluation as we practice it today can be conveniently divided into two areas; namely, evaluation of achievement and evaluation of aptitudes. The former is the larger of the two and, in many ways, much more complex.

Evaluation of Achievement

Pupil achievement is subdivided into three categories or domains: cognitive, affective, and psychomotor. The first is typically called academic achievement, the second the development of personal-social adjustment, and the third the development of motor skills.

Academic achievement means pupil achievement in all curriculum areas except physical development, emotional development, and ethical behavior. It has a very heavy verbal and mathematical orientation. Hence its evaluation procedures include a wide variety of paper-and-pencil tests, performance tests, and nontesting procedures. Evaluation of academic achievement should be as broad and varied as the educational objectives from which it springs, yet in practice it relies heavily on paper-and-pencil tests, most of which are classroom rather than standardized tests. Improving these tests by significant degrees is one of the most serious tasks of the classroom teacher.

The importance of the evaluation of academic achievement cannot be overestimated. Considerable attention has been given to achievement evaluation problems by measurement specialists, and properly so. Tens of standardized achievement test batteries have been developed for all grade levels with the exception of the primary grades. Their popularity with teachers and counselors has steadily increased in recent years.

Evaluating a pupil's personal-social adjustment is not the same as evaluating his personality. Personality is an all-encompassing entity, the sum total of all the individual's psychological characteristics. Thus it includes his abilities, emotions, motives, attitudes, interests, and whatever remains of all his past experiences. Evaluating a pupil's personality, then, includes evaluation of the other two categories of achievement and evaluation of aptitudes. In contrast, the evaluation of personal-social adjustment is intended to represent a miscellaneous category containing those evaluation activities not included in the classifications mentioned.

Useful techniques in the evaluation of personal-social adjustment include attitude inventories, interest inventories, any teacher ratings of such pupil characteristics as "emotional maturity," and "cooperativeness," any paper-and-pencil personality inventories, sociometric devices, and self-rating scales. Projective techniques, such as Murray's *Thematic Apperception Test* (often called the *TAT*) and the *Rorschach Inkblot Test*, definitely belong in this category, but receive minor mention in this book because they are essentially clinical instruments. Home visitations, interviews, and analyses of autobiographies and anecdotal records are also a part of this area of evaluation.

Evaluation of Aptitudes

An aptitude is a person's capacity to learn. Hence, the instruments included in the evaluation of aptitude are designed to predict the achievement that would occur if a pupil were given proper training. Both general and specific aptitudes have been the focal points of testing attempts, many of which produced paper-and-pencil instruments. Tests of general mental ability are the most common of the general aptitude tests; a clerical aptitude test, a nursing aptitude test, or a musical aptitude test typify testing for a much more specific aptitude.

Occasionally there is some confusion about the titles of aptitude tests. For instance, when considered in a broad sense, the expression "scholastic aptitude" cannot be considered as synonymous with the expressions "general mental ability" or "general intelligence." However, within the realm of paper-and-pencil aptitude testing, the expressions "scholastic aptitude test," "general mental ability test," and "general intelligence test" can be considered as essentially the same. They often have highly similar content and the same primary purpose, namely, to predict future academic success in school work.

Also, there is some doubt about the difference between scholastic aptitude and academic achievement tests. In terms of the definitions, the evaluation of scholastic aptitude and the evaluation of academic achievement are distinctly different. Whereas the purpose of the latter is to reveal a pupil's accomplishments as of a particular moment, the purpose of the former is to predict those that the pupil can achieve with suitable training. From this point, the differentiation becomes fuzzy. For instance, the difference between an achievement test and an aptitude test in terms of *test content* is virtually nonexistent. The best way to predict how well a pupil will perform in the future in a given area is to adopt the time-proven procedure of examining how well he performed in the past in that area or a similar area. Thus a scholastic aptitude test designed to predict future academic achievement might contain test items that could be found in an arithmetic achievement test or an English vocabulary test. Moreover, it is evident that a given test could serve both functions. For example, a reading test measuring speed comprehension may be used as an achievement test for sixth-grade pupils or as an aptitude test to predict their achievement in junior high school in such subjects as English and social studies. In short, aptitude tests differ from achievement tests in terms of purpose, but not necessarily in content. Both measure what a pupil has learned, and they often measure with similar process and content (Wesman, 1968).

Today we have tests designed to measure verbal and quantitative aspects of scholastic aptitude, others designed to measure primary mental abilities, such as memory, reasoning, and word fluency, and still others to measure differential aptitudes such as verbal reasoning, numerical ability, mechanical reasoning, and clerical speed and accuracy. Add to these the many stenographic, artistic, musical, and mechanical aptitude tests, as well as aptitude tests for academic subject matter areas such as reading and mathematics, which often are identified as readiness tests or prognostic tests. Such is the list of tools available to help the teacher know his pupils better. Such great strides during considerably less than one hundred years are indeed remarkable.

The Evaluation Movement Today

The principal developments that have contributed to pupil evaluation today have occurred since 1900. This fact more than any other clearly reveals the relative immaturity that characterizes the evaluation movement in psychology and education. Admittedly, modern efforts are less accurate and consistent than we might wish. The physical sciences far outstrip the behavioral sciences in ability to measure the phenomena being studied. Now time can be measured by means of a thallium-beam clock, which is even more accurate than the cesium-beam clock developed only a few years ago. Lasers can make automatic length measurements with an accuracy of 1.8 parts in 10^9. Such refinements as these allow us to make even greater technological advances in the space age. Educational advances are less impressive by far. Yet, instead of being disappointed in the inability of behavioral sciences to match physical sciences in measuring, we should be impressed by the fact that evaluation in the behavioral sciences has progressed so far in so short a time.

Pupil evaluation is now an important activity of the school and of most teachers who compose its permanent staff. No one knows how many standardized tests are administered each year in the schools of the United States, but we are certain that the number exceeds 150 million per year and is rapidly approaching 200 million. The number of teacher-constructed tests given annually cannot even be estimated, but must be many times the foregoing figure.

The merits of pupil evaluation are by no means universally acclaimed today. The history of the movement displays the familiar "pendulum" process. The popularity and general acceptance of the movement wax and wane, and the net result is that well-read teachers have come to realize that these tools are but means to an end and are imperfect even though indispensable. Thorough knowledge of the basic principles of evaluation is not only a necessary prerequisite to understanding and capitalizing on today's tools but also a necessary preparation for tomorrow's progress.

Problems

14. Beginning with World War I, trace the role of the armed services in the development of standardized aptitude tests of all kinds (Linden and Linden, 1968).

15. Do you think that the general public is well informed about general mental ability testing? What are the attitudes of various social groups toward this type of testing? Compare your opinions on the foregoing with data from two national surveys that explored American beliefs in this area (Brim, Glass, and Neulinger, 1969).

SUMMARY

Educational evaluation is the systematic process of determining effectiveness of educational endeavors in the light of evidence. Its four principal uses are (1) to appraise academic achievement of the individual pupil, (2) to diagnose his learning difficulties, (3) to appraise the effectiveness of educational programs and products, and (4) to assess the educational progress of a large population. The first two uses constitute pupil evaluation.

The nature of pupil evaluation and its function stem from individual differences. The fact that pupils can and do differ from each other in terms of physiological and psychological traits automatically makes it necessary for a teacher to be familiar with the kinds and amounts of such differences to be able to teach successfully.

The purposes of pupil evaluation are twofold: first, it helps the teacher evaluate the degree to which educational objectives have been achieved; secondly, it helps the teacher know his pupils to such a degree that educational experiences can be planned according to their varied interests, aptitudes, and prior experiences. Ideally, educational objectives should be stated in terms of the nature of the specific pupil behavior that will be displayed when they have been achieved.

The procedures used in pupil evaluation are varied. They include paper-and-pencil tests, ranking and rating scales, performance tests, anecdotal records, questionnaires, interviewing techniques, autobiographies, and sociometric procedures. The purpose of these and other evaluative methods is to provide information so that decisions can be made as to whether the changes in pupil behavior that have occurred are compatible with pertinent educational objectives.

Educational measurement and educational evaluation are not synonymous expressions. Measurement is the process that attempts to obtain a quantitative representation of the degree to which a pupil reflects a trait. Educational evaluation is a process in which a teacher commonly uses information derived from many sources to arrive at a value judgment. The information may be obtained by using measuring instruments and also other techniques that do not necessarily yield quantitative results, such as questionnaires and interviews.

Seventeen different types of tests are briefly described. They are divided into seven subdivisions, each of which contains two or three contrasting types. The subdivisions are: individual and group tests; classroom and standardized tests; oral, essay, and objective tests; speed, power, and mastery tests; verbal, nonverbal, and performance tests; readiness and diagnostic tests; and norm-referenced and criterion-referenced tests. A given test can be simultaneously classified in more than one of these subgroups. For example, an achievement test may be a group, standardized, objective, power, verbal test.

Educational measurement methods can be characterized by two features. First of all they are primarily indirect rather than direct. The pupil traits are appraised in terms of their effects, rather than in terms of the traits themselves. Secondly, measurement procedures are not remarkably accurate in terms of any absolute standards, but are dependable enough to be usable. The classroom teacher repeatedly discovers that his measuring instruments, inaccurate as they may be, reveal more information about pupils than any other techniques at his disposal.

Pupil evaluation can be conveniently divided into two areas: evaluation of achievement and evaluation of aptitudes. Evaluation of achievement includes those techniques designed to measure the degree to which educational objectives have been achieved. Included are objectives pertaining to the cognitive, affective, and psychomotor domains. Aptitude evaluation is designed to predict achievement that would occur if the pupil were given proper training.

Suggested Readings

Brim, O. G., Jr., D. C. Glass, and J. Neulinger. *American beliefs and attitudes about intelligence.* New York: Russell Sage Foundation, 1969.
> Two national surveys—one of adults and one of secondary school pupils—were conducted in order to determine attitudes toward intelligence and intelligence testing. Various group comparisons are reported. In general, the public lacks information about intelligence testing.

Chauncey, Henry, and J. E. Dobbin. *Testing: its place in education today.* New York: Harper & Row, 1963. Chapters 1, 2, and 3.
> The purpose of this book is to provide a broad picture of what testing in schools is all about. The first three chapters deal with the history of the testing movement, the nature of mental ability tests, and the nature of achievement tests. These chapters are comparatively brief and well written.

Cronbach, L. J. *Essentials of psychological testing.* (3rd ed.) New York: Harper & Row, 1970. Chapters 1 and 2.
> The first chapter is devoted to a brief discussion of the use of psychological tests. The second chapter includes a definition of a psychological test and a classification of tests into main types.

Ebel, R. L. Inventories and tests. *Education,* 1960, 81, 67–99.
> Eight critical questions about the use of tests are posed. These deal with instruments for measuring achievement, aptitude, and personal-social adjustment. Answers to the questions have been prepared by six testing experts and are summarized in eight separate articles, each devoted to one of the eight questions.

Ebel, R. L. Measurement in education. In R. L. Ebel (ed.), *Encyclopedia of educational research.* (4th ed.) London: Macmillan, 1969. Pp. 777–785.
> This article has broad scope. Included in it are such subtopics as history of educational measurement, measurement literature, nature and method of measurement, and public and professional attitudes toward measurement in education. A useful bibliography of 170 references has been compiled.

Linden, K. W., and J. D. Linden. *Modern mental measurement: A historical perspective.* Boston: Houghton Mifflin, 1968.
> Using slightly more than one hundred pages, the authors describe the history of educational testing in a reasonably comprehensive manner. The development of mental ability tests and their use receive considerable attention.

Thomas, R. M., and S. M. Thomas. *Individual differences in the classroom.* New York: David McKay, 1965. Chapters 1, 2, and 3.

The general problem of individual differences in the classroom is treated in the first two chapters. The next seven chapters deal with intellectual differences among pupils. Chapter 3 is the first of this group and is a discussion of the recognition and measurement of these differences.

Tyler, L. E. *Tests and measurement.* (2nd ed.) Englewood Cliffs, N.J.: Prentice-Hall, 1971. Chapter 1.

The first chapter of this paperback has two major topics: the need for quantification in the study of human behavior and the four levels of measurement. The discussion of each is brief but effective.

Tyler, R. W. *Basic principles of curriculum and instruction.* Chicago: University of Chicago Press, 1949 (1969 impression).

This book is a classic. Although written more than two decades ago, it still is considered a most lucid statement of the nature of educational objectives, the organization of learning experiences in terms of them, and the evaluation of the effectiveness of these learning experiences.

Tyler, R. W. (ed.) *Educational evaluation: New roles, new means.* Sixty-Eighth Yearbook of the National Society for the Study of Education, Part II. Chicago: University of Chicago Press, 1969. Chapters 2, 3, 13, and 16.

The topic of evaluation is treated in the broadest terms in this volume. A historical review is given in Chapter 2, whereas certain theoretical issues are reviewed in Chapter 3. Chapter 13 is a description of the National Assessment of Educational Progress. Lastly, ways of strengthening program and product evaluation are considered in Chapter 16.

References Cited

Anastasi, Anne. *Psychological testing.* (3rd ed.) London: Macmillan, 1968.

Bloom, B. S. Learning for mastery. UCLA CSEIP *Evaluation Comment,* 1968, 1, No. 2.

Brim, O. G., Jr., D. C. Glass, and J. Neulinger. *American beliefs and attitudes about intelligence.* New York: Russell Sage Foundation, 1969.

Campbell, V. N., and D. G. Nichols. National assessment of citizenship education. *Social Education,* 1968, **32**, 279–281.

Cronbach, L. J. Evaluation for course improvement. *Teachers College Record,* 1963, **64**, 672–683.

Cronbach, L. J. *Essentials of psychological testing.* (3rd ed.) New York: Harper & Row, 1970.

Finley, C. J. National assessment begins. *Education Summary,* March 1, 1969, 5–6.

Fors, G. (ed.) *Science guide.* Bismarck, N.D.: North Dakota Department of Public Instruction, 1969.

Gagné, R. M. *The conditions of learning.* (2nd ed.) New York: Holt, Rinehart and Winston, 1970.

Glaser, R., and A. J. Nitko. Measurement in learning and instruction. In R. L. Thorndike (ed.), *Educational measurement.* (2nd ed.) Washington: American Council on Education, 1970. Chapter 17.

Hand, H. National assessment viewed as the camel's nose. *Phi Delta Kappan,* 1965, **47**, 8–13.

Hively, W., H. L. Patterson and S. H. Pope. A "universe-defined" system of arithmetic achievement tests. *Journal of Educational Measurement*, 1968, **5**, 275–290.

Katzman, M. T., and R. S. Rosen. The science and politics of national educational assessment. *Teachers College Record*, 1970, **71**, 571–586.

Levine, H. G., and C. McGuire. Role-playing as an evaluative technique. *Journal of Educational Measurement*, 1968, **5**, 1–8.

Linden, K. W., and J. D. Linden. *Modern mental measurement: A historical perspective*. Boston: Houghton Mifflin, 1968.

Merwin, J. C., and F. B. Womer. Evaluation in assessing the progress of education to provide bases of public understanding and public policy. In R. W. Tyler (ed.), *Educational evaluation: New roles, new means*. Sixty-Eighth Yearbook of the National Society for the Study of Education, Part II. Chicago: University of Chicago Press, 1969. Pp. 305–334.

Milton O. "What it is . . . I measure I do not know." *Educational Record*, 1968, **49**, 160–165.

Popham, W. J., and T. R. Husek. Implications of criterion-referenced measurement. *Journal of Educational Measurement*, 1969, 6, 1–9.

Saylor, G. National assessment: Pro and con. *Teachers College Record*, 1970, **71**, 588–597.

Scriven, M. The methodology of evaluation. *AERA Monograph Series on Curriculum Evaluation*, 1967, No. 1. Pp. 39–83.

Selltiz, C., and others. *Research methods in social relations*. (Rev. ed.) New York: Holt, Rinehart and Winston, 1959.

Stake, R. E. The countenance of educational evaluation. *Teachers College Record*, 1967, **68**, 523–540.

Stoddard, G. D. On the meaning of intelligence. *Proceedings of the 1965 Invitational Conference on Testing Problems*. Princeton: Educational Testing Service, 1966. Pp. 3–11.

Stufflebeam, D. L. *Evaluation as enlightenment for decision-making*. Columbus: Evaluation Center, Ohio State University, January 19, 1968.

Trow, W. C. Grades and objectives in higher education. *Educational Record*, 1968, **49**, 85–91.

Tyler, R. W. The objectives and plans for a national assessment of educational progress. *Journal of Educational Measurement*, 1966, **3**, 1–4.

Tyler, R. W. *Basic principles of curriculum and evaluation*. Chicago: University of Chicago Press, 1949 (1969 impression).

Wesman, A. G. Intelligent testing. *American Psychologist*, 1968, **23**, 267–274.

CHAPTER 2

Educational Objectives
in Pupil Evaluation

In one of his many public statements, Oliver Wendell Holmes once mused:

> . . . Men often remind me of pears in their way of coming to maturity. Some
> are ripe at 20 . . . and must be made the most of, for their day is soon over.
> Some come into their perfect condition late, like the autumn kinds, and they
> last better than the summer fruit. And some, that, like Winter-Nelis, have been
> hard and uninviting until all the rest have had their season, get their glow and
> perfume long after the frost and snow have done their worst with the orchards.
> Beware of rash criticisms; the rough and stringent fruit you condemn may be an
> autumn or a winter pear, and that which you picked up beneath the bow in
> August may have been only its worm-eaten windfalls.

So it is with the achievement of life's goals. Each of us organizes his life
around them. A few are attained comparatively early in life, some later, and
still others not at all.

The sources of these goals are difficult if not impossible to trace. It is
clear, however, that they stem from the needs that each of us experiences. The
goals are direct outgrowths of social needs, such as the need for recognition,
prestige, power, security, and companionship. The physiological needs such as
hunger and thirst must also be included.

The nature of personal goals and also their relative importance will vary
among individuals, but practically all can be classified into categories such as
vocational, recreational, social, educational, and religious. This should not suggest that a goal in one category is independent of goals in any other. For
example, an educational goal of acquiring a bachelor's degree from a first-class
university may be closely related to a vocational goal of becoming a licensed
physician. Again, a recreational goal of raising a bowling average to 175 pins
per game may well be a part of a social goal of enlarging one's circle of friends.

At least for his more important goals each person organizes, formally or informally, programs that should lead him ever closer to them. Some may have tentative termination dates; others may not. They may differ in terms of the degree to which they are structured. Programs for educational and vocational goals are, for the most part, based on formal schooling. Those for recreational and social goals may be designed by the individual and quite casual.

It is only reasonable that a person following a program would be concerned about his progress toward the intended goal. He may search for evidence that will identify his present position. For example, in the case of the educational goal mentioned, evidence would include number of college credit hours accumulated and the grade-point average achieved; in the case of the bowling goal, it would be the bowling average for the past several games. With pieces of evidence such as these in mind, he can compare his present position with his initial position when the program began and with his goal. These two reference points allow him to evaluate the growth he has made.

Elementary and secondary schools contribute in a very substantial and basic way to the attainment of goals by the pupils enrolled in them. Educational objectives are established on the basis of pupils' needs that have been identified. School programs are designed to help pupils reach these goals and thereby learn how to satisfy their needs. Lastly, the teacher and the pupil evaluate the degree to which the pupil has achieved the educational objectives. Evaluation reveals the status of the pupil to him, his teacher, and his parents, and also contributes to any attempt to improve the school's program.

To appreciate fully the importance of pupil evaluation and the complexity of its mechanics, one should examine with some care the other aspects of the teaching process associated with it. Full treatment of these topics can be found in many books devoted to curriculum development, methods of teaching, and educational psychology. It is appropriate here, however, to review briefly one of these topics—the identification of the needs of youth and the society in which they live, and the manner in which these serve as sources of educational objectives (Tyler, 1964). Only after this can a discussion of the degree to which pupils have achieved educational goals be meaningful.

IDENTIFYING THE NEEDS OF YOUTH

The needs of youth have been repeatedly investigated by psychologists and educators. Although the particular methods of inquiry used have varied appreciably, each can be classified under one of two general categories, the individual approach and the social approach (Low, 1953, pp. 30–38). The first category includes methods that concentrate on a study of each youth as an individual, whereas the second category includes methods that try to identify the needs of youth by first analyzing the democratic society in which they live. The differences between the two categories are not so great as superficial inspection would lead one to believe.

Individual Approach

The methods in the individual approach attempt to identify the needs of youth by first studying the child as he is at a given moment and comparing his development with the behavior society expects him to display as an adult. The differences between his status of immaturity and society's standards for adulthood constitute his needs, whether or not he recognizes them at the moment. Studies of the status of youth at various ages have often been longitudinal in design and have characterized young people with regard to their physical, intellectual, and social development. From these findings has come a picture, inadequate as it may be, of the behavioral patterns and levels of maturation of typical children of a stated age with respect to these kinds of development.

To discover the kind of adult that society believes each child should become is no less difficult. Nevertheless, statements of authoritative tone have been formulated by a number of state, regional, and national organizations. The contents of the various statements resemble each other more than they differ, which may be due in part to the fact that some may have influenced others. A considerably more potent influence toward similarity is that all statements reflect to a substantial degree their authors' belief in a democratic society in which the individual is the dominant element.

Social Approach

The methods of inquiry included in the social approach attempt to discover the needs of youth by identifying first the present status of the democratic society in which the individual lives, and then the goals that this society is to reach. The differences between the present position and the desired goals represent the needs of society and thus the needs of society's youth. This approach is based on the assumption that each member of a democratic society must perpetuate and improve that society. His needs, then, can be traced to any deficiencies in his behavior patterns that in turn would prevent the democratic society from achieving its goals.

Evident at this point is the difficulty of separating the personal needs of youth from the needs of a democratic society. Personal needs are, after all, guided and molded by society. Youth living in a democratic society will have needs different from those of youth living in some other type of society. More-over, it can be argued that a democratic society achieves its goals only insofar as the needs of its members are appropriately satisfied. In other words, the members of a democratic society are obligated to serve it, and the society exists to serve them. The personal needs of youth and the broader needs of a democratic society are thus reciprocal in nature (Brink, 1953, p. 4).

Needs of Youth

Whether based upon the individual or upon democratic society as a frame of reference, the various statements of the needs of youth do not differ appreciably. Every child needs food, shelter, and rest. He also has needs related to preparation for his vocation, utilization of his leisure time, his responsibilities as a citizen, and his future role as a homemaker and parent. Furthermore, each child has needs related to the acquisition of attitudes and values that will allow him to live in harmony with himself and other members of his society. Such needs are common to all youth.

Needs of the Individual

Identification of the primary needs of youth, as those listed in the foregoing paragraph, offers a basis for identification of the individual needs of each child. Although it is true that the needs of each child are similar in many respects, studies of the needs of youth would be badly oversimplified if allow-ances were not made for other pertinent factors. One of these factors is that all children do not recognize the relative importance of each need in the same way. An almost complete unawareness of some needs may exist, for a variety of reasons. For instance, needs related to vocational goals might easily be ignored insofar as children in the primary grade levels are concerned. A second factor is the degree to which the child has already learned to satisfy his own needs. Whereas one child may fail to realize that a need exists even though it actually does, another child of similar age may be equally indifferent about that area of need because he has already learned to meet them for the most part. A fortunate amalgam of environmental influences such as the combination of home, religious, and educational environmental influences, plus an unusual amount of innate talent possessed by the individual may have been sufficient to show him how to satisfy some of his needs at an abnormally early age. Thirdly, the state of readiness of the individual is a factor. At a particular age, is he prepared to begin an educational program aimed at a given set of objectives? Is his background adequate?

Existence of these factors in no way refutes the claim that all children in a democratic society have certain general areas of need. Their influence simply accounts for the fact that, at a given moment, one individual may recognize his needs and their relative importance differently from his peers, even though all have common needs. Thus the needs of each child, although highly individualized, still fit into a pattern common to all youth.

Problems

1.   Select two school systems that you know well, preferably one in a metropolitan center and one not in such a center, and compare them in terms of the role the schools must play in the process of helping pupils learn how to satisfy their needs.
2.   Since children learn to satisfy some of their needs because of the experiences provided by agencies other than schools, and the number, type, and effectiveness of these agencies vary from community to community and state to state, on what basis can one defend a relatively rigid "state curriculum" or a "national curriculum," perhaps developed along the lines of those in some foreign countries?

TRANSLATING NEEDS INTO EDUCATIONAL OBJECTIVES

At one time the primary purpose of formal education was to teach each new generation all the knowledge that had been accumulated by all previous generations. This conception resulted in a highly rigid school curriculum that made the textbook the strongest single element in the classroom. At the present time this concept of the primary purpose of formal education has been largely superseded by another: to train pupils in such a way that they are better able to satisfy their needs (Tyler, 1953, p. 216). The kernel of this idea has been expressed by other writers in various ways. For instance, one writer said that "schools were created for the sole purpose of helping children to grow up properly" (Havighurst, 1953, p. 159). Another stated that the "major function of education is to foster, develop, and preserve democracy as a way of life" (Ahrens, 1953, p. 104). All three statements say in effect that the objectives of American schools must be derived from the needs of youth living in a democratic society.

The pertinent needs of youth are translated into educational objectives by identifying the new patterns of behavior that they must acquire to satisfy their needs. These involve development of new knowledges, intellectual abilities and skills, affective patterns, and psychomotor skills. Knowledge includes pupil behaviors that emphasize the remembering, either by recognition or recall, of ideas, material, or phenomena (Bloom, 1956, p. 62). If a pupil can comprehend the meaning of the pieces of information to the point that he can grasp the relationships among them, restate them in his own words, and take action intelligently on the basis of them, then he has developed his intellectual abilities and skills to an important degree. Affective patterns include changes in interests, attitudes, and values. These pertain to a pupil's predisposition to react in a particular manner to certain ideas, objects, people, and events. He now has "points of view"; he has feelings of attraction or aversion toward aspects of his environment. Finally, psychomotor skills are motor skills of the kind that are so vital to achievement in physical education, music, art, and industrial education, and vocations based on them.

The foregoing delineation of behavioral patterns can be neatly summarized. For purposes of convenience, the entire array of educational objectives is divided into three domains—cognitive, affective, and psychomotor; the new patterns of behavior are presented in the foregoing paragraph in that order. Taxonomies for classifying objectives have been established for each domain (see page 45) and greatly assist in reducing communication problems so often associated with objectives.

Classroom teachers and other education specialists have to examine each area of need and decide the nature of the new behavioral patterns that each pupil must develop to be able to satisfy his needs. Then they must make decisions as to how and when each pupil will be taught. Such decisions must be based on well-established principles gleaned from study of the psychology of learning. These decisions should produce a curriculum in which attainable goals, carefully keyed to the maturity levels and various backgrounds of the pupils in question, have been selected for each area of instruction. Whether goals should be established for each grade level of each curriculum area is another question, since the grading system can be thought of as little more than a convenient administrative device for grouping pupils. In any event, within a framework of educational goals every teacher should still find sufficient flexibility so that he can exploit to the best of his abilities all the learning possibilities in his field, and can do so in terms of the individual needs of his pupils as he recognizes them.

The goals of education are pupil-oriented rather than teacher-oriented. The manner in which they are stated should reflect this fact. In the not-too-distant past, educational objectives were stated in terms of the activities that the teacher was to perform. A certain topic was to be taught at a certain time in a certain manner. This was the objective, emphasizing subject matter content and the sequence in which it was to be presented. The modern way of stating educational objectives reflects the fact that they stem from pupil needs. To be consistent, therefore, educational objectives must be stated in terms of desired pupil behavior rather than in any other way.

Types of Objectives

Efforts to translate the needs of youth into educational objectives are typically directed toward producing precise statements that identify the observable changes in pupil behavior that should take place if the learning experience is successful. Unquestionably, such objectives are excellent starting points for development of the curriculum, planning of teaching strategies, and construction of testing and nontesting instruments. Nevertheless, we must recognize that the very preciseness that is so valuable may also be detrimental, in that it is difficult to identify measurable pupil behaviors in certain subject matter areas like the fine arts.

Recognition of this possibility causes some to feel that, in reality, two types of objectives exist, namely, instructional and expressive (Eisner, 1969, pp. 14–17). The former specify unambiguously the particular pupil behavior to be acquired as a result of learning. The latter do not. Expressive objectives describe "educational encounters," for instance, a situation in which pupils are to work or a problem they are to solve. These encounters are, in essence, tasks that yield pupil products—a poem, art object, or report.

Unsurprisingly, expressive objectives are most common in curriculum areas such as art, music, drama, dance, creative writing, and speech. Illustrative of this type of objective are the following:

1. The pupil will compose a poem depicting his personal impression of a brilliant sunset over the desert.
2. The pupil will interpret the meaning of Alexander Pope's *Essay on Man* and prepare a written summary of his interpretation.
3. The pupil will build an original mobile having at least five moving parts.

In each instance, the primary means of evaluating pupil performance would be the evaluation of the merits of the product he develops.

Both types of objectives are needed. On the one hand, the teacher may find that expressive objectives provide a kind of outreach for his teaching efforts that is exciting to him and his pupils. On the other hand, instructional objectives are the solid base on which he can plan his teaching and pupil evaluation. As educational outcomes become prescribable, expressive objectives are not needed and instructional objectives receive their proper emphasis. In this and the following chapters, instructional objectives are given primary attention.

Problems

3.   In a statement about the formulation of educational objectives, Louise Tyler (1969) suggests that a psychoanalytic framework be used both as a source of and

as a screen for objectives. Explain her point of view and compare it with that held by Ralph Tyler (1964).

4. In your opinion, are instructional objectives or expressive objectives more important in each of the following teaching situations:
   a. Elementary school science unit on climate.
   b. Junior high school carpentry shop.
   c. Senior high school English literature class.
   d. Senior high school marriage and family living class.

TAXONOMY OF EDUCATIONAL OBJECTIVES

Educational objectives have been classified into three domains, namely, the cognitive, affective, and psychomotor. The cognitive domain includes those educational objectives related to the recall of knowledge and the development of intellectual abilities and skills. The affective domain includes those objectives concerning changes in a pupil's emotional state, or degree of acceptance or rejection of some entity—it is the domain of personal-social adjustment. The psychomotor domain includes objectives that involve primarily muscular or motor skills, some manipulation of material and objects, or some act that requires a neuromuscular coordination (Krathwohl and others, 1964, p. 7).

Cognitive Domain

The taxonomies organized for each domain represent well the hierarchical nature of each. In the case of the cognitive domain, the main organizing principle used is degree of complexity of the cognitive process involved in the objective. Comparatively simple cognitive behaviors could combine with others of a similar nature and yield more complex pupil behaviors.

The taxonomy for the cognitive domain contains six subdivisions, and these in turn are subdivided as needed. The subdivisions are as follows (Bloom, 1956, pp. 201–207):

KNOWLEDGE

1.00 KNOWLEDGE
   The recall of specifics and universals, the recall of methods and processes, or the recall of a pattern, structure, or setting. The knowledge objectives emphasize most the psychological processes of remembering.
   1.10 Knowledge of specifics
      1.11 Knowledge of terminology
      1.12 Knowledge of specific facts

     1.20 Knowledge of ways and means of dealing with specifics
          1.21 Knowledge of conventions
          1.22 Knowledge of trends and sequences
          1.23 Knowledge of classifications and categories
          1.24 Knowledge of criteria
          1.25 Knowledge of methodology
     1.30 Knowledge of the universals and abstractions in a field
          1.31 Knowledge of principles and generalizations
          1.32 Knowledge of theories and structures

INTELLECTUAL ABILITIES AND SKILLS

2.00 COMPREHENSION

A type of understanding or apprehension such that the individual knows what is being communicated and can make use of the material or idea being communicated without necessarily relating it to other material or seeing its fullest implications.

2.10 Translation
2.20 Interpretation
2.30 Extrapolation

3.00 APPLICATION

The use of abstractions in particular and concrete situations. The abstractions may be in the form of general ideas, rules of procedures, or generalized methods.

4.00 ANALYSIS

The breakdown of a communication into its constituent elements or parts such that the relative hierarchy of ideas is made clear and/or the relations between the ideas expressed are made explicit. Such analyses are intended to clarify the communication, to indicate how the communication is organized, and the way in which it manages to convey its effects, as well as its basis and arrangement.

4.10 Analysis of elements
4.20 Analysis of relationships
4.30 Analysis of organizational principles

5.00 SYNTHESIS

The putting together of elements and parts so as to form a whole. This involves the process of working with pieces, parts, elements, etc., and arranging them in such a way as to constitute a pattern or structure not clearly there before.

5.10 Production of a unique communication
5.20 Production of a plan or proposed set of operations
5.30 Derivation of a set of abstract relations

6.00 EVALUATION

Judgments about the value of material and methods for given purposes. Quantitative and qualitative judgments about the extent to which material and methods satisfy criteria.

6.10 Judgments in terms of internal evidence
6.20 Judgments in terms of external criteria

The claim that the six levels represent a hierarchical order, that is, vary from the simple to the complex, has some empirical support (Krathwohl and Payne, 1970). Evidence verifies the ordering of the first three levels better than that of the last three.

Affective Domain

The main organizing principle used to develop the affective domain taxonomy is the process of internalization. This process is defined as "incorporating something within the mind and body; adopting as one's own the ideas, practices, standards, or values of another person or of society" (English and English, 1958, p. 272). In the case of the taxonomy, internalization is viewed as a process through which there is at first an incomplete and tentative adoption of only the overt manifestations of the behavior in question and later a more complete adoption. Hence the taxonomy represents a continuum of the behaviors implied by objectives in this domain (Krathwohl and others, 1964, pp. 29–35).

Five chief categories have been identified, each of which has two or three subdivisions as follows (Krathwohl and others, 1964, pp. 176–185):

1.00 RECEIVING (ATTENDING)
The sensitization of the learner to the existence of certain phenomena and stimuli. He is willing to receive or to attend to them. This is the first and crucial step if the learner is to be properly oriented to learn what the teacher intends that he will.
1.10 Awareness
1.20 Willingness to receive
1.30 Controlled or selected attention

2.00 RESPONDING
Pupil responses that go beyond merely attending to the phenomenon. The pupil is sufficiently motivated that he is not just willing to attend but to attend actively. This is the category that many teachers find best describes their "interest" objectives.
2.10 Acquiescence in responding
2.20 Willingness to respond
2.30 Satisfaction in response

3.00 VALUING
Recognition that a thing, phenomenon, or behavior has worth. This abstract concept of worth is in part a result of the individual's own valuing or assessment, but it is much more a social product that has been slowly internalized or accepted and has come to be used by the pupil as his own criterion of worth. This category is appropriate for many objectives using the term "attitude" and, of course, "value."
3.10 Acceptance of a value

3.20 Preference for a value
3.30 Commitment (Conviction)

4.00 ORGANIZATION
The beginnings of the building of a value system. As the learner succes-sively internalizes values, he encounters situations for which more than one value is relevant. Thus necessity arises for (a) the organization of the values into a system, (b) the determination of the interrelationships among them, and (c) the establishment of the dominant and pervasive ones.
4.10 Conceptualization of a value
4.20 Organization of a value system

5.00 CHARACTERIZATION BY A VALUE OR VALUE COMPLEX
Integration of beliefs, ideas, and attitudes into a total philosophy or world view. The values already have a place in the individual's value hierarchy, are organized into some kind of internally consistent system, have con-trolled the behavior of the individual for a sufficient time that he has adapted to behaving this way; and an evocation of the behavior no longer arouses emotion or affect except when the individual is threatened or challenged.
5.10 Generalized set
5.20 Characterization

The utility of the affective taxonomy is influenced by a number of factors. One of these is the lower level of emphasis often placed on these objectives as compared with cognitive ones. This is perplexing since, in keeping with the major objectives of education, we want pupils not only to have cognitive skills, but also to *want* to use them. Another factor is the comparatively limited knowledge we have about the affective domain in general. Such terms as *attitude, adjustment, appreciation,* and *interest* are used without being precisely defined. The range of meaning for each is so great that objectives using such terms may be classified in a variety of categories in the taxonomy (Krathwohl and others, 1964, pp. 36–38).

Psychomotor Domain

The taxonomy for the psychomotor domain is less well developed than the other two taxonomies. A significant effort made in this regard is based on the chief organizing principle of degrees of complexity in psychomotor behavior, with attention given to the sequence involved in the performance of the motor act (Simpson, 1966–67, 1969).[1] Seven major subdivisions are included.

1.00 PERCEPTION
The process of becoming aware of objects, qualities, or relations by way of the sense organs. It is a necessary but not sufficient condition for motor

[1] Reproduced by permission of Elizabeth Simpson.

activity, and is basic in the situation–interpretation–action chain leading to motor activity.

1.10 Sensory stimulation
      1.11 Auditory
      1.12 Visual
      1.13 Tactile
      1.14 Taste
      1.15 Smell
      1.16 Kinesthetic
1.20 Cue selection
1.30 Translation

2.00 SET
Preparatory adjustment or readiness for a particular kind of action or experience.
2.10 Mental set
2.20 Physical set
2.30 Emotional set

3.00 GUIDED RESPONSE
An early step in the development of skill. Emphasis is on the abilities that are components of the more complex skill. Guided response is the overt behavioral act of an individual under the guidance of the instructor or in response to self-evaluation where the pupil has a model or criterion against which he can judge his performance.
3.10 Imitation
3.20 Trial and error

4.00 MECHANISM
Achievement of a certain confidence and degree of proficiency in the performance of the act. The act is a part of the learner's repertoire of possible responses to stimuli and the demands of situations where the response is an appropriate one.

5.00 COMPLEX OVERT RESPONSE
Attainment of skill. The individual can perform a motor act that is considered complex because of the movement pattern required. The act can be carried out smoothly and efficiently.
5.10 Resolution of uncertainty
5.20 Automatic performance

6.00 ADAPTATION
Altering motor activities to meet the demands of new problematic situations requiring a physical response.

7.00 ORIGINATION
Creating new motor acts or ways of manipulating materials out of understandings, abilities, and skills developed in the psychomotor area.

Further refinement of the foregoing taxonomy is expected. This is not surprising since this one is not as "clean" as the other two, particularly the cognitive. Cognition can occur with a minimum of motor activity, and perhaps little feeling. In contrast, psychomotor activity involves both cognitive and affective influences. This seriously complicates work in the third domain (Simpson, 1966–67, pp. 117–118).

Value of the Taxonomies

The impact of the taxonomies on educational thinking is indeed powerful. As foreseen, they do assist appreciably in the task of helping teachers and other educational specialists discuss their curricular and evaluation problems with greater precision. We gain a better perspective of the relative importance of our objectives and their interrelationships by using the taxonomies as classification schemes. Also, terminology is standardized to a greater degree than ever before.

The three taxonomies represent the total framework of educational objectives for all types of educational institutions. They also represent, therefore, the total framework within which evaluation procedures are functioning. Hence, after careful study, a teacher can classify objectives pertinent to his teaching in appropriate categories, and devise a set of measurement procedures, some of which are tests, to obtain appropriate data on the basis of which evaluations can be made. Use of the taxonomies in this way adds meaning to the educational objectives and defines more sharply the limits of the scope of the pupil evaluation attempted.

Learning Hierarchies

For some purposes, the taxonomies are not sufficiently precise. For instance, the categories of the cognitive taxonomy deal with mental processes and do not recognize other significant aspects of a well-stated instructional objective. Such an objective identifies the specific overt behavior to be performed by the pupil, the conditions under which he is to perform, and the criteria of acceptable performance. Other tools than the taxonomies are needed if this kind of objective is to be formulated easily.

A categorizing system with a finer mesh has been designed by Gagné (1970, pp. 35–65). He identifies eight types of learning—eight sets of conditions under which changes in pupil behavior are brought about. They are ordered as follows:

1. Signal learning
   Making a general, diffuse response to a signal.
2. Stimulus-response learning
   Acquiring a precise response to a discriminated stimulus.

3. Chaining
   Combining two or more stimulus-response connections.
4. Verbal association
   Learning chains that are verbal.
5. Discrimination learning
   Learning to make n different identifying responses to as many different stimuli, which may resemble each other.
6. Concept learning
   Acquiring a capacity to make a common response to a class of stimuli that may differ from each other widely.
7. Rule learning
   Acquiring a chain of two or more concepts.
8. Problem solving
   Learning that requires thinking; combining two or more previously acquired rules to produce a new capability of a higher order.

The hierarchical nature of the breakdown is unmistakable. Achievement in each class depends on learning the preceding one. Thus these varieties of learning can serve as a means of conceptualizing a wide range of educational objectives.

This and other works by Gagné are basic to the preparation of a "learning hierarchy," that is, a set of component tasks that lead to the achievement of a certain educational objective. In other words, the behavioral pattern of a "major" objective of an instruction program is analyzed in terms of the pattern of tasks that must be mastered by the pupil. The tasks are ordered to form a hierarchy that can then guide teaching and pupil evaluation. Observe that the hierarchy of component tasks can be considered a hierarchy of specific objectives. We know "what comes first" when the pupil behaviors identified are ones known to exist among the pupils when instruction is to begin. Certainly this type of backward analysis is highly useful for pupil placement and for diagnosis and remediation of learning difficulties. In this regard, criterion-referenced tests are able to play a significant role (Glaser and Nitko, 1970).

The analysis of learning hierarchies, otherwise known as component task analysis, is highly complex. Its rewards are well illustrated by the results of its application in an elementary school science program known as *Science—A Process Approach* (Walbesser, 1968). The author has listed "action verbs" to be used in the formulation of instructional objectives in science. They are:

1. Identify
   Select the correct object from a set of objects.
2. Name
   Specify what an object, event, or relationship is called.
3. Order
   Arrange three or more objects or events in a sequence based on some stated property.

4. Describe
   State observable properties sufficiently to identify an object, event, or relationship.
5. Distinguish
   Select an object or event from two or more with which it might be confused.
6. Construct
   Make a physical object, drawing, or written or verbal statement.
7. Demonstrate
   Carry out a sequence of operations necessary for a stated task.
8. State a rule
   Provide a relationship or principle that can be used to solve a problem or complete a task.
9. Apply a rule
   Determine the answer to a problem by using a relationship or principle.

Use of these nine terms serves to sharpen the thrust of instructional objectives in traditional subject matter areas. It can be argued that only six are needed, namely, *identify, name, describe, construct, order,* and *demonstrate,* provided such highly specific verbs as *add, spell,* and *conjugate* are also used when appropriate (Sullivan, 1969). Be that as it may, the intent of action verbs is to focus attention directly on pupil behavior. The list should be so heterogeneous that practically every pupil behavioral pattern with heavy cognitive features could be classified under one of the terms.

Problems

5. Classify each of the following objectives in terms of the six principal levels of the taxonomy for the cognitive domain:
   a. The pupil can distinguish between related scientific concepts such as speed and acceleration, kinetic and potential energy, and mass and weight.
   b. The pupil can list the order of the steps normally followed for a bill to be passed by the U.S. Congress and become law.
   c. The pupil can apply the Pythagorean principle to practical problems such as those in carpentry.
6. Classify each of the following objectives in terms of the five principal levels of the taxonomy for the affective domain:
   a. The pupil finds pleasure in the investigation of natural phenomena such as the activity of an ant colony or tankful of tropical fish.
   b. The pupil develops awareness of aesthetic aspects of his style of dress.
   c. The pupil voluntarily reads for pleasure articles in magazines designed for his age group.
7. Classify each of the following objectives in terms of the seven principal levels of the psychomotor domain:
   a. The pupil can type "smooth-copy" prose at a minimum speed of 40 words per minute (after adjustment for errors) using an electric typewriter.
   b. The pupil can assume the proper bodily stance for driving a golf ball.
   c. The pupil can prepare a small two-cycle gasoline engine for use and start it.

LEVELS OF EDUCATIONAL OBJECTIVES

Even the most casual examination of educational objectives reveals that they vary widely in terms of their degree of specificity. Some are "general" objectives, that is, statements of the main aims or ultimate goals of the educational system. One example is the goal that every pupil become a good citizen and function as such throughout his life. In contrast to the global nature of this, consider the myriads of sub-objectives that such a goal can generate. These can be highly specific as in the case of those dealing with a pupil's ability to distinguish among *to, too,* and *two,* or to add accurately any combination of two integers, neither of which is greater than ten.

At least three main levels of objectives can be established (Krathwohl and Payne, 1970). The first is the most abstract and deals with long-term goals like vocational efficiency or self-realization. The second level, derived from the first, is more concrete and represents objectives to be attained by pupils successfully completing a course of study. For example, "the pupil can distinguish among a chemical element, compound, and mixture." Finally, the third level contains highly specific objectives derived from ones at the second level, which state not only the pupil performance desired, but also the situation that initiates the performance, the criteria of acceptable performance, and, if appropriate, any special conditions related to the performance. For example, "the pupil distinguishes among *to, too,* and *two* with 90 percent accuracy when provided short written sentences that can be completed by inserting one of the three words at a designated position."

First-Level Objectives: General Objectives

A number of the attempts to formulate first-level objectives have been quite ambitious. Committees as well as individuals have produced impressive lists most often delineating the ultimate goals of the educational system without direct reference to traditional subject matter areas. The following are illustrative of these efforts:

Cardinal Principles of Secondary Education.   Of the many attempts to define the general objectives of secondary education, perhaps the most widely quoted is that formulated by the Commission on the Reorganization of Secondary Education, which was appointed by the National Education Association. These objectives are commonly called the "Seven Cardinal Principles of Secondary Education" (1918) and have unquestionably influenced the majority of all subsequent attempts of this kind. Briefly stated, they are as follows:

Good health
Command of fundamental processes
Worthy home membership
Vocational efficiency
Good citizenship
Worthy use of leisure time
Ethical character

Purposes of Education in American Democracy. The Educational Policies Commission of the National Education Association classified the objectives of secondary education in four categories (1938):

Self-realization
Human relationship
Economic efficiency
Civic responsibility

Within each of the four categories of objectives are listed many specific ones. The objectives of self-realization include skills in reading, writing, and arithmetic, intellectual and aesthetic interests, physical health, good character, and many others. Included in the category of human relationships are respect for humanity, appreciation of the home, and skills in homemaking. The objectives of economic efficiency are appreciation of good workmanship, consumer skills, and knowledge of occupations and their requirements. Within the category of objectives of civic responsibility are an understanding of democratic processes, respect for law, appreciation of social justice and tolerance, and many others.

Developmental Tasks as Educational Objectives. The lessons or tasks that each individual must learn as he grows in his society are called *developmental tasks*. Havighurst defined a developmental task as "a task which arises at or about a certain period in the life of the individual, successful achievement of which leads to his happiness and to success with later tasks, while failure leads to unhappiness in the individual, disapproval by the society, and difficulty with later tasks" (Havighurst, 1953, p. 2). Some tasks may seem relatively easy to an individual; others extremely difficult. They are spread throughout the lifetime of each person.

Havighurst and others have attempted to list the developmental tasks common to all persons in the American society. Havighurst began by subdividing the life span into age periods, two of which are pertinent here: middle childhood and adolescence. Then on the basis of the evidence he had gathered he listed the developmental tasks for each period.

Middle Childhood
(Ages 6 to 12 or 13 years)

1. Learning physical skills necessary for ordinary games.
2. Building wholesome attitudes toward oneself as a growing organism.
3. Learning to get along with age-mates.
4. Learning an appropriate masculine or feminine social role.
5. Developing fundamental skills in reading, writing, and calculating.
6. Developing concepts necessary for everyday living.
7. Developing conscience, morality, and a scale of values.
8. Achieving personal independence.
9. Developing attitudes toward groups and institutions (Havighurst, 1953, pp. 25–41).

Adolescence
(Ages 13 or 14 to 18 years)

1. Achieving new and more mature relations with age-mates of both sexes.
2. Achieving a masculine or feminine social role.
3. Accepting one's physique and using the body effectively.
4. Achieving emotional independence of parents and other adults.
5. Achieving assurance of economic independence.
6. Selecting and preparing for an occupation.
7. Preparing for marriage and family life.
8. Developing intellectual skills and concepts necessary for civic competence.
9. Desiring and achieving socially responsible behavior.
10. Acquiring a set of values and an ethical system as a guide to behavior (Havighurst, 1953, pp. 111–158).

Developmental tasks that have been accurately determined for various age levels can be most useful in the determination of the objectives of education. They alert the teacher to the problems with which typical children of each age group are struggling, and in so doing, help the teacher improve the nature and the timing of the teaching process. Education should help each pupil achieve each of his developmental tasks when he is physiologically and psychologically ready and the pressures of his society are evident.

Primary Objectives for National Assessment. In the late 1960s, advisory committees composed of educators and subject matter specialists wrote the primary objectives for the National Assessment of Educational Progress in more than a dozen curriculum areas. Classroom teachers and lay consultants assisted each committee. Panels of laymen then reviewed their work and suggested revisions.

The foregoing procedure was used to insure that every objective should meet three criteria, namely, (1) it is considered important by scholars, (2) it is accepted as an educational task by the educational system, and (3) it is considered desirable by laymen. The following are samples of this work from four areas (Norris, 1969a, 1969b).[1]

Citizenship

1. Show concern for the welfare and dignity of others.
2. Know the main structure and function of our governments.

Science

1. Possess the abilities and skills needed to engage in the processes of science.
2. Have attitudes about and appreciations of scientists, science, and the consequences of science that stem from adequate understandings.

Music

1. Perform a piece of music.
2. Read standard musical notation.

Writing

1. Write to communicate adequately in a business or vocational situation.
2. Appreciate the value of writing.

To be sure, this work is not complete. In some ways, such primary objectives as these are moving targets. Therefore, review and revision of them occurs every testing cycle of about three years.

Second-Level Objectives: Sub-Objectives

The first important subdivisions of first-level objectives are often called subobjectives. Illustrations of them are countless. Here are several widely used examples representing both elementary and secondary education.

Elementary Education. A prominent statement of objectives at the second level for elementary education is the one prepared by Mid-Century Committee on Outcomes in Elementary Education (Kearney, 1953). Each objective included in the list is thought to be attainable by average children at some time prior to age fifteen or sixteen. No matter how defensible a proposed objective might have been on a purely philosophical basis, it was not included unless it was also deemed attainable during the first fifteen years of the child's life, regardless of whether the school, the home, or some other community agency was instrumental in helping the child reach this goal.

Nine curriculum areas are considered. They are:

[1] Reproduced by permission of the National Assessment of Educational Progress.

Physical development, health, and body care
Individual social and emotional development
Ethical behavior, standards, and values
Social relations
The social world
The physical world
Esthetic development
Communication
Quantitative relationships

Within each curriculum area, four types of behavioral patterns are cited:

Knowledges and understandings
Skills and competences
Attitudes and interests
Action patterns

The objectives of elementary education are not listed for each grade level. Instead, three points in time, called age-grade periods, are selected somewhat arbitrarily and the objectives are listed for each. The primary period corresponds to the end of the third grade, the pupils having attained an age of about nine years. The intermediate period corresponds to the end of the sixth grade, or an age of about twelve years. The upper-grade period corresponds to the end of the ninth grade, or an age of about fifteen years.

To illustrate the nature of the intermediate-period objectives reported (Kearney, 1953, pp. 68–73, 113–120), a few from two curriculum areas are listed below:

Ethical behavior, standards, and values

A. Knowledges and understandings
   1. The pupil develops an awareness of property rights and of truth and falsehood.
   2. The pupil understands the basic principles of giving value in return for value received.
B. Skills and competences
   1. The pupil is able to like a person in spite of disliking his behavior in specific instances.
   2. The pupil's conception of "property" enables him to refrain from taking what does not belong to him.
C. Attitudes and interests
   1. The pupil is interested in altruistic club activities.
   2. The pupil protects other pupils, particularly the "underdog" or the handicapped.
D. Action patterns
   1. The pupil tends to be analytical in evaluating behavior.
   2. The pupil habitually acts in accord with a system of ethical values, although these are not always the same as adult values.

Quantitative relationships

A. Knowledges and understandings
  1. The pupil knows how numbers apply to time, weight, and dry and liquid measures.
  2. The pupil sees the relationship of division to fractions, and understands decimals as fractions or as small units or parts of larger units, with their places held by a decimal point and zeroes or columns.
B. Skills and competences
  1. The pupil can add, subtract, and multiply decimals.
  2. The pupil performs the four fundamental processes, including long division, with whole numbers with a high degree of accuracy.
C. Attitudes and interests
  1. The pupil respects accuracy and arithmetical orderliness.
  2. The pupil enjoys estimating, playing with "shortcuts," and number magic.
D. Action patterns
  1. The pupil is able to search for meaning behind the number of numerical relationships he uses.
  2. The pupil can interpret scale drawings, and can construct and read line and bar graphs.

These objectives are not designed to be minimal objectives for some or all of the pupils. The members of the committee expected that all pupils would not achieve all objectives to an equal degree or at the same rate. Furthermore, it is apparent that, for each curriculum area, the difficulty of the objectives varies within each of the three age-grade periods as well as among them. Within each period, there are objectives to be attained relatively early and hence they seem to be quite simple. With these are other objectives to be attained relatively late, and hence they seem more difficult.

Secondary Education.   Similar to the foregoing effort, a study was made of the objectives of the secondary school (French and associates, 1957). Only the objectives for the general education program in the secondary school are included in this report. The basic purposes of this program are to help pupils realize their fullest potentialities and meet civic responsibility.

The lists of educational objectives are classified under three maturity goals and four areas of behavioral competence. The maturity goals are:

1. Growth toward self-realization. Self-realization is described as the development of "the common kinds of behaviors indicative of such personal growth and development as will enable them [the pupils] within the limits of their native environments, to live richer, more satisfying, more productive lives consonant with our ethical, aesthetic, and social standards and values."
2. Growth toward desirable interpersonal relations in small groups.
3. Growth toward effective membership or leadership in large organizations.

The four areas of behavioral competence are:

1. Attainment of maximum intellectual growth and development.
2. Cultural orientation and integration.

3. Physical and mental health.
4. Economic competence.

Combining the three maturity goals and the four areas of behavioral competence establishes twelve broad groups of behavior. In other words, a chart with twelve cells is formed. Each cell contains a group of related educational objectives. The cells are not considered mutually exclusive.

The educational objectives given below are classified under the maturity goal of self-realization within the area of behavioral competence called attaining maximum intellectual growth and development. These objectives are typical of those mentioned in the three major subgroups (1.11, 1.12, and 1.13) included in this cell (French and associates, 1957, pp. 92–102).

1.111 (d) The pupil uses common sources of printed information efficiently; e.g., dictionary, encyclopedia, *Readers' Guide*, card catalog in a library.

1.121 (a) The pupil adjusts his reading rate and his method of reading to the material at hand.

1.123 (f) The pupil demonstrates that he can read and understand mathematical reports, charts and graphs, and simple statements of financial accounts.

1.131 (e) The pupil analyzes a problem and can follow the recognized steps involved in scientific thinking.

1.133 (c) The pupil recognizes the unsoundness of drawing generalizations from insufficient evidence.

These objectives are designed to be reasonable goals for the most mature high school seniors. This means that, for each pupil, some of them will seem to be too high a standard. To assist the teacher in those instances in which they may seem to be too high, "developmental equivalents" are provided for each of the major subgroups of educational objectives. These are less mature behavioral patterns; they are indicative of the stages of development that we would expect as the younger pupils progress toward the mature behavior of the older pupils.

Sub-Objectives for National Assessment.   For each of the main objectives prepared for the National Assessment of Educational Progress, second-level objectives were also prepared. The following are illustrative of these from both the citizenship and science areas (Norris, 1969a, 1969b).[1]

Citizenship

First Level: Show concern for the welfare and dignity of others.
Second Level: Treat all individuals with respect; do not condemn others on the basis of irrelevant personal or social characteristics.
Consider the consequences for others of their own actions.

---

[1] Reproduced by permission of the National Assessment of Educational Progress.

Guard safety and health of others.

Help other individuals voluntarily.

Are loyal to country, to friends, and to other groups whose values they share.

First Level: Know the main structure and functions of our governments.

Second Level: Recognize the purposes of government.

Recognize the main functions and relations of governmental bodies.

Recognize the importance of political opposition and diverse interest groups.

Recognize that democracy depends on the alertness and involvement of its citizens, and know how citizens can affect government.

Science

First Level: Possess the abilities and skills needed to engage in the processes of science.

Second Level: Possess the ability to identify and define a scientific problem.

Possess the ability to suggest or recognize a scientific hypothesis.

Possess the ability to propose or select validating procedures, both logical and empirical.

Possess the ability to obtain requisite data.

Possess the ability to interpret data.

First Level: Have attitudes about and appreciations of scientists, science, and the consequences of science that stem from adequate understandings.

Second Level: Recognize the distinction between science and its applications.

Have accurate attitudes about scientists.

Understand the relationship between science and misconceptions or superstitions.

Are ready and willing knowingly to apply and utilize basic scientific principles and approaches, where appropriate, to everyday living.

Are independently curious about and participate in scientific activities.

Often the sub-objectives are further refined for each of four age levels, namely, nine, thirteen, seventeen, and adult. These refinements are a series of suggestions of the kinds of pupil behavior that, if present, indicate that the sub-objectives and hence the primary objectives are being achieved. Typically the suggested behaviors serve as a fine introduction to third-level objectives.

Third-Level Objectives: Specific Instructional Objectives

The various published statements of educational objectives at the first and second levels are most helpful to the classroom teacher. They point out the kinds of goals that should be achieved by all American youth, regardless of the family of which they are members, the schools in which they are enrolled, or the communities in which the schools are located. In so doing, these statements tend to keep the curriculum of all schools more or less aligned without necessarily specifying the nature of all of its parts.

The formal statements of educational objectives cited in the preceding sections have at least two common characteristics not mentioned previously.

None of the statements suggests the relative importance of the objectives listed. The order in which they are mentioned is not intended to reflect their order of importance. Nor do any of them suggest the particular objectives that are to guide the instruction by a specific teacher on a stated day with a certain group of pupils.

As a result, the teacher becomes the most prominent person involved in the process of identifying instructional objectives for the classroom. It is he who must amalgamate the first-level and second-level objectives with a variety of pertinent local factors to arrive at the proper third-level objectives for his class, and to give each its proper emphasis. Local factors usually considered are the instructional objectives of the courses previously completed by the pupils, their success in achieving these objectives, the educational philosophy of the school, the facilities of the community, the vocational goals of the pupils, and the nature of their homes. In other words, difficult as it is, the teacher must become acquainted with the individualized needs of the pupils in his class. The influence of all local factors should yield a set of realistic and pertinent third-level objectives for classroom use.

Third-level objectives are highly specific. One can imagine literally thousands of them. Certainly the teacher needs for each learning experience a series of very concisely stated objectives that are direct outgrowths of second-level objectives, which in turn are direct outgrowths of those from the first level. Then a high degree of consistency will exist. When this occurs, we are truly able to understand and interpret all levels of interrelated objectives.

How does a classroom teacher go about preparing his own third-level objectives? Considerable attention has been given to this question (Mager, 1962; Gronlund, 1970). Mager (1962, p. 12) believes that three basic steps must be taken to prepare the specific objectives. These are the following:

1. Identify specifically the kind of pupil behavior which is acceptable as evidence that he has achieved the objective in question. In other words, the objective must state explicitly what the pupil must be able to *do* in order to achieve it.
2. Describe the important conditions which influence pupil behavior. In other words, any support provided the pupil or any restrictions placed upon him when he must demonstrate his competence should be mentioned.
3. Specify the criteria of acceptable performance by describing at least the lower limit of such performance.

An illustration of the results of this procedure is the following taken from an elementary mathematics unit:

> When provided with accurate drawings of a variety of triangles, each having all needed dimensions shown, the pupil can compute the area of each correctly to the nearest whole number, at least 75% of the time.

Note that an attempt has been made to follow each of the three steps. First of all, the pupil behavior is concisely described; that is, he must "compute the area of each correctly to the nearest whole number." Secondly, a condition is introduced; that is, the pupil is "provided with accurate drawings of a variety of triangles, each having all needed dimensions shown." Finally, the lower limit of performance is established; that is, answers must be correct to the nearest whole number "at least 75% of the time."

A properly designed instructional objective should communicate the intent of the teacher quickly and completely to pupils and parents alike. An effective way of testing the wording of an objective is to present it to another teacher interested in the subject matter and see if he can select successful pupils in terms of it. These should also be acceptable to you, the author of the statement.

The manner of preparation here described will produce specific instructional objectives of considerable utility, especially in the cognitive domain. As one fractionates first- and second-level objectives in order to formulate third-level ones, he gains an excellent insight into the problems of providing good instruction and designing sensitive measuring instruments.

Problems

8.   In the statement of objectives in elementary education are cited "determining conditions," that is, the biological and sociological context in which children and the schools carry on together (Kearney, 1953, p. 36). In what way is this concept of "determining conditions" related to the basic thinking behind the developmental tasks as proposed by Havighurst?

9.   Suggest reasons why the second-level objectives in elementary and secondary education cited in this chapter are organized in noticeably dissimilar patterns.

10.   Using the NAEP second-level citizenship objective "Recognize the main functions and relations of governmental bodies," formulate a third-level objective for each of three age levels: nine, thirteen, and seventeen years.

EVALUATING IN TERMS OF EDUCATIONAL OBJECTIVES

Does a fourth level of objectives exist? Yes, in a sense it does. Have you heard of "mini-objectives"? They are statements "representing performances observed when an individual is responding to a particular frame in an instructional test or program" (Smith and Shaw, 1969, p. 137). Often each can be represented by a single test item. In other words, test items and instructional materials can be thought of as the fourth and most specific level of all. They are direct expressions of objectives and, in reality, are operational definitions of them (Krathwohl and Payne, 1970). Thus, using testing and nontesting procedures in the process of evaluating pupil behavior is a logical extension to the development and use of specific instructional objectives.

Eliciting Pupil Behavioral Patterns

Rarely is it a simple matter to determine the degree to which a pupil's behavior has changed so that it conforms more closely to that defined in an objective. In the first place, the pupil must be given an opportunity to demonstrate that he has or has not reached the goal. Secondly, this demonstration must occur under circumstances that will allow critical evaluation in terms of the appropriate objectives. To accomplish this, a trained observer equipped with suitable measuring tools is needed. This is the only truly meaningful way of evaluating pupil growth. All other methods are indirect and, by this very fact, tend to be somewhat inadequate. The practical importance of these inadequacies varies considerably. In some cases they are so serious that the measurement results are practically worthless; in other cases their presence only modestly reduces the effectiveness of the measuring methods.

Behavior in a Natural Situation.   The first step requires that goal behavior by a pupil be elicited within a natural situation. The pupil involved feels no compulsion to say the "proper" thing or to behave in the "proper" manner. He is behaving as he truly has learned to, rather than in a feigned manner he might adopt if required to exhibit a pattern of behavior for teacher evaluation. In the natural situation, the true, unvarnished products of his educational experiences are voluntarily displayed.

This description of natural situations actually points out one of the chief difficulties encountered in pupil evaluation. Since the very essence of natural situations prevents the teacher from controlling them, his efforts at evaluation are often hampered. Some natural situations will not occur in the classroom; in fact, some will not occur until after the formal education of the pupil has been completed. For example, it is reasonable to expect that pupil behavior related to aspects of educational objectives pertaining to citizenship, home membership, and vocational proficiency is best shown in natural situations, most of which occur outside the classroom. The natural situations that do occur during the pupil's elementary and secondary school career may take place at haphazard times and sundry places. Needless to say, the teacher should capitalize on them whenever possible, although evaluative efforts in natural situations are at times impractical, if not impossible.

To be sure, direct observation of pupil behavior in a natural situation can be made of the degree to which pupils have achieved some of the specific objectives of education. For example, a teacher can observe with relative ease and frequency whether a pupil consistently covers his nose and mouth with a handkerchief when sneezing or coughing, whether he can tell time and make change with accuracy, whether he enjoys active games, whether he uses conventional courtesies in his oral communications, whether he can read silently with little or no lip movement, or construct charts and graphs with only minor errors. These and other direct observations of pupil behavior can be made in lifelike situations outside the classroom or in connection with normal classroom routine. Class projects, teacher-pupil interviews, field trips, social functions, and other activities may be suitable opportunities for observation even though not necessarily designed for them.

Skillful Observation.   Although direct observations may be made in an informal atmosphere, the observation process cannot be as casual if it is to be successful. The skilled observer is intimately familiar with the goals to be reached, the characteristics of pupil behavior that fall short of the goal to various degrees and in various ways, and the methods of reporting observations. This suggests that he should have a full knowledge of human development, psychology of learning, methods of educational evaluation, and subject matter areas in which instruction takes place. The observer must know what he is looking for and must be able to search for it as systematically and objectively as possible. Vague "impressions" are not enough. Ranking and rating procedures, check lists, anecdotal records, and even sociometric devices are tools that can be used.

Artificial Situations and Evaluation Methods.   Evaluative attempts conducted in artificial situations are far more common than those conducted in natural situations. The teacher establishes artificial situations as similar to the natural situations as time and convenience will allow. It is hoped that the behavior exhibited by the pupil in the artificial situation is closely related to that he would have exhibited in a comparable natural situation if given the opportunity. Evaluation devices used in these situations are frequently paper-and-pencil achievement tests, but could be performance tests, written assignments, or work samples of a multitude of types.

The artificial situations and the evaluative devices used with them vary greatly in the degree to which they elicit pupil behavior closely related to that found in the corresponding natural situation (Lindquist, 1951, pp. 146–152). Some are quite successful in this respect. For example, paper-and-pencil tests, such as reading speed and comprehension tests, and performance tests, such as typing and shorthand tests, allow the pupil to demonstrate whether he has acquired the behavioral patterns described as objectives, and to do so in rather realistic settings. The same is true of performance tests given pupils in home economics classes, industrial art classes, and vocational agricultural classes. The products of the pupil's behavior as well as the behavior itself can be evaluated. A typed business letter, a meat roast, a wooden bookcase, or a welded wagon frame could serve this purpose. Note that in these instances the teacher does not wait until the pupil's behavioral patterns occur in the natural course of events, nor is he certain that the material involved in the evaluation is completely representative of that present in the natural situation.

On the other hand, there are countless other evaluation attempts involving artificial situations that do not elicit pupil behavior essentially the same as that the pupil would display in a natural situation. The teacher must make a rather shaky assumption that a sizable relationship exists. For example, attitude and interest inventories allow the pupil to indicate how he would (or should) behave in situations described to him, but do not actually place him in the situations so that he can overtly display his behavior. Is there a strong relationship between what he says he would do and what he actually would do if given the opportunity? Probably not, and so these inventories are unsatisfactory.

Additional illustrations of the importance of the foregoing assumption are easily found. For instance, paper-and-pencil tests are sometimes used as a basis for evaluating the pupil's ability to perform laboratory and shop activities. In a physics class, test items may describe the apparatus and materials necessary for laboratory experiments in electricity and magnetism. After the steps of the experiments have been recounted, the pupil is required to predict the outcome of each experiment and give reasons why this is the case. In an auto mechanics class, the test items may describe symptoms of an automobile engine that is not functioning properly. The pupil is required to diagnose the trouble by interpreting the symptoms, then select from a list of tools those necessary to repair the engine, and list the steps he would follow when making repairs. In an English class, artificial situations have been used to evaluate a pupil's writing ability. Rather than ask the pupil to write a composition, the teacher gives him a poorly written passage that he must improve by deleting or adding words, phrases, and punctuation marks.

In each of the three examples mentioned above, the response to the artificial situation is not the same as that which would have been elicited in a natural situation. The test items in physics and in auto mechanics do not allow the pupil to display his skill in the actual manipulation of laboratory apparatus and tools. It is conceivable that he could answer the test items correctly and still not be able to perform the tasks. The same is true of the English composition test. Writing ability involves more than correcting the punctuation and rearranging the words of a passage written by someone else. It also includes selection and arrangement of ideas and style of expression. Elements of originality so important in superior writing ability are scarcely tapped by the test. Nevertheless, in the case of all three examples the teacher must make the assumption that the abilities of the pupil measured by the paper-and-pencil test items are related to his abilities to perform the tasks as they occur in natural situations.

Pupil evaluation should be planned as an integral part of the teaching process. As the teacher examines each of his objectives and designs experiences for his class, he should also design the method of evaluation to be used. It is not surprising to discover that methods of evaluation vary markedly from one kind of behavioral change to another. Knowledges and intellectual abilities and skills are usually evaluated on the basis of test results yielded by paper-and-pencil tests, both teacher-constructed and standardized. Motor skills are customarily evaluated on the basis of results yielded by performance tests and the systematic use of ranking and rating devices. Attitudes and interests are sometimes evaluated in terms of paper-and-pencil inventory results, ranking and rating results, reports of teacher-pupil and teacher-parent interviews, anecdotal records summarizing direct observations, and, to a limited extent, sociometric results and other information from the pupil's peers.

Planning the Paper-and-Pencil Achievement Test

No doubt the most common measurement method used in schools today is the paper-and-pencil achievement test. In several respects its prominence is undeserved. Nevertheless, it shows the way in which measuring methods are designed in terms of a set of selected instructional objectives.

The teacher need take relatively few steps when constructing a paper-and-pencil achievement test. First of all, he must separate from among his objectives those that have verbal and mathematical aspects, thereby excluding many objectives of considerable merit. Secondly, he must determine the relative importance of the verbal and mathematical objectives, a purely subjective process. Teachers with the same objectives differ noticeably with respect to the relative importance they assign to each. As the relative importance varies from teacher to teacher, so does the nature of the instruction. The relative emphasis that an objective receives in the process of instruction is a crude but effective indicator of the emphasis to be given that objective when an achievement test involving it is constructed. Finally, the teacher must build a group of test items, either of the essay or objective type, that constitute a representative sample of all subject matter topics and behavioral patterns included within the objectives. This can be summarized by means of a two-way grid or table of specifications (see following section). The importance of each cell in the table is roughly equivalent to the number of test items related to it, the difficulty of these test items, the amount of credit allotted to right answers to the test items, or several or all of these simultaneously.

Tables of Specifications.   As an illustration of the foregoing process, consider the case of the secondary school chemistry teacher who is conducting his educational program in terms of a number of second-level objectives, three of which are the following:

1. The pupil can remember certain facts, definitions, laws, and theories of chemistry.
2. The pupil can comprehend the scientific method in its relations to the theories and principles of chemistry.
3. The pupil can apply the principles of chemistry in making predictions, explanations, and inferences.

When teaching a unit devoted to oxygen and some of its common compounds, he stresses the first and third objectives insofar as this subject matter is concerned. From these he derives a large series of third-level objectives, each of which establishes, for the most part, the criterion behavior which the pupil must display if he has achieved the objective, any restrictions placed on him when he demonstrates his competence, and the lower limit of acceptable performance. The following three statements, based on the first second-level objective, show the kind of objectives used.

1. When given a list of twenty common compounds containing oxygen, the pupil can properly classify at least fifteen of them as to whether each, at normal temperature and pressure, is a gas, a liquid, or a solid.
2. Of the ten oxides studied, the pupil can accurately identify each as an acidic oxide or a basic oxide at least 70 percent of the time.
3. When provided with an incomplete equation showing the ingredients and the conditions needed to synthesize each of twenty common compounds containing oxygen, the pupil can complete the equation and balance it properly at least 60 percent of the time.

The next step is to group the specific objectives as needed. Notice that the foregoing three deal with recall of chemical information, but each is concerned with a different subject matter topic. Although each deals with common compounds of oxygen, the first speaks of their physical properties, the second of their chemical properties, and the third of their preparation.

A convenient way of gathering and organizing the specific objectives is a table of specifications. In its simplest form, the table of specifications is a two-way table, one dimension of which is a breakdown of behavioral changes, and the other of subject matter topics. The behavioral changes can be classified into many categories, for example, the six principal categories of the taxonomy of educational objectives for the cognitive domain. Less than six are commonly used in teacher-constructed tests. For the chemistry test, three categories were considered significant, namely, the first three principal categories of the cognitive domain taxonomy—knowledge, comprehension, and application.

The subject matter topics are subdivisions of the verbal and mathematical material included in the unit. Normally, many topics are listed. For example, the unit devoted to oxygen and some of its common compounds might be first subdivided into general topics—their physical properties, chemical properties, preparation, and uses. Each of these topics could be again subdivided into as many minor topics as the classroom teacher deems necessary.

To build a table of specifications the teacher must decide the relative importance of the behavioral changes and the topics and represent them as percentages. The following decisions may be reached for the oxygen unit:

I. Behavioral changes
    1. Knowledge   35
    2. Comprehension   35
    3. Application   30
       Total   100

II. Subject matter topics
    1. Physical properties of oxygen and its common compounds   20
    2. Chemical properties of oxygen and its common compounds   30
    3. Preparation of oxygen and its common compounds   10
    4. Uses of oxygen and its common compounds   40
       Total   100

The two breakdowns and the assigned percentages are then combined into a simple table, as illustrated in Table 1. The entries in the twelve cells of the table are based on the best judgment of the teacher, and are arranged so that the row and column totals are not changed.

TABLE 1   Table of Specifications for a Chemistry Unit Devoted to Oxygen and Its Common Compounds.

Subject Matter Topic	Behavioral Changes			Total
	Knowledge	Comprehension	Application	
Physical properties	6%	10%	4%	20%
Chemical properties	10	10	10	30
Preparation	6	4	0	10
Uses	13	11	16	40
Total	35	35	30	100

The percentages included in the table are rough approximations of the importance of each behavioral change in each topic. Therefore, if an objective test is to be constructed, the percentages could be used as rough approximations of the percentage of test items in the test devoted to the behavior changes of each topic. In actual practice, however, circumstances force the test builder to deviate somewhat from this point of view. For instance, a given test item may refer to more than one cell in the table. On the other hand, items for some cells might be extremely difficult to construct. Because of the short supply that results, the test may not reflect the designated importance of each cell as accurately as we might hope. Finally, it must be remembered the percentage weights in the table are, at best, very crude. As the test is being constructed, the builder will sometimes gain better insight into his table of specifications and change it accordingly. The end result is a realistic view of the testing situation. The teacher knows which ideas are measurable and which are not, and thus what the test scores *do and do not* reveal about pupil behavior. After undergoing this agonizing appraisal, more than one teacher has *contracted* the scope of his interpretation of classroom test scores!

In spite of the crudeness of a table of specifications and the difficulty of constructing a sufficient number of test items for all of its cells, the use of such a table for building paper-and-pencil achievement tests produces tests vastly superior to those yielded by a casual, unsystematic skimming of lesson plans and textbooks. Furthermore, the effort invested in the development of a table of specifications can pay dividends for a prolonged period of time. With revision as needed, the table may materially assist the construction of paper-and-pencil achievement tests for a number of years.

To use the percentage weights contained in the table of specifications, the teacher must first decide how many essay or objective items the test will contain. This in turn depends on the time available for testing, the type of test item to be used, and the anticipated difficulty of those items. The time factor is frequently determined by the administrative routine of the school. A class period may be the maximum amount of time available. The maturity level of the pupils and the possibility of the test's causing excessive fatigue may be sufficient reasons for the teacher to reduce the time interval even more. In any event, knowing the testing time available, the teacher can estimate on the basis of past experience the number of test items of a given kind and difficulty that pupils can answer in the number of minutes allotted.

The techniques for constructing test items of various types are described in detail in the following chapters. Strict adherence to the rules given will yield test items of good technical quality. In spite of this, you will find that objective test items are difficult to build for the analysis, synthesis, and evaluation levels of the cognitive taxonomy (see pages 45–46). Essay tests, performance tests, and even product and procedure evaluation are used to supplement objective test items.

Content Validity.   Clearly, the central purpose of the procedure just described for building paper-and-pencil achievement tests is to develop a high-quality test, that is, one that will satisfactorily serve the purpose or purposes for which it is intended. An achievement test such as the oxygen test has the purpose of determining as of the moment it is administered how well a pupil recalls, comprehends, and applies the cross section of the total amount of subject matter studied that it contains. The degree to which the achievement test serves this purpose is its content validity (French and Michael, 1966, pp. 12–16). This is one of three types of test validity (see pages 278–279).

The degree of content validity of a test rises and falls in accordance with (1) the extent to which its table of specifications accurately reflects the relative importance of the various subject matter topics in relation to the various pupil behavioral changes stemming from verbal and mathematically oriented instructional objectives, and (2) the degree to which the test items built on the basis of the table of specifications accurately mirror the balance of the cells. A high degree of content validity is customarily attained when carefully contrived tables of specification, or some similar device, are used, and when the many rules of test item construction described in Part Two are conscientiously followed.

Instructional Objectives Exchange

The conscientious teacher who fully accepts his responsibilities for pupil evaluation is a very busy person. He must design innumerable third-level objectives and for each prepare a data-gathering method. This is a herculean job. To help him, a system for exchanging objectives is available. The Instructional Objectives Exchange (IOX) is a clearinghouse for this purpose. It collects and develops properly formulated instructional objectives with the goal of making available collections in all fields for all grade levels, kindergarten through twelfth grade. Significantly, measuring techniques suitable for assessing the attainment of each objective are also developed and distributed with it (Popham, 1969).

Successful use of the exchange permits the classroom teacher to study comprehensive collections of objectives and their corresponding measuring techniques and then to *select* those that are appropriate. Of course, his measurement plans are not completed at this point. For instance, no matter how imaginative the suggested measuring technique, if it is a paper-and-pencil device—and it usually is—he still must decide which nontesting approaches he can use. Happiness is a versatile, balanced evaluation plan.

Role of Paper-and-Pencil Tests

The true role played by paper-and-pencil tests in pupil evaluation is quite obvious at this point. The acknowledged purposes of elementary and secondary education have expanded greatly since the turn of the century. As they increased, the usefulness of the traditional paper-and-pencil test as a measuring instrument has steadily declined. For a curriculum based on the idea that a school must, above all, serve as a vehicle for transmitting to the new generation all of the knowledge accumulated by previous generations, this kind of test would serve admirably. For a curriculum based upon the idea that a school must help a pupil learn how to meet his many needs as a member of a democratic society, this kind of test still is of major importance, but by no means should it dominate pupil evaluation to the degree that it now does.

The unjustified popularity of paper-and-pencil tests as measuring instruments can be most disconcerting to pupils, parents, and teachers alike. After everyone assures everyone else that the objectives of education should reflect the needs of the "whole" child, the teacher evaluates the behavioral patterns of his pupils on a highly restricted basis. The pupil and his parents are understandably confused; the teacher usually feels unduly frustrated. No doubt he recognizes the possibility of injustices when this method is followed, but he also knows that he does not have sufficient data-gathering tools and that many of those he has lack the respectability of paper-and-pencil tests.

This dilemma in which teachers repeatedly find themselves has no convenient solution. To use paper-and-pencil instruments to the point where most other techniques are ignored, however, is not the answer to the problem. Instead, consider the following (Lindquist, 1951, p. 157):

> For many objectives of the type suggested, measuring or observational devices concerned with the student's overt behavior while he is yet in school, even though of a rough and opportunistic character, are perhaps much more worthwhile than any written type of tests. The actual behavior of the student in school elections, for example, however fragmentary or limited in sampling, may provide a better clue to his future behavior than anything he professes that he will do in a written test; books actually read by the pupil in his free time may constitute a truer indication of his literary tastes than his score on a literary appreciation test; anecdotal records may be more meaningful than scores on personality tests; etc. The problem of deriving comparable measures from such opportunistic observational data now seems to present almost insuperable difficulties, but perhaps no worse than have been resolved before through determined and persistent effort.

The foregoing remarks should not be interpreted as a general denunciation of written tests or a recommendation that they be abandoned completely. On the contrary, paper-and-pencil tests should be a sizable part of any pupil evaluation program. These tests should be used in conjunction with, rather than in the absence of, other methods. The very nature of many educational objectives requires that this be so. Paper-and-pencil tests can do a commendable job of determining the degree to which certain objectives have been achieved, but are totally inappropriate in the case of many others. Unfortunately, the results of such tests have also been used as estimates of the degree to which the pupil has achieved educational objectives far removed from the original ones. This has occurred in spite of the fact that the degree to which a pupil attains one educational objective is not necessarily the same as the degree to which he attains any other.

Problems

11.   Prepare several third-level verbal and mathematical objectives of a unit you are teaching or soon will be teaching. On the basis of these objectives, build at least one table of specifications suitable for the construction of a classroom achievement test.

12.   Using the cognitive and affective taxonomies, Metfessel, Michael, and Kirsner (1969) developed verbal guidelines for formulating specific instructional objectives. For each taxonomic category, behaviorally oriented infinitives (for example, *to recognize, to translate,* or *to classify*) and direct objects (that is, subject matter properties like *facts, terminology,* and *theories*) are given. Study these "key words" and use combinations of them to prepare three cognitive and three affective third-level objectives for a teaching situation you know well.

13.   Imagine that you are a member of a team of teachers who are to devise an achievement test to be administered at the end of a unit concerning the federal government that all are independently teaching to separate classes. How would you proceed to plan the test to guarantee a high degree of content validity for each class?

14.   Attempts have been made to use the cognitive taxonomy to build sets of test items that hold content constant and systematically vary process from simple (that is, knowledge) to complex (that is, evaluation). Evaluate the eight interrelated test items in the physical sciences prepared by Smith (1968) and suggest changes, if any, that you would make.

SUMMARY

Each child has needs that he must be able to satisfy to live a happy and productive life in a democratic society. Common to all youth are organic needs, such as food, liquids, and rest. Each individual also has needs related to preparation for a vocation, utilization of leisure time, responsibilities as a citizen, role as a homemaker, and personal-social adjustment. The areas of need are identified by studying intensively both youth and the democratic society in which they live.

There are many agencies that can help youth learn how to satisfy their needs. Their families, churches, and clubs are important factors. However, the school is most important in practically all instances. The primary purpose of formal education is to teach youth in such a way that they are better able to satisfy their needs. The objectives of education are developed on this premise.

The needs of youth are translated into educational objectives by identifying the new patterns of behavior the individual must acquire in order to satisfy his needs. The objectives involve the development of new knowledges, intellectual abilities and skills, affective patterns, and psychomotor skills. Thus the objectives of education are pupil-oriented rather than teacher-oriented and are stated in terms of desired behavioral patterns in the pupil. Taxonomies for objectives in the cognitive, affective, and psychomotor domains are now being used.

Educational objectives vary in terms of their degree of specificity. Three levels are present. The first level contains statements of major goals. The second level is a refinement of the first, whereas the third level includes highly specific instructional objectives. A number of formal statements of objectives have been prepared by committees for the first and second levels. Third-level objectives are direct outgrowths of these, and are usually prepared by teachers.

Having taught pupils with the guidance of his instructional objectives, of course the teacher must evaluate their achievement in terms of them. Ideally this should be done by direct observation of the pupil's behavior in a natural situation. At times this is impractical, if not impossible. Instead, the teacher establishes artificial situations that are as similar to natural situations as time and convenience will allow, and evaluates the pupil's achievement indirectly within these situations by means of a variety of data-gathering devices.

The artificial situations and the data-gathering devices used with them vary greatly in the degree to which they elicit pupil behavior closely related to that found in the corresponding natural situation. Performance tests are quite successful in this respect, as some paper-and-pencil tests are. However, many paper-and-pencil tests are considerably less successful, obvious illustrations being tests designed to measure pupil behavior in many areas in the affective and psychomotor domains.

The construction of a paper-and-pencil achievement test involves three steps. First, the educational objectives with verbal and mathematical aspects must be separated from all others. Secondly, the relative importance of these objectives and their subparts must be identified. Finally, a group of test items must be constructed. These should constitute a representative sample of all subject matter topics and behavioral patterns included within the objectives. The second and third steps can be facilitated by using a table of specifications, and a high degree of content validity can be attained.

Evaluating pupil behavior in terms of educational objectives is a complex task. Many methods are used. Knowledges and intellectual abilities and skills are usually evaluated on the basis of test results from paper-and-pencil tests, both classroom and standardized. Motor skills can be evaluated on the basis of results yielded by performance tests and the use of ranking and rating devices. Attitudes and interests are sometimes evaluated in terms of paper-and-pencil inventory results, ranking and rating results, reports of teacher-pupil interviews and anecdotal records. Pupil evaluation is ordinarily centered around paper-and-pencil tests to an unrealistically high degree.

Suggested Readings

Ammons, Margaret. Objectives and outcomes. In R. L. Ebel (ed.), *Encyclopedia of educational research.* (4th ed.) London: Macmillan, 1969. Pp. 908–914.
>A review of the historical development of objectives, the sources of them, and the manner of expressing them. The last two sections are devoted to behavioral objectives and taxonomies, followed by an extensive bibliography.

Bloom, B. S. (ed.) *Taxonomy of educational objectives: Cognitive domain.* New York: David McKay, 1956.
>This book provides an excellent basis for building evaluation instruments in the cognitive domain. By classifying objectives, it offers a framework for improving the chances that achievement tests in this area will have acceptable content validity. Illustrative objectives and test items are shown.

Bloom, B. S. Some theoretical issues relating to educational evaluation. In R. W. Tyler (ed.), *Educational evaluation: New roles, new means.* Sixty-Eighth Yearbook of the National Society for the Study of Education, Part II. Chicago: University of Chicago Press, 1969. Pp. 26–50.
>The controversy about the degree to which objectives should be stated specifically is reviewed. Also, careful consideration is given to the positive and negative effects of testing as formative and summative evaluation procedures.

French, W., and associates. *Behavioral goals of general education in high school.* New York: Russell Sage Foundation, 1957.
>This is a report of the second-level objectives of the general education program in the secondary school. Although organized in a different manner, it is, in a sense, a companion volume to *Elementary School Objectives* by Kearney. Part III contains lists of behavioral outcomes classified according to three maturity goals and four areas of behavioral competence.

Kearney, N. C. *Elementary school objectives.* New York: Russell Sage Foundation, 1953. Parts 2 and 3.
>Part 2 lists the second-level goals for the elementary school years as recommended by the Mid-Century Committee on Outcomes in Elementary Education. Their implications for educational practice, research, and measurement are treated in Part 3.

Krathwohl, D. R., B. S. Bloom, and B. B. Masia. *Taxonomy of educational objectives: Affective domain.* New York: David McKay, 1964.
>The first part of this book is an explanation of the rationale behind the taxonomy of educational objectives in the affective domain, including a discussion of internalization, the major organizing principle underlying the taxonomy. The second part contains a full description of the taxonomy and illustrative educational objectives and evaluation procedures classified in the various levels.

Krathwohl, D. R., and D. A. Payne. Defining and assessing educational objectives. In R. L. Thorndike (ed.), *Educational measurement.* (2nd ed.) Washington: American Council on Education, 1970. Chapter 2.
>A well-written chapter providing significant information regarding levels of ob-

jectives, their sources, and their taxonomies. Suggestions are given for utilizing third-level objectives.

Mager, R. F. *Preparing instructional objectives.* San Francisco: Fearon Publishers, 1962.

Techniques for stating objectives explicitly in behavioral terms are presented. Three considerations are: (1) identifying the terminal behavior that the pupil must demonstrate, (2) describing the conditions under which this behavior will be expected to occur, and (3) describing how well the pupil must perform in order to demonstrate mastery. Examples of well stated and poorly stated objectives are included.

Popham, W. J., E. W. Eisner, H. J. Sullivan, and L. L. Tyler. Instructional objectives. AERA *Monograph Series on Curriculum Evaluation,* 1969, No. 3.

The four chapters often take quite different views about the sources of objectives and the manner in which they are stated and used. Discussions among the four authors follow each chapter and are enlightening. The monograph ends with four epilogues well worth reading.

References Cited

Ahrens, M. R. Developing a plan of action for improving programs for youth. In N. B. Henry (ed.), *Adapting the secondary-school program to the needs of youth.* Fifty-Second Yearbook of the National Society for the Study of Education, Part I. Chicago: University of Chicago Press, 1953. Pp. 102–117.

Bloom, B. S. (ed.) *Taxonomy of educational objectives: Cognitive domain.* New York: David McKay, 1956.

Brink, W. C. The youth-needs motive in secondary education. In N. B. Henry (ed.), *Adapting the secondary-school program to the needs of youth.* Fifty-Second Yearbook of the National Society for the Study of Education, Part I. Chicago: University of Chicago Press, 1953. Pp. 1–21.

Cardinal principles of secondary education. *U.S. Office of Education Bulletin,* No. 35, 1918.

Educational Policies Commission. *The purposes of education in American democracy.* Washington: National Education Association and the American Association of School Administrators, 1938.

Eisner, E. W. Instructional and expressive objectives: Their formulation and use in curriculum. *AERA Monograph Series on Curriculum Evaluation,* 1969, No. 3. Pp. 1–31.

English, H. B., and A. C. English. *A comprehensive dictionary of psychological and psychoanalytical terms.* New York: David McKay, 1958.

French, W., and associates. *Behavioral goals of general education in high school.* New York: Russell Sage Foundation, 1957.

French, J. W., and W. B. Michael. *Standards for educational and psychological tests and manuals.* Washington: American Psychological Association, 1966.

Gagné, R. M. *The conditions of learning.* (2nd ed.) New York: Holt, Rinehart and Winston, 1970.

Glaser, R., and A. J. Nitko. Measurement in learning and instruction. In R. L. Thorndike (ed.), *Educational measurement.* (2nd ed.) Washington: American Council on Education, 1970. Chapter 17.

Gronlund, N. E. *Stating educational objectives for classroom instruction.* London: Macmillan, 1970.

Havighurst, R. J. *Human development and education.* New York: David McKay, 1953.

Kearney, N. C. *Elementary school objectives.* New York: Russell Sage Foundation, 1953.

Krathwohl, D. R., B. S. Bloom, and B. B. Masia. *Taxonomy of educational objectives: Affective domain.* New York: David McKay, 1964.

Krathwohl, D. R., and D. A. Payne. Defining and assessing educational objectives. In R. L. Thorndike (ed.), *Educational measurement.* (2nd ed.) Washington: American Council on Education, 1970. Chapter 17.

Lindquist, E. F. Preliminary considerations in objective test construction. In E. F. Lindquist (ed.), *Educational measurement.* Washington: American Council on Education, 1951. Pp. 119–158.

Low, C. M. Determining the nature of the needs of youth. In N. B. Henry (ed.), *Adapting the secondary-school program to the needs of youth.* Fifty-Second Yearbook of the National Society for the Study of Education, Part I. Chicago: University of Chicago Press, 1953. Pp. 22–43.

Mager, R. F. *Preparing instructional objectives.* Palo Alto, California: Fearon Publishers, 1962.

Metfessel, N. S., W. B. Michael, and D. A. Kirsner. Instrumentation of Bloom's and Krathwohl's taxonomies for the writing of educational objectives. *Psychology in the Schools,* 1969, 6, 227–231.

Norris, E. L. (ed.) *National assessment of educational progress citizenship objectives.* Ann Arbor, Michigan: Committee on Assessing the Progress of Education, 1969a.

Norris, E. L. (ed.) *National assessment of educational progress science objectives.* Ann Arbor, Michigan: Committee on Assessing the Progress of Education, 1969b.

Popham, W. J. *Instructional objectives exchange.* Los Angeles: UCLA Center for the Study of Education, 1969.

Simpson, E. J. The classification of educational objectives, psychomotor domain. *Illinois Teacher,* 1966–67, **10,** 110–144.

Simpson, E. J. Schema for classification of educational objectives, psychomotor domain. Unpublished manuscript, 1969.

Smith, R. B. A discussion of an attempt at constructing reproducible item sets. *Journal of Educational Measurement,* 1968, **5,** 55–60.

Smith, T. A., and C. N. Shaw. Structural analysis as an aid in designing an instructional system. *Journal of Educational Measurement,* 1969, 6, 137–143.

Sullivan, H. J. Objectives, evaluation, and improved learner achievement. *AERA Monograph Series on Curriculum Evaluation,* 1969, No. 3. Pp. 65–99.

Tyler, L. L. A case history: Formulation of objectives from a psychoanalytic framework. *AERA Monograph Series on Curriculum Evaluation,* 1969, No. 3. Pp. 100–129.

Tyler, R. W. Translating youth needs into teaching goals. In N. B. Henry (ed.), *Adapting the secondary-school program to the needs of youth.* Fifty-second Yearbook of the National Society for the Study of Education, Part I. Chicago: University of Chicago Press, 1953. Pp. 215–229.

Tyler, R. W. Some persistent questions on the defining of objectives. In C. M. Lindvall (ed.), *Defining educational objectives*. Pittsburgh: University of Pittsburgh Press, 1964. Pp. 77–83.

Walbesser, H. H., Jr. *An evaluation model and its application, a second report.* AAAS Miscellaneous Publication 68-4. Washington: American Association for the Advancement of Science, 1968.

PART TWO

Measuring Achievement in the Classroom

For the homeowner, the do-it-yourself movement usually dominates such activities as carpentry, painting, and landscaping. The novelty of being your own designer, contractor, and artisan contributes to the popularity of this movement. The self-satisfaction experienced at the completion of a project is virtually matchless.

The do-it-yourself idea is a familiar one to the teacher, both within the scope of his professional position and outside of it. Early in his training program he discovers that recipes for teaching are few, that prefabricated teaching techniques do not exist, and that hiring someone to perform part of his duties is seldom possible. In short, he learns that he must rely on his own skill and ingenuity practically all of the time. The unique characteristics of each teaching situation are too important to permit a standardization of the teaching art.

As one step in the teaching process, pupil evaluation offers an excellent opportunity for a teacher to display his skill and ingenuity. Although outside assistance is available in the form of standardized measuring instruments and measurement specialists who serve as consultants, the lion's share of the evaluation program must be shouldered by the classroom teacher. Frequently it is he who must design the instrument, administer it, score it, interpret the results, and, finally, appraise the worth of these activities. His responsibilities here are as clear as those related to the identification of his educational objectives and, on the basis of them, the determination of suitable learning experiences for his pupils.

The teacher's measuring efforts are often centered around the paper-and-pencil achievement test, either objective or essay type. Chapter 3, "Measuring

Knowledge Objectively," is devoted to discussions of the construction and use of objective test items to be used as a classroom achievement test, with emphasis on those test items that measure recall of information. Chapter 4, "Measuring Complex Achievement Objectively," emphasizes those test items that measure the pupil's ability to use his fund of knowledge. Successful performance means that the pupil can locate appropriate information and manipulate it to solve new problems. Chapter 5, "Preparing Essay Achievement Tests," identifies the role of essay test items in achievement testing and compares it with that of objective test items. Chapter 6, "Appraising Classroom Achievement Tests," contains descriptions of various methods of appraising paper-and-pencil tests, particularly those that are objective in nature.

Not all of the data-gathering instruments built by the classroom teacher are paper-and-pencil tests. Many are ranking and rating scales, check lists, product scales, and the like, that are used to evaluate pupil performance. Chapter 7, "Judging of Procedures and Products," describes and illustrates these methods.

The classroom teacher generally cannot build measuring instruments as technically perfect as those produced by teams of testing specialists. On the other hand, he has a decided advantage over the specialists in that he is far better informed concerning the quality of the pupils whose achievements are to be measured and the nature of the learning experiences they have had. This in turn means that the classroom instruments that he builds with care will often compare favorably with standardized instruments designed to accomplish the same purpose.

Instead of being discouraged about the likelihood of building useful measuring instruments, you should be optimistic. The expenditure of reasonable amounts of effort coupled with careful observance of a group of simple rules is all that is really needed. If you have a creative flair, the task is simpler and the product better.

CHAPTER 3

Measuring Knowledge Objectively

As consumers, each of us repeatedly samples various products on the market and, on the basis of our reaction, we draw conclusions about the quality of the product. Consider for a moment any of the purchases of food we commonly make. Suppose that we enter a supermarket to buy three items—candy, bakery goods, and breakfast cereal. In the first instance we select a pound of gum drops. Within the pound are individual pieces of a variety of colors. A nibble of one of each color may quickly convince us to favor the green gum drops over those of all other colors and to avoid the black ones at all costs. For the second purchase we choose one dozen glazed doughnuts. These we find to be fresh and tasteful, and, as a result, our opinion of the bakery is favorable. Finally, we select a well-known brand of breakfast cereal. If at breakfast on subsequent mornings we conclude that, as advertised, the cereal is indeed a "taste treat" and gives us that additional "go-power," we probably will continue to buy the product; if not, we will no doubt refuse to buy another box no matter how persuasive the exhortations of well-known motion picture personalities and professional athletes.

How sound are these judgments? This question is difficult to answer. To the degree that our taste sensibilities are reasonably normal at the time we tested the product, and to the degree that the sample of the product we consumed is reasonably representative, the judgments are sound. If these two conditions are not met, the soundness of the decision is certainly in doubt. For example, had we been ill shortly before or during the trial, the first condition would very likely not be satisfied. Had the gum drops, doughnuts, or breakfast cereal been accidentally contaminated in some way, they would hardly be representative of these products when properly handled, and the second condition would not be satisfied.

When acting as a consumer of food products, the classroom teacher samples and judges them just like anyone else. When evaluating the achievement of his pupils, he follows essentially the same procedure. He is actually making the same two basic assumptions. In the first place, just as he assumes that his testing faculties are normal when he judges food products, he believes that the ability of his pupils to reveal the knowledges and more complex intellectual skills they possess and their willingness to do so are not seriously impaired by any unusual factors. Such factors might be emotional disturbances, greatly reduced teacher-pupil rapport, physical fatigue, or any of a multitude of minor distractions.

Secondly, just as he assumes that the food products eaten are representative of similar ones in the supermarket on that day or any day, he concludes that the samples of pupil behavior that he observes are typical of much unobserved pupil behavior both present and future. In the case of achievement testing, the samples of pupil behavior are elicited by the questions or tasks included in a test. Hence, to obtain a representative sample of all of the possible variations of the pupil behavior in question, the teacher tries to find a representative sample of all of the possible questions or tasks that might be presented to the pupil.

The justification for the use of samples for evaluating food products as well as achievement is essentially one of practicality. It is not feasible or necessary that a person eat all gum drops in sight before deciding that the green ones are the most pleasing. In the same manner, it is not feasible or necessary that a teacher ask a pupil all possible questions or provide opportunities for him to perform all possible tasks to determine the degree to which he has achieved certain educational objectives.

The teacher would of course like to be confident that these two assumptions are fulfilled every time he tries to evaluate pupil achievement. He can never attain complete certainty. He can take steps, however, that improve the likelihood that both assumptions will be satisfied. As far as achievement tests are concerned, useful procedures for assuring that a pupil is responding willingly and to the best of his ability are discussed in Chapter 16. In addition, useful procedures for assuring that a representative sample of pupil behavior is being judged are mentioned in many parts of this book.

PRELIMINARY PREPARATION FOR THE OBJECTIVE TEST

Demanding that a paper-and-pencil achievement test contain a representative group of test items is equivalent to demanding that the test have a high degree of content validity. Notice again that content validity is inherently tied to educational objectives; in the case of paper-and-pencil achievement tests, it is tied to specific objectives with verbal and mathematical aspects. Thus, procedures such as the use of a table of specifications that are known to improve the degree of content validity of a paper-and-pencil test are important to us here.

A table of specifications is a miniature view of the test; it is actually a crude but helpful blueprint used by the teacher to devise a test, just as a contractor's blueprint is used by a carpenter. The relative weights the teacher attaches to each cell are his guides to building a test with representative items. As test items are written, they are identified with one or more of the cells, and this information recorded. The tendency to overrepresent or to underrepresent any cell or group of cells is greatly minimized by this procedure.

Tables of specifications in paper-and-pencil achievement tests guarantee that the subject matter will be properly sampled and all pertinent behavioral changes appropriately emphasized. Sometimes more than one table is required. If so, the test may be subdivided into several main parts, which in turn could be separately timed and scored.

Problems

1. Stodola (1961, pp. 3–13) describes the plans and procedures of four teachers, each teaching at a different grade level and in a different subject matter area, for constructing an informal achievement test to meet a particular need. Several tables of specifications are shown. Evaluate the test construction efforts of the teachers in the light of their stated needs and the tables of specifications to be used.

2. Writing test items often helps to clarify the table of specifications. This may cause one to modify table headings and even cell percentages while in the middle of his efforts to build test items (Tinkelman, 1970). In your opinion, does the failure of the table to remain fixed tend to reduce or increase the degree of content validity of the resulting achievement test?

TYPES OF OBJECTIVE TEST ITEMS

An efficient and convenient way to measure the pupil's ability to recall the information identified by a table of specifications is to build and administer a series of pertinent objective test items. An objective test item is one that can be scored in such a way that judgment is for all practical purposes eliminated when determining the correctness of a pupil's answer. To be sure, this is a broad definition. It is not surprising, therefore, to find many different types of test items identified as objective test items yet seemingly quite dissimilar in form. A broad classification of types followed by a description of the most popular variations is sufficient in a book of this kind.

Objective test items may be usefully designated as the supply type of item or the selection type of item (Wesman, 1970). When responding to a supply type of item, the pupil has to provide the words, numbers, or symbols. Possible answers are not listed as part of the item. An illustration of the supply type is the short-answer item, two varieties of which are shown below:

Short-answer question:

DIRECTIONS: Within the space provided, write the word or phrase that correctly answers the question.
What is the name of the author of the novel entitled *Pickwick Papers?* (Charles Dickens)

Completion test item:

DIRECTIONS: Within the space provided, write the word or phrase that correctly completes the statement.
The name of the author of the novel entitled *Pickwick Papers* is (Charles Dickens).

The selection type of item allows the pupil to choose the correct response from the information provided. The well-known true-false test item, multiple-choice test item, matching test item, and countless variations of them typify this category.

True-false test item:

DIRECTIONS: Determine whether each of the following statements is true or false. If the statement is true, circle the "T" preceding the statement; if the statement is false, circle the "F."
Ⓣ F 1. The novel entitled *Pickwick Papers* was written by Charles Dickens.

Multiple-choice test item:

DIRECTIONS: For each of the following questions choose the correct answer from among the four possible answers listed. Write the number of your choice in the blank to the left of the question.
(2) 1.   Who wrote the novel entitled *Pickwick Papers?*
                    (1) William Thackeray
                    (2) Charles Dickens
                    (3) Anthony Trollope
                    (4) George Eliot

Matching test item:

DIRECTIONS: Match the title of each novel with its author by writing the letter identifying the author in the blank to the left of the title. It is possible that some authors have written more than one of the novels listed.

	Novels	Authors
(F)	1. *Barchester Towers*	A. Jane Austen
(B)	2. *David Copperfield*	B. Charles Dickens
(B)	3. *Great Expectations*	C. Alexandre Dumas
(B)	4. *Oliver Twist*	D. George Eliot
(B)	5. *Pickwick Papers*	E. William Thackeray
(A)	6. *Pride and Prejudice*	F. Anthony Trollope
(D)	7. *Romola*	
(B)	8. *Tale of Two Cities*	
(E)	9. *Vanity Fair*	
(F)	10. *The Warden*	

The similarities and differences in form among these types of objective test items are obvious. There are, however, important similarities and differences in ease of construction, applicability, and ease of scoring. These and related topics are discussed and illustrated in the following sections.

Problems

3.   Some teachers argue that the differences among the various types of objective test items are seemingly large but actually small. In the case of the three chief variations of the selection type of item, defend their point of view.

4.   Many mathematics teachers build and use "computation" tests, that is, tests in which the pupil must arrive at numerical answers as the result of following certain computational procedures. Are these objective tests? Give reasons for your answer.

CONSTRUCTING OBJECTIVE TEST ITEMS

Building a paper-and-pencil test in terms of tables of specifications is, as we have seen, an important step toward assurance that the test will have high content validity. The value of this procedure, however, is noticeably lessened if the test items are carelessly devised. Even though the item may be carefully classified in terms of the subject matter topics and behavioral changes listed in the table of specifications, the test as a whole may lose some content validity if the teacher fails to apply properly a myriad of relatively simple, obvious, and seemingly unimportant rules when he builds the test items. Many "dos and don'ts" govern the construction of objective test items.

If a teacher is intimately familiar with his educational objectives, his own tables of specifications, and the backgrounds of his pupils, then you would expect that adhering faithfully to the spirit and letter of the suggestions for item construction would be a guarantee of good test items. This expectation is not totally justified. The writing of test items has been properly called an art—an art demanding the utmost degree of creativity, ingenuity, and persistence on the part of anyone who practices it. Knowledge of the steps to be followed is not enough. Excellence in item construction requires judgment and practice, and in large amounts!

Supply Test Items

The supply test item can be crudely defined as an essay test item demanding a highly abbreviated answer. This answer is often only a single word or number, seldom more than several words or numbers. The pupil responds to a direct question or incomplete declarative statement by writing his answer in the space provided. Notice that there is little difference between these two. By means of a simple rearrangement of words a short-answer question becomes a completion test item, or a completion test item becomes a short-answer question. They are sometimes haphazardly intermixed in classroom achievement tests; however, a better practice is to separate them, especially when young pupils are being tested.

Suggestions for Constructing Supply Test Items. *Design the supply test item so that it has only one correct answer, which is short and definite.* This is unquestionably the most difficult problem a teacher encounters when building supply test items. Although he has but one short and definite answer in mind for each item, he will be amazed at the pupils' facility for thinking of synonyms or near-synonyms of his answers, which in many instances must be considered as correct answers. For example, consider the following test item written in two different ways. It is intended for use in an achievement test in basic arithmetic for elementary school pupils.

Poor: In the mixed number 7⅔, the "2" is the (numerator).

Improved: In the mixed number 7⅔, which digit is the numerator? (2)

The first version of the item will elicit a variety of responses. Answers such as "top number," "even number," "smallest number," or "numerator" certainly will be given. In a sense, all of them are correct. Some are clearly better than others. Since the purpose of the test item is to see if the pupil can identify the numerator of a mixed number, the second version of the test item is an improvement. There is no doubt about the correctness of any answer given to this question.

The first version of the test item shown above can be quickly identified as a poor one. However, test items that, at a first glance, appear quite satisfactory can be equally inadequate. The following is such an item:

Poor: The novel entitled *Pickwick Papers* was written by (Charles Dickens).

Improved: The name of the author of the novel entitled *Pickwick Papers* is (Charles Dickens).

The first version of this completion test item could elicit such responses as "a man," "an Englishman," "an adult," a "novelist," or "a genius." All of these are technically correct, but none is the answer expected—"Charles Dickens." If a teacher wishes to avoid much needless quibbling over answers, he must exercise great care in the development of test items. Some proposed supply test items cannot be conveniently changed to avoid wrong or half-wrong answers—the desired answer might be too obvious and the item practically worthless because of too low level of difficulty. Changing the item form from a supply to a selection type sometimes helps in these cases.

Avoid removing statements verbatim from textbooks or other sources and trying to use them as short-answer test items. This practice will, of course, give an advantage to that pupil who can somehow detect a textbook expression and select his answers at least partially on the basis of whether they have a textbook flavor. Moreover, the use of verbatim statements may make the item ambiguous. For example, the first of the following statements is taken directly from a history textbook and one word is deleted to make it a completion item.

Poor: The power to declare war is vested in (Congress).

Improved: In the United States the power to declare war is vested in (Congress).

Since the test covered aspects of the governments of many other countries, the pupils were understandably confused by the first version of the test item. Obviously, the teacher quickly recognizes the trouble when it is called to his attention; however, he is less likely to anticipate this problem if he continually takes statements out of context and uses them as short-answer test items. In summary, each test item should be able to stand alone unless deliberately related to other items.

When building completion test items, avoid mutilating the statement until its meaning is all but lost. In an effort to increase the level of difficulty, or test for several pieces of information by means of one item, some teachers greatly increase the number of blanks in a completion item. The temptation to do so is rather strong at times, but seldom is the procedure successful. Using a relatively small number of well-chosen blanks is more satisfactory. Notice how the following item is improved by reducing the number of omitted words:

Poor: The (process) by which (petroleum) is separated into various component (parts) having different (boiling points) is known as (fractional distillation).

Improved: The process by which petroleum is separated into various component parts having different boiling points is known as (fractional distillation).

To the pupil, the second version is a well-defined problem, whereas the first is not. In fact, the first statement would discourage anyone but the person who originally deleted the words.

When building completion test items, try to place the blank or blanks near the end of the statement rather than the beginning, and provide sufficient space for pupil answers. Often it is a simple matter to place the blanks at either the beginning or end of the test item. Placing the blanks at the end prevents the test item from acquiring a noticeable awkwardness, as well as a degree of artificial difficulty. The following items illustrate the point:

Poor: (Ecology) is the name given to the study of the interrelationship of organisms among themselves and with their environment.

Improved: The study of the interrelationship of organisms among themselves and with their environment is known as (ecology).

Some pupils will need more time to arrive at the correct answer when confronted with the first version than with the second. This is particularly true of elementary school children.

Avoid the use of extraneous hints designed to help the pupil identify the correct answer. On occasion teachers try to help the pupil find the correct answer to a short-answer test item by inserting the first letter of each word of the answer, by drawing the length of the line indicating the omitted word so that it approximates the length of the answer, or by drawing several lines of appropriate length when the correct answer contains several words. The following short-answer test item in an elementary school geography test is typical of this procedure:

Poor: In which state is the most important seaport on the eastern seaboard located? N(ew) Y(ork)

Improved: In which state is the most important seaport on the eastern seaboard located? (New York)

The first version of the test item encourages guessing more than the improved version. In addition, offering such hints as these is not realistic; if a pupil were required to recall this information outside of the testing situation he undoubtedly would not be offered this assistance. The difference between the testing situation and the natural situation is increased, and therefore the form of the test item is open to criticism.

Also, the hints help him to use processes of elimination otherwise unavailable. In attempting to answer the test item, a pupil not knowing the correct answer could quickly eliminate possibilities by remembering that "N——" must mean "New" or "North." Therefore, the correct answer is New Jersey, New Mexico, New York, New Hampshire, North Dakota, or North Carolina. Of these states, only New York has the second word beginning with the letter "Y." This, then, is his answer.

Always indicate the units in which the answer is to be expressed for those supply test items that could have several answers depending upon the units chosen. For computational exercises this can be an annoying problem for both the pupils writing the test and the person who must later score it. For instance, the correct answer to the following exercise can be expressed in three different ways.

Poor: A four-foot piece of wire is to be cut into two pieces so that one
             piece will be six inches longer than twice the length of the second
             piece. What is the length of the longer piece? (2 ft., 10 in.)

Improved: A four-foot piece of wire is to be cut into two pieces so that one
           piece will be six inches longer than twice the length of the second
           piece. What is the length of the longer piece? Ans. (2) ft. (10) in.

The correct answer is 34 inches, $2\frac{5}{6}$ feet, or 2 feet and 10 inches. Demanding one type of unit rather than another can change the difficulty level of the
exercise as well as the amount of time needed to solve it.

Advantages and Limitations of Supply Test Items.   There are two advantages in using the supply test item rather than other kinds of objective test
items. First of all, the supply form minimizes the likelihood that the pupil
will guess the correct answer. Whereas in the case of the selection form, he
need only recognize the correct response from among a relatively small number
of given possibilities, in the case of the supply test item, he is confronted
with a situation that is not so highly structured. The likelihood of guessing
the correct response in the second instance is a less important consideration
than in the first. As a result, some pupils argue that this type of item is more
difficult for them.

A second advantage often attributed to supply test items is that they are
relatively easy to construct. This is, in a sense, a deceptive statement. Although
some teachers find them easier to build than the selection type of item, supply
test items are by no means so simple to construct as a casual investigation
might indicate. The foregoing suggestions for constructing supply test items
offer ample supporting evidence.

Of all of the limitations of using supply test items usually cited, two are
outstanding. In the first place, such items are more difficult to score than
other kinds of objective test items. Despite the best efforts of the teacher
building such a test item, often a variety of answers are totally or partially
correct. Assigning total or partial credit can only be done by someone intimately familiar with the test items, the background of the pupils, and the
teaching situation. In other words, it must be done by the teacher, and even
he finds it to be a difficult and time-consuming task. The scoring of pupil
responses is complicated by legibility of handwriting and faulty spelling. The
latter may or may not be sufficient cause for reducing the amount of credit a
pupil receives for an otherwise correct response. If one of the purposes of the
test is to determine whether a pupil can spell the correct answer after he has
recalled it, then loss of credit can be justified. If this is not the case, loss of
credit for faulty spelling cannot be defended.

The second limitation is the kind of behavioral change involved in the
item. Typically these items demand only recall of information rather than
more complex aspects, such as the application of principles in new situations.

This tendency is traceable in part to the fact that no matter what type of objective test item is to be used, test items requiring only recall of information are usually easier to construct. When building supply test items, the teacher strives to find items with correct answers that are short and clear, and in so doing, he often selects test items involving primarily factual details. Vocabulary is heavily emphasized.

On balance, supply test items leave something to be desired. They cannot be considered a versatile, efficient means of measuring a wide variety of pupil achievements. As a result, they are not commonly used except for teacher-built tests, and even for those their popularity is less than that of selection test items.

Problems

5. In the light of the foregoing suggestions to be followed when constructing supply test items, improve each of the following:
  a. A hogan is an almost round structure with walls made of (logs) and (mud plaster).
  b. Selling price equals cost plus (profit).
  c. (Sun) is the source of most of our heat.
  d. A diameter that is (perpendicular) to a chord (bisects) the chord.
6. Engelhart (1964, p. 13) labels supply test items as "semiobjective." Defend his position.

True-False Test Items

The true-false test item is nothing more than a declarative statement to which the pupil responds in one of two ways—the statement is true or it is false. Occasionally, the statement is so worded that it is more convenient to ask the pupil to respond with "Right" or "Wrong" rather than "True" or "False." Moreover, changing the declarative statement to a question need not necessarily increase the number of possible responses. In these instances, the question can be phrased so that a "Yes" or "No" response is requested.

The most common type of true-false test items has already been illustrated. Less common variations are the following:

Correction variety:

DIRECTIONS: Determine whether each of the following statements is true or false. If the statement is true, circle the "T" following the statement. If it is false, circle the "F" and write in the blank provided the word or words that, when substituted for the word underlined, will make the statement true.
  1. The earth is essentially spherical in shape.   Ⓣ F
  2. The sun is a planet.   T Ⓕ (star)
  3. The earth spins on its axis once each month.   T Ⓕ (day)

Cluster variety:

DIRECTIONS: The following statements pertain to the location of various European countries. Determine whether each statement about each country is true or false. If it is true, circle the "T" following the statement. If it is false, circle the "F."

    1. Switzerland has a common border with

        a. Italy on the south.   Ⓣ F

        b. France on the west.   Ⓣ F

        c. Austria on the east.   Ⓣ F

        d. Czechoslovakia on the north.   T Ⓕ

T-F-CT-CF variety:

DIRECTIONS: Determine (1) whether each of the following statements is true or false, and (2) whether the converse of the statement is true or false. If it is true, circle the "T" preceding the statement; if it is false, circle the "F." If the converse of the statement is true, circle "CT"; if the converse is false, circle "CF." *Two correct answers must be given for each statement.*

Ⓣ F CT ⒸF   1. A square is always a quadrilateral.

Ⓣ F ⒸT CF   2. An equilateral triangle is also an equiangular triangle.

T Ⓕ CT ⒸF   3. A right triangle is necessarily an isosceles triangle.

T-F-TF variety:

DIRECTIONS: Determine whether each of the following statements is true, false, or true under some circumstances and false under other circumstances. If the statement is true under all circumstances, circle the "T" preceding the statement; if it is false under all circumstances, circle the "F"; if it is true under some circumstances and false under others, circle the "TF."

T F ⓉF   1. The length on the earth surface of one degree of longitude is more than 69 but less than 70 statute miles.

T F ⓉF   2. If a person is living at a latitude of 40° he is living north of the equator.

Ⓣ F TF   3. The prime meridian is an imaginary line at 0° longitude.

Suggestions for Constructing True-False Test Items. *When constructing a test item requiring a response of either "True" or "False" and only that, search for statements that are true or false without additional qualifications.* All too commonly a true-false test item is *essentially* true or false rather than *absolutely* true or false. This is perplexing to the pupil. Should he mark statements as true only if they are true under all possible circumstances, and mark all others false even though some might be essentially true? On the other hand, should he mark those statements true that are in general true and those false that are in general false, thus ignoring specific and perhaps minor qualifications that might be pertinent? If his method of attack fails to be the one the teacher has in mind, his answer will be wrong even though his knowledge of the subject matter is superior.

The following test item illustrates the problem. The intended answer *is* "True."

Poor: The water vapor in the air will condense when the air is cooled.
Improved: If the temperature of the air in this room is progressively lowered, a temperature will ultimately be reached at which the water vapor in the air will start to condense.

The first version of the test item may trouble the pupil because the degree of cooling, the amount of water vapor in the air, and the temperature of the air are not stated. Slight cooling may or may not cause condensation; drastic cooling probably would. Hence, the statement is true under certain circumstances and false under others. A pupil who knows the information normally required to answer the test item correctly may fail to receive credit for his knowledge because he remembers too many facts. He judges the statement to be false. When confronted with the second version of the test item, he would mark it as "True." Incidentally, copying statements verbatim from textbooks or study guides customarily produces true-false test items that are not absolutely true or absolutely false.

Avoid the use of specific determiners. Specific determiners are words or expressions that frequently identify a statement containing them as true or false. Words often found in false statements are "only," "never," "all," "every," "always," "none," and "no." Those often found in true statements are "usually," "generally," "sometimes," "customarily," "often," "may," "could," and "frequently." The testwise pupil recognizes the situation. If he does not possess the knowledge necessary to answer correctly a true-false test item, he searches for a specific determiner. Should he find one and answer accordingly, his chances of having identified the correct answer are good. Consequently, the test item may discriminate among pupils on a basis other than their ability to recall information, and thus its usefulness is impaired.

In an effort to construct true-false test items that are absolutely true or absolutely false, teachers repeatedly resort to the use of specific determiners. The weakening of the test item that customarily occurs is illustrated in the case of the following:

Poor: None of the people of Switzerland is engaged in farming.
Improved: The mountains of Switzerland prevent the Swiss people from raising grain extensively.

A clever but ill-prepared pupil would quickly mark the first version of the test item as false. Even though he may know nothing of the farming problems of Switzerland, he is confident that at least one Swiss citizen is engaged in farming. The second version demands a knowledge of the geography of the country as well as the nature of its agriculture. It contains no specific determiners to provide hints as to its correct answer.

The teacher need not always avoid the use of such words as "all," "never," and "usually" because they can serve as specific determiners. On the contrary, they can be deliberately used, and with success, by including them in true-false test items that have correct answers the opposite of those suggested by the words in question. For example:

1. All planets revolve around the sun of our solar system.
2. The sum of the angles of a plane triangle is always 180°.
3. Each molecule of a given compound is chemically the same as every other molecule of that compound.
4. The galvanometer is the instrument usually used for the metering of electrical energy for determining the cost of electrical service in a home.

In these instances, the words "all," "always," "every" and "usually" are no longer specific determiners.

Try to keep the true-false test items reasonably short, and restrict each to one central idea. True-false test items that are extremely long require undue amounts of response time. The pupil must search out the truth or falsity of each phrase and dependent clause. Moreover, long true-false test items are more often true than false since the length is sometimes caused by the qualifying remarks needed to make the statement true. Strive to balance the true-false statements in terms of length. If lengthy statements are used, they should be false about as often as they are true.

A serious problem that is sometimes accentuated by lengthy true-false items is that several ideas become involved. The pupil has to answer the test item in terms of whether the statements made about all ideas are true or false. If one part of the test item is true, whereas another part is false, he customarily labels the test item as false. But this can be confusing to the pupil not only when he responds to the test item but also when he reviews his test at a later time. Misinformation may result.

An illustration of a true-false test item that is partially true and partially false is shown below:

Poor: Although today the members of the United States House of Representatives are elected by popular vote of the people of the districts they represent, the members of the United States Senate are selected by the state legislatures of the states they represent.

Improved: The members of the present Senate of the United States were selected by the state legislatures of the states they represent.

The length of the first version of this item makes it a forbidding thing indeed; it can be shortened easily. The clause at the beginning of the statement is unnecessary and should be eliminated, as illustrated by the second version of the test item. This deletion serves the additional purpose of reducing the scope of the item to one central idea, which can be judged as true or false.

If true-false tests are used regularly, be certain that the percentage of test items requiring a "True" answer, and hence the percentage of test items requiring a "False" answer, are not relatively constant from test to test. Some pupils quickly sense any tendency on the part of a teacher to maintain approximately the same percent of true and false statements from test to test. This is true regardless of whether an even balance between the two statements is maintained or an overbalance of one type is used. If a noticeable consistency is detected, the pupil may use it as a basis for guessing the answers of some of the test items that baffle him. Moreover, some pupils quickly discover any pattern that the correct answers may take, such as, F-T-F-T-F-T or T-T-F-F-T-T. Occasionally a teacher arranges the test items so that the correct answers form a systematic pattern, thereby simplifying scoring. Such an arrangement also simplifies the task of the alert pupil when he responds to the test items. An otherwise good true-false test can be seriously damaged by this procedure.

Advantages and Limitations of True-False Test Items.   The advantages accrued by using true-false test items are outweighed by the limitations. The popularity of these test items is unjustified—a popularity that can be traced primarily to the fact that true-false test items allow the teacher to sample widely a large amount of subject matter without needing a great amount of testing time. Most pupils can respond quickly to well-constructed items of this type. Even pupils in the primary grades can respond to them without requiring prohibitive amounts of time. A second and less obvious advantage sometimes cited in the case of true-false test items is that they are essentially a realistic task for the pupil. Frequently, in everyday life, he is called upon to judge a statement as true or false in the manner required of him by the test items. A third advantage of even more doubtful merit is the claim that true-false test items are easy to build. As in the case of the supply test items, the true-false test item is by no means so easy to construct as you might suppose.

One of the most serious limitations of the true-false test item is that many are concerned only with small, relatively unimportant pieces of information. Like the supply test item, the true-false item serves best as a means of measuring the pupils' ability to recall information. Because of the teacher's efforts to find statements that are absolutely true or false, the information needed to answer the items correctly is frequently highly specific. It is difficult to build good true-false test items that involve generalizations, broad principles, and relationships, all of which may be notably more important than the pieces of information involved in the usual true-false test items.

A second serious disadvantage is that true-false test items encourage some pupils to try to guess the correct response. They argue that, after all, they have a fifty-fifty chance of identifying the right answer without even bothering to read the statement. The use of specific determiners, the tendency of long statements to be true statements, and the practice of arranging the correct responses in a systematic pattern encourage guessing and increase the likelihood of that guessing being successful. Means of correcting for guessing are discussed later in this chapter (see page 124).

Finally, true-false test items can be criticized on the basis that many of them are ambiguous. Careful construction of a set of true-false test items reduces ambiguity, but does not necessarily eliminate it. Words like "several," "many," "some," "frequently," "important," and "principal" can hardly be avoided. But what do they mean? Variations in the meanings of these and similar terms can mean variations in the pupils' responses to the statements containing them. Hairsplitting distinctions may be necessary, to the distress of teacher and pupil alike.

Problems

7. Evaluate the usefulness of true-false test items used for the purpose of measuring pupil knowledge in the (a) elementary school and (b) the secondary school.
8. Suppose that the improved version of the true-false test item concerning Swiss agriculture on page 92 were changed to read:
> The terrain of Switzerland retards the development of a diversified agricultural program in that country.

Criticize this version of the test item.
9. In the light of the foregoing suggestions to be followed in construction of true-false test items, improve each of the following:
   a. If we feel heat traveling through a steel bar at a certain rate, we can assume that heat will travel through another kind of bar at that rate.
   b. Heat can do work.
   c. The *Reader's Guide* is the best source to use when looking for current material on a subject.
   d. If (+) times (+) equals (+), then (−) times (−) equals (−).

Multiple-Choice Test Items

A multiple-choice test item is one in which a direct question or incomplete statement is presented and a number of possible responses or options are given. The pupil chooses the response that is the correct (or best) answer to the question or that is the correct (or best) expression for completing the statement. The question or incomplete statement introducing the test item is known as the *stem*. Any undesired answer is called a *distracter* or *foil*. Generally four or five responses are listed and all but one is a distracter.

Some multiple-choice test items require a correct answer, others a "best" answer. This difference can be traced to the subject matter. For instance, when selecting the name of the author of a book among four names listed, the pupil searches for the correct answer; all distracters are completely wrong. However, when selecting the principal reason from among four possible reasons that Ulysses S. Grant was elected to the presidency of the United States, the pupil searches for the "best" answer. It should be clearly the most outstanding of those listed. As you can easily see, in this illustration the distracters can be actual reasons, but relatively unimportant. Both of these kinds of multiple-choice test items are commonly used.

Introducing a multiple-choice test item by means of an incomplete statement seems to be equally as satisfactory as introducing it by means of a direct question. Often the factor governing the choice of stem is the length of the test item. If the direct question approach yields a short, easily understood test item, it is customarily used; should it not do so, the incomplete statement approach replaces it. For a person inexperienced in building multiple-choice test items, however, the direct question is recommended, since fewer technically weak items result (Wesman, 1970). Both types of stems are popular and can be used regardless of whether a correct or "best" answer is desired.

There are numerous variations of the multiple-choice test item. The most familiar form is that illustrated earlier in this chapter. Three additional variations are shown below.

Negative variety:

DIRECTIONS: For each of the following questions, select from among the four responses listed that which is *not* the correct answer. Write the number of your choice in the blank to the left of each question.

(1)   1. Which of the following cities in the United States are located west of the Mississippi River?
       (1) Chicago
       (2) Denver
       (3) Los Angeles
       (4) Salt Lake City

Multiple-response variety:

DIRECTIONS: For each of the following questions, select the correct answer or answers from among the four listed. Note that for each question there may be as few as one and as many as four correct answers. Write the number(s) of your choice(s) in the blank to the left of the question.

(2, 3)   1. Which of the following compounds are gases when at room temperature and under normal pressure?
       (1) Benzene
       (2) Ammonia
       (3) Carbon dioxide
       (4) Silicon dioxide

Incomplete-response variety:

DIRECTIONS: Solve each of the following mathematics exercises and express your answer in the units designated. Identify the digit of your answer that occupies the second place to the left of the decimal point. Find that digit in the list of five shown with each exercise. Write the letter identifying it in the blank to the left of the exercise.

(D)   1. Four neighbors are to be assessed by their city for special repairs to the street in front of their houses. The amount to be paid is to be prorated among the neighbors according to the property frontage of each (i.e., the width of property along the street). The total assessment is $690, and the respective frontages are 50, 50, 60, and 70 feet. How much (to the nearest dollar) will the owner of the 60-foot frontage have to pay?

(A) 1
(B) 2
(C) 7
(D) 8
(E) 9

Combined-response variety:

DIRECTIONS: Each of the following exercises contains a group of objects, people, or events, the members of which are to be arranged in proper order according to the principle stated. Select the correct order for those listed and write the number of your choice in the blank to the left of the exercise.

(*1*)   1. Arrange the following British statesmen in terms of the dates of their careers, starting with the most recent.

a. Robert Walpole
b. Stanley Baldwin
c. William Pitt, Jr.
d. Winston Churchill
(1) d, b, c, a
(2) b, d, a, c
(3) b, a, d, c
(4) d, c, b, a

Suggestions for Constructing Multiple-Choice Test Items. *Select the distracters so that all of them are reasonably plausible and appealing to those pupils who do not possess the knowledge demanded by the item.* Your experiences as an examinee are no doubt sufficient to convince you of the importance of this suggestion. When you are confronted with a multiple-choice item to which you do not know the answer, you probably attack by a process of elimination. Any response that appears to be extremely unlikely you eliminate, even though you may have little or no knowledge of it. Often you are able to reduce the number of possibilities to two, sometimes to only one. If some of the distracters are implausible, the possibility of identifying the correct answer is greatly improved. Many a pupil arrives at the correct answer to a multiple-choice item by this means, yet he does not possess the knowledge required.

The following test item shows the ease with which the correct answer to a multiple-choice test item can be found when the distracters are implausible or appealing.

Poor: Which of the following men was at one time the Chief Justice of the Supreme Court of the United States?
(1) Charles Evans Hughes
(2) Nikolai Lenin
(3) Chiang Kai-shek
(4) John Paul Jones

Improved: Which of the following men was at one time the Chief Justice of the Supreme Court of the United States?
(1) Charles Evans Hughes
(2) William E. Borah

(3) Oliver Wendell Holmes
(4) William Jennings Bryan

If a pupil does not know the answer to the test item as stated in the first instance, a few miscellaneous pieces of information can help him find it. After all, responses 2 and 3 are unlikely possibilities. Names such as these hardly sound "American," so they probably should be eliminated. Response 4 sounds "American" enough, but John Paul Jones will no doubt be remembered as a military hero, perhaps as a Revolutionary War naval hero. Since it seems improbable that a military hero would ever be elevated to the position of Chief Justice of the Supreme Court, this response is eliminated. Response 1 is therefore correctly selected despite the fact that the pupil knows nothing of Charles Evans Hughes, Nikolai Lenin, and Chiang Kai-shek, and very little about John Paul Jones and the Supreme Court.

The second statement of the test item is greatly improved. All of the persons listed were citizens of the United States and were prominent in public life. They were also contemporaries. All had sufficient qualifications to be considered for such a post as Chief Justice; one of them, Oliver Wendell Holmes, was a prominent associate justice of the Supreme Court but never the Chief Justice of that body. This should be a plausible and attractive distracter to the partially informed pupil. The distracters used in the second version of the test item are more homogeneous than those used in the first version.

It is possible to build a third version of the test item having even more homogeneous responses. For example, the distracters could be the names of prominent associate justices who served with Charles Evans Hughes. As you would expect, most pupils will find this version more difficult than the second version, just as they found the second more difficult than the first. Thus, increasing the homogeneity of the responses tends to increase the difficulty of the multiple-choice test item. This is a useful rule to remember, but it must be tempered with the reminder that, whether the responses are considered homogeneous or heterogeneous, each distracter must seem plausible to any inadequately prepared pupils.

Plausible distracters are often difficult to find. What is plausible to the teacher may not seem so to the pupils, yet the teacher must decide which distracters are used. With sufficient planning however, an alternative technique can be used. By tabulating wrong answers to supply test items, the teacher can amass much helpful information for determining plausible distracters for future testing. Multiple-choice questions can be substituted for supply test items and wrong answers from earlier classes used as distracters.

Vary the number of options included in the multiple-choice test item as needed, anticipating that ordinarily there will be at least three and not more than five. How many options should the typical multiple-choice item have? To answer this question, consider first the test-sophistication of the pupils.

Four-option and even five-option test items are commonly used in achievement tests for pupils at the junior high school level and above. Certainly this is too many for pupils in the primary grade levels. Often two-option or three-option test items are used in an effort to avoid reading problems and excessive fatigue.

Another important factor influencing the number of options is the quality of distracters available. Sometimes we slavishly adhere to a fixed number of distracters for all multiple-choice items in a given test. This is unnecessary. The effectiveness of the distracters rather than their number determines the quality of the test item (Wesman, 1970). Instead of having a fixed mold (for example, one correct answer plus three distracters for each item), reduce the number of distracters when few good ones are available. Distracters that are nothing but "fillers" complicate the testing effort without improving our ability to differentiate among pupils in terms of achievement.

If the number of options varies somewhat from item to item in a test, the pupils should be told about it at the beginning of the test. Should variation occur frequently, group the test items according to the number of options they have, or even consider changing the item form, for example, to one of the true-false varieties.

Be certain that the length of the responses of a multiple-choice test item is not related to their tendency to be the correct (or best) answer. Because of the need to qualify to make one response the correct (or best) answer, the desired answer would regularly be the longest unless precautions are taken. Notice how obvious this is in the following illustration:

Poor: Sliced oranges are an excellent source of
    (1) protein.
    (2) starch.
    (3) vitamin A.
    (4) vitamin C, if the oranges are freshly sliced.
Improved: Freshly prepared orange juice is recommended for the diet because it is an excellent source of
    (1) protein.
    (2) starch.
    (3) vitamin A.
    (4) vitamin C.

If given the first version of the multiple-choice test item, the ill-prepared pupil will select repsonse 4 more frequently than any other. Its length probably means that it is the correct answer. When confronted with the second version, he has no such irrelevant clue to help him.

If a multiple-choice test item requires a "best" answer, make certain that one and only one is clearly the best. "Hairsplitting" is a problem in practically all objective test items. This is especially true of "best" answer multiple-choice test items, for a judgment is involved. It is a matter of opinion as to which of many reasons is the most important why a phenomenon occurred, or which of many is the chief result for a given cause. There are many counterparts to such possibilities, and they all too frequently appear in otherwise respectable multiple-choice tests.

Every multiple-choice test item should have a response that is clearly the best. For example:

Poor: The most serious health problem in the United States today is
        (1) cancer.
        (2) mental illness.
        (3) heart disease.
        (4) the common cold.
Improved: Of the following diseases, which hospitalizes the most people at the present time?
        (1) pneumonia.
        (2) mental illness.
        (3) poliomyelitis.
        (4) tuberculosis.

On the basis of the prevalence of the illness, the possibility of its being fatal, or the difficulty of relieving it, any one of the responses to the first version of the test item can be judged the "best." Unanimity or even near unanimity of opinion may be difficult to obtain. However, the test item as revised offers no such problem. Although all the diseases listed are health problems today, mental illness is the best answer here.

Whenever convenient, design the multiple-choice test item so that the stem includes as much of the item as is possible. Multiple-choice test items are usually improved if the stem is relatively long and the responses are relatively short; then the stem more clearly defines the problem on which the test item is based, and less response time is needed by most pupils. On the other hand, remember that it is sometimes awkward to build each multiple-choice test item with a long stem and short responses. The rule can be ignored to insure clarity.

Examination of the following two versions of a multiple-choice item from a sixth-grade social studies test shows the advantages of relatively long stems coupled with short responses.

Poor: Yugoslavia
        (1) is larger in area than France.
        (2) borders on the Adriatic Sea.
        (3) is located in western Asia.
        (4) contains the Ural Mountains.
Improved: In which of the following continents is Yugoslavia located?
        (1) Europe
        (2) Asia
        (3) Africa
        (4) South America

The first version is more difficult to understand than the second. The pupil may read it several times before he recognizes that the item is designed to test his knowledge of the geography of Yugoslavia. With the revised version, based on a single problem explicity stated in the stem of the item, the pupil should have no trouble grasping the problem and can devote his time to selection of the correct answer.

Express the responses to a multiple-choice test item so that grammatical consistency is maintained. In other words, if the stem of the multiple-choice item is an incomplete sentence, each response must be worded so that it is a grammatically correct completion of the introductory statement. If the stem is a direct question, the responses should be suitable though brief statements of parallel construction. Failure to maintain grammatical consistency is often due to carelessness; happily, this defect can be easily corrected in most instances. The following test item illustrates this point:

Poor: If the north pole of one bar magnet is brought very near the south pole of another bar magnet, the two poles will
    (1) repel each other.
    (2) attract each other.
    (3) no effect.
    (4) an electric spark will be produced.
Improved: If the north pole of one bar magnet is brought very near the south pole of another bar magnet, the two poles will
    (1) repel each other.
    (2) attract each other.
    (3) have no effect on each other.
    (4) produce an electric spark.

The two versions of this test item make it clear that the teacher can avoid grammatical inconsistency by simply checking each response with the stem. If this is done and any appropriate changes in wording are made, the test item is not only more impressive from a grammarian's point of view but it is also less confusing from a pupil's.

Minimize the use of negative expressions in a multiple-choice test item. Such expressions reduce the clarity of an item and may artificially add to its difficulty. This problem can become serious for less mature pupils. For instance, consider the following:

Poor: Which of the following is <u>not</u> true of Puerto Rico?
    (1) It is an island.
    (2) Its principal language is Spanish.
    (3) It is <u>not</u> a state in the U.S.A.
    (4) It does <u>not</u> have a warm climate.
Improved: What is the political status of Puerto Rico?
    (1) It is a state in the U.S.A.
    (2) It is an independent country like the U.S.A.
    (3) It is an unincorporated territory of the U.S.A.
    (4) It is a commonwealth under the U.S. government.

The intended correct answer to both versions is the fourth response. In the case of the first version, notice how awkward—and time-consuming—it is to arrive at this conclusion and to confirm it. The second version is much more straightforward and aims directly at one central point, namely, the political status of Puerto Rico. No negative expressions are needed or desired.

Advantages and Limitations of Multiple-Choice Test Items.   The advantages of multiple-choice test items are much more impressive than the limitations. The outstanding feature of the multiple-choice item is its versatility. It can be used to determine how well a pupil can recall the most specific pieces of information as well as his ability to apply the most important principle in a novel situation.[1] Moreover, it can do so without introducing the problems of subjective scoring, which weakens the short-answer test items, or ambiguity, so noticeable when true-false test items are used. Successful guessing by the pupils is reduced but not eliminated. Any teacher with a reasonable amount of patience and ingenuity can build and use multiple-choice items with favorable results. As illustrated by the various test items concerning novelists (see pages 83–84), he can often convert supply, true-false, and matching test items to multiple-choice form without undue difficulty.

Multiple-choice test items are used at all grade levels with the possible exception of the primary. Even there they can be orally administered if practice test items correctly answered are shown. Multiple-choice test items can also be successfully used in all subject matter areas when verbal and mathematical aspects are being tested. An objection is occasionally raised, however, to the use of these items in testing achievement in mathematics. A pupil may correctly answer the test item by using the four or five responses given as a basis for solving the problem backwards. This can be circumvented by using a variation of the standard multiple-choice form, such as the incomplete-response variety already illustrated.

Multiple-choice test items are not, of course, the panacea for the difficulties of achievement testing. They have distinct limitations, some of which have been mentioned in earlier discussions. They are difficult to build, and suitable distracters are hard to find. Although a teacher's ingenuity can produce many, and others can be found among the wrong answers given to supply test items administered to preceding classes, surpluses are rare. More often than not the teacher lacks at least one distracter. He may try to fill the void by adding the response "none of the foregoing," "not given," or "can't tell." These cannot be used for "best" answer multiple-choice test items; also, they customarily weaken the correct answer variety if used consistently as a distracter, since they are recognized by the pupil as more often the wrong answer than the correct one. Such responses need not be avoided but they must be carefully presented. For instance, do not use them as the *answer* to an item when it may include a *large number of incorrect responses* as in the case of

---

[1] The usefulness of objective test items for measuring a pupil's ability to apply information and principles in a novel situation is discussed in Chapter 4.

most questions requiring mathematical computations to arrive at a numerical answer.

Another limitation of multiple-choice test items is the response time they require. For a given amount of testing time, pupils can complete fewer multiple-choice test items than true-false items. This is particularly noticeable when the multiple-choice test items demand fine discriminations and fundamental understandings.

Problems

10.   Attempts to improve the quality of "best" answer multiple-choice test items may actually change the test item to the "correct"|answer variety. Examine the test item concerning diseases on page 100 and decide whether this has occurred.

11.   Do important differences exist between the multiple-response variety and the combined-response variety of multiple-choice items? Defend your answer with illustrations of both varieties.

12.   Study the following scoring system and criticize it as a measurement device and as an instructional device: According to a procedure known as probability scoring, the pupil not only selects his answer to a multiple-choice test item, but also reports his degree of uncertainty with respect to his choice; then he is scored in such a way that the more honest he is in reporting his uncertainty, the higher his score tends to be (Cronbach, 1970, pp. 58–59).

13.   Hughes and Trimble (1965) studied the use of complex alternatives in multiple-choice test items such as "All of the above are correct," "Both 1 and 2 above are correct," or similar combinations. Do these complex alternatives increase or decrease the difficulty of the test item?

Matching Test Items

The matching test item in its simplest form consists of two lists of items and a set of instructions for matching each of the items in the first with one in the second. The first is known as a list of *premises*, the second as a list of *responses*. The instructions explain how the pupil is to match each premise with one or more of the responses. Premises and responses may be statements, names of people or places, titles of works of art, dates, formulas, symbols, or even parts of a picture or drawing. They may vary greatly but will tend to be homogeneous within a given list. Usually the length of each premise or response is (and should be) relatively short, perhaps no longer than a word or two.

In some matching exercises, the number of premises and responses is the same and each response can be used only once; this is a "perfect matching" exercise. In other instances, some of the responses do not match any of the premises; this is an "imperfect matching" exercise. An "imperfect matching" exercise can be constructed by making the list of responses longer than the list of premises or, if the lists are of equal length, by including some responses that must be used more than once. Earlier in this chapter an example is given of an "imperfect matching" test item having a shorter list of responses than premises; two responses are used more than once and one is not used at all.

In addition to the types of matching test items mentioned in the foregoing paragraph, there are a number of other variations. Two promising ones are illustrated here:

Compound matching variety:

DIRECTIONS: Below is a list of nineteenth century and early twentieth century novelists. For each novelist identify the title of one of his works that is listed in the second column by writing the letter opposite the title in the first of the two blanks to the left of the author's name. Identify his nationality from among those listed in the column below by writing the number opposite it in the second blank.

Authors			Novels
(H) (3)	1.	Alexandre Dumas	A. The Adventures of Tom Sawyer
(G) (2)	2.	George Eliot	B. Barchester Towers
(F) (3)	3.	Victor Hugo	C. Call of the Wild
(C) (1)	4.	Jack London	D. David Copperfield
(E) (1)	5.	Herman Melville	E. Moby Dick
(J) (2)	6.	William Thackeray	F. Notre Dame of Paris
(B) (2)	7.	Anthony Trollope	G. Romola
(A) (1)	8.	Mark Twain	H. The Three Musketeers
			I. Uncle Tom's Cabin

Nationalities

    J. Vanity Fair
    K. War and Peace

1. American
2. English
3. French

Classification variety:

DIRECTIONS: Each of the following statements is a complete sentence. Determine whether the sentence is a simple, complex, compound, or compound-complex sentence. Using the list below, find the letter corresponding to your choice and write it in the blank to the left of the sentence.

    A. simple sentence
    B. complex sentence
    C. compound sentence
    D. compound-complex sentence

(C) 1. During the winter the days are short and the nights are long.
(A) 2. Jane rode to school on her bicycle.
(B) 3. If Mary Lou had been home she could have visited with her grandparents and their friends.
(B) 4. Mother unpacked the picnic basket while I gathered wood.

Suggestions for Constructing Matching Test Items.   *Make lists of premises and responses as homogeneous as possible.* Each list should be confined to one type of subject. For example, it may be composed entirely of dates, names of people, or mathematical symbols. A title including every member can be placed above the list. In contrast, some poorly constructed matching test items are unnecessarily heterogeneous. Suppose that a certain list of premises contained names of inanimate objects, insects, animals, and people. For many pupils this simplifies the task of answering the test item correctly. They can eliminate many of the possible responses to a given premise not because they know much about the premise and response, but because there is no conceivable basis for matching some responses to a given premise.

Notice how this process of elimination is possible in the first version of a matching test item intended for use in a junior high school social studies achievement test.

Poor:

DIRECTIONS: Match each description in the first column with one of the names in the second column by writing the letter identifying the name in the blank to the left of the description.

	Descriptions	Names
(C)	1. A river in southeastern Europe	A. Bucharest
(F)	2. One of the largest countries in the world	B. Czechoslovakia
(G)	3. Mountains in Russia	C. Danube
(D)	4. A level country	D. Poland
(A)	5. The capital of a country near Czechoslovakia	E. Romania
		F. Russia
		G. Ural

Improved:

DIRECTIONS: Match each river with the body of water into which it flows by writing the letter identifying the body of water in the blank to the left of the name of the river. It is possible that several of the rivers flow into the same body of water.

	Rivers	Bodies of Water
(C)	1. Danube	A. Adriatic Sea
(G)	2. Rhine	B. Bay of Biscay
(F)	3. Rhone	C. Black Sea
(E)	4. Seine	D. Caspian Sea
(G)	5. Thames	E. English Channel
(F)	6. Tiber	F. Mediterranean Sea
		G. North Sea

Both lists of the first test item are quite varied in content. The premises describe a river, two countries, a range of mountains, and a city. The responses are name a city, four countries, a river, and a range of mountains. This lack of homogeneity certainly will help the relatively uninformed pupil find correct answers by a process of elimination. Moreover, the statement of some of the premises is poor. For example, premise 5 is "the capital of a country near Czechoslovakia." No matter how little a pupil might know about the geography of Europe, rarely would he choose the response "Czechoslovakia" as the answer.

The revised version of the matching test item is greatly improved. Notice that the titles "rivers" and "bodies of water" are much more accurate and definitive than those used in the first version. Any pupil, especially one with only sketchy knowledge of the topic, would find it difficult to use the process of elimination in this test item. Additional matching items dealing only with the location of various European cities, mountain ranges, or countries can also be constructed. In other words, several matching test items are needed to lessen the variation of the premises and responses in the first version without excluding any of that information from the test.

Always indicate as clearly as possible the basis on which the matching of premises and responses is to be made. Every effort should be made to clarify the task the pupil is asked to perform by improving the directions and the titles of the lists. It is not the purpose of a matching test item to find out if a pupil understands the basis for matching, but rather to see if he can accurately match each premise with a response after he understands the basis of matching.

Below is a matching test item intended for an achievement test in elementary school science. Although it is not mentioned in the first version of the test item, the teacher wants the pupil to match each animal with the kind of food it ordinarily eats.

Poor:

DIRECTIONS: Match each animal with grass, insects, or other animals. Write the number in the box next to the name of the animal.

1	cow	1. grass
1	sheep	2. insects
3	fox	3. other animals
3	lion	
2	robin	

Improved:

DIRECTIONS: Here is a list of animals. Each of these animals eats many different things each day. However, each animal will most often eat grass, or insects, or other animals. If an animal most often eats grass, write "1" in the box next to the animal's name. If it most often eats insects, write "2" in the box next to the animal's name. If it most often eats other animals, write "3" in the box next to the animal's name.

Animals		Food
1	cow	1. grass
1	sheep	2. insects
3	fox	3. other animals
3	lion	
2	robin	

When confronted with the faulty version of this test item, even the most sophisticated elementary school pupil will at first be uncertain as to how the

matching should be done. Some of the less sophisticated may never understand it and consequently skip the test item; or they may unknowingly
establish a false yet semi-plausible basis for matching. For instance, several
will choose the response "other animals" each time, arguing that each animal
is more like other animals in terms of its activities and structures than it is
like insects or grass.

The directions accompanying the improved version of the test item are
long and may need to be read to the pupils. Perhaps an illustration of one
animal correctly matched with the food it ordinarily eats should be shown.
Either or both of the steps should be taken if the teacher suspects that the
pupils are confused about the mechanics of the test item.

Arrange the premises and responses in a logical order. If the premises or
responses are names or titles, they should be arranged alphabetically. If they
are dates, they should be in chronological order; if numbers, they should be
arranged according to size. Unless there is an excellent reason for doing otherwise, any logical order should be followed. This will noticeably reduce the
amount of response time needed for answering matching test items.

In the following versions of a matching test item, the pupils are asked to
identify the 25-year period in which certain western states were admitted to the
Union.

Poor:

	States	Time periods
(E)	1. Utah	A. 1900–1924
(A)	2. New Mexico	B. 1825–1849
(D)	3. Missouri	C. 1850–1874
(C)	4. Kansas	D. 1800–1824
(A)	5. Arizona	E. 1875–1899
(E)	6. Colorado	
(C)	7. Nevada	
(E)	8. Washington	

Improved:

	States	Time periods
(E)	1. Arizona	A. 1800–1824
(D)	2. Colorado	B. 1825–1849
(C)	3. Kansas	C. 1850–1874
(A)	4. Missouri	D. 1875–1899
(C)	5. Nevada	E. 1900–1924
(E)	6. New Mexico	
(D)	7. Utah	
(D)	8. Washington	

Notice how much more rapidly a pupil can find the matching response in
the second version than in the first. In addition, notice how the second version

allows the pupil to check his answers with greater speed and certainty at a later time.

In every matching test item always include responses that do not match any of the premises, or responses that match more than one premise, or both. In other words, always construct "imperfect matching" test items rather than "perfect matching" ones. The latter have the serious disadvantage of increasing the likelihood of the uninformed pupil guessing one of the correct responses. Since in the "perfect matching" test item there are as many responses as premises, and each response can be used only once, the pupil answering it can determine the last response by a process of elimination.

The following is a "perfect matching" test item; each elementary school pupil is to identify each word in terms of the part of speech it normally is.

	Words	Parts of Speech
(E)	1. with	A. Noun
(B)	2. am	B. Verb
(C)	3. red	C. Adjective
(A)	4. car	D. Adverb
(D)	5. always	E. Preposition
(F)	6. and	F. Conjunction

Should a pupil have trouble matching a response with such a premise as "always," he can pair all other premises and responses, thereby discovering that it matches the fourth response. Of course this is not possible if additional premises are included and hence some responses used more than once.

Keep the list of responses relatively short. When attempting to answer matching test items, the pupil reads a premise and searches the list of responses. If this list is long, he may spend considerable time in spite of the fact that he may have a rather clear notion as to what the response should be. Thus, valuable test time is wasted. Incidentally, observe that a lengthy list of premises may likewise increase the amount of time needed by the pupil to respond to a matching test item. This cannot be called wasted time, however, unless some of the premises cannot be justified.

There is no well-established limit to the list of responses; however, the following is a good rule of thumb: Allow the list to exceed ten only when the maturity of the pupil and the nature of the subject matter in the test item permit; for younger pupils restrict the list to about half of this number. Should you find the list of responses becoming almost endless, consider the possibility of constructing more than one test item. This will allow you to sample a number of different subject matter topics and will simplify the job of finding lists of homogeneous premises and responses.

Advantages and Limitations of Matching Test Items. The primary advantage of using matching items in an achievement test is that a lot of factual information can be included in the test without much testing time being required. Such items are useful for seeing if a pupil can associate words with their definitions, events with their places and dates, results with their causes, concepts with their designated symbols, authors with their published works, statesmen with their countries and contemporaries, and so forth. Although it is not commonly done, matching test items can be used to measure a pupil's ability to apply the information he has learned. Notice the illustration given on page 104 in which the premises are a list of novel sentences that the pupil is to classify as simple, complex, compound, or compound-complex sentences. The classification variety can be successfully used to measure products of learning other than simple recall of information.

The main limitation in measuring achievement with matching test items is that good items are difficult to build. Sometimes the subject matter is insufficient in quantity or not well suited for matching test items; in either case, homogeneous premises and responses are extremely hard to find. In others, the subject matter may seem to lend itself to this type of test item but the teacher has great difficulty in finding plausible but wrong responses as well as correct responses that are not completely obvious because of the terminology used.

Problems

14. Design a matching test item involving two lists in which several responses are, in at least one instance, matched with a single premise.
15. Design a compound matching test item involving three lists in which several responses in two of the lists are, in at least one instance, matched with a single premise.

APPRAISING AND EDITING OBJECTIVE TEST ITEMS

Before any newly constructed objective test items can be incorporated into an achievement test, they should undergo a critical reexamination—essentially an appraising and editing procedure. It consists in verifying the relationship between each test item and the table of specifications, rechecking it for any ambiguity or irrelevant clues, and estimating its level of difficulty and reading load. The reexamination of test items in terms of these characteristics may simply reconfirm the worth of many well-constructed items; in some cases, it may reveal grammatical weaknesses; in others, it may uncover glaring faults in test items previously thought to be sound. Regardless of the outcome, the procedure is profitable. When building the test item, the teacher is often preoccupied with details and in the process loses sight of basic features. A later review customarily allows the teacher to see with a new perspective, so he can readjust any features out of balance.

Appraising and editing objective test items can be done by the person who constructed the test items or, preferably, by someone competent in the subject matter. If the second possibility is not feasible, then the original item builder should make the review, but only some time after the building of the items.

No matter who is involved, a useful technique for appraising and editing is for that person to administer the test items to himself. He is now playing the role of the pupil. The answers he gives should then be compared to the answers as originally listed. Any lack of agreement between any two answers is a certain danger signal. It no doubt means that the test item is ambiguous. Perhaps a qualifying statement is missing, or some of the phraseology should be changed. Disagreement between two answers may be traced to the excessive difficulty of the test item. This flaw may be minor and easily corrected; it could be so serious that the item must be discarded.

The fact that the original answer to a test item and an independent answer later determined are the same, on the other hand, is no guarantee that the item is satisfactory. There may be other flaws in it that may not affect the answers arrived at by a reviewer but that could seriously affect the role of the test item in a test and the pupil's response. The teacher should therefore review each test item by checking it in terms of five questions:

1. Is the test item properly identified with one or more cells of the table of specifications?
2. Is the test item ambiguous in any respect?
3. Does the test item contain any irrelevant clues?
4. Does the test item have an appropriate level of difficulty?
5. Does the test item have a suitable reading level?

After a test item has been so examined and any differences corrected, a smooth copy of the test item is made. A highly useful and successful procedure is to type each test item on a 5 × 8-in. card. Generally there is ample room on the card to add additional pertinent information such as the correct answer to the test item, the name and page of the section of any book or outline on which it is based, and, at a later date, a summary of the responses pupils made when answering it. As a result, the teacher has all important information neatly summarized in a single place, and his test item file is enlarged (see page 203).

Relationship Between Test Item and Table of Specifications

When building test items, the teacher uses his tables of specifications as blueprints to guide his selection of subject matter and behavioral changes to be included in each test item. The relationship between each test item and the part of the table of specifications from which it arose can be recorded by means of a simple coding technique. For example, the cells in the table are numbered, and the numbers of those related to the test item are listed on a card containing a statement of the test item. The numbers of the cells are listed in the order of their importance. In other words, the number of the cell to which the test item is primarily related is written first; the numbers of any cells to which it is secondarily related follow.

The first attempt to establish the relationship between a test item and the cells of a table of specifications is usually successful. Since the teacher began to build the test item with one or more cells in mind, he has little difficulty cross-referring it and the cells. However, practically all test items undergo revisions. Perhaps the technical imperfections are corrected without regard to the manner in which these corrections might affect the relationship between the test items and the table of specifications. Sometimes they do not disturb this relationship. Many times they do. For instance, recall the differences between the two versions of many of the test items shown earlier in this chapter. Correcting a technical imperfection repeatedly may have necessitated a fundamental change in the test item. After revision, the test item may be primarily related to a different cell in the table of specifications.

Clearly, if these changes are numerous and go unnoticed, the test loses much content validity. To prevent this, the teacher must recheck the relationship between each test item and the cells in the table of specifications after all known technical imperfections have been removed.

Presence of Ambiguity

Many suggestions for constructing objective test items concentrate on one central weakness—ambiguity. The dangers of using verbatim quotes from textbooks and the difficulty pupils encounter when denied some relevant qualifications have already been stressed. Proper phraseology in the test item as well as in the directions to the pupil is also important.

Individually, these suggestions for avoiding ambiguity can usually be followed with ease. Yet they must be applied in harmony with other suggestions not directly concerned with the problem—not always easy to do. In some instances, a teacher building an objective test item will find two suggestions working more or less at cross purposes. Following one by making a certain revision violates another. Escape from the dilemma may be difficult. No doubt a more common situation is the automatic adoption of the most recently considered suggestion. If the revision happens to violate another suggestion, this is not noticed.

Since ambiguity is one of the chief weaknesses of objective test items, the teacher should make a final check by rereading each test item with one question in mind: Is it possible to word this test item more clearly and directly? In trying to answer his own question, the teacher may find himself improving test items he previously thought to be as polished as he could make them. After this, he can feel confident that he is using words and expressions that have precise meaning in the eyes of the typical pupil, and that he has at the same time eliminated any that are awkward or nonfunctional.

The importance of avoiding ambiguity in objective test items is primary. The pupil should never experience difficulty in trying to understand the question. We are trying to find out if a pupil can answer a question he understands, not if he understands the question.

Presence of Irrelevant Clues

Another weakness of objective test items is their tendency to include irrelevant clues. Such clues are those characteristics of the test items that allow some, perhaps most, of the unprepared pupils to answer correctly even though they do not possess the knowledge or understanding required. In other words, they reduce the value of the test item by changing the basis upon which it discriminates among the pupils to whom it is administered. Ideally, a test item should indicate whether they can do such things as recall one or more pieces of information or apply one or more principles to a new situation. Those who can do these things will answer a well-constructed test item correctly; those who cannot will respond incorrectly. It the test item contains irrelevant clues, the situation is changed. Some pupils who would normally respond incorrectly can give the right answer by properly interpreting the irrelevant clue.

There are many kinds of irrelevant clues. The suggestions for building objective test items reveal a number of them. Rechecking objective test items on the basis of these suggestions is generally not difficult work and the time is well invested.

Testwiseness.   A pupil's ability to capitalize on the characteristics and format of a test and/or a testing situation to obtain a high score is called testwiseness (Millman and others, 1965). Some aspects of testwiseness are independent of the test builder or the purpose of the test, for example, the pupil's ability to distribute effectively the testing time available among the various test items, to pay attention to directions, and to adopt a good guessing strategy based on the method of scoring. Others are directly dependent on the mistakes of the teacher when building test items, for example, the pupil's ability to identify correct answers on the basis of any consistent idiosyncrasies or specific determiners used by the teacher.

The second category emphasizes the potentially influential role of irrelevant clues. This must be reduced at all costs.

The existence of pupil testwiseness is a simple fact of life with which a teacher must contend. Reasonably even amounts of this trait within a given group of pupils can actually simplify test planning since the teacher can anticipate with some accuracy the kind of test format, terminology, time limits, and so forth, that are appropriate for an achievement test. Of concern are wide differences among pupils in this regard, which can cause important test scores differences not related to pupil achievement.

Proper Level of Difficulty

An important characteristics of objective test items sometimes overlooked by the teacher is the level of difficulty. Obviously this is not determined exclusively by the idea on which the test item is based, for the manner in which it is stated is also important. A single variation of a word or phrase can change it noticeably. Obtaining the proper level for each item and then the test as a whole is a perplexing problem.

The first consideration for the teacher about level of difficulty is the type of test he is building. In a mastery test the level of difficulty is uniformly low; in a power test, it varies somewhat, but concentrates in a zone around the 50 percent level of difficulty after correction for chance. In other words, this is the level at which half of the pupils have responded correctly to a test item after allowance has been made for successful guessing (see page 124). For a number of reasons, the target zone should be slightly above 50 percent rather than below.

A highly successful way of obtaining estimates of the level of difficulty of test items is to pretest them on a group of pupils similar to those for whom they are designed. Their answers to the test items can be tabulated and analyzed. On the basis of this analysis, the level of difficulty of each test item is determined. Unfortunately, this procedure is frequently impossible. Without pretesting data, the teacher must depend on his subjective judgment.

Subjective judgment is by no means precise. In reality it yields a rough approximation, even when the teacher is completely familiar with the situation, the maturity of the pupils, and many of their past experiences. At best, he can rate the test items on only a five-point scale: "very difficult," "moderately difficult," "average," "moderately easy," and "very easy." Sometimes a three-point scale of "difficult," "average," and "easy" is all that is appropriate. The principal reference point is the "average" category. Test items so rated are considered suitable for typical pupils in the class under consideration. When making such judgment, the teacher must weigh as best he can the nature of the test item, all pertinent factors related to the teaching situation, and whatever experience he has had in the past with similar test items and pupils.

Although crude, subjective judgment is useful. In the devising of norm-referenced tests, for example, subjective judgment can prevent any test item from being so easy that all pupils respond correctly or so difficult that none do. Since the purpose of these tests is to differentiate among pupils in terms of their achievement, both extremes should be avoided.

Reading Level

Because test items are constructed by adults they regularly include words and expressions more typical of adults than children. This happens despite the most conscientious efforts of the teacher and can be a severe problem in the case of objective test items designed for elementary school pupils. After all, to the teacher these words and expressions seem to express the thought behind the test item very clearly. To the pupil, however, this probably is not true. If he were constructing the test item, he would no doubt choose different words. Often he would use more of them, thereby creating another difficulty. Since there is much to read, the pupil needs more response time for each test item. Consequently, fewer can be included, and the breadth of the sampling of the subject matter decreases.

A pupil with a slow reading rate or a modest vocabularly should not be appreciably penalized in a typical objective achievement test. To prevent any penalty, needlessly difficult terms appearing in the test items should be replaced with simpler synonyms. Complex arrangements of words should be simplified and unnecessary words or phrases removed. Also, ample testing time must be allowed.

Test items must be carefully reread to eliminate improper vocabulary and cut excessive length. It is not easy to play the role of the pupil in this case. Yet, if appropriate adjustments are not made, the pupil with superior reading ability and vocabulary may have an undue advantage over his less fortunate fellow pupil. Superior reading ability and vocabulary help him to understand more of the questions more quickly and, as a result, he has more time in which to concentrate on obtaining the correct answers. When such items are included in a poorly timed test, they may actually measure the pupil's reading speed and comprehension more than his achievement in a chosen subject matter area such as science or social studies; the basis on which the test items are differentiating among the pupils has changed.

Problems

16. Goslin (1967, 1967–68) evaluated a number of criticisms of objective tests designed to measure pupil aptitude and achievement, four of which are the following:
   a. They are unfair for "deep thinkers."

b. They are unfair for culturally disadvantaged pupils.

c. They are unfair for individuals who lack experience in taking them.

d. Test scores yielded by them are poor predictors of subsequent performance, e.g., post-academic performance.

Prepare your reaction to these criticisms and compare them with those of Goslin.

17. A group of test items have been assembled and discussed in terms of the tactics used by testwise pupils to raise their achievement test scores (Millman and others, 1965). Study these illustrations and state your opinion with respect to two of the questions raised by the authors.

a. At what grade level do we usually find evidence of testwiseness among pupils?

b. How can we more nearly equalize the degree of testwiseness among pupils?

ORGANIZING THE OBJECTIVE TEST

So often it is said that a group of test items cannot necessarily be called a test. How true! After each of a group of objective test items has been appraised and edited in the manner described in the foregoing sections, that part of the group that appropriately reflects the balance among the subject matter topics and the behavioral changes established in the table of specifications is organized into an achievement test. For this to be done, we must decide the order in which the items are presented to the pupils and the number to be included. We must also formulate directions for the pupils and draw up a scoring key. Each of these steps must be taken carefully if the test items are to realize their maximum value.

Arranging Objective Test Items

Objective test items should not be arranged haphazardly in an achievement test. Instead, they should be organized on the basis of one or more of three characteristics: the type of item, the subject matter, and the level of difficulty.

When the items of an objective test are grouped according to type, all supply test items are placed together, as are all true-false, multiple-choice, and matching test items. This simplifies the directions given to the pupils. The number of times that new directions must be given is minimized. Furthermore, the pupil can no doubt complete a test so arranged more quickly. He acquires a mental set for each type of item and need not change it until all such items have been answered, speeding his progress through the test. Incidentally, it is advisable to restrict the number of different types to as few as conveniently possible.

Arranging the test items according to the subject matter means that the test items are grouped according to a set of subject matter topics, or perhaps according to the cells in a table of specifications. This appeals to the pupil because he sees the test as a miniature of the materials he learned. It is an integrated, orderly whole to him rather than a disorganized mosaic of unrelated questions. This arrangement may be attractive to the teacher, too, since it may help to reveal any stress or underemphasis in the test.

Objective test items can be grouped according to their levels of difficulty if they happen to vary appreciably, that is, the easy ones first, the more difficult next, and the most difficult last. Such an arrangement has advantages for the average and below average pupil. With this kind of test he uses the time allowed more efficiently, and his morale is improved. If the difficult test items appear first, many pupils of average or low achievement will waste a great deal of time trying to answer them. They may fail to answer easier items later in the test because so much time was spent on the first ones. Moreover, they may quickly become discouraged or even hostile. On the other hand, if the easier items are listed first, these same pupils will at first make smooth progress in the test, and consequently feel encouraged. When they later encounter the more difficult test items, they no doubt will have time to attack them. Even if they fail to answer some of them, as will very likely happen, the resulting disappointment will be moderated by the knowledge that they already have answered others correctly.

Certainly we cannot expect to use all three ways of arranging test items simultaneously. In reality, all a teacher can hope to do is find the best possible compromise among the three. Sometimes he can escape partially or wholly from the dilemma by eliminating one of the possibilities. For example, suppose that only one type of test item is used. Now the test can be designed so that the items are grouped according to major subject matter topic, and within each group they can be arranged in order of ascending difficulty. As a second example, suppose that the teacher is building a mastery test, or perhaps a norm-referenced test using test items with levels of difficulties which cluster in a comparatively small zone slightly above the 50 percent level. Now the level of difficulty is unimportant as a basis for arranging test items and should be ignored.

If test items are grouped according to major subject matter topics and, within each group, subdivided according to type of item, the teacher may wish to consider each subject matter group as a subtest. The items in such subtests can be independently numbered and, to assure that each receives proper emphasis, separate time limits can be imposed.

Length of Objective Achievement Tests

Ideally, the length of an achievement test should be determined by two key factors, representative sampling and reliability. The test should contain as many items as necessary to sample all the verbal and mathematical aspects of the educational objectives on which the table of specifications is based. The smallest sample of test items (in other words, the shortest test) that can be used without jeopardizing reasonable representation varies with the nature of this table. If the subject matter topics and behavioral changes in the table are heterogeneous, then a larger sample is needed. If they are very much alike, a smaller sample can be used. Remember that too short a test may be unsatisfactory because it is impossible to include items based on some less important cells of the table of specifications. Consequently, the degree of content validity is lessened.

The second key factor is that the length of the test is also related to its reliability, that is, the consistency of its results (see pages 304–306). In general, shortening the test decreases its reliability. If, therefore, the use of the test results demands a high degree of test reliability, the length of the test has to be increased. Test results used to diagnose an individual pupil's strengths and weaknesses in an area must be more reliable than those used only to determine differences between groups of pupils in terms of their achievement. In the first case, the test may be so long it is administered in parts and requires several hours. In the second, it may be so short that only one class period or less is needed.

In addition to these two factors governing the length of the classroom achievement test, there is another and very practical one: the time available for the administration of the test. Although this factor lacks the theoretical justification of the first two, it is just as important. Indeed, it often influences the length of the test more than factors of content validity or reliability, because the teacher often has so little control over it. Ordinarily, he must administer the test during a regularly scheduled class period which usually lasts forty to sixty minutes. To change the length would, in the eyes of the school administrator at least, create havoc. Thus, time becomes the primary factor.

In this connection, remember the importance of pupil fatigue. Writing achievement tests can be an exhausting task. For this reason, it is doubtful that time periods longer than one hour should be used for achievement testing even if they were available. Certainly time periods of more than two hours should be discouraged. The maximum length will of course vary with the maturity of the pupil and the environmental conditions at the time of the test administration. Any time pupil fatigue is suspected of being a noticeable influence on test performance, the test should be broken into parts with rest periods permitted between them.

The teacher customarily determines the length of his achievement test in a somewhat backward manner. First, he notes the maximum amount of time that administrative routine will allow for giving the test. Then he estimates the number of items to which the pupils should be able to respond in the time allotted. Finally, he selects this number from among those he has constructed. He selects these in such a way that, as a group, they reflect the established relative importance of the various cells of the table of specifications.

The first step is seldom a problem. The amount of time allotted is well known to the teacher. However, the second can be difficult. How many objective test items of a given type can the typical student answer in a given amount of time? The answers to this question vary. For example, some say that a mature pupil can answer about one hundred true-false test items or about sixty-five multiple-choice test items in a fifty-minute period. Such statements as these are not too helpful. After all, how mature is this pupil? Maturity here means testwiseness, and this is hard to assess. Moreover, what is the nature of the test items being used? Items requiring only recall of information can generally be answered much more quickly than those measuring more complex achievement. Those that are short or that have a low vocabulary load require less reading time, hence less response time. In the last analysis, therefore, the teacher has to rely on his own judgment. On the basis of his experience with his pupils and various kinds of objective test items, he must decide how many to include in the test. Remember that if it is a power test, its length must be restricted so that at least 90 percent of the pupils will have sufficient time to attempt all the items.

As the restrictions on testing time limit the number of items to be included in the test, so also do they weaken its content validity and reliability. All too frequently, there is no convenient way of overcoming this progression of troubles. Instead, the teacher must recognize the situation for what is is, build his achievement test accordingly, and temper his use and interpretation of the results to compensate for whatever degree of content validity and reliability is lost.

Directions for Pupils

To perform to the best of his ability, the pupil must be completely oriented to the achievement test. Otherwise stated, he must know the purpose of the test and must be thoroughly familiar with its mechanics. The teacher therefore formulates directions that the pupil reads or that are read to him before he responds to any of the test items.

The purpose of most classroom achievement tests is quite clear to the pupils. No doubt the initial announcement of the test is supplemented with remarks concerning the reasons why it is being administered; or, perhaps it is one of a series and the pupils are well aware of its purposes. In both of these instances, the directions need not include statements concerning the purposes of the test. If, however, the teacher doubts for any reason the completeness of the pupil's understanding of the purposes of the test, he should devote the first part of the directions to a brief statement about them. Failure to do so when the pupils are unacquainted with the purposes can cause an unnecessary loss of motivation.

The mechanics of the test typically command much more attention in the directions than the purposes. The pupil needs a complete knowledge of the "ground rules" under which he will operate. This means that he must be aware of the time allowed, the manner in which he is to select and record his answers, and the scoring system to be used. He should even be instructed in test-room etiquette if circumstances dictate.

Directions for Selecting Answers.   Directions for selecting answers must be carefully written. Notice that the sample instructions of this kind given earlier assume that the pupil knows nothing about objective test items. This of course is an extreme assumption and, for the most part, an unnecessary one. Yet, stating the directions with too much detail is far less an evil than stating them with too little. The first procedure assures us that any pupil who has read the directions will not be penalized by lack of familiarity with the objective test items. This point is particularly important when novel or seminovel items are being used.

For assurance that these directions are understood, practice test items may be included. These may consist of a typical item correctly answered in terms of the directions, as well as one or more to be answered by the pupil before beginning the test itself. He is told the correct answers to practice test items so that he can verify his understanding of the directions. Such items can be helpful when testing either elementary or secondary school pupils. The use of this procedure with the former group is quite common. Only after the pupils have independently solved the practice test items will many elementary school teachers begin the test.

Directions for Recording Answers.   How the pupil is to record his answer is another small detail that cannot be overlooked. When the answer is to be written on the same sheet as the question, this is less of a problem. It is necessary to prepare directions such as those already illustrated, and to design a layout of the test items that allows generous space for circling letters, writing numbers, and filling blanks. When separate answer sheets are used, the directions are not so simple. The relationship between the test copy and the answer sheet must be explained and also any features of the answer sheet that would speed or impair the marking of responses selected or that would increase or decrease the accuracy of scoring.

If separate answer sheets are used, teachers usually design their own. A typical one is shown in part in Figure 2. Notice that it can be used with a test having several types of objective items. These have been grouped according to type and each is numbered independently. The manner in which the pupil uses the answer sheet is described in the directions provided.

For many years, the most popular commercial answer sheets have been

Date _____	Name _____

Subject _____

Scores: Part A _____
            Part B _____
            Part C _____
            Part D _____
              Total _____

DIRECTIONS: Read with care the general directions at the beginning of the test and the directions preceding each subpart. Then read each test item and decide which answer is correct. Indicate your answer by filling the blank or circling the number or letter provided below. Be certain that the number of the test item corresponds exactly with the number on the answer sheet when you record each answer.

A: SUPPLY		B: TRUE-FALSE		C: MULTIPLE-CHOICE		D: MATCHING	
Item	*Answer*	*Item*	*Answer*	*Item*	*Answer*	*Item*	*Answer*
1	_____	1	T F	1	1 2 3 4 5	1	_____
2	_____	2	T F	2	1 2 3 4 5	2	_____
3	_____	3	T F	3	1 2 3 4 5	3	_____
4	_____	4	T F	4	1 2 3 4 5	4	_____
5	_____	5	T F	5	1 2 3 4 5	5	_____

FIGURE 2. Section of a Teacher-Designed Answer Sheet.

those distributed by the International Business Machines Corporation, usually IBM Form I. T. S. 1000 B 108. Space for responses to 150 true-false or multiple-choice test items is provided on each side of the answer sheet. With an electrographic pencil, the pupil carefully marks the space corresponding to his choice for each test item. The answer sheet is then scored electronically by a scoring machine to which most schools have access.

Other methods of machine scoring are also being used, for instance, those employing the IBM Optical Mark Scoring Reader or the Optical Mark Page Reader and answer sheets designed for them. An answer sheet is shown in reduced size in Figure 3. It strongly resembles the original IBM answer sheets although the spaces for pupil responses are arranged horizontally instead of vertically. However, it is much more versatile. In addition to true-false and multiple-choice test items, it can be used for matching test items. The pupil marks his responses with an ordinary soft or medium lead pencil. The scoring machine optically reads the marks at an extremely high rate and prints part and/or total scores. Various scoring formulas (for example, formulas for correcting for guessing) can be applied by the scoring machine. Also, multiple-

Reproduced by permission of the International Business Machines Corporation.
FIGURE 3. An International Business Machine Answer Sheet, IBM 1230 Document No. 509.

response test items can be scored. Finally, it is possible to transfer test score information directly into a computer, which in turn can provide a wide variety of summary data about the test score distribution; for instance, the arithmetic mean of the scores.

Tests involving separate test copies and answer sheets can be successfully fully administered to pupils as inexperienced as those in the fourth grade.

However, if they are used with elementary school pupils, a training period is necessary prior to testing. Even after this, the pupils cannot handle the separate answer sheet efficiently. No doubt the time limits should be expanded for them. Secondary school pupils familiar with separate answer sheets lose very little time using them.

Directions for Scoring Answers. The pupil should be informed of the scoring procedure when it is conveniently possible. He is entitled to ask how much credit he will get for each right answer. Usually this can be easily included in the directions because it is constant for each objective item within the subtests or possibly the total test.

Allowing the same number of points for each item is somewhat illogical. After all, they may vary in difficulty and importance, and thus more credit should be allowed for some correct answers than for others. However, attempts to weight the test items in terms of these characteristics tend to be highly subjective. Moreover, research has shown that scores made on an objective achievement test graded with a constant number of points for a right answer correlate very highly with scores obtained on the same test when the right answers are weighted in what is seemingly a more defensible manner. This means that, no matter which scoring procedure is used, the relative position of the pupils within the class remains unchanged in practically all cases. In view of this, most objective achievement tests are scored by means of the simpler method, which is to allow a constant amount of credit for each correct response to a given type of objective test item.

The directions should also include a statement about correction for guessing (see pages 124–126). Since the possibility of successfully guessing the correct answers appeals to some pupils, teachers may choose to discourage such attempts by penalizing the pupil for any wrong answers he makes. This is known as a correction for guessing. The pupil has the right to know whether one of these methods is to be used. This information could greatly affect his willingness to omit a test item or try to guess the correct answer with little or no information.

Presenting Directions Orally. Writing clear and explicit directions is of little help if the pupil refuses to read them or reads them carelessly. Therefore, a number of teachers read the directions aloud as the pupils read them silently. Any questions the pupils might have are answered, and then the test begins. This is wise procedure with elementary school pupils. With the primary grade levels it must be carried one step further. Copies of the directions for any objective test items are not given to the pupil. Instead, he is given an answer sheet that is meticulously tailored to the test. After the directions are read and explained, practice exercises are completed. Then the teacher reads the questions one by one, allowing time for a response to each. At the conclusion of the test, he might repeat some or all if time allows. Administering tests in this way removes a serious obstacles to the use of objective test items with elementary school pupils—the reading speed and comprehension problem.

Scoring the Objective Test

To many classroom teachers the least exciting task of achievement testing is the scoring of the pupil responses. To handle this task the pupils are sometimes asked to score their own papers or their neighbors'. Considering the importance of accurate scoring, the limitations of this procedure are obvious. Should the teacher score the papers himself, he commonly takes a blank copy of the test, fills in the correct responses, and compares this key with the responses on the test copy returned by each pupil. The number of correct responses by each pupil is determined and recorded. The total operation may not require much time, but being essentially clerical in nature, it is often viewed with distaste by those who must do it.

Various attempts have been made to reduce the time required for scoring objective tests. Such reduction means less boredom and fatigue for the scorer and, as a result, more accurate scores. These attempts have taken the form of scoring keys designed to assist in hand-scoring individual test copies or separate answer sheets containing the pupils' responses, and machine-scoring procedures using separate answer sheets.

Scoring Keys for Hand-Scoring. A number of the more successful scoring keys for hand-scoring have been described and illustrated by Traxler (1951). Prominent among these are the fan key, the strip key, and the cut-out key.

The fan key is a sheet of paper on which the correct responses are written in a series of columns. The sheet of paper is the same size as the test copy or the separate answer sheet. Each column corresponds to a page of the test or a column on the answer sheet, and the correct responses are spaced in the column as the pupil responses are spaced on the page of the test or the column on the appropriate answer sheet. The key is folded along vertical lines separating its columns, thus taking the appearance of a fan. It is superimposed on the appropriate page of the test copy or placed next to the appropriate column on the answer sheet and matched with the corresponding responses.

The strip key is similar to a fan key except that the various columns are strips. Each strip is usually mounted on cardboard. It is used like a fan key.

The cut-out key is also a sheet of paper of the same size as the test copy or answer sheet. However, windows are cut in appropriate positions to reveal the correct responses if they are made. The key is superimposed on a page of the test copy or the separate answer sheet and the pupil's responses are scored. For a supply test item, the scorer sees only the pupil's written response and can quickly compare it with the correct response written on the key in a space immediately adjacent to the window. For a true-false or multiple-choice test item, the window corresponds to the letter or number of the response to be circled. If no circle appears in the window, the scorer marks the pupil's response as incorrect.

Machine-Scoring. The machine-scoring procedure now becoming popular for scoring informal objective tests utilizes the IBM Optical Mark Scoring Reader. If the separate answer sheets shown in Figure 3 are properly marked, the teacher can, if he chooses, turn over his task of scoring to a skilled clerk operating this machine. Under ideal conditions, the speed and accuracy of scoring can be superior.

The disadvantages of machine-scoring of this type are well known. First of all, it cannot be used with supply test items under any circumstances. Secondly, the pupils must be trained in the procedure of marking the answer sheets. The marks in the spaces must be reasonably heavy. Erasures must be complete and stray pencil marks avoided, because they might be recorded by the machine as wrong answers. A third disadvantage is the availability of the machine. Unless one is available on relatively short notice, machine-scoring may prove to be more trouble than it is worth as far as classroom achievement tests are concerned. Finally, there is no indication on the answer sheet as to whether an answer to a given test item is correct or incorrect. The pupil cannot identify his strong and weak areas by examining his answer sheet alone.

Correcting for Guessing. A persistent problem encountered with objective achievement tests is the tendency of the pupil to guess when he does not know the correct answer. Sometimes this guess is based on partial knowledge, other times on misinformation, and still other times on no information at all. In the last instance, he may not even have read the test item or, if he did, its answer is a total mystery to him. In either case, his chances of guessing the correct answer are greater in a true-false test than in a multiple-choice or matching test.

If the score is the number of correct responses, any success the pupil had when he guessed will raise it. Obviously, this is not a defensible situation. The test score should reflect his achievement only, rather than this plus the pupil's willingness to guess and the amount of success he happened to have in this case. Therefore, some teachers argue that the pupil must be discouraged from wild guessing and be penalized if he does.

The formula for correcting for guessing in the case of the most common varieties of selection type objective test items is as follows:

$$S = R - \frac{W}{n-1},$$

where
$\qquad S =$ the test score;

$R =$ the number of correct responses;

$W =$ the number of incorrect responses;

$n =$ the number of suggested responses from which one is chosen.

R is often called the number of "rights," whereas W is thought of as the number of "wrongs."

For a true-false test, n is two and the formula reduces to

$$S = R - W.$$

For a multiple-choice test having four suggested responses, the formula becomes

$$S = R - \frac{W}{3}.$$

If the multiple-choice test items have five suggested responses, the formula becomes

$$S = R - \frac{W}{4}.$$

Notice that to use the formula in any of these cases, you need only determine the number of correct and incorrect responses. The number of omitted test items is ignored.

These formulas assume that all incorrect responses and a chance proportion of the correct ones are the result of wild guessing. This is, of course, not fully justified. The pupils are often taking "calculated risks" when selecting their responses. Rather than making wild guesses they are making more or less intelligent guesses based on sound but incomplete knowledge. The pupil hopes, and legitimately so, that his chances of selecting the correct response are much better when he makes an intelligent guess than when he makes a wild guess. Testwiseness is a definite factor.

Because the foregoing assumption is not completely satisfied, the formulas will overcorrect in some instances and undercorrect in others. Consequently, they are persistently criticized by teachers and pupils alike.

There is another disadvantage when a correction for guessing formula is applied. Informing the pupil that such a correction will be made customarily acts as a deterrent, but its effectiveness varies with the pupil. Some are willing to gamble no matter what the penalty and guess wildly no matter what correction formulas are used. Others are cautious. A correction for guessing will cause them to answer only when they are certain of the correct response, and even intelligent guesses are not ventured. Hence, many more test items are omitted. More often than not, the first type of pupil gains higher test scores than the second. Thus, an extraneous personality factor unduly influences achievement tests designed to measure verbal or mathematical ability.

If sufficient time is allowed for the test so that every pupil can attempt every item, and if every pupil then answers every test item, no correction for guessing is needed for norm-referenced tests. Determining the test score by counting the number of correct responses is perfectly acceptable. Despite the fact that the test scores are different in size when corrected than when not corrected for guessing, the relative position of each pupil in the class is the same in both cases. The relationship between the uncorrected and corrected test scores under these conditions is perfect. If the purpose of an achievement test is to determine the relative position of each pupil in the class, the simpler test score may as well be used.

To assure that all pupils will answer all test items, they must be instructed to guess when they do not know the answer, even if they must guess wildly. Needless to say, these instructions can hardly be considered good pedagogy. The pupil may lose respect for objective achievement testing, possibly even for the subject matter or the teacher. The full impact of these instructions is difficult to measure. Admittedly unsavory, they probably have no lasting effect upon most pupils.

Problems

18.   What is your opinion of the practice of having pupils score their own test papers? Respond to this question both from the point of view of scoring accuracy and accepted principles of learning.

19.   Demonstrate empirically that the relative position of each pupil in a class is the same whether or not the test scores are corrected for guessing by doing the following:
   a. Randomly list the words "True" and "False" ten times. Consider this to be the test key.
   b. Have a group of pupils do the same independently. Consider these to be pupil answer sheets.
   c. Score the answer sheets with and without a correction for guessing.
   d. Determine the relative rank of each pupil on the basis of both scores.

20.   Branch-testing or tailored testing is a procedure whereby, with the aid of a computer, the test items to which a pupil is to respond next are determined by his responses on preceding items (Glaser and Nitko, 1970). Hence he is administered a test tailored to his pattern of achievement. Study this procedure and react to it in terms of its potential value in conserving testing time, measuring achievement in depth, and improving educational diagnosis.

SUMMARY

An objective test item is one that can be scored so that subjective judgment is practically eliminated when determining the correctness of a pupil's answer.

There are two types of objective test items, the supply type and the selection type. When responding to the supply type, the pupil has to provide the words, numbers, or symbols necessary. Possible answers are not listed as part of the item. In contrast, the selection type allows the pupil to choose the correct response from the information it provides.

Illustrations of the supply type are the short-answer question and the completion test item. Those teachers who use supply items in achievement tests do so because the likelihood of a pupil's guessing the correct answer is minimized and because of their ease of construction over the selection type. However, they also find that pupil responses to supply test items are more difficult to score, and that often the items measure only the pupil's knowledge of factual details.

True-false, multiple-choice, and matching test items all illustrate the selection type. The true-false item in its simplest form is a declarative statement that the pupil must judge as true or false. A test containing this type can sample widely a large amount of subject matter without requiring much testing time. On the other hand, the true-false test item involves only trivial pieces of information and, because one of two responses must be correct, pupils not knowing the right one frequently guess.

A multiple-choice test item is one in which a direct question or incomplete statement is presented and a number of responses are given. The pupil is to choose the correct (or best) answer to the question or expression for completing the statement. This type of objective test is widely used in standardized as well as classroom achievement tests because it is so adaptable. It can be used to measure recall of information or application of a principle in a novel situation in practically any subject matter area with all but the most naive pupils. The principal disadvantage teachers experience when they attempt to use multiple-choice test items is that they are relatively difficult to build. A sufficient number of suitable distracters is sometimes hard to find.

The typical matching test item consists of two lists of items and a set of instructions for matching each in the first list with one in the second. Like the true-false test item, the matching item can include large quantities of factual information without requiring a proportionately large amount of testing time. However, some subject matter is not well suited for matching test items. Homogeneous lists may be difficult if not impossible to develop.

After a group of objective test items have been constructed, they must be appraised and edited prior to being organized into an achievement test. This process involves rechecking the relationship between each item and the table of specifications, removing any ambiguity or any irrelevant clues that still remain, establishing relative level of difficulty, and correcting any feature that seriously increases the amount of time needed by the pupil to read and understand it.

Organizing the objective items into an achievement test is a more complicated task than commonly supposed. For instance, the arrangement of the items within the test must be determined. This may be based on the type of objective item, the level of difficulty, or a logical arrangement of the subject matter included. The length of the test must be established; generally the time available for testing is the key factor. Also, directions must be formulated and a scoring key prepared. In this connection, decisions must be made as to the use of a separate answer sheet and a correction-for-guessing formula for any selection type items the test contains.

Suggested Readings

Coffman, W. E. Achievement tests. In R. L. Ebel (ed.), *Encyclopedia of educational research.* (4th ed.) London: Macmillan, 1969. Pp. 7–17.
  This is a good overview of achievement testing. Attention is given to the history of achievement testing, types of test items, and test construction problems.
Dressel, P. L., and others. *Evaluation in higher education.* Boston: Houghton Mifflin, 1961. Chapters 4, 5, 6, and 7.
  These four chapters deal with evaluation in the social sciences, the natural sciences, the humanities, and communication skills. Each has been written by a different author. The role of objective test items is described in detail.
Ebel, R. L. *Measuring educational achievement.* Englewood Cliffs, N.J.: Prentice-Hall, 1965. Chapters 3, 5, 6, and 7.
  In four chapters, the planning of a classroom achievement test, the construction of true-false and multiple-choice test items, and the administration and scoring of achievement tests are discussed. Numerous faulty true-false and multiple-choice test items are shown and criticized.
Engelhart, M. D. *Improving classroom testing.* What Research Says to the Teacher, No. 31. Washington: National Education Association, 1964.
  All of the basic steps to be followed in the construction of classroom achievement tests are described, at least briefly, in this short pamphlet. Primary emphasis is given to the use of objective test items.
Schoer, L. A. *Test construction: A programmed guide.* Boston: Allyn and Bacon, 1970.
  For those who wish to improve their knowledge of achievement test construction without benefit of outside help, this programmed book will help. It covers all of the chief steps of building classroom achievement tests.
Stodola, Quentin. *Making the classroom test, a guide for teachers.* (2nd ed.) Educational Testing Service Evaluation and Advisory Service Series, No. 4. Princeton, N.J.: Educational Testing Service, 1961.
  In relatively few pages, the basic rules of test-making for both objective and essay tests are developed and illustrated. Elementary and secondary school examples are given.
Tinkelman, S. N. Planning the objective test. In R. L. Thorndike (ed.), *Educational measurement.* (2nd ed.) Washington: American Council on Education, 1970. Chapter 3.
  In a well-organized manner, the author discusses the steps followed in the development of a table of specifications and the planning for the types of test

items, their number, and their level of difficulty. Sound recommendations are given.

Wesman, A. G. Writing the test item. In R. L. Thorndike (ed.), *Educational measurement*. (2nd ed.) Washington: American Council on Education, 1970. Chapter 4.

Of the materials available of less than book length that deal with objective test items, this is one of the best. It contains many illustrations of the various forms of objective test items and numerous suggestions for building them properly.

Wood, Dorothy A. *Test construction, development and interpretation of achievement tests*. Columbus, Ohio: Charles E. Merrill, 1960. Chapters 5, 6, and 7.

This is a short book devoted to achievement testing by means of objective tests; only brief mention is made of essay tests. The three chapters cited concern the preparation of objective test items.

References Cited

Cronbach, L. J. *Essentials of psychological testing*. (3rd ed.) New York: Harper & Row, 1970.

Engelhart, M. D. *Improving classroom testing*. What Research Says to the Teacher, No. 31. Washington: National Education Association, 1964.

Glaser, R., and A. J. Nitko. Measurement in learning and instruction. In R. L. Thorndike (ed.), *Educational measurement*. (2nd ed.) Washington: American Council on Education, 1970. Chapter 17.

Goslin, D. A. What's wrong with tests and testing—Part I. *College Board Review*, 1967, No. 65, 12–18.

Goslin, D. A. What's wrong with tests and testing—Part II. *College Board Review*, 1967–68, No. 66, 33–37.

Hughes, H. H., and W. E. Trimble. The use of complex alternatives in multiple-choice items. *Educational and Psychological Measurement*, 1965, **25**, 117–126.

Millman, J., and others. An analysis of test-wiseness. *Educational and Psychological Measurement*, 1965, **25**, 707–726.

Stodola, Quentin. *Making the classroom test, a guide for teachers*. (2nd ed.) Educational Testing Service Evaluation and Advisory Service Series, No. 4. Princeton, N.J.: Educational Testing Service, 1961.

Tinkelman, S. N. Planning the objective test. In R. L. Thorndike (ed.), *Educational measurement*. (2nd ed.) Washington: American Council on Education, 1970. Chapter 3.

Traxler, A. E. Administering and scoring the objective test. In E. F. Lindquist (ed.), *Educational measurement*. Washington: American Council on Education, 1951. Pp. 329–416.

Wesman, A. G. Writing the test item. In R. L. Thorndike (ed.), *Educational measurement*. (2nd ed.) Washington: American Council on Education, 1970. Chapter 4.

CHAPTER 4

Measuring Complex
Achievement Objectively

Some years ago a delightful book was published that contained countless "boners" made by pupils in the classroom (Abingdon, 1952). As nearly as can be determined, all that are listed are authentic errors made by pupils in examinations, themes, and occasionally in correspondence. The following are typical entries:

> In one instance, a pupil attempting to define the term "adolescence" asserted that it is "the stage between puberty and adultry." Another pupil was asked to explain the effect of heat and cold and to give an illustration. His response is a classic: "Heat expands; in the summer the days are long. Cold contracts; in the winters the days are short." Finally, an English teacher was offered this unique differentiation between an active and a passive verb: "An active verb shows action, as, 'he kissed her'; and a passive verb shows passion, as, 'she kissed him.'"

Aside from the humor present, these and other parts of the anthology make an important contribution. They reveal the pathetically inadequate grasp that some have of simple concepts, meanings, and relationships. Excessive verbalism is common. Words are only partially understood and, as a result, the pupil commits what might be called "logical errors." In other words, some parts of the pupil's verbal or mathematical achievements are at best superficial.

There are numerous less extreme illustrations of the same problem. In a science class it is generally possible to find a pupil who can quickly and properly define pH as the negative logarithm of the concentration of the hydrogen ion in gram atoms per liter, yet does not know what a logarithm or a hydrogen ion is or of what usefulness pH can be when a farmer tests his soil before deciding whether to spread lime on it. Another pupil can freely quote Newton's laws of motion but fails to see a connection between any of them and the fact that children of various weights travel varying distances when using the same sled on the same hill. A pupil in a modern language class can conjugate a French verb perfectly, but fails persistently to use the proper form of this verb when translating an English passage to French. In a social studies class we find a pupil who can recognize the relationship between latitude and climate north, but not south, of the equator. In a geometry class there are usually several pupils who have difficulty recognizing two parallel lines unless they are drawn vertically or horizontally, or who have trouble solving problems with right triangles if the right angle is not the lower left-hand angle.

These are but a few of many frustrating situations confronting the classroom teacher almost daily. The achievement of the pupil does not reach desired levels. Within a restricted situation, he can recall partially or totally correct information, but it has little meaning for him. The pupil seems incapable of restating it in his own words or using it in a novel situation.

These deficiencies have a far-reaching impact on achievement testing. If a test measures only the pupil's ability to recall information, some of the pupils responding to the items may succeed admirably even though they comprehend the subject matter only superficially. Moreover, the teacher may erroneously assume that any pupil who can recall the information is also capable of using it properly, but the consistency of relationship between these two abilities is not large enough to justify this assumption. To identify more closely the perimeters of the pupil's verbal and mathematical achievements, the tests must include items that measure complex cognitive achievement as well as knowledge. Both essay and objective test items can be used for this purpose.

TESTING FOR KNOWLEDGE AND MORE COMPLEX ACHIEVEMENT

For the purposes of this book, a pupil's knowledge is composed of those pieces of information that he commands. He can recall them when he wants to do so. According to this definition, the pupil may, but not necessarily, have some grasp of the meanings, implications, or significance of his knowledge. In other words, all the facts about people, places, events, and things that he acquired by rote and that he can still recall are a part of his knowledge, whether or not he grasps their meanings.

More complex cognitive achievement, on the other hand, is based on the acquisition of meanings. The pupil gains this when he comprehends the meaning of parcels of knowledge to the point that he can restate them in his own words, grasp the interrelationships among them, and take action intelligently on that basis. Complex achievement is knowledge with its meanings, implications, and significance attached. Now the pupil is able to meet the changing situations thrust upon him every day and to attack intelligently the problems they contain. In other words, we are talking about the five levels of the cognitive taxonomy (Bloom, 1956) called intellectual abilities and skills, that is, comprehension, application, analysis, synthesis, and evaluation.

Testing for Knowledge

Testing for verbal and mathematical knowledge with objective test items is illustrated in the preceding chapter. Most of the test items can be correctly answered by any pupil willing to memorize. If he fails to gain meaning as he memorizes, little is lost as far as these items are concerned.

Consider for a moment the matching test item in which a pupil must identify the twenty-five-year period in which certain western states were admitted to the Union (see page 107). Certainly he can memorize the admission date of every state and thereby answer the test item correctly. Any significance to the sequence in which the states were admitted or any factors determining the time at which a particular state was admitted are not needed to answer the test item. Quite possibly the pupil knows less about these than he does about the dates of admission.

Since testing for knowledge is comparatively easy, it receives considerable attention in the classroom. The teacher experiences little difficulty in constructing test items requiring the pupil to recall an isolated fact or a series of facts. Consequently, classroom achievement tests and many standardized achievement tests are heavily overbalanced in this direction. This in turn has a profound influence on learning and teaching. Pupils quickly discover the advantages of concentrating on topics on which they are tested. They orient their learning procedures accordingly. Sometimes the teacher is no less susceptible to this pressure, particularly if his pupils are a part of a citywide or statewide testing program. When the tests stress recall of information, he generally teaches accordingly so that the class test results will compare favorably with those of the other classes. In brief, the educational objectives dealing with knowledge become the primary objectives.

The overemphasis on recall of information found in achievement tests today should not be replaced with a fault equally as serious: an underemphasis on testing for knowledge. Knowledge is the raw material for developing more complex achievement. Before a pupil can acquire the latter, he must have all pertinent knowledge at his disposal. A severe deemphasis on educational objectives dealing with knowledge could be as damaging as the present overemphasis.

Testing for Complex Achievement

In knowledge testing, the material the pupil learns is essentially, if not exactly, the same as that included in the test items. Novel material is virtually non-existent in the test. Appreciably novel test items require more of the pupil than simple recall of information.

It follows that evidence of a pupil's complex cognitive achievements can be obtained by asking him questions about a carefully contrived situation that is new to him. Within this situation he is to apply the appropriate part of his total store of knowledge. To do so successfully, he must know the meanings of his knowledge and be able to reorganize them within a strange but plausible situation. By using a novel situation, the teacher can be confident that the pupil is doing more than merely parroting memorized material.

An illustration of the use of novelty in testing can be found in the test item on tax assessment shown in the preceding chapter (see page 96). Assume that this situation is new to the pupil but the mathematical procedures involved have been studied. To answer it correctly he must recognize that the amount to be paid by each property owner is proportional to the frontage of his property. Therefore, he can proceed as follows:

$$\frac{230 \text{ feet}}{\$690} = \frac{60 \text{ feet}}{X}.$$

Thus, the pupil selects from his mathematical knowledge the part appropriate to this fictitious but realistic situation and applies it correctly.

What the Test Item Measures

There are instances when we are uncertain as to whether the test item is measuring a pupil's knowledge or a higher order of learning. This is particularly true when the purpose of the test item is to measure knowledge. The teacher building the test item has no intention of measuring anything except recall of information and, as far as most members of the class are concerned, he succeeds. Consider, however, the pupil who for some reason did not acquire the knowledge in question, yet arrives at the correct answer by a process of deduction based upon related knowledge. For him, more complex achievement is measured.

The multiple-choice test item shown below is an example:

In Shakespeare's *Hamlet* the following quotation appears:
"This above all: to thine own self be true,

And it must follow, as the night the day,
Thou canst not then be false to any man."
Which of the following characters speaks these lines?
(1) Claudius
(2) Hamlet
(3) Horatio
(4) Laertes
(5) Polonius

If the class studied the passage, the test item measures recall of information. No doubt most pupils memorized the fact that Polonius spoke these lines when giving advice to his son Laertes. To answer the question, they simply recall that fact. Yet a pupil who did not learn this as such but who is very familiar with the play may also arrive at the correct answer. He may do so on the basis of his knowledge of the play's plot and of the motives of the five characters listed. His response may be a reflection of his ability to interpret *Hamlet*, in which case the response represents a higher level of achievement than simply acquiring knowledge.

A similiar line of reasoning may be used to answer the matching test item concerning the dates of admission of certain western states into the Union. The item is also intended to test recall of information. However, a pupil who cannot recall that Missouri was admitted in 1821 might be sufficiently familiar with the economic, political, and social aspects of this country in the nineteeth century to know that it was admitted some time after 1800 and before 1825. In other words, he may be able to arrive at the correct answer by analyzing the knowledge he has of the arguments concerning slavery, the balance of the free and slave states in the Senate, the Missouri Compromise, and the rate of growth in population and wealth of the Mississippi valley. His answer may be a direct indication of his ability to interpret American history in the first half of the nineteenth century.

Test items designed to measure complex achievement may measure only recall of information. If the situation on which the test item is based is familiar to a pupil, the teacher cannot be certain which aspect of the pupil's achievement is reflected in his answer. For example, it is possible in the case of the tax assessment item that a pupil had previously memorized the problem and perhaps the answer itself. Certainly under these conditions he needs only to recall this information to handle the test item successfully. Comprehension might be minimal.

Tests of Knowledge and Complex Achievement Compared

The similarities and differences between tests measuring knowledge and those measuring complex achievement have been repeatedly investigated and reported. The studies have tried to answer two questions:

1. Are the gains made by pupils as measured in terms of tests of complex achievement more permanent than those measured in terms of tests of knowledge?
2. Is there a relationship between pupil performance as measured by tests of complex achievement and as measured by tests of knowledge?

The answer to the first question is an affirmative one. Studies of secondary school and college academic achievement (Tyler, 1934; Wert, 1937; Weitman, 1965) have shown with remarkable consistency that, as the months pass following instruction, pupils retain more of the materials included in a test of complex achievement than those in a test of knowledge. In some studies, tests of both types were administered to classes as pretests at the beginning of the school year and as final tests at the end of the period of instruction. The difference between the score for each pupil was defined as his gain. Then, without an opportunity to review and relearn the subject matter, the pupils were retested one, two, and sometimes three years later. The gains in knowledge shrank alarmingly; however, the gains in areas of complex achievement showed no such loss. On the contrary, in some instances they actually increased somewhat.

The relationship between pupil performance as measured by tests of complex achievement and by tests of knowledge has been found to be positive and somewhat low (Tyler, 1936). Otherwise stated, the pupil who acquires knowledge in a subject matter area ordinarily acquires more complex learning outcomes too, but this tendency is so imperfect that the second cannot be satisfactorily predicted on the basis of the first. More complex achievement cannot be assessed indirectly by measuring knowledge in a subject matter area; instead, tests specially designed for various levels of the cognitive domain must be used (Solomon, 1965; Smith, 1968).

Problems

1. Ebel (1966) believes that (1) any complex achievement in the cognitive domain can be measured by testing separately the pieces of knowledge that compose it, and (2) simple achievement test items are usually more efficient than complex ones. Is this a strong argument against the use of complex test items based on novel situations? Why?

2. If a teacher of a class well known to you built a series of objective test items according to the six principal levels of the cognitive taxonomy, do you think that, working independently, you could properly classify almost every test item according to its intended level (Stoker and Kropp, 1964)? Even if you and the teacher agree as to the classification, have you necessarily identified the cognitive process that each item is intended to measure?

3. Give possible explanations why, as reported by Weitman (1965), tests composed of items that place little emphasis on rote learning will provide a good basis for predicting long-term learning by pupils.

BUILDING AND SCORING TEST ITEMS
MEASURING COMPLEX ACHIEVEMENT

Data concerning complex pupil achievement can be gathered in many different ways. The daily observation of pupil behavior by the teacher can provide a wealth of evidence. Observation can take place in the classroom, on the playground, or in the pupil's home, and the information acquired can be organized by anecdotal records or rating scales. Pupil work products are also useful. An original theme for an English class, a collection or exhibit for a science class, a painting or clay model for a fine arts unit, an apron for a home economics class, or a bookcase for an industrial arts class will quickly reveal some of the pupil's more complex achievements. Also helpful are teacher-pupil interviews, diaries of out-of-class activities, and, of course, paper-and-pencil tests.

The wide variety of possible ways of gathering such evidence is shown in the *Forty-Fifth Yearbook of the National Society for the Study of Education, Part I* (1946). This is one of the better discussions of the measurement of complex achievement. Illustrative procedures are shown for every major school subject. Considerable space is devoted to a measuring technique that is often overlooked: the objective test item. Although by no means a universal solution for the problems of measuring complex achievement, it can be extremely effective in science, social studies, mathematics, and the language arts. In such subjects as agriculture, home economics, and industrial arts, objective test items are used less frequently, but still provide much-needed information.

Procedure for Constructing Test Items

To construct test items that measure more complex pupil achievement, two basic steps must be taken. First, the teacher must decide which pattern of pupil behavior is to be measured. Behavioral patterns include the pupil's ability to apply facts and principles to new situations, and his ability to interpret data and recognize cause-and-effect relationships and assumptions underlying conclusions. Another way to think of these is in terms of the last five levels of the cognitive taxonomy, namely, comprehension, application, analysis, synthesis, and evaluation. Of course only those levels that are important are included in the table of specifications on the basis of which the test is being developed.

Secondly, the teacher must devise a novel but realistic situation with questions that, to be answered correctly, require the pupil to display the pattern of behavior being considered. The situations can be completely original or based on some convenient source such as newspaper or magazine articles or even research reports unfamiliar to the pupils. If possible, they should resemble the everyday environment familiar to the pupil. He is generally impressed with the fairness of a testing approach that requires him to use what he has learned in school to answer questions about situations similar to his out-of-school experiences.

Combining an appropriate pattern of pupil behavior with a suitably novel situation is not simple. Initially, the teacher may be hard pressed to find the situation he wants and then experience difficulty in reducing it to an objective test item. Finding the situation is a matter of a teacher's sensitivity to the application of what he teaches in the world about him; reducing it to an objective test item is largely a matter of following many of the suggestions for constructing objective test items described in Chapter 3.

In his search for a novel situation, the teacher starts, of course, with a clear notion of the pattern of pupil behavior with which he is concerned. For example, in a mathematics class the pupils have mastered many theorems, one of which is the Pythagorean theorem. To see if they can use this information, the teacher may, in a test item, give them the outer dimensions of a baseball diamond and ask them to compute the distance that the ball must travel when the catcher throws it from home plate to second base. In an elementary school arithmetic unit, the pupils have studied simple areas. Therefore, the teacher might have them compute the number of square pieces of candy of 2×2-inch size that could be cut out of a 8×10-inch rectangular pan. In a science class the pupils learned of the law of refraction. Hence, the teacher builds a test item in which they must tell how they would judge the position of a rock at the bottom of a fish pond if they, standing on the bank, were to retrieve it. In a home economics class the pupils have completed a unit concerning nutrition. The teacher may wish to measure their ability to use this information for maintaining a balanced diet. The test item may list the foods eaten by a hypothetical pupil for breakfast and for lunch, and some of those selected at a cafeteria for dinner. The pupil must apply his knowledge by selecting one salad from among those on the menu that this person should eat, and giving reasons for this choice. Certainly these and many similiar illustrations in other subject matter areas are realistic, challenging problems to the pupils.

Single-Response Objective Test Items.   Some teachers prefer to ask only one question concerning the novel situation selected. It can be phrased to conform to any of the types of objective test items already described. Condensing the description of the novel situation and the question concerning it into a single test item can sometimes be accomplished without lengthening the test item excessively. For instance, in elementary school arithmetic the following short-answer and yes-no test items are typical.

Mrs. Johnson had 1½ pounds of butter in her refrigerator. She used ⅓ of it while baking this morning. How many pounds did she use?

Answer (½)

Yes (No) Joan had 25¢ with which to buy cookies. The cookies she wished
to buy cost 36¢ per dozen. Did she have sufficient money to buy
¾ of a dozen?

In a secondary school English class the teacher may want to check on the
pupil's skill in the proper use of the words *who, whose, whom, which,* and
that. To do this he could give the pupil a series of sentences like those below
and ask him to select the correct word from the two given, then write it in
the space provided at the right.

1. The man (which, who) is speaking is our president.   1. (*who*)
2. Do you know the boy (who's, whose) model air-   2. (*whose*)
   plane is broken?

Sometimes not one but several questions can be asked about the novel
situation. These questions can be more or less independent of each other—
the response to one does not influence appreciably the response to any other.
Each correct response may require the pupil to reveal a different aspect of his
ability to use his knowledge.

The following novel situation is one on which a series of test items is constructed. These test items are intended to measure the ability of pupils in a
home economics class to apply certain rules for meal planning. Typical menus
are shown and proposed changes are to be accepted or rejected by the pupils.
The pupils are also to identify the rule that supports the changes that are
accepted. Since the rules are summarized for the pupil, these test items demand
less recall of information than some of the others included in this chapter.

DIRECTIONS: Listed below are the menus of meals for two days and certain meal
planning rules. Study them carefully.

Breakfast

A. Pear sauce   D. Orange slices
   Poached egg on milk toast   Soft cooked egg on toast
   Coffee   Cocoa

Lunch

B. Tomato soup   E. Chicken soup (broth)
   Bacon, lettuce, and tomato   Cherry jello salad
   sandwich   Orange
   Peaches and cookie   Tea
   Milk

Dinner

C. Fried pork chops   F. Pea soup
   French fried potatoes   Meat loaf
   Spinach   Baked beans
   Mince pie   Rolls and butter
   Coffee   Custard pie
                                           Coffee

Meal planning rules

1. Balance the different types of foodstuffs in each meal.
2. Do not serve the same food twice in the same meal, even in a different form.
3. Do not use many rich or hard-to-digest foods in one meal.
4. Combine bland or soft foods with those of more pronounced flavor or different texture.
5. Plan meals in which the colors harmonize and are appealing.
6. Plan at least one food in each meal that has high satiety value.

DIRECTIONS: Keeping in mind the above rules, consider the following changes. If the change would not improve the meal, place a zero in the blank. If the change would improve the meal, write the number of the rule supporting your decision in the blank opposite the change. Judge each change independently of all others.

(4) 1. Substitute scrambled egg and cinnamon toast for poached egg on milk toast in Menu A.

(2) 2. Substitute cream of mushroom soup for tomato soup in Menu B.

(3) 3. Substitute broiled steak for the fried pork chops in Menu C.

(0) 4. Substitute pecan pie for mince pie in Menu C.

(0) 5. Substitute half of grapefruit for orange slices in Menu D.

(6) 6. Substitute cream of chicken soup for chicken soup in Menu E.

(1) 7. Substitute baked potato for baked beans in Menu F.

Observe that the description of the novel situation is quite long. This is to be expected, since it provides ample material for a series of test items. Also observe that the objective test items following the description can be any one of several types. The true-false and multiple-choice types are commonly used.

Building test items such as the foregoing involves a series of revisions if a high-quality product is to be obtained. The teacher begins by writing a description of the novel situation, then constructs test items on the basis of it. It is soon apparent that revision of the description will strengthen one or more of the proposed items. Minor deletions or additions of material may result in a wealth of new test item possibilities. Thus, the construction of test items suggests changes in the description, and changes in description suggest new or better test items. Persistent efforts along these lines by the teacher will produce a description of the novel situation that is virtually unambiguous and that contains no nonfunctional portions of any consequence; with this description will be a series of test items exploiting practically all the possibilities for measuring complex pupil achievement in terms of the situation used.

Multiple-Response Objective Test Items. Multiple-response objective test items are also used to measure pupil understandings. A common instance of this occurs when the teacher wishes to measure the pupil's ability to apply facts and principles to new situations. In this case the situation is described in some detail. A paragraph or more may be needed. The basic problem within the novel situation is defined and a question asked about it. The pupil answers the question by selecting the correct response from among several listed. Finally, he selects from among many reasons listed those that support his answer. In a sense he views each reason as he does a true-false test item. He must decide whether it is sound or faulty.

An illustration of the above is the following test item intended for use in a secondary school science class.[1] A knowledge of the principles of reproduction, how they operate in plants, and an ability to apply this information in a novel situation are measured by this test item.

A visitor to a rural area noticed that each apple orchard of any size had beehives located in it. This puzzled him, so he asked one of the local farmers why this practice was followed.

DIRECTIONS: Immediately following are given three possible answers to the question asked above. Check the *one* that *best* answers the question.

_____A. The bees will be able to get good nectar.
___✓__B. The number of apples formed on each tree will increase.
_____C. The apple blossoms will be self-pollinated.

DIRECTIONS: Following is a list of statements that are suggested as reasons for the above answer. Check the statements that are *good* reasons for the *answer* you selected above.

_____ 1. Yield of apples is increased if bees are present.
___✓__ 2. Fertilization makes possible the development of mature fruits.
_____ 3. Cross-pollination is necessary for the production of a good apple crop.
_____ 4. Cross-pollination frequently results in desirable variations.
_____ 5. Many fruit growers keep bees in their orchards.
_____ 6. The apple blossoms contain the most desirable type of nectar that can be used in commercial honey.
___✓__ 7. Flowers from which insects have collected nectar are usually pollinated.
_____ 8. The only completely satisfactory location for beehives is in the orchard from which they can get nectar.
___✓__ 9. Even though self-pollination is possible in a flower, it frequently fails to occur.
_____10. Bees pollinate apple blossoms in order to aid in the production of a good crop.
_____11. All insect-pollinated flowers are cross-pollinated.
_____12. Double fertilization increases the yield.

The construction of test items like the above is, unfortunately, not a simple task. Even after the difficulties of finding a suitable situation and identifying the central problem have been overcome, the teacher must still find two or more plausible answers, each of which is supported by a group of logical reasons. The latter are the most difficult to find. One way of simplifying the task is to submit the situation to groups of pupils as an essay test item, then

[1] This test item was adapted with modifications from materials prepared in the College of Sciences and Humanities of Iowa State University (1949).

screen their answers for attractive but wrong answers and logical reasons for them. These answers can be restated so that an objective test item results.

Two additional features of this kind of objective test item deserve mention. Observe that the pupils do not know how many of the suggested reasons are good reasons, and that some that are not relevant to the correct answer are nevertheless essentially true statements. An example of this is the fifth reason listed: "Many fruit growers keep bees in their orchards." To avoid confusion these two points are sometimes mentioned in the directions to the pupils.

Scoring the Multiple-Response Test Item

When a series of more or less independent questions are asked about the same novel situation, the pupil responses can be weighted and scored in essentially the same manner as any other objective test items of the same type; however, when pupil responses to one point of the test item are in some way dependent on responses to another part, the weighting and scoring become more complicated. In the scoring of many of these test items, two questions can be asked:

1. How much credit should a pupil receive if he answers one part of the item incorrectly and, because of this, responds incorrectly to other parts dependent on the first?
2. When the pupil is not told how many responses to make, how are his responses scored if he makes too few or too many, some of which are correct and some of which are wrong?

Both of these questions can be discussed in terms of the multiple-response objective test item concerning beehives in an apple orchard. The pupil must select one of three alternatives as the principal advantage of placing bees in an apple orchard, and then indicate which of the twelve reasons listed support his answer. Suppose a pupil selects the wrong alternative and defends his choice well by checking appropriate reasons for it. How much credit should he receive? According to the scoring key, his responses are totally wrong. He argues, however, that only his first response is wrong. He did check the correct reasons for the wrong alternative. What should the teacher do? Although practices vary, one of the more popular is to allow no credit for any of the reasons checked if the correct alternative is not selected.

The second question deals with the case in which the pupil checks the correct alternative and receives whatever points are allowed for this answer, but does not check the proper reasons. Possibly he checks too many reasons, including the correct ones. Or possibly he checks too few reasons, yet those selected are correct. In either case, how should his choice of reasons be scored? Again, there is no single, widely accepted answer to this question. Sometimes teachers take the point of view that the pupil should be penalized if he checks any unacceptable reasons. Moreover, a pupil who indiscriminately checks *all* reasons should receive no credit.

According to this view, the penalty for any reason erroneously checked will be determined by the total number of reasons listed and the number correct. In the beehives test item, four of twelve reasons are listed on the key as acceptable. Hence, if one point were allowed for each correct reason checked, then one-half of a point would be deducted for every incorrect reason. In this way a pupil who checks all reasons will receive four positive points and four negative points, a net of zero. If more than one point is allowed each correct reason checked, the penalty for each incorrect reason is proportionally increased.

Problems

4.   On the basis of each of the following principles in science, describe a novel situation and construct test items concerning it which will measure a young pupil's ability to apply that principle.
  a. Water tends to seek its own level.
  b. An object floating in water will displace water equal to its weight.
  c. The theoretical mechanical advantage of a lever used in conjunction with a fulcrum is related to the position of the fulcrum.
  d. The earth rotates on its axis once a day and circles the sun once a year.

5.   Using a table of specifications in a subject matter area of interest to you, design one or more test items that measure comprehension, application, or analysis. Then cross-refer each test item with the table, that is, indicate the cells in the table with which it is primarily related and those with which it is secondarily related (for example, cells concerning knowledge).

6.   Design an original method of scoring the multiple-response test item concerning beehives shown on page 140.

OBJECTIVE TEST ITEMS BASED ON PICTORIAL MATERIALS

A picture is said to be worth ten thousand words. This is just as true in achievement testing as in any other aspect of everyday living. Consider for a moment a teacher who regularly discovers that he needs a large number of words to develop a sufficiently unambiguous test item. Many words, he realizes, increase the pupil's reading load and the time required to answer the test item. Hence, he asks the logical question: Could a diagram, map, photograph, picture, or even a table of data be used to construct the test item? When this is done, the number of words needed to make the item specific and understandable is generally reduced, sometimes to less than half that required when no pictorial or tabular material is used. Furthermore, a well-chosen photograph or table serves as an excellent means of describing a novel situation on which the item is based.

Suggestions for Constructing Pictorial Test Items

Use pictorial material only when it makes a unique and sizable contribution to the quality of the test item. The pictorial material must be functional in an important way. It should represent a central idea much better than words can.

Consider the following junior high school test item designed to measure the pupil's ability to use his knowledge of angles in a new situation.

A real estate agent buys the city block shown in the diagram below and divides it into ten lots as indicated by the dotted lines. The lines CD, EF, GH, and IJ are parallel to the streets AB and KL. Street BL meets street AB at an angle of 72°.

1. What will the agent find to be the size of angle BDC? (108) degrees.
2. What will the agent find to be the size of angle IJL? (72) degrees.
3. Will the lots facing street AK have more, less or the same frontage as the corresponding lots facing street BL? (less)

Certainly it would be most difficult to construct test items of this kind without including a diagram. Furthermore, the number of test items based on the diagram can be increased easily, for example, by adding questions about the areas of the lots.

The pictorial material should be no more complicated than needed to accomplish its purpose. Some of the problems experienced in this regard are illustrated in the following test items designed for primary-level pupils. Their knowledge of insects is being measured by responding to questions about drawings of insects which they are given. The teacher reads each question at least once and pauses while the pupils draw a line through the answer each selects.

Teacher: *Draw a line through the number that tells you how many legs this insect has.*

2
4
6
8
10

Teacher: *Draw a line through the number that tells you how many feelers this insect has.*

2
4
6
8

Teacher: *Draw a line through the number that tells you how many wings this insect has.*

0
2
4
6
8

Teacher: *Draw a line through the number that tells you how many eyes this insect has.*

2
4
6
8

It is difficut to know whether too little or too much detail is included in drawings such as these. The amount used seems to be appropriate, but we cannot be sure of this point without studying pupil responses and questioning the class members about their incorrect answers.

When necessary, use explanatory statements to clarify the meaning of the pictorial material. Often the pictorial material can stand alone, or virtually so. On the other hand, efforts to avoid complex material can produce ambiguities for some pupils. The following is an example of how this might happen.

DIRECTIONS: Carefully study the map below. Do not consider it to be any particular place. The dots represent cities. Each city is identified by a letter. For each of the questions following the map, choose the correct city from among the four listed. Write the letter of that city in the blank provided.

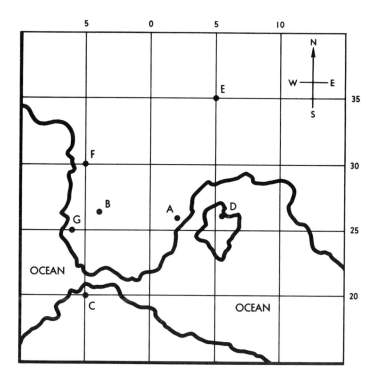

(C)   1. Which city is nearest the equator?
       City C
       City D
       City E
       City G

(A)   2. Which city is nearest the prime meridian?
       City A
       City B
       City D
       City F

(D)   3. Which city has the greatest east longitude reading?
       City C
       City D
       City E
       City G

The purpose of the items is to measure the ability of elementary school pupils to interpret unfamiliar maps. This purpose might not be realized if pupils fail to understand the symbolism used. Also, they are cautioned not to consider the region shown to be any particular place. Since the drawing vaguely resembles the western end of the Mediterranean Sea, a pupil who considers it to be that area may believe the cities to be actual localities, thereby adding confusing features to the multiple-choice questions.

Integrate the test items with the pictorial materials so as to reduce the complexity of test items as much as possible. This suggestion is followed in all of the pictorial items shown. Notice that the questions are comparatively short, particularly in the case of the map interpretation items. In addition, the pupil responds to these items by using the letter of the city he selects; numbers for the responses are not provided, thereby streamlining each test item still more.

Problems

7. Suppose that, in the case of the second multiple-choice test item concerning map interpretation, the distracter "City B" is changed to "City C." Would this improve the test item? Why?

8. Excellent illustrations of the use of pictorial and tabular materials as a part of test items to measure more than recall of information have been published by the Educational Testing Service (1963). Select one from this publication and analyze it with respect to the pupil behavioral changes probably involved.

ADVANTAGES OF MEASURING COMPLEX ACHIEVEMENT WITH OBJECTIVE TESTS

The advantages gained by measuring complex cognitive achievement with objective test items are in part the same as those obtained by any other means. In other words, their use enlarges the scope of the achievement evaluation program, which in turn increases the attention paid by both pupils and teachers to the role of educational objectives dealing with a higher order of learning.

Moreover, pupils ordinarily find that objective test items designed to reveal more complex achievement are challenging and practical. Pupil interest can reach the point where more than a few will voluntarily admit that this type of testing is enjoyable and meaningful, a situation particularly probable when pictorial material represents the novel situation. Often we can simulate a natural situation quite well and thereby reduce the degree of artificiality present in the testing situation.

Objective test items measuring complex pupil achievement have several additional advantages. Teachers skilled in objective testing who use it for measuring pupil knowledge find this technique a convenient extension of familiar testing procedures that covers other parts of the table of specifications without sacrificing objectivity of scoring. Unlike the evaluation of pupil work products, for example, the objective test items provide highly structured problems to which the pupils are to react. Each pupil is confronted with the same novel situation and responds in terms of the same list of possible answers. This allows comparisons of pupil performances to be made more easily. Incidentally, the structuring of the problem may also limit the usefulness of objective test items. Complex pupil achievement is reflected in the originality of pupil performance. Responses to objective test items do not reveal this originality, whereas a creative work product does.

Problem

9.   Compare the value of information from objective test items with that gained by examining creative pupil products when the degree of complex pupil achievement in the cognitive domain is being evaluated in a subject matter area of interest to you.

LIMITATIONS OF MEASURING COMPLEX ACHIEVEMENT WITH OBJECTIVE TESTS

There are three important limitations in the measuring of complex pupil achievement with objective test items. First, the methods tend to be more difficult to devise and execute than those for measuring pupil knowledge. They demand considerable ingenuity on the part of the teacher, especially if he focuses his efforts at the upper levels of the cognitive taxonomy. Secondly, the time needed for pupil response may be excessive. Finally, the results yielded by this procedure cannot be attributed to one—and only one—pupil trait. Instead, they are the products of a combination of pupil traits; prominent among these are ability to recall information and scholastic aptitude.

Difficulty of Construction

The value of the objective test item in the measuring of complex achievement depends directly on the novel situation selected and the description or pictorial material provided. It is already apparent that the selection of the situation is a painstaking operation. After identifying the cognitive level to be incorporated in the test item, the teacher must find a reasonably simple, understandable, practical, and yet novel situation that illustrates it. Many possibilities are considered before one is selected.

The description of the situation and any pictorial material used must be prepared with equal care. Since the pupils answering the test items cannot add or change any features of the description, it must be complete and, above all, unambiguous. Several rewritings of the description or reconstructions of the pictorial material are ordinarily necessary before this is accomplished. Needless to say, the teacher must also strive to maintain an appropriate vocabulary level and reasonable brevity.

Another factor that complicates the problem of construction is the relationship between the description of the novel situation and the basic question contained in the test item. These two parts must be clearly interdependent if the test item is to measure complex pupil achievement. In brief, it must be so designed that it can be answered correctly only if the pupil recalls appropriate facts and uses them in terms of the information contained in the description. Building this interdependence into the test item sounds like a relatively simple task, but it is not. The following is an illustration. This is a part of a group of test items designed to measure the pupil's comprehension of certain aspects of our legal system.

A janitor saw a strange man walking near the high school on the same night that a door was smashed and $400 stolen. He reported this to the police who promptly arrested the man on a burglary charge. Although the man claimed he was innocent, he was held without bail. A fellow prisoner suggested that he should try to obtain a writ of habeas corpus.

⊤ F 1. A writ of habeas corpus is a writ inquiring into the lawfulness of the restraint of a person who is imprisoned.

⊤ F 2. When a person who is arrested is held without bail, he is allowed to confer with his lawyer.

Observe that it is possible to answer both true-false test items correctly without reading the introductory material. They are measuring the pupil's ability to recall information rather than his ability to recall it and then use it effectively. As appropriate as the description of the stranger's troubles seems to be, it is nothing but window-dressing in the test.

Suppose that the last sentence of the introductory material were deleted and that the following two test items replaced the original pair:

⊤ F 1. An effective way to help the stranger would be to obtain a writ of habeas corpus.

T Ⓕ 2. The manner in which the stranger was held (i.e., without bail) is a violation of the Tenth Amendment of the Constitution.

It is difficult if not impossible for the pupil to answer the above questions correctly without reading the description of the novel situation. These changes make the introductory material functional and greatly improve the degree to which the responses reflect higher levels of the cognitive taxonomy rather than knowledge alone.

No doubt a number of teachers would have found the second pair of test items more difficult to construct than the first, for reasons not easy to trace.

It may be that the item builder would not have a clear idea of the cognitive level of concern to him, or possibly it would be difficult to break the habit of building completely self-contained test items. In any event, obtaining the proper relationship between the introductory material and the question is still another factor that lengthens the process of constructing appropriate items.

Response Time Needed

Class time is a precious commodity. The classroom teacher will be pleased with any measuring procedures that require less time and effort than the techniques already known to him, and concerned about any that seem less efficient. Objective test items for measuring complex achievement are usually placed in the latter category.

No doubt you are impressed with the length of many of the objective items in this chapter, especially the multiple-response type. The first reading consumes plenty of time, but the several that are usually required dangerously lengthen the response time. Unfortunately, attempts to shorten test items are only partially successful. The description of the novel situation can be abbreviated only so much. Any inappropriate reading load will penalize the poor reader. This reduces the effectiveness of these objective test items, particularly in the elementary school.

Another factor that increases a pupil's response time is lack of confidence in his answer. Unlike his responses to recall-of-information test items, his answers do not carry the conviction that he is correct. Hence, he rechecks. His relative lack of confidence carries over from item to item and tends to slow his pace.

The limitation of extended pupil response time may have acquired exaggerated importance in some quarters. Although it is true that these objective test items often consume unduly large amounts of testing time and at best reflect a small sample of complex pupil achievement, the teacher can hardly justify not using them on this basis alone, unless he has better means of obtaining as much or more information about these pupil traits. An increase in testing time is, after all, a small price to pay when the reward is a measurement program broadened to obtain evidence of highly important educational outcomes.

Interpretation of Results

Interpretation of results yielded by test items measuring complex achievement is clouded by a variety of traits contributing to the pupil's response. Examination of test items in this chapter shows us that behavioral changes at several levels of the cognitive taxonomy are probably intermixed. After all, knowledge is the building material for more complex cognitive achievement. Therefore a correct pupil response means that several correct steps have been taken. Failure to answer a test item correctly means that the pupil failed to perform one or more steps correctly. Yet the teacher does not know which these are. In a simple case, the teacher might ask whether the pupil failed to give the right answer because he could not recall the necessary information correctly or could not use it in terms of the novel situation after he recalled it.

The manner in which the objective test items discussed here are constructed does not give the teacher any appreciable information with which to answer this question. Nor does it allow him to determine the full meaning of a correct response. If a pupil responds correctly, does this mean that he simply followed a correct procedure, or that he followed the *most efficient* correct procedure? A correct response does not mean that the pupil has full command of the steps required any more than an incorrect response means that he has no command of them.

Testing techniques have been developed that reveal in greater detail the procedures that the examinee follows as he attempts to solve a problem. Prominent among these are the tab item technique reported by Glaser and his associates (1960), a card technique reported by Rimoldi (1955, 1963), and simulation exercises developed by McGuire and Babbott (1967).

The tab item described is designed to measure a technician's proficiency in detecting the defective unit in a television set that is not operating properly. He is provided with a description of the malfunction, a diagram of the television set, a list of check procedures that might be employed to determine the cause, and a list of possibly defective units. Opposite each check procedure is a tab, under which is a verbal or diagrammatic description of the results the examinee would have obtained if he had actually performed the procedure. The examinee tries to locate the defective unit by making as few check procedures as possible. He begins by selecting one, tearing off the tab, and uncovering the information produced if the procedure is actually followed. He continues to do this until he has diagnosed the difficulty. The pattern of removed tabs reveals all of the steps he had to take; the sequence of the steps can also be recorded.

The card technique is similar to the tab item. The examinee is given a problem, such as the complaints made by a patient upon admission to a hospital. The examinee has to solve the problem by asking questions that he thinks necessary for its solution. The questions that he might be expected to ask are written on cards; the answers are written on the back of the card. The examinee selects a question and reads the answer. He continues to do this until he has solved the problem. The examiner records the order in which the questions are asked and thus knows the steps followed in the solution of the problem.

Simulation exercises have also been based on medical problems. They are designed to test the skill of medical students in gathering data about a patient and making judgments for correcting his ailments. A brief verbal description or a short color film is provided, in which the patient's complaints are recounted. The examinee then chooses one of several starting points to be used to alleviate the difficulty, and records his choice by erasing the opaque overlay on an answer sheet. Now he is confronted with a list of possible medical interventions that provide additional information about the patient. He selects those that seem appropriate, again recording his choice by erasing the proper section of the overlay. The results of each of his interventions are reported to him in a realistic verbal, visual, or auditory manner. On the basis of the new data he continues the treatment until his efforts result in the patient's recovery, referral to a specialist, or in some cases death.

Clearly, the simulation exercises differ from the other two techniques in one important way, namely, the problem is modified by the intervening steps taken by the examinee. For this reason these are called *branched* exercises. Several routes may lead to an acceptable outcome. In the first two techniques the same problem is presented to all examinees and it remains the same. This is known as a *linear* exercise.

Certainly none of these techniques has been developed to the point where a teacher can conveniently use them in classroom achievement testing, nor have attempts to establish their worth utilized elementary or secondary school pupils. Nevertheless, these techniques and their variations may appreciably influence future developments in measuring complex pupil achievement. Many superior pupil evaluation techniques have been developed from starting points such as these.

A final question that is frequently asked is whether objective tests that measure higher-order achievement are appreciably different from tests of mental ability. In other words, are these tests achievement tests at all? Certainly the pupil's mental ability plays an important role; there is evidence, however, that these are not the same as tests of mental ability (Furst, 1950; Glaser, 1941). The results yielded by the two types of tests are positively related, but not to a perfect degree by any means.

Problems

10. Study the scheme prepared by Ebel (1954) for classifying test items on the basis of the knowledge or ability which the test item requires of the pupil. Is it possible accurately to classify test items designed to measure complex pupil achievement when the mental processes involved in solving them are not clearly known and may vary from pupil to pupil?

11. Using the card technique, build a test item for measuring pupil ability to apply principles in new situations in a subject matter area of interest to you.

12.   Different types of secondary school physics curricula produce different cognitive preferences by pupils (Heath, 1964). The cognitive preference test consists of four-option multiple-choice test items, frequently containing a diagram or graph in the stem. Since all options are correct answers, the pupil selects the one he prefers. Analyze this effort to evaluate curricula by means of an achievement test.

OPEN-BOOK TESTING

Teachers typically administer closed-book tests. The pupil has no source materials at his disposal that would provide him with the correct answers to any of the test items. He depends exclusively on his memory and his ability to manipulate successfully what he remembers. Occasionally the teacher modifies the rules slightly; although access to the textbook and many reference books is forbidden, a restricted number of source materials is allowed. For example, in some mathematics tests the pupils are permitted to use tables of logarithms, tables of trigonometric functions, or tables of squares, square roots, and reciprocals. During science tests the periodic table of elements is prominently displayed, and various chemical, zoological, and botanical handbooks are available to the pupils. In social studies tests, the pupils are sometimes allowed to refer to certain maps and charts. Furthermore, English teachers approve the use of a dictionary during some of their tests. Perhaps these should be called limited closed-book tests.

If the test being administered measures only pupil knowledge, the use of the traditional closed-book approach can be effectively defended. After all, an open-book administration with ample time limits may tell us little more about a pupil's achievement than whether he can use his textbook and other reference materials to find the correct answers to a list of questions. If the test being administered measures primarily complex pupil achievement, however, the use of the traditional closed-book procedure seems to be an unnecessary restriction. An open-book administration is much more realistic. Since a basic purpose of this type of test is to discover whether the pupil can use his knowledge in everyday living, the test situation should simulate the natural situation as much as possible and allow the pupil the use of the normal tools and aids he would have in the natural situation.

The debate on closed- or open-book testing procedures gets complicated when we try to establish the degree to which the test or test item measures primarily complex achievement. It is clear from inspection of the sample test items included in this chapter that a number of levels of the cognitive taxonomy are involved in each, that the relative amount of each varies from item to item, and that this balance can be controlled by the person building it. Furthermore, no matter what the test item may seem to measure on the surface, the learning experiences of the pupils answering the test item must also be known before the behavioral patterns it measures can be determined.

The final decision is, of course, in the hands of the classroom teacher. If he believes that tests for knowledge should be the traditional closed-book procedure and that tests for complex achievement should be open-book, then on the basis of his knowledge of the test items, the pupils, and their experiences, he may separate his test items and administer them accordingly. For those test items about which he is in doubt, he must decide which evidence of a pupil behavioral change is more important and classify the item accordingly.

Building Open-Book Tests

Constructing test items for an open-book test is probably more difficult than constructing those for a closed-book test. Some of the suggestions for constructing objective test items already discussed must be followed with great care. For example, efforts to avoid textbook terminology should be redoubled. Copying verbatim from a textbook, even when designing test items for a closed-book test, is dangerous; for those items to be included in an open-book test it is very damaging.

Above all, the teacher must construct each test so that the textbook or reference materials will be used in much the same manner as they would be in a similar problem in a natural situation. Although this requirement cannot be fully satisfied, attempts to meet it typically yield good results. For instance, in a mathematics test the textbook may be of little direct help to a pupil as he decides which formula to use to solve the problem, but it does provide an accurate statement of any formula selected. In a social studies test an encyclopedia to which the pupil can refer may serve a similar function. The pupil need not trust his memory here any more than he would in a similar everyday situation in which he wanted to use a given formula or historical fact. In other words, the materials to which the pupil has access in a test should play a supporting role only. The test item should be designed to effect such a condition.

Administering Open-Book Tests

If pupils are to be given an open-book test, they should be forewarned. The reference materials they can use should be carefully listed for them. Perhaps there will be no restrictions, or as some teachers prefer, the list may include only those materials that might be used in a typical out-of-class situation. In any event, the availability of the materials listed will greatly influence the manner in which the pupil prepares for the test. Quite possibly he will concentrate less on factual details and more on broad principles and relationships (Feldhusen, 1961). Moreover, he may try to become familiar with the reference materials, their content and organization.

Teachers sometimes argue that if an open-book test is to be used and no restrictions placed on the reference materials, class time need not be used for its administration. Instead, the pupil can write the test at home. Although the so-called take-home test has some merit, it suffers from two serious disadvantages. First, the teacher has no certainty that the pupil will work independently. Any assistance destroys the worth of the test results. Secondly, the pupil writing the test at home does not have an opportunity to ask legitimate questions about the items or procedure. Since tests are rarely so well constructed that no questions are necessary, the pupil should not be denied the chance to ask pertinent questions.

Problems

13.   Do open-book tests necessarily measure different pupil abilities from those measured by closed-book tests (Kalish, 1958)?

14.   One study of college students showed that, in their opinion, they performed about as well on open-book achievement tests as on closed-book tests (Feldhusen, 1961). Is this finding surprising? Why?

SUMMARY

A paper-and-pencil achievement testing program measuring only the pupil's knowledge is quite inadequate. Where possible, a testing program should be extended to measure his more complex cognitive achievement as well. In other words, it should determine whether the pupil knows the meaning of his knowledge, grasps the interrelationships among different parts, and can take action intelligently on the basis of them. With enough ingenuity and care, the classroom teacher can construct objective test items capable of eliciting these behavioral patterns from the pupil.

When a pupil acquires higher-order achievement, he can use his knowledge effectively. Therefore, evidence of this fact can be obtained by asking him questions about a carefully contrived situation that is new to him. To answer these questions correctly he must recall the appropriate part of his total store of knowledge and use it in terms of the novel situation described. If he can do so, he has achieved important, complex educational goals.

The novel situations are difficult to develop. First, they must involve one or more of the upper levels of the cognitive taxonomy in which the teacher is interested. Secondly, they must be realistic, relatively commonplace, and plausible. Finally, they should require only a short description and/or comparatively simple pictorial material to be understood. Quite often, at least one of these requirements cannot be completely satisfied.

The question or questions concerning the novel situation can be presented as one or more objective test items. Any type of objective item can be used. The suggestions described in Chapter 3 can be followed in building them, although minor variations are occasionally necessary. Integrating the test items with the pictorial material or description of the novel situation requires special care. Objective test items for measuring complex achievement have the principal advantage of offering the teacher a convenient extension of familiar testing procedures to cover other parts of the table of specifications without sacrificing objectivity of scoring. The principal limitations are that the test items are difficult to build, the pupils need considerable time in which to respond, and the test results are hard to interpret.

The administration of the objective test to measure complex achievement is much like that of an objective test to measure knowledge. The possibility of using an open-book testing procedure should be seriously explored when more than knowledge is being measured, for such a procedure simulates realism. Since a basic purpose of the test is to discover whether the pupil can use his knowledge in everyday living, the pupil should be allowed to use the tools and aids normally available to him.

Suggested Readings

Commission on Undergraduate Education in the Biological Sciences. *Testing and evaluation in the biological sciences.* Publication No. 20. Washington: Author, 1967.
　　After carefully designing a table of specifications, a committee of biologists assembled a large number of test items representing a broad spectrum of both behavioral changes and subject matter. Each item is cross-referred with a cell in the table of specifications. Novel situations are repeatedly used as a basis for item construction.

Educational Testing Service, *Multiple-choice questions: A close look.* Princeton, N.J.: Author, 1963.
　　For the purpose of dispelling the myth that objective test items require no thought or insight by the pupil who responds, twenty-two test items in a variety of subject matter areas are reproduced in their entirety. Explanations of each and a description of the kinds of responses often given are provided.

Hedges, W. D. *Testing and evaluation for the sciences in the secondary school.* Belmont, Calif.: Wadsworth, 1966.
　　A short, practical book aimed directly at the problems associated with constructing objective test items in general science, biology, chemistry, and physics. Repeated use of the various levels of the cognitive taxonomy yielded many illustrations of items measuring more than recall of information and suggestions for designing them.

Henry, N. B. (ed.) *The measurement of understanding.* Forty-Fifth Yearbook of the National Society for the Study of Education, Part I. Chicago: University of Chicago Press, 1946.

> This is an outstanding presentation of the methods of measuring complex achievement in the elementary and secondary schools. Of particular interest are Chapter 3, in which the nature of complex achievement is discussed, and Chapter 4, in which methods of obtaining evidence of complex achievement are described. In Section II are separate chapters devoted to the measurement of complex achievement in social studies, science, elementary school mathematics, secondary school mathematics, language arts, fine arts, health education, physical education, home economics, and agriculture. Methods other than the use of objective test items are also explained.

Smith, R. B. A discussion of an attempt at constructing reproducible item sets. *Journal of Educational Measurement,* 1968, **5,** 55–60.

> Central to this article is a set of eight objective test items based on a novel experiment dealing with the reflection and absorption of light. Each of the six levels of the cognitive taxonomy is represented by at least one item. Study of these items is quite helpful.

Solomon, R. J. New directions in assessing achievement. *Proceedings of the 1965 Western Regional Conference on Testing Problems.* Princeton, N.J.: Educational Testing Service, 1965. Pp. 45–51.

> Current trends in achievement testing are reviewed with particular attention given to measuring complex cognitive achievement. Emphasis is given to broadening the testing program to the same degree as the educational objectives.

Wesman, A. G. Writing the test item. In R. L. Thorndike (ed.) *Educational measurement.* (2nd ed.) Washington: American Council on Education, 1970. Chapter 4.

> The last portion of this chapter concerns "context-dependent" objective test items, including items based on pictorial or tabular materials. Suggestions for constructing such items and also illustrations of them are provided.

References Cited

Abingdon, Alexander (pseud.). *Bigger and better boners.* New York: Viking Press, 1952.

Bloom, B. S. (ed.) *Taxonomy of educational objectives: Cognitive domain.* New York: David McKay, 1956.

College of Science and Humanities. *Testing for more than memorization.* Unpublished manuscript. Ames, Iowa: Iowa State University, 1949.

Ebel, R. L. Procedures for the analysis of classroom tests. *Educational and Psychological Measurement,* 1954, **14,** 352–364.

Ebel, R. L. Some measurement problems in a national assessment of educational progress. *Journal of Educational Measurement,* 1966, **3,** 11–17.

Educational Testing Service. *Multiple-choice question: A close look.* Princeton, N.J.: Author, 1963.

Feldhusen, J. F. An evaluation of college students' reactions to open book examinations. *Educational and Psychological Measurement,* 1961, **21,** 637–646.

Furst, E. J. Relationship between tests of intelligence and tests of critical thinking and knowledge. *Journal of Educational Research*, 1950, **43**, 614–624.

Glaser, E. M. *An experiment in the development of critical thinking.* New York: Teachers College, Columbia University, 1941.

Glaser, R., D. E. Damrin, and F. M. Gardner. The tab item: A technique for the measurement of proficiency in diagnostic problem-solving tasks. In A. A. Lumsdaine and R. Glaser (eds.), *Teaching machines and programmed learning: A source book.* Washington: National Education Association, 1960. Pp. 275–285.

Heath, R. W. Curriculum, cognition, and educational measurement. *Educational and Psychological Measurement*, 1964, **24**, 239–253.

Henry, N. B. (ed.) *The measurement of understanding.* Forty-Fifth Yearbook of the National Society for the Study of Education, Part I. Chicago: University of Chicago Press, 1946.

Kalish, R. A. An experimental evaluation of the open book examination. *Journal of Educational Psychology*, 1958, **49**, 200–204.

McGuire, C. H., and D. Babbott. Simulation techniques in the measurement of problem-solving skills. *Journal of Educational Measurement*, 1967, **4**, 1–10.

Rimoldi, H. J. A. A technique for the study of problem solving. *Educational and Psychological Measurement*, 1955, **15**, 450–461.

Rimoldi, H. J. A. Rationale and application of the test of diagnostic skills. *Journal of Medical Education*, 1963, **38**, 364–373.

Smith, R. B. A discussion of an attempt at constructing reproducible item sets. *Journal of Educational Measurement*, 1968, **5**, 55–60.

Solomon, R. J. New directions in assessing achievement. *Proceedings of the 1965 Western Regional Conference on Testing Problems.* Princeton, N.J.: Educational Testing Service, 1965. Pp. 45–51.

Stoker, H. W., and R. P. Kropp. Measurement of cognitive processes. *Journal of Educational Measurement*, 1964, **1**, 39–42.

Tyler, R. W. The relation between recall and higher mental processes. In C. H. Judd and others, *Education as cultivation of the higher mental processes.* London: Macmillan, 1936. Pp. 6–17.

Tyler, R. W. Some findings from studies in the field of college biology. *Science Education*, 1934, **18**, 133–142.

Weitman, M. Item characteristics and long-term retention. *Journal of Educational Measurement*, 1965, **2**, 37–47.

Wert, J. E. Twin examination assumptions. *Journal of Higher Education*, 1937, **8**, 136–140.

CHAPTER 5

Preparing Essay Achievement Tests

A skilled trial lawyer in action is a pleasure to watch. With great precision and organization, he carefully extracts information from witnesses—information that, of course, he hopes will be beneficial to his client. He may do this in such a way as to capitalize on any dramatic effects that are present, and he may later summarize the testimony presented to accentuate whatever casts a favorable light on his case and to deemphasize whatever does not. In drawing a parallel between the foregoing and teaching, we are most interested in the lawyer's preparation of questions to ask the witnesses.

It is difficult to imagine the amount of preliminary preparation that a lawyer must make before he ever appears in court. Even the framing of the questions to be presented to the witnesses must be carefully planned. The questions need not reveal all the information the witness can recall. Most of this information is irrelevant; some of it may even be damaging to his case. Framing and presenting helpful questions without resorting to leading questions, which the judge might disallow, is a genuine art.

The classroom teacher trying to measure academic achievement with essay tests might tear a page from the lawyer's book. The teacher is also asking questions of reasonably cooperative subjects; he, too, is interested in soliciting certain kinds of information and no other. Therefore, it seems reasonable to expect that the task faced by the teacher as he frames questions for his pupils is essentially the same as that faced by the lawyer as he prepares to cross-examine a witness. Each has in mind distinct purposes that his questions are to serve. If the questions are to serve the respective purposes, they must be prepared deliberately.

Unfortunately, the teacher's questions designed to reveal pupil achievements are usually only partly successful. Consider for a moment oral questioning. Notice how frequently the pupil attempting to answer a question must ask his own questions to clarify his task. He may want to know the definition of some of the terms, or whether a certain basic assumption should be made when answering, or how much detail is desired. Only after this confusion has been dispelled can the original question be answered. The cost in time and frustration is sometimes considerable.

The essay test items included in a paper-and-pencil achievement test are generally a distinct improvement in this respect. Their preparation is much more systematic. Yet there is still unnecessary pupil confusion. In spite of the fact that few questions about the test or none are asked when it is administered, a review of the pupils' responses customarily reveals considerable uncertainty about one or more questions. Sometimes this review may even lead one to believe that the pupil would have written a correct answer if he had understood the question. In such cases, the questions are clearly not serving the purpose for which they were intended.

It has been said that to construct a good essay achievement test one need only be able to compose clear questions. This sounds simple. In reality, when compared with the procedures for constructing objective items, those for constructing essay items do seem simple. Nevertheless, as the skilled trial lawyer learns at an early stage, you cannot question anyone with consistent success unless the questions are planned. The fact that essay test items are deceptively simple in appearance and hence in construction is the reason why many of their potential values have not been entirely realized.

CHARACTERISTICS OF ESSAY TEST ITEMS

An essay test item is one for which the pupil supplies, rather than selects, the correct answer. More specifically, an essay item demands a response composed by the pupil, usually in one or more sentences, of a nature that no single response or pattern of responses can be listed as correct, and the accuracy and quality of which can be judged subjectively only by a person skilled and informed in the subject, customarily the classroom teacher (Stalnaker, 1951, p. 495). The important features of this description are the freedom of response allowed the pupil, and the difficulty of scoring the responses. The first is used as a basis for classifying essay items; the second indicates the most perplexing problem associated with essay items, a problem treated in detail later in this chapter.

Freedom of Response

The freedom of response allowed the pupil may vary appreciably from one essay test item to another. Consider the following items, both of which are designed for use in a secondary school, the first in an American history achievement test, and the second in an English and world literature achievement test.

> In your opinion is the federal government of the United States more or less democratic today than it was at the end of the eighteenth century? Give reasons for your answer.

> Explain how the study of English and world literature can help a person to understand better the political, economic, social, and religious aspects of past ages, and how it can influence his present understanding of and attitudes toward modern ways of life.

Both of these test items demand extended responses from the pupils. In fact the typical pupil reaction to each would be ". . . but I could write a book about it." This is justified in both instances. Both items are tapping a higher order of learning than some objective test items; only those pupils who can recall what they have learned, evaluate it in terms of the question, and then organize it into a suitable answer will succeed.

In contrast, examine the following items, one of which is taken from an elementary school test dealing with a health unit, the second from a junior high school general science test.

> Bill and Tom are pupils in the sixth grade. They try to take good care of their teeth. Both brush them immediately after their morning and evening meals, but do not brush them after their noon meal or after eating between meals. Both have the dentist inspect their teeth every six months. However, Bill's teeth decay more easily than Tom's. Give possible reasons why this is true.

> An athlete wishes to know the amount of time he needs to run 100 yards. He stations one man at the starting line with a revolver and a second at the finish line with a stop watch. In order to time the athlete accurately, should the man at the finish line start the watch at the moment he sees the flash of the revolver or the moment he hears the sound of the shot? Why?

In terms of freedom of response, these two essay items represent the opposite extreme. The correct responses are now quite specific; notice also that, if the two situations described are novel, more than recall of information is required of the pupil.

The variations in freedom of response allowed the pupil offer a crude but useful means of classifying essay test items into types. At least two principal types can be established: the *extended response* type, as illustrated by the first pair of test items, and the *restricted response* type, as illustrated by the second pair.

Extended Response. The extended response has much to be said in its favor. It can be extremely challenging to pupils. To respond correctly, pupils must display such traits as their ability to organize, evaluate, write clearly, and be creative. Thus, the responses to these test items show how well the pupils have achieved important educational goals.

There is some evidence that this type of essay item can serve as a projective technique (Sims, 1948), that is, as a relatively free expression by the pupil that can be analyzed to gain information about his motives, values, interests, modes of adjustment, and the like. For instance, suppose that a general science teacher presented the following test item to his pupils:

Write a short composition on the topic "What Conservation Means to Me."

The pupil responses to such a test item are more complex and varied than those to essay test items of the restricted response type. Presumably they contain helpful information about the pupil's difficulties and patterns of thought that can be used as a partial basis for remedial instruction. The latent content of the response can be separated from the manifest content and interpreted; even the style of presentation and any omissions detected have possible significance.

The value of the extended response essay test item as a projective technique is not clearly established. Whether or not this type of item is considered a projective technique, the scoring of pupil responses is difficult and the reliability low. This reason more than any other has restricted the use of extended response items. Although ample justification for the use of these test items can be found, especially in terms of the important educational objectives they reflect, their practical value is limited by the teacher's inability to score them reliably. This in no way detracts from their use as a teaching device.

Restricted Response.   The restricted response essay item is of greater concern to us in the measurement of pupil achievement except as a measure of his writing ability. This type of essay item differs from the first in that the perimeter of pupil response is better defined. A specific problem is presented. It requires the pupil to recall the proper information, organize it in a suitable manner, arrive at a defensible conclusion, and express it in his own words. In several important respects, it requires the pupil to reveal abilities much like those required by a satisfactory answer to an extended response essay test item; however, this display must occur within well-defined restrictions. These restrictions simplify the scoring problem, thereby greatly improving the reliability of the scoring.

Observe that the restricted response essay item is far removed from the supply type of test item described in Chapter 3. In the first place, it differs in the amount of freedom of response allowed the pupil. Although the restricted response essay sets limits in this respect, it does not confine the response to a word or two; on the contrary, a paragraph or more is usually needed if the question is to be answered properly. Secondly, it differs in terms of the behavioral changes reflected. The short-answer test is almost invariably used as a means of measuring pupil knowledge; the restricted response essay item can be used for this purpose or designed to measure more complex pupil achievement. The latter is a very important function of the essay item.

Problems

1.   Construct a supply item for an objective test and a restricted response item for an essay test. Design the latter so that it overlaps the scope of the objective test item. Compare the two in terms of the cognitive levels of the pupil behavioral patterns required to respond correctly.

2.   Differentiate between essay items designed to measure a pupil's achievement in a subject matter area and those designed to measure his ability to write (Coffman, 1970). Construct a test item of each type.

CONSTRUCTING ESSAY TEST ITEMS

Essay test items are quite popular in the classroom as a method of measuring educational achievement. Objective items are heavily used in standardized achievement tests, but not to the point of excluding the essay type. Essay questions in various subject matter areas dominate the *Advanced Placement Program* of the College Entrance Examination Board (CEEB), and are an important component of the National Assessment of Educational Progress. Essay items measuring pupil writing ability have been used as a part of the *Sequential Tests of Educational Progress (STEP)* and the achievement test series for college admission administered by CEEB.

Preparing and scoring writing ability tests have received considerable attention from teachers and testing specialists (French, 1962; Diederich, 1965, 1967). To measure writing ability, objective and semi-objective items are being used alone and in conjunction with essay items that often require between 20 to 40 minutes of testing time. Combinations of these testing methods seem to be satisfactory means of measuring writing ability (Godshalk and others, 1966). Methods of evaluating essays are described in Chapter 7.

With the possible exception of those cases in which evidence of writing ability is desired, the extended-response essay item has limited value as a measuring tool. Therefore, the remainder of this chapter is devoted to the restricted-response type.

Teachers usually consider essay items relatively easy to construct since they require less time and technical skill than objective items. The task, however, is not a simple one. Five important considerations confront the teacher as he constructs essay items:

1.   Relating the essay item to one or more cells of the table of specifications.
2.   Sampling the pertinent subject matter adequately.

3. Adapting the essay item to fit the academic background of the pupils to whom it is to be administered.
4. Determining the amount of freedom of response to be allowed the pupil.
5. Establishing a suitable time allotment for the pupil's response.

The five categories overlap each other to some degree and are not of equal importance. However, each is sufficiently important that it cannot be ignored in the process of constructing essay items and arranging them as parts of a test. Failure to comply with the suggestions stemming from any one of the categories will cause otherwise well-designed essay items to fail.

Relating Essay Items to the Table of Specifications

As in the case of the objective test item, the essay test item is a direct outgrowth of one or more cells of the table of specifications. In other words, the fundamental relationship between the table and the test item is the same in both cases. Yet the objective and the essay test items do not merely duplicate each other. Like a station wagon and a sports car, they both perform all the functions demanded, but not with equal ease and efficiency.

As you know, objective test items can be used to measure pupil knowledge with considerable success. Using them, the teacher can sample broadly with a minimum expenditure of time. Measuring complex cognitive achievement with objective test items is an effective approach but not to the same degree as measuring knowledge. The difficulties of item construction and the length of response time pose problems. The essay item, on the other hand, presents a different picture. It is not as efficient a means of measuring pupil knowledge as an objective test, one reason being that the scoring of the answers is a demanding task. As a means of measuring complex pupil achievement, however, it offers many encouraging possibilities. Such test items can be developed without spending the inordinate amounts of time often required when objective items are built for this purpose.

For these reasons, objective test items are often developed primarily in terms of the cells of the table involving knowledge, and the essay test items in terms of cells involving other levels of the cognitive taxonomy. This means that the achievement test frequently will be composed of both types of items. Such tests offer the pupil some variety. They also distribute the teacher's work load. The construction of the objective item requires more of his time before the test, and the scoring of the essay item requires more of his time after the test.

In addition to differing in the kind of cells of the table of specifications with which they are associated, the objective and essay items commonly differ in the number with which they are associated. Most often, the objective item is primarily related to one cell and perhaps secondarily to another. The essay item quite frequently is related to several in both cases. It deals with a larger whole than the objective item. The correct response to it has several subparts. These may easily involve one group of cells in the table of specifications in a primary manner and another in a secondary manner.

Care must be exercised if we are to maintain a high degree of content validity in an achievement test containing essay items. For instance, suppose that a teacher using an essay item for measuring complex pupil achievement finds that it is primarily related to several cells pertaining to the upper levels of the cognitive taxonomy as well as cells pertaining to knowledge. In addition, it may be secondarily related to still other cells. If this is true, any objective test items included in the same test for measuring pupil knowledge must be readjusted accordingly. Only when the various subparts of the correct response to an essay test item are identified and analyzed can the relationship between that item and the table of specifications be determined. The contribution of the item to the content validity of the test obtaining it can then be established.

The true function of the essay item in achievement measurement is to reveal the pupil's progress toward the more complex educational goals. Pertinent pupil behavioral changes are the abilities to apply principles, form generalizations, make inferences, interpret data, evaluate evidence critically, and recognize and use cause-and-effect relationships. Involvement of these mental processes in essay items will favorably influence study habits and teaching procedures. Both pupil and teacher will find themselves concentrating on the basic aspects of a field of study, the relationship between these and other fields, and their applications in everyday living. Thus, the proper use of essay items can have a profound effect on the teaching-learning procedure.

In summary, the teacher follows these steps as he builds essay test items according to the table of specifications. First, he must select the cell or group of cells dealing with complex cognitive achievement (and some dealing with knowledge) to which the item is to be related. With these in mind, he starts his search for suitable item content, most likely a novel situation. When the situation is identified, he frames one or more questions on its basis. Finally, he composes the correct response, separates it into its subparts, and cross-refers them with the cells in the table of specifications. He may discover that the cells he originally had in mind are not involved in the test item in exactly the manner initially intended. Therefore, he may alter the item to support his first plan, or he may expand or contract in an appropriate manner other essay and objective items to be included.

Sampling Subject Matter Adequately

The problems of sampling subject matter for an achievement test are essentially the same as those of a public opinion pollster or a reader selecting a novel in the library. A basic problem in all cases is the size of the sample. How large must it be to guarantee that generalizations based on it will truly represent the population from which it came? All three situations have practical restrictions on the size of the sample. The test cannot have more than a certain number of test items because of limited time. The pollster does not have the financial resources to draw huge samples. The reader thumbing pages at random will not scan endlessly because it requires too much time and may spoil the novel when he reads it in entirety.

The variety of the population sampled also affects the size of sample needed. For example, sampling a homogeneous mixture, such as a bottle of milk or a bag of well-mixed inorganic fertilizer, is comparatively simple; a relatively small sample will no doubt be sufficiently representative. On the other hand, sampling a heterogeneous mixture such as subject matter and complex mental processes is difficult. Inevitably, large samples are needed if one is to have confidence in the breadth of the sample.

In the light of this discussion, the inadequate subject matter sampling of the essay test comes into focus. The typical essay achievement test contains only a handful of test items; therefore, despite the fact that each item may have a number of subparts, the test is a distressingly small sample when the variety of most subject matter is considered. The possibility that the sample is unrepresentative is increased. Otherwise stated, its content validity is quite possibly less than satisfactory. There is greater likelihood that a well-prepared pupil might have the misfortune to find that one or more test items touch on his weak areas; hence he responds poorly, and the total test results underestimate his true achievement.

Restrictions on testing time may cause a classroom achievement test dominated by essay items to seem very narrow in scope when judged in light of the table of specifications used. Under such restrictions, it is advisable to replace each essay item requiring a long response with several requiring shorter responses. A careful adjustment will cause the degree of content validity and reliability of the test to rise appreciably.

Use of Optional Test Items. Some teachers try to reduce the sampling limitation of the essay item with optional items. For instance, twelve test items might be listed, and the pupil allowed to answer any eight of them. Rather than improve the sampling, this procedure weakens it. Since many pupils will make partially different selections, they are, in effect, confronted with partially different samples. The content validity depends on the particular combination the pupil chooses, since test content and the meaning of the score varies from pupil to pupil. A direct comparison of the various test scores cannot be defended.

A different use of optional test items is that in which a series to be answered by all pupils is first presented, and a series of paired items follows. The pupil is to choose one of each pair. The members of each pair are considered to be equivalent test items; they are of the same level of difficulty, require approximately the same response time, are based on the same combination of cells in the table of specifications, and so forth. Thus, ideally, the content validity would be the same for all practical purposes no matter what choices the pupil made; yet the test is somewhat more flexible.

The last-mentioned use of optional test items is much more defensible than the first described. Nevertheless, it cannot be recommended. It doesn't relieve the basic difficulty, which is that certain cells of the table of specifications are not represented in the test. The pairs are merely independent test items representing the same combinations of cells. Building equivalent test items is, of course, no simple task. Moreover, they increase the scoring labor because the scorer has a greater variety of items to score.

Adapting Essay Items to the Pupils' Backgrounds

"How much detail should I give?" is a common question asked by a pupil confronted with an essay test item. The answer is particularly important to him if he is well aware of the fact that his response will be scored in terms of exactly what he writes; that is, no credit is allowed for what he seems to have written or for statements that are essentially correct but not pertinent. He recognizes that he will waste valuable testing time by making a very detailed response if detail is not required or that he will lose significant amounts of credit for his response if he erroneously assumes that the teacher allows no credit for minor but important detail.

The teacher also is penalized by any pupil uncertainty as to the amount of detailed information that the correct response should contain. If he expects a great deal but does not make this fact explicitly known, the pupils who did not include the details, but could have, will complain when penalized. If the teacher expects only the major elements but does not make this fact explicitly known, some pupils will include unnecessary information, thus lengthening their responses greatly, and complicating the scoring task.

The problem is illustrated by the following essay test item constructed by a physics teacher for use in a unit examination concerning electricity:

> A customer telephones your electrical shop concerning his doorbell, which will not ring when the door button is depressed. He wants to know what the trouble might be. Assuming that the electric current has not failed, describe to him two possible causes of this difficulty and how they could be corrected.

To answer this question the pupils will undoubtedly use such terms as *contact points, armature, magnetic field, hammer, gong,* and so forth. Should they define these terms, or merely use them with the assumption that the teacher will consider proper use of the expressions to signify that the definitions are also known? With the test item stated in its original form the pupils will vary in their answers.

Suppose that the teacher wants somewhat limited detail; he is willing to assume that proper use of the expressions means comprehension of their meaning. In this event, he could improve the item by adding the following statement:

> Assume that the customer is familiar with the basic principles of electricity and magnetism as well as the names and functions of all parts of the common doorbell.

If he did not wish to make this assumption, he could add a statement such as the following:

> Assume that the customer has no knowledge either of the basic principles of electricity and magnetism or of the common doorbell. Be certain, therefore, that you define all technical expressions you use.

This illustration emphasizes a broad issue: adapting the essay test item to the academic background of the pupils. Pupils often have a large body of general knowledge. Asking them to reveal this knowledge in a response to an essay test item does nothing but demonstrate that they have it. No differentiation among the pupils has been accomplished. The teacher must decide on how much of this common knowledge is important in the correct response.

If the purpose of a test item is to serve as a means of differentiating among pupils, it is difficult to defend any test item that requires the pupil to repeat great quantities of this so-called common knowledge. Instead, the test item should be built so that the pupils devote most of their response time to, and hence acquire most of their credit from, those aspects that will differentiate among them. This procedure shortens the response time needed and should result in a more efficient use of the testing time.

All these points have a direct bearing on the level of difficulty of the essay item's various parts and, therefore, of the item as a whole. Objective test items are quickly recognized as inadequate if their level of difficulty is very low or very high, a condition not so easily recognized in the case of essay test items. One or more subparts of the essay item may have suitable levels of difficulty but the remainder may not. Adapting the essay item to the academic background of the pupil is equivalent to minimizing those parts of the essay test item that are so easy or so difficult that they do not provide a basis for differentiating among the pupils responding.

Determining the Amount of Freedom of Response

How "restricted" is the response to a restricted response essay item? No definite answer can be given. The illustrations given earlier suggest that the responses are fairly brief. However, they can exceed these limits and still be perfectly acceptable.

The suggestions for the adaptation of the essay item to the background of the pupils indicate some ways in which the freedom of response is restricted. These suggestions help the pupil sort the important elements in the response from the unimportant; nevertheless, the pupil is still confronted with the question of which important elements are wanted. Perhaps the essay test item can be answered from more than one point of view. Although all types of response based on each of several points of view may be correct in a sense, only one is intended.

The essay item must be so framed that each pupil will easily recognize exactly the task he is to perform. He should understand the question in the same way that all other pupils understand it. Any confusion or uncertainty that he may experience should be attributed to his inability to answer correctly rather than his failure to understand the purpose of the test item.

To achieve this clarity in an essay test item is often difficult. On the other hand, violations of this principle can be easily identified and corrected, at least partially. For instance, consider the following essay item, intended for use in a secondary school social studies test:

> Today both major political parties of the United States include members representing practically every shade of political conviction between arch conservatism and extreme liberalism. Suppose that a rearrangement of membership took place so that the Republican Party acquired a truly conservative philosophy, and the Democratic Party, a truly liberal philosophy. What would happen to the political situation in this country?

Imagine the great variety of responses that this test item would elicit. The impact of such a drastic rearrangement of the political parties could be discussed in terms of the changes in the sizes of the parties, their financial resources, leadership, appeal to the general public, platforms, and control of state legislatures, governorships, the presidency, and Congress. One pupil could have written successfully about several of these topics, another about several different topics, and yet both could have missed the point of the test item and consequently lost credit. In short, the task to be performed by the pupil is not clearly defined and, as a result, even the well-informed pupil will very likely be penalized.

Suppose the question at the end of the test item is replaced by the following:

> Compare the present platforms of the two parties with the platforms that you think the parties would adopt after the rearrangement of membership. Restrict your comparison to the areas of:
> 1. civil rights legislation
> 2. public works legislation
> 3. environmental improvement legislation

Now the task is better identified. It is only in terms of certain aspects of the platforms that comparisons are to be made between present and hypothetical party composition. A framework for the pupil's response is established. Incidentally, notice that the test item still requires the pupil to select information, organize it properly, and present it as an integrated whole. Although the framework restricts the pupil's freedom of response, it does not do so to the point where the test item elicits only an extremely specific response dealing with superficial knowledge.

Attempts to clearly define the pupil's task have contributed to the general decline in the use of expressions such as "discuss," "tell about," and "give your opinion of." In their place have come a series of different expressions that, when used individually or in combination, tend to clarify the intent of the test item. Typical of these expressions are the following (Stalnaker, 1951, p. 527): "explain," "relate," "interpret," "compare," "discriminate," "select significant ideas," "contrast," and "state the conclusion." The list is suggestive only.

Establishing Suitable Time Limits

Suitable time limits for essay tests are even more difficult to establish than those for objective tests. First, some teachers find it more difficult to estimate the level of difficulty of essay items and overestimate or underestimate the response time needed. Secondly, pupils vary in terms of the speed at which they can write and, as the test progresses, their susceptibility to fatigue. Third, a well-designed test item forces the pupil to marshall his facts and organize them in a suitable manner. To do so he may sketch out the preliminary notes or even a complete outline, then write his answer on the basis of such notes. The amount of time needed for this is another uncertain variable. Finally, if the pupil's response is to be scored partly in terms of organization, spelling, and grammatical accuracy, he will need more response time.

There is a tendency to allow too little response time for essay tests. The pupils must rush through at top speed if they hope to finish. The immediate results are, of course, a steady deterioration in the legibility of the handwriting and the organization of the answer, with consequent complication of the task of scoring.

Suitable time limits can be determined by pretesting the items on a similar group of pupils under normal conditions, and any needed adjustments made on the basis of this trial. Since this can rarely be done, the teacher must rely on his past experience with similar test items and pupils, or he might note the time he needs to write a complete model answer for each item. Estimating time allotments for each item and listing them on the test copy helps him pinpoint his judgments. When in doubt, the teacher should allow too much rather than too little time. It is better to have fewer or shorter responses and not have to worry about a speed factor.

Problems

3. Would the essay item concerning the two political parties (see page 168) be strengthened by stipulating what is meant by a *truly conservative philosophy* and a *truly liberal philosophy?* Why?

4. On the basis of a table of specifications in a subject matter area of interest to you, build an essay item which will measure complex pupil achievement. Identify the cells in the table to which it is primarily and secondarily related.

5. Criticize and strengthen as you see fit the following essay items which were included in a ninth grade social studies test administered at the completion of a unit devoted to government organization, functions, and services.

    a. An amendment was proposed in the Congress to have the electoral college vote proportionately, according to actual vote of the people.

       1. How would this change the present system?

       2. Would this proposal strengthen the democratic control of the people and would it lead to a probable increased vote? Give reasons for your answers.

    b. The Supreme Court has nine members. Do you feel this number is too large, too small, or just right to carry the responsibilities of the court? Give reasons.

    c. In recent years the Federal government has given aid to the farmer. Therefore we are faced with the parity problem.

       1. What is parity?

       2. What is the soil bank program?

       3. Do you favor either or both, and why?

ADMINISTERING THE ESSAY TEST

The administration of the essay test involves many of the same principles and procedures described in the two preceding chapters in connection with objective tests. Hence, these need not be repeated here. Two features of test administration that deserve additional comment for essay tests are the directions to the pupils and the use of open-book testing.

Unlike the directions given in objective tests, those for essay tests are quite simple. Most often the test items are sufficiently self-contained so that few pupils need any additional information to formulate satisfactory responses. The directions are sometimes omitted, or, if given, are no more complicated than the following:

> DIRECTIONS: Answer the following questions in as brief a manner as possible. Only a few sentences will be necessary in order to cover the important points needed to answer each.

Special features of the test must be mentioned in the directions. For example, a brief description of the basis for scoring is sometimes included. The classroom teacher can point out if he plans to add or subtract credit for penmanship, style of writing, grammar, or spelling. He should also mention any restrictions on the time allowed or the type of paper to be used, the amount of space on the paper allowed for the response, or the use of pen or pencil.

Using the essay test item primarily as a means of measuring complex achievement suggests an open-book test. If this point of view is accepted, then the question is raised as to whether the pupils could write the answers at home rather than in the classroom. The open-book, take-home administration of essay tests is somewhat common. The task may now fall under the classification of "homework" rather than a test, but, with the proper design of the questions and the cooperation of the pupils, it still can serve as a test with generous time limits.

SCORING THE ESSAY TEST

The scoring of the pupils' responses to an essay test item is unquestionably the most disagreeable task related to the use of these items. In the first place, the teacher is understandably reluctant to allot the great quantities of time that are needed if the job is to be done properly. Also, he is concerned about his ability to recognize the variation of quality in the responses. He suspects that his judgments are highly subjective. Perhaps his state of mind or the name of the pupil at the top of the page are more powerful factors in his determination of the quality of the response than the response itself. These and other doubts cause the scoring problem to be an important one.

The problem is also complicated by the testwiseness of the pupil. This is the same element that reduces the effectiveness of objective achievement tests, but it manifests itself in a different manner here. An imaginative method of faking responses to the essay test item is to practice the art of "precise vagueness." The pupil takes great pains to write at length in a flowing, colorful style. He also takes great pains not to commit himself; he skirts the issue as closely as he can without actually facing it. In short, he wants to impress the scorer without revealing his ignorance. An illustration of this technique is the following response by a pupil to a test item requiring him to evaluate the causes of the fall from power of Napoleon Bonaparte.

There was a day when Napoleon Bonaparte was at the pinnacle of success. People admired him and respected him. He was the outstanding leader in Europe. But this could not last forever. Difficulties arose. These difficulties were political, economical, social, and, of course, military. Moreover, they were not always obvious. Indeed, some were so subtle that even Napoleon himself was not aware of them. Nevertheless, obvious or subtle, these difficulties were sufficiently powerful that, in combination, they toppled him from power.

The relative importance of these difficulties is hard to determine. It would seem that some were clearly more important than others. This is to say that some contributed more directly to Napoleon's fall than did others.

Paragraph after paragraph, perhaps page after page, the pupil continues to string one vague sentence to the end of another. Each rings of accuracy. Yet the true worth of such an answer is elusive; like a puff of smoke, it seems to disappear as you reach for it. The foregoing response is essentially empty. Yet, in the face of its impressive length and style, it would require a teacher well-schooled in the art of scoring responses to essay test items to recognize this and score accordingly.

Testing specialists have devoted considerable attention to simplifying the task of scoring responses to essay test items and to improving the reliability of the scoring process. Their efforts have been somewhat successful. Well-established general suggestions have been formulated and several methods of scoring have been devised and used.

Improving the Scoring of Essay Items

There are four general suggestions for improving the scoring of essay items.

Score the pupils' responses anonymously. It has been demonstrated that the "halo effect" can appreciably reduce objectivity of scoring. Because a certain pupil has written the response, the teacher expects a certain quality of response and has, in effect, prejudged it. The identical response written by a pupil with a decidedly different reputation will receive a different amount of credit.

The scoring of a response should be based exclusively on what is written and never should be influenced by knowledge of the identity of the pupil who wrote it. To conceal the identity of the examinee is not easy. If the teacher is familiar with the penmanship or style of writing of the pupils, it is virtually impossible. Should this not be the case, the use of numbers, rather than names, to identify the responses, or the practice of having the pupil's name written on the back of the paper, will provide a simple but effective means of maintaining anonymity.

Score all responses to each test item at one time. Only when this is done, and one item is completely finished, should the responses to any other item in the test be examined. This means that, instead of the responses to all test items by one pupil being scored at one time as is most often true of an objective test, the responses to one test item by all of the pupils are scored at one time.

Two advantages are thereby gained. First, it is easier to maintain a constant or near-constant set of standards on the basis of which each response is to be judged. All details of the completely correct responses can be remembered, and comparisons between and among various pupil responses can be made. Secondly, any "halo effect" that might modify the scoring of all responses by one pupil in a test tends to be minimized. In other words, the way in which a pupil answers one test item will not influence the judgment of the teacher when he scores the pupil's response to a second test item that is more or less independent of the first. There is an unjustified feeling that, because the response to one test item by a pupil is poor or good, the responses to all other test items in the same test by that pupil must necessarily be of similiar quality.

If the spelling, penmanship, grammar, and writing style of the responses are to be scored, it should be done independently of the subject matter content. In other words, how a pupil writes should be judged apart from what he writes. You can easily imagine instances in which one might be of a very different quality from the other, and instances in which the quality of one affects the teacher's judgment of the quality of the other. An all too common occurrence is the case in which accurate spelling, legible handwriting, and pleasant style upgrade the rating of the quality of the content of the response, whereas substandard spelling, handwriting, and style function in the opposite direction (Marshall and Powers, 1969).

The question is frequently asked whether the quality of grammar, spelling, handwriting, and style should be scored at all. The answer is simple. If any or all of these are a part of the educational objectives and hence the table of specifications on which the test is based, they should be scored. If they are not, any deficiencies in these respects can be noted and any superlative achievements can be acknowledged, but no loss or gain of credit can be given. In view of this it is easy to understand why in other tests than those of the language arts, such aspects as grammar, spelling, and writing style are seldom scored, or are scored on a restricted basis. An example of restricted scoring is the marking of spelling for technical words but not for nontechnical words.

If the results of the test are extremely important, have at least one other person score the responses independently. If this is not possible, score them a second time yourself, doing so without knowledge of your first judgments. The time-proven method of improving the scoring of responses to essay items is to average independent judgments made by competent scorers guided by the same set of standards. The feasibility of this practice is questionable. The next best substitute is the procedure in which two independent judgments are made by the same teacher.

Any radical discrepancies between the scores yielded by independent judgments should be immediately investigated and resolved. Perhaps the services of a third scorer are needed. If the differences cannot be resolved, then the opinion of the person who knows the teaching situation best, the classroom teacher, should be followed.

Methods of Scoring Essay Items

A number of different methods of scoring the responses to essay test items have been developed; only two are discussed here. The first is called the *analytical method;* the second is known as the *rating method.*

Analytical Method.   To use the analytical method of scoring, the teacher must first write out the perfect response to each test item, that is, the answer that would receive the highest possible score. Then it is analyzed and its component parts identified. The total number of raw-score points allowed for the correct response is distributed among the various subparts. The points may be distributed equally or unequally among the parts, depending on the teacher's feelings about the matter and the importance of the cells in the table of specifications on which the subpart is based. Finally, each pupil's response to the test item is read, the various subparts of the correct response that it contains are noted, and the raw score determined accordingly. As far as the scoring is concerned, any extraneous material in the pupil's response is ignored, whether it is accurately stated or not. Note that this procedure does not prevent the teacher from marking any inaccuracies in the statements containing unnecessary information. Indeed, he should mark them. The steps of the foregoing procedure are then repeated for each of the other essay items.

The division of the correct response of an essay test item into its component parts and the assignment of raw-score points to each subpart are two key steps in the analytical method of scoring. A simple illustration of these procedures is the test item concerning possible reasons for the differences in incidence of tooth decay of two sixth-grade boys (see page 160). The teacher may decide that the correct response should contain three elements thought to be of approximately equal importance. Therefore, each is allotted one raw-score point.

1. Recognition that the nature of the boys' diets influences incidence of tooth decay.
2. Recognition that heredity factors can partly account for incidence of tooth decay.
3. Recognition that all factors causing tooth decay are not known; hence differences between the two boys in terms of these unknown factors could account partly for variations in the incidence of tooth decay.

A more complex illustration of the analysis of the correct response is the following. It is based on an essay test item designed for an achievement test to be administered to agriculture pupils completing a unit concerning dairy cattle. The item is in three parts.

A farmer is undecided whether two of the dairy cows in his herd should be fed the same or different amounts of a concentrate mixture he is using. The following information is available concerning the two cows:

Cow	Breed	Weight	Age	Milk Production	Butter-fat Content	Months in Calf
A	Guernsey	1000 lb	4 yr	37 lb/day	5.1%	4
B	Holstein	1200 lb	5 yr	49 lb/day	3.5%	2

Both cows are fed adequate amounts of the same roughage.
1. Cite reasons why Cow A should be fed more concentrate mixture than Cow B.
2. Cite reasons why Cow B should be fed more concentrate mixture than Cow A.
3. Evaluate all the information and decide whether the farmer should feed more concentrate mixture to Cow A than to Cow B, or more to Cow B than to Cow A, or the same amount to both.

To answer the essay test item correctly, the pupil must recall that the amount of concentrate mixture fed a dairy cow is noticeably influenced by the cow's size, amount of butterfat produced per day, and stage of pregnancy, but is not appreciably influenced by differences in breed and age such as are shown in the chart. Then he must use this information accordingly.

If eight raw-score points were allowed for the correct response, one possible way of subdividing them among the subparts is as follows:

Subpart 1
    Total points: 3
      A. (2 pts.) Amount of butterfat production is greater for Cow A (1.9 lb/day) than for Cow B (1.7 lb/day).
      B. (1 pt.) Cow A is in a more advanced stage of pregnancy than Cow B.
Subpart 2
    Total points: 1
      A. (1 pt.) Cow B weighs more than Cow A.
Subpart 3
    Total points: 4
      A. (1 pt.) If only the differences in breed and age are considered, both cows should be fed the same amount of concentrate mixture.
      B. (3 pts.) The two reasons for feeding more concentrate mixture to Cow A than Cow B overbalance the reason for feeding more to Cow B than Cow A.

With this analysis of the correct response firmly in mind, the teacher should be able to score pupil responses more quickly and consistently. Moreover, later discussion of the test item, which would include a review of the pupils' responses and the scoring of items, is greatly facilitated when based on such an analysis as the foregoing. Both teacher and pupil are much more certain that the scoring is fair, and, in addition, they have isolated any gaps in each pupil's achievement revealed by the test item.

The analytical method offers several excellent advantages. In the first place, the analysis of the so-called perfect response will quite frequently cause the teacher to redesign the statement of the test item. He may realize that the item as originally stated will not necessarily elicit the response he desires, even when the pupil is very well informed. Any reframing of the test item and re-adjustment of the time limits that result from analyzing the correct response are generally distinct improvements. Secondly, the analytical method used by a conscientious grader can yield very reliable scores. This is true when the essay test item is of the restricted rather than extended response type.

Attempts have been made to train pupils to score essay items using the analytical method. The results are encouraging. In one attempt (Nealey, 1969), the responses for each essay item were separated from the others and those for a specific item were given to several examinees along with criteria for judging the correctness of the responses. Thus, small groups of pupils scored all responses to a given item. Since their pooled evaluations corresponded closely to those of the instructor, it seems reasonable to explore further the possibility of teaching this scoring technique to secondary school pupils, thereby realizing pedagogical gains as well as conserving the teacher's time.

Rating Method.   The rating method (sometimes called the global method) also requires that a so-called perfect response be written for each test item; however, this is not subdivided as such. The wholeness of the response is emphasized; the scorer attempts to grasp its complete scope. With this in mind, he reads the pupil's responses. On the basis of the wholeness of each response, he classifies it in one of three or one of five categories. The categories represent levels of quality such as, in the first case, good, average, or poor, and in the second case, very good, good, average, poor, or very poor. Although the use of five categories is common in classroom testing, as many as nine can be used with good success (Coffman, 1970).

Once the scorer has read and classified all responses, he reads them a second time, possibly even a third. The answers in each category are compared with each other. Those that don't fit are shifted to a more suitable category. Homogeneity in each category is desirable, even though the scorer realizes that it depends on the number of categories used. The fewer categories used, the more variability exists within each.

When the scorer is completely satisfied that each response is in its proper category, it is marked accordingly. Total, partial, or no credit is allowed, depending on the category checked. The entire process is then repeated for all other essay items in the test.

The rating method of scoring essay items is a distinct improvement over the single hasty reading in the absence of a clearly understood correct answer that some teachers use as a means of scoring pupil responses. On the other hand, it has not yielded the high scorer reliabilities of the analytical method. A scorer often has difficulty differentiating between the various categories and may even find that his basis for differentiating is changing at times.

Computer Scoring.   Incredible as it sounds, efforts to use a computer to score essay items measuring writing ability have been rather successful (Page, 1966, 1967). As a point of departure, a differentiation was made between intrinsic and proximate variables in an essay. The former are characteristics recognized by the teacher and presumably used in his evaluation. Examples are word usage, spelling, and complexity of sentences. Proximate variables are any which, for whatever reason, happen to correlate with expert judgments of writing quality. These vary widely and include such aspects as the number of commas, apostrophes, dashes, relative pronouns, and prepositions present. As many as thirty of these have been used by a computer as it scans essays and assigns scores to each statistically. Believe it or not, these scores based on proximate variables corresponded closely to those for overall quality based on intrinsic variables used by judges.

Furthermore, evidence exists that a computer can detect the presence or absence of a high degree of opinionation, vagueness, or specificity in an essay (Hiller and others, 1969). For instance in the case of vagueness, it counted the number of times the examinee used any of sixty key words such as *probably, sometimes, usually,* etc. Computer-derived scores on vagueness correlated negatively with essay scores on characteristics such as content, organization, and style as determined by judges. This is the kind of correlation one would expect.

Can computers be used to score restricted response essay items in a subject matter area? Undoubtedly. While awaiting better research data on which to base their techniques, a few teachers are moving ahead on a tentative basis. Typically they administer essay items requiring only a three- or four-sentence answer. The pupil prints his answer on a special answer sheet that is converted into a punch card and fed into a computer. Key phrases for each question are specified and assigned various scores so that the computer can compute a total score as it scans each pupil's response. As a check the teacher selects a small random sample of the responses and gives these intensive personal study. Usually, these checks verify the scores assigned by the computer.

Unreliability of Scoring

Research shows that seemingly competent scorers frequently cannot agree with themselves, much less with each other, concerning the amount of credit to be allowed a pupil's response to an essay item. The subjectivity in the scoring process varies according to the nature of the item but is typically large. When the test item approaches the extended response type, subjectivity increases and reliable scoring becomes an extremely difficult problem. Unfortunately, the pupil does not always graciously accept any inconsistencies in the teacher's scoring efforts.

The general suggestions for improving scoring that are given in the preceding sections can increase scorer reliability. For this to occur, three conditions must be met. First, the responses must have been elicited by carefully framed test items, which present the pupil with a well-defined task. The problem here resembles that encountered when designing supply items. For instance, consider the plight of the teacher who posed the question: "What is the difference between a king and a president?" One young pupil responded: "The king has to be the son of his father. The president doesn't."

Secondly, the teacher using the analytical or rating method should master and apply it carefully. Among other things, this may mean practicing the method by scoring pupil responses several times independently, then analyzing whatever differences have occurred. He may also wish to tackle his scoring problems in cooperation with his fellow teachers. Such ventures can be profitable (Diederich, 1967). Thirdly, ample time must be allowed. The teacher must be an alert, discerning judge at all times, which is a role he cannot play properly if pressed for time.

Problems

6.   Even though a teacher decides to score responses to essay items on the basis of content without consideration of writing style, he may be influenced, consciously or subconsciously, by the quality of writing (Marshall and Powers, 1969). To what degree do you think this is true? Does the intensity of this problem depend in part on the subject matter used in the item?

7.   After an essay test, some teachers ask their pupils to record the reasons for their answers on a 3 × 5-inch card. This information is then used for diagnosing pupil difficulties and strengthening similar future test items. Identify the advantages and limitations of this procedure.

COMPARISON OF ESSAY AND OBJECTIVE TESTS

At this point, we can identify a number of sizable differences between the essay and objective test as a means of gathering information on which pupil achievement can be evaluated. Seven general characteristics used as a basis for differentiating between the two types of items are as follows:

Difficulty of preparing the test item
Adequacy of the sampling of the subject matter
Relative ease with which knowledge and complex achievement are measured
Study procedures followed by the pupil as he prepares for the test
Originality of the response the pupil must make to the test item
Relative success of guessing correct responses
Difficulty of scoring the pupil responses

The differences between essay and objective tests in terms of these seven characteristics are summarized in Table 2. This table reveals the fallacy of the argument that one type of test item is unquestionably superior or inferior to the other. Each has peculiar advantages and limitations. There are testing needs for which each is particularly well suited.

TABLE 2.   Comparison of Essay and Objective Tests.

Characteristic	Essay test	Objective test
Preparation of the test item.	Items are relatively easy to construct.	Items are relatively difficult to construct.
Sampling of the subject matter.	Sampling is often limited.	Sampling is usually extensive.
Measurement of knowledge and complex achievement.	Items can measure both; measurement of complex achievement is recommended.	Items can measure both; measurement of knowledge is more common.
Preparation by pupil.	Emphasis is primarily on larger units of material.	Emphasis is often on factual details.
Nature of response by pupil.	Pupil organizes original response.	Except for supply test items, pupil selects response.
Guessing of correct response by pupil.	Pupil is less prone to guess.	Pupil is more prone to guess.
Scoring of pupil responses.	Scoring is difficult, time-consuming, and somewhat unreliable.	Scoring is simple, rapid, and highly reliable.

No one should needlessly restrict his measurement program by adhering to one type or the other. Recognizing this situation, many classroom teachers build and administer achievement tests containing both types of items. In these cases, pupils generally prefer to answer the objective items first and the essay items later, thereby making better use of their testing time. This is the order followed in the National Assessment of Educational Progress and the CEEB *Advanced Placement Program*.

The choice of whether to build an objective or essay test is usually influenced by one additional consideration, namely, the number of pupils to be tested. If the group is small, less effort may be needed to construct, administer and score an essay test than an objective one. Sometimes the labor needed to build high-quality objective items can only be justified if they are incorporated in a test file and used several times (see page 203).

Problems

8. On the basis of your experience, compare the additional time required to build an objective test rather than an essay test with that required to score the essay rather than the objective test.

9. Stodola (1961, p. 17) says that essay tests encourage the pupil to learn how to organize his own ideas and express them effectively, whereas objective tests encourage him to build a broad background of knowledges and abilities. Evaluate this comparison.

SUMMARY

An essay test item demands a response composed by the pupil, usually in the form of one or more sentences. The quality of the pupil's response can be judged subjectively by an informed scorer. This person is customarily one who instructed the pupil and built the test item, that is, the classroom teacher.

The freedom of response allowed on an essay item can vary appreciably. In one case, few restrictions are placed on the nature of the pupil's response; such a test item is an extended response essay test item. Other test items define quite specifically the task to be performed by the pupil; these are restricted response essay test items. Because of the extremely difficult task of scoring answers to extended response essay test items, their value as a method of measuring subject matter achievement is curtailed. On the other hand, the restricted response type plays an important role in achievement testing, since its answers can be scored reliably.

Five important considerations face the teacher when he builds essay test items. First, he must relate the item to one or more cells in the table of specifications; those to be emphasized involve complex cognitive achievement. Second, he must sample the subject matter broadly, favoring those essay items that require comparatively short answers and thereby using more items for a given testing period. Third, he must adapt the item to the academic background of the pupils. Fourth, he must determine the freedom of response to be allowed the pupil. Finally, he must establish suitable time limits.

Scoring responses to an essay item is usually difficult. To help simplify this task and, at the same time, improve the reliability of the scoring process, four general rules should be followed. First, score the pupils' responses anonymously. Second, score all responses to each test item at one time. Third, if spelling, penmanship, grammar, and so forth are to be graded, score them independently of the subject matter content. Last, if possible, have another person go over them; if this is not possible, score them a second time yourself.

Two prominent methods of scoring essay test items are the analytical method and the rating method. In the analytical method, the teacher breaks the correct response into subparts, assigns raw-score points to each, and awards points for a pupil's answer insofar as each subpart of the correct response is or is not included. In the rating method, the teacher tries to grasp the complete scope of the right answer, and then, on the basis of the wholeness of a pupil's response, to classify it into one of three or five categories representing various levels of quality.

It is highly appropriate to use both objective and essay items in the same achievement test. If this is done, the objective items should be administered first, followed by the essay items.

Suggested Readings

Coffman, W. E. Essay examinations. In R. L. Thorndike (ed.), *Educational measurement.* (2nd ed.) Washington: American Council on Education, 1970. Chapter 10.
    This is a superior discussion of the value of essay test items as a means of measuring pupil achievement. In it are described the limitations of this type of test item, its potential value, suggestions for improving it, and reliable methods of scoring pupil responses.

Diederich, P. B. Cooperative preparation and rating of essay tests. *English Journal,* 1967, **56,** 573–584.
    It is the author's opinion that evaluation of pupil writing ability by individual teachers is a failure. A team approach is needed. Five possible objections to the idea are discussed, following which a plan for cooperative efforts by teachers is provided.

Ebel, R. L. *Measuring educational achievement.* Englewood Cliffs, N.J.: Prentice-Hall, 1965. Chapter 4.
    The differences and similarities between objective and essay items are recounted, and suggestions are given for the preparation, use, and scoring of essay tests.

LaFave, L. Essay vs. multiple-choice: Which test is preferable? *Psychology in the Schools,* 1966, **3,** 65–69.
    A forceful statement condemning the multiple-choice test as a measuring tool because it is "superficial." Essay tests are held as desirable replacements since they have the potential to be standardized and still measure more than trivial aspects of pupil achievement.

Page, E. B. Imminence of grading essays by computers. *Phi Delta Kappan,* 1966, **47,** 238–243.

Initial efforts show that a computer can grade pupil essays about as well as classroom English teachers. These promising results are leading to the study of the use of the computer to score limited response essay items dealing with subject matter. These and other considerations are reviewed in a nontechnical way.

Palmer, O. Seven classic ways of grading dishonestly. *English Journal*, 1962, **51**, 464–467.

Although these remarks are directed to English teachers, they are equally telling when considered by any teacher. With slight modification, the ways of grading dishonestly can be applied to the problem of improving the scoring of essay items.

References Cited

Coffman, W. E. Essay examinations. In R. L. Thorndike (ed.), *Educational measurement*. (2nd ed.) Washington: American Council on Education, 1970. Chapter 10.

Diederich, P. B. Reading and grading. In A. Jewett and C. E. Bish (eds.), *Improving English composition*. Washington: National Education Association, 1965. Chapter 11.

Diederich, P. B. Cooperative preparation and rating of essay tests. *English Journal*, 1967, **56**, 573–584.

French, J. W. School of thought in judging excellence of English themes. *Proceedings of the 1961 Invitational Conference on Testing Problems*. Princeton, N.J.: Educational Testing Service, 1962. Pp. 19–28.

Godshalk, F. I., and others. *The measurement of writing ability*. New York: College Entrance Examination Board, 1966.

Hiller, J. H., and others. Opinionation, vagueness, and specificity-distinctions: Essay traits measured by computer. *American Educational Research Journal*, 1969, 6, 271–286.

Marshall, J. C., and J. M. Powers. Writing neatness, composition errors, and essay grades. *Journal of Educational Measurement*, 1969, 6, 97–101.

Nealey, S. M. Student-instructor agreement in scoring an essay examination. *Journal of Educational Research*, 1969, 63, 111–115.

Page, E. B. Imminence of grading essays by computers. *Phi Delta Kappan*, 1966, 47, 238–243.

Page, E. B. Grading essays by computer: Progress report. *Proceedings of the 1966 Invitational Conference on Testing Problems*. Princeton, N.J.: Educational Testing Service, 1967. Pp. 87–100.

Sims, V. M. The essay examination is a projective technique. *Educational and Psychological Measurement*, 1948, 8, 15–31.

Stalnaker, J. M. The essay type of examination. In E. F. Lindquist (ed.), *Educational measurement*. Washington: American Council on Education, 1951. Pp. 495–530.

Stodola, Q. *Making the classroom test, a guide for teachers*. (2nd ed.) Educational Testing Service Evaluation and Advisory Service Series, No. 4. Princeton, N.J.: Educational Testing Service, 1961.

CHAPTER 6

Appraising Classroom Achievement Tests

The use of measuring instruments in our commercial, scientific, and even recreational pursuits is commonplace. This would be a strange world indeed if the desk rulers, bathroom scales, water meters, clocks, thermometers, speedometers, and electrical meters were suddenly removed. These and countless other measuring instruments are constantly feeding information to us that we use to make decisions. Without such information, a significant part of our modern civilization would cease to function.

An interesting result of the dominance of measuring instruments is the great confidence we have in their accuracy. True, we may doubt the readings of an ancient wristwatch or an inexpensive outdoor thermometer, but only infrequently do we entertain doubts as to whether the desk ruler is twelve inches long and divided into twelve equal parts, or whether the water and gas meters are measuring volume properly, or whether the speedometer in our automobile is registering as it should. We assume that, for our purposes, their accuracy is sufficient.

Fortunately our confidence in such instruments is well-founded. Extensive efforts are made by the federal government as well as by industrial and scientific organizations to maintain accurate measuring instruments. For example, the United States Bureau of Standards works actively in this field. Among other functions, it maintains fireproof vaults in which platinum-iridium meter bars and kilogram weights are carefully stored; they are the standards against which some of the instruments for measuring distance and weight can be checked. Governmental officials known as sealers conduct systematic checks of devices such as the scales used in food stores and the meters used in gasoline stations, thereby protecting the consumer. Also, scientists are constantly recalibrating the thermometers, burets, and weights used in their work to be certain that the accuracy of their measurements is maintained.

The perpetual vigilance in commercial, industrial, and scientific fields should be copied by the classroom teacher. He makes numerous measurements and, in so doing, uses instruments in which he has notably less confidence than in the scales and meters mentioned. This is particularly true when classroom achievement tests are used. Although the product of much time and effort, they no doubt contain numerous unsuspected flaws. After all, many tentative decisions are made as they are constructed. Decisions concerning item difficulty, the attractiveness of distracters, or the length of the test, to name just a few, are made on the basis of inadequate evidence and could be at least partially wrong. The teacher will not know the success or failure of these decisions unless the test is carefully reexamined after its administration. Then and only then will he know how worthwhile it was and how meaningful the scores.

In addition to determining the worth of a classroom achievement test after it has been given, reexamining test results has other values. For instance, any errors or inadequacies discovered can serve as warnings to the teacher when he constructs other achievement tests. Although the methods and material used in a class may change from year to year, the important educational objectives are generally stable. Therefore, the classroom achievement testing program changes from year to year but seldom drastically. In view of this, any past failures and successes can assist the teacher immeasurably in future achievement test construction. Furthermore, a careful inspection of pupil responses to individual test items or groups of items has diagnostic value. The areas of strength and weakness for each pupil—or the class as a whole—can be identified.

ITEM ANALYSIS METHODS

Reexamining each test item to discover its strengths and flaws is known as *item analysis*. Item analysis usually concentrates on two vital features: level of difficulty and discriminating power. The former means the percentage of pupils who answer correctly each test item; the latter the ability of the test item to differentiate between pupils who have done well and those who have done poorly.

Essay or objective items from open-book or closed-book tests can be subjected to item analysis. However, it is most useful to us when the items are a part of a power test, rather than of a mastery or criterion-referenced test. In other words, the purpose of the test is to measure the level of performance of each pupil; the scores are to be used as a basis for ranking pupil achievement. The purpose of a mastery test, on the other hand, is to separate the pupils into two groups, those who have achieved at least as high as a certain level and those who have not. Consequently, the level of difficulty and discriminating power of its items are much less important considerations. The remainder of this chapter is devoted to the analysis of power test items.

Methods of item analysis are essentially mathematical and can take many forms. Various statistical techniques are used, many of them requiring a considerable amount of computing. In addition, the relative merits of these methods are not clearly established. Testing specialists do not always agree as to which method should be used even though they produce results that seem to be more similar than dissimilar.

The methods described in the following sections are, in contrast to many, relatively simple. They are quite satisfactory for classroom teachers. Since teachers do not have the time, facilities, or number of cases often demanded by the more elaborate methods, such methods are of little practical value although widely used in the construction of standardized achievement tests.

Item Difficulty

It is easy to determine a test item's level of difficulty. First a tabulation is made of the number of pupils who successfully answer the item. This figure is then divided by the total number of pupils attempting the item, and the quotient is multiplied by 100. These steps are summarized in the following formula:

$$P = \frac{N_R}{N_T} (100),$$

where

P = percentage of pupils who answer the test item correctly;
N_R = number of pupils who answer the test item correctly;
N_T = total number of pupils who attempt to answer the test item.

Suppose that an item in a classroom achievement test is answered correctly by eighteen of the twenty-eight pupils who attempt to answer it. Then the level of difficulty of this test is found as follows:

$$P = \frac{18}{28} (100) = 64.$$

In other words, 64 percent of the pupils who attempted the test item answered it correctly.

The formula shown does not alert the teacher to two questions that are often raised about the determination of item difficulty. In the first place, is the number of pupils who attempt to answer the item the same as the total number who are administered the test? If the time limits are too restrictive, it is conceivable that some pupils did not have an opportunity to answer test items appearing near the end. Hence, the number of pupils who attempt to answer the test item is less than the number to whom the test was administered. Secondly, is the number of pupils who know the correct answer the same as the number who answer it correctly? In the case of objective test items, successful guessing may cause the two numbers to be different and thus, to some degree, destroy the value of the computation of item difficulty.

The first question is seldom a problem to the classroom teacher. Sufficient time is allowed for the administration of the test so that each pupil attempts each item. Therefore the denominator of the formula is the same for each test item. Of course it is sometimes difficult to determine whether a pupil has attempted to answer an item. Failure to record an answer does not necessarily mean that the pupil did not try to do so. The rule usually followed is that the pupil is considered to have attempted to answer a test item if he records an answer to either this or any subsequent item. As you can see, the assumption underlying this rule is that the pupil works systematically through the test, mentally trying to answer all items up to and including the last one for which an answer is recorded.

The second question is the source of widespread debate among measurement specialists. Simply stated, it is: Should a correction for guessing be made when the levels of difficulty of test items are being computed? Obviously the question concerns itself with objective test items of the selection type. Successful guessing of the answer to one of these test items will cause the number of pupils who answer it correctly to exceed the number who actually know the correct answer. Adjusting the former number with correction-for-guessing formulas appreciably improves the situation in the opinion of some measurement specialists. Others are disturbed by the fact that the conventional formulas may either overcorrect or undercorrect for successful guessing, and believe that such an adjustment creates about as many problems as it solves.

The arguments for and against correcting for guessing are concisely summarized elsewhere (Henrysson, 1970). For our purposes it is not necessary to use formulas for computing item difficulty that incorporate a correction for guessing. In the first place, the added computational burden, though not serious, can be troublesome. Also, the assumptions underlying the formula are not fully satisfied, and the pupils' reaction to the warning that a correction for guessing is to be made are so varied that extraneous personality factors influence the achievement test scores. Finally, the teacher ordinarily does not need a very accurate measure of item difficulty. Rough approximations are usually sufficient.

For these reasons, the formula for determining item difficulty contains no provision for correcting for successful guessing. To the degree that successful guessing has occurred, the value of P yielded by the formula will be too large.

Item Discriminating Power

The discriminating power of a test item is its ability to differentiate between pupils who have achieved well (the upper group) and those who have achieved poorly (the lower group). To determine the discriminating power of a test item we must first specify the characteristics of the upper and lower groups. Here we have considerable latitude. We may wish to use an independent criterion to classify the pupils. Such a criterion might be the score from a standardized test thought to measure the same aspects of achievement as the classroom test containing the item in question. Or we may wish to use final marks in the same or similar achievement areas, these having been determined without knowledge of the scores yielded by the classroom test. On the other hand, an internal criterion may be used, such as the total scores from the classroom achievement test, the items of which are being studied.

In most cases, the internal criterion is used. This is done not only because independent criteria are customarily unavailable, but also because they are not good measures of the aspects of achievement involved in the classroom test. Achievement tests are, in a sense, "self-defining," that is, the test itself defines what it is to measure. Therefore, the independent criteria such as those mentioned are automatically inappropriate to some degree, perhaps a large one. Incidentally, the use of the total test scores as the criterion for classifying pupils into upper and lower groups, followed by the use of these groups to determine an index reflecting the discriminating power of individual test items, is known as the *internal-consistency* method of computing indices of item-discriminating power.

When the total test scores are used in this manner, a decision must be made as to which part of the distribution of scores is the upper group and which part is the lower group. Some choose the upper and lower halves, others the upper and lower thirds with the middle third discarded, and still others the upper and lower 27 percent with the middle 46 percent discarded. The last has received a great deal of support by testing specialists, and a number of tables designed to assist item analysis are based on this division. However, for the classroom teacher analyzing his own test, use of the upper and lower thirds is probably a suitable compromise. Fewer cases are lost than when the upper-lower 27 percent method is used, and a more distinctive separation between the groups is provided than in the case of the upper-lower halves method.

The rationale behind the scheme for computing an index of item-discriminating power is quite simple. A test item with maximum discriminating power would be one which every pupil in the upper group would answer correctly and every pupil in the lower would answer incorrectly; in short, it can discriminate between every pupil in the upper group and every pupil in the lower group. Thus, this test item produces a maximum number of correct discriminations. Of course, we cannot expect items to discriminate perfectly. The typical test item will yield some correct discriminations—part of the upper group will respond correctly and part of the lower group incorrectly—and will yield some incorrect discriminations in that the remainder of the upper group will respond incorrectly and the remainder of the lower group correctly.

The discriminating power of a test item is the difference between the number of correct and incorrect discriminations expressed as a percentage of the maximum possible correct discriminations. Several reports based on this idea have appeared (Johnson, 1951; Ebel, 1954; Findley, 1956). In simplified form, the formula to compute an index of discriminating power based on this idea is the following:

$$D = \frac{U - L}{N},$$

where

D = index of item discriminating power;
U = number of pupils in upper group who answer the test item *correctly*;
L = number of pupils in the lower group who answer the test item *correctly*;
N = number of pupils in each of the two groups.

To use this formula conventionally, one must first find the total raw scores on the test for all pupils. Then the test papers are ranked according to the raw scores, and the top and bottom thirds of the raw-score distribution are found; the middle third is ignored. For each test item, the number of pupils in the upper and lower groups who respond correctly are tabulated. Appropriate substitutions are then made in the formula. For instance, suppose that ten of twelve pupils in the upper third of the raw-score distribution answer an item correctly, and five of twelve in the lower third answer it correctly. The index of discriminating power for this test item is:

$$D = \frac{10 - 5}{12} = +0.42.$$

It is evident that the maximum size of the index is $+1.00$ and the minimum size is -1.00. In the first case, maximum discrimination occurs in the desired direction; in the second, in the opposite direction. Any negative value means that the test item discriminates—to some degree—in the wrong direction. Hence, the discriminating power of the test item is unsatisfactory. Positive values show that the test item discriminates in the desired direction, even though it may not be completely satisfactory. The larger the positive value the better. Although it is difficult to establish a suitable minimum positive value below which the discriminating power of a test item is considered faulty, certainly values less than +0.20 indicate that the discriminating power of the test item is questionable. A reasonably good achievement test item should have an index of at least +0.30.

Difficulty Levels Near Fifty Percent

It has long been known that the discriminating power of an item is influenced by the difficulty of the item. The manner of influence depends on the relative intercorrelation of the items, that is, the degree to which each test item is correlated with every other. In the case of tests containing items that have low intercorrelation, those composed of items with levels of difficulty near 50 percent will display more discriminating power than those composed of items with widely varying levels of difficulty. In the case of tests containing items with high intercorrelations, the reverse is true. The reasons are beyond the scope of this book; further discussion can be found in any of several standard references (Henrysson, 1970).

Since achievement tests rarely are composed of highly intercorrelated items, the recommendation is frequently made that they include only those test items with midrange levels of difficulty, between 40 and 70 percent (Ebel, 1954). This recommendation often disturbs teachers who feel that a wide distribution of levels of item difficulty is necessary to test very good and very poor pupils properly. To separate the very good, the good, the average, the poor, and the very poor pupils from each other, an achievement test with superior discriminating power is needed. To obtain this, it is necessary, strange as it may seem, to avoid the use of test items with widely varying levels of difficulty.

Problems

1. Using data obtained from an objective test which you have either administered or taken yourself, determine P values and D values for all test items. Interpret the results of your computations.

2. The statement has been made that homogeneous grouping of pupils often reduces the likelihood of sharp discriminations by test items, and also the need for such discriminations (Katz, 1961, p. 269). Describe situations for which this statement is true.

3. By means of a simple experimental study, Ebel (1965, pp. 360–364) demonstrated empirically that an inverse relationship exists between the spread of item difficulties and the spread of test scores. Study the three test score histograms shown. Are the differences among them striking?

4. Do you think that teachers can study multiple-choice test items and success-fully predict the level of difficulty and discriminating power of each? Compare your opinion with the findings of a study in which secondary school mathematics teachers were asked to make such predictions (Ryan, 1968).

USING ITEM ANALYSIS RESULTS

The results of item analysis can serve two main purposes. The first and more obvious one is that they provide important information concerning the problems encountered when classroom achievement tests are built. Such information can give the teacher a much better view of the worth of the test he built and used; he can also profit by his mistakes in that he should be able to construct noticeably better tests in the future. The second use can be summarized in a single word: diagnosis. By examining the data from item analysis, the teacher can detect learning difficulties of individual pupils or the class as a whole, and can plan more suitable remedial programs. Studying the strengths and weaknesses of pupil achievement will also help him to evaluate more accurately the effectiveness of various parts of the learning situation (see Chapter 14).

Improving Classroom Achievement Tests

As he administers each achievement test, the classroom teacher is usually plagued by countless questions. Will the distracters of the third multiple-choice item be attractive? Is the ninth item so worded that the superior achievers may misunderstand its intent and respond incorrectly, yet, paradoxically, the poor achievers will not be misled and will tend to respond correctly? Is the last item too difficult? The answers to questions such as these can cause a teacher to view the test results with confidence or doubt.

Levels of Item Difficulty.   As a first step in the process of answering questions such as the foregoing, item difficulties can be computed. A quick scanning of these data reveals all items to which 100 and 0 percent respond correctly. Since the purpose of a power test is to yield scores that will differentiate among the pupils, neither type of item is suitable. They contribute nothing in terms of differentiation and can be considered unnecessary "padding." On the other hand, a possible use of one or two test items to which 100 percent responded correctly would be to place them at the beginning, thereby letting them serve as a gentle introduction to the remainder of the test.

All items of extremely high or low levels of difficulty should be carefully scrutinized. Since any test items with levels of difficulty that are not in the general vicinity of 50 percent (that is, between 40 and 70 percent) tend to reduce the discriminating power of the test, these can be viewed with suspicion. Their indices of discriminating power should be checked since an item which is extremely easy or difficult cannot possibly have a large *D* value.

Further inspection of the item difficulties will reveal how closely the arrangement of the test items corresponds crudely to an order of ascending level of difficulty. Also, the gross failure of certain test items to approximate the anticipated level of difficulty may be information of great value to the teacher. Is the item poorly designed? Is the effectiveness of the learning experiences far different from that expected? If so, why? Is the level of difficulty of this test item affected by the presence of other items in the test? If so, which items? These and other avenues of explanation can be explored.

Indices of Discriminating Power.   The second step that can partly answer some of the questions posed by the teacher is to compute and interpret indices of discriminating power. Any *D* values above +0.40 can be considered very good, any between +0.40 and +0.20 satisfactory, and any between +0.20 and zero poor. It is clear that negative values identify items that differentiate among pupils in the wrong way. Ebel (1954) suggests that, in a well-built classroom achievement test composed of objective test items, more than 50 percent of the test items should have *D* values exceeding +0.40, less than 40 percent should have values between +0.40 and +0.20, less than 10 percent should have values between +0.20 and zero, and none should have negative values. Obviously, these are only guides and can be changed at the discretion of the teacher.

Examining All Responses to an Item.   An even closer inspection of the effectiveness of test items can be obtained by tabulating and comparing all of the responses of the pupils in the upper and lower groups. For example, in the case of a multiple-choice test item, the responses to each of the distracters— as well as the correct response—are counted. Incidentally, this tabulation can be made quickly and accurately by a test-scoring machine or a computer if the proper answer sheets have been used (Miller and others, 1967; English and Kubiniec, 1967).

To see the kinds of information that can be obtained by scrutinizing all responses, let us examine several multiple-choice items. For instance, the following item was included in an achievement test administered to thirty-six pupils completing a percentage unit in arithmetic.

Mr. Miller purchased a dress shirt from a department store. The retail cost was $4.40, and the sales tax 5%. What was the total cost of the shirt which Mr. Miller must pay?
(1) $0.22
(2) $4.18

(3) $4.40
(4) $4.62

The responses to all options by the pupils in the upper and lower thirds are shown below. Option 4 is the correct response.

Option	Upper third	Lower third
1	0	0
2	3	6
3	0	1
4	9	5
(Omits)	0	0
Total	12	12

Although the item is discriminating fairly well ($D = +0.33$) the attractiveness of the distracters is extremely unbalanced. The first option is chosen by no one, whereas the third is selected by only one pupil. Clearly these distracters are not sufficiently attractive. If this or a similar item were to be used again, perhaps changing the first to $4.45, that is, $4.40 + 0.05, and the third to $4.42, that is, $4.40 + 0.02, would improve the situation. No doubt these changes would make the item more difficult; they would also provide a better basis for determining whether the pupils are committing some of the more common mistakes in percentage computations.

Some teachers will estimate the level of difficulty of the test item by using the data from the upper and lower groups. Since fourteen pupils out of twenty-four marked the item correctly, P is estimated to be 58 percent. Such estimates are usually fairly accurate for our purposes. The middle third often divides itself between correct and incorrect answers much as the other two-thirds combined.

Although the first and third options of the arithmetic test item are criticized because they attracted practically no response, it cannot be said that the ability of a distracter to attract responses is necessarily a sign that a distracter is performing effectively. It must do more than this. A good distracter should have a differential attractiveness, that is, it should be more attractive to the lower group than the upper group. In this way it contributes to the discriminating power of the test item.

This point is illustrated by the following item from a general science test. The correct response is the first option.

Which of the following diseases may be readily contracted from water that is polluted with sewage?
(1) typhoid fever
(2) rickets

(3) rheumatism
(4) heart disease

The responses of the upper and lower groups are:

Option	Upper third	Lower third	Difference $(U - L)$
1	9	4	+5
2	3	2	+1
3	1	4	−3
4	1	4	−3
(Omits)	0	0	
Total	14	14	

Observe that the discriminating power of the test item ($+0.36$) and its level of difficulty (46 percent estimated) are satisfactory.

The relative power of each distracter is shown in the far right-hand column. Notice that the second option is as attractive as the other two distracters but not in the same way. Any properly functioning distracter will yield a relatively large negative value in this column. Therefore, if changes are to be made and the item reused in a modified form, the second option should be replaced. This conclusion must be tempered by the fact that the estimate of differential attractiveness is quite unreliable owing to the small number of pupils used in the analysis.

A third illustration of some of the kinds of information produced by a close scrutiny of pupil responses to test items is one administered to an English class concerning library skills.

If you wish to find quickly the page on which a particular topic or subject appears in a reference book, to which of the following would you refer?
(1) the appendix
(2) the subject index
(3) the table of contents
(4) the bibliography

The responses of the pupils in the upper and lower groups are as follows:

Option	Upper third	Lower third
1	0	1
2	10	8
3	1	2
4	0	0
Omits	0	0
Total	11	11

This test item is too easy, the estimate of P being 82 percent. Moreover, its discriminating power is poor, D being $+0.18$.

Quite possibly, the weakness in the test item is due to the inclusion of the word "subject" in the second option. This may be a clue to the correct response so obvious that the pupils quickly notice it and choose their answer accordingly. The uninformed pupil will profit more by such a clue than the informed pupil who didn't need one in the first place. If this word were deleted, it is conceivable that the differential attractiveness of the distracters would increase, thereby improving the level of difficulty of the item and its discriminating power.

A final illustration is a test item with a satisfactory level of difficulty but negative discriminating power. It appeared in an elementary school social studies test. The first option is the correct response.

The capital of Switzerland is
    (1) Bern
    (2) Zurich
    (3) Lucerne
    (4) Geneva

The responses of the pupils in the upper and lower groups are as follows:

Option	Upper third	Lower third
1	5	6
2	2	3
3	1	1
4	5	3
(Omits)	0	0
Total	13	13

The estimated level of difficulty is 42 percent and the index of discriminating power is -0.08.

We can only speculate as to why more pupils in the lower group than in the upper responded correctly and so many of the pupils in the upper group selected the fourth option. Possibly their familiarity with the League of Nations and the many important international conferences that were held in Geneva caused the pupils in the upper group to think of Geneva as the most important city in Switzerland and thus the capital of the country. The pupils in the lower group, on the other hand, may not have known this about Geneva and therefore were not misled by it. Having no preconceived ideas about the importance of these four cities, almost half of them learned that Bern is the capital and responded accordingly. Perhaps the relative importance of the cities of Switzerland and their relationship to each other and the world are not well taught. Certainly these data indicate that further clarification of the status of Bern is needed.

The four previous illustrations make it clear that a rich fund of information concerning his test is available to the teacher who takes the trouble to examine all responses to the test items. Although only multiple-choice items are shown, similar information can be obtained from other types of objective test items and even essay test items of the restricted response type. At the very least, this information should give the teacher a much more realistic view of the value of his test. Ideally, it should also warn him of some of the pitfalls encountered in achievement test construction and suggest means of overcoming or circumventing these. With item analysis information, the teacher should be able either to improve older test items if he wishes or to build better new ones. Without it we can fully expect that, with rare exceptions, the flaws present in a classroom test will be found in succeeding tests constructed by the same teacher.

Diagnosing Inadequacies in Achievement

As informative as a pupil's total raw score can be in many respects, it does not provide very much information about the sources of his successes and failures. In other words, the raw score of a pupil or the arithmetic mean of the raw scores of a class may be interpreted to mean that one or more pupils are having trouble, but such scores will not tell what the trouble is or where it is located. To locate the nature of the trouble, an item-by-item inspection of the test is necessary.

The first step in diagnosing inadequacies in achievement is to build a chart showing the item-by-item performance by each pupil. A section of such a chart based on an objective achievement test is shown in Table 3. The plus signs indicate correct responses, the negative signs incorrect responses, and the zeros omitted responses. Incidentally, some teachers have their pupils participate in the construction of such a chart as this; others use printed reports prepared by computers (Miller and others, 1967).

The totals listed at the bottom of the table reveal the number of pupils who responded correctly and incorrectly to each test item. The totals pinpoint the areas of difficulty for the pupils as a class. Notice that, of the first ten test items, these seven pupils found items 2, 3, 4, 6, and 8 to be relatively easy, whereas they found 1, 5, and 10 to be moderately difficult, and 7 and 9 quite difficult. Now the strengths and weaknesses in the achievement of the pupils can be quickly found by examining the areas of achievement involved in the test items identified and noting the cells of the table of specifications on which

TABLE 3.   Sample Chart for Analyzing Pupil Responses to Each Item in an Achievement Test.

| Name of Pupil | Test Item Number | | | | | | | | | | Total score |
	1	2	3	4	5	6	7	8	9	10...60	
1. Steve	+[a]	−[b]	+	+	+	−	−	+	−	+	+	39
2. Mary	−	+	+	−	+	−	+	−	−	+	0[c]	21
3. Dick	−	+	+	+	−	+	−	−	+	−	−	18
4. Carol	+	−	−	+	+	+	+	+	−	−	−	37
5. Becky	+	+	+	−	−	+	−	+	−	+	+	41
6. June	+	+	+	+	−	+	+	+	+	−	+	55
7. Sheri	−	+	−	+	+	+	−	+	0	+	−	44
Total No. correct	4	5	5	5	4	5	3	5	2	4.... 3	
Total No. wrong	3	2	2	2	3	2	4	2	4	3.... 3	
Omissions	0	0	0	0	0	0	0	0	1	0.... 1	

[a] Correct response
[b] Incorrect response
[c] Omitted response

they are based. Discussing this information with members of the class immediately following the administration of the test can be most enlightening to them.

Very likely the teacher will wish to study the test items that cause difficulty before those that do not. After satisfying himself that there is nothing technically wrong with such a test item and its scoring, he can pose questions as to the reasons why it is difficult: Is little emphasis placed on the point of the test item during the period of instruction? If so, is this lack of emphasis deliberate or accidental? Is there widespread misunderstanding among the pupils in spite of the fact that careful instruction is given? If so, what is the nature of the misunderstanding? Should the learning experiences related to the areas of difficulty be changed in any way? Do the pupils omit the test item frequently? If so, is this because the test might be too long?

There is profit as well in examining test items that the class found to be easy. Again, after a search for technical imperfections fails to reveal any defects, the teacher can raise questions about why the test items are relatively easy: Are the items found to be easy those that primarily measure recall of information rather than more complex cognitive achievement? If so, does this indicate that undue emphasis is being placed on the objectives related to knowledge with a corresponding deemphasis on those involving other levels of the cognitive taxonomy? Can the idea behind one or more of the relatively easy test items be traced to a particular learning experience? If so, is there some feature of that learning experience such as a visual aid or supplementary instructional material that is responsible for the pupils' successes and that should be reused with subsequent classes? Is extreme success with a test item caused by unwarranted hints given before or during the administration of the test? If so, should the test be rescored with this item omitted?

After these questions have been answered to his satisfaction, the teacher can turn to the responses of each individual pupil. Just as he attempted to analyze the areas of strength and weakness for the class as a whole, he can now do the same for each pupil. Following a thorough examination of the item-by-item performance of the pupil, other records of his achievement can be consulted, observations of his study habits made, and, in many instances, a teacher-pupil conference held. In this manner, many additional pieces of information come to light as to why the pupil is successful or unsuccessful. These details can be used along with the initial information concerning what the areas are as a basis for building a remedial program. Such a program is individually tailored to the needs of the pupil. If it succeeds, it will not only correct his past inadequacies but also provide him with the means of preventing a number of future difficulties.

Sampling Problem.   Analyzing the item-by-item performance of each pupil has one serious weakness that must be recognized. This is the problem of adequate sampling—the same problem we encounter with other aspects of educational measurement. According to the procedures outlined in the foregoing paragraphs, the teacher may regularly make decisions concerning the pupil's achievement on the basis of his response to one or perhaps several test items. Frequently these are very small samples of the achievement areas in question; consequently, the probability that they do not present an accurate picture of the pupil's accomplishments is uncomfortably large. This means that the information gleaned from the item-by-item analysis must be considered suggestive rather than definitive.

The sampling problem can be corrected in part without destroying all of the diagnostic features of the analysis by modifying Table 3 slightly. Instead of listing the test items individually across the top of the table, we can organize them into meaningful groups and list them in place of the individual items. For instance, in an arithmetic test the test items may be grouped in four categories: those requiring addition, subtraction, multiplication, and division. The number of correct and incorrect responses to each group of items by each pupil can be tabulated.

A recommended scheme for organizing the test items into groups is to use the table of specifications. Items representing the same or similar cells may be combined into one group. The number of groups used, as well as their size, are determined by the teacher and, of course, can vary widely. However, to make the grouping process effective, the two extremes should be avoided.

If only two groups are used, little information is gained that cannot be obtained from inspection of the total test scores. If the number of groups is only slightly less than the number of test items, the process will not sufficiently relieve the sampling problem to justify the work it entails.

Problems

5. Study the steps described by Katz (1961, pp. 266–268) with which the teacher prepares a homemade answer sheet for objective achievement tests having selection test items, which will reduce the effort required to complete an item analysis of the test. Demonstrate this procedure with an achievement test to be used in a class you are now teaching or attending. Evaluate the demonstration.

6. Study the steps described by Diederich (1964, pp. 2–8) in which an item analysis is completed by the pupils to whom an achievement test was administered. They performed most of the work involved in the item analysis by raising their hands in response to instructions from the teacher. Demonstrate this procedure with a class which you are now teaching or attending. Evaluate the demonstration.

7. Compare the Katz item analysis procedure and that proposed by Diederich in terms of their feasibility and accuracy.

8. A properly programmed computer can identify the test item missed by each pupil and provide him with printed suggestions as to the material he should review (Miller and others, 1967). Study the illustrations provided. Are the computer print-outs specific enough to help both pupil and teacher? How could the table of specifications on which the test was based assist in this effort?

LIMITATIONS OF ITEM ANALYSIS

Although item analysis data are useful for evaluating an achievement test and diagnosing weaknesses, several serious limitations exist in application of the techniques. In the first place, whereas the internal-consistency method is suitable for tests containing items that measure somewhat the same mental functions, achievement tests generally contain test items that are relatively heterogeneous in this respect. Second, the classroom teacher frequently must base his item analysis on a small number of pupils, forming judgments on limited evidence. Third, analysis of responses to essay test items is less informative than that of responses to objective items. This lessens the utility of the techniques for the teacher using these items. Finally, item analysis results are more relative than some teachers realize. The level of difficulty and discriminating power of a test item are influenced by the test in which the item appears, the conditions under which the test is administered, and the quality of the pupils.

Use of Internal-Consistency Methods

The internal-consistency method for computing indices of item discriminating power is appropriate when the pupil traits measured by the total test scores are homogeneous for all practical purposes. Successful items in a test of this kind are those that are closely related to each other and, of course, that tend to measure whatever the total test scores measure. They will have large positive *D* values. As any test items with low discriminating power are eliminated or changed so that their discriminating power increases, the resulting test will become more and more homogeneous. In other words, it is becoming more and more internally consistent; all test items are reflecting the same unitary pupil trait.

The total scores of achievement tests typically represent heterogeneous rather than homogeneous aspects of the pupils. They contain test items that measure several different kinds of behavior (that is, various levels of the cognitive taxonomy) in unequal amounts. The total score is actually a composite representation of these behaviors. The biggest part contributes greatly to the size of the total test score and will, in a sense, dominate the results of the discriminating power determinations. In other words, if one pupil trait stands out in the total test scores, well-constructed items that reflect it will have satisfactory indices of discriminating power. On the other hand, test items reflecting less important and somewhat unrelated traits, even though they are well constructed in many technical respects, will tend to have low indices of discriminating power.

This problem can be easily illustrated. Suppose that an achievement test contains forty-five recall-of-information items that are fairly homogeneous and five application-of-principles items that are noticeably unlike the first group. The total score is found by counting the number of correct responses, regardless of which type of test item is being scored. All other factors being equal, we would expect that the items in the larger group would have markedly higher indices of discriminating power than those in the smaller group, if the internal-consistency method of computation is used.

Effect on Content Validity. The true significance of the foregoing statements comes into focus when the problem of content validity is considered. Certainly maintaining high content validity in each achievement test is the primary goal of the teacher who designs and builds it. Yet indices of discriminating power may actually encourage him to reduce the degree of content validity of future tests. This would occur if, in the illustration of the 50-item achievement test, the teacher wishes someday to use it again and either eliminates the items with low indices of discriminating power or modifies them in the hope that the indices will improve. In both cases, large or potentially large changes in content validity could take place. Obviously more is lost than gained.

Indices of discriminating power based on the internal-consistency method must be interpreted with some caution. We are continually faced with the prospect that a test item may have a low index of discriminating power not because it is faulty but because it measures a trait making a secondary contribution to the total test score. Of course the problem is largely corrected if it is possible to break down an achievement test in homogeneous subtests with reasonably reliable scores and to use each as the internal criterion for computing indices of discriminating power for items within that subtest. Although this is regularly done with standardized achievement tests, such is not the case with classroom achievement tests because it is often impracticable.

Inadequate Numbers of Pupils

Item analyses for standardized achievement tests are often based on hundreds of cases. Contrast this with the usual class size, which places a limit on the number of cases available to a teacher at one time. His sample is extremely small.

Reexamine for a moment the distributions of the responses made by pupils in the upper and lower groups to the four test items shown earlier in this chapter. Note how a shift of one response from one option to another can change your opinion of the power of a distracter, or how it might even change the P or D value noticeably. Remembering that some of the reasons why a pupil selects one option rather than any of the other three can be vague and obscure, you can imagine how easily a shift in choice could have taken place. All of this means that the profile of pupil responses to an item must be considered tentative as long as the number of pupils is so small.

The teacher's alternatives are simple. Either he bases his item analysis on an inadequate number of pupils or he must continue to build and interpret his achievement tests without item analysis data. His choice is obvious. Tentative item analysis information followed by tentative judgments based on it is clearly better than no information at all. Although the fact that only a few cases are available weakens the value of item analysis data, it does not totally destroy it.

Analyzing Responses to Essay Test Items

Item analysis technique can be applied to the responses to essay items as well as to objective items; however, it is definitely more difficult, and the results are sometimes considered less meaningful. The difficulty is traced to the problems of reliable scoring of essay responses and tabulating the incorrect responses. Both of these activities are time-consuming. The relative lack of meaning of the data is attributed to the fact that the various subparts of the correct response are frequently related to each other. The level of difficulty of one subpart may affect the level of difficulty of another; the correctness or incorrectness of a pupil's response to one part may affect the correctness or incorrectness of his response to a subsequent part. These are the principal reasons why responses to essay items are analyzed so infrequently.

The analysis of responses to essay items is most successful if they are of the restricted-response type and are scored by the analytical method. If at all possible, each subpart should be separately considered. This is equivalent to considering each an independent test item with its own level of difficulty and discriminating power. When some or all subparts cannot be logically separated, they should be combined as necessary and the composites treated as separate test items. An analysis based on the internal-consistency method can be used here as it is with responses to objective items.

Relative Nature of Item Analysis Data

We should like to believe that data from item analysis are completely accurate and meaningful. Clearly this is not justified, both because of the limitations introduced by the use of an internal criterion and a small sample of pupils and because of the special circumstances surrounding every test item as it is administered.

Some of those special circumstances relate to the pupils as they respond to the item—their alertness, motivation, and emotional tone. Some relate to the environment in which the test is given—the time of day, the amount of extraneous noise, the temperature of the room, and the ventilation. Some relate to the test containing the item in question—its length, the levels of difficulty of the other items, and the order in which they are arranged. Yes, even the attractiveness of a distracter in a multiple-choice item is influenced by the other distracters with which it is used.

It is hard to determine how much these factors influence item analysis data. The influence might be slight, but in a given instance it could be prominent. Regardless of which it is, a qualification must be added to every interpretation of item analysis data. It must be understood that the P value and the D value are merely representations of the level of difficulty and discriminating power of an item as it appeared in a certain test administered under specific circumstances to one group of pupils. It is clear that if the test or environment is changed, the values can and do change.

General Considerations

The foregoing sections point out many of the functions of item analysis and the limitations commonly incurred. However, at no point is notice taken of a somewhat strange misconception that is occasionally found concerning the relationship between item construction and analysis. Some teachers believe that a careful analysis of test results somehow makes careful construction of items less important. This is not true. The many suggestions given in Chapters 3, 4, and 5 for improving test items should be followed, regardless of whether techniques for the analysis of items are later used. Item analysis results can be successfully used to improve subsequent measurements of pupil achievement but do not improve the test being analyzed. Even in this subsequent use, item analysis operates imperfectly since all flaws in a test item have not necessarily been revealed by analysis. Bear in mind, therefore, that item analysis in no way relieves the teacher of the responsibility of building the best achievement test possible.

Persistent attempts to follow the suggestions for improving test items should directly and indirectly help produce test items with encouraging item analysis data. There is no guarantee, however, that this will happen. Very careful construction and even ingenious revision based on item analysis data may fail to improve the P and D values of a test item satisfactorily. This creates a dilemma: considerations of content validity make it necessary to include the material in the test, yet item analysis suggests that the related items are inferior in some respects. Preference must be given to the content validity. Items based on the material must be included and repeated efforts made to improve their quality. If this fails, then the table of specifications can be changed so that the material can be properly excluded from the test. As a result, the meaning of the total score is changed and evaluation of pupil achievement in the area omitted must be made by other methods, that is, nontesting procedures such as rating methods, product scales, and check lists. These are discussed and illustrated in the following chapter.

Problems

9.   It can be shown that, to obtain multiple-choice test items with good discriminating power, it is more efficient to revise faulty ones on the basis of item analysis data than to design new ones (Lange and others, 1967). On the basis of your experience, what would you estimate the time savings to be? Compare your estimate with that reported by Lange.

10.   For classes of about 30 pupils or less, item analysis data are rather undependable. Demonstrate the degree to which P values and D values will change by

systematically altering the response of one pupil in the upper third and one in the lower third of the test item concerning Switzerland (see page 194), and recomputing the two values each time.

TEST ITEM FILE

The teaching notes maintained by many classroom teachers are voluminous. A syllabus, a variety of outlines, numerous references, several study guides, and a quantity of newspaper clippings and miscellaneous pamphlets are usually a part of this collection. Each assists the teacher as he pursues his instructional duties. Some of these are highly prized; they are considered to be proven teaching aids. Although other notes may be of more doubtful value, the practicing teacher would rarely be willing to part with them.

The portion of this mass of teaching notes that often receives the least attention is the evaluation section. Usually it consists of a copy or two of each of the classroom achievement tests administered during the past year or so, and possibly the tables of specifications on which they were based. Nevertheless, more complete materials concerning these techniques could easily simplify the teacher's measurement functions as much as teaching notes simplify his instructional functions. A highly successful means of organizing much of the pertinent information on classroom achievement tests is a test item file.

Item Data Card

A test item file is nothing more than a series of cards that record a great deal of the information obtained by item analysis procedures. Usually the file contains as many cards as there are test items, although sometimes the length of the item or the nature of the information about it requires several cards. The cards are customarily 5 × 8 inches in size and are arranged in any order the teacher desires.

The front of a sample item data card is shown in Figure 4. Notice that the multiple-choice test item shown is typed so that ample space is allowed for revision. Interlinear notations can be made if the item is to be changed; new options can be written to the right of the original ones if desired. Notice also that the item is cross-referenced with the cells of the table of specifications on which it is based. Each cell is identified by the row (the Arabic number) and the column (the English letter) of the table that intersect to form it. Additional useful information is the page or chapter number of a book or other reference directly related to the subject matter of the item. This allows the teacher to check quickly any detail that might be questioned.

No. 143
___

If both the President and the Vice President of the United States are unable

to serve, which of the following officials will act as President?

    (1) Secretary of State

    (2) Speaker of the House of Representatives

    (3) Secretary of Defense

    (4) President pro tempore of the Senate

Cells in table of specifications:			*Reference(s):*
Table No.	*Primary*	*Secondary*	Doe and Colofort
2	4B	—	American Government Today, Revised Ed. 1970, pp. 273–274.

FIGURE 4.   Front Side of Item Data Card.

    The reverse side of the item data card is shown in Figure 5. Space is allowed for summarizing the item analysis data for as many as three separate administrations of the test item or a revision of it and for any appropriate comments made by teacher or pupils. For each administration the name of the test, the class to which it was administered, its size, the date of administration, the test item number, and the type of administration are noted. Below these, the responses to all options by the upper and lower third of the class, and the P and D values of the test item are recorded.

    Clearly, maintaining item data cards is a serious clerical problem. Fortunately it is not insurmountable. Item data cards such as the one shown can be easily prepared with a mimeograph or ditto machine. Once an ample supply is available and the necessary item analysis tabulation is completed, the item data card can be filled out rather rapidly. Regular attention will prevent a backlog of unrecorded data from accumulating and provide a smooth, permanent, and up-to-date record for every test item used.

    Some teachers reduce the clerical load by using less elaborate cards. For instance, the data concerning the name of the test, the class to which it was The advantages of maintaining a test item file are obvious if the teacher in- administered, its size, and the type of administration are omitted. If the cards

Test	Unit 2					Comments:
Class	11th grade					4-22-71—Pupils are confused about the meaning of the expression "unable to serve." Possibly this should be changed to "die while in office."
Date	4-22-71					
Item No.	18					
N_T	33					
Type of Adm.	Closed book					

Options	Upper	Lower	Upper	Lower	Upper	Lower
1	2	4				
2	⑦	②				
3	0	2				
4	2	3				
5	–	–				
Omits	0	0				
P (Est.)	41%					
D	+0.45					

FIGURE 5.   Reverse Side of Item Data Card.

for each test are filed in a separate group, this information need be recorded only once. Others do not fill out cards for all the test items they use. Instead, only very promising test items are filed.

Advantages of a Test Item File

tends to use his test items again. On the basis of the item analysis information and the comments made, he can revise the item. A quick check of the table of specifications will reveal whether the relationship between the item and the table of specifications has changed. The fact that the items are on cards facilitates separating and counting them in terms of the cells in the table of specifications. In this way, the degree of content validity of the total test can be estimated. Having the items on cards also simplifies the reproduction of the test. Since the test is built by accumulating a pack of cards, the arrangement of the items in the test can be changed by simply rearranging the cards, and the final copy of the test can be typed directly from them.

Much can be said in favor of using test items again. By constantly reworking his test items and adding new ones as needed, the conscientious classroom teacher can develop some excellent achievement tests. In this way, the teacher's investment of time and effort in maintaining a test item file becomes reasonable and profitable. However, he cannot use test items again if there is any chance that pupils in succeeding classes will be familiar with them before the test is given. To prevent this, some teachers withhold the test copies and answer sheets after the test.

Withholding test materials, however, is neither fair to the pupils nor good teaching procedure. The pupil who is aware of his successes and failures can take action to improve his deficiencies and gain a much more realistic view of his achievements. His attitudes toward school work are also affected. It is difficult, to say the least, to provide the pupil with a true and complete record of his achievements if he is not allowed to keep his test materials. Therefore, the teacher must, if at all possible, return them and discuss the results with him.

Reusing test items, therefore, becomes considerably more difficult. Only after a teacher has developed a large pool of test items over a period of years should he use any of them again. Under these conditions it is unlikely that any pupils will have any unfair advantage worth mentioning. After all, the vast majority of the previous test copies have been discarded or lost. On the other hand, even if a pupil had access to all of them, the task of studying them would be more forbidding than preparing for a test in the normal manner. Finally, the test items that are used again are usually revisions of the original items. Even when the revision is minor, it helps prevent a pupil who may have studied the original item and memorized the answer from gaining a tremendous advantage over others.

Maintaining a test item file also offers advantages to teachers who do not intend to use any of them again. Restudying test items used in the past can provide helpful hints for constructing new ones. The new item may be totally original yet based on the same idea as one in the file, or it might be such a drastic revision of an older test item that its relationship to it is not easily recognized by the pupils.

In addition, restudying the results of earlier tests can alert the teacher to those cells in the table of specifications that very often are the basis of successful test items and those, if any, that are the basis of unsuccessful test items. If cells of the latter type are found, efforts at item construction can be focused on them. Likely weaknesses of a new test can be detected before it is given.

Limitations of a Test Item File

One of the chief limitations of maintaining a test item file has already been mentioned, the great clerical involvement. Another limitation is that the method of recording the data is not equally applicable to all types of test items.

Although the form shown in Figure 4 can be used for many different items, that shown in Figure 5 cannot. It is suitable for the common multiple-choice and true-false test items but must be modified if short-answer or some of the longer matching items are used. The essay item presents even more problems, since the scoring and analyzing of the responses are so difficult.

Still another possible limitation is that maintaining a test item file will actually have an adverse effect on the teacher's instructional and measurement efforts. The first part of the argument goes this way: if teachers are very familiar with past test items, and if the same or similar test items are used in the future, they may teach toward the test without knowing it. In reality, they may be coaching the pupils; the instruction may slavishly follow the achievement tests instead of the reverse. The second part is that intimate knowledge of the old test items will tend to dull the teacher's creativity when building new test items. In other words, the teacher falls into a testing rut. The new test items strongly resemble old ones, novel types are typically ignored, and, as a result, the classroom achievement tests become stereotyped.

Certainly these adverse effects are possible. It is difficult to believe, however, that the discerning teacher would tolerate any of them for any length of time. The advantages gained by maintaining a test item file far outweigh these limitations.

Problems

11. Design a data card for a restricted-response essay test item.
12. Can the data card be used successfully with multiple-response objective test items designed to measure complex pupil achievement, for example, the item concerning beehives in an apple orchard shown on page 140? Give reasons for your answer.

SUMMARY

Since many tentative decisions are made during construction of classroom achievement tests, teachers are understandably concerned about the worth of the test. They want to know its strengths and weaknesses so that they can interpret the results more properly. Each test item must be reexamined to discover its strengths and weaknesses in an item analysis.

Item analysis concentrates on two vital features: level of difficulty and discriminating power. The former means the percentage of pupils who answer each test item correctly; this is expressed in terms of P values. The latter means the ability of the test item to differentiate between pupils who achieve well and those who achieve poorly; this is expressed in terms of *D* values. The pupils who achieve well and those who achieve poorly are usually identified by the internal-consistency method. The total scores on the test containing the items to be analyzed serve as the criterion. Those pupils in the upper third of the raw-score distribution are said to achieve well; those in the lower third are said to achieve poorly.

Results of item analysis can serve two significant purposes. In the first place, they provide important information concerning the problem encountered in the construction of achievement tests. On the basis of this information, the teacher can gain a much better idea of the value of the test he has built, and he should also be able to construct noticeably better tests in the future. The second use is diagnosis. By examining the data from item analysis, the teacher can detect learning difficulties of individual pupils or of the class as a whole. He can plan more suitable remedial programs.

There are four prominent limitations in the application of item analysis. Firstly, the internal-consistency method is suitable for tests containing items that measure somewhat the same mental functions. Achievements typically are not of this type. Secondly, only a very small sample of pupils is available for the analysis. Thirdly, it is difficult to analyze pupil responses to essay items. Lastly, item analysis data are relative in that they are influenced by the remainder of the test in which the item appears and the particular conditions under which it is administered.

A convenient means of organizing much of the pertinent information yielded by item analysis is a test item file. This file is a series of 5 × 8-inch cards on which are typed the item, information about the test administration, and the item analysis data. Although maintenance creates a difficult clerical problem, a file can greatly assist the teacher who wishes to use some or all of his original test items in later tests, and also the teacher who plans to build new test items and, in so doing, wants to capitalize on past experiences.

Suggested Readings

Anastasi, A. *Psychological testing*. (3rd ed.) London: Macmillan, 1968. Chapter 7. Item difficulty and discriminating power are treated in a complete fashion. Of special interest are the item characteristic curves showing the relationship between the test item and the criterion—in this case, the total scores on the test containing the item. Curves are shown for items with good and poor discriminating power.

Cox, R. C. Item selection techniques and evaluation of instructional objectives. *Journal of Educational Measurement*, 1965, 2, 181–185. Empirical evidence is presented indicating that item analysis data may inadvertently cause objective test items related to some educational objectives to be disproportionately eliminated from an achievement test. The first four categories of the cognitive domain taxonomy were used to classify the educational objectives.

Diederich, P. B. *Short-cut statistics for teacher-made tests.* (2nd ed.) Educational Testing Service Evaluation and Advisory Service Series, No. 5. Princeton, N.J.: Educational Testing Service, 1964. Pp. 2–8.

All needed instructions are given for completing an item analysis of an achievement test by pupils' "show of hands" in the classroom. It is possible to complete an item analysis of a one-period test in ten to twenty minutes of class time, thereby conserving much teacher time and effort.

Ebel, R. L. *Measuring educational achievement.* Englewood Cliffs, N.J.: Prentice-Hall, 1965. Chapter 11.

The rationale underlying the *D* index is explained. Illustrations are given of the use of item anaysis data for improving faulty multiple-choice items.

Engelhart, M. D. A comparison of several item discrimination indices. *Journal of Educational Measurement*, 1965, **2**, 69–76.

In this somewhat technical report, the *D* index is found to compare favorably with other measures of discriminating power such as tetrachoric coefficients of correlation, phi coefficients, and biserial and point biserial coefficients of correlation.

Henrysson, S. Gathering, analyzing and using data on test items. In R. L. Thorndike (ed.), *Educational measurement.* (2nd ed.) Washington: American Council on Education, 1970. Chapter 5.

The first part of this chapter is a well-written, nontechnical presentation of the methods and principles of item analysis. In contrast, the second part deals with special problems and methods and has a stronger statistical emphasis.

Katz, M. Improving classroom tests by means of item analysis. *Clearing house*, 1961, **35**, 265–269.

Detailed instructions are given for the teacher who wishes to prepare an item analysis for his achievement tests. The method described is very useful and is based in part on the rationale for the *D* index.

References Cited

Diederich, P. B. *Short-cut statistics for teacher-made tests.* (2nd ed.) Educational Testing Service Evaluation and Advisory Service Series, No. 5. Princeton, N.J.: Educational Testing Service, 1964.

Ebel, R. L. Procedures for the analysis of classroom tests. *Educational and Psychological Measurement*, 1954, **14**, 352–364.

Ebel, R. L. *Measuring educational achievement.* Englewood Cliffs, N.J.: Prentice-Hall, 1965.

English, H. H., and C. M. Kubiniec. An objective test analysis program utilizing the IBM 1230 optical mark scoring reader. *Educational and Psychological Measurement*, 1967, **27**, 165–170.

Findley, W. G. A rationale for evaluation of item discrimination statistics. *Educational and Psychological Measurement*, 1956, **16**, 175–180.

Henrysson, S. Gathering, analyzing and using data on test items. In R. L. Thorndike (ed.), *Educational measurement.* (2nd ed.) Washington: American Council on Education, 1970. Chapter 5.

Johnson, A. P. Notes on a suggested index of item validity: The U–L index. *Journal of Educational Psychology*, 1951, **42**, 499–504.

Katz, M. Improving classroom tests by means of item analysis. *Clearing house*, 1961, **35**, 265–269.

Lange, A., I. J. Lehmann, and W. A. Mehrens. Using item analysis to improve tests. *Journal of Educational Measurement*, 1967, **4**, 65–68.

Miller, C. D., and others. Scoring, analyzing, and reporting classroom tests using an optical reader and 1401 computer. *Educational and Psychological Measurement*, 1967, **27**, 159–164.

Ryan, J. J. Teacher judgment of test item properties. *Journal of Educational Measurement*, 1968, **5**, 301–306.

CHAPTER 7

Judging of Procedures and Products

The full extent of our achievements cannot always be predicted on the basis of information about part of them. For instance, an investor may reveal widespread knowledge about the economic laws of supply and demand, the histories of prominent industrial companies, and the characteristics of economic cycles in the United States and the world, but still fail to realize anything more than an occasional modest profit when playing the stock market. An avid football fan can no doubt quote at length the rules of the game, recall accurately outstanding contests of past seasons, and even diagnose a quarterback's offensive strategy and plan effective defenses to contain it, yet be unable to play the game himself on a par with his twelve-year-old son. The music critic may command extensive knowledge of the musical score, the instruments played, and perhaps the life of the composer, but not be able to play a single note. Likewise, the mechanical engineer may be completely familiar with the principles of an internal combustion engine, the transmission and the suspension system of a modern automobile, yet not be able to drive or repair it with ease.

There are obvious parallels in formal education. A pupil studying general science may be able to cite accurately the laws on which an experiment is based and even draw schematically the apparatus needed to conduct the experiment, yet experience great difficulty when trying to set up the apparatus and reproduce the results of the original experiment. In the language arts, a pupil may quote the rules of English grammar without hesitation, spell a great variety of words, and command a large vocabulary, but be unable to write an acceptable original theme. Pupils in a home economics class may know many facts and principles about food preparation, yet fail in their attempts to prepare a baked custard that is suitable to serve.

It is clear that attempts to predict the quality of a performance involving physical activity on the basis of verbal and mathematical knowledge are often unsuccessful, not only in everyday experiences but also in the classroom. For information about the pupil's ability to perform, direct inspection of that performance is called for. This means that the pupil must be given an opportunity to perform under suitable conditions.

Evaluation of pupil performance all too often is accorded a secondary place in the pupil evaluation program. A quick study of educational objectives reveals, however, that such an attitude is unjustified. Sprinkled liberally throughout the listings of elementary and secondary school educational objectives are those directed toward development of motor skills, ability to create products of approved quality, ability to perform services efficiently, and so forth. These are a part of the psychomotor domain.

Note that some of the objectives of physical and biological science require that the pupil be able to manipulate apparatus and create products such as drawings of specimens, logs and diaries, precipitates, and operational mock-ups. In physical education, driver education, art, and music, many of the most important objectives are not verbal or mathematical in nature. The vocational programs, such as business, agriculture, industrial arts, and home economics, also are dominated by educational objectives that stress pupil performance. Finally, in the language arts, handwriting skill and speaking ability are integral parts of the program.

The importance of these objectives cannot be overestimated. Quite regularly, pupil success or lack of success in reaching such goals as these reveals the nature of his higher-order learning. Paper-and-pencil achievement tests are a useful but somewhat limited means of measuring complex pupil achievement. They need to be supplemented. Systematic examination of pupil performance is often an excellent means of doing this. Instead of being restricted to primarily verbal and mathematical aspects, the pupil behavior elicited can also involve nonlanguage features such as motor skills. It can incorporate originality, creativity, and the ability to organize and coordinate many parts of past achievements.

No doubt the principal reasons that a relatively small part of the teacher's evaluative effort is directed toward the study of pupil performance are that (1) the techniques tend to be more subjective and less dependable than paper-and-pencil achievement testing, and (2) they are aimed at more complex aspects of pupil behavior, and hence are difficult to administer, score, and interpret. In spite of these two problems, a number of highly useful instruments have been developed in this area. Some are directed primarily toward the procedure displayed by the pupil, whereas others are directed toward a product yielded by that procedure. Therefore, as a first step in examining these measurement efforts, it is convenient to divide pupil performance into two parts— procedures and products.

PROCEDURES AND PRODUCTS

Procedure and product are clearly interdependent, yet in terms of their description they are easily distinguished. Procedures are the sequences of movements executed by the pupil; products are the results of these procedures. A good illustration can be found in typing. The procedure learned by the pupil involves assuming a proper posture, placing the fingers on certain keys before beginning, watching the material to be typed rather than the keyboard, and striking only designated keys with each finger, doing so with the proper stroke. The product can be a typed business letter or several paragraphs or pages of prose. Similar illustrations can be found in art, mechanical drawing, handwriting, home economics, agriculture, and industrial arts.

In some educational areas, however, it is difficult to separate the two. Some of the objectives in music, physical education, and speaking are so stated that procedure and product are inextricably intermixed. The procedures could be singing a song, dribbling a basketball, or reciting a poem. The corresponding products are identified in the same manner.

Measurable Characteristics of Procedures

The complex nature of many procedures prevents a teacher from measuring all their subtle aspects. Indeed, he often feels fortunate if he can record sufficient data on just their major features. Since the time available is generally short, and a number of the characteristics of many procedures defy measurement for all practical purposes, the teacher is generally faced with a difficult task.

The characteristics that virtually defy measurement may be extremely important. For example, speaking ability should be evaluated in terms of such attributes as rhythm of talking, variety of word usage, and appropriateness of pitch and tone of voice. Shop procedures should display, among other things, an adaptability by the pupil when unforeseen difficulties arise. Performance in a physical education class should often be characterized by grace, ability, and coordination. Since these are essential features of a pupil's performance, they must be judged. But how? Clearly, the teacher must, on the basis of training and experience, establish standards for such features as these and then, in a subjective manner, classify the performance by comparing it with the standards.

The characteristics of measurable procedures can usually be classified in one of two categories—those related to the efficiency of the procedure and those related to its accuracy. Efficiency suggests a smoothness of action coupled with rapidity and a general economy of effort. Very often key data in this category are the speed of performance, as in a typing exercise, or the identification of the sequence of steps followed, as in the use of a microscope. Accuracy means that few errors are committed; moreover, those committed are relatively unimportant. For example, tabulations can be made of the number of words mispronounced and grammatical errors made during a speech. In a singing or instrumental exercise, a similar count could be made of the instances in which the pupil misjudges the pitch of a note or its duration, or the length of a rest. Clearly it is possible for a given pupil performance to have some but not all of the characteristics in each category.

Measurable Characteristics of Products

Since the quality of a product is basically a reflection of the quality of the procedure that yielded it, the tendency of a product to be complex varies directly with the complexity of its related procedure. Again, this factor increases the difficulty of the measurement. On the other hand, the time available is an important difference. Seldom does the teacher feel the extreme pressure of time limitation when examining products, as is often the case with procedures. Moreover, some products can, if necessary, be broken down into their component parts and each part analyzed; many can be subjected to rigorous measurement of various types without such a breakdown—all at a relatively leisurely pace, which simplifies the process.

The study of pupil products is highly subjective. For instance, the teacher must answer questions such as the following: Is the drawing of the biological specimen sufficiently accurate? How "light" must a cake be before it is a good product? Is the woodworking project in question esthetically attractive? What must a typing exercise look like before one can say that it is "professional" work? These and a myriad of similar questions can only be answered by the teacher applying his standards in the same subjective manner as in the case of procedure evaluation.

Measurable characteristics of products are typically numerous. For example, laboratory products from a chemistry course can be measured in terms of their volume or weight; a cake in terms of its height or volume; a woodworking project in terms of its length and weight; a typing exercise in terms of its length and the number of errors. Notice that these characteristics of the products tend to be specific rather than general, and that the measurement of them is often quite reliable.

Importance of a Natural Situation

Procedures and products are usually studied in a natural situation or one very much like it. This is one of the great strengths of these methods. The elaborate equipment found in the gymnasium, the science laboratories, the industrial and agricultural shops, the art and music studios, the business education rooms, and the home economics kitchens and sewing quarters of the modern school offer realistic settings in which to teach and also to evaluate pupil growth. Certainly samples of pupil behavior concerning procedures and products are being observed in a much more natural situation and much more directly when these facilities are used than when paper-and-pencil tests based upon the same specific educational objectives are administered.

The realism of these observation settings is a function of several factors, one of which is the nature and amount of equipment available. For instance, in vocational education or science courses, the equipment may differ greatly from that later used by the pupil when he leaves secondary school for a job or college. Close liaison with business, industry, and colleges plus a flexible budget for purchasing can prevent any serious gap.

Observation Techniques

The instruments used in the observation of procedure and product are primarily of the nontesting type. In other words, they can but do not necessarily yield quantitative information. Instead, they commonly include qualitative information coupled with personal impressions or opinions. Many times they function as recording devices. They provide a convenient means of organizing and summarizing the teacher's observations of pupil performances and his reaction to them.

The most widely used techniques for procedure and product observation are ranking and rating methods, check lists, product scales, and anecdotal records. Of these, teachers often rely on ranking and rating methods more than any of the others.

Ranking.   Ranking is one of the lower levels of measurement. All that is attempted in an ordering of the pupils according to the merits of the procedures they displayed or the products according to their excellence. Under certain circumstances, ranking can be fairly reliable, that is, consistent. This is usually true when a competent judge is ranking a procedure or product on the basis of only one of its characteristics. Thus, members of a driver training class may be reliably ranked according to their ability to brake properly, or the drawings of a mechanical drawing class in terms of the uniformity of thickness of the straight lines. The more clearly defined the characteristic, the more likely that the ranking will be reliable.

As the basis for the ranking broadens, its reliability tends to drop. Rankings of general merit of a procedure or product in which not one but several characteristics are simultaneously considered, can be quite unreliable. Certainly the ranking of pupils' general driving ability (including posture, starting, steering, and stopping) and the general quality of their drawings (including lettering, dimensions, accuracy, and neatness) are no doubt less reliable than the rankings of single characteristics described. This drop in reliability can be traced to two causes. First, it is difficult to define clearly the meanings of these many characteristics. Second, the relative importance of each characteristic in terms of its contribution to the composite rank is rarely, if ever, completely established. Thus, it is clear that successful ranking normally must be based on a single well-defined characteristic. Moreover, if possible, the ranking should be repeated by the same (but without knowledge of the results of the first attempt) or other competent observers.

Rating.   Rating scales, which take many forms, are popular devices for summarizing procedure and product information. One of the most common is the continuum form. The basic steps followed in its construction and use are as follows. Characteristics of the performance or product are identified, and a continuum representing degrees of merit is established for each characteristic. The continuum may be divided into as few as two positions or as many as ten or more, each position representing a different degree of merit or quality. The various positions along the continuum are often identified by number and, in the case of the graphic scale, a brief description of the corresponding degree of merit. The observer then rates each characteristic of the procedure or product in question by checking the number or description that corresponds most closely to the degree of merit observed. Illustrations of this type of rating scale are included in the following sections.

Rating based on overall general merit is as difficult a process as ranking on that basis. The failure to define clearly the characteristics to be included and to establish definitely the relative importance of each reduces the worth of this type of rating. Again, successful rating, like successful ranking, usually should be based on a single well-defined characteristic and should be repeated.

Check Lists.   Check lists are highly serviceable instruments for recording pupil procedures. Usually they list a series of actions, whether desirable or not, that are a part of a typical pupil's performance. These are arranged in a convenient manner, usually in the order in which you would expect them to occur. For instance, in the case of the check list for softball batting form shown in a following section, the sequence is: (1) grip of the bat, (2) preliminary stance, (3) stride, (4) pivot, and (5) swing.

The type of response for each entry in the check list can vary. Very often, it is simply a check mark indicating that the action listed had occurred. In other cases, a "yes-no" response is required, the "yes" response meaning that the action had been performed in a satisfactory manner, the "no" response meaning the opposite. A third type of response is one in which numbers are placed after the actions. The numbers, starting with "1," indicate the sequence in which the actions occurred. In other words, the completed check list is a step-by-step summary of the procedure followed by a particular pupil.

The development and use of check lists sensitizes the teacher to the subparts of each procedure. In this way, he gains a better view of the totality of the procedure and a more reliable technique for reporting information about it.

Product Scales.   A product scale is a carefully selected series of products representing various levels of quality. Each product in the scale is usually identified by a number or letter. Generally each scale is composed of five or more products, and an attempt is made to select these so that they are evenly spaced along an "inferior-superior" continuum of quality.

The application of a product scale is quite simple. Each pupil prepares a product of the kind included in the product scale. This is then compared with those of the scale and as close a match as possible is made. The pupil's product is then assigned the letter or number of the one in the scale it most closely resembles. An excellent example of this procedure is found in the case of handwriting, which is described in a following section.

Teachers can build product scales without great difficulty. For instance, pupil products such as drawings involving orthographic projection, sewing samples of hemming, basting, and backstitching, woodworking samples of sawing and nailing, and typing products such as a business letter, can be accumulated over a period of a few years. No doubt their quality will vary widely. Repeated independent attempts to arrange them by quality in equal-appearing intervals will eliminate many products that are near-duplicates or about which there is disagreement. The remainder can serve as a product scale.

Anecdotal Records.   Anecdotal records are the most informal of the five techniques mentioned here. The teacher does little more than summarize in writing the major actions of a procedure performed by a pupil. A definite attempt is made to produce a factual report. A single such record may mean little; however, a series of related anecdotal records can contribute appreciably to the study of pupil procedures.

Anecdotal records are used most frequently when so little is known about the procedures in question that its characteristics cannot be well defined. Thus, suitable check lists and rating scales cannot be constructed. Anecdotal records are fittingly used in those cases in the fine arts, physical education, social studies, and home economics in which the teacher is interested in expressive educational objectives.

Problems

1. Identify the measurable aspects of each of the following procedures:
    a. Shooting free throws in basketball.
    b. Bending a piece of glass tubing to form a right angle.
    c. Parking an automobile parallel to the curb.
    d. Hemming a dress.

2. Identify the measurable aspects of each of the following products:
    a. A map that is an enlargement of a professionally drawn map.
    b. A short poem.
    c. An apron.
    d. A set of wooden whatnot shelves.
3. Five main types of rating scales cited by Wrightstone (1960, pp. 929–931) are descriptive scales, graphic scales, product scales, man-to-man rating scales, and numerical scales. Study each type and determine its merits as a means of gathering data about pupil achievement.
4. Time samples are defined as the observation of a pupil's behavior for definite, short periods of time and the recording of the occurrence or nonoccurrence of specific types of pupil behavior during each (Wrightstone, 1960, p. 928). How might this technique be used to determine the degree to which pupils have achieved specific social studies objectives in the affective domain?

OBSERVATION OF PROCEDURES

Techniques most often used in observation of procedures are ranking procedures, rating scales, check lists, and anecdotal records. Among the many variations of these techniques that have been developed are the following: (1) rating scales for evaluating speaking, (2) a check list for evaluating softball batting form, (3) a check list for recording skill in the use of a microscope, (4) a check list for reporting pupil behavior when engaged in group work, and (5) a sample anecdotal record concerning achievement in social studies.

Rating Scales for Speaking

The characteristics of speaking have been defined quite clearly. Among those usually listed are enunciation, pronunciation, loudness, word usage, rhythm, pitch, rate, and posture and movements. The skilled observer can separate one from another without much difficulty and, with appropriate rating scales, can record his judgments of the quality of a pupil's performance.

Typical of the graphic rating scales constructed and used by teachers are the pair shown in Figure 6, the first pertaining to enunciation and the second to pronunciation. Here only a three-point scale is used. If desired, they could be expanded to five points and appropriate descriptions added as required.

The descriptions beneath each number, though brief, are helpful. They add meaning to the numbers; as a result, the rating scales are improved. The space for comments is often an invaluable addition to the scale. Much useful specific information for evaluation and also remediation can be added. If desired, a tally of the frequency of a flaw in procedure can be added as in the case of the "agin" for "again" error in Scale B.

When a pupil is to deliver a prepared speech, some teachers prefer rating

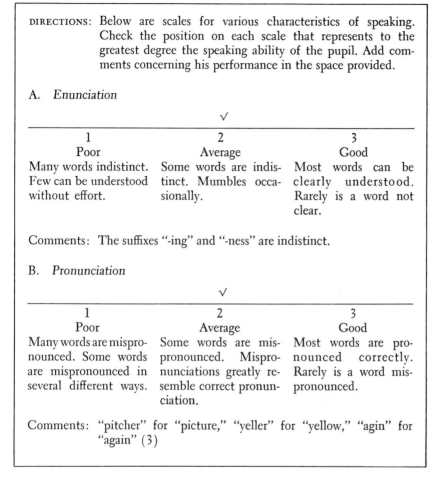

DIRECTIONS: Below are scales for various characteristics of speaking. Check the position on each scale that represents to the greatest degree the speaking ability of the pupil. Add comments concerning his performance in the space provided.

A.   *Enunciation*

1	2	3
Poor	Average	Good
Many words indistinct. Few can be understood without effort.	Some words are indistinct. Mumbles occasionally.	Most words can be clearly understood. Rarely is a word not clear.

Comments: The suffixes "-ing" and "-ness" are indistinct.

B.   *Pronunciation*

1	2	3
Poor	Average	Good
Many words are mispronounced. Some words are mispronounced in several different ways.	Some words are mispronounced. Mispronunciations greatly resemble correct pronunciation.	Most words are pronounced correctly. Rarely is a word mispronounced.

Comments: "pitcher" for "picture," "yeller" for "yellow," "agin" for "again" (3)

FIGURE 6.   Sample Rating Scales for Judging Speaking Ability

scales tailored more closely to this activity than a series such as that in Figure 6. For example, scales can be constructed for judging the effectiveness of such elements of the speech as the introduction used by the pupil, the body of the speech, the transition from topic to topic, and the conclusion. Added to these might be scales for judging of gestures and movements, eye contact, voice, and so forth.

Check List for Batting Form

Check lists and rating scales may not differ as much as descriptions of them would suggest. The "comments" sections frequently included in rating scales

Date   Rater's initials   Player's name _____
_____   _____   Captain's name _____

INSTRUCTIONS: Rate the player each time he bats. Place a tally mark in
the space which precedes the best description of play-
er's form in each of six categories. Indicate your observation of errors in the right-hand half of the page, again
with a tally mark. Write in any additional errors and add
comments below.

1. Grip   Errors
   _____ good   _____ Hands too far apart
   _____ fair   _____ Wrong hand on top
   _____ poor   _____ Hands too far from end of bat

2. Preliminary stance
   _____ good   _____ Stands too near plate
   _____ fair   _____ Stands too far away
   _____ poor   _____ Rear foot closer to plate than
                         _____   forward foot
                         _____ Stands too far forward
                         _____ Stands too far backward
                         _____ Bat not in readiness position

3. Stride or footwork
   _____ good   _____ Fails to step forward
   _____ fair   _____ Fails to transfer weight
   _____ poor   _____ Lifts back foot from ground

4. Pivot or body twist
   _____ good   _____ Fails to twist body
   _____ fair   _____ Fails to wind up
   _____ poor   _____ Has less than 90° of pivot

5. Arm movement or swing
   _____ good   _____ Arms held too close to body
   _____ fair   _____ Rear elbow held too far up
   _____ poor   _____ Bat not held parallel to ground

6. General (Eyes on ball, judgment of pitcher, etc.)
   _____ good   _____ Jerky action
   _____ fair   _____ Tries too hard
   _____ poor   _____ Poor selection of bat
                         _____ Lacks confidence

From Scott and French, 1945; reproduced by permission of A. S. Barnes and Company.

FIGURE 7.   Sample Check List for Softball Batting Form

allow space in which the observer can note specific features of the pupil's behavior; in a check list the most common of these features would be listed and, hence, checked only when appropriate. On the other hand, some check lists include crude representations of continua much like those found in rating scales.

An illustration of a check list that is based in part on a series of rating scales is that shown in Figure 7. This is designed to record observations of batting form (Scott and French, 1945, p. 168). Each time a pupil bats, an observer checks "good," "fair," or "poor" with respect to his grip, stance, stride, pivot, and swing. Then the observer checks in the right-hand column the errors that are committed. The list of errors is expanded if necessary. An experienced observer can complete such a check list as this very quickly and with acceptable accuracy.

Check List for Operation of a Microscope

One of the most widely known check lists is that devised by Tyler (1930) for use in reporting a pupil's ability to use a microscope. It is shown in Figure 8. Although the check list as such may have only limited application in a secondary school science program, it is interesting because it represents a high degree of development in the use of check lists and can serve as a pattern for the construction of additional lists.

The teacher observes operation of a microscope by a pupil who is attempting to find a specified substance present in a culture. All needed materials such as slides, cheesecloth, and lens paper are provided. As the pupil attacks the problem, the teacher records the sequence of actions by numbering them as they occur. He also checks the most obvious characteristics of the pupil's behavior and his mount and the skills in which he needs further training.

The numbers and checks in Figure 8 serve as a description of the pupil's efforts to complete the exercise. Not only does the teacher know that the pupil failed in this case, but he also knows the errors he made. All important desirable and undesirable actions that he made and the order in which he made them are a matter of record. Also shown are some of the intervening directions that he might have been given, such as "Find the object under low power" (see aaa in Figure 8).

Check List for Behavior in Group Work

Teachers frequently want to determine whether their pupils are acquiring and practicing desirable social habits and attitudes. Some of these are revealed when the pupils are engaged in committee and group work. Of interest in these instances are such pupil behaviors as willingness to cooperate, volunteer-

	Student's actions	Sequence of actions
a.	Takes slide	1
b.	Wipes slide with lens paper	2
c.	Wipes slide with cloth	
d.	Wipes slide with finger	
e.	Moves bottle of culture along the table	
f.	Places drop or two of culture on slide	3
g.	Adds more culture	
h.	Adds few drops of water	
i.	Hunts for cover glasses	4
j.	Wipes cover glass with lens paper	5
k.	Wipes cover with cloth	
l.	Wipes cover with finger	
m.	Adjusts cover with finger	
n.	Wipes off surplus fluid	
o.	Places slide on stage	6
p.	Looks through eyepiece with right eye	
q.	Looks through eyepiece with left eye	7
r.	Turns to objective of lowest power	9
s.	Turns to low-power objective	21
t.	Turns to high-power objective	
u.	Holds one eye closed	8
v.	Looks for light	
w.	Adjusts concave mirror	
x.	Adjusts plane mirror	
y.	Adjusts diaphragm	
z.	Does not touch diaphragm	10
aa.	With eye at eyepiece turns down coarse adjustment	11
ab.	Breaks cover glass	12
ac.	Breaks slide	
ad.	With eye away from eyepiece turns down coarse adjustment	
ae.	Turns up coarse adjustment a great distance	13, 22
af.	With eye at eyepiece turns down fine adjustment a great distance	14, 23
ag.	With eye away from eyepiece turns down fine adjustment a great distance	15
ah.	Turns up fine adjustment screw a great distance	
ai.	Turns fine adjustment screw a few turns	
aj.	Removes slide from stage	16
ak.	Wipes objective with lens paper	
al.	Wipes objective with cloth	
am.	Wipes objective with finger	17
an.	Wipes eyepiece with lens paper	
ao.	Wipes eyepiece with cloth	
ap.	Wipes eyepiece with finger	18
aq.	Makes another mount	
ar.	Takes another microscope	
as.	Finds object	
at.	Pauses for an interval	

Student's actions	Sequence of actions
au. Asks, "What do you want me to do?"	
av. Asks whether to use high power	
aw. Says, "I'm satisfied"	
ax. Says that the mount is all right for his eye	
ay. Says he cannot do it	19, 24
az. Told to start new mount	
aaa. Directed to find object under low power	20
aab. Directed to find object under high power	

Skills in which student needs further training

a. In cleaning objective	√
b. In cleaning eyepiece	√
c. In focusing low power	√
d. In focusing high power	√
e. In adjusting mirror	√
f. In using diaphragm	√
g. In keeping both eyes open	√
h. In protecting slide and objective from breaking by careless focusing	√

Noticeable characteristics of student's behavior

a. Awkward in movements	
b. Obviously dexterous in movements	
c. Slow and deliberate	√
d. Very rapid	
e. Fingers tremble	
f. Obviously perturbed	
g. Obviously angry	
h. Does not take work seriously	
i. Unable to work without specific directions	√
j. Obviously satisfied with his unsuccessful efforts	√

Characterization of the student's mount

a. Poor light	√
b. Poor focus	
c. Excellent mount	
d. Good mount	
e. Fair mount	
f. Poor mount	
g. Very poor mount	
h. Nothing in view but a thread in his eyepiece	
i. Something on objective	
j. Smeared lens	√
k. Unable to find object	√

From Tyler, 1930; reproduced by permission of the Bureau of Educational Research and Service, Ohio State University.

FIGURE 8.   Check List for Reporting Skill in Using a Microscope

	BEHAVIOR	YES	NO	UNCERTAIN
DIRECTIONS:	Below are eight kinds of behavior that a pupil might display when participating in committee or group work. Check "Yes" if it occurred; check "No" if it did not. If the evidence available is insufficient or conflicting, check "Uncertain."			

BEHAVIOR	YES	NO	UNCERTAIN
1. Starts working promptly			
2. Volunteers for assignments			
3. Displays interest			
4. Cooperates with other pupils			
5. Displays cheerfulness			
6. Makes worthwhile suggestions			
7. Is a follower occasionally			
8. Is a leader occasionally			

FIGURE 9.   Sample Check List for Reporting Pupil Behavior in Group Work

ing for duties, making worthwhile suggestions, and displaying democratic leadership. To provide a situation in which these behaviors can be displayed, a committee of pupils is formed to perform some tasks, such as drawing a map of the playground or planning class observance of a national holiday. The behaviors displayed can be recorded on a check list.

A sample check list of the kind that might be used in these situations is shown in Figure 9. Eight kinds of behaviors are listed. The teacher is to check whether each occurred. Should the evidence be insufficient or conflicting, he checks the category labeled "Uncertain." Observe that this category is not a middle position between "Yes" and "No." Instead it is a position that indicates that the teacher is unable to make a judgment for any number of reasons. Perhaps the pupil has no opportunity to display the behavior in question throughout the period that the committee is at work. Perhaps the teacher is unable to observe the pupil as long as he desires. Perhaps the pupil behaved inconsistently. The last might be the subject of anecdotal records that would then supplement the check list.

Anecdotal Record in Social Studies

Recording observations of spontaneous procedures is seldom an easy task. Yet much of this behavior is very indicative of learning already acquired, and hence it cannot be ignored. The anecdotal record reports the principal details of the procedures observed, and when a series of them is available concerning related procedures, interesting insights into learning can be gained.

The sample anecdotal record shown in Figure 10 concerns a comparatively shy junior high school boy who surprised his teacher by insisting that he make his oral report to a social studies class as scheduled, even though he had accidentally left his written notes at home. His level of performance revealed an unusual degree of knowledge and interest in his topic and offered possible clues with regard to ways to involve him to a greater degree in future classroom discussions. Notice the factual nature of the description of the incident as contrasted with the interpretive nature of the comments that follow it.

This case of pupil behavior differs from those previously considered in this chapter. In speaking, batting, and microscope skill, the observer is interested in the efficiency and accuracy with which the procedure is executed. These, too, might be the subjects of anecdotal records. Here, however, the observer is primarily concerned with the fact that this behavior happened at all. In other words, a helpful insight into a pupil's achievement in social studies is obtained by noting what he did and how he reacted to it rather than the level of quality of specific features of his behavior. For example, whether he enunciated clearly or had well-organized material for his oral report is not so important.

Problems

5. Construct a graphic rating scale to use as a basis for reporting a pupil procedure in a subject matter area of interest to you.

6. Would the check list for reporting pupil behavior in group work shown in Figure 9 be improved if a column entitled "Sometimes" were inserted between the "Yes" and "No" columns and the directions changed appropriately? Why?

7. Using the anecdotal record shown in Figure 10 as an example, list the inherent limitations present in this reporting technique.

JUDGING OF PRODUCTS

Ranking procedures, rating scales (including score cards), and product scales are popular means by which pupil products are studied. As illustrations of some of the many possibilities offered by these techniques, four instruments are shown here: (1) rating scales for theme analysis, (2) rating scales for judging pupil success in fastening pieces of wood with nails, (3) score cards for food products, and (4) product scales used for judging handwriting specimens.

ANECDOTAL RECORD FORM

Date: November 16, 1971   Pupil's Name: Fred Burke

Observer: R. S. Rover

Description of Incident:

Fred was scheduled to make an oral report to the class concerning cattle branding. Although he forgot his notes, he did not want a postponement. He specifically requested that he report as planned.

He spoke extemporaneously and used the blackboard repeatedly to sketch the various brands he mentioned. Much information was presented, including references to the history of the American West. The class was unusually attentive.

Comment:

This was by far the best report he has given. For the first time he was visibly pleased with his efforts. He evidently knows much about the history of the early West, and enjoys talking about it.

FIGURE 10.   Sample Anecdotal Record Pertaining to Achievement in Social Studies.

Rating Scales for Themes

Many subjects occasionally require a largely original written product of the pupil. English courses are—and should be—especially demanding in this respect. The well-known English theme calls upon the pupil to select a topic, arrange its subparts in a suitable manner, and develop them in appropriate written form. From a measurement point of view, a theme is both an important and a complex product.

The complex nature of a theme makes its evaluation difficult. To overcome this problem, some teachers divide the characteristics of a theme into two categories, content and matters of form and style. The content categories include the selection of the topic (if topics are not assigned), organization, and the quantity and quality of investigation. The form and style category includes the elements of grammar, punctuation, vocabulary, spelling, capitalization, division of words, documentation, and so forth.

The relative importance of the two categories and their respective subparts no doubt varies radically from teacher to teacher, depending on the purpose of the theme and the maturity of the pupil. For example, themes in a social studies class should be scrutinized more carefully in terms of content than form and style. The reverse may be true for most themes in an English class. In addition, the subparts of a category, such as the quantity and quality

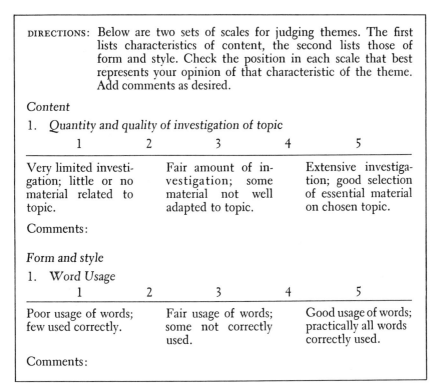

DIRECTIONS: Below are two sets of scales for judging themes. The first lists characteristics of content, the second lists those of form and style. Check the position in each scale that best represents your opinion of that characteristic of the theme. Add comments as desired.

Content

1. *Quantity and quality of investigation of topic*

    1   2   3   4   5

Very limited investigation; little or no material related to topic.	Fair amount of investigation; some material not well adapted to topic.	Extensive investigation; good selection of essential material on chosen topic.

Comments:

Form and style

1. Word Usage

    1   2   3   4   5

Poor usage of words; few used correctly.	Fair usage of words; some not correctly used.	Good usage of words; practically all words correctly used.

Comments:

FIGURE 11.   Sample Rating Scales for Judging Themes.

of investigation of the topic and the documentation of the theme, will probably lose importance when one is judging themes from lower grade levels.

Sample rating scales for themes are shown in Figure 11. Only two are shown, one from each category. Notice that these are five-point scales although only three descriptions are included. An observer vacillating between two of the positions for which descriptions are available may want to select the intermediate position. A series of similar scales for other characteristics in each category can be developed.

Further suggestions for analyzing themes have been prepared by Dressel and Mayhew (1954), whose handbook contains themes of varying quality together with analyses of them. In addition, principles for analyzing themes are discussed. These include: (1) judging a theme according to the nature of the assignment, (2) judging it in terms of the pupil's purposes, and (3) judging it according to neglected opportunities for more effective writing. Although this handbook is oriented toward higher education, it can be helpful to secondary school teachers.

Diederich (1964) suggests two sets of five-point rating scales that could be used for judging English compositions. One category deals with general merit and has four scales: (1) quality and development of ideas, (2) organization, relevance, and movement, (3) style, flavor, and individuality, and (4) wording and phrasing. The other deals with mechanics, and its four scales are (1) grammar and sentence structure, (2) punctuation and capitalization, (3) spelling, and (4) handwriting and neatness.

Some doubt exists as to the need for sets of criteria such as those mentioned in this section. There is little evidence that they are consistently used (Fostvedt, 1965). Moreover, other investigations have established that a fast impressionistic reading of essays by several qualified readers is a reliable method of measuring pupil writing ability (Godshalk, 1966). This method requires the readers of themes and essays to make "global or holistic" judgments of each paper rather than analytical judgments. The theme is read quickly for total impressions and given one of three ratings: a score of "3" for a superior paper, "2" for an average paper, and "1" for an inferior paper.

Attempts to grade essays by means of a computer are described in connection with procedures for scoring responses to essay test questions (see page 177). This work is promising. If the computer can consistently appraise writing ability as well as competent judges or better, we have made a significant breakthrough in our ability to evaluate this important work product.

Rating Scales for Shop Products

Many shop products must conform to prescribed dimensions and, as a result, mechanical devices can be used as one means of determining their quality. For instance, rulers, combination squares, calipers, and gauges of various kinds are employed in this process. In a very direct manner, one or more measurements are obtained that reveal the success or failure of the pupil to develop a product of a certain size, with certain proportions, or within certain tolerance limits.

Helpful as mechanical devices are, they are not capable of measuring all of the important characteristics of a shop product. Anyone who has carefully examined wood, metal, or plastic shop products realizes that two such products may have nearly identical dimensions, but still differ noticeably in workmanship. Characteristics such as esthetic attractiveness, strength, finish, design, and neatness must be judged by other techniques.

A set of numerical rating scales reported by Adkins (1947, p. 231) for fastening edges of pieces of wood with nails is shown in Figure 12. Many of these scales are related to the characteristics of strength, attractiveness, and neatness mentioned in the foregoing paragraph. For example, the splitting, spacing, and utility scales are a part of the strength characteristic; the hammer marks and depth scales are a part of the attractiveness and neatness characteristics.

(1)	Straightness	1	2	3	4	5	6	7	8	9	10
		Are nails driven straight, heads square with wood, no evidence of bending?									
(2)	Hammer marks	1	2	3	4	5	6	7	8	9	10
		Is wood free of hammer marks around nails?									
(3)	Splitting	1	2	3	4	5	6	7	8	9	10
		Is wood free of splits radiating from nail holes?									
(4)	Depth	1	2	3	4	5	6	7	8	9	10
		Are depths of nails uniform and of pleasing appearance?									
(5)	Spacing	1	2	3	4	5	6	7	8	9	10
		Are nails spaced too close or too far apart?									
(6)	Utility	1	2	3	4	5	6	7	8	9	10
		Will the nails hold?									

From Adkins, 1947; reproduced by permission of D. C. Adkins.

FIGURE 12.   Sample Rating Scales for Fastening.

Notice that a ten-point scale is given for each factor. It is quite possible that a teacher will find that he is unable to identify this many degrees of quality. If he finds that fewer than ten points will suffice, the scale should be so revised. Also notice that, unlike the other rating scales included in this chapter, these scales contain a question as a part of each scale and no brief descriptions of the positions. Whether this format is an improvement is for you to decide. Perhaps both techniques could be used to advantage.

Scorecards for Food Products

An extensive study of pupil achievement in home economics programs has been done by Arny (1953). Since food preparation is an important part of these programs, and since food products are excellent representations of a pupil's achievement, she and others developed a set of food scorecards.

There are 57 different cards in each set. Practically every food product

		1	2	3	Score
		MUFFINS (Plain)			35
Appearance	1.	Not symmetrical	Symmetrical		1. _____
	2.	Peaked or knobbed top	Definitely rounded top		2. _____
	3.	Smooth surface	Pebbled surface		3. _____
Color: Exterior	4.	Dark brown, pale, or uneven	Golden brown		4. _____
Interior	5.	Yellow spots or evidence of unmixed flour	Creamy white		5. _____
Moisture Content	6.	Dry or soggy	Slightly moist		6.
Texture	7.	Large holes or tunnels or very compact	Medium size, fairly uniform holes		7.
Lightness	8.	Heavy	Light		8.
Tenderness of Crust	9.	Hard or tough	Tender		9.
Taste and Flavor	10.	Flat or unpleasant flavor of certain ingredients	Pleasing flavor		10. _____

SCORE _____

From Arny, 1946; reproduced by permission of the University of Minnesota and the Educational Testing Service.

FIGURE 13.   Scorecard for Plain Muffins.

that a pupil might prepare in the foods laboratory is included. Typical of the scorecards is that for plain muffins shown in Figure 13.

The muffins are judged on the basis of seven important characteristics, one of which has three subparts, another two. Each characteristic or subpart is rated in terms of a three-point scale; thus ten scores are obtained. The two extremes of each scale are described, one based on an improperly prepared product, the second on a standard product. After the ten scores have been determined, they are added to obtain a total score. The scorecards increase the objectivity of the study. In addition, they require very little scoring time. Finally, they can be used as a teaching device in that the pupils can, by studying the cards, learn the important characteristics of a standard product.

Product Scales for Handwriting

Two styles of writing are generally taught in the elementary school. One is the manuscript style, in which the letters are disconnected and made in a form similar to printed letters. The other is the cursive style, in which the letters of each word are connected. The general practice is to teach manuscript writing first, and then change to cursive writing at about the third grade.

The easiest way to gather information about pupil achievement in handwriting, whether manuscript or cursive style, is to examine specimens that have been obtained under controlled conditions. Both speed and quality can be determined. The speed or rate at which pupils write is the more easily measured of the two. Quality can be defined in many ways. Thorndike, who built the first scale for measuring quality of handwriting, interpreted quality to mean beauty, legibility, and character. Ayres, whose scale is shown in part in Figure 14, considered quality to mean legibility only.

Speed of handwriting can be measured by a teacher-made test if it is carefully administered. First the teacher selects a simple statement such as "Mary had a little lamb" or "The quick brown fox jumps over the lazy dog." The statement should be so simple that it can be easily memorized; it should have no unusual words or expressions that will in any way hinder the pupil in his speed test. After the statement has been memorized by the pupils, they are told that, when given a signal, they should start to write the statement as well and as rapidly as they can, and continue to do so until told to stop. Either two or three minutes are allowed. The number of letters written by each pupil is counted and divided by the number of minutes allowed.

One of the most widely used scales for measuring the quality of handwriting is the *Ayres Measuring Scale for Handwriting, Gettysburg Edition* (1915). Before the scale can be used, the pupils must be thoroughly familiar with the first three sentences of Lincoln's Gettysburg Address. Then they are given two minutes in which to copy them. To determine quality, each pupil's handwriting specimen is then compared with a scaled series of printed samples. There are eight samples in all, four of which are included in Figure 14. The comparison is made by sliding each specimen along the scale until a printed sample of the same or very similar quality is found. The number above this sample is the value assigned to the pupil's specimen. The numbers increase as the quality of the specimen improves. This scale is designed for elementary school pupils and contains only cursive writing samples. Rate scores can be obtained in the same manner as described earlier.

Teachers have not been able to get consistent results when using product scales to study handwriting samples (Feldt, 1962). To improve this situation, at least three handwriting samples should be obtained independently from each pupil and the ratings averaged. This can be repeated each time pupil growth is to be checked in this area of achievement.

Problem

8. Seventh-grade pupils in social studies were required to draw a map showing the principal rivers and lakes in their home state. They were allowed to refer to, but not copy directly, printed maps. The following graphic rating scales were to be used first by each pupil and then by the teacher to judge the product of his efforts. Revise these scales in any manner that, in your opinion, will strengthen them.

MEASURING SCALE FOR HANDWRITING

20	40	70	90

Russell Sage Foundation
130 East 22d Street, New York 10, N.Y.
SCALE BY LEONARD P. AYRES

FIGURE 14.   Sample Scales from Ayres Measuring Scale for Handwriting.

From Ayres, 1915; reproduced by permission of the Educational Testing Service.

RATING SCALE

5	4	3	2	1
Very neat	neat	fairly neat	somewhat messy	messy
Words are printed not written	printed	some words might not be printed	written	written
Has title and key	Both title and key	Might lack correct title or key	Might lack title or key	Lacks both
Has shown rivers and lakes most clearly	Has shown all rivers and lakes	Lacks one or two required items	Lacks several items	Lacks a lot of items
Turned in at required time	Turned in at required time	One day late	More than one day late	More than one day late

RELIABILITY OF JUDGING PUPIL PERFORMANCE

It is clear that judging pupil performance is an integral part of the total pupil evaluation program conducted by a teacher; it is also one of the most difficult. It is typically less objective and organized than paper-and-pencil testing, and sometimes less satisfying to both teacher and pupil. Many of these problems are associated directly with a serious weakness of judging performance, that is, its relatively high degree of unreliability. A high degree of unreliability means that the procedures frequently yield inconsistent results.

This can be traced both to the performance evaluated and to the observer. In other words, the reliability of the process is directly related to the degree of successful sampling of pupil performance and the consistency of the observer in judging that performance.

Sampling Pupil Performances

Sampling pupil performances is necessarily limited in scope. How many times is it possible for a pupil to deliver a prepared speech, build a pair of bookends, or cut out and sew an apron? The teacher may have only one or two opportunities to observe these performances, and they may not take place under conditions that he can control as much as he would like. Yet he must assume that they are typical representations of pupil achievement.

Some pupil products require considerable quantities of both class and out-of-class time in which to be completed. As a result, unauthorized assistance by a second party is likely. The product then becomes much less useful in terms of judging pupil achievement in that it is a poor sample of his work.

Ideally, then, the teacher should have at least several opportunities to observe an important pupil performance. Such samples should truly reflect the pupil's achievement and his alone, and should take place under suitable conditions.

Observer Reliability

Fatigue, boredom, and indifference can destroy the worth of the observer's attempts to examine pupil performance. To eliminate these factors, the teacher can preplan his observations as much as possible, being certain that he spreads them out over a reasonable period of time. On the other hand, since these and other factors can never be eliminated, multiple observation is desirable. This means that, in the case of judging of procedures, several competent teachers should observe independently, then reconcile any differences that exist. In the case of judging of products, several persons can participate, or one can judge the product more than once without knowledge of earlier decisions.

Unfortunately, consistent results yielded by efforts to judge a pupil's performance do not necessarily mean that a proper analysis has been made. After all, the observer or even a team of observers could be consistently wrong. This, of course, is unlikely if the observers are reasonably competent. On the other hand, such factors as the well-known "halo effect," so often present in efforts of this kind, can make the analyses more consistent but less accurate. For improvement of observer reliability, well-defined reference points are needed. In the case of procedures, these may be careful descriptions of the important aspects of various degrees of quality; in the case of products, they may be a variety of specimen products of known quality.

Use of Performance Tests to Improve Reliability

Performance tests of considerable complexity are sometimes used for improving the quality of procedures and product evaluation. These are tests in which some criterion situation (for example, a job) is simulated to a higher degree than is represented by the usual paper-and-pencil test (Fitzpatrick and Morrison, 1970). On the basis of a careful analysis of the educational objectives in question, a great effort is made to design a realistic situation for the examinee within which he can demonstrate his skills.

As mentioned in Chapter 4, considerable success in this regard has been achieved in medical education (see page 150). Furthermore, standardized group situations and observational techniques are being used for evaluation purposes as a part of the National Assessment of Educational Progress (Campbell and Nichols, 1968).

With thorough planning, we can design highly useful performance tests in physical education, foreign languages, industrial arts, music, and many areas of vocational education. Such tests typically combine appropriate equipment arranged in a true-to-life environment with a set of explicit instructions to the examinee. These permit a trained observer to use specially designed rating scales or check lists to report the quality of performance with a comparatively high degree of reliability. The improved reliability is well worth the effort.

Problems

9. It has been recommended that, as an aid in judging of pupil compositions properly, files of various sorts of pupils' writing should be kept from year to year (Burrows, 1959, pp. 27–28). Speculate as to how this system might be organized. Do you think that this procedure would improve the reliability of judging writing ability to any appreciable degree?

10. The closer that a performance test approaches the real criterion situation it simulates, the more likely that the reliability of the measurement of pupil performance will *decrease* (Fitzpatrick and Morrison, 1970). What causes this?

JUDGING BY PUPILS

Pupils as well as teachers can judge performances—their own and also those of their classmates. For example, an audience of pupils can rate a speaker, and he can rate himself. In a food laboratory, all pupils including the cook can examine the roast that is prepared. A pupil who submits a specimen of handwriting can arrive at his own judgment of its merits by following the same procedures the teacher follows.

Much can be said for this type of multiple evaluation as a learning experience. When both pupils and teacher use the same instruments to judge the same performance simultaneously, and the results are examined, the pupils gain a much better perspective of the important features of the performance and the teacher's standards concerning them. Particularly informative is the comparison of the self-evaluation by the pupil with that made independently by his teacher. Certainly the diagnosis of defects and their causes as well as remediation can be based on such a conference. Most important to the pupil is the realistic view of his achievement that he gains.

From the point of view of sound principles of evaluation, there are serious objections to using the pupils' judgments or a composite of them in reporting pupil achievement. Certainly we cannot assume that the average pupil is as competent a judge of the quality of another's performance or of his own as the teacher. This automatically reduces the value of pupil observations to a point where they are normally of minor importance. The successful observer has a maturity of judgment and sense of impartiality rarely found in pupils. Pupils should be regularly allowed to gain experience in observing, but they should not be expected to make sound judgments with great consistency unless carefully trained.

Problem

11. Some teachers believe that, as pupils become skilled in self-evaluation, they actually raise the standards on which evaluations are made. Do you agree? Why?

SUMMARY

Some of the educational objectives for elementary and secondary school are such that paper-and-pencil measuring instruments cannot reveal the degree to which pupils have achieved them. These goals pertain to pupil performances such as the ability to deliver a speech, write a paragraph, conduct an experiment, or hem a garment. Generally they are quite complex, involving both language and nonlanguage aspects, and are a part of the psychomotor domain.

Judgments of pupil performance can be based on the procedure displayed by the pupil or the products yielded by the procedure. Both have some characteristics that lend themselves readily to measurement and some that do not. Efficiency and accuracy are the easiest procedure characteristics to measure. Product characteristics can often be measured more easily; in fact, mechanical devices are available for this purpose for such articles as shop products.

The instruments used in judging procedures and products are primarily of the nontesting type. For procedures, ranking and rating methods, check lists, and anecdotal records are frequently applied. Illustrations of these are rating scales for speaking, a check list for softball batting form, a check list for the operation of a microscope, a check list for pupil behavior during group work, and an anecdotal record reflecting achievement in social studies. For products, ranking and rating methods and product scales are used. Illustrations of these are rating scales for theme analysis, rating scales for determining pupil success in fastening pieces of wood with nails, score cards for food products, and product scales for handwriting specimens. In all cases a competent observer is needed.

Performance evaluation is not always reliable because pupil performance is not always successfully sampled and the observer not always consistent. Repeated sampling of pupil performances and independent observations by one or more qualified teachers increase the reliability of the process. When pupils judge their own performances or those of their classmates, they gain excellent experience in this process, although their attempts seldom produce superior evaluative data.

Suggested Readings

Ahmann, J. S., M. D. Glock, and H. L. Wardeberg. *Evaluating elementary school pupils.* Boston: Allyn and Bacon, 1960. Chapters 11, 12, and 13.
  The three chapters cited deal with appraisal in the language arts, mathematics, and the content areas, respectively. A number of rating scales and check lists to be used with elementary school pupils are shown.

Arny, C. B. *Evaluation in home economics.* New York: Appleton-Century-Crofts, 1953. Chapter 7.
  Techniques suitable for judging pupil performance in home economics are discussed in this chapter. They include rating scales, check lists, and anecdotal records. Illustrations are given of one or more of these techniques in the areas of foods and nutrition, textiles and clothing, and family relationships.

Dressel, P. L., and others. *Evaluation in higher education.* Boston: Houghton Mifflin, 1961. Chapter 7.
  Rating scales for judging pupil writing and speaking ability are shown. Ranking techniques are mentioned briefly.

Fitzpatrick, R., and E. J. Morrison. Performance and product evaluation. In R. L. Thorndike (ed.), *Educational measurement.* (2nd ed.) Washington: American Council on Education, 1970. Chapter 9.
  Performance tests to measure achievement are described, and a wide variety of illustrations of them is given. Steps for developing and scoring performance tests are presented.

Godshalk, F. I., and others. *The measurement of writing ability.* New York: College Entrance Examination Board, 1966. Chapters 1 and 2.
  The first two chapters of this research report describe the problem of measuring writing ability and the measuring devices to be tested. Of particular interest are the illustrations of the objective test items and interlinear exercises used to measure writing ability indirectly. A short description of the "global" or "holistic" method of scoring essays is included.

Madaus, G. F., and R. M. Rippey. Zeroing in on the STEP writing test: What does it tell a teacher? *Journal of Educational Measurement,* 1966, **3**, 19–25.
  An attempt was made to determine the degree of validity of the STEP writing test by comparing scores on it with scores on writing assignments. The seven composition rating scales used are included in the report.

Wrightstone, J. W. Observational techniques. In C. W. Harris (ed.), *Encyclopedia of educational research*. (3rd ed.) London: Macmillan, 1960. Pp. 927–933.
  Research on observational techniques of all kinds is summarized. Separate sections are devoted to time samples, rating methods, and anecdotal records.

References Cited

Adkins, D. C. *Construction and analysis of achievement tests*. Washington: U.S. Civil Service Commission, 1947.

Arny, C. B. *Evaluation in home economics*. New York: Appleton-Century-Crofts, 1953.

Arny, C. B., and others. *Minnesota food scorecards*. (Rev. ed.) Minneapolis: University of Minnesota, 1946.

Ayres, L. P. *Ayres measuring scale for handwriting, Gettysburg edition*. Distributed by the Cooperative Test Division of the Educational Testing Service, 1915.

Burrows, A. T. *Teaching composition*. What Research Says to the Teacher, No. 18. Washington: National Education Association, 1959.

Campbell, V. N., and D. G. Nichols. National assessment of citizenship education. *Social Education*, 1968, **32**, 279–281.

Diederich, P. B. Problems and possibilities of research in the teaching of English. In *Research design and the teaching of English*, Proceedings of Conference of National Council of Teachers of English. Champaign, Ill.: National Council of Teachers of English, 1964.

Dressel, P. L., and L. B. Mayhew. *Handbook for theme analysis*. Dubuque, Iowa: Wm. C. Brown, 1954.

Feldt, L. S. The reliability of measures of handwriting quality. *Journal of Educational Psychology*, 1962, **53**, 288–292.

Fitzpatrick, R., and E. J. Morrison. Performance and product evaluation. In R. L. Thorndike (ed.), *Educational measurement*. (2nd ed.) Washington: American Council on Education, 1970. Chapter 9.

Fostvedt, D. R. Criteria for the evaluation of high school English composition. *Journal of Educational Research*, 1965, **59**, 108–112.

Godshalk, F. I., and others. *The measurement of writing ability*. New York: College Entrance Examination Board, 1966.

Scott, M. G., and E. French. *Better teaching through testing*. New York: A. S. Barnes, 1945.

Tyler, R. W. A test of skill in using a microscope. *Educational Research Bulletin*, 1930, **9**, 493–496.

Wrightstone, J. W. Observational techniques. In C. W. Harris (ed.), *Encyclopedia of educational research*. (3rd ed.) London: Macmillan, 1960. Pp. 927–933.

PART THREE

Characteristics of a Good Measuring Instrument

An unknown wit of several generations ago remarked that the only good thing about error was that it created jobs. The truth of this can be demonstrated in many areas including pupil evaluation. All of our measuring instruments are somewhat inadequate, a number of them to an appreciable degree. To reduce error, the builders of these instruments are striving constantly to refine their products; this is, in a sense, an endless job. These efforts in turn complicate the problems of those who must choose from among many available measuring instruments the ones that are best suited for a particular need. Each new instrument means a repetition of the job of selection by anyone needing an instrument of that type.

The classroom teacher may find himself cast in either or both of the following roles: in one case, he may be constructing a paper-and-pencil achievement test to measure the academic achievement of his pupils; in a second, he may be a member of a teacher committee organized to select a scholastic aptitude or standardized achievement test to be used as a part of the school testing program. In either case the teacher needs standards. He must be familiar with the characteristics of a good measuring instrument and the methods of determining the degree to which a given instrument may possess them.

The characteristics of a good measuring instrument can be classified in many different ways. Here they are grouped under three headings: norms, validity, and reliability. These three headings identify the three chapters that compose Part Three. In Chapter 8, "Using Test Scores and Norms," the need for an instrument to yield information that is easily understood and utilized is discussed. This need is ordinarily satisfied by the computing of norms, that is, by identifying the relative performance of a pupil in terms of a group of pupils much like him. Chapter 9, "The Validity of Measurement Methods," is devoted to the most important of the three characteristics. A measuring instrument is valid to the degree that it serves the purpose or purposes for which its use is intended. In Chapter 10, "The Reliability of Measurement Methods," the need for an instrument to yield consistent or dependable information is discussed. An instrument that strongly reflects this characteristic will yield virtually the same information each time it is used in an unchanging situation.

Some statistical methodology must be introduced to describe these characteristics and how they are measured. The arithmetic mean, the median, the standard deviation, and the product-moment coefficient of correlation are discussed at appropriate points in Part Three. In Appendix A is an additional explanation of these statistical measures, as well as a step-by-step description of the easiest means of computing each. Although classroom teachers are seldom required to compute such values, they are often required to interpret them in connection with the validity, reliability, and norm determinations found in test manuals and educational literature.

The purpose of Part Three is to identify the characteristics of a good measuring instrument, to illustrate the most common methods of determining how strongly a specific instrument reflects them, and to provide an adequate background for those statistical techniques commonly used in such determinations. The importance of Part Three can hardly be overemphasized.

CHAPTER 8

Using Test Scores and Norms

Early every morning, practically every radio station in the United States broadcasts a summary of the weather conditions in the locality at that moment and as they probably will be for the remainder of the day. Typical of the kind of announcement that might be heard on a morning in mid-April is the following:

> The temperature at 7:00 A.M. this morning was 50° F., the barometric pressure was 29.8, the wind velocity was 10 to 20 miles per hour from the northwest, and the relative humidity was 70 percent. Today will be cloudy and mild, with a high temperature of about 60° F. The probability of measurable precipitation today is 5 percent.

To most listeners, this report, brief as it is, is useful. As he prepares for the day's activities the informed citizen can readily decide such questions as whether he should wear a spring topcoat rather than a winter overcoat, make his son of preschool age button his woolen sweater before leaving the house, or plan an early season golf or tennis match.

The teacher, while he has the common interest in the weather report, may well ponder two additional features of this interpretation to the public of meteorological conditions. These features are involved in the teacher's attempts at describing a pupil to a parent.

In the first place, the complexity of the entity being described is almost overwhelming. A one-word description in either case would be unhappily inadequate. Multiple measurements are involved in a weather report or well-designed school testing program.

The second feature is the meaning of the measurements when they are reported to a relatively uninformed audience. Here the meteorologist has an advantage over the educator. Each of us learns at a tender age that temperatures in the vicinity of 70° F are comfortable, whereas those in excess of 90° F and less than 60° F tend to be uncomfortable unless appropriate adjustments in dress or physical activity are made. A barometric pressure is almost automatically compared to 30 inches of mercury, the ordinary barometric pressure at sea level. Wind velocities of less than 10 miles per hour are conceded to be practically unnoticeable; velocities between 30 and 75 miles per hour are called gales. Little more need be said to prepare most individuals for the weather. These facts are understood.

Teachers may envy the meteorologist's ability to present succinct, understandable descriptions of something as intricate as the weather. Although the meteorologist has not achieved perfection in his efforts, he can point to notable success. A teacher may well question whether those same individuals who seem to comprehend so much of a brief report on the day's weather would understand comparable amounts of a report on the academic achievement of their child that day in school.

Although the comparison of the teacher's position with that of the meteorologist may appear far-fetched, it is thought-provoking. Certainly one of the reasons why the teacher has difficulty is that his units of measurement are not so meaningful as degrees Fahrenheit or miles per hour. In order to make their measurements more meaningful, people seriously concerned with pupil evaluation pay considerable attention to the nature of test scores and their interpretation.

RAW SCORES

The difficulty of meaningfully presenting the results yielded by educational measurement has many illustrations. Assume, for example, that a battery of standardized achievement tests is administered to the pupils in all of the tenth grades of a city school system. One is a vocabulary test composed of 100 words, the meanings of which have to be identified by each pupil. The success of each pupil is then expressed in terms of the number of words correctly identified. Therefore, for each of the 360 pupils who wrote the vocabulary test, a numerical representation of his effort is available, and it can be no smaller than zero nor larger than 100.

Let us consider for a moment the position of a teacher whose pupils are involved in the testing program. One of his pupils correctly identified the meaning of 58 of the 100 words. Hence the teacher records a "58." This he properly calls a *raw score*, that is, the quantitative report that is the immediate end product of scoring the test. In the case of this test and many others like it, each pupil is credited with one point for every correct answer and zero points for any wrong or omitted answer. To be sure, the amount of credit could have varied for each right answer, increasing to two points or more as the words became more difficult. Furthermore, correction for guessing on the part of the pupil could have been made by subtracting points for wrong answers. Had either or both of these procedures been used, the result of the scoring process would still be called a raw score.

Simply labeling the "58" as one of many raw scores does not answer other questions concerning this representation of degree of success. For example, the teacher may wonder whether 58 indicates that this pupil's vocabulary of words is twice as great as that of a pupil whose score on the same test is only 29. Certainly it is tempting to assume that this is true. Yet the whole idea, in reality, is absurd. Such a comparison of the raw scores cannot, unfortunately, be made unless the units of measurement possess certain characteristics, that is, the characteristics of a ratio scale. Principal among these is the requirement that a raw score of zero represent a total absence of knowledge of word meanings. Of course, such total absence could not be true in this case.

Absolute Zero

The failure of the raw score of size zero to indicate zero knowledge of vocabulary is equivalent to saying that it is not an absolute zero. In other words, unlike the customary measurement of height and weight, the units of measurement of the vocabulary test are relative. Relativity is a common characteristic of test scores.

Like many achievement tests, the vocabulary test is deliberately constructed in such a way that a score of zero is not an absolute zero. If for no reason other than economy of time and energy, such simple words as *dog*, *house*, and *bicycle* are not included in the test, since they do not differentiate among pupils of a typical tenth-grade class. On the other hand, words like *immaculate*, *predicament*, and *conscientious* may very likely be of acceptable difficulty for the class and hence are included in the test. Instruments such as the vocabulary test are generally designed to have a relatively small, carefully chosen, difficulty spread so that all pupils to be measured will be represented on the scale rather than somewhere below or above it. Hence raw scores of zero and 100 will be virtually nonexistent. The test then differentiates among pupils even though absolute zero has not been identified.

This idea can be translated into a diagram such as Figure 15. Although this figure is but an approximate representation of the relationship between the raw scores of the vocabulary achievement test and its level of difficulty, it nevertheless illustrates two noteworthy points. First of all, it is evident that a raw score of zero differs from absolute zero by some large and unknown distance. Obviously, the distance between a raw score of 58 and absolute zero

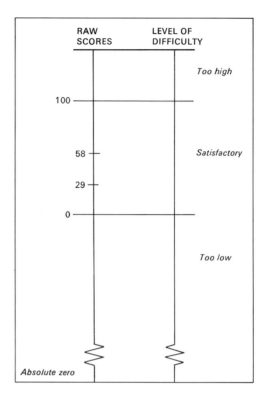

FIGURE 15.   Raw Scores and Level of Difficulty of an English Vocabulary Test for Tenth-Grade Pupils.

is not twice the distance between a raw score of 29 and absolute zero. The
second point concerns the level of difficulty of the instrument. Of course, the
satisfactory level of difficulty for this achievement test varies with the group
of pupils for whom it is designed. It would move up the scale for twelfth-
grade pupils and down for eighth-grade pupils. If the test is carefully constructed, its raw-score spread will fall directly opposite the satisfactory level of
difficulty as illustrated. Previous test results are invaluable aids in identifying
the test items that are useless for a specific achievement test because they are
too easy or too difficult. Note again that the position of absolute zero is of no
direct concern to the test builder as he identifies the proper level of difficulty.

Figure 15 resembles the situation that might exist if a school nurse
wished to obtain the relative rather than the absolute heights of a group of
secondary school girls. To do so she could nail a yardstick vertically to the wall
at a position such that every girl would be found to be at least as tall as the
distance between the floor and the lower edge and no taller than the distance
between the floor and the upper edge of the yardstick. Her knowledge of

typical heights of girls of this age group would help her to make a satisfactory approximation of the position. After the yardstick is in place, each girl stands barefooted at a point beneath the yardstick and a reading can be made.

There are two similarities between this determination of relative height and the vocabulary test. In the first place, the relative heights would be very acceptable information for differentiating among the girls in terms of height, just as the vocabulary test scores can differentiate among the tenth-grade pupils. Ratios between these heights, however, like ratios between the test scores, defy interpretation. Certainly a girl with a relative height of 22 inches is not twice as tall as a girl with a relative height of 11 inches. Thus, as in the case of the test scores, the zero point of the yardstick differs from an absolute zero by some unknown distance. Secondly, determining a suitable position on the wall at which to nail the yardstick is essentially the same as selecting the vocabulary test items of satisfactory difficulty. In both cases, changes would be made if different groups of subjects were measured. For example, if elementary school girls were used in the determination of relative height, the yardstick would be lowered; if sixth-grade pupils were tested, less difficult vocabulary test items would be used.

The failure of educational measuring instruments to have an absolute zero is not as serious as it may first seem. The continued successful use of the Fahrenheit and centigrade scales to measure temperature is ample evidence that scales without absolute units still have superior utility. The absence of absolute units simply means that ratios between raw scores lack meaning when generalizations about the attribute measured are being made. To question whether one pupil's vocabulary is twice that of another pupil's is no different from questioning whether a room at 100° F is twice as warm as a room at 50° F.

Differences Between Raw Scores

As the teacher examines the raw scores reported for his class, he may find himself grappling with other uncertainties. He notices, for example, that another pupil received a raw score of 59 in contrast to the first pupil's 58. Does this pupil in fact surpass the first in terms of the vocabulary test? When answering this question remember that this test, like all tests, is somewhat unreliable. In other words, it does not yield completely consistent results. Test unreliability forces us to interpret each score as an interval rather than a point. These intervals, sometimes called *confidence intervals* or *bands*, are found by using the standard error of measurement (see pages 316–318).

Unequal Units.   Further examination of the vocabulary raw scores may reveal a situation such as the following:

Pupil	Raw score
Sheri	88
Carol	68
Arthur	37
Donald	17

Since the raw-score difference between the two members of each pair is 20 in both instances, can it be said that Sheri surpasses Carol in terms of the vocabulary test by the same amount that Arthur surpasses Donald? If the raw-score units are equal, the question can be answered affirmatively. In all likelihood, however, the difference of 20 raw-score units between the two girls is not exactly the same as the difference of 20 raw-score units between the two boys. It is all too true that educational measurement habitually yields somewhat unequal units. A specified difference, such as 20 raw-score units, cannot be identified at any position along the range, as 5 inches can be isolated in any position on an accurate yardstick. Hence the requirements of an interval scale are imperfectly met.

In all probability, increasing a raw score in a vocabulary test from 68 to 88 represents greater accomplishment than increasing a raw score from 17 to 37. Hence, Sheri surpasses Carol to a greater degree than Arthur surpasses Donald. It is typical of achievement tests to find the "rubber units" contracted at the lower end of the raw-score distribution and expanded at the upper end.

Interpreting Raw Scores

The individual most vitally concerned about the 58 his teacher wrote in the record book is the pupil himself. When informed of his achievement, he is understandably puzzled. Obviously he lacks reference points against which to compare his information. He needs a raw-score counterpart of "70° F" to help him interpret "58" the way "70° F" helps him interpret temperature reports.

His first reaction might be to convert the number of correct responses to a percent. However, to know that he correctly identified 58 percent of the words is not particularly helpful. If the test were composed of simple words, 58 percent might indicate inferior achievement. If the test were composed of difficult words, on the other hand, 58 percent might indicate superior achievement for a tenth-grade pupil.

No doubt the pupil requests information concerning the number of words correctly identified by the other class members. If all other class members correctly identified fewer than 58 words, he would certainly be elated about his achievement; however, if all other class members correctly identified more than 58 words, he may very well be downcast. If the average number of words correctly identified by his classmates is reported, then he can describe his position as " above average" or as "below average" in terms of the vocabulary test.

Three helpful reference points are now available to the pupil. They are the maximum number of words correctly identified by any classmate, the minimum number of words correctly identified by any classmate, and the average number of words correctly identified by the entire class. Meager as this information is, it nevertheless provides the pupil with the opportunity to interpret his "58" in much the same manner as he would a reported temperature. Both numerical reports have some meaning in terms of certain relative criteria.

Frequency Distribution.   To provide the pupil with information that will help him interpret his raw score, the teacher must follow several steps. Initially he explains that, in view of the similarity of curriculum and educational environment in general, it is reasonable to compare the raw score of 58 not only with those of other members of his class at his school, but also with those of all 360 pupils of the tenth-grade classes in all schools in the city. Then he decides to show his pupil the scores of all other pupils tested. Needless to say the columns upon columns of unarranged raw scores (often called the ungrouped data) are hardly informative. On the other hand, the raw scores can be grouped into intervals and a *frequency distribution* constructed. The procedure is illustrated in Table 4. The total spread of the scores from 15 (the lowest raw score) to 94 (the highest raw score) is arbitrarily subdivided into 16 intervals of a constant size of five raw-score units. This procedure forms the first column of Table 4, which is called the raw-score intervals column. Then each raw score is tallied in the proper interval, as indicated by the vertical marks adjacent to the intervals. Counting the tallies yields the frebeing the pupil in question.

The interpretation of the values of the frequency column is by no means difficult. It is clear that three of the pupils have raw scores somewhere between 15 and 19 inclusive, whereas five have raw scores between 20 and 24 inclusive. Forty-six have raw scores between 55 and 59 inclusive, one of these being the pupil in question.

To help the pupil understand even more clearly his relative position in the group of 360 pupils, Table 4 is changed to Table 5. Now two columns of percentages are available, one based on cumulative frequencies. Approximately 13 percent of the tenth-graders fall within the same interval as the pupil we are considering, and 47 percent fall within the intervals below his. Thus about 40 percent of the pupils fall within intervals above the one containing his raw score.

Constructing a Graph.   A further step the teacher may take in his attempts to improve the meaningfulness of the pupil's raw score would be to convert the frequency distribution to graphic form. It is common practice to plot the

TABLE 4.   Work Table for Determining a Frequency Distribution of 360 Vocabulary Raw Scores.

Raw-score intervals	Tallies	Frequency
90–94	IIII	4
85–89	ℍℍ I	6
80–84	ℍℍ ℍℍ II	12
75–79	ℍℍ ℍℍ ℍℍ ℍℍ	20
70–74	ℍℍ ℍℍ ℍℍ ℍℍ ℍℍ III	28
65–69	ℍℍ ℍℍ ℍℍ ℍℍ ℍℍ ℍℍ ℍℍ I	36
60–64	ℍℍ ℍℍ ℍℍ ℍℍ ℍℍ ℍℍ ℍℍ ℍℍ	40
55–59	ℍℍ ℍℍ ℍℍ ℍℍ ℍℍ ℍℍ ℍℍ ℍℍ ℍℍ I	46
50–54	ℍℍ ℍℍ ℍℍ ℍℍ ℍℍ ℍℍ ℍℍ ℍℍ III	43
45–49	ℍℍ ℍℍ ℍℍ ℍℍ ℍℍ ℍℍ ℍℍ IIII	39
40–44	ℍℍ ℍℍ ℍℍ ℍℍ ℍℍ ℍℍ II	32
35–39	ℍℍ ℍℍ ℍℍ ℍℍ IIII	24
30–34	ℍℍ ℍℍ III	13
25–29	ℍℍ IIII	9
20–24	ℍℍ	5
15–19	III	3
Total		360

data included in Table 4 by spacing the raw-score intervals along a horizontal axis and the frequencies along a vertical axis. In this manner, Figure 16 is constructed. The frequency of each interval is plotted directly above the midpoint of that interval.

The curve in Figure 16 is fairly characteristic of those resulting from similar plotting of the scores yielded by many different kinds of measuring instruments used in education and elsewhere. Had the pupils involved been infinite in number and unselected with respect to vocabulary, it is expected that the curve would be smooth and symmetrical rather than erratic. The group of 360 pupils somewhat approximates these conditions, and thus the line resulting approximates a smooth symmetrical curve. Measurements made on smaller groups such as the typical class often yield a very erratic curve.

Normal Curve.   The curve in Figure 16 is shaped, for all practical purposes, like a *normal* curve. The normal curve is distinctively bell-shaped, with the peak of the curve above a point on the horizontal axis corresponding to the average score of the distribution. From the peak, the curve drops rapidly on

TABLE 5.   Frequency Distribution of 360 Raw Scores.

Raw-score intervals	Frequency	Per cent	Cumulative frequency	Cumulative per cent
90–94	4	1.1	360	100.0
85–89	6	1.7	356	98.9
80–84	12	3.3	350	97.2
75–79	20	5.6	338	93.9
70–74	28	7.8	318	88.3
65–69	36	10.0	290	80.6
60–64	40	11.1	254	70.6
55–59	46	12.8	214	59.4
50–54	43	11.9	168	46.7
45–49	39	10.8	125	34.7
40–44	32	8.9	86	23.9
35–39	24	6.7	54	15.0
30–34	13	3.6	30	8.3
25–29	9	2.5	17	4.7
20–24	5	1.4	8	2.2
15–19	3	0.8	3	0.8
Total	360	100.0		

either side, yielding a symmetrical tapering as it approaches either end of the raw-score distribution.

The fact that the raw scores from the vocabulary test tend to be normally distributed assists considerably in their description. It is immediately possible to say that few pupils have high raw scores, few pupils have low scores, whereas many have scores clustering around the average raw score. The statement can be appreciably strengthened by wording it in terms of the standard deviation and the arithmetic mean of raw scores. If the standard deviation is added to and subtracted from the arithmetic mean, points along the horizontal axis are found between which fall a fixed percentage of the scores.

Mean and Standard Deviation.   The arithmetic mean is often called the "average." It is a measure of central tendency, that is, a point at or near which the test scores are clustering. With ungrouped data, it is computed by adding all the scores and dividing by the number of scores. However, this procedure cannot be followed when they are arranged in a frequency distribution since, in these instances, the exact test score for a particular pupil is unknown. A modified formula for computing the arithmetic mean of scores in a frequency distribution is shown in Appendix A (see pages 573–575). When this formula is applied to the 360 vocabulary raw scores, an arithmetic mean of 55.7 is found.

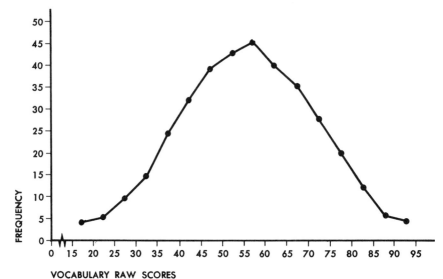

VOCABULARY RAW SCORES

FIGURE 16.   Distribution of 360 Vocabulary Raw Scores as Presented in Graphic Form.

Like the range, the standard deviation is a measure of the variability or dispersion present in a distribution of test scores. It is a distance expressed in test-score units rather than a point such as the arithmetic mean. Relatively small standard deviations are obtained when the test scores of a distribution are clustered in the vicinity of the arithmetic mean. As the test scores of a distribution spread widely above and below the arithmetic mean, the size of the standard deviation increases.

As in the case of the arithmetic mean, the standard deviation can be computed for test scores that are ungrouped or for test scores arranged in a frequency distribution. Appropriate formulas are shown in Appendix A (see pages 575–578). For the 360 vocabulary test scores shown in Table 4, a standard deviation of 15.3 was computed.

We can add and subtract the standard deviation (σ) from the arithmetic mean (M) in the following manner:

$$M + \sigma = 55.7 + 15.3 = 71.0$$
$$M - \sigma = 55.7 - 15.3 = 40.4$$

and

$$M + 2\sigma = 55.7 + (2)\,(15.3) = 86.3$$
$$M - 2\sigma = 55.7 - (2)\,(15.3) = 25.1.$$

Because the distribution is approximately normal, about 68 percent of raw scores are higher than 40.4 but no larger than 71.0. Of the 360 pupils, we should estimate that roughly 245 have scores between 41 and 71 inclusive. On the other hand, about 95 percent of the raw scores are larger than 25.1 and smaller than 86.3. Consequently, we should estimate that approximately 342 pupils have scores between 26 and 86 inclusive. Only when a normal distribution exists can the foregoing estimates be made.

Because finite groups of raw scores never conform to a perfect normal distribution, it is common to speak of the 68 percent of the scores falling between $M + \sigma$ and $M - \sigma$ as the "middle two-thirds" of the distribution. Thus the two remaining tails of the distribution are identified as the "upper one-sixth" and the "lower one-sixth," respectively. Rough as this subdivision is, it is quite useful. For example, the teacher confronted with these almost normally distributed vocabulary raw scores can quickly add the standard deviation to the arithmetic mean, then subtract the standard deviation from the arithmetic mean, and visualize an ideal diagram such as the one in Figure 17. He can accordingly classify any raw score above 71 as in the upper one-sixth of the distribution, any raw score larger than 40 but no larger than 71 as in the middle two-thirds of the distribution, and, finally, any raw score of 40 and below as in the lower one-sixth of the distribution. Although the teacher may be wrong in his classification of raw scores in the immediate vicinity of 71 and 40, he will very likely classify all other raw scores correctly. For example, 58 is clearly within the middle two-thirds of the distribution.

Scores from Teacher-Built Tests.   In the case of classroom achievement tests, the teacher typically deals with 25 to 35 raw scores rather than groups as large as the 360 used here. This means that we cannot safely expect a close approxi-

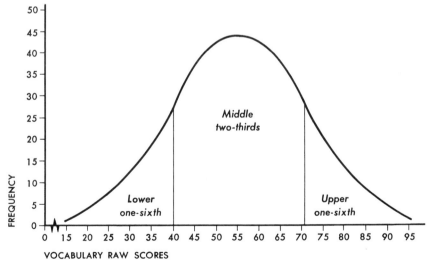

FIGURE 17.   Theoretical Normal Distribution of Vocabulary Raw Scores.

mation to the normal curve to exist, and thus interpretation of the test scores in terms of it is largely lost. Depending on the situation, we may wish instead to interpret these scores primarily in terms of their frequency distribution, mean, range, and highest and lowest values. Furthermore, for such small groups of scores, it is not reasonable to convert them routinely to derived scores like percentile ranks or standard scores.

Problems

1.   On the basis of data shown on page 246, the statement is made that Sheri surpasses Carol in terms of the vocabulary test to a greater degree than Arthur surpasses Donald. Suppose that it required Carol two weeks of study to raise her score 20 points to 88, whereas it required Donald only one week to raise his score 20 points to 37. Ignoring possible measurement errors, can we now say that the difference in vocabulary achievement between the two boys is about half of that between the two girls, even though the raw-score difference is 20 in both cases? (For further elaboration regarding this line of reasoning, see Angoff, 1970.)

2.   In addition to the arithmetic mean, what other measures of central tendency are commonly computed for raw-score distributions?

3.   For the distribution of 360 vocabulary raw scores, find the range, that is, the difference between the highest and lowest raw scores. How many times larger is the range than the standard deviation? Do you expect that this relationship between the sizes of the two measures of variability would change appreciably when determined for other groups of normally distributed raw scores? Why?

IDENTIFYING RELATIVE PERFORMANCE

Attempts to identify the relative performance of a pupil in terms of a test have been numerous. Furthermore, these attempts have yielded procedures that are vastly less cumbersome and casual than the manipulations of the raw-score distribution described above. The gist of the problem of simplifying the identification of relative performance is to convert the raw scores yielded by a test to some kind of derived scores that have, by their very nature, considerably greater interpretability. The many variations of derived scores are classified under the heading of *test norms*.

Test norms are representations of average or common performance, based on the results of testing a normal group of pupils. This group is usually large and supposedly representative of those pupils for whom the test is designed. The test is of course administered under the conditions specified by its author.

Test norms are sometimes confused with test standards. The two expressions are not synonymous. Test norms represent *actual* performance of certain groups of pupils. In contrast, test standards represent *desired* performance in terms of a specific test. In the case of the vocabulary test, for example, the average number of words correctly identified is 55.7, or slightly more than one-half of the total number of items. This value is an indication of average or common performance on the part of the tenth-grade pupils and hence falls within the notion of test norms. However, it is possible that the teachers feel that any raw score below 60 is unsatisfactory. If this position is taken, the teachers have obviously established a standard. Such a standard may coincide with a value such as the mean raw score, and then again it may not. Presumably, standards are based on the considered judgment of teachers and supervisors who are intimately familiar with the teaching environment related to the characteristic measured by the test and with the talent of the group of pupils tested.

The most common types of norms can be classified into four groups:

Quartiles, deciles, and percentiles
Standard scores
Grade equivalents
Age equivalents

The very length of this list suggests that none seems to be completely satisfactory. It is common to find test authors and consumers reporting several kinds of norms for the same test. Thus, each type of norm deserves a separate, though brief, description.

Quartiles, Deciles, and Percentiles

Quartiles, deciles, and percentiles are points in a distribution of test scores below which specified percentages of the scores fall. The quartiles are three points dividing the distribution into four equal parts in terms of the number of test scores; deciles are nine points dividing the distribution into ten equal parts; percentiles are ninety-nine points dividing the distribution into one hundred equal parts.

The interpretation of a quartile, decile, or percentile is quite uniform. The first quartile, often identified as Q_1, is the point below which 25 percent of the scores fall. The first decile, D_1, is the point below which 10 percent of the scores fall. The first percentile, P_1, is the point below which 1 percent of the scores fall. In a similar manner, the remaining quartiles, deciles, and percentiles are identified symbolically and interpreted. In other words, in the case of the quartile, 25 percent of the scores fall below Q_1, 25 percent between Q_1 and Q_2, 25 percent between Q_2 and Q_3, and 25 percent above Q_3.

By definition, equalities have been established between certain quartiles, deciles, and percentiles. For example,

$$Q_1 = P_{25}$$
$$Q_3 = P_{75}$$
$$D_1 = P_{10}, \ldots .$$

The most notable equality is

$$Q_2 = D_5 = P_{50}.$$

Interestingly enough, the point in question, namely, the point below which 50 percent of the scores fall, is not known as Q_2, D_5, or P_{50}, but as the median. The median also plays a role in other types of norms described in this chapter.

The computation of any quartile, decile, or percentile can be based on a frequency distribution of raw scores such as the distribution of vocabulary scores shown in Table 5. The formula necessary for the determination of any of these values is shown in Appendix A (see pages 582–584). Repeated application of this formula yields the raw-score equivalents of all of the quartiles, deciles, and percentiles; these values for the first 25 percentiles are listed in the fourth column of Table 6.

The fact that quartiles, deciles, and percentiles are points and nothing more is reemphasized by examination of the raw-score equivalents. Consider D_1 for a moment. Its raw-score equivalent is 35.8. This value, like the others, is arbitrarily rounded back to one decimal since additional decimal places are of little value. Furthermore, like a great majority of its fellow values, it is not an integer. Hence we can say that a raw score of 35 is slightly below D_1, whereas a raw score of 36 is slightly above. No raw score exactly corresponds to D_1. Note that it is not correct to say that any raw score of less than 36 is *in* the first decile. Quartiles, deciles, and percentiles are points, not parts. Raw scores can be above a given one of them, below it, occasionally at it (for example, $P_{65} = 62.0$), but never in it. To refer carelessly to Q_1 as the lowest quarter, or to D_1 as the lowest tenth of the distribution is inaccurate and unnecessarily confusing.

The raw-score equivalents of the quartiles, deciles, and percentiles as presented in Table 6 lack utility to some degree. We might now ask, for example, what statement can be made about the raw score of 43. Can it be reported that it fell somewhere between P_{21} and P_{22}? Certainly this is true, but it is an awkward way to identify relative performance. Simplification of the wording is not possible if it is necessary to speak of percentiles. However, if *percentile ranks* are to be used, the statement reduces itself appreciably.

Percentile Ranks.   Quartile ranks, decile ranks, and percentile ranks are not points, but ranges of raw scores. In the case of percentile ranks, these ranges are customarily quite small. By definition, any raw score of the same size as P_1 or

TABLE 6.   Percentiles and Percentile Ranks for the Bottom Fourth of a Distribution of Vocabulary Scores.

Percentile	Decile	Quartile	Raw-score Equivalent	Percentile Rank	Raw Scores
25		1	45.0	25	45
24			44.6	24	
23			44.0	23	44
22			43.4	22	43
21			42.9	21	
20	2		42.3	20	42
19			41.8	19	
18			41.2	18	41
17			40.6	17	
16			40.1	16	40
15			39.5	15	39
14			38.8	14	
13			38.0	13	38
12			37.3	12	37
11			36.5	11	36
10	1		35.8	10	
9			35.0	9	35
8			34.0	8	33, 34
7			32.7	7	32
6			31.3	6	30, 31
5			29.9	5	29
4			28.1	4	27, 28
3			26.1	3	24, 25, 26
2			23.7	2	21, 22, 23
1			20.1	1	20 and below

less is given a percentile rank of one. Symbolically, this is PR_1. Any raw score larger than P_1 but no larger than P_2 is given a percentile rank of two, that is, PR_2. The process continues until PR_{100} is reached. Any raw score larger than P_{99} is so identified. Thus the distribution is divided into one hundred percentile ranks.

The last two columns of Table 6 list the percentile ranks and the corresponding raw scores. The former are found simply by inspecting the size of the raw-score equivalents of the percentiles and applying the definition of percentile ranks. A less laborious means of determining percentile ranks is by reading them from an accurately plotted ogive curve, that is, the curve resulting when cumulative percentages are plotted against the raw scores (Cronbach, 1970, pp. 90–91).

The relationships among raw scores, percentiles, and percentile ranks are worth examining in some detail. Figure 18 facilitates the discussion; the lower

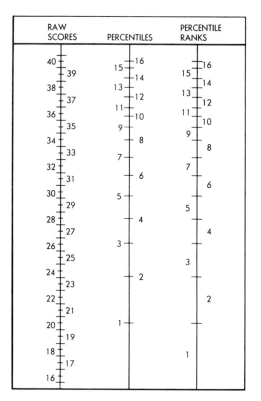

FIGURE 18.   Relationships among Raw Scores, Percentiles, and Percentile Ranks.

part of the raw-score distribution from the vocabulary test is reproduced on the left-hand vertical line, the corresponding percentiles on the center vertical line, and the percentile ranks on the right-hand vertical line. The raw scores are represented as the midpoints of tiny theoretical ranges, the size of the range being a function of the sensitivity of the measurement. Since, in the case of the vocabulary test, the characteristic is measured to the nearest whole number, a raw score such as 16 is considered to be the midpoint of a tiny theoretical range between 15.5 and 16.5. The size of the range is unity throughout these raw scores. Because percentiles are defined as points, the identifying numbers in the center vertical line are placed opposite the appropriate mark. In contrast, the percentile ranks are ranges, and are numbered on the right-hand vertical line by centering the numbers midway in the proper interval.

Clearly, Figure 18 is nothing more than a graphic presentation of most of the data included in Table 6. It is a suitable adjunct to the table in that it shows strikingly that raw scores are equivalent to theoretical ranges, percentiles are points, and percentile ranks are ranges of raw scores isolated by consecutive percentile points. Notice that the size of the ranges of the percentile ranks does not remain constant.

Percentile ranks are more commonly reported and used than percentiles. Tables converting raw scores to percentile ranks are standard equipment in many test manuals. Although the last two columns of Table 6 perform the conversion function, they are probably not shown in that fashion. Rather, the two columns are rearranged so that the raw-score column is first and the percentile-rank column is second, as in Table 7.

Table 7 shows the percentile rank equivalent for each raw score. As you can see, a raw score of 58 is equivalent to a percentile rank of 56. This means that a pupil with a score of 58 on this vocabulary test ranks fifty-sixth from the bottom in a standard group of one hundred tenth-grade pupils.

Utility of Percentile Norms. The use of percentiles and percentile ranks to represent relative performance is extremely popular. Authors of standardized tests seldom fail to include these norms in their test manuals. Now that teachers, pupils, and even parents have been educated to a point that the term "percentile" has become almost a household word, test authors capitalize on the situation and view percentile norms as a convenient way of communicating with a large, heterogeneous audience.

There is a second reason for the continued use of percentile norms: the tables of norms can always be interpreted exactly no matter what the nature of the distribution of raw scores from which they are derived. Because the percentiles and percentile ranks discussed in this chapter are based on an almost normal distribution of raw scores, we may have been tempted to generalize that only when raw scores are so distributed can these norms be computed and interpreted as described. This is not true. The distribution of raw scores can vary immensely from a normal distribution without changing the interpretation of percentile norms.

The disadvantages of using percentile norms for representing relative performance of pupils are, however, somewhat damaging. Firstly, and most important of all, the size of units of percentiles and percentile ranks is not constant. Differences between percentiles are not equivalent to differences between raw scores. The failure of the percentile norm to reflect the characteristic measured in the same manner as the original raw score is serious indeed.

Inspection of Table 7 and Figure 18 reveals this situation in a typical case. Certainly the percentiles and percentile ranks are hiding large differences between raw scores when they occur at either the high or low extremity of the raw-score distribution, and also are enlarging small differences between raw scores when they occur near the center of the distribution. A pupil with a raw score of 15 is no different in terms of percentile rank from a pupil with one of 20. Both are at the first percentile rank. Similarly, a pupil with a raw score of 94 is no different in terms of percentile rank from a pupil with a raw score

TABLE 7.   Percentile Rank Equivalents of Vocabulary Raw Scores.

Raw Score	Percentile Rank	Raw Score	Percentile Rank	Raw Score	Percentile Rank
95	100	68	78	41	18
94	100	67	76	40	16
93	100	66	74	39	15
92	100	65	72	38	13
91	100	64	70	37	12
90	99	63	68	36	11
89	99	62	65	35	9
88	99	61	63	34	8
87	99	60	61	33	8
86	98	59	59	32	7
85	98	58	56	31	6
84	97	57	53	30	6
83	97	56	51	29	5
82	96	55	48	28	4
81	95	54	46	27	4
80	95	53	43	26	3
79	94	52	41	25	3
78	93	51	39	24	3
77	92	50	36	23	2
76	90	49	34	22	2
75	89	48	32	21	2
74	88	47	30	20	1
73	86	46	28	19	1
72	85	45	25	18	1
71	83	44	23	17	1
70	82	43	22	16	1
69	80	42	20	15	1

of 91. Both have a percentile rank of 100. On the other hand the raw score of 58 yields a percentile rank of 56. With the present system of scoring the vocabulary test, it is not possible for a pupil to have a percentile rank of 54 or 55.

Percentile norms have "rubber units." The extent to which the units have been "rubberized" depends on the nature of the distribution of the raw scores. If that distribution is normal or nearly normal, the amount of distortion is large, as in the illustration. In Table 7 notice that a pupil at PR_{96} is much farther away from a pupil at PR_{86} in terms of raw-score units than a pupil at PR_{56} is from a pupil at PR_{46}. The difference in raw-score units is nine in the first instance and four in the second. In short, percentile norms form ordinal scales, not interval scales.

The second objection is less serious than the first and sometimes of little concern to teachers. Simply phrased, it states that percentiles and percentile ranks as such cannot be treated arithmetically and a meaningful end product obtained. One cannot legitimately compute an arithmetic mean of these values or correlate them with other measurements by means of a product-moment coefficient of correlation. Percentiles and percentile ranks are, in effect, terminal values. Once computed they can be interpreted; then their utility is virtually exhausted. Test norms such as standard scores do not suffer from this limitation.

Standard Scores

Another popular system for representing relative performance on a test is the standard score. The intent of the standard score is to transform the raw-score distribution to a derived-score distribution having a desired arithmetic mean and standard deviation. If the arithmetic mean and standard deviation are known, and if the derived-score distribution is normal, identification of the relative performance of individual pupils is a simple matter. The same approach is used here that is described in connection with Figure 17 when normally distributed raw scores were involved.

z-Scores.   There are many types of standard scores, each with its own arithmetic mean and standard deviation. The "parent" of the group is the well-known z score. From this base have sprung the others, three of which are commonly encountered and are described below.

The z scores are computed from the formula

$$z = \frac{X - M}{\sigma},$$

where

z = standard score;
X = any raw score of a given distribution;
M = arithmetic mean of the raw-score distribution;
σ = standard deviation of the raw-score distribution.

Examination of the formula reveals that any raw score smaller than the arithmetic mean of the raw scores yields a z score with a negative sign, whereas any larger than the arithmetic mean yields a z score that is positive. When a raw-score distribution is transformed into z scores, the arithmetic mean of the resulting z scores is zero, and their standard deviation is unity.

To change a raw score to a z score, a table of norms similar to that used for percentile ranks is consulted. Such a table is Table 8, the second column of which is constructed by successively solving the z score equation for all obtained raw scores ($M = 55.7$, $\sigma = 15.3$) resulting from the administration of the vocabulary test. Any raw score can be readily converted to a z score merely by glancing at the table. For example, a z score of $+0.15$ corresponds to the raw score of 58. Note that the practical limits of the z score distribution do not exceed $+3.00$ and -3.00.

Other Multiple-Digit Standard Scores.   Because z scores have negative signs and decimal points, their usefulness decreases. Clerical errors too easily and too often create havoc when test results are reported. To avoid these difficulties, linear transformations of the original z scores are made and an entire family of standard scores is automatically born. One such transformation is

$$\text{Standard score} = 10\,(z) + 50.$$

This equation produces a distribution of standard scores with an arithmetic mean of 50 and a standard deviation of 10. In Table 8 these standard scores are listed opposite the corresponding z score and vocabulary test raw score. It should be noted that this type of standard score is often called a *T* score, although the original *T* score as proposed by McCall (1939) is somewhat different.

Another transformation is

$$\text{Standard score} = 20\,(z) + 100.$$

Now the arithmetic mean of the standard scores is 100 and the standard deviation is 20. This type of standard score is used with the *Army General Classification Test* administered during and after World War II.

Also, the equation can read

$$\text{Standard score} = 100\,(z) + 500.$$

The arithmetic mean of these standard scores is 500, whereas the standard deviation is 100. Standard scores of this type are used in connection with the *College Entrance Examination Board Tests.*

The above information is summarized in the following table. In addition to the arithmetic means and standard deviations, the practical limits of the standard score distribution are given. The practical limits are the points that are three standard deviation units above the arithmetic mean and three below it.

The interpretation of any standard score of any type depends directly on the knowledge of the arithmetic mean of the standard-score distribution and its standard deviation. If the distribution of standard scores is normal, the interpretation is not difficult; if it is not normal, the interpretation is quite uncertain.

To assume that standard scores are always normally distributed simply because they are standard scores is a common mistake. If the raw scores are

TABLE 8.   Standard Scores of Raw Scores Based upon 360 Tenth-Grade Pupils.

Raw score	z	Standard score $(M = 50, \sigma = 10)$	Raw score	z	Standard score $(M = 50, \sigma = 10)$
94	2.50	75	54	−0.11	49
93	2.44	74	53	−0.18	48
92	2.37	74	52	−0.24	48
91	2.31	73	51	−0.31	47
90	2.24	72	50	−0.37	46
89	2.18	72	49	−0.44	46
88	2.11	71	48	−0.50	45
87	2.05	71	47	−0.57	44
86	1.98	70	46	−0.63	44
85	1.92	69	45	−0.70	43
84	1.85	69	44	−0.76	42
83	1.78	68	43	−0.83	42
82	1.72	67	42	−0.90	41
81	1.65	67	41	−0.96	40
80	1.59	66	40	−1.03	40
79	1.52	65	39	−1.09	39
78	1.46	65	38	−1.16	38
77	1.39	64	37	−1.22	38
76	1.33	63	36	−1.29	37
75	1.26	63	35	−1.35	36
74	1.20	62	34	−1.42	36
73	1.13	61	33	−1.48	35
72	1.07	61	32	−1.55	34
71	1.00	60	31	−1.61	34
70	0.93	59	30	−1.68	33
69	0.87	59	29	−1.75	32
68	0.80	58	28	−1.81	32
67	0.74	57	27	−1.88	31
66	0.67	57	26	−1.94	31
65	0.61	56	25	−2.01	30
64	0.54	55	24	−2.07	29
63	0.48	55	23	−2.14	29
62	0.41	54	22	−2.20	28
61	0.35	54	21	−2.27	27
60	0.28	53	20	−2.33	27
59	0.22	52	19	−2.40	26
58	0.15	52	18	−2.46	25
57	0.08	51	17	−2.53	25
56	0.02	50	16	−2.60	24
55	−0.05	49	15	−2.66	23

			Practical limits	
Type	Arithmetic mean	Standard deviation	High	Low
z	0	1	+3.00	−3.00
10 (z) + 50	50	10	80	20
20 (z) + 100	100	20	160	40
100 (z) + 500	500	100	800	200

normally distributed, then the standard scores computed from them are auto-matically normally distributed. The standard-score distribution is the same as the distribution of raw scores on which it is based. Since quite a few raw-score distributions are for all practical purposes normally distributed, the inter-pretation of many standard scores is based on the normal curve.

In interpretation of standard scores based on normally distributed raw scores, it is helpful to think of a diagram such as Figure 17. For z scores, the middle two-thirds of the distribution falls between +1.00 and −1.00, whereas the upper one-sixth is composed of z scores that exceed +1.00 and the lower one-sixth contains z scores that fail to reach −1.00. For the other three types of standard scores, the following reference points are available:

Standard score characteristics		Middle two-thirds	Upper one-sixth	Lower one-sixth
M	σ	Between	Greater than	Less than
50	10	40 and 60	60	40
100	20	80 and 120	120	80
500	100	400 and 600	600	400

Unlike the percentile rank procedure, no attempt is made here to inter-pret more exactly the relative performance of each pupil. Occasionally, per-centile ranks are criticized for leaving a largely artificial impression of exact-ness. In any event, the normal curve can be broken into more segments than the three mentioned. Should this be desirable for whatever reason, a table of areas under the normal curve can be consulted. Such a table, along with a description of its functions, can be found in most of the available textbooks devoted to statistical methodology (for example, see page 461 of Dixon and Massey, 1969).

Stanines.   The outstanding single-digit standard score used today is the stanine (pronounced stay-nine). This word was originally derived from the expression "standard *nine*-point scale," which is a system of standard scores developed during World War II. At that time, a simple and workable type of norm was sought. The stanine scale was found to be satisfactory since it employs a single digit to represent relative performance and yet is precise enough for many practical testing problems. It is used for both standardized and teacher-constructed tests.

When stanine norms are used, raw scores are converted to one of nine stanine scores, which vary from a low of 1 to a high of 9. The mean of the stanine distribution is 5 and its standard deviation 2. On the other hand, when large numbers of pupils are involved, some measurement specialists will subdivide the two extreme positions on the scale, thereby creating an eleven-point scale with a low of zero and a high of ten.

The determination of stanine scores is simple (Durost, 1961). For example, when working with raw scores from smaller groups of pupils, a teacher can arrange the raw scores from high to low, then determine the median of the distribution, and, with this as a starting point, apply the theoretical percentages of the stanine subgroups. These percentages are as follows:

Stanine	1	2	3	4	5	6	7	8	9
Percentage of Pupils	4	7	12	17	20	17	12	7	4

The median is theoretically in the center of the middle 20 percent of the distribution. This subgroup is given a stanine of 5. By working upward and downward from this subgroup the remaining subgroups are found and the stanines assigned. Certain minor adjustments of the subgroups are usually necessary to bring the actual percentages into the closest possible agreement with the theoretical percentages. This is necessitated by the principle that every pupil having the same raw score will, of course, have the same stanine score.

One word of caution: Remember that the percentages used are derived from the normal curve. Therefore, if the stanine scale is to be used, one must be willing to assume that the trait measured follows this curve reasonably well for the pupils tested.

Utility of Standard Score Norms.   After comparing the interpretation of the vocabulary raw scores with that for standard scores based upon those raw scores, you may wonder what advantages standard scores have over raw scores. One is the fact that standard scores have a specified arithmetic mean and standard deviation. Raw-score distributions have a habit of producing arithmetic means and standard deviations that have somewhat quaint sizes and are seldom integers. On the other hand standard-score distributions have arithmetic means that are easily remembered—0, 5, 50, 100, or 500—and a standard deviation that can be speedily added to or subtracted from that mean. In the case of the vocabulary test, it would be faster to manipulate the standard-score distribution with its arithmetic mean of 50 and standard deviation of 10 than the raw-score distribution with its arithmetic mean of 55.7 and standard deviation of 15.3. Also, fewer arithmetical errors would occur.

The two disadvantages of percentile norms cannot be attributed to standard-score norms. Because multiple-digit standard scores are nothing but a linear transformation of raw scores, they are a direct reflection of them, both in terms of size of unit and shape of distribution. No "rubber units" are generated as in the case of percentile ranks. Furthermore, standard scores can be treated arithmetically. Finding the arithmetic mean or standard deviation of standard scores is just as legitimate as finding those values for raw scores.

Another important advantage of standard scores is the ease of comparison of scores for a pupil who has been given several tests, and the ease of determining a composite score if desired. For instance, reporting each of a battery of achievement test scores in a subject matter area in terms of stanines permits the teacher to compare levels of achievement from one test to another for a specific pupil, as when a graphic profile of stanines is prepared. He can also combine these stanines to obtain a composite score representing the overall achievement of the pupil. Such a composite score is often the arithmetic mean of the stanines in question. Finding the arithmetic mean weights each test score equally. If desired, various weights can be assigned the stanines before the arithmetic mean is computed.

Percentiles and all types of standard scores are interrelated if the raw-score distribution from which they are computed is normal. The normal distribution restriction is highly important. In Figure 19 these relationships are shown in part (Seashore, 1955). Before the relationships shown in this figure can be considered useful, there must be statistical evidence that the distribution of raw scores is essentially a normal one.

The main disadvantage of standard scores is that they are difficult to interpret when they are not normally distributed. This fact, plus the general public's lack of familiarity with them, somewhat restricts their use.

Grade Equivalents

Representing the relative performance of pupils with grade equivalents is still another popular method. A grade equivalent of a particular raw score is the grade level of those pupils whose median (or arithmetic mean) is the same as the raw score in question. In other words, if the median raw score happened to be 63 for a test administered to sixth-grade pupils just beginning that grade level, all raw scores of 63 have a grade equivalent of 6.0.

The generally accepted way of reporting grade equivalents is in terms of two numbers. The first of the two numbers is designed as the year and second

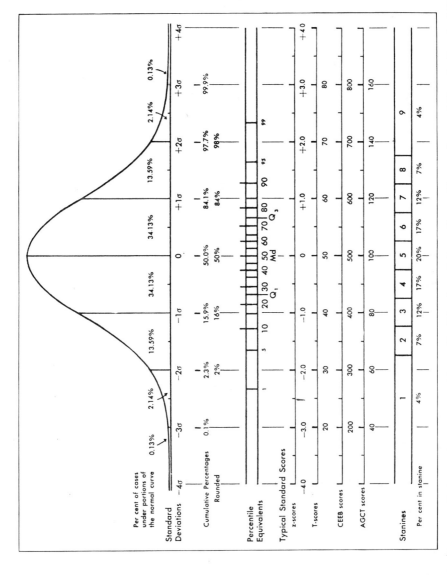

FIGURE 19. Relationships among Normally Distributed Raw Scores, Percentiles, and Certain Standard Scores.

as the month. For example, a grade equivalent of 5.4 is the median raw score of pupils tested at the fourth month of the fifth grade. Note that the calendar year is divided into ten parts, nine representing the academic year and one representing summer vacation months.

The process of computing grade equivalents is systematic but not unusually impressive. In the first place, the test is administered to large groups of pupils in consecutive grade levels. This takes place at the same time of year for all pupils. The median raw score of each grade level is found and plotted, on ordinary graph paper, against the grade level. Then the "best-fitting" curve is passed through the points, and sometimes extended (extrapolated) dangerously far beyond the upper and lower grade levels involved in the initial testing. The grade equivalents of raw scores are read directly from the curve.

The weaknesses of this method of determination are apparent. The "best-fitting" curve is a matter of judgment. So is the extension of the curve to grade levels not included in the testing. Furthermore, the smoothness of the curve suggests regular and gradual pupil growth throughout the academic year, and summer vacation growth comparable to one month of growth during the academic year. These assumptions are more easily attacked than defended.

Utility of Grade Equivalents.   Despite the limitations in the plotting procedure for computing grade equivalents, these scores are amazingly well received, especially in the elementary grade levels. Grade equivalents are easily understood. Contrast these derived scores with standard scores or even percentile ranks. Comparing a pupil's actual grade level with his grade equivalents yielded by tests in various subject matter areas is definitely more comprehensible to many teachers, administrators, and parents than standard scores and percentile ranks. Moreover, grade equivalents offer convenient units for plotting profiles of pupil achievement. Such profiles are graphic representations of a pupil's test scores and typically emphasize the areas of overachievement and underachievement. Again, the reference point most useful for interpreting the profile is the present grade level of the pupil.

Several basic restrictions of grade equivalents must be remembered if they are to be properly used and interpreted. The most important of these is that a grade equivalent cannot always be taken at face value. When the "best-fitting" curve used to determine the grade equivalents of raw scores has been extended to grade levels higher and lower than those used in the initial testing, this trouble becomes pronounced. Suppose, for example, that a pupil beginning the fifth grade is given a fifth-grade arithmetic test and receives a grade equivalent of 8.0. This does not necessarily indicate that he has mastered all of the arithmetic subject matter in the fifth, sixth, and seventh grades. Although he is displaying superior arithmetic achievement when compared to the typical fifth-grade pupil, in all probability he is not sufficiently well trained at that moment to compete successfully in arithmetic with pupils beginning the eighth grade. In other words, had he been tested by an *eighth-grade* arithmetic test, he very likely would have fallen well below the grade equivalent of 8.0.

A second restriction limits the highest grade level to which equivalents may extend. Grade equivalents should not extend beyond the ninth grade since, with the exception of English, there is no continuous and systematic instruction beyond the ninth grade for those subject matter areas taught in elementary school. Remember that the plotting method of determining grade equivalents assumes regular and gradual pupil growth over the period of time selected. Since this does not occur in secondary school in such areas as reading, arithmetic, and spelling, grade equivalents like 10.3 and 11.0 are meaningless. Standard scores or percentile ranks should be used to represent relative performance of secondary school pupils.

Finally, grade equivalents suffer from that ancient malady we call "rubber units." There is no assurance that a given difference between two grade equivalents is comparable to the same difference betwen two other grade equivalents, even though the same test is involved. However, the seriousness of this difficulty varies with the subject matter area being tested. Within the elementary school levels, grade equivalents yielded by tests in areas such as reading, arithmetic, and spelling tend to have equal units. This is true because the subject matter areas are given a consistent emphasis throughout a relatively long period of time. For other subject matter areas, we should expect grade equivalents to have units of decidedly unequal size.

On balance, one must argue that grade equivalents should be used with great caution. Their simplicity is deceptive; their meaning is often unclear. In many instances standard scores and percentile ranks are superior to them as representations of relative performance by pupils.

Age Equivalents

Age equivalents are very similar to grade equivalents. Years of age have simply replaced grade levels in the method of computation and interpretation. It follows then that an age equivalent of a particular raw score is the chronological age of those pupils whose median (or arithmetic mean) raw score is the same as the raw score in question. For example, a pupil who received a raw score of 48 on a certain test finds, on consulting a table converting raw scores to age equivalents, that it corresponds to an age equivalent of 10–4. The median (or arithmetic mean) raw score of pupils ten years and four months of age is therefore 48.

The foregoing illustration lists the age equivalent by means of two numbers separated by a dash, a typical way of reporting these values. The first number represents the number of years, whereas the second represents the number of months. Unlike grade equivalents, the calendar year is divided into twelve parts, so that the second number varies from a minimum of zero to a maximum of eleven.

Computing age equivalents strongly resembles the computation of grade equivalents. Both processes utilize plotted points to determine a "best-fitting" smooth curve from which derived scores are read off for any raw score. Both processes commonly extend the curve rather liberally beyond the limits of the data and thereby automatically inject serious possibility of error for derived scores in the regions of the extended curve.

Utility of Age Equivalents.   Many of the remarks concerning the utility of grade equivalents can be attributed to age equivalents. For instance, age equivalents are most suitable for the chronological years covered by the elementary grade levels. Also, they are based on the assumption that the represented characteristic changes continually and smoothly during the years spanned by the norms. They are simple to grasp and convenient to talk about, just as grade equivalents are.

On a number of occasions, the authors of tests list both age and grade equivalents as suitable derived scores for their achievement tests. The choice of the score the teacher is to use may or may not be difficult. If the pupils in question are members of an elementary school that practices automatic promotion based on chronological age, and the teachers recognize this in their teaching, the two types of norms will differ little from each other. If this is not the case, then the nature of the characteristic measured by the test plays a more important role.

Age equivalents are suitable for representing characteristics that change as a part of the pupil's general development. In other words, age equivalents have, in the last analysis, a biological base. For this reason physiological traits like height and weight can be appropriately represented by age equivalents. Of the psychological traits, general intelligence is sometimes expressed in terms of age equivalents.

In contrast, it is logical to represent relative performance of pupils in terms of grade equivalents when the characteristic measured is influenced primarily by the formal educative processes of school systems. Subject matter areas such as arithmetic, spelling, nature study, and reading fall in these categories, even though certain gains take place outside the classroom. As far as summer vacation is concerned, the grade equivalent tries to compensate for the change by allowing one month for the period. This probably undercompensates for the amount of change, especially in such an area as reading. Age equivalents consider every month to be the same as all other months and thus undoubtedly overcompensate for the amount of change occurring during summer vacation in the subject matter areas mentioned.

The age equivalents obtained by measuring a pupil are most readily interpreted by comparing them with his present chronological age. If the age equivalent noticeably surpasses his chronological age, he is considered to be above average; if the two are approximately the same, he is average; if the age equivalent is definitely lower than his chronological age, he is below average.

Like grade equivalents, age equivalents can be misleading. They are helpful when used with pupils at ages at which the trait measured is known to increase noticeably year by year. In other instances they are inferior to standard scores and percentile ranks.

Problems

4.   Teachers are often interested in pupil growth or improvement in achievement in a given subject matter area and will administer the same test before and after a period of instruction hoping that the difference between the two scores will measure pupil growth. Identify the principal measurement problems present in this process (Angoff, 1970). How successfully can the various types of norms reflect pupil growth (Tiedeman, 1951)?

5.   Construct an ogive curve based on Table 5 and determine several percentile ranks by means of it (Cronbach, 1970, pp. 90–91). Check your results against those shown in Table 7.

6.   When using grade equivalents, a teacher will sometimes confuse norms and standards by saying that his pupils are progressing satisfactorily if they are performing "up to the norm." What does he mean by this statement? What questions would you raise if you were to challenge it?

7.   A differentiation is made between "normative" standard scores and a "nonnormative" scale called "content" standard test scores (Wesman and others, 1962). On what basis is this differentiation made and of what significance is it to classroom teachers?

STANDARDIZATION GROUPS

When the pupil's raw score of 58 was compared with those of all the other members of his class, undoubtedly no one seriously complained about the fairness of the procedure. After all, in terms of formal education, he and his classmates probably had similar opportunities and goals. In addition, his class represented a small geographic area within a city, and thus a smaller socioeconomic range than in the city at large, certainly a smaller range than in the state or nation. If these conditions existed, it is likely that the range of scholastic aptitude among the pupils of his class was somewhat restricted in comparison with the range in the entire city or state. Very possibly the class was relatively homogeneous in many other respects. If so, one might ask whether there is a group of pupils to whom he might more suitably be compared than these tenth-grade classmates, many of whom were his neighbors and had attended the same classes with him for at least several years.

Throughout the discussion of derived scores, repeated mention is made of the standardization or norm group, that is, the group of pupils whose raw scores are used to identify the raw-score equivalents of the derived scores. The standardization group consists of pupils for whom the test is designed and who are given the test under conditions recommended by its author. For our illustration, this group is more than the tenth-grade class; it is the 360 tenth-grade pupils within the city school system. The appropriateness of interpreting achievement in the light of the results of this larger group must be established before taking the trouble to compute any of the derived scores.

A regularly observed principle is that the expression of a pupil's relative standing in terms of derived scores is meaningful when the standardization group used to determine them resembles that pupil in terms of any of a variety of salient characteristics. It follows, therefore, that comparison of a pupil's vocabulary with that of the 360 pupils is suitable since, within a single city school system, there is appreciable similarity in amount and quality of instruction in any subject matter area among the various component schools, and similarity in the pupils' ability to profit from that instruction.

It is only rarely appropriate to compare a pupil's vocabulary achievement to that of a seemingly very different group. Hence to support the use of the 360 pupils as a standardization group, they should be described in terms of the amount of their previous formal schooling in the area tested, their age distribution, scholastic aptitude distribution, socioeconomic ratings, and so forth. Since the averages of these measures do not differ greatly from the pupil's position, the comparison of his achievement with theirs would seem to make sense. Should the 360 pupils as a group be vastly unlike him, the interpretation of his performance relative to those of this group is less useful, barring unusual reasons.

Sampling Problem

The problem so often faced by teachers who wish to use test norms is that their pupils are not a part of the standardization group. Hence, the teacher must know whether his pupils can be considered a part of the population of which the standardization group is a cross-sectional sample. Unless they can be considered a part of such a population, the tables of norms cannot be used.

The sampling problem with test norms has been vastly underestimated in some instances. Tables of norms that are labeled "national" or "regional" without bothering to specify the manner in which the nation or region is sampled, are contributing by omission to the fuzzy notion that the worth of a sample is determined only incidentally by the method of obtaining it. More often than not, the size of the sample is impressive and is noted with pride, notwithstanding the fact that it is incidental to the method of selecting its members.

The whimsical nature of some methods of sampling pupils to be used as standardization groups can be neatly illuminated by changing the scene slightly. Suppose you want to find the average body temperature of human adult males. This is a norm, of course, and you already recognize that, if you use the thermometer-under-the-tongue technique, the answer is 98.6° F. In any event, assume that this information is unknown, even though the measurement technique has been perfected. Had you attacked the problem as some test authors attack the problem of norms, you would immediately search for a group (preferably large) of readily available and unusually cooperative subjects. What better place is there to find them than in the local hospitals? Hospital authorities will probably cooperate because it means an inexpensive way of acquiring more information about their patients; the patients can't complain; nurses can be quickly trained to measure temperature reliably. You proceed happily with your research and discover the average body temperature of human adult males to be 100.2° F.

There is a remarkable parallel between the foregoing illustration and the procedure sometimes used in the past for establishing norms of educational tests. However, results of the temperature measurements are summarily rejected by the medical profession and for good reason. The method of measurement is not questioned, but the accurate representation of the sample certainly is. On the other hand, in educational measurement, tables of norms yielded by equally faulty sampling procedures are sometimes accepted uncritically. Those pupils that serve as standardization groups because they are conveniently available are more likely atypical than typical of the regional and national population that they are supposed to represent.

The task of satisfactorily sampling a group of pupils is admittedly difficult and highly expensive. If there is no evidence to the contrary, national norms should include, in proportion to their numbers, boys and girls, some white and some colored, native-born and foreign-born, intelligent and not intelligent, some who live in cities, some in suburban areas, and some in rural areas, those who are wealthy and those who are poor, who attend large schools and small schools, and public and private, and who have received superior and inferior instruction. Even this list is not complete. Any factor that could conceivably affect the test results to an appreciable degree should be considered in the selection of the sample. In recent years, test authors have redoubled their efforts to draw suitable national and regional samples, and the representativeness of their standardization groups has correspondingly increased.

A number of test authors strengthen the utility of their tables of norms by publishing not one but several such tables, each designed for a relatively homogeneous population. If the sexes are found to differ in terms of a test, such as a paper-and-pencil personality inventory, separate tables of norms for boys and girls are listed. In some instances, separate tables are shown for rural schools and urban schools, for schools in different geographical regions, for various levels of scholastic aptitude within a grade level, and for pupils specializing in various types of secondary school curricula. For each group of pupils so used, the author then reports data concerning the group's age, educational status, and the like. Every pertinent piece of information characterizing the standardization group helps a teacher decide whether his pupils logically belong in the population sampled by the standardization group.

Local Norms.   Even though a variety of tables of norms is available, consideration should be given to the possibility of constructing local norms. These are usually expressed in terms of percentile ranks or standard scores. If several hundred or more test scores from a certain test are available, and if future use is to be made of that test, local norms should be found, and should be revised from time to time as additional raw scores become available. After all, a particular raw score on a test may be equivalent to a standard score of 60 in terms of national norms, 57 in terms of regional norms, 58 in terms of local norms based on one city, or 52 in terms of local norms based on one school. All these indications of relative performance may be helpful, depending on the purpose of the testing and hence the educational decisions about the pupil to be made.

Problems

8.   A senior whose percentile rank on a scholastic aptitude test was 85 had a percentile rank of 60 on an achievement test in advanced mathematics. His mathematics teacher concluded that he was underachieving. What information must you know about the standardization groups used before you can evaluate the teacher's conclusion on that basis?

9.   Study the description of procedures used to select a standardization group and the description of the standardization group finally used for the *Iowa Tests of Basic Skills*. Compare this with similar information provided by any other achievement test battery for the elementary school.

10.   In addition to norms for pupil scores, manuals of the *Iowa Tests of Educational Development* provide information concerning norms for school averages. Evaluate the worth of the school norms.

11.   An attempt has been made to develop norms for a test by administering only a few of its items to each pupil in the standardization group (Owens and Stufflebeam, 1969). What practical gains are realized by this technique?

SUMMARY

The results yielded by measuring instruments frequently lack meaning. For instance, raw scores, which are the immediate quantitative end product of scoring a test, defy interpretation until suitable reference points are known. Three such reference points are the arithmetic mean of a group of raw scores and the values of the largest and smallest raw scores. Other reference points can be readily located if the distribution of raw scores is normal or practically normal. When this is true, the standard deviation of the raw scores can be successively added to and subtracted from the arithmetic mean to identify distribution points including fixed percentages of raw scores.

Raw-score distributions are habitually characterized by two inadequacies. In the first place, a raw score of zero does not correspond to absolute zero. This is not a serious deficiency in terms of lessening raw-score interpretability. Secondly, raw-score distributions tend to have "rubber units," that is, unequal units. This deficiency is considerably more serious but hardly disastrous in well-constructed instruments.

There have been many efforts to improve the meaningfulness of raw scores. Raw scores are changed to derived scores, which more readily show the relative performance of a pupil in terms of the test. Derived scores (better known as norms) are obtained by giving a test to a group of pupils for whom it is designed under conditions recommended by the author and, with a distribution of raw scores available, applying the necessary formulas or plotting the necessary graphs. The group of pupils so used is called a standardization group.

The most common norms in educational measurement are quartiles, deciles, and percentiles; standard scores; grade equivalents; and age equivalents. Quartiles, deciles, and percentiles are points in a distribution below which specified percentages of raw scores will fall. Standard scores are derived scores with known arithmetic means and standard deviations. Grade equivalents represent average test performance of pupils of various grade levels, whereas age equivalents represent average test performance of pupils of various chronological ages.

The standardization group used to compute tables of norms must be carefully chosen. It is a sample of a population of pupils and, ideally, should be selected in accordance with the sampling procedures designed by a competent statistician. Before tables of norms can be used, a teacher must be convinced that his pupils can legitimately be considered a part of the population represented by a standardization group. Many test manuals contain several tables of norms representing various populations, since, for most purposes, norms become more meaningful as the standardization group used to determine them more closely resembles the pupils involved in the comparison. This resemblance should occur for any and every characteristic known to influence test performance. The need for similarity between a pupil and the standardization group with which he is being compared contributes heavily to the importance of local norms.

Suggested Readings

Anastasi, A. *Psychological testing.* (3rd ed.) London: Macmillan, 1968. Chapter 3.
    This chapter includes sections dealing with age norms, percentiles, and standard scores. It concludes with a discussion of normative samples and nonnormative scales, for example, content standard scores.

Angoff, W. H. Scales, norms, and equivalent scores. In R. L. Thorndike (ed.), *Educational measurement.* (2nd ed.) Washington: American Council on Education, 1970. Chapter 15.
    Each of the principal types of norms is reviewed in terms of its purposes, computation, and utility. Considerable attention is given to the problem of selecting suitable standardization groups. Parts of the material presented are somewhat technical.

Cronbach, L. J. *Essentials of psychological testing.* (3rd ed.) New York: Harper & Row, 1970. Chapter 4.
    The interpretation of raw scores and various derived scores is systematically considered. Attention is given to the normal curve and the relationships between standard scores and percentile ranks when raw scores are distributed in this manner.

Downie, N. M. *Types of test scores.* Boston: Houghton Mifflin, 1968.
    The seven chapters in this booklet cover a wide range of topics related to norms. One deals with descriptive statistics, the others with various types of popular norms. All are succinct and well written.

Durost, W. N. *The characteristics, use, and computation of stanines.* Test Service Notebook, No. 23. New York: Harcourt, Brace & World, 1961.
    All aspects of stanines that are important to classroom teachers are covered in this bulletin. Illustrations are given of their computation and uses.

Lyman, H. B. *Test scores and what they mean.* Englewood Cliffs, N.J.: Prentice-Hall, 1963. Chapters 5 and 6.
    Written for individuals such as classroom teachers who must interpret test scores, this book covers its topics well. Chapter 5 concerns norm tables and standardization groups, and Chapter 6 types of derived scores. A thirteen-page glossary of testing terms ends the book.

McLaughlin, K. F. *Interpretation of test results.* Washington: U.S. Government Printing Office, 1964. Chapters 8 and 9.
    Classroom interpretation of test scores is the topic of Chapter 8, whereas Chapter 9 is devoted to the interpretation of test results to parents. Both chapters are short and clearly stated.

Ricks, J. H., Jr. *On telling parents about test results.* Test Service Bulletin, No. 54. New York: Psychological Corporation, 1959.
    The principle of informing parents about the test scores of their children is

warmly supported. Suggestions for explaining intelligence quotients, grade equivalents, standard scores, and percentile ranks are given.

Wesman, A. G., and others. Symposium: Standard scores for aptitude and achievement tests. *Educational and Psychological Measurement*, 1962, **22**, 5–39.

The virtues and limitations of various kinds of standard scores are compared and evaluated. Five testing specialists contributed to the symposium.

References Cited

Angoff, W. H. Scales, norms, and equivalent scores. In R. L. Thorndike (ed.), *Educational measurement*. (2nd ed.) Washington: American Council on Education, 1970. Chapter 15.

Cronbach, L. J. *Essentials of psychological testing*. (3rd ed.) New York: Harper & Row, 1970.

Dixon, W. J., and F. J. Massey, Jr. *Introduction to statistical analysis*. (3rd ed.) New York: McGraw-Hill, 1969.

Durost, W. N. *The characteristics, use, and computation of stanines*. Test Service Notebook, No. 23. New York: Harcourt, Brace & World, 1961.

McCall, W. A. *Measurement*. London: Macmillan, 1939.

Owens, T. R., and D. L. Stufflebeam. An experimental comparison of item sampling and examinee sampling for estimating test norms. *Journal of Educational Measurement*, 1969, **6**, 75–83.

Seashore, H. G. *Methods of expressing test scores*. Test Service Bulletin, No. 48. New York: Psychological Corporation, 1955.

Tiedeman, D. V. Has he grown? *Personnel and Guidance Journal*, 1951, **30**, 106–111.

Wesman, A. G., and others. Symposium: Standard scores for aptitude and achievement tests. *Educational and Psychological Measurement*, 1962, **22**, 5–39.

CHAPTER 9

The Validity of Measurement Methods

Some years ago, so it is reported, an anthropologist studying the culture of a primitive community wanted to determine the number of children of each age living there. Since birth records were available for only a few children and parental reports were quite undependable, the anthropologist decided to measure the heights of the children to obtain an estimate of their ages. He did this by first measuring the heights of those few children whose ages were known. Then, by comparing the heights of children of unknown age with the heights of children whose ages were available, he estimated the unknown ages on the basis of height. This maneuver by the anthropologist was probably received sympathetically by his colleagues. It is possible that, had he not estimated ages from heights, he would have departed with no information about ages.

The anthropologist's action is not unlike that of a high school senior in his search for a university; he may assess the quality of a university's academic offerings on the basis of the size of its undergraduate student body, or perhaps the number of games won by its football team, or both. In somewhat the same category is the political pundit who evaluates the popularity of his party's agricultural program in terms of the number of unsolicited favorable letters received from the public at large, and also the economic soothsayer who describes the economic health of the nation solely in terms of the rise and fall of the stock market.

Each of the foregoing illustrations may be cynically interpreted by discerning observers. The causes for such cynicism can be traced to such questions as the following: Do differences in heights of children always indicate differences in age? Is the quality of a university's academic program necessarily a function of its size? Do unsolicited letters received at a political party's headquarters represent a cross section of voter opinion? Is the stock market completely sensitive to all of the subtle changes in the economic

276

structure? These and similar questions would undoubtedly tend to yield nothing more than hesitant answers surrounded by embarrassment.

The individuals using the foregoing measurement methods in such potentially dangerous fashions are possibly somewhat innocent. The very accessibility of such data as height, enrollment, number of letters, and stock market reports tempts most investigators. Furthermore, the accuracy of these data is generally considered good. For instance, height can easily be measured to the nearest one-fourth of an inch. The difficulty then is not centered in the accuracy of the data involved, but rather in the interpretation of them. To argue that unwarranted interpretations have been made is to argue that validity, to some degree, is absent.

DEFINITION OF VALIDITY

In educational measurement, validity is often defined as the degree to which a measuring instrument actually serves the purposes for which it is intended. A scholastic aptitude test is a valid measurement of scholastic aptitude if it truly measures scholastic aptitude. An achievement test in spelling is valid to the extent that it assuredly measures achievement in spelling. In the illustrations just cited, it is obvious that the data concerning height, enrollment, favorable letters, and stock market fluctuations are valid insofar as they are used in measuring height, enrollment, favorable letters, and stock market fluctuations, respectively. This statement sounds needlessly repetitious. Nevertheless it reemphasizes the idea that a measurement of height by means of an accurate tape measure applied under controlled conditions is unquestionably a valid measurement of height, but a doubtful measure of age. Likewise, scores yielded by a scholastic aptitude test may very well be valid indicators of degrees of scholastic aptitude but inadequate representations of emotional stability. An excellent test measuring achievement in spelling most certainly will yield scores that do not reflect individual differences in finger dexterity.

Validity is clearly the most important characteristic of a measuring instrument. No matter what other characteristics an instrument may possess, if it does not adequately serve the purposes for which its use is intended, it is of no value whatsoever.

Problems

1. Perhaps you have heard someone make statements such as the following: "The test that I am using measures general mental ability. General mental ability means that pupil trait which this test measures." Are these statements meaningful in terms of a discussion of test validity? Why?

2. The claim is made that some definitions of validity are virtually synonymous with that of test value (Ebel, 1961). If this is true, then ease of administration, adequacy of norms, reliability, etc., become aspects of validity. Should the definition of validity be this encompassing? Give reasons for your answer.

TYPES OF VALIDITY

The definition of validity already stated is useful, but still inadequate. To say that a measuring instrument is "valid" in the sense that validity has been defined is not enough. The statement is too vague. An instrument is valid in terms of its purpose or purposes. Examples already have been presented that vividly illustrate the fact that results yielded by a measuring instrument may be highly valid for one purpose and not at all for another. Since the relative validity of an instrument indicates the degree to which its purposes or aims are being achieved, and since the aims of tests vary, somewhat different types of validity are under consideration in various measuring instruments. The types of validity differ with the aims.

The aims of measurement methods are divided into three categories (French and Michael, 1966, p. 12):

1. To determine how well a pupil performs today in a certain type of situation or subject matter, a cross-sectional sample of which is present in the measuring instrument. For example, a teacher might administer a spelling test to his class to determine how much they know at that moment about spelling. In all likelihood, the test would include only a sample of all the words for which the pupils are responsible.

2. To predict a pupil's future behavior or to estimate his present standing with respect to some characteristic not directly measured by the instrument. For example, in the case of future behavior, a scholastic aptitude test could be given to pupils completing junior high school to predict their academic success in senior high school. In the case of a pupil's present standing, a teacher can administer a paper-and-pencil arithmetic test composed of addition and subtraction problems involving representations of pennies, nickels, dimes, quarters, half dollars, and dollar bills. The size of the test score is intended to show the accuracy with which each pupil can make change when purchasing articles from retail stores.

3. To infer the strength of a pupil trait or quality as reflected in the results yielded by the measuring instrument. For example, a teacher might give a memory test to a class to make inferences about each pupil's scholastic aptitude.

There are certain similarities and dissimilarities among the three aims of measuring instruments. These may be conveniently examined after each of the aims has been translated into its corresponding type of validity. The three types of validity are commonly identified as content validity, criterion-related validity, and construct validity.

Each can be defined as the degree to which a measuring instrument accomplishes the aim associated with that type. Of course, an instrument may be designed to meet more than one of the three aims, and hence the person who develops and uses it must investigate more than one type of validity. Also, some types of validity tend to be more vital in certain kinds of tests. For example, content validity plays a key role in achievement testing and criterion-related validity in aptitude testing. To examine these and other ramifications resulting from the classification of validity types, separate consideration of each type is necessary.

Content Validity

Finding the content validity of a measuring instrument is equivalent to showing how well it samples certain types of situations or subject matter. The instrument claiming high content validity clearly attempts to include a cross-sectional sample of a great variety of items representing the area in which the pupil's performance is being measured.

You recall that the primary purpose of achievement measurement is to discover how well pupils have achieved educational objectives. Prominent educational objectives are those concerning mastery of specific facts and general principles related to the subject matter already covered. These are the objectives toward which many measurement efforts are directed. For example, a teacher may wish to know how well his pupils can add whole numbers, or how rapidly they can read. Another may want to determine how much information his class retains from prolonged discussions and readings about the political, economic, and social causes of World War II. Still another teacher may want to know how well his pupils comprehend and apply the Pythagorean theorem. These and countless similar illustrations typify the rather well-defined areas of subject matter and behavioral changes in terms of which classroom and standardized achievement tests are constructed. The validity of such a test is determined by the representativeness of its contents. Since all possible questions cannot be included, the test is necessarily a sample. To the degree that the sample is not representative, the test lacks content validity.

Content validity is a useful characteristic of measuring instruments other than achievement tests such as scholastic aptitude tests and personal-social adjustment inventories. In each of these types of instrument it is generally true that content validity is secondary to another kind. In scholastic aptitude tests criterion-related validity is paramount, yet content validity is involved in the identification of the great variety of possible test items from which those used are selected. The methods used to arrive at these decisions are vital.

Criterion-Related Validity

Criterion-related validity can be divided into two parts, namely, the validity of instruments designed to predict future performance, and that of instruments designed to estimate present status with respect to a characteristic different from the test. In the past, the former was known as predictive validity and the latter as concurrent validity. The principal difference between these two classifications is the time at which the pupil displays the behavior in question. In the first case we wish to predict the future. In the second instance we want to gain information about present performance by using information obtained indirectly.

Instruments Predicting Future Performance. The foregoing discussion of content validity has already indicated the importance of criterion-related validity in aptitude measurement. The fact that aptitude tests are designed to predict what a pupil can accomplish with training is another way of saying that aptitude tests, by definition, are fundamentally dependent on the establishment of a high degree of criterion-related validity. The uses of scholastic aptitude scores for sectioning classes, anticipating success in reading, estimating the likelihood of graduating from secondary school, or guiding a pupil toward a career in law, amply illustrate the use of a test score or scores to infer tomorrow's successes and failures. This criterion-related validity of a measuring instrument depends on the accuracy of its predictions of future pupil behavior.

In spite of the fact that achievement tests are constructed for the primary purpose of determining how much a pupil knows or how well he can perform as of that moment, another and less common use is forecasting subsequent achievement. For instance, reading tests are used to section classes in various subject matter areas and to predict academic success in secondary school and college. In these cases, high criterion-related validity is unquestionably necessary (Hansmeier, 1960).

Instruments Estimating Present Standing. Some measuring instruments try to determine a pupil's present standing indirectly. The pupil behavior elicited by this type of instrument is thought to correspond closely to a certain external behavior criterion. If it does, the instrument has acceptable criterion-related validity of the concurrent type.

Like content validity, this type is usually a necessary attribute of achievement-measuring instruments. Consider, for example, the measurement of the quality of a pupil's handwriting. General quality may be broken down into elements such as correctness of letter formation, spacing, and uniformity of size and slant. A specimen of the pupil's handwriting might then be compared with a series of specimens of increasing merit with respect to the foregoing elements, and an estimate of the quality of his handwriting obtained. It seems reasonable to argue that this is useful only if it shows the quality of the pupil's handwriting when he writes a letter to his grandmother to thank her for a birthday present or copies the grocery order as dictated by his mother. If, therefore, the data resulting from the measurement of the quality of handwriting are closely related to the quality of handwriting in somewhat less formal simultaneous attempts, then there is sufficient criterion-related validity of this type.

Since paper-and-pencil achievement tests tend to measure a characteristic indirectly rather than directly, additional illustrations of criterion-related validity in achievement testing are readily found. A reading comprehension score from a test might be interpreted as the pupil's reading comprehension when he reads for pleasure. The results of an arithmetic test may be interpreted as related to the accuracy with which a pupil can compute his hourly wages when he shovels snow after school. A teacher may wish to interpret scores on a language usage test as closely correlated with a tabulation of the pupil's actual verbal usage at the time.

Criterion-related validity is also important when considering the validity of instruments in personal-social adjustment, particularly so when they are used to classify pupils in groups. For example, an interest inventory may reflect one or more differences between pupils who have hobbies involving manual skills and those who do not. Also, pupils in need of immediate counseling may be detected by personal-social adjustment inventory scores and other evidence.

Construct Validity

To describe construct validity, it is first necessary to establish the meaning of the term "construct." A construct is a characteristic assumed to exist to account for some aspect of human behavior. In psychology many constructs are used, such as cautiousness, tendency to conform, rigidity, insecurity, dominance, and ability to apply principles. These terms serve the useful purpose of providing a convenient means of identifying the psychological concepts they represent. By themselves, however, they do not explain the concept or any theory underlying it.

Whenever a measuring instrument is believed to reflect a particular construct, its construct validity must be investigated. This amounts to determining how well certain constructs account for pupil performance as measured by the instrument. To make a suitable investigation possible, the construct should be sufficiently well defined so that verifiable inferences can be drawn from it. Testing the accuracy of the inferences with a measuring instrument is a way of confirming or denying the claim that a certain construct accounts for variations in the performance elicited by the instrument. If the instrument has a high degree of construct validity, its findings will vary from one kind of individual to another, or from one situation to another, as the theory underlying the construct would predict. In many ways, establishing construct validity is the same as validating the theory that defines the construct (Cronbach and Meehl, 1955).

Examples of the importance of construct validity can be found in the measurement of achievement, aptitude, and personal-social adjustment. In the case of achievement measurement, construct validity is a pertinent characteristic of those tests claiming to measure study skills and ability to reason. Is there any proof that the tests actually measure study skills or reasoning ability as defined by the authors of the tests? Aptitude tests can be challenged by questioning whether evidence is available that can describe the complete meaning of the aptitude measured. A teacher using a general mental ability test may demand of its author an explanation of his concept of general mental ability and how the pupil's activities as he writes the test correspond to that concept. Finally, when a personal-social adjustment inventory is thought to reveal the composition of the pupil's personality, the inventory must have a high construct validity.

Problems

3.   Give illustrations of cases in which a teacher might be concerned about the content validity of (a) a paper-and-pencil personality inventory and (b) a paper-and-pencil test of clerical aptitude.

4.   Cite arguments for and against the statement that content and construct validity have little in common with criterion-related validity, as well as little in common with each other (Ebel, 1961, p. 640).

5.   Cronbach (1970a, p. 125) believes that the central question asked when the construct validity of a test is being determined, is the following: "How can scores on this test be explained psychologically?" What is the full meaning of this question? Illustrate.

6.   In the last analysis, the responsibility for valid use of a test rests on the individual who interprets it (Cronbach, 1970b). Do you agree? If so, what are the responsibilities in this regard for authors of standardized tests?

DETERMINATION OF DEGREES OF VALIDITY

Since validity is classified into three types for descriptive purposes, it is appropriate to discuss the determination of the validity of measuring instruments in terms of the same classification. It has already been shown that, as the purposes of instruments vary, so do the types of validity. Furthermore, a given instrument may have more than one purpose, and thus should be characterized by more than one type of validity. The demonstration of high validity, then, is commonly a multiple approach rather than a single attempt.

These facts are of vital concern to the builders of measuring instruments. After all, acceptable validity is the most critical quality an instrument can have. Thus the author is obliged to examine carefully the aims of his instrument and, for each aim, present evidence that the instrument can validly perform that function. This information can be of immeasurable help to those who wish to use the test for a particular purpose and, most important of all, interpret its scores in the most precise manner possible.

Content Validity

Because content validity is oriented toward achievement testing, which is such a formidable part of pupil evaluation, this section is restricted to achievement testing. Achievement tests are developed on the basis of educational objectives with verbal or mathematical aspects and are designed to show how well pupils have achieved those objectives. Therefore, to construct a test with high content validity, the teacher must begin with the same educational objectives that guided his classroom instruction. On the basis of the objectives chosen, tables of specifications are built, which in turn guide the selection of test items.

When a skilled teacher devises an achievement test for his own class, the probability increases that the level of content validity will be acceptable. Who knows better than he which of many proposed test items are probably "trick" or "unfair" items? Such test item labels, when attached after considered thought by either teacher or pupil, can be regarded as vernacular expressions equivalent to saying that the test items, and hence the test as a whole, lack content validity to some degree. The teacher's knowledge of the class and its educational objectives are the most important factors accounting for the superior content validity of carefully constructed classroom tests.

Standardized Achievement Tests. To some teachers standardized achievement tests are unknown quantities. The impressive titles of the tests, coupled with sometimes equally impressive authorship and precisely stated directions for administration, tend to add to, rather than subtract from, their doubts. Yet these instruments typically resemble classroom tests a great deal, although they are more highly refined. They usually represent the thinking of teachers, supervisors, subject matter specialists, and others, and have withstood a rigorous statistical assault by professional testing specialists.

The educational objectives of a course of study and their tables of specifications, which are so important in the identification of the content validity of teacher-built achievement tests, are equally important in the identification of the content validity of standardized achievement tests. Hence, for a standardized achievement test to have high content validity when measuring pupil achievement resulting from a given teaching effort, it must be constructed in terms of the table of specifications evolving from the learning experiences guided by that teacher in that instance. Beyond question, this rarely happens.

Since his test is to be used by not one teacher but hundreds, and since each teacher has his own peculiar set of educational objectives and tables of specifications, despite much common ground in many subject matter areas, the author can hope only to orient his instrument toward those educational objectives that appear to be most prevalent. Each teacher who proposes to use a standardized achievement test is automatically obliged to find convincing evidence that the educational objectives and tables of specifications involved closely correspond to his own.

To aim a standardized achievement test at popularly held educational objectives, the test builders do considerable investigation. A year or more may be spent in the laborious process of scanning lesson plans, state study guides, and widely used textbooks covering the subject matter in question and also in interviewing teachers and supervisors directly involved in the selected field. The process finally yields a core of reference materials thought to be most representative, and possibly a panel of subject matter specialists thought to be well-informed. On the basis of these sources of information, test items are constructed.

If the reference materials are identical with or closely related to those used by a teacher, the possibility of the standardized achievement test having high content validity for that teacher's use is considerably improved. Obviously, the textbooks and courses of study composing the reference materials should be identified for the potential test user. Some, but by no means all, manuals accompanying standardized achievement tests include complete titles and dates of publication of each of the reference materials. If a panel of subject matter specialists in the field is used, either independently of or in conjunction with the reference materials, they should be identified by name and pertinent facts about their professional qualifications listed.

Unfortunately, detailed information about the reference materials and any panel of specialists is not given in some test manuals. The inquiring teacher finds only glib statements about the "careful selection" of the test items and the "popular modern textbooks" that were consulted. This is meager fare indeed for any astute reviewer.

Regardless of the limited data of this kind that might be offered in the test manual, at least two other avenues relative to content validity should be explored. In the first place, manuals usually supply ample statements about the purposes of the test and its limitations in terms of subject matter covered. These statements bear careful perusal for evident reasons. Secondly, the test items themselves should be carefully scrutinized. It is highly recommended that a teacher play the role of pupil and write the answers under similar conditions. Then there should be an additional item-by-item examination. For each item the question must be asked: In view of my educational objectives, the tables of specifications derived from them, and the method of teaching I followed, is this test item appropriate for my pupils this term? Answers will be regularly affirmative if there is acceptable content validity.

The item-by-item examination should not be a casual operation. On the contrary, it should be tied directly to the teacher's educational objectives and his tables of specifications. A tabulation should be made by copying each item number opposite the cell of the table of specifications with which it is associated. If a test item is related to more than one cell, it should be tabulated accordingly. If it is primarily related to one cell of the table and secondarily related to another, a simple coding scheme can identify these differences. Although this process is lengthy, it is necessary if the content validity of a standardized achievement test is to be assessed.

Some standardized achievement tests simplify the tabulation process by including with the test materials a printed outline summarizing the various subject matter areas covered and listing opposite each the numbers of the test items primarily related to that area. An illustration of this can be found in the manual of the *Dunning-Abeles Physics Test* (1967, p. 5). In addition, the 50 items are classified according to subject matter topic and pupil behavioral change. This is summarized in Table 9 for *Form E*. Note the comparatively heavy emphasis on the traditional topics of mechanics, electricity, and magnetism, and the comparatively light emphasis on recall of information (that is, knowledge) about each topic.

TABLE 9.   Classification of Test Items in the *Dunning-Abeles Physics Test (Form E)*.

| Subject Matter Topic | Behavioral Changes | | | |
	Knowledge	Compre-hension	Application	Total
Mechanics	1	9	6	16
Electricity and Magnetism	3	4	5	12
Atomic and Nuclear Physics	3	2	1	6
Wave Motion and Light	1	7	2	10
Kinetic-Molecular Theory	0	5	1	6
Total	8	27	15	50

From Dunning and Abeles, 1967; reproduced by permission of Harcourt, Brace & World, Inc.

The balance among the cells in Table 9 may or may not be agreeable to a secondary school physics teacher for a given testing situation. Even if it is, it may not be acceptable one term or one year later. The relative emphasis teachers place on various combinations of topics and behavioral changes is a moving target. It shifts with time. Ideally a standardized achievement test must keep pace, step by step. Content validity can be fleeting.

Problems

7. Unlike Table 9, the table of specifications for the *Dunning-Abeles Physics Test* lists the number of each test item in the cell in which it is classified. Select five test items from the test at random and, without referring to the item numbers in the table, assign each to a cell. Explain the reasons for your classification and any differences between your decisions and those of the authors.

8. The *Cooperative Primary Tests* are designed to measure "understandings" in verbal and mathematical areas at the three primary grade levels. Study the table of specifications for each of these tests that are included in the manual. Does a high degree of content validity seem to exist in each case?

9. Dizney (1965) has found evidence that pupil comments on the fairness of the items do little to improve achievement tests. Do you agree?

Criterion-Related Validity

The degree of criterion-related validity for various types of tests can be determined by using aptitude tests as illustrations. The practical value of tests designed to measure mechanical aptitude, clerical aptitude, scholastic aptitude, musical aptitude, and similar areas is centered in the accuracy with which a teacher can make predictions on the basis of their scores. It is logical, then, to take a longitudinal approach to the problem of determining criterion-related validity. A scholastic aptitude test can be administered to a group of pupils today and predictions of future academic achievement can be made in one or more subjects. Actual academic success can be measured at that future time by achievement tests or, possibly, final marks. Finally, predicted achievement can be compared with actual achievement, and the criterion-related validity of the scholastic aptitude test as applied in these prediction situations can be evaluated.

Predictions of future academic achievement can also be made in terms of the same units as those of the achievement measurement criterion, but are not always made in this manner. With statistical techniques beyond the scope of this book, a teacher or administrator may be able to say, for example, that a pupil whose scholastic aptitude test score is 117 should be expected to score in the vicinity of 82 on a particular English test. However, the predictions usually made are informal, thus making it awkward to compare predicted and actual achievement. They are often equivalent to saying that pupils who do well on the scholastic aptitude test will probably achieve well in school, whereas those who do badly will probably achieve poorly. In view of this, comparison of the scholastic aptitude scores and the measures of academic success would yield information concerning criterion-related validity.

Some of the basic steps in establishing the validity of an aptitude test can be examined most directly with an illustration. Suppose that an eighth-grade teacher of social studies wishes to know how satisfactorily achievement in that class can be predicted from scholastic aptitude test scores from a test given one year earlier. For the sake of simplicity, he is willing to define achievement in the social studies in terms of the scores of a comprehensive achievement test given at the end of the term. The result is a double measurement of each pupil, the data from which may be compiled in a fashion similar to Table 10.

TABLE 10.   Scholastic Aptitude Test Scores and Achievement Test Scores of Eighth-Grade Social Studies Pupils.

Name	Scholastic Aptitude Test Fall Term, Seventh Grade		Social Studies Test Fall Term, Eighth Grade		Difference in rank
	Score	Rank	Score	Rank	
Jim	135	1	66	9	8
Sam	130	2	90	1	1
Ruth	120	3	68	8	5
Mary	117	4	85	3	1
John	116	5	81	4	1
Louise	114	6	47	17	11
Ralph	113	7	69	7	0
Mae	112	8	77	5	3
Quinton	111	9	65	10	1
Sandra	109	10	56	15	5
Larry	107	11	89	2	9
Norma	106	12	49	16	4
Frank	101	13	57	14	1
Milton	100	14	58	13	1
Dave	97	15	71	6	9
Joe	95	16	60	11	5
Bill	94	17	38	19	2
Sally	90	18	31	20	2
Margaret	88	19	40	18	1
Sue	87	20	59	12	8

The twenty pupils are arranged according to their scores on the scholastic aptitude test. Their achievement scores are listed opposite the scholastic aptitude scores. To facilitate interpretation, both sets of scores are ranked from 1 to 20 according to the position of the pupil in the class with respect to each test. If the scholastic aptitude test possesses high validity, the rank of any pupil in the scholastic aptitude test should be approximately the same as his rank in the achievement test. Table 10 shows that the aptitude and achievement ranks of some pupils do not differ by more than one. These cases support the contention that the scholastic aptitude test can predict achievement in eighth-grade social studies. Since other pupils, however, have differences of eight or more, these cases tend to refute the contention concerning the validity of this test.

The foregoing analysis is casual, if not crude. A precise statement of the validity of the test is still lacking. Figure 20 was prepared to give a more comprehensive picture of the entire class of twenty pupils. In this figure are plotted twenty points, one for each pupil. The position of a point is found by locating on the vertical axis the scholastic aptitude test score of that pupil, and moving to the right, parallel to the horizontal axis, until his achievement in social studies is located. The points are numbered in terms of the ranks of the pupils on the scholastic aptitude test.

A moment of thought will indicate that, if the scholastic aptitude test has high criterion-related validity in this example, the points should arrange themselves in a straight line. Thus, the greater the tendency of the points to approximate a straight line, then the greater the validity. All points in Figure 20 obviously do not fall in a straight line, yet the eye can detect a definite elongated pattern that certainly suggests linearity. It is interesting now to observe the positions of points representing the five pupils whose ranks differ so greatly. The points are numbered 1, 6, 11, 15, and 20, and are represented by squares rather than circles. It is not surprising that they are all found along the perimeter of the pattern, and that their deletion would strengthen the impression that the points tend to form a straight line.

Figure 20 strongly suggests, as Table 10 did, that the scholastic aptitude test has at least some validity in this situation. To identify the degree even more precisely, another step is necessary. This is the computation of the *Pearson product-moment coefficient of correlation*, often known as simply the *correlation coefficient*, and represented by the letter r.

The Correlation Coefficient.   The correlation coefficient is a number representing the straight-line relationship between the values of two variables, such as the values of the two variables resulting from double measurement of the pupils listed in Table 10. If points are plotted, as in Figure 20, and all of them fall in a straight line, the value of r will be 1.00. As the points deviate from a straight line, the value of r decreases to zero. In addition,

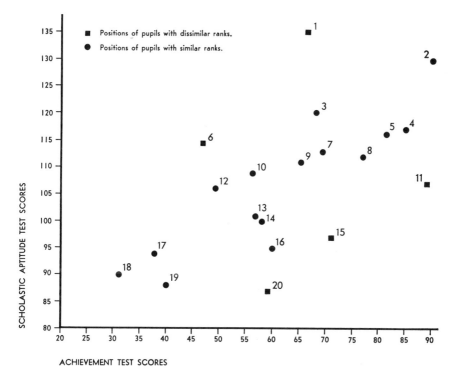

FIGURE 20.   Scatter Diagram of Scholastic Aptitude Test Scores and Achievement Test Scores.

when high values of one variable are associated with high values of the second variable, and low values of one variable are associated with low values of the other, as in the data in Table 10, the relationship is called positive and the r value carries a positive sign. If high values of one variable are associated with low values of the other, and low values of the first are associated with high values of the second, the relationship is called negative and the r value carries a negative sign. Thus, r values vary from -1.00 to $+1.00$. The number is indicative of the degree to which the points form a straight line, and the sign reveals the direction of the relationship. It should be noted that positive r values are much more common than negative values in educational evaluation.

The computation of an r value provides a succinct representation of the validity of the scholastic aptitude test in this instance. The extent to which the points plotted in Figure 20 tend to form a straight line determines the r value computed from the data, and also shows how efficiently the scholastic aptitude test predicts the eighth-grade achievement in social studies.

Computation of the correlation coefficient is somewhat lengthy, but simple. One formula of r that can be applied to the data in Table 10 is shown in Appendix A (see pages 578–581). With the formula is a complete description of the manner in which the values in Table 10 are summarized and substituted into the formula. An r value of 0.61 is found.

The interpretation of this value has, in reality, already been given. It represents the degree to which the points fall into a straight line or, stated differently, the rate of change in social studies achievement test scores compared with a given change in scholastic aptitude test scores. Unfortunately, some uninitiated observers try to improve on the interpretation by considering the r value as a percent. The fact that r values, with the sign ignored, vary from 0.00 to 1.00 undoubtedly encourages this error. In any event, the reasoning follows essentially this path: An r value of 1.00 results from data that, when plotted, yield a perfectly straight line. Hence, prediction of achievement on Test Y from scores from Text X will be 100 percent accurate. On the basis of this evidence, the accuracy of the prediction decreases as the r value decreases in such a fashion than an r value of 0.61 would mean that estimates of social studies achievement test scores based upon scholastic aptitude test scores will be 61 percent accurate. This latter argument is not true.

Although it is correct to say that an r value of 1.00 indicates a prediction of 100 percent accuracy, the decrease in prediction accuracy is not proportional to the decrease in the r value. Table 11 shows the percentage reductions in the margins of prediction error of scores on Test Y from scores de-

TABLE 11.   Forecasting Efficiency of Product-Moment Coefficients of Correlations of Various Sizes.

Coefficient of correlation	Index of forecasting efficiency (per cent)
1.00	100.0
0.99	85.9
0.97	75.7
0.95	68.8
0.90	56.4
0.80	40.0
0.70	28.6
0.60	20.0
0.50	13.4
0.40	8.4
0.30	4.6
0.20	2.0
0.10	0.5
0.00	0.0

rived from Test X as the correlation between the two sets of scores changes. This percentage reduction is known as the *index of forecasting efficiency*. Instead of being 61 percent, the forecasting efficiency of an r value of 0.61 is slightly greater than 20 percent. In other words, predicting social studies achievement test scores on the basis of scholastic aptitude test scores will have a margin of error about 80 percent as great as the margin of error that would occur if we predict social studies achievement test scores *without* knowledge of the scholastic aptitude test scores. The reduction in the margin of error is about 20 percent, which can be considered the percentage of improvement over chance. As the correlation increases, so does the reduction in the margin of error of prediction (Guilford, 1965, pp. 376–379).

Care must be exercised when using the index of forecasting efficiency to interpret correlation coefficients representing the predictive validity of a test. It is all too easy to underestimate the effectiveness of the prediction instrument (Angoff, 1968). For instance, when we wish to select from a large group those pupils who will be academically successful, it is likely that a scholastic aptitude test will produce results vastly superior to random selection. An example is the selection of a freshman class for a highly selective university from a large number of high school seniors who apply. Here the aptitude test is far more useful than suggested by the index of forecasting efficiency associated with its validity coefficient.

Although they represent by no means the only method, product-moment coefficients of correlation are popular representations of the criterion-related predictive validity claimed for a test. Other types of coefficients of correlation, discussions of which can be found in many textbooks of statistical methodology, are also used, but in a minority of instances. The computation of some of these is quite simple and rapid. One is the rank-difference correlation coefficient, otherwise known as the Spearman rho. It uses the differences between two sets of ranks such as those in Table 10 as a basis for its computation (see pages 580–581). In the case of the data in Table 10, the rho value is 0.60, a close approximation of the r value. We cannot always expect such a high degree of agreement.

It is clear, certainly, that an adequate grasp of the demonstration of criterion-related validity is highly dependent on an adequate grasp of the meaning of the correlation coefficient. Although teachers generally do not find themselves confronted with computations of an r value, they are regularly obliged to interpret them.

Expectancy Tables.   Computing product-moment coefficients of correlation and interpreting them in terms of the information on forecasting efficiency in Table 11 is an investigation of the relative validity of an instrument when its data are used for making very fine "pinpoint" predictions. Note that the scholastic aptitude scores in Table 10 are to be used to predict the *exact* social studies achievement test scores. Often such close prediction is unnecessary. Rather than try to predict in this manner, many teachers wish to predict only in terms of broad categories: they may wish to predict whether a pupil will achieve "above average," "average," or "below average" in his class. If this is the intended use of the scholastic aptitude test, the predictive validity of the instrument can be much more realistically appraised by *expectancy tables* (Wesman, 1949, 1966).

An expectancy table is merely a condensed version of plotted data similar to that in Figure 20. In the figure, each gradation of the scores of each test is shown; in an expectancy table, the scores are grouped into a convenient number of intervals. Table 12 is an expectancy table based on the data in Table 10 in which each set of test scores is grouped into three intervals. The number within each cell of the table represents the number of pupils who have scholastic aptitude and social studies achievement scores within the limits indicated.

The interpretation of Table 12 is straightforward. For instance, we can say that none of the pupils whose aptitude score is "below average" (less than 95) has an achievement score that is "above average" (greater than 75). Moreover, none of the pupils with "above average" aptitude scores (greater than 115) receives a "below average" achievement score (less than 55). More inclusive statements could be made in a slightly different manner. Pupils with aptitude scores of 95 or greater rarely (2 out of 16) receive achievement scores of less than 55.

Generally the interpretation of the expectancy table is simplified if percents are used. This requires a larger number of cases than twenty but can be illustrated by using the data from Table 12. By computing percents for each row separately, as in Table 13, we can estimate the probability of different levels of success in social studies for pupils having a given level of

TABLE 12.   Expectancy Table for Scholastic Aptitude and Social Studies Achievement Test Scores.

Scholastic aptitude test scores	*Social Studies Achievement Test Scores*			
	Below average (Below 55)	*Average* (55–75)	*Above average* Total	(Over 75)
Above average (Over 115)	0	2	3	5
Average (95–115)	2	7	2	11
Below average (Below 95)	3	1	0	4
Total	5	10	5	20

scholastic aptitude. For example, if a pupil has "average" scholastic aptitude, the probability of his having "below average" achievement in social studies is 18 in 100. His probability of having "average" achievement is 64 in 100; for "above average" achievement, it is 18 in 100.

TABLE 13.   Expectancy Table Based on Percents.

Scholastic Aptitude		Number of Cases	Social Studies Achievement Test Scores		
Category	Test Score		Below Average	Average	Above Average
Above Average	Over 115	5	0	40	60
Average	95–115	11	18	64	18
Below Average	Below 95	4	75	25	0

Degrees of Criterion-Related Validity.   It is certainly clear at this point that the scholastic aptitude test in question does not have the greatest possible predictive validity. On the other hand, although the r value is no larger than 0.61 and the expectancy table shows some pupils classified in cells other than the ones desired, we cannot automatically say that the validity of the instrument is unsatisfactory. On the contrary, the instrument may be judged as useful for prediction purposes if, in spite of its inaccuracies, it can predict future achievement of these pupils better than other means.

Actually the r value of 0.61 is comparatively large in this case. When attempting to predict future academic achievement we often must work with scholastic aptitude tests with lower r values. This does not mean that they are extremely poor. On the contrary, tests yielding r values as low as 0.30 can be quite useful for screening groups of candidates for an educational program or a job. Oddly enough, we have a good deal of confidence in such everyday predictions as those concerning quality of one's physical health and the outcome of athletic contests, and yet there is reason to believe their degree of validity is less than that of the scholastic aptitude test.

Predictions of future achievement based on aptitude test data must be viewed in much the same manner as the predictions of life expectancy made by insurance companies and of deaths due to automobile accidents made by national safety organizations. Life insurance companies can predict with striking accuracy the percentage of thirty-year-old men who will be living twenty-five or fifty years from now; yet they cannot predict with similar accuracy which members of the group will be alive or dead at these future dates. The number of deaths in automobile accidents during a Fourth of July weekend can be predicted with small error, but the identity of the victims cannot be predicted with the same minimum of error. This is true of achievement predicted from aptitude test data. If predictions are made for a group, the accuracy is customarily quite good; a prediction made for an individual member of that group may be distressingly inaccurate.

Test Manual as a Source of Information.   The primary source of information for most teachers as they investigate the validity of standardized aptitude tests and personal-social adjustment inventories is the test manual. Although this compilation is usually highly abbreviated, it regularly provides sizable amounts of data about the author's attempts to establish acceptable validity and perhaps lists references to research conducted by other interested investigators. Examination of the test manual by the potential test purchaser is always sound practice.

The test author who wishes to present the most comprehensible discussion of his test's validity is certain to find it an exacting task. Among other things, he must carefully describe the criterion with which his test is correlated and the nature of the pupils who cooperated in the validation attempt. Both of these descriptions emphasize the fact that the determination of validity as it is outlined is relative to the criterion used and the pupils measured. To the degree that the criterion is weak or the standardization group inadequate in any way, the determination of validity becomes less meaningful.

In the illustration summarized in Table 10, the scholastic aptitude test has some validity in terms of the social studies test as administered to eighth-grade pupils. If this illustration were a formal attempt to determine the relative validity of the scholastic aptitude test, the author of that test should report in the test manual such characteristics of the social studies achievement test as its length, level of difficulty, the nature of its items, and its content validity. Furthermore, the test author would identify the pupils tested as to their sex, age, level of education, socioeconomic status, and any pertinent factor that would help the teacher decide whether this group of pupils was similar to those for whom the author's test is designed and in turn similar to the pupils which he, the teacher, plans to test.

Problems

10.   What is cross validation (Anastasi, 1968, pp. 181–184)? Of what significance is it in the determination of the relative validity of a scholastic aptitude test? Give an illustration to support your answer.

11.   When homogeneous groups of pupils are used, the predictive validity of aptitude tests is low. In other words, the r values are small compared with those for

the same test used with heterogeneous groups. Explain why this is so (see Cronbach, 1970a, pp. 431–432).

12.   What is a standard error of estimate (Guilford, 1965, pp. 360–361)? Of what use is this value when a validity determination is being made for a scholastic aptitude test and its results interpreted?

13.   What major types of expectancy tables are being used? Study the illustrations shown by Schrader (1965) and compare them with Tables 12 and 13.

Construct Validity

Many of the methods used to determine the relative validity of the first two types are also suitable when construct validity is being investigated. An analysis of construct validity is supported by total available knowledge of the validity of the instrument in question. In other words, demonstrating what constructs account for variations in the performance elicited by a measuring instrument is a difficult task. It involves many methods, some of which can also be properly used in connection with other types of validity.

The basis on which the investigation of construct validity proceeds is provided by the theory underlying the construct supposedly involved in the measuring instrument. On the basis of the theory, predictions are made: one group of individuals will differ from another in terms of the data yielded by an instrument involving the construct, or individuals will or will not change in terms of an instrument involving the construct after they have experienced certain environmental conditions. The measuring instrument is then used to test the predictions. If the predictions and the data produced by the instrument concur, evidence in support of the construct validity has been found. If they do not, a state of uncertainty exists. Either the instrument does not involve the construct, or the theory is not sound. In any event, the degree of construct validity is in doubt (Cronbach and Meehl, 1955).

Comparisons with Other Instruments.   One method of determining construct validity is to correlate the data from the instrument under study with a second instrument thought to measure the same construct. This is sometimes done with group tests of general mental ability of the type regularly used in elementary and secondary schools. For example, an experimental group test of general mental ability and the *Stanford-Binet Scale, Form L-M,* are administered to a sample of pupils. The scores from the experimental test and the *Stanford-Binet* test are then correlated. If the *Stanford-Binet* test is an acceptable measure of general mental ability, and its scores are closely correlated with those of the experimental test, the experimental test is said to have high construct validity.

Since complete agreement is seldom obtained as to the quality of the test serving as a standard, the correlation process is often repeated with several tests. When a group test of general mental ability is being studied, the standards are usually individual tests or well-known group tests of this trait. In areas other than general mental ability testing there is a similar tendency, rightly or wrongly, to use popular tests reputed to measure the same construct as the test under investigation.

Comparisons with Judges' Ratings.   The use of judges is another means of assessing construct validity and has been used in connection with a variety of tests. For example, suppose that a paper-and-pencil inventory has been constructed to measure the social adaptability of junior high school pupils. Each of the 100 items included in the inventory requires the pupil to select one of the five alternatives that best approximates his behavior should he be confronted with the social situation described. The author defines social adaptability as the ability of a person, when participating in a social situation, to adjust his behavior in accordance with the nature of the situation and to do so easily.

To discover whether this inventory actually measures social adaptability, the author may employ a group of judges who are to observe independently— and somewhat surreptitiously—the social behavior of a group of pupils. The judges are, of course, ignorant of the pupils' scores determined by the paper-and-pencil inventory. They may use rating scales and check lists to record each pupil's behavior at such events as a school dance, a class picnic, a basketball game, and a concert. If the scores correlate well with the ratings, then the paper-and-pencil inventory has acceptable construct validity.

Serious doubts have been raised about the use of ratings of individuals as criteria against which to validate test scores (Guilford and others, 1962). These ratings are thought to be valid in that it is assumed that the raters know what they are measuring. Unfortunately, ratings regularly measure different traits from those intended.

Problems

14.   When two testing instruments are compared to estimate the construct validity of one of them, and the second is considered a standard, is the investigator engaging in a "circular" argument?

15.   Select a well-known paper-and-pencil personality inventory and suggest procedures that might be useful for establishing its construct validity.

General Considerations

Determining the relative strength of any one of the three types of validity in a measuring instrument is sometimes frustrating. If the instrument is commercially distributed, the teacher may faithfully scan the test manual and doggedly sift the references to articles in professional journals in which the instrument is mentioned. Yet it often happens that even this effort leaves the investigator unsatisfied. The information gleaned from the process is often too vague and too limited.

Vague Terms.   The complaint of vagueness is traceable in part to the widespread use of a handful of terms that are not as meaningful as often supposed. Expressions such as "face validity," "statistical validity," and "curricular validity" fall into this category. Even the expression "validity coefficient" is applied too generally to contribute much to a discussion of validity.

A paper-and-pencil test has "face validity" when it seems to be valid to someone reading it. In other words, if a person unsophisticated in achievement measurement is handed an English vocabulary test for high school seniors and, after reading it, agrees that it appears to be a "valid" vocabulary test for that group, "face validity" is claimed. Admittedly, this is important to the pupils writing a test. Certainly they will tend to cooperate more readily if they sense that the nature of the items logically corresponds to the overall purpose of the test. Nevertheless, a flat claim for "face validity" of an instrument does not release its author from the responsibility of establishing the relative strength of one or more of the three types of validity. Also, the presence of "face validity" does not guarantee that the test has enough validity of any type.

"Statistical validity" is not a meaningful expression. As the title suggests, validity determinations in which correlation coefficients of some kind are computed are labeled determinations of "statistical validity." Within this loose framework are many determinations of validity, particularly criterion-related and construct validity. The expression is, therefore, unnecessary.

The coefficients of correlation resulting from computations of "statistical validity" are known as "validity coefficients." This is a more helpful expression than "statistical validity," but still cannot be applied in isolation. The "validity coefficient" indicates how much criterion-related or construct validity an instrument possesses. Thus, unless a "validity coefficient" is described in terms of one of these types, it is not definitive.

The expression "curricular validity" suggests the same type of validity as content validity. In achievement measurement both are acceptable. In aptitude and personal-social adjustment measurement, however, "curricular validity" becomes an awkward identification because the term "curricular" suggests only that an academic curriculum is implicated in some fashion. To speak of content validity does not inject any such restrictions. Therefore, the expression "curricular validity" is not so flexible and thus less satisfactory than "content validity."

Limitation of Evidence.   The validity of an instrument often appears to be based on limited evidence. Reflection will show that determining the strength of any one of the three types of validity is noticeably time-consuming and expensive in all but a minority of cases. Even the most conscientious author cannot exhaust all the possible avenues of approach or use many varieties of groups of pupils for his validation attempts. Also, evidence that a certain type of validity is *not* present in an instrument is rarely listed in a test manual. In many cases, however, it is reported in educational or psychological journals or test reviews in other publications.

The Mental Measurements Yearbooks.   Fortunately, there is a yet unmentioned source of information about standardized instruments of all kinds. This helps fill the voids mentioned in the preceding paragraphs, and is known as *The Mental Measurements Yearbooks*, the first volume of which was published in 1938. Additional volumes are published at fairly regular intervals. The largest section of each of the *Yearbooks* is entitled *Tests and Reviews* and contains—among other items—materials related to validity. This section assists in appraisal of measuring instruments by providing frank, critical reviews of them and comprehensive bibliographies of references concerning each. For a given instrument, it is common to find such information as its complete title, age or grade levels of the individuals for whom it is designed, date of publication, cost, time limits, and the names of the author and the publishing company. In addition, one or more reviews is usually included, and the author identified. Pertinent references are listed without comment and may be numerous, in a few instances as many as one hundred. These contain information on the construction, validity, use, and limitations of the instrument.

The magnitude of the yearbooks is somewhat startling. For instance, *The Sixth Mental Measurements Yearbook* (Buros, 1965) alone contains 1219 test and inventory titles, 795 critical reviews of them, and 8001 references. When it is remembered that this yearbook supplements rather than supplants the preceding five volumes, it is eminently clear that these volumes along with *The Seventh Mental Measurements Yearbook* (Buros, 1971) form a colossal body of material.

Several significant companion volumes to the *Yearbooks* have been published. The first was *Tests in Print* (Buros, 1961), which contains information about currently available tests and is cross-referred with the *Yearbooks*. Later two monographs were issued, *Reading Tests and Reviews* (Buros, 1968) and *Personality Tests and Reviews* (Buros, 1969). These contain a wealth of information about reading tests and personality inventories respectively, part of which appeared originally in the *Yearbooks*.

Counselors, supervisors, and research workers, as well as classroom teachers, find the *Yearbooks* and their companion volumes of inestimable value in their instrument appraisals. As a readily accessible compilation of facts about, and considered criticisms of, measuring instruments, they are unmatched. Certainly no validity appraisal other than a teacher-constructed instrument is complete without including whatever information the *Yearbooks* can provide.

Problems

16. Study the reviews in *The Mental Measurements Yearbooks* of two tests or test batteries of interest to you in the area of (a) academic achievement, (b) scholastic aptitude, and (c) interest patterns. On the basis of the evidence presented, compare each pair of tests or test batteries in terms of their various kinds of validity.

17. What is differential content validity (Hopkins and Wilkerson, 1965)? How is this concept related to the methods used to establish high content validity for achievement tests?

SUMMARY

Validity, the most vital attribute of any measuring instrument, is commonly defined as the degree to which that instrument actually serves the purposes for which it is intended. Since the purposes of measurement are divided into three categories, validity is classified into three types: (1) content validity, (2) criterion-related validity, and (3) construct validity.

Content validity is defined as the degree to which an instrument can be used to measure the present performance of a pupil in a certain type of situation or subject matter of which its items are a cross-sectional sample. Criterion-related validity exists (1) to the extent that it can be used to predict a pupil's future performance, and (2) to the degree that the behavior elicited by a measuring instrument corresponds to external but concurrent pupil behavior. An instrument has construct validity if a specified construct accounts for the variations in pupil performance it elicits.

The demonstration of a measuring instrument's validity is almost invariably a lengthy and laborious task. It may be necessary, for example, to ascertain whether a given instrument is characterized by more than one of the three types of validity, perhaps all three. Furthermore, suitable criteria and samples of pupils must be found before the validity determination can be completed. This is particularly true of criterion-related validity investigations. Lastly, the end product of a validity determination may or may not be quantitative in nature. Studies of content validity typically do not yield quantitative evidence, whereas studies of criterion-related and sometimes construct validity do yield quantitative evidence, such as a product-moment coefficient of correlation.

Before a teacher uses any measuring instrument, he is obliged to conduct a thorough investigation of its validity. Not only must he decide that his purposes are the same as those for which the instrument is designed, but also he must convince himself that its author has acceptable evidence that the instrument can accomplish the purposes claimed. A teacher's appraisal of the validity of a standardized instrument commonly utilizes the material presented in the instrument's manual, the information provided by *The Mental Measurements Yearbooks* and their companion volumes, and the considered judgment of the teacher.

Suggested Readings

Anastasi, A. *Psychological testing.* (3rd ed.) London: Macmillan, 1968. Chapters 5 and 6.
> Chapter 5 includes descriptions of various types of validity and is nonquantitative in nature. In contrast, Chapter 6 emphasizes quantitative representations of validity and their interpretation. One section deals with expectancy tables, another with the net gain in selection accuracy resulting from the use of a test.

Angoff, W. H. Written test scores and prediction of success in college: A reply. *School and Society,* 1968, 96, 282–283.
> Illustrations given show that the effectiveness of a prediction instrument can be underestimated by interpreting its validity coefficient in terms of the index of forecasting efficiency. In a given situation, the use of a test to select pupils who will be successful can yield a pronounced improvement over random selection.

Campbell, D. T. Recommendations for APA test standards regarding construct, trait, or discriminant validity. *American Psychologist,* 1960, 15, 546–553.
> The background of the debate concerning construct validity is reviewed. Objections raised by various testing specialists are listed, each of which is followed by a brief evaluation by the author.

Cronbach, L. J. *Essentials of psychological testing.* (3rd ed.) New York: Harper & Row, 1970. Chapter 5.
> Within this chapter are discussions of the three types of validity. Steps for computing a product-moment and a rank difference coefficient of correlation are given.

Cronbach, L. J. Validation of educational measures. *Proceedings of the 1969 Invitational Conference on Testing Problems.* Princeton: Educational Testing Service, 1970.
> Validation problems associated with educational tests are considered. Primary emphasis is given to content and construct validity. A useful summary of types of validation is given in table form.

Ebel, R. L. Must all tests be valid? *American Psychologist,* 1961, 16, 640–647.
> This is a provocative article. The author argues that all tests need not be "valid" if the term "valid" is not to be made synonymous with the term "good," and if validity is a clearly defined concept that can be quantified by correlating test scores and data from an independent criterion.

French, J. W., and W. B. Michael. *Standards for educational and psychological tests.* Washington: American Psychological Association, 1966. Pp. 12–24.
> This bulletin is the result of the second important attempt by the American Psychological Association and other organizations to develop an authoritative statement concerning test standards. Content, criterion-related, and construct validity are defined carefully and illustrations are provided.

Wesman, A. G. *Double-entry expectancy tables.* Test Service Bulletin, No. 56. New York: Psychological Corporation, 1966.
> Since predictions of future achievement are often made on the basis of two predictors rather than one, a double-entry expectancy table is needed. In this bulletin, such tables are described and one is developed for the relationship between college grade-point average and a combination of scholastic aptitude scores and rank in high school graduating class.

References Cited

Anastasi, A. *Psychological testing.* (3rd ed.) London: Macmillan, 1968.

Angoff, W. H. Written test scores and prediction of success in college: A reply. *School and Society,* 1968, 96, 282–283.

Buros, O. K. (ed.) *Tests in print.* Highland Park, N.J.: Gryphon Press, 1961.

Buros, O. K. (ed.) *The sixth mental measurements yearbook.* Highland Park, N.J.: Gryphon Press, 1965.

Buros, O. K. (ed.) *Reading tests and reviews.* Highland Park, N.J.: Gryphon Press, 1968.

Buros, O. K. (ed.) *Personality tests and reviews.* Highland Park, N.J.: Gryphon Press, 1969.

Buros, O. K. (ed.) *The seventh mental measurements yearbook.* Highland Park, N.J.: Gryphon Press, 1971.

Cronbach, L. J. *Essentials of psychological testing.* (3rd ed.) New York: Harper & Row, 1970a.

Cronbach, L. J. Validation of educational measures. *Proceedings of the 1969 Invitational Conference on Testing Problems.* Princeton: Educational Testing Service, 1970b.

Cronbach, L. J., and P. E. Meehl. Construct validity in psychological tests. *Psychological Bulletin,* 1955, 52, 281–302.

Dizney, H. Characteristics of classroom test items identified by students as "unfair." *Journal of Educational Measurement,* 1965, 2, 119–121.

Dunning, G. M., and S. Abeles. *Manual, Dunning-Abeles Physics Test.* New York: Harcourt, Brace & World, 1967.

Ebel, R. L. Must all tests be valid? *American Psychologist,* 1961, 16, 640–647.

French, J. W., and W. B. Michael. *Standards for educational and psychological tests.* Washington: American Psychological Association, 1966.

Guilford, J. P. *Fundamental statistics in psychology and education.* (4th ed.) New York: McGraw-Hill, 1965.

Guilford, J. P., and others. Ratings should be scrutinized. *Educational and Psychological Measurement,* 1962, 22, 439–447.

Hansmeier, T. W. The Iowa Tests of Educational Development as predictors of college achievement. *Educational and Psychological Measurement,* 1960, **20,** 843–845.

Hopkins, K. D., and C. J. Wilkerson. Differential content validity: The California Spelling Test, an illustrative example. *Educational and Psychological Measurement,* 1965, **2,** 413–419.

Schrader, W. B. A taxonomy of expectancy tables. *Journal of Educational Measurement,* 1965, **2,** 29–35.

Wesman, A. G. *Expectancy tables—a way of interpreting test validity.* Test Service Bulletin, No. 38. New York: Psychological Corporation, 1949.

Wesman, A. G. *Double-entry expectancy tables.* Test Service Bulletin, No. 56. New York: Psychological Corporation, 1966.

CHAPTER 10

The Reliability of Measurement Methods

Prodded by his teenage son, the proud owner of a near-new automobile decided to determine the number of miles that it traveled for each gallon of gasoline consumed. During a week in early May he carefully tabulated the gasoline consumption and the miles traveled, and computed the gasoline mileage to be 15.2 miles per gallon. Later that same month the owner selected another week, determined the gasoline consumed and miles traveled, and found that the gasoline consumption was 15.0 miles per gallon. The procedure was repeated during the first week of June, and a gasoline mileage of 15.4 miles per gallon demonstrated.

It is not surprising that the gasoline mileages varied by only small amounts. Because the three one-week periods were separated by relatively short periods of time, and because such factors as weather and traffic conditions were, for all practical purposes, uniform during all three trials, it seemed reasonable that the results should be consistent if these measurements of gasoline mileage were at all accurate. No doubt the owner ignored the minor differences among the three values and concluded that the gasoline mileage produced by his automobile under the existing traffic and weather conditions was fairly well identified. He might have even averaged the three measurements, and then used this value as the final product of his investigation.

Had he known that the true gasoline mileage had remained unchanged during the three trial periods and was really 15.3 miles per gallon, he would not have been dismayed. On the contrary, he might have been quite pleased with the accuracy of his estimates. Furthermore, if he had been pressed for an explanation as to why his three estimates varied although the true value did not vary, he might have shrugged his shoulders and attributed the small fluctuations to "chance" errors.

The chance errors that he had in mind are many. First of all, the measurement of the gasoline delivered by the pump might have been in errror. Thus, exactly ten gallons of gasoline drawn from the pump might not necessarily have been registered on the meter as exactly ten gallons. Quite possibly in one case it might have been measured as slightly more than ten gallons and in another as slightly less. Secondly, the reading of the meter introduced a possibility of error. The gasoline was measured to the nearest one-tenth of a gallon, and since the amount necessary to fill the tank probably fell somewhere between two such points, it had to be estimated to the nearest one-tenth of a gallon. Overestimates and underestimates are distinct possibilities. Thirdly, the attendant might have filled the gasoline tank to varying degrees of "fullness" each time the owner began and completed the measurement of the gasoline mileage. Haste and carelessness might have caused slightly different amounts of gasoline to be contained within the tank when it was classified as "full." Lastly, the odometer might not have registered the miles traveled with perfect accuracy, and the reading of it also might have involved certain amounts of estimation.

Despite these possibilities of error, the gasoline mileages were fairly consistent. Such consistency of measurement is equally desirable in education. A good measuring instrument must yield dependable information; in other words, if it is possible to use it repeatedly in the same unchanging situation, the information yielded by each administration of the instrument should be similar to that yielded by any other administration. For instance, the typing teacher who gives a speed test to his pupils on Friday would hope that the typing rates determined would be the same, for all practical purposes, as those obtained from such an exercise administered on Monday, if the pupils did not study or practice during the weekend. Likewise, the scholastic aptitude scores yielded by a test given to pupils at 10:30 A.M. on September 18th are assumed to be essentially the same as those that would be obtained were the test administered at 9:30 A.M. on September 19th.

Should there be no assurance that tests such as these do yield reasonably consistent results, their value would be severely limited. Before any measuring instrument should be used, therefore, the question might be asked: If repeated attempts are made to obtain information about an unchanging pupil attribute with this instrument, will the results tend to duplicate each other? The question can be stated much more simply: Is the measuring instrument highly reliable?

DEFINITION OF RELIABILITY

Reliability means consistency of results. This is equivalent to saying that a highly reliable instrument can be used repeatedly in an unchanging situation and produce constant or near-constant results. When, on the contrary, a measuring instrument is applied again and again and yields results that vary greatly, even though the situation has not changed, the instrument is highly unreliable. Unfortunately, all instruments are somewhat unreliable.

Chance Errors

To say all measuring instruments are somewhat unreliable is the same thing as saying that all measurements are subject to some *chance error*. Chance errors, or compensating errors as they are sometimes called, have one vital characteristic; they have a tendency to cancel each other when the instrument is used many times. There are a number of possibilities of chance error in the gasoline mileage determinations, one of which can be traced to the meter on the gasoline pump. Although a given withdrawal of precisely ten gallons from the pump may be recorded on the meter as slightly more than ten gallons, a second attempt might be recorded as slightly less. Were the process to be repeated an infinite number of times and the tendency to over-estimate and underestimate found to be equal, then the error is a chance error and affects the reliability of the measurement.

There still remains, of course, the possibility that the meter consistently overestimates or consistently underestimates; no canceling takes place no matter how many measurements are made. This is obviously an error of measurement, but not a chance error. It does not lessen the reliability of the measurement, but does lessen the validity. Thus, the degree of validity of the gasoline mileage measurement is reduced if the readings on the gasoline meter were always, say, one percent less than the actual amount of gasoline delivered by the pump. In the case of the typing speed test and the scholastic aptitude test, similar errors are possible. Either one could have yielded erroneous measurements to the extent that, say, every typing rate is seven percent too low or every scholastic aptitude score is four percent too large. In contrast to compensating (chance) errors, which are important in the reliability of measuring instruments, these errors are classified in the second group of errors called *biased errors*, or *constant errors*, and affect only the relative validity of these instruments. These errors do not tend to cancel each other when an instrument is used many times.

Pupil-Centered and Instrument-Centered Factors.   Many factors affect the reliability of measuring instruments. Some are associated with the pupils themselves, whereas other factors arise from the instrument itself. Pupil factors ordinarily mentioned are state of health, fatigue, motivation, emotional strain, and the like. Two factors associated with the instrument itself are prominent in the paper-and-pencil test. First of all, the test is only a sample of an immense number of possible test items; secondly, the scoring of the test, particularly those with essay test items, may not be consistent, a factor known as lack of scorer reliability. Many additional factors related both to the pupils and to the instrument and its administration have been listed elsewhere (Thorndike, 1951).

Certainly the importance of these factors as they affect the information yielded by a measuring instrument is not uniform from pupil to pupil or instrument to instrument. The pupil-centered factors may easily fluctuate from day to day, perhaps from forenoon to afternoon, and, for many pupils, play only a small role in terms of influencing an instrument's results. Instrument-centered factors tend to be less damaging when, for example, a paper-and-pencil test is lengthened by adding suitable items and when the scoring becomes more objective. Trivial as some of the sources of trouble may seem to be, they can drastically reduce the value of a measuring instrument.

Perhaps it is disconcerting to find such factors as those listed classified as the originators of chance errors. Admittedly they may not fit as neatly into the scheme as the gasoline meter and its errors do. Yet we can argue that the errors from the sources listed would cancel out if it were possible to measure an unchanging pupil attribute many times with each of many tests for this attribute, tests in turn scored independently by many judges.

Problems

1. On the basis of your experiences, order the following in terms of the degree of reliability that probably exists:
   a. Using a common yardstick to measure the height of basketball players.
   b. Using a stopwatch to measure the time needed to run 100 yards.
   c. Using a quart bottle to measure volume of bath water.
   d. Using a bathroom scale to measure the weight of loaded suitcases.
2. Suppose that you were confronted with the problem of estimating the degree of reliability with which a small group of English literature teachers could score pupil answers to a certain limited-response essay test item. Describe the steps you would take to meet the problem.

DIFFERENTIATING BETWEEN VALIDITY AND RELIABILITY

The terms "validity" and "reliability" have too often been used as though they are synonymous or nearly so. Though the concepts are somewhat related, they are by no means identical. The validity of a measuring instrument is the degree to which it actually serves the purposes for which its use is intended; the reliability of an instrument is its capacity to yield consistent information regardless of whether it serves the purposes in question. Thus a highly reliable instrument is not necessarily an equally valid instrument. For example, the heights of male college seniors majoring in education can be measured with considerable reliability. Yet this fact would in no way support the statement that the tall male college senior will be a better class-room teacher in future years than a short one. Educational tests may likewise have superior reliability and still be woefully lacking in validity. An arith-metic achievement test used to measure qualities of leadership is one of many possible examples.

It is timely to reemphasize that high validity is the most important characteristic of an instrument. The role of reliability is a vital but secondary one when a measuring instrument is being appraised. The importance of both characteristics can be summarized in the statement that the perfect in-strument must serve the purpose or purposes for which it is intended and, in doing so, must produce consistent information.

DETERMINATION OF DEGREES OF RELIABILITY

Testing specialists concerned with methods for estimating the validity of a measuring instrument often search for external evidence and try to appraise the instrument's validity in terms of such evidence. Reliability determination, on the other hand, is not based on evidence of this kind. Instead, the instru-ment is compared with itself or some equivalent form. These procedures can be illustrated readily in the case of paper-and-pencil tests.

The determination of test reliability is based on one central method. The instrument to be investigated is used (perhaps in conjunction with an equivalent form) to obtain one or more attribute measurements of each member of a group of pupils. Each measurement identifies the position of each pupil in terms of the attribute measured. The consistency with which he maintains his position within the group from measurement to measure-ment is a reflection of the reliability of the test. This consistency can be translated into a product-moment coefficient of correlation, called a *coefficient of reliability*. Moreover, a coefficient of reliability can often be interpreted more easily by converting it to a *standard error of measurement*. This is an attempt to estimate the size of the errors of measurement caused by the unreliability of the test.

Determination of Coefficients of Reliability

Coefficients of reliability can result from four separate processes known as the stability method, the equivalence method, the stability and equivalence method, and the internal-consistency method. According to the stability method, a test is administered once, then a short period of time is allowed to pass and it is administered a second time to the same pupils. A coefficient of reliability is computed from the two sets of test scores. The equivalence method requires two equivalent forms of the test. They are given consecutively to a group of pupils, and a coefficient of reliability is computed. If a time interval of some size (for example, one week) occurs between the administration of the two equivalent forms, then the reliability determination follows the stability and equivalence method. Lastly, it is possible to analyze the data obtained from a single administration of a test and compute a reliability coefficient. This is the internal-consistency method.

In the past, the coefficients of reliability resulting from the application of the four methods have been identified as the coefficient of stability, coefficient of equivalence, coefficient of stability and equivalence, and coefficient of internal consistency respectively. Although these are useful labels, they do not adequately describe the kind of reliability determination that yielded the coefficient of correlation (French and Michael, 1966, pp. 26–27). It is recommended that in their place more complete statements be used to describe the coefficient of correlation such as "coefficient of reliability representing stability of measurements obtained by administering two different forms of the test one week apart."

Stability Method.   We can easily determine the reliability with which we can assess such dimensions as the length or weight of a block of wood. Repeated measurements of the object are made and compared. A similar procedure is sometimes applied when the reliability of educational measuring instruments is under study. Suppose that a test author constructs a 100-item test designed to measure eleventh-grade pupils' knowledge of American history, and that this test has satisfactory content validity. To determine the reliability of his instrument, the author may give the test to a sample of eleventh-grade pupils, tabulate the results, allow an interval of time to pass, and finally readminister the instrument to the same pupils under the same conditions as before. Unless there is evidence to the contrary, it is assumed that the group has not changed with respect to their knowledge of American history during the time interval. Ideally then, each pupil would receive the same test score the second time as the first. In reality, the most the author can hope for is that pupils who received high scores on the first test administration will receive high scores on the second test administration and that those who received low scores the first time will receive low scores the second time.

Plotting the results of the two test administrations is most profitable. Figure 21 is a partial reproduction of the kind of configuration that might occur if the test were highly reliable. Many more cases (perhaps 200 or more) would be used than are shown in Figure 21. Observe that in this figure, as in the case of Figure 20 shown in Chapter 9, the points arrange themselves in an elongated manner so as to approximate a straight line. If the test were very unreliable, the points would scatter considerably, even to the extent that no straight line could satisfactorily represent the total number of points.

Once again the product-moment coefficient of correlation is the most convenient and suitable means of representing the degree to which the points conform to a straight line. The scores of the two test administrations are substituted in the appropriate formula (see page 579) for the coefficient of correlation, and a coefficient of reliability is computed. For a test such as described in this illustration, the r value might be 0.90 or more. A value of 1.00 would represent perfect test reliability in terms of this method, whereas a value of 0.00 would represent no test reliability.

Further examination of Figure 21 reveals another noteworthy feature of the data. Observe that the straight line that seems to fit the points as plotted will not, if extended, touch the point at which the score resulting from each administration is zero. Instead it will intersect the vertical axis slightly above the zero point. This commonly occurs when the reliability of achievement tests is determined by test-retest procedures. The scores from the second test administration are generally slightly higher than those from the

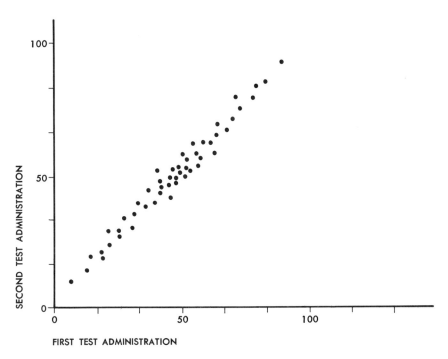

FIGURE 21. Scatter Diagram of Achievement Test Scores Resulting from Two Test Administrations.

first test administration, because of the practice effect that results from the first test administration. Unlike a block of wood, which can be measured endlessly without any noticeable effect on the block, a pupil will probably change as a result of the measurement. In the case of achievement tests, the change is customarily slight but discernible.

The length of time allowed between test administrations is critical and must be selected with care. If it is too short, pupils will remember the answers given at the first test when they answer the questions the second time; if it is too long, the pupils may change with respect to the characteristic measured. In many cases, a week or two is judged to be an appropriate compromise. Obviously there is no single, widely accepted time interval suitable for all types of test with all varieties of pupils.

The stability method is not considered the most defensible for establishing test reliability. Some of its weaknesses have been mentioned. Three apparent defects are the practice effect that may result from the first test administration, the difficulty of establishing a suitable interval of time between test administrations, and the failure to have identical testing conditions both times. More serious in the eyes of some, however, is the fact that the coefficient of reliability reflects pupil-centered chance errors but not one of the most vital instrument-centered chance errors, namely, the fact that tests are samples of an immense number of possible items. Repetition of a test at different times will reveal inconsistent pupil behavior, but, since the same test is used twice, the sampling of the items is held constant. Consequently, an important instrument-centered chance error is ignored and the coefficients of reliability tend to be unduly *high*. Some writers recommend that these coefficients not be computed for achievement tests.

Equivalence Method.   Rather than involve administration of the same test twice to a group of pupils, as in the case of the stability method, the equivalence method utilizes the scores from each of a pair of equivalent tests. The two equivalent tests are given to a suitable group of pupils with little or no time allowed between the two administrations. For each pupil two scores are available, one from each form of the test. When the scores are correlated, a coefficient of reliability results. If the two forms of the test were administered with an intervening time interval as in the test-retest method, then the stability and equivalence method is being followed. In many such cases, the time interval is at least a day and no longer than a week.

The requirement that a measuring instrument be available in two equivalent forms is, of course, a severe limitation. Equivalent forms of classroom tests are seldom found. Teachers usually do not construct them except in the case of "make-up" tests, which are supposed to be equivalent to the tests they replace. Standardized tests, on the other hand, are often published with two equivalent forms, sometimes more. Suppose that the test author who developed the 100-item achievement test in American history wants to construct an equivalent form. The problem he faces is not incidental. One danger to be avoided is the designing of the equivalent form to be so "equivalent" to the original that it is essentially identical. Then he still has but one test in spite of his efforts. The second danger is to design the equivalent form to be so "unequivalent" that it is measuring something at least slightly different from the original. A satisfactory equivalent form is somewhere in between.

The problem of building an equivalent form of the American history achievement test can be attacked systematically. First of all, as emphasized in the discussion of content validity of achievement tests, the test author must have identified certain specific educational objectives and developed one or more tables of specifications on the basis of them. To measure the degree to which these selected objectives have been achieved, he had to compose a vast number of test items. Pretesting the items at various times with appropriate pupils has helped screen them. In all likelihood, only part of the surviving items are included in the original form of the test. The balance are available for an equivalent form. Then the test author might dip into this supply in search of a second cross-sectional sample of test items that represent the same level of difficulty and the same relative importance of the cells of the table of specifications as the set of test items composing the original form. Evidence concerning the equivalence of the two forms can be obtained by methods beyond the scope of this book (Wilks, 1946; Gulliksen, 1968).

Assume that the test author completes an equivalent form of the American history test and labels it Form B. The original test, now called Form A, and Form B can be administered consecutively to a group of 200 eleventh-grade pupils for whom the test is designed. The result is a pair of scores for each pupil, which in turn can be plotted and will yield a scatter of points very much like that in Figure 21. A coefficient of correlation computed from the data is a coefficient of reliability and will of course fall somewhere between 1.00 and 0.00. An r value of 0.91 is found in the case of the history test.

This coefficient of reliability is clearly not the same representation of test reliability as the coefficient yielded by the stability method. The chance errors involved in the two methods are different. In the equivalence method, the pupil-centered chance errors are not reflected in the coefficient of reliability. This is because the time interval between the two test administrations is virtually nonexistent. On the other hand, the instrument-centered chance error, associated with the fact that the test is necessarily a sample, is manifest in this method. Each form of the test is assumed to be a cross-sectional sample of the same group of items. The opposite is true in the case of the stability method: the pupil-centered chance errors are operative, whereas the instrument-centered chance error is not.

The use of two equivalent forms of a test is a recommended way of computing an estimate of test reliability. The test author may choose to give the two forms consecutively to an appropriate group of pupils, or he may choose to allow a time interval between the two tests. By the latter process, many pupil-centered as well as instrument-centered chance errors will influence the reliability estimate. Therefore, since reliability is defined as the relative absence of chance errors in the measurement results, the most logical procedure for estimating test reliability is to give equivalent forms with a time interval between the test administrations, and then compute a coefficient of reliability. Remember that this type of coefficient of reliability represents stability of performance by the pupil over a short period of time. This is essential information, since we often want assurance that the pupil would have obtained a similar test score had he been tested on a different day or with an equivalent instrument.

Internal-Consistency Method.   The practical difficulties in the test-retest and equivalent-forms methods of determining reliability emphasize the desirability of estimating test reliability with a single administration of a single form of the test in question. The savings in time and labor are obvious. In this undertaking, however, new formulas are necessary and new assumptions must be made.

There are two basic procedures for analyzing the results of a single administration of a test to assess the reliability of the instrument. The first, sometimes known as the split-half procedure, arbitrarily divides the total test into two halves, scores them separately, thereby yielding two scores per pupil, and correlates the pairs of scores. The resulting coefficient of correlation is a coefficient of reliability of one-half of the test rather than the total test, and is adjusted to be applicable to the total test. The second procedure, sometimes known as an analysis-of-variance procedure, involves examination of the responses to each test item in terms of the number of pupils who successfully answered the item and the number who failed it.

Usually the first controversy concerning the application of the split-half procedure is centered around the selection of the two halves. Imagine the number of possible halves that could be obtained by splitting the 100-item achievement test in American history previously mentioned. The most satisfactory set of all possible halves would be that pair composed of the two most equivalent members. In other words, the level of difficulty of the test items and the manner in which the items reflect the relative importance of the cells of the table of specifications involved should be the same in both halves. Dividing a test haphazardly into halves without thought of equivalence reduces the split-half process of reliability determination to busy work of dubious value.

If two equivalent halves of a test are to be found in the same way as two equivalent forms of a test are constructed, little has been gained in terms of conserving time and labor when the split-half method is used. Therefore, some compromises generally are made. Again the achievement test in American history can illustrate a typical situation. Let us assume that this achievement test, like most achievement tests, follows two general principles of construction. In the first place the level of difficulty of the test items for the most part increases slightly from the beginning to the end of the test so that the least difficult items are found at the beginning of the test and the most difficult are found at the end. Secondly, the test items are crudely grouped according to content; items relating to each cell in the table of specifications are clustered in a systematic fashion. Under these conditions, a convenient way of selecting two halves that would tend to be equivalent is to separate the odd-numbered items from the even-numbered items. The level of difficulty of the items in the odd half will approximate the level of difficulty of those in the even half. So also will the content of the test items in the odd half approximate that of the items in the even half. Note that had the author decided to divide his test so that the items numbered from 1 to 50 composed one half, whereas the items numbered from 51 to 100 composed the second half, the second would be somewhat more difficult than the first and would sample different material. The lack of equivalence would be striking.

The odd-even division is a popular method of separating a test into two halves of approximate equivalence. If the test author chooses to use this method, the remainder of the reliability determination is simple. First he gives the complete test (with odd and even test items in their proper order) to a representative group of eleventh-grade pupils for whom the test is designed. Then he separately scores the odd- and even-numbered items. Plotting the two scores for each pupil produces a diagram much like Figure 21, if the performance of the pupil tends to be consistent. The degree to which the points fit a straight line can again be represented by a correlation coefficient, which can be computed by substituting the odd-half and even-half scores into the appropriate formula. The correlation coefficient between their scores is 0.73. This is the coefficient of reliability for one-half of the test rather than for the total test. To estimate the expected coefficient of reliability of the total test, and adjustment formula known as the Spearman-Brown "Prophecy Formula" (Spearman, 1910) is used.

In modified form the fomula is

$$r_{xx} = \frac{2\, r_{oe}}{1 + r_{oe}},$$

where

r_{xx} = coefficient of reliability of the total test;
r_{oe} = coefficient of correlation between the odd-half scores and the even-half scores.

In the case of the American history achievement test the coefficient of reliability is

$$r_{xx} = \frac{(2)\ (0.73)}{1 + 0.73} = 0.84.$$

Observe in this case the noticeable increase in the size of the coefficient of reliability as the length of the test is doubled.

The principal assumption underlying the applicability of the Spearman-Brown formula is that the two halves are indeed equivalent. As the two halves fail to be ideally equivalent, so the coefficient of reliability of the total test as yielded by the Spearman-Brown formula is an underestimate. Since the equivalence of the two halves is probably somewhat inadequate, the coefficients of the Spearman-Brown formula are conservative estimates of test reliability.

Computation of a coefficient of reliability by an analysis-of-variance method most often utilizes one of the Kuder-Richardson formulas (Kuder and Richardson, 1937). This formula, identified as K-R #20, is relatively easy to apply, although its derivation is intricate and beyond the scope of this book. An important category of information necessary for solution of the formula is the proportion of pupils passing and failing each test item. This procedure estimates test reliability on the basis of consistency of pupil performance from item to item within the test. In the case of achievement tests, the r values computed are usually smaller than expected because the item content of this type of test is not homogeneous.

The Kuder-Richardson and Spearman-Brown formulas are appropriate only for power tests, which are so administered that practically all pupils have an opportunity to attempt every test item. The r values that will result from use of these formulas with a single administration of a pure speed test will be inflated, perhaps substantially. The amount of overestimation is difficult to establish, but tends to decrease as the number of unattempted test items becomes smaller. The preferred procedure for determining the reliability of a speeded test is the stability and equivalence method.

You can readily see that, no matter which of the two methods of computation is used, the coefficients of reliability do not reflect chance errors associated with day-to-day variations of the pupils tested. Stated otherwise, pupil-centered chance errors are ignored in this type of reliability coefficient; however, the instrument-centered chance errors, arising from the fact that the test is but a sample of many possible test items, are reflected.

Comparison of Coefficients of Reliability. The various coefficients of reliability can be compared in two different ways. First of all, the similarities and dissimilarities in their methods of determination can be tabulated. In

TABLE 14. Test Forms and Number of Administrations Required by Various Methods of Determining Coefficients of Reliability.

	Number of Test Administrations		
		Two test administrations	
Test forms needed	One test administration	Same day	Different days
One form	Internal Consistency		Stability
Equivalent forms		Equivalence	Stability and Equivalence

the second place, they can be compared on the basis of the chance errors they reflect. Both comparisons can be summarized by tables such as Table 14 and Table 15.

In Table 14 the methods of determination are considered. For each coefficient of reliability, the need for one or more forms of the test and the number of test administrations required are listed. It is apparent again that the coefficient or reliability most easily found is that yielded by the internal-consistency method, whereas the one found with greatest difficulty is that yielded by the stability and equivalence method.

TABLE 15. Chance Errors Reflected in Various Coefficients of Reliability.

		Chance Errors	
Method of determination	Procedure	Pupil-centered	Instrument-centered
Stability	Same test form given on different days	X	
Stability and Equivalence	Equivalent test forms given on different days	X	X
Equivalence	Equivalent test forms given on same day		X
Internal Consistency	Split-half procedure		X
Internal Consistency	Kuder-Richardson procedure		X

Two important types of chance errors and their relationship to each coefficient of reliability are shown in Table 15. Pupil-centered and instrument-centered chance errors are reflected only in the stability and equivalence method.

Problems

3.   To what degree would one expect the problem of the "practice effect" to reduce the value of a coefficient of reliability from the stability method as a representation of the reliability of a test? Is "practice effect" also a problem when the equivalence method is used? Explain your answer.

4.   Serious objections have been raised with respect to the usefulness of the test-retest correlations as representations of degrees of reliability (Cureton, 1969, p. 795). Do these objections justify the position that this type of reliability determination should be avoided?

5.   It is argued that, in spite of evidence presented by the test author, so-called equivalent forms of an achievement test may be far from equivalent for a particular pupil population, and therefore comparisons based on these forms of the test may be distorted (Howell and Weiner, 1961). Study this argument and the supporting data. Of what significance are they in terms of the equivalence method?

6.   Differentiate between K-R #20 formula and K-R #21 formula for determining a coefficient of reliability for classroom tests (Cureton, 1966).

Determination of the Standard Error of Measurement

Since every test is somewhat unreliable, each score obtained for a pupil must be considered as an estimate of his "true score," which would have been found had the test been totally reliable. Useful as the coefficients of reliability are when test reliability is being appraised, they do not directly offer an estimate of the actual magnitude of the error in a test score for a given pupil, that error having been caused by test unreliability. The standard error of measurement, on the other hand, attempts to do this. In other words, the standard error of measurement affords the test consumer some indication of the size of the difference (resulting from the fact that the test is unreliable to some degree) between an obtained score for a pupil and his "true score" on the test. This difference is expressed in the same units as the test scores are. Observe that, when using the expressions "obtained score" and "true score" in the description of the standard error of measurement, considerations of validity are temporarily ignored.

Computing Standard Errors of Measurement.   The computation of the standard error of measurement is not difficult. Its formula is

$$S.E._{\cdot m} = \sigma\sqrt{1 - r_{xx}},$$

where

$S.E._m$ = standard error of measurement;
σ = standard deviation of total test scores;
r_{xx} = coefficient of reliability.

The standard error of measurement of the achievement test in American history is 3.2. To obtain this value, we use the coefficient of equivalence of 0.91 along with the standard deviation, which is computed in accordance with a formula shown in Appendix A (see pages 575–578). The standard deviation value of 10.5 and the coefficient of equivalence are substituted in the standard error of measurement formula as follows:

$$S.E._{\cdot m} = \sigma\sqrt{1 - r_{xx}} \quad = \quad (10.5) \quad \sqrt{1 - 0.91} \quad = \quad 3.2.$$

Interpreting Standard Errors of Measurement.   It is *not* appropriate to say that, in the case of the American history achievement test, a pupil's "true score" differs from his obtained score by no more than 3.2 raw-score points. Rather, it can be said that the "true scores" will not differ from their respective obtained scores by more than 3.2 raw-score points in approximately two-thirds of the measurements we might make with this test. Or, the standard error of measurement can be doubled and the statement made that the "true scores" will not differ from their respective obtained scores by more than 6.4 raw-score points in approximately 95 percent of the measurements we might make. Finally, we could triple the standard error of measurement and say that the "true scores" will not differ from their respective obtained scores by more than 9.6 raw-score points in approximately 99 percent of the measurements.

Although the foregoing interpretations still do not offer a direct, unequivocal statement of the error caused by test unreliability in a given pupil's obtained score, teachers still consider the standard error of measurement to be a highly meaningful measure of test reliability. The fact that it is expressed in the same units as the test scores contributes greatly to its popularity. Teachers repeatedly argue that it offers a good basis for judging how satisfactory the reported test reliability is for a given testing function. In general, of course, it is pleasing to find low standard errors of measurement and most distressing to be confronted with large values. As the standard error of measurement increases, the confidence in obtained scores as estimates of "true scores" correspondingly decreases.

Because of test unreliability, scores must be interpreted as regions rather than as points. Such regions, often known as "bands," are determined by the standard error of measurement of the test. Since a pupil's "true score" does not differ from his obtained score by more than the standard error in approximately two-thirds of the measurements we make, it is customary to find the limits of the "band" by adding the standard error of measurement to and subtracting it from the obtained score. Suppose that a pupil obtained a test score of 70 on a test with a standard error of measurement of 3. The "band" often used would have a lower limit of 67 and an upper limit of 73. A pupil with a score of 75 would have a 72–78 "band." By the way, because the two "bands" overlap, we can say that there is probably no difference between the two pupils in terms of this test. Should the two "bands" fail to overlap, there probably is a genuine difference between the pupils in question. This use of the standard error of measurement, crude as it is, serves to inject caution into the interpretation of small differences between raw scores.

Problems

7. Study the procedure for scoring and interpreting the *School and College Ability Tests*. Why does the width of the percentile bands vary?
8. The standard error of measurement is a standard deviation. Identify the theoretical distribution of which it is the standard deviation (Anastasi, 1968, pp. 94–95).
9. Describe a practical classroom situation in which knowledge of the standard error of measurement would be useful to you. Using layman's terms, how would you explain to a pupil that his test score should be interpreted as a region (or band) rather than as a point?

APPRAISING ESTIMATES OF RELIABILITY

The test manual accompanying the standardized achievement test and *The Mental Measurements Yearbooks* are extremely valuable sources of information in a study of reliability determinations, as they are in connection with the topic of validity. One or both sources often provide sufficient information to allow the teacher to make at least tentative judgments. Particular attention needs to be given those aspects of the determination that may influence negatively the interpretability of the reliability coefficient or standard error of measurement reported.

Coefficients of Reliability

With statistical results, a simple judgment based upon the statistical value alone is probably foolhardy. Careful scrutiny of the source of the value generally produces an enlarged view of it. In the case of coefficients of reliability, careful scrutiny most often includes a prolonged look at (1) the test itself, (2) the characteristics of the group of pupils involved in the reliability determination, and (3) the testing conditions. The enlarged view embodies shrewd guesses as to why the reliability coefficient is the size it is and whether the test scores are sufficiently free of chance errors to permit the test to be satisfactorily applied in a specific situation.

Characteristics of the Test.   Examination of the test itself to find helpful evidence for appraising a coefficient of reliability requires attention to at least three characteristics. These are the tendency of the test to be speeded, the homogeneity or heterogeneity of its content, and the length. The role of speededness as it affects the size of coefficients yielded by the internal-consistency method and the role of homogeneity of test content when the Kuder-Richardson formula is applied are mentioned earlier. The importance of test length in determining the size of coefficients of reliability is dramatically illustrated by the Spearman-Brown formula. If the number of items in a test is increased by adding items equal in quality to the original ones, the reliability of the test will improve noticeably. With use of the Spearman-Brown formula, it is necessary to assume the items added are indeed equal in quality to the originals. Unfortunately this assumption is not always remembered, and an overgeneralized statement results, namely, the longer the test, the more reliable it is. Although it is true that longer tests tend to be more reliable in repeated instances, lengthening a test does not automatically assure us of greatly improved reliability.

Characteristics of the Pupil Group.   The group of pupils cooperating in the reliability determination is a second source of information. As in the case of the determination of criterion-related validity, the test author should characterize this group as to any attribute conceivably related to the dimension being measured. For example, the 200 eleventh-grade pupils involved in the experimental use of the American history achievement test should be identified as to grade level, average scholastic aptitude score on some well-known instrument, previous training in history, and geographic location. These and other pieces of information will help the teacher immeasurably in reaching his decision as to whether the 200 eleventh-grade pupils are comparable to his class for whom the test is being selected. If his class and the 200 eleventh-grade pupils seem to be the same, he can assume that the reliability estimates listed accurately reflect the reliability of the measurements he will make. If his class is vastly dissimilar, the reliability estimates based on the test scores of the 200 pupils may well be meaningless for him.

The variability of the 200 eleventh-grade pupils with regard to the attribute being measured by the achievement test must never be ignored. A key value in describing the variability of the group in terms of this test is the standard deviation, in this instance 10.5. As the variability in American history achievement increases, so will the standard deviation. Moreover, as the variability increases, so will the coefficient of reliability. An extreme illustration involving the achievement test under consideration can readily illuminate the problem. Suppose that the 200 pupils had been drawn in about equal numbers from tenth, eleventh, and twelfth grades, in spite of the fact that the test is designed for eleventh-grade pupils who are completing a course in American history. The tenth-grade pupils may know relatively little about the material covered in the test; the eleventh-grade pupils know more; the twelfth-grade pupils, now having completed both American history and probably world history courses, supposedly command even more knowledge. If this is true, the new group of 200 pupils is extremely variable in terms of American history achievement, and the standard deviation will exceed 10.5. Hence the coefficient of reliability will be larger. Obviously the robust size of a coefficient of reliability based on a highly variable group of pupils does not indicate the reliability of measurements made on a more uniform group. Therefore, to interpret a coefficient of reliability, one should study the standard deviation of the test scores. Coefficients of reliability become more and more interpretable as the standard deviation of the standardization group, the 200 eleventh-grade pupils, approaches that of the teacher's class.

Standardization of Testing Conditions.   The uniformity or lack of uniformity of the testing conditions is another point of concern when reports of reliability determination are appraised. Certainly the testing conditions at the time the standardization group is measured must be essentially the same as those recommended by the test author. This prerequisite is generally attained without difficulty. A persistent problem, however, is pupil motivation. An appropriately oriented pupil who is to be given the test only once may be highly motivated throughout the measurement process. In contrast, a pupil who is the unwilling victim of double measurement, be it by test-retest or equivalent forms, and who is measured at some inopportune time for no reason known to him, is undoubtedly less motivated. These differences introduce error. They will, for example, tend to lower the coefficients of stability that might be computed.

Minimum Coefficients of Reliability.   Thoughtful consideration of the test itself, the characteristics of the standardization group used, and the testing conditions inevitably lead to a more intimate grasp of the meaning of the coefficient of reliability. The question is often posed, however, as to what minimum a coefficient of reliability must attain before the test can be used under any condition. The answer is not straightforward. For instance, tests whose reliability coefficients are near 0.50 are used. Either the teacher applied an instrument of limited reliability or he did not measure at all, since, as happens periodically in the measurement of personality traits, no other more satisfactory instruments exist. Needless to say, interpretation of scores from instruments with such low reliability coefficients must be made with extreme caution.

There is no single mimimum size a coefficient of reliability must reach, since the minimum alters with the purpose for which the test scores are to be used. The minimum size is comparatively low when the level of group accomplishment is being measured. It rises for the measurement of the level of *individual* accomplishment. In any event, coefficients of reliability of about 0.85 and higher are regularly found for many standardized achievement and aptitude tests distributed by well-known publishing companies. Values for personality inventories vary considerably but frequently are lower.

Reliability of the Difference Between Two Measurements.   An important sidelight of the problem of appraising coefficients of reliability is revealed when the purpose of the measurement is to identify differences between two measurements rather than to interpret each measurement as such. Determining the difference between two measurements is relatively common. A teacher may wish to know how much progress his pupils made as a result of a particular learning experience. He could measure the class before the learning experience, then again after it, and interpret the difference between the two scores. In another case, a test battery composed of three, four, or more achievement and aptitude tests may have been given to a class. Then a test profile for each pupil is found. Among others, the question might be raised as to whether a pupil or a class is more competent in English than in general science. Differences between the scores of the two appropriate tests would be most helpful.

Although the coefficient of reliability indicates the reliability of individual measurements, it does not directly show the reliability of the difference between two measurements. This, however, can be computed when we know the coefficients of reliability of the two tests involved in the determination of the differences in question, and the intercorrelation between these tests.

It is unfortunately true that, if there is any important correlation between the two tests yielding scores from which difference scores are obtained, the reliability of these difference scores is substantially lower than average reliability of the two tests in question. All users of tests should be keenly aware of this fact. In Table 16 notice the striking drop in the reliability of the difference scores as the correlation increases between the two tests used.

If the correlation between the two tests is zero, the reliability of the difference scores is the same as the average of the coefficients of reliability of the two tests. In other words, relatively uncorrelated tests are needed if suitable difference scores are to be obtained.

TABLE 16. Reliability of Difference Scores for Tests Having Various Degrees of Reliability.

Coefficient of reliability		Correlation between Test A and Test B	Reliability of difference scores
Test A	Test B		
0.90	0.90	0.60	0.75
		0.40	0.83
		0.00	0.90
0.80	0.80	0.60	0.50
		0.40	0.67
		0.00	0.80
0.70	0.70	0.60	0.25
		0.40	0.50
		0.00	0.70

Standard Errors of Measurement

The foregoing discussion of the coefficients of reliability is appropriate in part to the standard error of measurement. Appraising the significance of standard errors of measurement embodies a searching examination of the test itself, the characteristics of the standardization group of pupils, and the testing conditions. However, fluctuations in the variability of the group with respect to the characteristic being measured are considerably less important when standard errors of measurement are being considered instead of coefficients of reliability. Whereas differences in variability of the characteristic measured cause considerable fluctuations in the coefficients of reliability, the standard errors of measurement are, for all practical purposes, independent of fluctuations in the variability of the test scores. Hence, the standard error of measurement is a desirable way of comparing the reliability of a particular test administered to two different groups of pupils. This is precisely what happens when a teacher compares the reliability of a test given to a standardization group with its reliability when it is given to his class.

There are no readily applied suggestions as to how big a standard error should or should not be to insure that the test is useful for a given purpose. Since it is expressed in the same units as the test scores, and since these units typically vary from test to test, a standard error of measurement of a specific size may be considered small in the case of one test and large in the case of another. Consider for a moment the standard error of measurement of the American history achievement test, a value of 3.2. This can be interpreted to mean that the pupils' "true scores" will not differ from their respective obtained scores by more than 3.2 raw-score points in approximately two-thirds of the measurements made. Should the teacher feel that a difference of 3.2 raw-score points does not represent a serious amount of variation in terms of the characteristic measured, then the test is judged to have satisfactory reliability. Evaluation of standard errors of measurement is largely centralized in the teacher's concept of the importance of score difference in terms of the purposes for which the test has been administered. If a test author reports more than one standard error of measurement and identifies them as being applicable to certain different score levels, the foregoing principle still holds.

Problems

10.   Study the procedure for scoring and interpreting the *Differential Aptitude Tests*. Relate the discussion of the question of a vertical distance of one inch on the individual report form (see page 399) to the foregoing discussion of the unreliability of difference scores.
11.   Identify the similarities and differences between a standard error of measurement and a standard error of the difference between two test scores (Anastasi, 1968, pp. 96–98). Explain why the standard error of the difference between two scores is larger than the standard error of measurement of either of the two scores.

SUMMARY

Reliability is defined as the tendency of a measuring instrument to yield consistent information. It is secondary to validity as a desirable characteristic, and highly reliable instruments may be virtually invalid. A test is reliable if chance errors do not influence the information produced when it is given. Common chance errors in educational measuring methods are (1) pupil-centered errors, such as fluctuations in level of health, emotional strain, and motivation, and (2) instrument-centered errors, which arise from the fact that, for example, a paper-and-pencil test is actually a sample of an immense number of possible items, and it may not be scored consistently. Unfortunately, all measuring instruments are somewhat unreliable.

Reliability is practically always expressed in quantitative terms, either as a coefficient of reliability or as a standard error of measurement. The coefficient of reliability, as discussed in this chapter, is a product-moment coefficient of correlation that can be determined in one of several ways. These are the stability method, the equivalence method, the stability and equivalence method, and the internal-consistency method. According to the stability method, the coefficient of reliability is computed when a test is administered twice (with an intervening period of time) to a group of pupils, and the pair of scores correlated. For the equivalence method, the coefficient of reliability is found by administering (with no intervening period of time) two equivalent forms of a test to a group of pupils, then correlating the pairs of scores. When a time interval is allowed, the stability and equivalence method is being applied. For the internal-consistency method, several procedures may be followed, the split-half method or an analysis of variance method. The split-half method may utilize the Spearman-Brown "Prophecy Formula." An analysis-of-variance method is described in terms of the Kuder-Richardson Formula #20.

The standard error of measurement affords some indication of the size of the error caused by test unreliability. In its computation, the size of the coefficient of reliability and the standard deviation of the test scores must be known. It is considered a useful indicator of test reliability because it is expressed in the same units as the test score and it is relatively independent of fluctuations in group variability in terms of the characteristic measured.

Suggested Readings

Anastasi, A. *Psychological testing.* (3rd ed.) London: Macmillan, 1968. Chapter 4.
    The chapter cited contains sections dealing with the types of test reliability, the reliability of speed tests, the dependence of test reliability upon the sample used, and the interpretation of the standard error measurement.
Cronbach, L. J. *Essentials of psychological testing.* (3rd ed.) New York: Harper & Row, 1970. Chapter 6.
    Strictly speaking, only part of this chapter is devoted to reliability (which the author prefers to call "generalizability"). Analysis-of-variance methods are stressed.
Diedcrich, P. B. *Short-cut statistics for teacher-made tests.* (2nd ed.) Educational Testing Service Evaluation and Advisory Service Series, No. 5. Princeton, N.J.: Educational Testing Service, 1964. Pp. 9–33.
    The three chief topics considered are the standard error of a test score, reliability, and correlation. Simple methods of computing needed statistical values are demonstrated.
Ebel, R. L. The relation of item discrimination to test reliability. *Journal of Educational Measurement*, 1967, 4, 125–128.
    An important generalization is demonstrated, namely, if one is to achieve a high degree of reliability for a test of a given length, use test items that are high in discrimination as measured by the *D* index.
French, J. W., and W. B. Michael. *Standards for educational and psychological tests.* Washington: American Psychological Association, 1966. Pp. 25–32.
    In this section, a brief general discussion of reliability is given, and essential information needed for evaluating any reported coefficients of reliability is cited.
Thorndike, R. L. Reliability. *Proceedings of the 1963 Invitational Conference on Testing Problems.* Princeton, N.J.: Educational Testing Service, 1964. Pp. 23–32.

(Also reprinted in A. Anastasi (ed.), *Testing problems in perspective*. Washington: American Council on Education, 1966. Pp. 284–291.)

Some of the main issues concerning test reliability are presented. Particular attention is given to problems related to samples and populations in reliability determinations.

Wesman, A. G. *Reliability and confidence*. Test Service Bulletin, No. 44. New York: Psychological Corporation, 1952. (Also reprinted in N. E. Gronlund (ed.), *Readings in measurement and evaluation*. London: Macmillan, 1968. Pp. 193–202.)

The purpose of this bulletin is to clarify some of the more important aspects of the reliability of measuring instruments. It includes discussions of reliability as an important characteristic of an instrument, factors affecting the interpretation of reliability coefficients, and some common misconceptions about the meaning of certain reliability determinations.

Womer, F. B. *Basic concepts in testing*. New York: Houghton Mifflin, 1968. Chapter 2.

Topics such as errors of measurement and the computation and interpretation of reliability coefficients are covered in a brief and straightforward manner.

References Cited

Anastasi, A. *Psychological testing*. (3rd ed.) London: Macmillan, 1968.

Cureton, E. E. Kuder-Richardson reliabilities of classroom tests. *Educational and Psychological Measurement*, 1966, 26, 13–14.

Cureton, E. E. Measurement theory. In R. L. Ebel (ed.), *Encyclopedia of educational research*. (4th ed.) London: Macmillan, 1969. Pp. 785–804.

French, J. W., and W. B. Michael. *Standards for educational and psychological tests*. Washington: American Psychological Association, 1966.

Gulliksen, H. Methods for determining equivalence of measures. *Psychological Bulletin*, 1968, 70, 534–544.

Howell, J. J., and M. Weiner. Note on the equivalence of alternate forms of an achievement test. *Educational and psychological measurement*, 1961, 21, 309–313.

Kuder, G. F., and M. W. Richardson. The theory of estimation of test reliability. *Psychometrika*, 1937, 2, 151–160.

Spearman, C. Coefficient of correlation calculated from faulty data. *British Journal of Psychology*, 1910, 3, 271–295.

Thorndike, R. L. Reliability. In E. F. Lindquist (ed.), *Educational measurement*. Washington: American Council on Education, 1951. Pp. 560–620.

Wilks, S. S. Sample criteria for testing equality of means, variances, and covariances in a normal multivariate distribution. *Annals of Mathematical Statistics*, 1946, 27, 257–281.

PART FOUR

Standardized Tests, Scales, and Inventories

The purpose of Part Four is to acquaint the reader with the nature and availability of various instruments designed to measure achievement, aptitude, and aspects of personal-social adjustment. Considerable attention is given to standardized measuring instruments. Chapter 11, "Standardized Achievement Tests," discusses the construction of such tests, attempts to give the reader an understanding of their general nature, and emphasizes the differences in construction and use from teacher-constructed tests. Selected achievement tests and batteries are used to illustrate their contribution to the evaluation program. These include both survey and diagnostic tests, and their roles in the evaluation program are explained.

Chapter 12, "Measuring Pupil Aptitudes," is devoted to an explanation of the various kinds of aptitude instruments. It discusses selected tests to clarify the different purposes for which each should be used, and outlines procedures for their effective use in the classroom and with individual pupils. A large part of the chapter is concerned with a discussion of scholastic aptitude and its testing both by individual and group instruments. The concepts of mental age and intelligence quotient, including the DIQ, are developed, and precautionary measures for their use discussed. Differential testing is also explored and its advantages are delineated. Certain questions are raised regarding the value of the "culture-fair" scholastic aptitude test. Those concerned with college admission will find a brief description of national aptitude tests.

Chapter 13, "Evaluating Personal-Social Adjustment," is devoted to the third general area of evaluation. Emphasis is laid upon the strengths and weaknesses of the personal-social adjustment inventories, and suggestions are given for their use in conjunction with less formal methods of evaluation, including observation with use of anecdotal records, rating scales, check lists, and interviews. There is some consideration of sociometric techniques, which provide helpful information about pupils' interaction with the group. Measurement of attitudes and interests is dealt with as an important aspect of understanding pupil growth.

CHAPTER 11

Standardized Achievement Tests

When a golfer "breaks seventy-five" for eighteen holes, he is considered an outstanding performer. The athlete who runs a mile in four minutes has finished a superlative race. The major league baseball player with a batting average of over 0.300 will be surpassed by relatively few. On the other hand, the golfer who requires more than 100 strokes to complete eighteen holes is considered a duffer and the miler who is clocked over 4′ 30″ would not be likely to make a good college track team. Certainly a baseball player whose batting average is below 0.225 isn't considered a good hitter.

These performances are evaluated in terms of norms generally accepted as representing various degrees of competence. It makes no difference whether the game is played or the mile run in Kansas City or Seattle. The performances are regulated by specific rules so that the degree of excellence is affected by the ability of the performer. Even though an athlete may be considered outstanding when compared with limited competition, his performance may be mediocre on a national scale.

A similar situation exists when standardized tests are administered. There are prescribed conditions for testing. Norms are established. It follows that the examinee's performance can be evaluated by comparing it with that of a large number of his peers from many schools.

If you have studied the foregoing chapters carefully, you already know a great deal about standardized achievement tests. To understand the concepts of validity, reliability, item analysis, test scores and norms, the place of educational objectives in testing, and the building and appraisal of classroom tests means that you already know about the framework on which standardized achievement tests are constructed.

STANDARDIZED VS. TEACHER-
CONSTRUCTED TESTS

The term *standardized* actually refers to specific instructions for administration and scoring. Norms are subsequently prepared that represent performance for similar groups. These give the teacher an independent yardstick for checking the achievement of his pupils. While his own tests can measure only the relative performance of the pupils in his class, norms provide the opportunity to compare their achievement with that of pupils in other schools. The college-bound pupil particularly needs to know how well he does in comparison with future competitors. The teacher, too, can use norms to judge the effectiveness of his teaching.

Most of the factors that distinguish standardized from classroom achievement tests relate to better test making. Planning and construction are probably more careful and thorough for achievement tests, which are handled by specialists, than for teacher-constructed tests. There is also a much more critical analysis of the objectives on which the measurement is based. Exacting procedures are followed in the construction and appraisal of individual test items for standardized tests, and extensive statistical analyses are applied to determine their level of difficulty and discriminating power. Often there are comparable forms of the instrument so the test can be administered periodically to measure growth.

In building a classroom test, teachers can take advantage of the individuality of the local community and the pupils in the classes, having pupils study that which best relates to their experiences. Appreciation of literature can be taught with different literary selections, and scientific method can be taught through different subjects. Obviously, individual variations in study materials cannot be considered on a test designed for wide use in many schools, and it becomes necessary to include the materials on which questions are based. This results in many short selections with a definite limitation on achievement measurement; it is impossible to ask an examinee to criticize complete literary works or determine his recall on wide reading. At the classroom level, however, teachers must be better trained in test construction so that they will avoid using assigned materials to measure memorization of content for its own sake; they should instead use these materials as a vehicle for evaluating the lasting results of instruction. Lindquist (1969, p. 352) points out that "there has been little or no experimentation with, or successful development of, new and improved types of tests or tests measuring hitherto unmeasured objectives, ..."

Problems

1.   What arguments might you, as a teacher, offer your school principal to justify using a standardized achievement test as a final examination in your course?

2.   Standardized tests are generally recognized as superior in planning and construction to tests prepared by classroom teachers. What techniques used by standardized-test builders could be easily and profitably used by the classroom teacher?

3.   A high school senior who hopes to enter a highly competitive university was given a standardized achievement test in mathematics designed for high school seniors. He and his parents were greatly encouraged because he received a percentile rank of 80 on this test. His counselor was less enthusiastic. Suggest reasons related to the test for his counselor's reaction.

USES OF STANDARDIZED TESTS

Standardized tests play an important role in strengthening the instructional program. One function is to provide the teacher with a criterion for checking his own emphasis in teaching. Of course, the use of norms implies that comparisons made between and among pupils or classes are restricted by the content of the test. If a class has a high mean score on an American history test, it has not necessarily achieved more in this subject matter area than another class with a lower score. Emphasis in one class may have been on facts and details, while the other stressed critical thinking and broad relationships. Test content must be analyzed before final judgment is made. However, when a test proves to include important and generally accepted areas of knowledge and skills, a teacher ought to make a critical evaluation of his own educational objectives and instruction if a class does poorly in relation to individual pupil ability.

A second use of standardized tests is for determining pupil progress. Generally there are comparable forms of the test, which allows the administering of one at the beginning of the year and another at the end. Although cautious interpretation should be made on the basis of individual test scores, group scores representing progress or the lack of it may reliably emphasize particular strengths or weaknesses.

It must also be remembered that pupils' mental ability is positively correlated with achievement. Effective teaching cannot always be inferred just because the class average is at the median. On the other hand, a class average below the median may actually represent excellent progress in one case, while in another achievement above the median may still be far below the potential of the group.

A third function of standardized tests is to provide a comparison of achievement between various subject matter areas and specific phases of a particular area. It is often desirable to determine how a pupil's arithmetic skill compares with his reading ability or to compare achievement in vocabulary, comprehension, and rate of reading. Obviously these comparisons can be made on an individual or group basis. If the group has a particular weakness, then an evaluation of class learning experiences is in order. When problems seem to relate to individual pupils, then the teacher must provide individual attention.

A fourth use of standardized tests is for diagnosis of difficulties in achievement. Often the source of pupil difficulty may be determined through one or a number of very effective standardized instruments. Because test items have been constructed on the basis of studies that have determined frequent sources of difficulty, it is possible to analyze the adequacy of performance in crucial areas. In diagnosing a reading disability, for example, one can discover whether the pupil knows the initial consonant sounds, whether he can break words into syllables, and whether he makes use of punctuation for improved comprehension. Naturally, the teacher will also use his own tests in diagnosis, but standardized tests are helpful in providing a systematic approach to diagnosis.

Finally, a fifth use is for purposes of selection and classification. Achievement tests can serve as aptitude tests predicting performance in a given subject area. Not only are achievement test results helpful in grouping for instruction, but scores are useful in determining whether pupils can be expected to do well or poorly in given courses.

Problems

4.   Before becoming elated or depressed over your pupils' scores on standardized achievement tests, what primary factors related to the tests and the pupils would you consider carefully?

5.   Mary James received a total percentile rank of 45 on a standardized arithmetic test. Part scores were as follows: Concepts: 65 PR, Computations: 35 PR, Problem Solving: 40 PR. What conclusion might you reach from these data? What further information would be valuable?

6.   A principal use of standardized tests is that of grouping pupils for instruction. Would you consider achievement or scholastic aptitude test results more appropriate for this purpose? Explain your choice.

STANDARDIZED TEST CONSTRUCTION

One may gain better understanding of standardized tests through a discussion of some of the important steps in their construction. The expense and effort involved in constructing these tests demand a very careful appraisal of the need for a particular kind of instrument. First, it may be determined whether there is a group of individuals that provides a potential test market. Ideally, there should be a need for an instrument and no satisfactory test available to meet this need. Unfortunately, the criterion for the construction of a new test sometimes becomes the soundness of the business venture, even though several good instruments that can serve the same purpose are available.

Nevertheless, once it has been decided that a new instrument will be constructed, representatives from the population of test consumers are consulted to formulate specifications for the instrument. The purpose of the test must be spelled out clearly. Is it to be a survey or a diagnostic test? Is it to be primarily for individual or group guidance? Will there be subscores or just a total score? For what population of pupils is the test to be designed? Is it for a group of homogeneous ages or for grades three through twelve? Does it require reading ability? What will be its general contents? All of this must be answered before actual test construction begins.

Pretest Construction and Administration

In the discussion of paper-and-pencil achievement tests in Chapter 2, three steps are outlined for construction: (1) identifying educational objectives with verbal and mathematical aspects, (2) developing tables of specifications reflecting the relative importance of the objectives, and (3) building the test items on the basis of the tables of specifications. A similar approach is used in developing standardized achievement tests, though test items are generally constructed by several subject matter specialists and examined by test specialists for technical considerations. Practical considerations, such as typical length of school class periods help determine test length. Although at times improving the reliability and validity of a test by increasing its length would be desirable, it is not always possible because test administration must be fitted into existing school schedules.

In the development of the better tests, more items are initially constructed than will be used in the final form of the test. These items are assembled into a form called a *pretest*. Before the pretest is administered, the individual items are carefully scrutinized by other subject matter specialists and test experts for inaccuracies and technical flaws.

Directions and accessory materials must be prepared and provision made for recording answers on either separate sheets or the test booklet itself. When the test has been cast into its final form, these accessory materials, including scoring stencils, must be revised to fit it.

Analysis of Pretest Data

When the pretest form is ready, it is administered to a group of pupils comparable to those for whom the test is being designed. The results of the pretest administration are studied to determine which items should be kept. If the test is to discriminate among pupils, the items should be neither so difficult that some will answer them all incorrectly, nor so easy that some can make a perfect score. In neither case is it possible to obtain a true measure of the individual's achievement. It is absurd to conclude that he has achieved nothing; it is equally erroneous to assume that an individual has achieved the ultimate or that two individuals with a perfect score have equal achievement. Therefore, the levels of difficulty of the test items retained should be such that both zero and perfect scores will rarely, if ever, occur.

Items should also be chosen on the basis of their power to discriminate between good and poor pupils. Therefore, those items are retained that are answered correctly by more good pupils than poor. By the same token, the distracters or foils should be chosen more often by the poor than the good pupils.

The total number of items selected for the final form of the test depends on how many can be answered by the pupils in a given amount of time. One general rule of thumb is that about 90 percent of an average class should have an opportunity to attempt all the items in the time allowed. If careful attention has been given to the level of difficulty of these items, an average pupil should answer somewhat more than 50 percent of them correctly (Educational Testing Service, 1965).

Developing Norms

On the basis of the criteria discussed above and the tables of specifications, items are selected for the final form of the test. It is then given to groups of pupils typical of those for whom the test is designed but who have not taken the pretest. Their scores provide the basis for setting up the norms of the test by which a teacher or school administrator can compare pupils' performances. These norms usually are standard scores, percentile ranks, age equivalents, or grade equivalents. Often several different kinds of norms are reported.

Equivalent, Parallel, and Comparable Test Forms

It is often helpful to have two or more forms of a test so that a pupil may be tested more than once—perhaps at the beginning and end of a term of instruction. A second test may be helpful at times when there is reason to doubt the validity of a pupil's first test score—because of illness, for example.

Parallel forms of a test may be developed simultaneously. This is sometimes done by constructing pairs of items that measure the outcome of specific objectives and are of approximately the same level of difficulty. Obviously, the administration procedures and format of both tests should be alike. Parallel forms administered to a large population of pupils and yielding scores with identical distributions are equivalent forms. Comparable forms of a test are illustrated by the various subtests of the Differential Aptitude Tests (DAT; see p. 397). Unlike the approach in equivalent forms, various mental traits are measured. In the DAT all comparisons are based on the same norm group. The raw scores of each test can be converted into the same type of derived scores.

Accessory Materials

In addition to the test booklet, there may be special scoring stencils and, with all of the better tests, a manual. A set of test standards (French and Michael, 1966) recommends that certain kinds of information be placed in the manual. Procedures in administration and scoring should be stated so that it is possible to duplicate the conditions under which the test was standardized. The directions should be clearly phrased so the examinee will understand how the author intended him to perform. Although most standardized tests can be scored objectively, whenever there is an element of subjectivity, scoring variations leading to error should be discussed.

Because the name of a test does not always clarify its purpose and sometimes may even misrepresent what the test actually measures, the manual should state the objectives to be measured and assist in the correct interpretation of test results. Competencies required in administration, scoring, or interpretations beyond the typical classroom teacher should be indicated.

Detailed information on reliability and validity should include evidence that can be used in judging whether it is pertinent to the teacher's and the examinee's problems. The method of determining the reliability coefficient should also be reported. Discussion of validity should be specific in terms of whether it is content, criterion-related, or construct validity (see Chapter 9). The nature of any validating criteria and their desirability for a specific test purpose should be reported fully. Statistical data for determining any validity coefficients should be so adequate that the test user may judge their worth.

The manual should contain a discussion of the development of the test norms. Norm groups must be defined, method of population sampling reported, and the time and conditions under which norm data were secured should be included. It is imperative that measures of central tendency and variability be reported.

Problems

7.   Assume that you are the chairman of the social studies department of a public school system. Your project for the school year is to construct an achievement test to be used as a final examination in social studies for ninth-grade pupils graduating from junior high school. The test is to sample seventh-, eighth-, and ninth-grade subject matter content and should reflect the philosophy of your department. Prepare a detailed, step-by-step outline of how you will proceed in this task and how you will evaluate the final product.

8.   You have an appointment with your principal to present a request to purchase and use a certain standardized achievement test. What specific information about this test should you have prior to the conference? What will be your chief selling point?

SELECTED STANDARDIZED TESTS

There are many standardized achievement and diagnostic tests available to the classroom teacher. They attempt to measure a wide variety of areas, including such skills as critical thinking, reading, and listening. There are also tests in subject areas such as arithmetic, physics, and history. A number of selected and illustrative tests are listed in Appendix C, and an extended discussion of a few selected tests and batteries is included here. The survey test, test battery, and diagnostic test are illustrated. The reader can thus become more familiar with standardized test construction and the general problems and approaches that apply to this type of instrument.

Survey Tests

Whether a test can be labeled as a survey test depends partly on the purpose for which it is used and also on the number of its subscores. Although generally a test yielding only one score is not thought of as being inherently diagnostic, it could well be used for diagnostic purposes if one were to analyze the performance of the examinee on individual questions. As the number of subtests is increased, the instrument begins to assume a diagnostic flavor.

Tests generally thought of as survey instruments are often used along with scholastic aptitude tests to determine whether pupils are retarded. For example, the retarded reader is one who does not read as well as he should for his ability. He may be reading above his grade level, but if he is a bright child, he still may be an underachiever. Likewise, a child who reads below his grade level is not necessarily retarded; his performance may be adequate for his mental capacity. The reading survey test actually provides a measure of the level of difficulty at which the pupil can read. In general it contains at least two measures, one of vocabulary and the other of comprehension. A measure of reading rate is often included.

Gates-MacGinitie Reading Tests.   The *Gates-MacGinitie Reading Tests* is a series of tests replacing the well-known *Gates Primary Reading Test, Gates Advanced Primary Reading Tests,* and the *Gates Reading Survey*. The plan of the tests is as follows:

Primary A—Vocabulary and comprehension for grade 1 (Forms 1, 2)
Primary B—Vocabulary and comprehension for grade 2 (Forms 1, 2)
Primary C—Vocabulary and comprehension for grade 3 (Forms 1, 2)
Primary CS—Speed and accuracy for grades 2 and 3 (Forms 1, 2, and 3)
Survey D—Speed, vocabulary, and comprehension for grades 4 through 6 (Forms 1, 2, and 3)
Survey E—Speed, vocabulary, and comprehension for grades 7 through 9 (Forms 1, 2, and 3)
Survey F–Speed, vocabulary, and comprehension for grades 10 through 12 (Forms 1, 2, and 3)

Both *Survey D* and *Survey E* contain thirty-six short paragraphs of approximately the same level of difficulty as in the *Speed and Accuracy Test*. These paragraphs end in a question or incomplete statement. From four words, the pupil chooses one that best answers the question or completes the statement. Vocabulary tests contain fifty items, each of which has a word to be defined from a choice among five other words. Items become progressively more difficult. The comprehension test contains twenty-one passages with fifty-two blank spaces. From five choices, the pupil picks the completion that best fits the passage meaning. In this test, too, difficulty increases progressively.

The vocabulary tests in *Primary A, Primary B,* and *Primary C* consist of items of four printed words and a picture that illustrates one of these words. *Primary C* has, in addition, items of a test word followed by four others, one of which means the same as the test word.

Comprehension tests are designed to measure a pupil's ability to read and grasp the meaning of whole sentences and paragraphs. In *Primary A* and *Primary B*, passages are matched with a four-picture panel, one of which best conveys the meaning of the paragraph. In *Primary C*, there are two multiple-choice test items for each paragraph.

Primary CS, Speed and Accuracy Test, is similar in construction to this kind of test in surveys *D* and *E*. Short paragraphs of uniform difficulty end in a question or an incomplete statement followed by four words, from which the pupil chooses one.

This series of tests appears to have corrected a serious criticism of the original *Gates Reading Survey*, which attempted to cover a range of eight grades (3–10). This range was too great to discriminate among pupils at every level of competency.

Additional information about the tests is available in a *Technical Manual*. Among other topics, there is a discussion of item selection, establishment of norms, reliability, and correlation between subtest scores and reading and IQ scores. Validity information is not given. Nor does the manual indicate how an interpretation of the score should be translated to classroom practice. Unfortunately such interpretation is seldom done for any reading test.

Cooperative English Test: Reading Comprehension.   These tests are available at two levels of difficulty and in three forms. *Test 2* is designed for pupils in grades nine through twelve. *Test 1* is intended for college freshmen and sophomores. However, *Test 1* is much more discriminating among the good readers in the eleventh and twelfth grades than *Test 2* is.

The authors of these tests have recognized the complexity of reading comprehension and the need to use selections and questions that sample the examinee's ability to think, manipulate verbal concepts, utilize his experience background, and apply various techniques of reading as they relate to purpose. They measure depth of comprehension rather than meaning alone. The following indicate some of the aspects of reading sampled: determining the meanings of words from contextual clues; construing the writer's meaning, tone, intent, point of view, and the reliability of his evidence; and applying conclusions to different situations.

The tests provide four scores: *Vocabulary, Speed of Comprehension, Level of Comprehension,* and *Total Reading Comprehension*. There are two parts to the test. *Part I* (vocabulary) is fifteen minutes long and *Part II* (reading) provides twenty-five minutes of working time. The vocabulary test includes sixty multiple-choice items with words chosen to provide a wide range of difficulty. The speed of comprehension score depends on the number of items answered correctly in *Part II*, which also contains sixty multiple-choice items, each based on a reading passage.

An interesting idea, labeled *Level of Comprehension*, is also built into the tests. Experience has shown that most pupils have time to try at least the first thirty items in *Part II*. Hence, the number of items the pupil answers correctly out of the first thirty in this part is primarily a power score, which represents level of comprehension. This score does not contribute to the *Total Reading Comprehension* score, which is computed by averaging the *Vocabulary* and *Speed of Comprehension* scores.

Problems

9. An elementary school principal has administered a reading survey test designed for grade levels 3–6. In the case of the sixth grade, 80 percent of the pupils scored above the 75th percentile. Why was the principal displeased with these results? How could this situation be remedied?

10. In the selection of a good general reading test, what kinds of information should the subtests yield? Which of these do you consider most significant?

Test Batteries

In any survey of pupil strengths and weaknesses, information is needed concerning relative achievement in the basic skills and the various subject areas. Does the pupil excel in reading but do poorly in arithmetic? Is he a high achiever in the physical and biological sciences but lacking information and skill in dealing with problems in the social studies? Standardized tests can provide information for evaluating a pupil's relative status. However, scores from single tests standardized on different populations are not necessarily comparable. For example, the standardization group for one test may have higher achievement or aptitudes than that for another, resulting in more exacting norms for the first test; representativeness of the normative sample may vary in terms of size of school, type of location (urban or rural), geographical area, and so forth. Norms may also vary according to time of year when the test was administered. Recency of norms also affects a pupil's standing. Since Sputnik, there has been a substantive improvement in national achievement and recent norms are more difficult. Therefore, a pupil would have to show better performance to avoid appearing deficient.

This limitation inherent in the use of separate tests is overcome through the use of test batteries standardized on the same population. By comparing subtest scores, it is possible to determine whether a pupil has any real differences in his achievement pattern.

Profiles.   We have seen that the raw scores pupils earn on a test may be expressed as derived scores that can be classified as test norms (see page 252). Four types of norms are discussed: (1) quartiles, deciles, and percentiles, (2) standard scores, (3) grade equivalents, and (4) age equivalents. If a battery of tests is given and a pupil gets twenty-five vocabulary questions right but only fifteen spelling questions correct, he may not necessarily be better in vocabulary than in spelling. The vocabulary test may be longer or more difficult, so that the two raw scores cannot be compared.

If these raw scores are changed to percentile rank norms based on the same standardization group, units may then be compared. This pupil may, for example, have a percentile rank of 80 in vocabulary and a percentile rank of 90 in spelling. It appears that his achievement in spelling is greater than that in vocabulary. But this is not necessarily so. Neither test has perfect reliability, and the reliability of the difference between two scores is less than the reliability of either test (see page 321). In the better standardized tests, information is included in the manual that will help the test user determine when real differences exist.

When the raw scores of a battery of tests are changed into common derived scores, the result is a pupil's score profile. Profiles may be reported in various ways. A number of batteries have a class record sheet on which all pupils in the class have their profiles presented in tabular form (see Figure 22). Also, they may provide profile sheets for individual pupils (see Figure 23).

Note that Alice White's profile (Figure 23) is recorded in percentile bands. She has earned a *Reading* score of 300. However, because this test, like others, is somewhat unreliable, we cannot be certain that she would earn this same score if she took the test again. On the other hand, we can say that approximately two-thirds of the time a pupil's "true-score" will lie within the percentile band. In the case of Alice White's *Reading* score, this band extends from the sixty-first to the eighty-second percentile rank. How then does one compare a pupil's standings in the various areas recorded on the profile? Can we infer that Alice White's score in *Reading* is significantly higher than her score in *Writing* or *Social Studies*? The answer would have to be "no," since these bands overlap. On the other hand, it is reasonable to infer that her scores in *Reading, Writing,* and *Social Studies* are probably greater than her scores in *Listening, Science,* and *Mathematics,* because there is no overlapping of the percentile bands of these two groups.

Elementary School Test Batteries.   There are a number of achievement test batteries available for elementary school use. Those batteries listed in Table 17 are widely used. The table presents a rough classification of the emphasis in the different areas or achievement for the intermediate grades. In some cases, this includes grades 4, 5, and 6, and in others, only grades 5 and 6. Time limits allotted to the various subtests are used in determining the percentages listed. Because the total time of test administration varies, caution should be exercised in comparing percentages between tests. They can best be used in noting the degree of emphasis. Another point in interpretation is that, in some batteries, areas were combined. For example, in the *Metropolitan Achievement Tests* we placed *Mathematical Concepts* and *Mathematical Computation* under *Mathematical Fundamentals.*

Note that the *California Achievement Tests* and the *Iowa Tests of Basic Skills* do not include social studies and science. Emphasis is placed on diagnosis in fewer areas. Only two of the batteries listed, the *Metropolitan Achievement Tests* and the *Stanford Achievement Test,* include subtests in social studies and science.

CLASS RECORD SHEET

Iowa Tests of Basic Skills

Grade 6   Semester (1st or 2nd) 2nd   County Cherry   School Building Pleasant View   Date May 3, 1971   Form 1

City, or District Chalsea, New York   State New York   Teacher Susan Allison

Names of Pupils	SEX (Write B or G)	AGE — Age in Years at Last Birthday	AGE — Months Since Last Birthday	TEST V Vocabulary	TEST R Reading Comprehension	L-1 Spelling	L-2 Capitalization	L-3 Punctuation	L-4 Usage	L TOTAL TEST L	W-1 Map Reading	W-2 Reading Graphs and Tables	W-3 Knowledge and Use of Reference Materials	W TOTAL TEST W	A-1 Arithmetic Concepts	A-2 Arithmetic Problem Solving	A TOTAL TEST A	COMPOSITE V, R, L, W, A
Adams, John				6.3 / 40	7.4 / 66	6.5 / 42	5.6 / 18	6.1 / 22	5.9 / 34	5.8 / 27	7.2 / 63	6.5 / 26	6.9 / 54	6.7 / 48	5.3	5.7 / 12	5.5	6.3 / 35
Baker, Alvin				8.4 / 80	7.0 / 56	6.5 / 42	7.6 / 64	6.6 / 47	9.7 / 93	7.6 / 67	8.0 / 85	6.5 / 44	7.1 / 60	7.2 / 68	6.5 / 40	6.9 / 55	6.7 / 46	7.4 / 68
Bell, Betty				8.5 / 82	8.6 / 88	8.4 / 86	7.6 / 64	9.5 / 91	10.3 / 97	9.0 / 89	7.8 / 80	8.1 / 89	9.5 / 98	9.2 / 98	9.8 / 98	7.6 / 80	8.2 / 93	8.7 / 93
Carter, Susan				8.2 / 77	7.6 / 70	5.8 / 23	8.8 / 83	8.6 / 47	8.1 / 97	7.5 / 65	6.5 / 40	8.1 / 89	8.0 / 82	7.5 / 76	7.8 / 86	7.4 / 74	7.6 / 81	7.7 / 76
Chenworth, Ellis				9.2 / 91	9.0 / 93	4.9 / 05	8.2 / 56	6.0 / 47	8.2 / 72	7.0 / 54	7.7 / 78	7.5 / 72	7.4 / 69	7.5 / 76	7.7 / 77	6.2 / 24	6.8 / 50	8.0 / 82
Corson, Margaret				8.7 / 87	6.8 / 68	8.0 / 79	9.8 / 98	10.4 / 98	9.1 / 86	9.6 / 95	4.0 / 83	9.0 / 83	8.5 / 91	7.8 / 78	9.4 / 98	9.4 / 89	9.4 / 98	8.5 / 91
Daig, Herbert				10.6 / 96	8.5 / 87	9.1 / 91	10.0 / 98	8.9 / 94	8.4 / 94	9.6 / 95	7.5 / 72	8.8 / 88	8.9 / 92	8.5 / 89	8.1 / 90	8.0 / 89	8.4 / 75	8.7 / 93
Dall, Amy				10.6 / 98	9.8 / 97	8.5 / 87	9.7 / 94	9.5 / 95	10.7 / 97	9.5 / 94	7.8 / 80	8.1 / 95	9.8 / 98	8.7 / 95	8.3 / 90	8.5 / 95	8.2 / 93	9.4 / 97
Fela, Ann				10.3 / 97	9.8 / 97	8.5 / 87	11.2 / 99	10.5 / 97	10.6 / 98	10.2 / 98	7.7 / 78	8.9 / 97	9.7 / 98	8.8 / 96	8.1 / 91	8.2 / 91	8.2 / 93	9.5 / 98
Green, Carter				5.6 / 25	6.2 / 35	5.2 / 15	6.8 / 50	6.5 / 27	6.5 / 44	6.2 / 36	6.3 / 34	5.9 / 26	6.7 / 48	6.3 / 33	5.9 / 54	6.6 / 35	6.6 / 42	6.2 / 32
Gould, Robert				6.2 / 38	6.3 / 43	7.1 / 71	8.2 / 74	7.8 / 68	9.6 / 96	8.0 / 80	6.3 / 34	7.1 / 71	7.7 / 76	7.1 / 64	9.1 / 91	8.4 / 75	8.4 / 95	7.5 / 75
Hall, William				7.0 / 54	7.0 / 56	6.5 / 42	5.3 / 11	5.1 / 22	6.5 / 44	5.7 / 27	7.7 / 77	7.6 / 64	7.5 / 74	7.5 / 76	7.3 / 73	5.1 / 24	6.7 / 46	6.8 / 51
Heald, Joe				8.4 / 80	8.5 / 87	8.0 / 79	8.2 / 81	8.2 / 73	9.1 / 86	8.4 / 81	8.0 / 85	8.9 / 97	7.2 / 70	8.0 / 86	7.0 / 75	8.5 / 95	6.8 / 90	8.3 / 88
Julson, Patricia				8.5 / 80	6.8 / 68	7.3 / 74	7.4 / 52	6.9 / 52	9.6 / 86	7.9 / 73	8.0 / 85	6.9 / 44	7.1 / 60	7.1 / 68	7.0 / 63	6.7 / 46	6.8 / 50	7.7 / 73
Larson, Alfred				6.9 / 52	6.4 / 41	5.5 / 15	5.9 / 27	6.2	8.8 / 82	6.7 / 47	6.0 / 26	7.4 / 71	6.9 / 54	6.8 / 52	6.7 / 26	6.7 / 46	6.4 / 34	6.6 / 45
Metz, Connie				7.8 / 70	7.0 / 60	8.3 / 83	9.0 / 89	8.4 / 73	5.6 / 30	7.8 / 71	7.8 / 80	7.1 / 71	8.0 / 82	7.6 / 80	7.3 / 73	7.8 / 80	7.4 / 75	7.3 / 73

HOUGHTON MIFFLIN COMPANY   BOSTON

Printed in the U.S.A.

From Lindquist and Hieronymous, 1955; reproduced by permission of Houghton Mifflin Company.

FIGURE 22. Class Record Sheet Showing Grade Equivalents and Percentile Ranks.

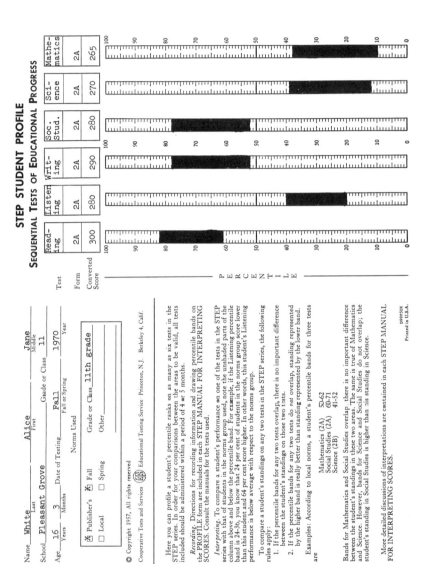

From Cooperative Test Division, 1957; reproduced by permission of the Educational Testing Service.

FIGURE 23. Pupil Profile Chart.

TABLE 17.   Elementary School Test Batteries and Percentages of Total Testing Time Allotted to the Various Areas.[a]

	California achievement tests	Iowa tests of basic skills	Metropolitan achievement tests	Stanford achievement test
Reading comprehension	14.0	19.7	9.2	11.2
Vocabulary	26.3	6.1	5.5	4.5
Fundamentals of arithmetic	12.2	10.7	22.2	20.6
Arithmetic reasoning	14.9	10.7	9.2	11.9
Language	23.6	19.7	18.5	17.9
Social studies	0.0	0.0	16.6	9.3
Science	0.0	0.0	12.9	9.3
Spelling	8.0	4.3	5.5	5.6
Study skills	0.0	28.7	0.0	9.3
Total working time (minutes)	114	279	270	267

[a] The *Contemporary Mathematics Test* (see Appendix C) has been designed to supplement the *CAT* battery. The instrument measures outcomes common to "new" mathematics programs. A modern mathematics concept test is also reported for use with the *Stanford Achievement Test* and the *Iowa Tests of Basic Skills*. The new revision of the *Metropolitan Achivement Tests* also includes tests on modern mathematics.

Note that content of test batteries is based on what is considered important on a national scale. Certain local objectives may be deemphasized or even omitted. For example, the "new" mathematics is taught by some schools but is not adequately sampled in the typical test battery. However, even though a school may teach the new mathematics, the objective of developing an understanding of the basic mathematical concepts found in the typical test battery would be maintained. A number of the test batteries now have supplementary tests for the "new" mathematics.

Iowa Tests of Basic Skills.   This is a multilevel edition test designed for grades three to nine and is representative of most available batteries. Its title is descriptive. By means of eleven separate tests, five areas of basic skills are emphasized: *Vocabulary, Reading Comprehension, Language Skills* (the mechanics of correct writing), *Work-Study Skills,* and *Arithmetic Skills.* Pupils of only one grade level take the same test. Although there is overlapping, the tests are designed for specific grade levels. The *Iowa* battery is the longest of the four named above, and provides analytical subtests in *Language, Work-Study,* and *Arithmetic Skills.* There are no tests in the content subjects. These are not course-oriented achievement tests.

The battery is unusual in that all levels are bound in a single booklet.

There are actually six batteries, one for each of grades 3 to 8; grades 8 and 9 use the same battery. Therefore, pupils at different grade levels can be tested simultaneously, since the time limits and directions are the same for all levels. Separate answer sheets for each grade level may be either hand-scored with a stencil or machine-scored with IBM equipment.

Instructions for administration are written very clearly, and the mechanics of the test booklet are simple. A test schedule of four sessions is suggested. Some schools administer the battery in four consecutive sessions, one each half-day. Others choose to give the test in the mornings of four consecutive days. The authors rightly recommend that under no circumstances should the entire battery be administered in one day.

The *Vocabulary* subtest is composed of items requiring the examinee to select from four choices a word having most nearly the same meaning as one designated in a brief context. As in all vocabulary tests of this kind, the examinee needs only to recognize a synonym superficially; there is no measure of the breadth and depth of his concepts.

Reading Comprehension is measured by series of multiple-choice questions on brief selections. The authors are to be commended for including a variety of questions unrelated to fact or detail. For example, there are a number of items on organizational pattern, main ideas, summarizing, and tone and intent. True measures of reading comprehension must determine whether the reader understands more than the sense meanings. Also, he must not be able to select the correct answer by a process of matching words in the test item with those in the selection. In some reading tests, questions can be answered from the reader's general background of information. In either case, a true measure of comprehension is not obtained through answers to the questions. The authors of this test have generally succeeded in eliminating these pitfalls. Another very strong point of this reading test is the variety of the subject matter and style of the chosen selections, which give a better over-all measure of comprehension than simple narrative material alone. Furthermore, the selections appear to be sufficiently difficult to provide for individual differences at each level.

A battery such as this should be considered analytical rather than diagnostic in nature. The difference lies in the thoroughness of sampling rather than in the methodology of the approach. The teacher needs more information than can be obtained from tests of this kind to make a thorough diagnosis.

The *Language Skills* test actually measures the skills of correct writing, spelling, capitalization, punctuation, and usage. The spelling test uses recognition items. There are five choices, the fifth one in each case being "No mistakes." The pupil's task is to determine if any word is misspelled, and if so, which one. The incorrect spellings are selected from children's frequent errors. Those who favor this approach to measuring spelling achievement should find that, in general, all words have been well chosen for each level.

The tests on *Capitalization, Punctuation,* and *Usage* have four choices in each item, the last choice being always "No mistakes." Pupils are directed to determine whether an error occurs, and if so, to indicate the choice where it is to be found. Various kinds of materials are used, such as letters and conversation. The skills chosen appear in general to be consistent with what is taught at the various levels.

Work-Study Skills are divided into three subtests—*Map Reading, Reading Graphs and Tables* and *Knowledge and Use of Reference Materials.* The subtests represent important aspects of reading skill in addition to development of vocabulary and comprehension of narrative material. The maps, graphs, and tables are clearly printed. No confusion should result from poor reproductions of drawings. Items in the map-reading test determine a pupil's knowledge of direction, distance, symbols, and specific concepts such as latitude, parallels, and elevation. Measurement of ability to read graphs and tables includes use of pictures; bar, circle, and line graphs; the calendar; and a various assortment of tables. The test is organized so that several items refer to one graph or table. In general, the material is meaningful and should result in greater pupil motivation.

Knowledge and Use of Reference Materials is concerned with those skills required in locating words in a dictionary, using an index and table of contents, using an encyclopedia, and locating information through the selection of correct references. There are also items on the interpretation of diacritical markings in the dictionary.

Arithmetic Skills are divided into two subtests, *Arithmetic Concepts* and *Arithmetic Problem Solving.* Among the concepts included are cardinal and ordinal numbers, directional orientation, geometric figures and component parts, telling time, our monetary system, linear measurement, reading a thermometer, size of fractional components, common denominators, Roman numerals, and some simple algebra. All of the items in *Arithmetic Problem Solving* are problems requiring the student to set up his own operations. The items have four choices, the last choice being "Not given." The problems require the pupil to use addition, subtraction, multiplication, and division for whole numbers and fractions. Items on percentage are also included. The various skills are introduced at the grade levels where they are generally taught. Problems tend in general to be related to the meaningful activities of children and their families. Readability is geared to the particular grade level for which the problem is designed. A supplementary modern mathematics test is available.

Two manuals are published with these tests. The *Teachers Manual* includes a discussion of the purposes of the test and preparations for testing, directions for test administration and scoring, suggestions for using the test results in the improvement of instruction, and the norm tables. The *Manual for Administrators, Supervisors, and Counselors* (Lindquist and Hieronymous,

1956) is more comprehensive, and explains in detail such technical considerations as data on validity, reliability, sampling, and scaling of scores.

The group on which this battery of tests is standardized represents an attempt to include a sampling of all elementary children in grades 3 through 8 who are in regular attendance in the public schools throughout the United States. A total of 74,174 pupils from 213 school systems in 46 states are included in the normative sample.

Grade and percentile norms are available for each of the eleven tests and for the composite of all tests. There are also percentile norms for interpreting individual pupil achievement and school averages. Norms for school averages are presented for the beginning, middle, and end of the year.

Both the coefficient of reliability and the standard error of measurement for each of the eleven tests and the composite of these are given. The split-half method was used to determine the reliability coefficients, and they range from 0.70 in *Map Reading*, grade 3, to 0.96 in *Reading*, grade 4, for the subtests. The coefficient for the composite is 0.98 for all grades except grade 3, which has a coefficient of 0.97.

A great deal of planning and careful consideration was given to the validity of this battery of tests. Instructional procedures, courses of study, and textbooks were analyzed. The skills tested and subject matter content included were identified and studied with considerable care. The manual includes a complete analysis. Proper grade placement received particular attention. Cruciality and discriminating power served as the main criteria for items finally selected, items that emphasize the pupils' ability to use the skills, in line with the test's objective. Tests are longer than usual to provide as adequate a sample in each area as was practically possible.

Secondary School Test Batteries.   Although achievement test batteries have been constructed for secondary school pupils, meaningful norms for the content subjects are difficult to develop. This is so because the populations are different for each subject area and often pupils included in the norm group have not studied the subject in question. Pupils enrolled in physics have not necessarily completed a course in ancient history. When the same pupils constitute the norm group for all subject areas whether or not they have received instruction in them, the norms are meaningless; the test is invalid for those who have not received instruction.

Two popular test batteries are the *Iowa Tests of Educational Development* and the *Sequential Tests of Educational Progress*.[1] The latter battery has an unusual approach in measuring achievement in the content fields. This series of achievement tests, known as *STEP*, was constructed to measure "the

[1] This discussion is concerned with *STEP I*, rather than *STEP II*, published in 1971. It is discussed on page 354.

critical skills in *application* of learning" in the fields of *Essay Writing, Listening and Reading Comprehension, Writing, Science, Mathematics,* and *Social Studies.* In each area there are tests at four educational levels:

Level 4—Grades 4, 5, and 6
Level 3—Grades 7, 8, and 9
Level 2—Grades 10, 11, and 12 of high school
Level 1—Freshman and sophomore years of college

Two forms of every test are available at each level with the exception of the *Essay* tests, which have four forms. All tests except the *Essay* tests are allowed seventy minutes of working time. They are broken up into two thirty-five-minute working periods, which may be given separately. The *Essay* tests have only one thirty-five minute section.

An important objective in the construction of these tests is to measure "the ability of students to use what they have learned in the classroom." A previous discussion pointed out that tests in the content areas emphasize the content of the subject rather than the overall result from the subjects being taught. For example, there is general agreement that one objective of a science course is to promote a scientific attitude, although teachers select different subject matter content to develop it. Therefore, an attempt to measure specific subject matter results in some items that are too difficult for pupils who have not had an opportunity to learn the information, whereas other items prove too easy. In addition to the difficulty of constructing discriminating items, subject matter tests of this kind do not measure the pupil's ability to solve new problems through the knowledge he has learned.

After querying hundreds of teachers and researchers about measurement of student achievement, the authors planning the *STEP* tests could set up the following directives for their construction (Cooperative Test Division, 1957, p. 3):

1. Tests must be long enough and broad enough for sound individual interpretation. Short tests are not adequate for measuring an individual student's development.
2. There must be continuity of measurement over nearly all the years of general education. The same skills should be measured over a long range of years on a single continuous score scale. Measurement begins with the early simple learnings and proceeds to the later complex skills. Shifting from one short-range test or battery to another results in loss of continuity.
3. The focus should be on the outcomes of instruction rather than on its content. The items must be centered on critical skills and understandings.
4. Ability to apply learning rather than just to "play it back" must be tested.

In this series, ability to write is measured by the *Essay Tests.* About 5000 student essays on eight topics of interest at each level were evaluated to provide scoring samples. The teacher uses these products as guides in grading his own pupils' papers. Quality is therefore evaluated on the basis of a national norm.

The following essay topic is for Level 3 (grades 7–9):

> If you knew that you were going to go blind twenty-four hours from now and that nothing could prevent it, what would you do with the time between now and this moment, this time tomorrow when you could see no more? Where would you go? What and whom would you try to see? Write an account of what you would do from the time you leave this room until your blindness strikes, explaining, if possible, the reasons for your actions.

In the *Listening Comprehension Tests*, the examiner reads the selection aloud once and then continues to read orally the multiple-choice questions and the possible answers. The pupil is given a booklet containing only the possible answers and an answer sheet. He marks his responses on the answer sheet. Each level contains twelve to thirteen selections chosen on the basis of listening requirements common to the pupil's experiences. They sample narration, exposition, directions, argument, poetry, and so on. Questions relate to four aspects of the selection: main idea, important details, organizational pattern, and word meaning. Three levels of understanding are measured: plain-sense comprehension, interpretation, and evaluation and application. Interpretation and evaluation represent higher-order skills, which go beyond determining the sense of the passage. They involve implied meanings and the validity of the communication. The importance of critical and selective listening is illustrated.

To standardize the examiner's reading of the passage to some degree, suggested time limits are given for each selection. The examiner is cautioned to practice reading the materials to present the author's ideas clearly and effectively. Below is a selection from Level 3 (grades 7–9). The reading time is one minute and thirty seconds.

The examiner reads:

> Here is the fourth selection. It is a speech by a student running for school office. "A students, B students, C students, D students, and my friends! As you know, I am running for the office of President of the Student Council. I'd like to tell you what I'll do if I'm elected. In the first place, I think several students ought to sit in on teachers' meetings. They settle too many things for us. I don't think that the teachers always know what's best for us.
>
> "In the second place, I'd like to see our Student Council do something. Take the business of the candy machine, for instance. Just because a couple of doctors and dentists don't like it doesn't mean we shouldn't have one. Candy is good for us. It gives us energy, and I, for one, don't think it hurts either your teeth or your appetite. And if it does, so what? You save the lunch money and can go out on a date.
>
> "Last, you know that my opponents—and you'll hear from them in a minute—are two girls. Now, everybody says girls are smarter than boys. That might be true—but just because they're smarter doesn't mean they'll make better

officers. In fact, I think girls are too smart and can't always get along with people because of that. Maybe we need somebody not so smart, but that can get along. That's me, fellow students—vote for me!"

One of the questions asked the examinee about the above selection follows:

20. It is likely that in the past the speaker has:
   E. disagreed with the teacher's decisions
   F. disagreed with the opinions he has stated
   G. agreed with the doctor about the candy machine
   H. agreed with his other opponents about decisions of teachers

Materials in the *Reading Comprehension Tests* were chosen from a wide range of content in order to test breadth as well as depth of comprehension. Questions may be answered from the reading matter. Five reading skills are tested:

1. Ability to understand direct statements made by the author.
2. Ability to interpret and summarize the passage.
3. Ability to see the motives of the author.
4. Ability to observe the organizational characteristics of the passage.
5. Ability to criticize the passage with respect to its ideas, purpose, or presentation.

The format of the test commonly used is a short reading selection followed by multiple-choice questions. Other reading tests that do an equally effective job of sampling reading skills are available. The merit of this test, therefore, lies in the fact that it is a part of a battery as well as one of a series of tests with different levels of reading maturity.

The format of the *Writing Tests* consists of a series of unedited selections written by children and followed with multiple-choice questions which suggest possible ways to edit the selections, thereby testing the following writing skills:

1. Ability to write logically.
2. Ability to organize materials.
3. Ability to write for purpose, occasion, and audience.
4. Ability to write effectively, concerning word choice, emphasis, details, reasons, examples, and so forth.
5. Ability to use the conventions of writing such as basic form, syntax, and word-form mechanics.

Note the following example for Level 2 (grades 10–12):

My Favorite Magazine
1. Many young people of today are taking a great interest in the magazine *Suburbia*. 2. It is of fairly large size with a considerable number of pages. 3. The publishers, Allen and Watts, are well known and reputable; thus providing young homemakers with ideas and practical plans for their present and future homes. 4. Because it also contains articles of family and community rela-

tions and hints on home improvement, it is most likely preferable reading to people who are seeking guidance on such matters. 5. The previously mentioned content explains why the advertisements would logically be about products and furnishings for the home. 6. The articles were well written, and all the features of *Suburbia* help to form an interesting and informative magazine. 7. I found one particularly interesting article, it was entitled "Families Are Using Spare Time to Broaden Their Horizons." 8. This article points out that leisure time should be spent in any activity other than usual work, instead of remaining in complete inactivity.

Among the questions asked is the following:

14. Which of these possible additions to the report would be most helpful?
    E. A listing of the advertisers making use of several issues of *Suburbia*
    F. A statement of the rates paid by the publishers for articles purchased
    G. A listing and brief description of the "departments" appearing in every issue, as distinct from the featured articles
    H. A statement, accompanied by authoritative references, of the credit rating of the company which publishes *Suburbia*

The *Mathematics Tests* were organized around the idea of the sequential organization for teaching mathematical concepts. Therefore, content is not confined to any one or a series of mathematics courses. Because there is not complete agreement as to the grade level at which concepts should be taught, there may be a need to shift to higher or lower levels depending on the group's progress. The *STEP* tests assess five skill areas essential to the understanding and application of mathematical concepts:

1. Number and operation: understanding of cardinal and ordinal numbers, the number system, fractions, kinds of numbers, fundamental processes, etc.
2. Symbolism: use and nature of symbols, algebraic symbolism.
3. Measurement and geometry: geometric nomenclature and relations, denominate numbers, significant digits and measurement, etc.
4. Function and relation: graphs, ratio, equations, scale drawing, etc.
5. Proof: deductive and inferential reasoning.
6. Probability and statistics: depicting trends, concepts of mean, median, correlation, sampling, data interpretation, etc.

Note the samples of test material drawn from the four levels of the battery.

Level 4 (grades four-six)
Situation: In Tom's school, some children ride bicycles, some walk to school, and some ride the school bus. The pupils on the safety patrol have to come early.
1. Two children from each class in the school were members of the safety patrol. To find how many patrol members there are altogether, what other facts would you need to know?
    A. The number of children in the school.
    B. The number of classes in the school.
    C. The number of children in each class.
    D. The number of street crossings.

Level 3 (grades seven-nine)
Situation: Mrs. Cain went to the power and light company to check on her electric bills and obtain information about electrical equipment.
1. Mrs. Cain wanted to buy an electric blanket. The office manager of the electric company told her that the blanket would cost 3 cents a night to use. If she used it 200 nights out of the 365 nights of the year, the yearly cost would be:
    A. $ 4.95
    B. $ 6.00
    C. $10.95
    D. $60.00

Level 2 (grades ten-twelve)
Situation: Mr. Jones has a dairy farm on which he also grows corn.
1. Mr. Jones has two fields of equal size on which he grows corn. If $7/8$ of field I and $8/9$ of field II are devoted to corn, which one of the following statements is true?
    A. Field I has more space devoted to corn.
    B. Field II has more space devoted to corn.
    C. Equal space is devoted to corn in both fields.
    D. The amounts of space devoted to corn cannot be compared.

Level 1 (grades thirteen-fourteen)
Situation: The Mill City Statistical Agency conducts opinion polls and surveys and performs related statistical research.
1. A new interviewer for the agency reported at the end of his first day that he had interviewed 100 people. He said that 42 of these were men, of whom 30 were Democrats, and that 49 were Republican women. The agency needed to know how many Democratic women he had interviewed but all that he could remember was that everyone had been either Democratic or Republican. From this information alone, it is possible to determine that:
    A. The data are contradictory
    B. There were 9 Democratic women
    C. There were 19 Democratic women
    D. There are still insufficient data for an answer

The *Science Tests* emphasize basic scientific concepts and applicational skills. These factors are tested in situational aspects related to economics, culture, social relations, and science in the home. Six skills are sampled:

The ability to:
1. Identify and define a scientific problem.
2. Suggest, screen, and test a hypothesis.
3. Design experiments and collect data.
4. Interpret data and draw conclusions.
5. Evaluate critically the printed and spoken word.
6. Reason quantitatively and symbolically.

The following example shows how items have been based on concepts and skills rather than specific textbook information:

Level 3 (grades seven-nine)
Situation: Tom planned to become a farmer and his father encouraged this interest by giving Tom a part of the garden to use for studying plant life.

Tom wanted to find out what effect fertilizer has on garden plants. He put some good soil in two different boxes. To box A he added fertilizer containing a large amount of nitrogen. To box B he added fertilizer containing a large amount of phosphorus. In each box he planted 12 bean seeds. He watered each box with the same amount of water. One thing missing from Tom's experiment was a box of soil with:
A. Both fertilizers added
B. Neither nitrogen nor phosphorus fertilizers added
C. Several kinds of seeds planted
D. No seeds planted

As in the *Science Tests*, the objectives of the *Social Studies Tests* are to measure long-term values rather than specific subject matter. The following basic skills are measured:

Ability to:
1. Read and interpret maps, charts, cartoons, pictures, diagrams, as well as the printed word.
2. Think critically, to distinguish fact from opinion, and to recognize propaganda.
3. Assess and interpret data.
4. Apply appropriate outside information and criteria.
5. Draw valid generalizations and conclusions.

Basic understandings must relate to past, present, and future. The authors list the following as measured by this test:

Basic understandings. Although the following understandings are stated in the present, a thorough appreciation of them will involve a realization of how the past has contributed, what the present situation is, and what the future may bring: With increasing insight and breadth of perception, the student should be able to understand:
1. The nature of social change and its effect on man's ways of living.
2. The profound effects of geographic environment on man's institutions and ways of living.
3. Control over the forces of nature as a major factor in accounting for the ways in which we live today.
4. The nature of a democratic society and the rights, privileges, and responsibilities of free men.
5. The means by which society directs and regulates the behavior of its members.
6. Man's economic wants and the ways of satisfying them.
7. The ways in which man attempts to understand and adjust to his environment and his place in the universe.
8. The interdependence among individuals, communities, societies, regions, and nations.
9. The sources of human nature and personality.

The example on page 353 suggests measurement of an important work-study skill and a long-term value. The pupil is provided with the monthly temperature and rainfall chart and is asked questions about it such as the two following the chart.

In addition to the care exercised in the selection of test content and the construction of items, the norm sample was carefully chosen for meaningful interpretation. Because there is evidence indicating a variance of achievement among the regions of the country, the battery was administered to a standardization group chosen from elementary and secondary schools representing nine regions in the United States. College norm groups were also selected by region as well as for junior or four-year colleges.

Percentile norms have been prepared for each of the six tests for individual pupils in grades 4 through 14. School mean norms for all tests, except *Listening*, in each of these grades are also available. Percentiles on each of the various tests can be compared, since they are based on groups of pupils with the same ability. Individual score norms are listed as percentile bands rather

1. Which of these cities are north of the equator?
     (A) I and III only
     (B) II and IV only
     (C) All of the cities
     (D) None of the cities
2. In which city would one need, the greatest variety of weights of clothing?
     (E) I (F) II (G) III (H) IV[1]

[1] These and all other test items from *STEP* included in this chapter are reproduced with the permission of the Educational Testing Service.

than as percentiles for a given earned score (see Figure 23). You will find the *STEP Teachers' Guide* (Cooperative Test Division, 1959) most helpful for interpreting test scores.

The relationship of the *STEP I* tests to the *School and College Ability Tests* (*SCAT I*) should be emphasized. The new form of *SCAT* (*SCAT II*) is discussed on pages 377–378; both *SCAT* tests are measures of verbal and quantitative skills. Like *STEP*, they are designed for continuity of measurement, having five overlapping levels of instruments extending from fourth grade through the college sophomore year. *STEP I* and *SCAT I* were developed at the same time and normed on the same population; the scores may be used to compare a pupil's achievement with his own ability to achieve. Norms are available to determine whether the pupil's *STEP I* scores correspond to his verbal and quantitative skills as measured by *SCAT I*. Likewise, *SCAT II* is normed on the same population as *STEP II* to provide similiar data for these tests. Furthermore, the *STEP I* and *II* tests are correlated, thus linking them together to provide continuity of measurement data. *STEP II* is also linked with the *Cooperative Primary Tests* in order to establish an interrelated testing program from grades 1 through 14.

A decision was made after a survey of those who use *STEP I* to construct a new edition measuring the same broad outcomes of education, but requiring less than seventy minutes for the administration of each test. This limitation is met with only a few exceptions. Of course as for *STEP I*, separately timed parts may be administered in separate sessions. None of these periods is more than sixty minutes in length.

The format of *STEP II* is very similiar to that *STEP I*. One substantial change is in the *Writing Test*. In contrast to *STEP I*, where the pupil responded to a set of questions based on a passage incorporating a wide variety of errors, the pupil responds to discrete items in *STEP II*. Also, there is no test of listening comprehension. Two mathematics tests rather than one are included in *STEP II*, namely *Mathematics Computation* and *Mathematics–Basic Concepts*. The content of the latter is similiar to the original mathematics test in *STEP I*.

STEP II is designed to exhibit the same content validity as is apparent in the old series. Various types of norms are provided in terms of a converted score scale. These include percentile bands, mid-percentile ranks, and stanines for individual interpretation and school mean norms for group interpretation.

Problems

11.   What, in your opinion, is the outstanding advantage of using the *Sequential Test of Education Progress* or the *Iowa Tests of Basic Skills* for the purpose of measuring pupil achievement in the elementary school?

12. Table 17 (page 343) compares four achievement test batteries for the elementary school. Which of these four appears most useful to you in your particular subject matter field? Why?

13.   In one study, third-grade norms on the *California Achievement Test* yield grade placements significantly higher than those for four other popular test batteries for the elementary school (Stake, 1961). What are the consequences of a difference such as this?

14.   Thelen (1960, p. 19) says that "our tests teach pupils that academic status, not learning, is the goal of education." Do you agree? Why?

Diagnostic Tests

Survey tests, whether individual or battery, help the teacher screen out those pupils who have serious learning disabilities. They provide some diagnostic information. The teacher, however, needs many more data on the specific difficulties of a pupil to be able to provide adequate remediation. Diagnostic tests serve this purpose.

Such tests must, therefore, be considerably longer than the typical survey tests to make the necessary subtests sufficiently reliable. Instead of the three scores typical of reading survey tests—vocabulary, comprehension, and rate—they may provide numerous scores. A reading diagnostic test may give scores in syllabication, knowledge of consonant sounds, blending, reversals, wrong beginnings, and endings. Whereas an arithmetic survey test may provide two scores, computational and reasoning, a diagnostic arithmetic test may provide information on the difficulties encountered by a pupil in each of the fundamental processes as well as in fractions and decimals. For example, one pupil may have difficulty in long division because he makes mistakes in subtraction. Another makes errors in multiplication that give him an incorrect answer. Still a third has difficulty in his placement of zeros in the quotient. A good diagnostic test will reveal to the teacher the source of the pupil's difficulty.

The more detailed diagnostic tests are individually administered and require greater administrative skill than survey tests. Interpretation is also more complex. Norms are not always provided. Although norms are useful, they are not nearly so important as the careful tabulations and analysis of the pupil's performance in the varied tasks presented.

Finally, because diagnostic tests often tend to be subdivided into numerous subtests, sampling is frequently limited, and doubt is thereby cast on the adequacy of their reliability. Such scores should be supported by further data if the test is to realize its potential usefulness.

Diagnostic Tests and Self-Helps in Arithmetic.   A good illustration of this type of test is the *Diagnostic Tests and Self-Helps in Arithmetic* for use in grades 4, 5, and 6. Three kinds of materials are provided: *Screening Tests,*

Diagnostic Tests, and Self-Helps exercises. Three screening tests enable the teacher to survey the pupils' achievement in whole numbers, fractions, and decimals. A fourth screening test, designed for use in grade 6 and above, is general in nature and contains more difficult examples than the other three. The author suggests that when a pupil makes one or more errors in a screening test, the proper diagnostic tests be administered.

There are twenty-three diagnostic tests in all:

Addition facts	Subtraction of like fractions
Subtraction facts	Addition of unlike fractions
Multiplication facts	Subtraction of unlike fractions
Division facts	Multiplication of fractions
Uneven division facts	Division of fractions
Addition of whole numbers	Addition of decimals
Subtraction of whole numbers	Subtraction of decimals
Multiplication of whole numbers	Multiplication of decimals
Division by one-place numbers	Division of decimals
Division by two-place numbers	Percent
Regrouping fractions	Operations with measures
Addition of like fractions	

The tests are also cross-referred to each other. For example, those related to *Multiplication of Whole Numbers,* Test 8, are Tests 1, *Addition Facts,* 3, *Multiplication Facts,* and 6, *Addition of Whole Numbers.* When a pupil makes a mistake in a problem such as 986×357, he may have one of several difficulties. He may place the products of the various steps incorrectly. Possibly he does not know how to carry. Perhaps he does not know his addition facts or understand how to do column addition. Some of these difficulties will be obvious after administering Test 8. By assigning the related tests, the teacher can locate the source of error.

The *Self-Helps* guide the pupil in overcoming his difficulties in a particular skill. Each diagnostic test has its companion self-help material. For example, if a pupil has difficulty in multiplying numbers with zeros in the multiplicand, there are exercises showing all the work required in this type of skill:

760	806	900
$\times$ 59	$\times$ 48	$\times$ 67
6840	6448	6300
38000	32240	54000
44840	38688	60300

The pupils are instructed to study the work to determine how the answers are found. They are then advised to cover the work and answers and solve the exercise on their own.

No coefficients of reliability or validity are reported. However, the author points out that rows of examples testing each step were included to increase reliability. For example, in testing a pupil's ability to deal with one-place multipliers where no carrying is involved, we have the following exercises:

$$
\begin{array}{ccc}
34 & 213 & 111 \\
\times\ 2 & \times\ 3 & \times\ 6 \\
\hline
\end{array}
$$

Content validity is stressed. The tests are based on an analysis of the underlying skills involved in the various operations. These are organized systematically in terms of the development of each skill.

Problem

15. Would a different type of validity be stressed in a diagnostic test than in a survey test of achievement? Explain.

SUMMARY

Standardized tests differ from teacher-constructed tests in that they have norms and, in general, exhibit greater care in construction of items and more attention to educational objectives. Both the standardized and teacher-constructed tests serve useful purposes. The strength of standardized tests lies in their use as an added criterion of measurement against which the teacher may judge the adequacy of his content selection and the effectiveness of the learning experiences he has organized.

In a testing program, survey tests are generally given first to identify areas of individual and group weakness. Although tests of this kind are numerous, the trend has been toward the use of test batteries for this purpose. In the past, batteries have been employed almost entirely in the elementary school. However, new batteries designed for the secondary school will probably result in more extensive use of these instruments at this higher level. A distinct advantage of the battery is the availability of a profile providing a more adequate interpretation of a pupil's strengths and weaknesses.

The diagnostic test can be administered to those pupils who do poorly on the survey test. Diagnostic tests include items sampling aspects of learning that have caused difficulty for large numbers of pupils. They therefore aid in analyzing areas of weakness.

The frontier in standardized testing lies in the development of instruments measuring complex cognition and affective behaviors rather than specific information taught. The teacher-made test can utilize the materials in a specific textbook or reference work as a vehicle for measuring the development of ability to apply scientific method, for example. However, in a standardized test, the authors cannot depend on all pupils having studied the same references and must therefore supply materials, a requirement which presents practical problems, particularly with regard to test length.

Suggested Readings

Anastasi, A. Psychological testing. (3rd ed.) London: Macmillan, 1968. Chapter 15.
> An excellent discussion of achievement tests in general and in special areas is presented. Uses and limitations of achievement tests and batteries and problems in construction are emphasized. A number of achievement tests in special areas are described, and some of the items are illustrated.

Blum, S. H. Group test administration: Promise and problems. *Educational Forum*, 1969, **33**, 213–218.
> An interesting, nontechnical, practical article on the important factors to consider in test administration.

Engelhart, M. D. What to look for in a review of an achievement test. *Personnel and Guidance Journal*, 1964, **42**, 616–619.
> As the title implies, the author discusses the salient factors that make a satisfactory achievement test. Validity and reliability are stressed.

Katz, M. *Selecting an achievement test, principles and procedures.* (2nd ed.) Educational Testing Service Evaluation and Advisory Service Series, No. 3. Princeton, N.J.: Educational Testing Service, 1961.
> This monograph is designed to help laymen make a more intelligent choice among the many available tests. The basis for test selection consists of certain universal elements, namely, pupil population, school objectives, purposes in testing, methods of accomplishing these purposes through tests, orientation and motivation of school personnel, and available time and money.

Merwin, J. C., and F. B. Womer. Evaluation in assessing the progress of education to provide bases of public understanding and public policy. In R. W. Tyler (ed.), *Educational evaluation: New roles, new means.* Sixty-Eighth Yearbook of the National Society for the Study of Education, Part II. Chicago: University of Chicago Press, 1969. Chapter 13.
> A historical review of the initiation of the National Assessment of Educational Progress and the bases from which it developed. Problems faced such as obtaining proper difficulty of items, means and place of administration, and correct language for phrasing items are discussed.

Shimberg, F. Standardized tests in industrial arts. *Industrial Arts and Vocational Education*, 1968, **57**, 24–25.
> The author gives the reader some insight into test development, and also orients him as to the availability of such tests in industrial arts.

Stake, R. E., and J. T. Hastings. Stanford achievement battery. *Personnel and Guidance Journal*, 1964, **43**, 178–184.
> This is an excellent critique of a standardized achievement test battery. It pro-

vides an insight into many aspects of test construction that determines the quality of the instruments.

Thompson, A. *Test giver's self-inventory*. New York: Harcourt, Brace & World, 1965.

A well-organized check list is presented for those who have the responsibility for the administration of standardized tests.

Traxler, A. Some misconceptions about standardized testing. *Education*, 1967, 87, 407–410.

The author discusses five misconceptions about testing. These involve the definition of psychological tests, the use of tests for screening purposes, the focus of interest on individual responses to specific questions, the meaning of the intelligence quotient, and limiting an individual's freedom of choice.

References Cited

Cooperative Test Division. *A Prospectus, Sequential Tests of Educational Progress*. Princeton, N.J.: Educational Testing Service, 1957.

Cooperative Test Division. *Sequential Tests of Educational Progress*. Princeton, N.J.: Educational Testing Service, 1957.

Cooperative Test Division. *Sequential Tests of Educational Progress. Teacher's guide*. Princeton, N.J.: Educational Testing Service, 1959.

Educational Testing Service. *ETS builds a test*. Princeton, N.J.: Educational Testing Service, 1965.

French, J. W., and W. B. Michael. *Standards for educational and psychological tests and manuals*. Washington: American Psychological Association, 1966.

Lindquist, E. F. Impact of machines on evaluation. In R. W. Tyler (ed.), *Educational Evaluation: New roles, new means*. Sixty-Eighth Yearbook of the National Society for the Study of Education, Part II. Chicago: University of Chicago Press, 1969. Chapter 15.

Lindquist, E. F., and A. N. Hieronymous. *Iowa Tests of Basic Skills*. Boston: Houghton Mifflin, 1955.

Lindquist, E. F., and A. N. Hieronymous. *Manual for administrators, supervisors, and counselors: Iowa Tests of Basic Skills*. Boston: Houghton Mifflin, 1956.

Stake, R. E. "Overestimation" of achievement with the California Achievement Test. *Educational and Psychological Measurement*, 1961, 21, 59–62.

Thelen, H. A. The triumph of "achievement" over inquiry in education. *Elementary School Journal*, 1960, 60, 190–197.

CHAPTER 12

Measuring Pupil Aptitudes

Visit any classroom with a democratic social climate and you will observe as many kinds of behavior as there are pupils. Within a fifth-grade class you find some pupils working arithmetic problems while another group turns, fascinated, to the production of a play they have written. One boy is building a model to illustrate the operation of a machine studied in a science unit; one of the girls is writing a poem. Other children are reading and seem to be totally absorbed in a story. You see one pupil staring out of the window; occasionally he will try to work at an assignment, but he seems to give up easily. Another child is buzzing around the room enjoying a series of social calls, and is soon called back to his seat.

You also notice that performance varies considerably. Some children seem adept at manipulating scissors or blocks. Others paint very well, though the art work of their peers seems immature. Certain pupils offer many ideas as they work with others; some tend to follow and do as they are told.

The many individual differences you observe reflect interests, attitudes, experience backgrounds, and innate ability. All of these factors form the basis for the pupil's ability to learn. His ability to learn is his aptitude; his achievement refers to what he has learned. As we shall see, tests that measure aptitude and achievement differ not so much in their content but in the functions they perform.

Certain inherited traits are basic to specific aptitudes. Early studies of individual differences revealed that some people react to stimuli more quickly than others. Take, for example, the case of a certain astronomer engaged in recording the instant at which he saw the images of stars as they crossed the field of his telescope. When a consistent time-lag appeared in his reports, his employers discharged him promptly, thinking him simply careless. This occurred before scientists discovered that individuals react to stimuli with varying rapidity. Those who react quickly have an advantage in some kinds of work. Certain manual skills require long fingers and a deftness of manipulation. In those areas an individual with short stubby fingers that he uses awkwardly will find himself at a definite disadvantage. In most instances, aptitude represents more than innate ability. Two individuals with identical inherited capacities, like identical twins, may have quite different aptitudes because their experiences have been different. One may learn or perform a task with ease; he has a high aptitude for that work. The other may find the task difficult; he is inept at improving his skill, and has little aptitude for the work. Theoretically, each could develop this special genetically based aptitude to the same degree, but this may not happen because of the important part achievement plays in aptitude potential.

High general ability is necessary for the development of superior specific aptitudes. The concert pianist has not only high musical aptitude, but high general ability as well. An individual with superior native endowment is also more likely to have a wider range of aptitudes than his peer who is less intellectually mature and may be talented in the graphic arts, exhibit physical prowess, and show high scholastic achievement.

Knowledge of a pupil's aptitudes is of value in counseling him on vocational plans and preparation for jobs in which he is likely to succeed. It is also helpful in organizing learning experiences for the individual. For example, low achievement may be the result of lack of effort or ability; we want to know how much a pupil can achieve. Of course, reliability of prediction is dependent on the stability of the aptitude. If an aptitude is unstable, it cannot be measured reliably and will have low correlation to achievement. The findings of research dealing with constancy of aptitudes indicate some disagreement among psychologists, but, in general, aptitudes seem to be fairly stable. Super (1962, p. 72) states that ". . . whether largely innate or largely acquired, the aptitudes about which we know something appear to become crystallized in early childhood and that after that they mature in a predictable way and are generally relatively constant."

In developing instruments for evaluating aptitudes, investigators have emphasized proceeding from general to "purer" aptitudes. Any list of aptitudes we choose will be arbitrary, depending on the extent to which we find measurement of discrete aptitudes helpful as opposed to lumping them together for practical purposes. For instance, it is often useful to know a pupil's mechanical aptitude in addition to having a measure of his general mental ability. Yet mechanical aptitude is a composite of spatial visualization, perceptual speed and acuity, and mechanical information. At the present time it is probably more generally useful to take a global approach to aptitude measurement than an "atomistic" one such as making a separate analysis of mechanical aptitude.

Thus the discussion that follows is centered around special groupings of the purer aptitudes. Those of particular importance to school personnel are classified under the headings scholastic and mechanical. There is also a discussion of the basis for differential aptitude testing and of instruments designed for this purpose. A selected list of tests that measure many different aptitudes is shown in Appendix D.

SCHOLASTIC APTITUDE

Someone once quipped that intelligence is what intelligence tests measure. Unfortunately most other definitions do little more to clarify the concept, and though many have been offered, they all fail in some sense. Since intelligence, unlike a muscle, cannot be described, definitions delineate an individual's inherited capacity. Because intelligence can only be inferred from the behavior of the organism, test scores imply a quantity or quality of intelligence rather than a direct measure.

In measuring achievement, we sample areas of learning, and if our test and testing situation are adequate, we can arrive at some fairly defensible conclusions about the pupil's skills. But in measuring intelligence, we must consider unequal educational opportunities. Since we cannot measure intelligence directly, we establish problem situations that represent important intellectual functions. Though we try to exclude problems whose solutions have been taught in school, the tools the pupil uses are learned. If he is to answer questions on a group intelligence test, he probably will have to know how to read. Some items will demand arithmetic; others, the development of specific concepts, such as rod, quarter, capital, civil war, and so forth. Because a pupil's ability to do well on these tests is so closely related to success in school, the commonly used measures of general intelligence are known as scholastic aptitude tests. There is a high correlation between scores on these tests and achievement tests. Test items are often difficult to differentiate. (See page 32.)

Glaser (1970) suggests that our scholastic aptitude tests are designed to predict achievement in situations where instruction is relatively nonadaptive; it is the kind of instruction directed at the total group that one finds in the average classroom; it isn't generally adjusted for maximum effectiveness on an individual basis. According to Glaser, nonadaptive instruction assumes that all pupils can develop a certain degree of proficiency in a given task. However, adaptive instruction demands a different approach to prediction. In essence, it involves determination of specific instructional methodology for each learner and prediction of success from each learner's characteristics. The reader will find that Glaser's discussion and bibliography will provide him a good background for this frontier thinking.

Individual Tests

The individual scholastic aptitude test, as the name implies, is designed for face-to-face administration to the individual pupil. Three commonly used instruments in this category are the *Stanford-Binet Scale, Form L-M, Wechsler Preschool and Primary Scale of Intelligence* (*WPPSI*), *Wechsler Intelligence Scale for Children* (*WISC*), and *Wechsler Adult Intelligence Scale* (*WAIS*).

Stanford-Binet Intelligence Scale, Form L-M. The 1960 revision of the *Stanford-Binet Intelligence Scale*, which is designated as *Form L-M*, differs from earlier revisions in both content and structure. Some of the content revisions have relocated or eliminated certain subtests and test items. Many of the nonscholastic items are omitted to put greater emphasis on word knowledge. Others clarify directions for test administration and scoring. By structural changes the authors have attempted to make the intelligence quotients comparable at the various ages, and have tried to correct an inadequacy of the 1937 revision of the scale, which yielded intelligence quotients with an arithmetic mean greater than 100. In addition, the intelligence quotient tables in the 1960 revision have been extended to include ages seventeen and eighteen.

Form *L-M* is grouped into twenty age levels. Beginning at Year II, the levels are placed at six-month intervals up to Year VI; that is, Year II, Year II–6, Year III, Year III–6, and so forth. This grouping allows for the rapid growth of preschool children. Each level has six tests; one month of credit toward the mental-age score is allowed for each test. From Year VI to Year XIV, twelve-month intervals are used. Since there are also six tests in each of these levels, each receives two months of credit. Topping the scale are four increasingly difficult levels, the Average Adult, the Superior Adult Level I, Superior Adult Level II, and the Superior Adult Level III. The Average Adult level has eight tests counting two months each. Each of the three Superior Adult levels has six tests. In Superior Adult Level I, each test counts four months, in Superior Adult Level II, five months, and in Superior Adult Level III, six months. Form *L-M* reflects the conclusions of longitudinal studies (Bradway & Robinson, 1961; Bradway & Thompson, 1962), that improvement in performance on the test continues after sixteen years of age. The new form recognizes improvement to age eighteen.

The tests demand both verbal and nonverbal performance. In some cases, simple memory is sufficient; in others, reasoning is necessary. The pupil must rely on his past experiences as well as his talent to solve problems in new situations. Test materials consist of toy objects, printed cards, a test booklet for recording responses, and the test manual.

Below are samples of some of the tests (Terman & Merrill, 1960, reproduced by permission of Houghton Mifflin Company) from various age levels:

Year II—*Identifying Objects by Name* (Alternate)
  Material: Card with dog, ball, engine, bed, doll, and scissors attached.
  Procedure: Show the card with the six small objects attached and say, "See all these things? Show me the dog." "Put your finger on the dog." "Where is the dog?"
Year VI—*Mutilated Pictures*
  Material: Card with mutilated pictures.
  Procedure: Show subject the card with mutilated pictures and pointing to each in turn, ask, "What is gone in this picture?" or "What part is gone?"
Year XIV—*Orientation: Direction I*
  Procedure: Read the following directions distinctly, emphasizing the critical words:
    (a) "Which direction would you have to face so that your left hand would be toward the east?"
    (b) "Suppose you are going west, then turn to your right; what direction are you going now?"
    (c) "Suppose you are going north, then turn to your left, then turn right; what direction are you going now?"
    (d) "Suppose you are going south, then turn left, then turn right, then turn left again; what direction are you going now?"
    (e) "Suppose you are going north, then turn left, then left again, then right, and then right again; what direction are you going now?"
Superior Adult III—*Reasoning*
  Material: Card on which problem is stated.
  Procedure: Let subject look at the card while you read the problem aloud and while he is solving it. "I planted a tree that was 8 inches tall. At the end of the first year, it was 12 inches tall; at the end of the second year it was 18 inches tall; and at the end of the third year it was 27 inches tall. How tall was it at the end of the fourth year?"

The authors emphasize three requirements for a valid test (Terman and Merrill, 1960):

1. The standard procedures must be followed.
2. The pupil's best efforts must be enlisted by the establishment and maintenance of adequate rapport.
3. The responses must be correctly scored.

The examiner must have special training in test administration and scoring before he can meet these criteria. He must also have background information in testing and a considerable amount of practice with the instrument to administer it well. Any variation of the standardized procedure invalidates the test results somewhat. Too much attention to details excludes continuing rapport with the pupil and may result in a less-than-adequate performance. Test administration is further complicated by the fact that scoring is simultaneous with administration. Cues for the next step in the procedure are dependent on the pupil's success or failure.

With younger children, testing is usually begun at an age level about one year below the anticipated mental age of the child. If all tests at this level are passed, that is known as the pupil's *basal age*, and the tests at the next higher age level are administered. If any tests are failed, the examiner drops down to the next lower level until a basal age is reached. Tests are then given through the higher age scales until a level is achieved at which the child fails all the tests. This is known as his *ceiling* or *maximal age*.

Year level	Number of tests passed	Months of credit per test	Total Credit	
			Years	Months
VI	6 (Basal Age)	—	6	0
VII	3	2	0	6
VIII	1	2	0	2
IX	0 (Ceiling Age)	2	0	0
Mental Age			6	8

This child's basal age is six, and his ceiling age is nine. His mental age is the sum of the various amounts of credit he earned.

At levels of Year VI and above, some examiners may begin with the vocabulary test. This is used for Years VI, VIII, X, and XIV, and all adult levels; the scoring standards change from level to level. The age level for further test administration is determined by comparing the number of words passed by the pupil and the number of correct word definitions necessary for success at a given level. The procedure for determining the basal and maximal ages is identical to that previously described.

It is obvious that no pupil takes all of the tests. He tries only those items that determine the upper and lower limits of his ability. Provision is made for the spoiling of tests by making an alternative test available at each of the age levels. About one hour is usually needed for test administration; the time required may vary from as little as thirty to forty minutes for younger children to an hour and one-half or more for older children.

The test manual specifies the desired performance on each test for credit at a particular level. For example, in *Identifying Objects by Name* for Year II, the child must correctly identify at least five of the six objects to pass. Scoring is on an all-or-none basis. The child who identifies three objects correctly receives no more credit than one who identifies two. Both children fail. Some tests are used at more than one age level and require higher standards of performance for success at the higher age levels. If a test is administered at a lower level, it is not given again at the higher level, but is scored and credited for the proper age level at that time. For example, in the *Opposite Analogies I* test of Year IV, the child needs to have only two of the items correct; however, if three or more are right, he is given credit for the same test in Year

IV–6. The items in this test follow (Terman & Merrill, 1960, reproduced by permission of Houghton Mifflin Company):

    a. "Brother is a boy; sister is a _____."
    b. "In daytime it is light; at night it is _____."
    c. "Father is a man; mother is a _____."
    d. "The snail is slow; the rabbit is _____."
    e. "The sun shines during the day; the moon at _____."

    The mental age of a child is determined by adding to his basal age the number of months he earned on those tests passed beyond this age. Traditionally, the intelligence quotient (IQ) had been found by dividing his mental age (MA) by the chronological age (CA) and multiplying by 100. However, this method prevents IQs having the same meaning at different age levels. At one CA an IQ of 120 may be the highest score of 85 percent of the age group while, for another age group, an IQ of 115 may be the top figure for the same percentage of that population. To overcome this problem, in *Form L-M* of the *Stanford-Binet*, a deviation or standard score IQ (sometimes known as DIQ) is found by entering a table with the proper MA and CA for the pupil in question. In essence, DIQs are standard scores with an arithmetic mean of 100 and a standard deviation of 16.

    Because *Form L-M* was constructed from items selected from *Forms L* and *M* of the 1937 revision, data from this earlier revision are still important. For example, *Forms L* and *M* were administered to a group of children with a time period between the two administrations, and a coefficient of reliability was obtained. Appreciable differences among the reliability coefficients for the various age groups were found, as can be noted from Table 18 (McNemar, 1942, pp. 62–63). Reliability of the scores of older children and scores of those having lower IQs tends to be greater. Most of the coefficients are about 0.90 or only slightly below for the total range, which is excellent considering the greater homogeneity of specific age levels. Reliability of most scholastic aptitude tests has been determined on far more heterogeneous groups.

    The validity of *Form L-M* is based on three factors. First, the best items borrowed from the two forms of the 1937 revision assure us that the 1960

TABLE 18. Reliability Coefficients of the Stanford-Binet Scale (1937 Revision) for IQ Intervals and Age Groups.

	Age Group		
IQ-Interval	2½ to 5½	6 to 13	14 to 18
140–149	0.83	0.91	0.95
60–69	0.91	0.97	0.98

revision measures whatever was measured by the previous one. Secondly, items were selected on the basis of an increasing percentage of success as the CA of the children increased. For example, based on both forms of the 1937 revision, a higher percentage of six-year-old children than five-year-olds should pass an item at Year VI. Thirdly, items were chosen on the basis of their relationship with the total score on each form, a criterion of internal consistency.

The criterion-related validity of an intelligence test is of interest to teachers. Scholastic achievement is the criterion generally used in investigations of this kind. Studies show that there is a high relationship between academic achievement and scores on the *Stanford-Binet,* with those courses emphasizing verbal skills tending to show the highest coefficients of correlation, for example, higher than 0.70. Though academic success is influenced by numerous unmeasured factors such as background, persistence, and personal-social adjustment, the *Stanford-Binet* scores are still very helpful to those planning a pupil's education.

Like any other aptitude test, the *Stanford-Binet* does not measure pure native capacity, but innate ability and the effect of learning. Only if we could assume that the test is completely valid and reliable and that influencing environments are identical could we infer that the pupils tested have the same native capacity. At that, it would be sounder to infer only that they had the same ability to learn. But no psychological test has perfect reliability or validity; rapport and effective tapping of a pupil's maximum potential are always problems. He may know the answer to a question and refuse to respond; he may give an incorrect answer for many reasons. Pupils with academic disabilities may have a particularly strong dislike or even a fear of the kinds of items included in the *Stanford-Binet.*

The improbability that children will experience the same environments extends even to siblings. The older children may be asked to assume more responsibility, to supervise younger brothers or sisters. Perhaps more sharing is demanded of them. Because older children serve as models of behavior, younger members of the family are likely to participate in certain activities at an earlier age than their older siblings.

Differences also exist among family environments. One home may provide a great deal of social interaction, another almost none. Reading may be a central interest of all members of one pupil's family; his classmate's family may lack even a daily newspaper. Bilingual homes present a special problem for children. Because the *Stanford-Binet* is highly verbal, a pupil from a bilingual home is likely to be severely affected by lack of verbal stimulation. Although he may have other types of ability, they are not effectively sampled by this test.

It should also be noted that the *Stanford-Binet* is not designed to differentiate among the various aspects of intelligence. There are no separate scores, only a composite.

Despite these limitations, the *Stanford-Binet* has proved over the years to be a valuable instrument. Although superior performance on the test is dependent on success in school, the test may also be the instrument for predicting such success, since verbal ability is an important factor in school success and this highly verbal test enables an examiner to assess the pupil's verbal facility. It also helps spot deficiencies in arithmetic, problem solving, and the fund of information.

During the administration of the *Stanford-Binet*, one can observe a child's reactions. Although the quality of his performance should be interpreted cautiously by an experienced examiner, a pupil's problem-solving ability, his work habits, and his reaction to success and failure can be examined. When he fails, the examiner seeks to determine whether he is disturbed, irritable, argumentative, or depressed. When he is successful, his reaction is also observed. Reaction time should be noted; it can be indicative of certain personality problems. Is it delayed, blocked, or irregular? Is there any indication of negativism, or are the responses given quickly and impulsively? On the basis of this and other evidence, the examiner can gain insights into the personality of the pupil.

Problem

1. Billy and Sally, both 8 years old, received IQs of 97 on the *Stanford-Binet*. However, the basal age for Billy was 5 and his ceiling age was 12. Sally's basal age was 7; her ceiling was 10. On the basis of this information, what differences might you expect in the pattern of abilities of these two pupils?

Wechsler Preschool and Primary Scale of Intelligence.   This is the newest scale in the series, published in 1967. The instrument was designed for use with children 4 to 6½ years old. Eight of the eleven subtests are downward-adapted extensions of the *WISC*, discussed in the next section. The remaining three tests were devised to replace *WISC* tests unsatisfactory for a child of this age. Only ten of the eleven tests are used in determining *Performance*, *Verbal*, and *Full Scale IQs*. The *Sentences* test may be used as an alternative or a supplement to one of the verbal tests; however, if it is utilized as a supplement, it is not used to determine the IQ.

The eleven-test scale is as follows, with the three newly devised tests identified with an asterisk:

Verbal tests	Performance tests
Information	Animal House*
Vocabulary	Picture Completion
Arithmetic	Mazes
Similarities	Geometric Designs*
Comprehension	Block Design
Sentences*	

The standardization sample was chosen with the same careful consideration that Wechsler used with all his tests. Factors governing stratification were age, sex, geographic region, urban-rural residence, color (white-nonwhite) and father's occupation. Eight groupings of occupations were employed.

The Spearman-Brown "Prophecy Formula" with odd and even scores gave reliabilities having medians of 0.82, 0.82, 0.82, 0.84, and 0.81 for the age groups of 4, 4½, 5, 5½, 6 and 6½ respectively. An exception is the *Animal House* test. Since this test is speeded, its reliability was determined by test-retest procedure; the retest was administered at the end of the testing period. The range of the *Verbal IQ* reliability coefficients was between 0.87 and 0.90, with an average of 0.89. For the *Performance IQ*, the coefficients ranged between 0.84 and 0.91, with an average of 0.88. For the *Full Scale*, the coefficients ranged between 0.92 and 0.93, with an average of 0.93. From data on standard errors of measurement and significance of the difference between scores, the author suggests that a difference between *Verbal* and *Performance IQs* of fifteen points is important enough for investigation. Stability over time, determined by retesting with a population of fifty kindergarten children over an average elapsed time of eleven weeks, resulted in reliabilities of 0.86, 0.89, and 0.92 for *Verbal IQ*, *Performance IQ*, and *Full Scale IQ* respectively.

Other data of interest include reported correlations between subtests for six age groups ranging between 0.28 and 0.73. There is further evidence of overlap indicated by the average correlation of 0.66 between *Verbal* and *Performance IQs*. The relationship of the *Full Scale IQ* with the *Stanford-Binet IQ* is reported as 0.75 for a group of five- and six-year-old children. *Verbal IQ* of the *WPPSI* correlates 0.76 and *Performance IQ* 0.56 with the *Stanford-Binet Test IQ*. In another study (Fogan and others, 1969) results indicate a correlation of 0.80 between the *Stanford-Binet* and *WPPSI* for a small group of lower-class children five years of age. IQs on the *Stanford-Binet* had a mean of 95.2, eight points higher than those of the *WPPSI*.

Problem

2. How might one account for the low correlations between scores on infant tests and later measures of intelligence in terms of validity?

Wechsler Intelligence Scale for Children.   Most of the items in the *WISC* have been taken from *Form II* of the earlier *Wechsler-Bellevue Intelligence Scale*. The most important change is the addition of easier items so that young children can be tested. It is planned for children of ages five to fifteen.

The *WISC* is organized by subtests rather than age scales as in the *Stanford-Binet* and is a series of point scales. That is, each test item is assigned points for a correct response. Points for each test represent raw scores, which are changed to scaled scores by means of a table. The respective tests in the *Verbal Scale* and the *Performance Scale* are added to secure the verbal and performance scores. By the use of tables, the intelligence quotients may be determined.

The pupil's IQ is found, therefore, by a comparison of the score representing his test performance with those scores earned by the individuals in the standardization sample of a single age group. If the standard deviation of IQs is held constant and the total mean score for each age group equated, the IQ is made comparable for pupils of different ages. An individual is assigned an IQ on the basis of the amount that he deviates from the average performance of those in his own age group.

The *WISC* actually has twelve subtests grouped under *Verbal* and *Performance Scales*. However, two of these, the *Digit Span* in the *Verbal Scale*, and *Mazes* in the *Performance Scale*, were omitted in establishing the IQ tables. *Digit Span* and *Mazes* (or *Coding*) may be used as either alternative or supplementary tests if time permits.

The ten-test scale is therefore as follows:

Verbal tests	Performance tests
General information	Picture completion
General comprehension	Picture arrangement
Arithmetic	Block design
Similarities	Object assembly
Vocabulary	Coding or mazes

Care must be exercised in interpreting differences among subtest scores, and we must anticipate many differences resulting from chance variations. Cohen (1957) concludes that only 86 percent of what a subtest measures is the result of common factors and error.

The *WISC Manual* emphasizes that the test examiner must be well-trained and have access to a quiet testing room and proper materials. The directions for test administration must be followed specifically. Rather than change the wording of the questions, the teacher should read the instructions from the manual. The conditions under which the child performs certain tasks have been carefully standardized; norms of performance have been prepared under the conditions of the instructions. As in the administration of the *Stanford-Binet*, the examiner has an opportunity to note any unusual behavior that bears on the child's personality.

The examiner must always be concerned with securing optimum performance, and very skillful questioning is required. Often the child's response needs clarification, which can be accomplished by nonevaluative querying. For example, the examinee may be asked "Please explain further," or "Tell more about it." Also, in maintaining rapport it is sometimes necessary to encourage with supporting statements, such as, "This is a little difficult; you will find it easier when you are older." One should not build up an expectancy for approval within the child, because he may come to interpret no comment as disapproval.

The scoring is partly clerical but also highly professional because interpretations must be made. Although the scoring of a certain test, such as *Arithmetic* and *Coding*, can be completely objective, the responses children give for *Vocabulary*, as in the case of the *Stanford-Binet*, are numerous and demand considerable judgment from the examiner. Test items correctly answered are accorded a certain number of points, and are then added to obtain a raw score, which, in turn, is changed to standard scores from tables provided. The IQs may then be found as previously explained.

Split-half reliability coefficients were determined for *Full, Verbal,* and *Performance Scales* for 7½, 10½, and 13½ year age groups. Subtest score reliabilities were also reported. *Full Scale* reliabilities were 0.92, 0.95, and 0.94 respectively, for these age groups. *Verbal Scale* reliabilities were 0.88, 0.96, and 0.96. The reliabilities on the *Performance Scale* were 0.86, 0.89, and 0.90. However, the subtest reliabilities were considerably lower. *Digit Span* was as low as 0.50 for the 13½ year group. Most of the values lie in the 0.60s, 0.70s, and 0.80s (Wechsler, 1949).

No interpretive data are presented in the manual on the validity of the test. However, many studies have compared performance on the *WISC* with that of the *Stanford-Binet*. Coefficients of correlations usually found vary between 0.60 and 0.80. Correlations based on the *Performance Scale* alone tend to be somewhat lower than those based on the *Verbal Scale* alone.

The *WISC* uses a standard deviation of 15 in contrast to the 16 used for *Stanford-Binet* scores. Therefore, if two bright pupils have numerically similar means on the two tests, the DIQ on the *Stanford-Binet* will be slightly higher than on the *WISC*. With comparably dull children, the DIQ on the *Stanford-Binet* will be a little lower.

The *WISC* is more easily administered than the *Stanford-Binet*. Moreover, the subject does not undergo the frustrating situation he experiences in the latter during the series of failures as he approaches his ceiling. Unlike the *Stanford-Binet*, which provides only one IQ score, the *WISC* has separate verbal and nonverbal IQs. This feature is often valuable in diagnosing educational problems of some pupils. One of the limitations of the *WISC*, however, is in testing retarded children; it does not yield an IQ below 45.

Wechsler Adult Intelligence Scale.   *Form I* of the original *Wechsler Intelligence Scale* was published in 1939 and was called the *Wechsler-Bellevue Intelligence Scale. Form II* was adapted from a scale developed during World War II. Scales of both forms were designed for adults rather than children. The tasks in existing instruments, such as the *Stanford-Binet*, do not hold enough interest to motivate many adults. In addition, the speed factor is particularly detrimental in assessing adult intelligence when a test is standardized on children.

The items in these scales reflect Wechsler's specific objective, namely, to construct an instrument that would enable him to understand better his adult patients at New York's Bellevue Hospital. Because he had to determine their intelligence and personality aberrations, he needed an instrument with diagnostic properties in addition to those measuring "global" intelligence.

These scales were used for ten to fifteen years, and during that time a considerable amount of research revealed certain limitations that warranted an extensive revision. This was undertaken, and in 1955 the *Wechsler Adult Intelligence Scale*, commonly called the *WAIS*, was published. The significant changes were more adequate norms, based on a broader population sampling, and an increase in the range of difficulty in the items of the subtests and in improved total scale reliability.

Like its two predecessors, the *Wechsler-Bellevue Intelligence Scale* and the *WISC*, the *WAIS* is a point scale designed to yield a deviation IQ. There are eleven tests in the *Full Scale* of the *WAIS*, six of which comprise the *Verbal Scale* and the remaining five are grouped into the *Performance Scale*. The same considerations for interpreting the differences between subtest scores and verbal and performance IQs mentioned in the previous section should be adhered to.

Verbal tests	Performance tests
Information	Digit Symbol
Comprehension	Picture Completion
Arithmetic	Block Design
Similarities	Picture Arrangement
Digit Span	Object Assembly
Vocabulary	

Problems

3.   Teachers usually look only for the actual IQ score when an individual psychological test has been administered. Few bother to read the detailed report prepared by the examiner. What dangers are inherent in this practice? What information should you as a teacher look for and expect to find in a psychological report? In what respects might a psychological report of a *Stanford-Binet* test differ from one on the *WISC* in terms of the kinds of information given?

4.   Prepare a summary of the main differences between the *Stanford-Binet* and the *WAIS* or *WISC*. Compare them in terms of test construction, computation of IQ, statistical data on reliability and validity, and the interpretation of the IQ score.

Group Tests

In most school situations, neither time nor trained personnel is available for the administration of the individual tests described. Group tests, therefore, are much more extensively used, since they may be administered to a large group by an examiner with minimum training. In general, they are verbal, and if they do not require reading, the examinee must at least be able to understand the verbal instructions of the examiner. Therefore great care must be taken in interpreting test scores, for a low score may indicate a lack of verbal facility rather than intellectual immaturity.

Although many good group intelligence tests are available for school use (see Appendix D), all of them cannot be discussed here. We take the logical alternative of examining several tests that represent somewhat different approaches to the measurement of mental ability. In addition, a summary of the important college aptitude tests is included.

Otis-Lennon Mental Ability Test. In 1918, publication of the *Otis Group Intelligence Scale* marked the development of the first group test of mental ability for school use. During the intervening years various forms and editions have been published. The *Otis-Lennon Mental Ability Test* represents the fourth principal edition. The authors continue to emphasize the g or general factor as the most meaningful assessment of scholastic aptitude. Therefore, a broad range of cognitive abilities is measured by the spiral omnibus form; instead of using subtests of homogeneous items, the designers introduce all easy items first, whatever the nature.

Six levels of tests have been developed for pupils in kindergarten through the freshman year in college. They are as follows:

Primary I Level (K)
Primary II Level (Grade 1)
Elementary I Level (Grades 2 and 3)
Elementary II Level (Grades 4–6)
Intermediate Level (Grades 7–9)
Advanced Level (Grades 10–13)

The first three levels measure the ability to classify, follow directions, reason quantitatively, conceptualize, and reason by analogy; items contain both pictorial and geometric material. *Primary I* and *Primary II* have the same content. They vary only in response called for. In kindergarten the pupil responds by circling the picture. In the first grade he fills in an answer oval beneath the picture. The authors indicate that the upper three levels contain verbal and nonverbal items that sample *fourteen* different mental processes designed for a power measurement of abstract reasoning. However, they present no factor-analytic evidence to support these claims.

The *Otis-Lennon* tests appear to be highly reliable. Median reliability coefficients for combined single-age and single-grade groups range from 0.87 to 0.95.

The authors attempt to support construct validity by high correlations with scores from other mental ability batteries. On the other hand, similar high correlations are reported with scores on achievement tests. Although this is not unusual for scholastic aptitude tests, it does raise a question about the degree to which the *Otis-Lennon* is measuring achievement.

The norms are based on the testing of about 200,000 pupils drawn from 117 school systems in all 50 states. The schools were selected on the basis of a stratified random-cluster sampling procedure to obtain a representative sample of the national elementary and secondary school population. The deviation IQs reported have a mean of 100 and standard deviation of 16. They provide an index of a pupil's relative brightness when compared with others of his own age regardless of grade. According to the authors, they "reflect, at a given point in time, the pupil's ability to deal with abstract relationships involving the manipulation of ideas expressed in verbal, numerical, figural, or symbolic form." The authors recommend that DIQs be translated into percentile ranks and stanine scores for proper interpretation.

California Test of Mental Maturity.   The 1963 edition of the *CTMM* (Long Form) is available for six levels: Level 0 (Kindergarten-Grade 1), Level 1 (Grades 1, 2, 3), Level 2 (Grades 4, 5, 6), Level 3 (Grades 7, 8, 9), Level 4 (Grades 9, 10, 11, 12), Level 5 (Grades 12–College and Adult). There are twelve subtests listed under five factors: *Logical Reasoning, Spatial Relationships, Numerical Reasoning, Verbal Concepts,* and *Memory.* Tests results yield a language, nonlanguage, and total IQ. Actually, here again nonlanguage is not accurate terminology since the examinee must understand the verbal instructions of the examiner in the nonlanguage tests.

Probably the total test IQ is the most valid measure to be derived from this instrument. The language and nonlanguage IQs, however, can aid in educational diagnosis. If the pupil is poor in reading, he is likely to make a lower language IQ score than a nonlanguage IQ on this test, and knowledge of this fact can help prevent wrong classification.

The reliability of the total IQ varies from 0.86 to 0.96. The variation for the language factors is from 0.71 to 0.95, and for the nonlanguage factors from 0.79 to 0.93. The deviation IQ has been adopted.

The manual contains an Intellectual Status Index for determining anticipated achievement for a pupil in his actual grade placement. This index enables one to predict, for example, whether a pupil can be expected to do average, below average, or above average work in accordance with his score on the *CTMM* series. When used with scores on the *California Achievement Test* it roughly indicates the status of a pupil's performance in various subjects.

A short form of the test is available for eight levels: Level 0 (Kindergarten–Lower First), Level 1 (Grades High First–Lower Third), Level 1H (Grades 3–4), Level 2 (Grades 4–6), Level 2H (Grades 6–7), Level 3 (Grades 7–8), Level 4 (Grades 9–12), and Level 5 (Grades 12–College and Adult). Language, nonlanguage, and total IQs are also available for this series. Four out of the five factors in the long form are included: *Logical Reasoning, Numerical Reasoning, Verbal Concepts,* and *Memory.* Total score reliabilities vary from 0.78 to 0.95, and the language and nonlanguage score reliabilities vary from 0.59 to 0.94. The short form requires only 34 to 43 minutes of actual testing time for administration while the long form demands 48 minutes to one hour and 23 minutes depending on the particular test level.

Short Form Test of Academic Aptitude.   Another instrument was derived from the *California Test of Mental Maturity (CTMM)* series and designated as the *Short Form Test of Academic Aptitude (SFTAA).* Four item types were selected for the *SFTAA* focusing on the kinds of verbal and inductive abilities related to school success. New materials were then developed, based on these item types found successful in the *CTMM* series. Content includes the following tests: vocabulary, analogies, sequences, and memory. Language, nonlanguage, and the total derived scores are available for five levels, Grades 1.5–12. The tests were standardized jointly with the 1970 edition of the *California Achievement Tests (CAT).* The *SFTAA* requires only 31 to 38 minutes of actual testing time.

Kuhlmann-Anderson Intelligence Tests.   The seventh edition of the *Kuhlmann-Anderson Tests* contains eight booklets that are designated by letters *K, A, B, CD, D, EF, G,* and *H* for use in kindergarten, grades 1; 2; 3 and 4; 4 and 5; 5, 6, and 7; 7, 8, and 9; and 9, 10, 11, and 12, respectively. Although there is overlapping between consecutive booklets, this has been somewhat reduced from the sixth edition. There are now eight tests in the booklets instead of ten, but each test has been lengthened. About 40 percent of the content of this edition has been changed. Booklets are now reusable for *H, G, EF,* and *D* batteries.

Changes also include tables of deviation IQs with stanine equivalents available. Grade percentile ranks are provided for the beginning, middle, and end of a school year for each test booklet (Kuhlmann and Anderson, 1963).

Although verbal (V) and quantitative (Q) scores may be derived from booklet *D* upward, the user is warned that these scores for the *D* and *EF* booklets are not to be used to predict differential success in these areas because they lack sufficient independence. This limitation has been overcome somewhat at the *G* and *H* levels and grade percentile ranks are available for the V, Q, and T scores. The users should interpret the differences between V and Q scores with caution, however.

The tests are easy to administer. They are of the speeded variety and are not corrected for guessing. Testwise pupils may increase their scores by random marking if they find they do not have time to finish the test.

Test reliability is determined in several ways. First, test-retest coefficients range from 0.83 to 0.92. Secondly, testing pupils on adjacent forms produced coefficients from 0.77 to 0.89. Split-half coefficients of reliability for booklets *K* to *CD* range from 0.93 to 0.95.

The validity of the sixth edition of the *Kuhlmann-Anderson Tests* was determined by its ability to discriminate among scores of subjects at successive levels of chronological age, by a comparison of scores of successful and unsuccessful pupils, and by intercorrelations among the subtests. The authors emphasize the test's capacity to discriminate between small increments of mental development. Subsequent studies show a substantial relationship between a pupil's achievement, individual intelligence test scores, and *Kuhlmann-Anderson* scores (Allen, 1944; Dearborn and Rothney, 1963). Acceptable validity for the seventh edition is claimed on the basis that the validity of the sixth edition was built into it. Item analyses were performed using the sixth edition as a criterion.

Schools should find this edition greatly improved over the preceding editions. The reusable booklets, the deviation IQ, excellent reporting of norms, and the very adequately written *Norms Manual* and *Technical Manual* attest to this improvement.

Problems

5. What advantages can you see in the *Kuhlmann-Anderson* that neither the *Otis-Lennon* nor the *CTMM* appears to have? What particular advantage does the first have for the intellectually superior child?

6. If you were given the choice among these three group tests of scholastic aptitude, which would you select for a sixth-grade class? Why?

Scholastic Aptitude Test. Hills (1970) lists and discusses five issues that institutions of higher education must consider in developing a sound selection program: the criteria, the source of applicants, the predictors, the means of combining predictors, and the cutting point for rejection. As more and more high school pupils become interested in going to college, many admissions offices are relying heavily on test scores (predictors) as one of the criteria for selecting students. To provide these scores, several independent testing agencies develop tests, arrange for their administration, score the answer sheets, and report information to the pupil and the college to which he wishes to gain admission.

The College Entrance Examination Board *Scholastic Aptitude Test* (*SAT*) is probably the oldest test for this purpose. Generally, the pupil takes these tests during his senior year in high school. However, because there were demands to have these test scores before the last high-school year, the *Preliminary Scholastic Aptitude Test* was made available to juniors in secondary schools.

The *SAT* is generally administered five times each year at designated centers throughout the country. Students apply to the College Entrance

Examination Board in order to register for the examinations. The *Scholastic Aptitude Test* has two parts, the *Verbal* and *Mathematical* sections. Items are of the best-answer multiple-choice type, requiring three hours of working time.

The candidate who has read widely, so that his vocabulary and skill are well developed, has a definite advantage in the verbal section over a peer with the same native ability but inadequately developed verbal skill. Performance on this test depends on developed skills rather than knowledge of specific information. The quantitative part of the test is also a measure of ability for dealing with concepts rather than mathematical achievement. Although a knowledge of elementary mathematics is necessary, emphasis is on the pupil's application of basic knowledge in the solution of problems. The ceiling of this test is high enough to discriminate among able pupils even though their training in formal mathematics may be limited.

The value of such a carefully constructed and secure test is found in the findings of an extensive research report (Hills, 1964). Twenty-seven thousand nine hundred and sixty-one students in nineteen colleges over a five-year period were involved in the study. Hills reports that the average correlation between high-school performance and first-year college grade-point average was 0.55. When he included the SAT scores the average multiple correlation was raised to 0.65.

American College Testing Program.   Another program for testing college-bound pupils has been developed under the auspices of the Measurement Research Center in Iowa. The American College Testing Program (ACT) offers a basic battery of four tests in the fields of English, mathematics, social studies, and the natural sciences. This battery can predict college success, and like other widely used scholastic aptitude tests it includes items sampling the intellectual skills of solving problems that require mathematical reasoning and interpreting of passages.

School and College Ability Tests.   *SCAT I* was developed to replace the *American Council on Education Psychological Examinations*. It is a scholastic aptitude test with a comparatively heavy emphasis on academic achievement. *SCAT II* replaces *SCAT I*. It is considerably shorter than *SCAT I*, requiring only forty to forty-five minutes compared to seventy minutes. Its stated purpose is to provide estimates of basic verbal and mathematical ability. There are four levels accommodating pupils from grades 4 to 14. Single verbal and mathematical subtests provide for three scores, the third being a total score. Analogy items comprise the verbal test, and computational and reasoning items are the basis of the mathematical test. The academic achievement emphasis may not be quite so great as in that of its predecessor, *SCAT I*.

Although reliability data for *SCAT II* appear to be satisfactory, information on validity is very meager. Undoubtedly these data will be supplemented.

The National Merit Scholarship Examination.   Still another college aptitude program was initiated in 1955. Under the auspices of the National Merit Scholarship Corporation, it has aroused public interest in scholarship aid for talented youth. At the beginning of each school year, all secondary schools in the United States and its territories are invited to select pupils to take the examination, which is administered through a private testing agency.

On the basis of scores from the selecting test, which measures both the aptitude and achievement of the student, semifinalists are named. Semifinalists then are administered the *SAT.* These data, along with school records, recommendations, work and outside activities records, and so forth, form the basis on which scholarships are awarded in each state roughly in proportion to the number of high school graduates in that state. In addition to the National Merit Scholarships, the Corporation also awards scholarships provided by industry, foundations, and individuals.

Preparing for the Tests.   Teachers wonder if they can prepare pupils for these tests by tutoring them. The effect of coaching for College Entrance Examination Board *Scholastic Aptitude Test* has been studied extensively (College Entrance Examination Board, 1968). Scores obtained by groups coached in private and public schools and by groups given intensive individual tutoring were compared with scores obtained by matched control groups with no special training. Results show that special coaching increased test scores only very slightly. On the average, the increase was ten points or fewer. Remember that the scale extends from 200 to 800; the gains in question are much less than the standard error of measurement of the test.

These findings are not strange. Scholastic aptitude tests require both innate ability and achievement. To demonstrate this fact, solve the problems below:

If 5 post cards cost y cents, how many cents will 15 post cards cost? (A) 3y (B) 15y (C) 5y (D) 75y (E) 16y.

The answer is 3y. However, the purpose of the problem is not to determine whether the pupil can multiply 3 by y, which is one computation that might be used in determining the answer, but to determine if he knows how to attack the solution of the problem—finding the cost of one post card and then 15. Nevertheless, it is obvious that if he cannot divide 15 by 5 correctly and then state the product of 3 and y, his answer will be wrong. Therefore, achievement in mathematics is basic to success in this test.

The following analogy is similar to those found in the *Verbal* section of the *SAT* (College Entrance Examination Board, 1965):

Trigger: Bullet::	(A) handle: drawer	(B) holster: gun
	(C) bulb: light	(D) switch: current
	(E) pulley: rope	

The purpose of the item is to determine the examinee's ability to see the relationship among these words rather than to measure his understanding of each. However, the examinee has to know the meanings of trigger, bullet, switch, and current to select response *D* as the correct answer.

Teachers can do nothing to increase the innate intellectual capacity of their pupils, but can do much to improve their effective intelligence. Verbal and mathematical facility are based on good intellectual ability, but poor achievement in language and mathematics precludes the use of this ability. If it were possible to select two pupils of equal capacity, the one who had read more widely, had a broader vocabulary, and had developed more critical skills in reading and thinking than the other would be at an advantage in taking the various scholastic aptitude tests. Pupils pay a penalty for a meager educational environment, since with their deficiencies they may not do so well in further school work, and are rightfully steered to other paths.

Individual vs. Group Tests

The individual intelligence test can be administered to only one person at a time. The only numerical limitation on a group intelligence test is the number of facilities and proctors available. Administering group tests is not difficult in most instances, although certain problems arise when young children are being tested.

The examiner must cope with their short attention span and their difficulties in following instructions. However, he can be trained rather quickly for group test administration. The same is not true for the individual test; special training is necessary if the examiner is to capitalize on the testing situation to learn something of the individual's work habits and personality. One of the most important factors in any test administration is motivating the examinee to optimum performance. It is much easier to obtain good motivation when the examiner's attention can be concentrated on one person. In group testing, disinterest, lapses of attention and effort are more difficult to determine.

Scoring of responses on individual tests tends to be more subjective than on group tests. Although scoring guides are furnished, the examiner must interpret the correctness of the response. For example, in the *Stanford-Binet Vocabulary* the examinee is asked, "What is an orange?". The response "tree" is listed as a correct answer but "lemon" is not. The *Memory for Designs* test at years nine and eleven requires the examinee to reproduce two designs after looking at them for ten seconds. In scoring, he is allowed full credit for the *A* designs but only one-half credit for the *B* designs shown in Figure 24. On the other hand, a group test is generally scored in terms of the number of items

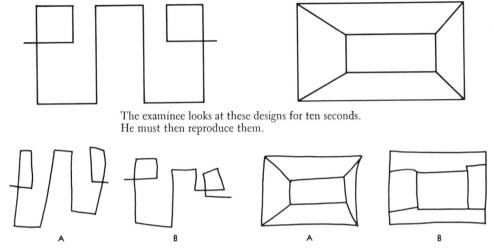

The examinee looks at these designs for ten seconds.
He must then reproduce them.

A   B   A   B

From Terman and Merrill, 1960; reproduced by permission of Houghton Mifflin Company.

FIGURE 24.   Memory for Designs—Stanford-Binet Scale Years IX and XI.

right and, in most instances, no such fine interpretation need be made. Ordinary clerical or machine scoring can be employed.

Each type of test has advantages and disadvantages. The group test is used more in the schools because it does not require highly trained personnel for administration and is more economical in time and cost to administer. An individual intelligence test should be administered when one suspects that group-test results are invalid. Because the group test emphasizes reading ability more than the individual test, considerable caution should be exercised lest a low score be interpreted as lack of native ability rather than as low reading achievement.

Problem

7.   Bill received an IQ of 107 on the *Otis-Lennon* and 107 on the *Stanford-Binet*. What justification can you see for the additional time and expense involved in the use of the individual test?

Verbal vs. Performance and Nonlanguage Tests

Performance tests generally require the subject to manipulate some object, put parts of a figure or picture together, set up a color design, and so forth. Generally they call for individual administration; they are often designed for those individuals with some physical anomaly, and are exemplified by speech or hearing tests for illiterates or those who cannot speak English. Scoring procedures vary. In some instances, only the time to complete the test is recorded. In other tests, the examiner scores the number of moves in addition to keeping a time record, and sometimes tabulates false movements.

Nonlanguage tests are paper-and-pencil tests designed for group administration. No knowledge of written or spoken language is necessary, and although some test instructions are given orally, they are very simple and can be translated into another language without affecting test validity. Pantomime is often used to clarify instructions. Test items may require a subject to complete paper-and-pencil mazes, determine the number of cubes in a pile, complete a series in which X's and O's have different patterns of arrangement, mark identical pairs of numbers, draw in missing parts of pictures, and solve a spatial relations test.

One test requires the examinee to determine which geometric figure cuts another into parts of a certain shape; find missing parts on reversed geometric figures; determine the resulting design of a pattern synthesis, in which two geometric figures are superimposed; determine the next position of a sequence of geometric figures in a movement sequence; determine spatial relations in a manikin test, in which the position of the manikin is changed and the correct figure in terms of hand placement must be determined; and identify, in paper folding, how the paper would look after it had been folded, cut, and opened again (Pintner, 1945).

It should be understood that both the performance and nonlanguage tests measure different aspects of intelligence from those measured by verbal tests. It is doubtful if they tap higher-order abilities, since the verbal tests demand the manipulation of verbal symbols through thinking. Performance and nonlanguage tests rely on spatial and perceptual abilities.

The tests are useful in supplementing data obtained from verbal tests on certain occasions. A child who has failed in school may not be motivated to do items on a verbal test so similar to school work. On the contrary, he may find the tasks in performance and nonverbal tests novel and exciting. Performance tests are also helpful to the clinician in his observation of a child's behavior, but require training beyond that of the average teacher. Despite certain limitations, the verbal test is a better instrument for prediction of academic success.

Problems

8. What place would you allocate to performance and nonlanguage tests in a public school testing program? Defend your answer.
9. In your opinion, what is the main drawback of the performance or nonlanguage test? Could this be overcome?

Culture-Fair Tests

This type of test is sometimes spoken of as a *culture-free* test, which, of course is not an accurate description. Every individual's development bears the imprint of some culture. The concern is that the typical scholastic aptitude test is unfair to those reared in a deprived environment. We often question whether our commonly used tests give a valid indication of a pupil's intelligence when he comes from an unstimulating environment where verbal communication is not valued.

Various kinds of items have been utilized in an attempt to avoid penalizing this kind of pupil. Mazes, symbol copying, classification of pictures, explaining the essence of a picture, and identification of similar drawings have been employed. Because speed is a cultural factor, it has been deemphasized. Tests placing a premium on quick recall have not been used.

Despite an attempt to eliminate cultural bias, studies in general show that lower-class children do not perform any better on this type of test than on other tests of mental ability.

Stroud (1957, p. 85) writes that:

> . . . We may find that the problem is really too big for the test author. It may turn out that the kinds of cultural impact associated with social class differences affect the course of *mental development* of children as well as their performance on intelligence tests.
>
> Social class differences are real differences, substantial psychological phenomena with which schools and society must deal. It may be that we cannot build valid intelligence tests which will not at the same time discriminate among the social classes. Or, if we start the other way round by designing tests which will not discriminate among social classes, we may find that the tests are poor predictors of academic achievement.

But there is another aspect to the use of scores from our typically culturally biased standardized tests. A number of children coming from "disadvantaged" environments and having values and classroom behavior at variance with that of their teachers, do well on the tests, in contrast to their daily academic performance. Without objective test results some of these nonconforming children would be categorized adversely by the typically middle class professional staff.

There is other evidence supporting the use of our commonly used standardized tests. If the criterion of validity of our scholastic aptitude tests is the prediction of academic success, then we can have some satisfaction in the findings of studies investigating the problem. Cleary (1966) studied the relationship of scholastic aptitude test scores and achievement in three integrated colleges. In two of these institutions there was no significant difference in over- or underprediction of academic success by the SAT. However, in the third college the SAT overpredicted grades of the black students.

However, Fishman and others (1964) urge us to look for the different meanings in the scores of minority children. They ask that we not use their scores as evidence of fixed potential but that we plan activities that will help to free the child from his handicaps. They state (1964, p. 143):

> We should depart from too narrow a conception of the purpose and function of testing. We should re-emphasize the concept of the test as an integral component of teaching and training whereby a floor of communication and understanding is established and *learning* capabilities are measured in repeated and cyclical fashion.

Because of government programs, such as Head Start, designed to improve the aptitude for learning of culturally disadvantaged children, there has been considerable discussion about the possibility of increasing mental ability and scholastic achievement. Jensen (1969a, 1969b) argues forcibly that compensatory education efforts have failed to make permanent gains on children's IQ and achievement. He questions the rationale on which these programs have been based—that variance of the environment and the cultural bias of scholastic aptitude tests are the main causes of IQ differences. Finally, he concludes that genetic factors are of greater importance in producing these differences than environmental influence is.

Six psychologists and a geneticist answered Jensen's arguments in the *Harvard Educational Review*. Kagan (1969) does not believe standardized tests reflect the potential of the disadvantaged. Hunt (1969) does not believe Jensen's conclusions about heritability are substantiated. Although Crow (1969), the geneticist, has some reservations and suggests qualifications, he agrees for the most part with Jensen's analysis. Bereiter (1969) agrees with Jensen's emphasis on the heritability of intelligence, but is even more pessimistic about the possible effects of the environment. He believes that, as varying environments are cancelled out, the effect of heritability will increase. Elkind (1969, p. 335) concludes that Piagetian psychology "provides no support either for those who advocate formal preschool instruction or for those who argue for new methods and materials to stimulate intrinsic motivation." Cronbach (1969) believes that Jensen oversimplifies individual differences in discussing heritability, although he agrees that performance is developed from a genotypic, inherited base.

How much then can we boost mental ability and scholastic achievement? Hunt (1969, p. 297) concludes: "As I read the evidence, the odds are strong that we can boost both IQ and scholastic achievement substantially, but we cannot know how much for at least two decades." Longitudinal studies (see *Untangling the Tangled Web of Education* in the Suggested Readings) will be necessary to answer the question.

Educational Loading

Cronbach (1970, p. 282) has constructed a chart for comparing various tests of scholastic aptitude (see Figure 25) by establishing a continuum ranging from those sampling schoolwork content directly to those utilizing analytic tasks. Those tests at the bottom of the chart sample trained abilities; they make few demands for adaptation or transfer. The analytic tasks at the other

From *Essentials of Psychological Testing*, 3rd ed., by Lee J. Cronbach (Harper & Row, Publishers, Inc., 1970). Reprinted by permission of the publishers.

FIGURE 25.   Spectrum for Comparing Tests of Scholastic Aptitude or General Aptitude.

(Note: Tests with which you are unfamiliar are discussed in Buros' *Mental Measurements Yearbooks*. Symbols in figure above represent the following tests: LT, *Lorge-Thorndike*; SAT, *Scholastic Aptitude Test*; ACT, *American College Testing Program*.)

end of the chart, however, require little use of specific knowledge and much transfer. Cronbach suggests that the scale be considered in terms of transfer of learning. Recall is required of the pupil when he must respond to a stimulus identical with one to which he has responded before. However, if the stimulus is modified or presented in varied contexts, the pupil must transfer his knowledge. The amount of transfer depends on the degree of similarity between the new stimulus and the old one. When the new stimulus is unfamiliar, then the pupil must transfer what he has learned. The skills and aptitude required to complete the tasks at the upper part of the scale have not been developed by direct training. Nevertheless, previously learned habits and mental structures are applied in their solution.

The *A* tasks in the spectrum seldom demand advanced knowledge; analysis and reasoning are required. Verbal concepts may aid the examinee but he doesn't need to understand the examiner's language. At the *B* level tasks, the subject is required to use familiar words in novel combinations. In the *C* or *D* categories the difficult items would just use rare words. Cronbach emphasizes that the spectrum is oversimplified. He discusses a more complex scheme on pp. 331 ff. of his book.

Mental Age

When buying clothing for school-age children, we do not ask for something to fit a ten-year-old; we ask for a definite size because children of the same age vary. Intelligence testing is the same; pupils of the same age do not have the same amount of intelligence. The outstanding feature of the *Stanford-Binet Scale* is that the tests are grouped according to the age at which a majority passed. For example, if a child passes the items at the ten-year level and fails those at the eleven-year level, he has a mental age of ten. If his chronological age is less than ten, he is bright; if his chronological age is greater than ten, he is duller than average. In actual testing practice, a child may receive a mental age of ten and yet miss some items in the scale below the ten-year level and pass some above this level.

Mental age may be determined in other tests from the raw score, such as the total number of items correct. The mean raw score earned by a particular age group in the standardization sample would represent the mental age for the group. If the group were seven-year-olds, the mental age would be seven. A child who makes a raw score equal to the average of seven-year-olds would, therefore, have a mental age of seven. It should be emphasized that the mental age in itself tells us nothing about the brightness of the child. It refers only to the level of mental development.

Other characteristics inherent in the concept of mental age make interpretation difficult. Unlike the measurement of height or weight, no absolute zero point exists, and it would be difficult to define the point of no intelligence in a human being. Moreover, mental age units are unequal. As the individual grows older, the mental age units represent decreasing development. Since the increase in mental age units compared to the increase in the CA is quite small, the concept of MA becomes meaningless for pupils in their late teens. Actually, the growth pattern is not unlike that for height. Between two and four years of age, there is a much greater increase than between the years of sixteen and eighteen. It is for this reason that percentile ranks and standard scores, rather than IQs, are used for older pupils.

Another problem is in the interpretation of identical mental ages of two pupils who have different chronological ages. If mental age is assumed to represent a pupil's level of mental capacity, than an MA of eight represents the same degree of intellectual maturity no matter if one child has a CA of six and another a CA of ten. However, these two pupils are quite different intellectually. Further difficulties in the interpretation of the MA must be dealt with when extrapolating to determine an IQ value for the superior pupil. How does one interpret a mental age of twenty-two obtained from the norm table when the mean adult mental age on the test is fifteen years?

We should not conclude from this discussion or from recent trends indicating use of the DIQ that the MA has no value. When the teacher recognizes the limitations, the concept of mental age can be of help in suiting a learning task to the pupil's ability. We know that the understanding of concepts of number, time, and distance requires a certain degree of mental maturity. Much research about teaching children to read has established that general intelligence is the most important factor in reading readiness; mental age is closely related to the pupil's success or failure. Harris (1970, p. 26) summarizes the evidence as follows:

1. There is a substantial relationship between mental age and ease of learning to read; most children who fail in reading in the first grade have mental ages below six years. The more mature children not only learn more easily but also retain what they learn better than the less mature children.

2. Most children who have IQs within or above the normal value and are free from special handicaps can be successfully taught to read in the first grade. However, a delayed start does these children no harm.

3. It is not possible to set a definite minimum mental age for learning to read because too many other factors are involved. Children with mental ages as low as five years can be taught to read first-grade materials. There seems to be no lasting advantage in such an early start, however, and many of these children fail to make any headway when the pace of instruction is geared to the progress of older or brighter children.

4. A program of systematic readiness training preceding the beginning of reading instruction enables some children to make faster and easier progress in reading when they do start, but is not needed by all children; many are ready before the first day of school. A delayed start without specific efforts to improve readiness has little to recommend it. Readiness training of a specific kind can also be continued after reading instruction has been started.

Intelligence Quotient

Information concerning a child's rate of mental development is also useful to the teacher. He needs to know whether the child is maturing more or less rapidly than the average child. If his mental age is greater than his chronological age, he is brighter and will eventually be more mentally mature than his duller peers. Other things being equal, he will be a more rapid learner.

Levels of intelligence have been classified in relation to IQ intervals, as listed in Table 19. These descriptive levels are helpful in communicating about individuals with different degrees of intelligence and in roughly predicting job success. It is well to remember that these classifications are useful guides, not rigid divisions.

Constancy of the IQ. How stable is the IQ of an individual? Does it effectively predict an individual's ability over a long period of time? This question is of great importance in educational and vocational planning. You will recall that intelligence is implied from an intelligence test score. Test intelligence demands achievement as a means for sampling innate ability; inherited capacity cannot be measured directly. Heredity and environment are also relatively important, and if heredity is more significant, and if we could meas-

TABLE 19. Distribution of Intelligence Quotients from the 1937 Revision of the Stanford-Binet Scale.

IQ	Percentage	Classification
160–169	0.03	Very superior
150–159	0.2	
140–149	1.1	
130–139	3.1	Superior
120–129	8.2	
110–119	18.1	High average
100–109	23.5	Normal or average
90–99	23.0	
80–89	14.5	Low average
70–79	5.6	Borderline defective
60–69	2.0	
50–59	0.4	
40–49	0.2	Mentally defective
30–39	0.03	

ure it accurately, it might yield a more stable score. If environment were more important, its influence could vary from time to time and change measurement. We have reason to believe that both heredity and environment influence effective intelligence. Someone has said that "heredity sets the limit, while environment determines how closely an individual approaches this limit." In other words, probably no individual fully develops his innate capacity; nevertheless, heredity is generally considered the more important of the two variables.

Unreliability of measuring instruments may result in the conclusion that the IQ is less stable than is really warranted. Even a test-retest on different forms of the *Stanford-Binet* administered very close together causes a considerable variance in scores for the same individual (Terman and Merrill, 1960). Another limitation of some tests is their lack of an adequately high top score for the brighter pupils in a recommended grade range (Stanley, 1951). The average college freshman has a mental age of around sixteen and one-half years; average college graduates test around eighteen. Graduate students have an average mental age of eighteen and one-half, and those who earn Ph.D.s in the natural sciences have a mental age of nineteen and one-half, which corresponds to a childhood intelligence quotient of about 130 (Wolfle and Oxtoby, 1952). Suppose John receives an IQ of 160 on the *Stanford-Binet* at nine years of age, which is equivalent to a mental age of about fourteen years and five months; if his IQ does not change, at age fifteen he will have a mental age of about twenty-four. When he is in the tenth grade, tests designed for this grade level are not difficult enough to measure his ceiling, and college tests have no norms for bright youngsters of his age. These tests would have more validity, however, than tests at his grade level (Stanley, 1954, p. 33).

Most upper-half tenth-graders in typical schools can be measured adequately by tests designed for Grades IX–XII. A crude but perhaps helpful way to determine the adequacy of a score is to note the number of points it falls short of the maximum possible score; this might well be at least three times the standard error of measurement of the test. If the difference is less than this amount, try administering a higher level of the test or a more advanced test to the student. Testing, like all other phases of teaching, must be individualized. Few instruments are adequate throughout the entire range of abilities found in typical classrooms. At least three different levels are usually needed for optimum assessment of differences among individuals in a single grade. For this reason, the actual range of talent within a class will often be greater than it appears on the basis of only one test. The least able students are crowding the "floor," while the ablest ones are bumping their heads on the "ceiling."

The results yielded by tests administered periodically over a number of years have shown that mental growth is uneven (Bayley, 1949; 1955; Freeman and Flory, 1937). Note the fluctuations in the individual mental growth curves of the five boys in Figure 26. Freeman and Flory (1937) point out that growth curves do not indicate which of several explanations cause these fluctuations. Possible causes could be transitory psychological or physical conditions, such as rapport between the examiner and the subject, or illness. On the other hand, the irregularities might reflect real changes in intellectual maturity.

Bayley's studies (1933; 1949) are in agreement with other longitudinal studies that provide correlational results with regard to a pupil's relative standing in a group. A pupil tends to change in his relative position in the group in relation to the amount of time between tests. Less shifting of relative position occurs with increasing age. Reporting the age of the pupil at the time of testing along with the name of the test is therefore important in considering the constancy of the IQ.

Pinneau (1961) emphasizes other considerations. Because standard deviations of conventional IQs for a given test vary from age to age, he draws certain conclusions. First of all, the same relative standing in a group may result from very different scores at different ages. He explains how, on the 1937 edition of the *Stanford-Binet*, a pupil's IQ might be 125 at age 6 and 140 at age 12. For the same reason another pupil may have an IQ of 75 at 6

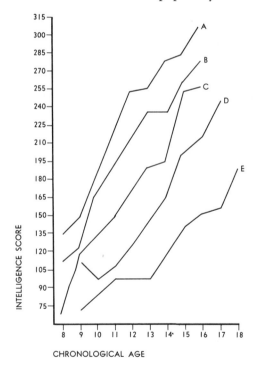

From Freeman and Flory, 1937, p. 56; reproduced by permission of the authors and the Society for Research in Child Development.

FIGURE 26. Mental Growth of Five Boys.

years and 60 at 12 years. Both pupils maintained the same relative position in their age groups, and change in their IQs was a result of changes in the size of the variability. Another conclusion is that the same change in IQ for two different pupils may indicate a different relative standing. Two six-year-olds may drop 15 points in IQ by the age of 12—one from 75 to 60 and the other from 125 to 110. The former does not change in relative position; the second drops from the 87th to the 69th percentile of his age group. Finally, the IQs of pupils who are tested at an age when the conventional IQ variabilities are large as compared with those of pupils tested at an age when these variabilities are small designate a different amount of change in relative position. Suppose two pupils have conventional IQs of 90 and they show a 20-point increase on a second test. If the first pupil was tested at the ages of 2 and 12, and the second at ages 5 and 17, the first child changes from the 31st to the 69th percentile, and the second from the 24th to the 76th percentile on the second test.

When an individual is tested with different instruments, the measured IQs are likely to differ. Hence, the report of an IQ should always include identity of the test from which it was derived, e.g., IQ (Otis-Lennon, Form J, Intermediate Level) = 93. For a given pupil, test scores from different scholastic aptitude tests may differ greatly.

Conclusions. We may conclude that the IQ of an individual is quite stable throughout his life if we consider it to be a rough classification. Certainly, the child with a high IQ will tend to remain an individual with considerable intellectual prowess. A pupil who has an IQ well below 100 will probably become an adult who functions on a lower intellectual level, unless the score is the result of poor academic efficiency. We are assuming also that the IQ is not based on an infant test since such tests are quite unreliable. Because of the numerous factors that may influence test scores, a teacher should never rely on the results of a single test. In addition to other test scores, data obtained through observation, for example, should be used to evaluate mental maturity.

Problems

10. An elementary school is grouping pupils in the intermediate grade levels according to MA as measured by a good standardized test. Is this defensible? Explain.

11. There is much current controversy concerning making school records available to parents, including the reporting of actual IQ scores. Should this be done? Can you justify your answer?

CREATIVITY

If tests operationally define creativity, it would have varied meanings. Thorndike (1963, p. 423) states:

> The data suggest that there remains some modest common core running through different tests and making for correlation among them, but this common core appears to play only a minor role so far as success on any given test is concerned.

In one of the most popular "creativity" tests there is a question as to whether it is measuring anything different from the typical scholastic aptitude instruments (see Wallach, 1968, in the Suggested Readings).

Among the most active workers in creativity research have been Guilford, MacKinnon, and Torrance. Guilford's work leading to the structure-of-intellect model (see page 395) produced a section on *divergent-production*, which is regarded as one aspect of creative thinking. Divergent thinking is required in responding to a question like "How many uses can you think of for a brick?" To answer the question "2 + 2 = ?" demands convergent thinking; a "correct" response is required. MacKinnon (1966) found significant differences in personality traits between creative and noncreative groups. Torrance's research (1959, 1962) within classrooms to discover experiences that foster creativity resulted in tests based on factors identified in Guilford's research.

In their intensive review of the literature, Gaier and White (1965) list four directions that creativity research has taken: (a) the nature and quality of the product created, (b) the actual expression of creative acts and the continuing intellectual process during the creation, (c) the nature of the creator, and (d) environmental factors that fostered creativity. The authors pointed out that unfortunately little empirical research is grounded in theory. Taylor (1964) concludes that biographical items and measures of past achievement appear to be better predictors of creativity than self-ratings, inventories, and traditional aptitude and general intelligence measures.

At this point, we should not overrate creativity tests at the expense of general intelligence tests. In their present state of development creativity tests would best be used for research purposes.

Problem

12. Some psychologists have suggested that it would be better for teachers to concentrate their attention on helping youngsters to be original rather than on measuring their creativity. Do you agree? Why?

MECHANICAL APTITUDE

Mechanical aptitude is actually made up of a number of quite specific aptitudes. Among those identified through research studies are perceptual, spatial, and mechanical reasoning ability. Manual dexterity should also be included. Moreover, mechanical aptitude is affected by knowledge of mechanical information and experience with mechanics.

Single tests used to measure mechanical aptitude do not sample all these factors. Also, jobs requiring mechanical skill differ in their demands for these specific aptitudes. Although certain tasks require a great deal of manual dexterity, others demand perceptual and spatial abilities. This fact explains in some degree why, in general, the current tests of mechanical aptitude cannot claim high predictive validity. The factors included in the tests as well as on the job must both be known. It is important that other means of evaluation, such as observation of performance in shops and a careful study of the record of experience, be used in counseling pupils on mechanical aptitude.

Minnesota Paper Form Board Test

Available tests for measuring mechanical aptitude may be classified either as paper-and-pencil or performance tests. They may also be categorized as measures of perceptual and spatial abilities, as assembly tests, or as tests of mechanical information. Various means are used to measure perceptual and spatial abilities, including construction puzzles, form boards, and paper-and-pencil tests. One of the most popular paper-and-pencil tests is the revision of the *Minnesota Paper Form Board Test*. It consists of items having two-dimensional diagrams cut into separate parts (see Figure 27). The subject chooses one figure out of five that he believes to be made up of the exact parts shown in the original diagram. Numerous validity studies have proved its usefulness in selecting personnel for various mechanical jobs. It possesses some validity for predicting academic success in art, dentistry, drafting, and geometry. It is particularly helpful in measuring an individual's ability to visualize and manipulate objects in space. Reliability coefficients vary between 0.80 and 0.92.

Minnesota Mechanical Assembly Test

In assembly tests the subject works with parts in putting a mechanical object together. One of the better known assembly tests is the *Minnesota Mechanical*

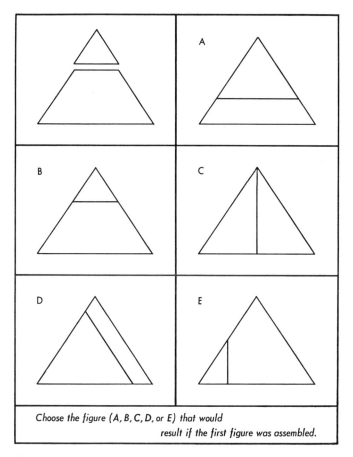

Choose the figure (A, B, C, D, or E) that would
result if the first figure was assembled.

Reproduced by permission of The Psychological Corporation.

FIGURE 27.   Sample Item from the Revised Minnesota Paper Form
Board.

Assembly Test, a revision of the *Stenquist Assembly Test.* The test consists of
a series of mechanical contrivances, such as a monkey wrench, hose clamp,
bicycle bell, spring clothespin, spark plug, flat iron, that can be easily assembled. Most individuals could be successful with the tests if they had enough
time. Therefore, time limits are rigidly controlled. Speed is a basic factor for
successful completion of the tests.

The instrument is designed for subjects eleven or older. It has not, however, proved particularly valid for women and girls, and mechanically apt men
find it too easy. Also, the test is less reliable for men than for junior high
school boys. The short form is considerably less reliable than the original test.

Bennett Mechanical Comprehension Test

The *Bennett Mechanical Comprehension Test* is a paper-and-pencil test that can be used with older adolescents and adults. The 1969 revision has norms for industrial applicants, employees in skilled trades, and eleventh and twelfth graders in academic and technical high schools. It measures an individual's understanding of mechanical and physical relationships. Items consist of pictures illustrating principles of mechanics, fluid pressures, and so forth. Questions related to the pictures have two or three alternatives. Various criterion-validity coefficients are reported involving both concurrent and predictive analyses. They vary over a considerable range. The authors point out that the reliability and authenticity of the criteria influence these fluctuations. Also the coefficients were determined with relatively small groups, which are subject to sampling error. They suggest that local validity studies are desirable with large enough populations and meaningful criteria. Incidentally, one of the tests in the *Differential Aptitude Test* battery, the *Mechanical Reasoning Test* (see page 397), is similar to the *Bennett*.

Problem

13.   For each of the three tests of mechanical aptitude discussed, describe a situation in a public school in which it might prove to be a useful tool.

PROGNOSTIC TESTS

Prognostic tests are designed to predict a pupil's success in a specific subject. At the elementary level, reading readiness tests may be classified in this category. In the secondary school, tests of prognosis for algebra, geometry, foreign languages, and shorthand have been developed. Although these tests are supposedly designed to contain material from the field in question, this has not always proved true. In general, prognostic tests for secondary school pupils have declined in use. Differential test batteries have proved more helpful to the counselor since it is impractical to administer prognostic tests to all pupils for every subject. Only when large groups of pupils are being tested to predict skill in a particular area for which other test results may be unavailable, are they of great importance. This is particularly true in an area such as shorthand.

Probably the prognostic tests most widely used in our schools are those classified as reading readiness tests. Although these tests are very similar to scholastic aptitude tests, their content demands abilities that are specifically related to elementary reading skills. For example, a lesson situation may be presented in which the pupil's ability to learn words is demonstrated. Other items may test his ability to give the names of letters. He may also be instructed to match sounds. Whether a scholastic aptitude test or a reading readiness test best predicts reading achievement is debatable. Some evidence shows that general intelligence tests may better predict ultimate reading achievement, because reading at higher levels requires considerable verbal ability as measured by many general intelligence tests. On the other hand, the reading readiness tests may better predict early reading success because of their higher content validity. Another factor to consider in a reading readiness test is its diagnostic value; teachers would do well to select tests with this attribute in mind in addition to the total test score.

Problem

14. In an elementary school faculty meeting, a lively dispute arose over the relative need and importance of various standardized tests. Miss Brown argued strongly for the use of reading readiness tests. Miss Johnson said that the present group mental ability tests could serve the same purpose and warned against the danger of overtesting. Which teacher would you support? Why?

DIFFERENTIAL TESTING

In his discussion of techniques for multiple measurements, Cooley (1970) suggests that the basis of multiple measurement is rooted in trait and factor psychology. He defines a trait as an enduring pattern of behaviors that is exhibited by everyone in varying degrees. Educators, he asserts, must use the multiple trait approach in studying individual differences. They are attempting to change behavior along several dimensions, for example, verbal as well as quantitative skills. Furthermore, the affective domain as well as the cognitive must be considered in predicting a pupil's performance. Motivation, to mention one such trait, is obviously a factor in achievement.

He continues his argument for multiple measurement by describing talent within the school. For example, if two traits are normally distributed in a group and correlate 0.50, about one-third of those in the top 10 percent on one trait will score similarly on the other. Even if the two traits correlate as high as 0.80, only about one-half of the students scoring in the top 10 percent on one trait will do so on the other.

One of the most interesting theoretical models classifying the factors of the intellect was proposed by Guilford (1959; 1965). His model shown in

Figure 28 provides for 120 cells, each corresponding to a potential factor. His threefold model includes the process of operation performed (cognition, memory, convergent thinking, divergent thinking, and evaluating), products (units, classes, relations, system, transformations, and implications), and contents (figural, symbolic, semantic, and behavioral). Although each cell has as yet not been identified, the model proves most helpful in aiding the formulation of hypotheses for further research designed to explore the nature of the intellect.

Theoretically, it may some day be possible to predict any behavior from Guilford's model whether it be performance in algebra or architecture. However, at the present time, validity of available aptitude tests enables us to predict criterion behavior only within certain limits. In some of the widely used instruments, the verbal and quantitative scores are still the best predictors of academic success.

However, useful insights into a pupil's strengths and weaknesses may be

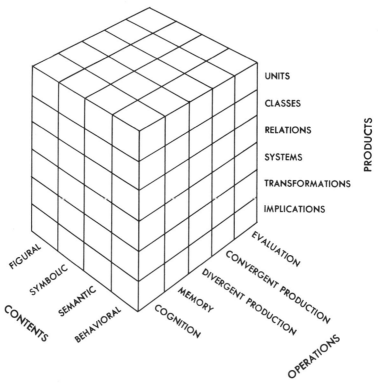

From Guilford, 1959; reproduced by permission of The American Psychologist.

FIGURE 28.   Theoretical Model for the Complete "Structure of Intellect."

found through a battery of tests standardized on the same population. A profile of aptitude scores can be determined and comparisons made among an individual's cognitive, perceptual, and sensorimotor aptitudes. Recently, batteries of tests standardized on the same population have made a comparison of scores more meaningful. Representative of this kind of test battery are the *Academic Promise Tests* (*APT*) designed for grades 6–9, the *Differential Aptitude Test* (*DAT*) for use in the secondary school, and the *General Aptitude Test Battery* (*GATB*) for ages sixteen and over. We shall discuss in some detail the *DAT* and the *GATB* to illustrate differential testing instruments.

Differential Aptitude Test Battery

The *Differential Aptitude Tests* is a battery of eight tests: *Verbal Reasoning, Numerical Ability, Abstract Reasoning, Space Relations, Mechanical Reasoning, Clerical Speed and Accuracy, Language Usage*. The last test has two scores, *Spelling* and *Grammar*. Norms are also available for the combined *Verbal Reasoning* and *Numerical Ability* scores. The tests are essentially power tests, except the one on *Clerical Speed and Accuracy*, which is actually a speed test. Figure 29 contains two sample test items illustrating the approach. The first represents the *Abstract Reasoning Test*; the second represents the *Space Relations Test*.

By means of statistical procedures, content overlapping is minimized in the various tests, and the level of difficulty is related to the particular age group. These tests are published in groups in the case of *Form L* and *Form M*. Two booklets are available, each containing four tests. A separate booklet containing only the *Verbal Reasoning* and the *Numerical Ability* tests is also used. Since IBM answer sheets are available, the test booklets can be reused.

Profile Chart.   The authors suggest the use of the profile chart in Figure 30, but they caution against interpreting the bars extending downward as negative and those upward as positive (Bennett and others, 1966, p. III–5):

> If only the top twenty percent on a given test are likely to succeed in a given course or job, it is not a "positive" sign to have a bar extending up to the sixty-fifth percentile. Conversely, if all but the lowest ten per cent may be expected to succeed, a bar extending down to the twentieth percentile mark is not "negative."

Through statistical formulas the authors arrived at a convenient method for approximating the significance of the differences between test scores by the use of a ruler on the Individual Report Form shown. The vertical distance between any two scores, as plotted on the form, can be measured. A real

Abstract reasoning

Study the position of the black dot. Note that it keeps moving around the square clockwise: upper left corner, upper right corner, lower right corner, lower left corner. In what position will it be seen next? It will come back to the upper left corner. Therefore, B is the answer, . . .

Space relations

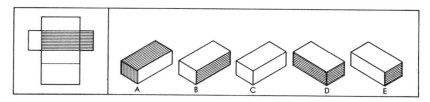

Notice—all the "boxes" made from this pattern are correct in shape, but the sides which you see are different. Some of these figures can be made from this pattern while others cannot. Let us look at them.

—Figure A is correct. If the large gray surface is shown as the top, then the end surface of gray can be shown facing towards you.

—Figure B is wrong. The long narrow side is not gray in the pattern.

—Figure C is correct. The two gray surfaces can both be hidden by placing the large gray surface at the bottom and the gray end to the back.

—Figure D is wrong. The gray end is all right, but there is no long gray side in the pattern.

—Figure E is correct. One can show the box so that the large gray surface is at the bottom (as it was in C), but with the gray end showing at the front. So, you see, there are three figures (A, C, and E) which can be made from the pattern, in example Y and two figures (B and D) which cannot be made from this pattern. Remember that the surface you see in the pattern must always be the OUTSIDE surface of the completed figure.

FIGURE 29.   Sample Items from the Differential Aptitude Tests.

DIFFERENTIAL APTITUDE TESTS [1963 EDITION]

G. K. Bennett, H. G. Seashore, and A. G. Wesman

Profiling Your DAT Scores

The numbers that tell how you did on each test are in the row marked "Percentiles." Your percentile tells where you rank on a test in comparison with boys or girls in your grade. These percentiles are based on test scores earned by thousands of students in numerous schools across the country. If your percentile rank is 50, you are just in the middle — that is, one-half of the students in the national group did better than you and one-half did less well. (If your school uses local norms, your counselor will explain the difference.)

In the columns below each percentile you can draw your aptitude profile. For each test make a *heavy short line* across the column at the level which corresponds to your percentile rank on that test.

Your aptitude profile will be more visible if you black in each column *up to* or *down to* the 50-line from the short lines

How Big a Difference Is Important?

Of course we do not want to over-estimate small differences in ability on tests because a test cannot be perfectly accurate, and your score might not be exactly the same if you could take the same test twice.

To estimate the importance of a difference between your scores on any two tests on this profile, use a ruler to measure how much higher on the chart one mark is than the other. It is the *vertical* distance ⤒ that counts, of course, *not* how far *across* the chart ⤢ or ⤡.

you have just made. The vertical bars on your profile show the strength of your tested aptitudes, *up* or *down* from the rank of the *middle student* of your grade and sex.

Think of "percentile" as meaning "per cent of people." In your case, the people are boys or girls in your grade in many schools across the country. The percentile shows what per cent of this group scored no higher than you did. If your percentile rank on one test is 80, you are at the top of 80 per cent of the group — only 20 per cent made higher scores than yours. If you scored in the 25th percentile, this would mean about 75 per cent of the group did better than you on the test. Thus, a percentile rank always indicates your relative standing among a theoretical 100 persons representing a large "norm" group — in this case, students of your sex and grade. It does not tell how many questions (or what per cent of them) you answered correctly.

If the distance is *one inch or greater*, it is probable that you have a real difference in your abilities on the two tests.

If a difference between the two percentile ranks is *between a half inch and one inch*, consider whether other things you know about yourself agree with it; the difference may or may not be important.

If the vertical distance between two tests is *less than a half inch*, the difference between the two scores may be disregarded; so small a difference is probably not meaningful.

FIGURE 30.   Sample Profile from the Differential Aptitude Tests.

difference may be assumed to exist if the distance is one inch or greater. Differences between one-half inch and one inch should be evaluated along with other evidence, as the significance of the difference may be doubtful. Probably no important difference exists if the vertical distance between any two scores is less than one-half inch. (The measurements mentioned do not apply to the reduced chart in Figure 30.)

In Figure 30, the difference on the actual profile sheet in the length of bars representing *Verbal Reasoning* and *Clerical* measures over one inch, and we may assume that this is significant. Likewise, the difference between the *Clerical* score and each of the other scores except *Grammar* is also significant. On the other hand, the measured difference between the *Space Relations* and *Mechanical Reasoning* bars is only about one-fourth of an inch and therefore probably insignificant. The measured difference between the *Verbal Reasoning* and *Abstract Reasoning* bars is between one-half and one inch, the value of which is in question.

It is important that the individual tests in a battery have high reliability; it is also essential, however, that tests do not correlate highly with each other if important differences among the abilities of an individual are to be determined. The following tests gave the highest intercorrelations: *Verbal Reasoning, Numerical Ability,* and *Grammar; Mechanical Reasoning, Abstract Reasoning,* and *Space Relations; Spelling* and *Grammar. Clerical Speed* and *Accuracy* gave the lowest correlations. The average intercorrelation coefficients range from 0.06 to 0.67 with the average being about 0.50 except for *Clerical Speed and Accuracy.*

Through a formula utilizing both test reliability and intercorrelations among tests, the differentiating power of the tests was determined. It is believed that tests having a differentiating power of less than 25 percent should not be used in differential diagnosis. When the formula was applied to all possible pairs among the eight tests for *Form L,* the 25 percent value was exceeded for all twenty-eight differences among the girls and for twenty-seven differences among the boys. The results for *Form M* were the same for boys and slightly less satisfactory for the girls, due primarily to the lower reliability of the *Mechanical Reasoning Test* when administered to girls.

Reliability. Reliability coefficients are available for each test, each grade, and for both sexes. These data, based on homogeneous and meaningful groups, are of basic importance for interpreting the test scores. The reliability coefficients for *Forms L* and *M,* varying from 0.79 to 0.94, were determined by the split-halves techniques except for the *Clerical Speed and Accuracy Test.* Average reliability coefficients varied from 0.87 to 0.94 for boys, and from 0.79 to 0.93 for girls. Both low coefficients, 0.87 and 0.79, are for the *Mechanical Reasoning Test.* So even though the intercorrelations among the tests are substantial, the adequate reliabilities make differential measurement possible.

Measurements made with the *DAT* are found to be consistent over an appreciable span of time. The authors point out that this consistency results only in part from test reliability. If the trait measured is not constant, then of course it is impossible to obtain consistency in test scores. In one instance, pupils were tested in the ninth grade and again in the twelfth. The test-retest coefficients for a large group of pupils varied from 0.59 to 0.86. *Verbal Reasoning* and *Spelling* were two tests that reflected unusually great constancy of performance. Over this period of time, these data indicate good stability for these tests.

Validity. Numerous validity studies resulting in over 4000 correlation coefficients have been reported on the *Differential Aptitude Tests* (Bennett and others, 1966). Investigations have included research in the prediction of course grades in secondary school and college, prediction of achievement test results, and prediction of vocational and educational success. An interesting graphic presentation in terms of the number of studies producing validity coefficients with a certain range is reported for final marks in English, mathematics, science, social studies, and history. Although a considerable range in these coefficients is reported for both boys and girls, certain patterns do stand out. The highest relationship with English final marks exists with the tests of *Verbal Reasoning* plus *Numerical Ability*, *Verbal Reasoning* alone, and *Grammar*. The test correlating most highly with mathematics is *Numerical Ability*. *Verbal Reasoning* plus *Numerical Ability*, *Verbal Reasoning* alone, *Numerical Ability* alone, and *Grammar* are all highly related to science achievement. Finally, scores from these same tests also seem to be highly related to achievement in the social studies. It is obvious that scores on *Verbal Reasoning* and *Numerical Reasoning* are the best predictors for all academic areas. These abilities are involved in most of the common scholastic aptitude tests.

A follow-up study reported in the manual produced interesting data showing relationships between scores attained by high school pupils on the *DAT* and the vocational or educational choice made as college students. Among the groups studied, premedical students were especially high in *Verbal Reasoning*, *Numerical Ability*, and *Spelling*. The science group was outstanding in *Numerical Ability*. Engineering students were superior in *Numerical Ability* and much higher in *Space Relations* and *Mechanical Reasoning* than other student groups. The various unskilled groups had overall low performance but average performance in *Mechanical Reasoning*. The skilled groups were below average in *Numerical Ability*, *Space Relations*, and *Abstract Reasoning*, but about average on the other tests.

In another follow-up study seven years later, the conclusions of the earlier report were reinforced. Profiles of high school pupils entering diverse occupational and educational careers varied widely from one another. For example, the engineers showed marked superiority in *Numerical Ability, Mechanical Reasoning,* and *Spelling;* on the other hand, the average of boys who entered the building trades was near the class average in *Abstract Reasoning, Space Relations,* and *Clerical Speed and Accuracy.*

The *Differential Aptitude Tests* represent a model of attention to detail of test construction and interpretation. The care that has been exercised in their development is so well presented in the four editions of the test manual that by studying these discussions, the reader can develop an understanding of the important considerations of test construction in general. However, despite this commendation, one must be aware that many of the reported validation coefficients are low and differential prediction of performance must be made carefully.

General Aptitude Test Battery

This multiple aptitude battery was developed by the U.S. Employment Service in the 1940s. It measures traits of value in predicting success in some 198 specific occupations or clusters of very similar occupations. The orientation is toward the world of work rather than toward formal education. The battery results from a statistical analysis (known as factor analysis) of numerous tests that had been used for civilian and armed forces jobs. In its present form, twelve tests are used to measure nine factors.

Factors of the *GATB* are as follows:

G factor (General Mental Ability): Determined from three scores, namely, *Vocabulary, Arithmetic Reasoning,* and *Three-Dimensional Space.*

V factor (Verbal Aptitude): Determined by a vocabulary test that requires a response differentiating between pairs of words that have the same or opposite meanings.

N factor (Numerical Aptitude): Determined by two tests, namely, *Computational* and *Arithmetic Reasoning.*

S factor (Spatial Aptitude): Determined by three-dimensional space test.

P factor (Form Perception): Determined by two tests, one in which the examinee must match tools. In the other he matches geometrical forms.

Q factor (Clerical Perception): Determined by matching names.

K factor (Motor Coordination): Determined by the placing of marks within a series of squares.

F factor (Finger Dexterity): Determined by two tests, *Assembly* and *Disassembly,* in which the examinee assembles and disassembles rivets and washers.

M factor (Manual Dexterity): Determined by two tests in which the examinee puts pegs into a board and then reverses them.

The *GATB* differs from the *DAT* in that it has no mechanical comprehension and language subparts. On the other hand, it has motor and form perception tests, which are missing in the *DAT*. Another important difference and limitation is that the *GATB* tests are highly speeded while those of the *DAT* are basically power tests.

The authors report reliability data on aptitude scores rather than on the individual tests from which these scores are determined. The coefficients are determined from test-retest procedures for periods of a week to a year; they range between 0.80 and 0.90. In addition, the amount of validity data is considerable. Most coefficients are based on concurrent validity designs, however. The range is 0.24 to 0.96 with a median near 0.65.

Although there is an assumption by a number of psychologists that, as the teenager matures, his general ability differentiates into highly specialized aptitudes, a very carefully controlled study with the *GATB* shows that this was not true. Werner (1964, p. 587) concludes that "there is no decrease in prominence of the general ability or intellective factor as a concomitant of increasing age in successive age groups from 14 to 54." Nevertheless, he also concludes that, in most instances, *GATB* scores can be of considerable value in the selection of personnel. The high school counselor can use them with the upper secondary school grade levels, however.

Problem

15. Figure 30 presents a *DAT* profile chart for a tenth-grade boy. Is this boy a potential college student? Can you predict areas of subject matter difficulty for him? What might a vocational counselor point out in discussing this chart with John and his parents?

USE OF APTITUDE TESTS
IN SCHOOL

The Scholastic Aptitude Test

The aptitude test most commonly used by the classroom teacher is the so-called "intelligence" or scholastic aptitude test. Whether a test measures aptitude or achievement depends not so much on its content as on its function. A test at one time may be used to measure present achievement and at other times to predict future achievement. There is a high correlation between the scores on achievement tests and the tests commonly used to determine academic aptitude. If one compares items on the two kinds of tests, he is struck by their similarity.

However, as we have indicated, the commonly used tests of scholastic aptitude differ greatly. Choosing the right test for a given purpose requires careful consideration. Test specialists are not agreed on their utility. Some believe that tests of general mental ability are of limited value, and argue that most of the uses to which they have been put can be better served by using properly constructed achievement tests of more specialized abilities (Davis, 1964, p. 137). Nevertheless, a pupil's academic potential must be determined and the scholastic aptitude test is helpful for this purpose.

Group, rather than individual, tests of verbal mental ability are probably the most useful and can provide helpful information in any school testing program. Because of their economy and practicality, they do not require a trained examiner, and yet they tend to be as reliable as individual tests. For school use their degree of validity is satisfactory.

It must be emphasized, however, that at times a pupil does not give his optimum performance, and this invalidates the score. If the score seems to deviate widely from other data available, a teacher may want a child retested on an individual basis with an instrument such as the *Stanford-Binet* or the *WISC*. In administering the individual test, the examiner can observe the pupil and better evaluate the validity of the test. If personnel trained for administering individual tests are unavailable, another form of the group test already used or a different group test should be administered. The non-language test is a helpful supplementary instrument for discovering pupils whose scores are affected by poor reading or general lack of verbal facility. Some tests give a language and a nonlanguage IQ in addition to a composite IQ, and are popular in some schools. However, in interpreting these scores, one must realize that differences may be due to measurement error.

Grouping

The classroom teacher and guidance staff can use the scores on the scholastic aptitude tests to understand the pupil better in teaching and in planning his educational and vocational goals. Likewise, the test scores may be administratively helpful in class grouping and occasionally for problems of promotion. Goslin (1967) reported that in a survey of 714 elementary schools about one-third used individual intelligence tests for grouping and about 40 percent used group intelligence tests. It should be emphasized, however, that no group determined by one criterion is homogeneous. A typical scholastic ability test contains both verbal and quantitative problems. Pupils making the same total score may vary considerably in their abilities. Pupils with identical scores also may have quite different motivations and interests. As one psychologist concluded, "The only way it is possible to have a homogeneous group is to have one pupil—and he continues to change." Grouping alone is not the answer to effective learning (see Yates, 1966, in Suggested Readings).

The teacher must plan in terms of materials and method to meet the needs and potential of each group. Furthermore, he must make special provisions for the deviate within a group, whether this individual is very bright or very dull, or has problems of an affective nature. Most schools are unable to organize special classes for these individuals.

It is perhaps easier to group for academic achievement in high school than in the elementary school. In the latter, many subjects are taught in one class. In high school, subjects are typically separated and an achievement test can be used along with an aptitude test for grouping.

Differential Testing

At the secondary school level, differential aptitude testing may provide some information for educational as well as vocational counseling; yet testing alone should not be used as the only criterion for determining the aptitude of boys and girls. The alert teacher is aware of their interests, their performance in and out of the classroom, the kinds of questions they ask, and so forth. Complete evaluation is necessary for valid interpretation.

An increasing number of secondary schools are realizing the importance of obtaining information about other aptitudes of their pupils. With the advent of differential testing, such instruments as the *Differential Aptitude Tests* have provided a means to identify the aptitude patterns in areas other than those most generally measured by the typical scholastic aptitude test. This added information provides many more data for the school to help all pupils plan their studies.

To be specific, a few of pupils' special problems more readily identified by differential testing are listed below:

1. The boy who is failing the verbally oriented courses, but who has excellent mechanical ability.
2. The boy from a bilingual home with few cultural opportunities who makes high scores on the *Numerical Ability, Mechanical Reasoning,* and *Space Relations* tests, but is failing in school.
3. The girl whose tested abilities are below average except for *Clerical Speed and Accuracy.*
4. The boy who aspires to be a physicist but whose numerical reasoning score is low.

The school must have adequate information about its superior pupils if it is to help them achieve. The gifted pupil is too often overlooked or unmotivated to continue his education. School authorities should identify such pupils and exercise every effort to appreciate and develop their talents.

It is also important to identify accurately the aptitude patterns of those who are less able. The common practice is to direct them into vocational courses without regard for any other criterion except that they are doing poorly in their academic classes. Yet, the chances of a pupil's succeeding in a commercial course are not good if his score on the *Clerical Speed and Accuracy Test* is valid and low. In addition, the mechanically inept are not served best in a shop course. It is necessary to assign courses that correspond with the interests and abilities of all students.

Overachievement and Underachievement

A concern of the teacher is determination of a pupil's achievement in terms of his ability. One may well question as to how a pupil can overachieve. The concept refers to a pupil achieving more than is predicted for a person of his academic ability. That is, he isn't achieving more than is possible for him to achieve but more than is expected of him based on the past performance of pupils with like ability. On the other hand, the underachiever is so labeled because his performance in comparison with others of his ability is not measuring up to expectations.

Before such conclusions are drawn about pupils, several considerations should be taken into account. First of all, prediction of achievement made from performance on a scholastic aptitude test score alone is insufficiently based. A teacher's final marks, by which academic success is generally evaluated, reflect bias of values relating to children's interest, cooperation, grooming, and courtesy. Secondly, although aptitude and achievement are not perfectly correlated, they are highly related and not at all independent; there is not a one-to-one relationship between ability and achievement. Thirdly, one must also consider that, in addition to this problem, tests measuring these components are not perfectly reliable; they contain errors of measurement.

A much more effective way to predict achievement, and thus determine whether pupils are performing adequately, is to judge achievement on the basis of achievement expected from an individual with his aptitude. In the past, teachers have attempted to estimate performance without any real basis for doing so. What they have done in many instances is to label pupils underachievers when they haven't measured up to the average performance of all pupils. This could be grossly unfair to a given pupil.

Some test publishers now provide a joint norms table that indicates the expected achievement of a pupil who performs at a given level on an aptitude test. The *Iowa Test of Basic Skills* is such an instrument; tables indicate the percentile rank equivalent for a grade equivalent score for pupils falling at various IQ levels on the *Lorge-Thorndike Intelligence Tests*. The *California Achievement Test* also has tables for relating achievement to ability. Nevertheless, one must interpret these norm tables with care because adequacy of achievement is determined by many factors and not the score on a scholastic aptitude test alone. It should also be remembered that when predictions are made from data on relatively homogeneous groups such as these, the reliability of the difference scores is not high.

The causes and characteristics of underachievement are suggested by a wealth of labels such as free-floating anxiety, negative self-value, hostility toward authority, high dependence-independence conflict, and negative interpersonal relations. Also, underachievement is usually defined arbitrarily by the investigator. As a result, depending on definition, underachievement is found among both gifted students (Ewing and Gilbert, 1967) and low-ability students (McGowan, 1968).

Problem

16. In advising pupils about curriculum choice, what relative weights would you assign to aptitude scores as compared with school marks?

SUMMARY

Schools are committed to help children develop according to their growth potential. It is therefore necessary to measure each child's aptitude to provide the best learning experiences for him. The results of using aptitude tests for grouping are contradictory. Grouping without provision to meet needs and abilities of the group is not sufficient. Aptitude testing has progressed from the general to the specific, and performance on general aptitude tests is closely related to schoolwork. Such tests are called scholastic aptitude tests; some can be administered to one pupil at a time, others to groups. One must exercise care in predicting achievement from aptitude test scores. Many factors determine achievement. Among the disadvantaged and minority children we must look for different meanings in the scores. It is best to use norms based on achievement of pupils at a given aptitude level.

Aptitude tests may be classified as verbal, performance, or nonlanguage tests. To perform successfully on verbal tests, the subject must understand oral and often written language. Performance tests emphasize the manipulation of objects rather than verbal skill and are individual tests. Although some oral instructions in the administration of a nonlanguage test may be required, in general, no written or spoken language is necessary to give correct responses. Instructions are simple and may even be translated to another language without invalidating the test. Nonlanguage tests are constructed as paper-and-pencil tests and, unlike performance tests, are designed for group administration.

Because aptitude is affected by achievement and innate ability, consideration has been given to the construction of tests that would deemphasize the role of the examinee's environment and are known as culture-fair tests. They vary in the degree to which they achieve their purpose, but there are substantial relationships between scores of these tests and the common scholastic aptitude tests.

The scores made by younger children on scholastic aptitude tests can be translated into mental ages or IQs. There is a trend toward the replacement of the ratio IQ by the deviation IQ. A rough classification of an individual's IQ generally holds throughout life; that is, dull, normal, and bright children tend to become dull, normal, and bright adults.

Test constructors seem not to agree on operational definition of creativity. At their present stage of development these instruments had best be used for research purposes.

Interest in special aptitudes has focused attention on the construction of various tests to measure such specific ones as artistic, musical, and clerical aptitudes. The difficulties in using these instruments are that the standardization population is different for each test, and the units of measurement are not comparable, so that it is impossible to construct a meaningful profile for the examinee. At present an attempt has been made to solve these problems through differential measurement; tests of a series are standardized on the same population so that scoring units are comparable. Low and high scores made on these tests are used to interpret the pupil's strengths and weaknesses.

Suggested Readings

Anastasi, A. Culture fair testing. *Educational Horizons*, 1964, **43**, 26–30. (Also reprinted in N. E. Gronlund (ed.), *Readings in measurement and evaluation*. London: Macmillan, 1968. Pp. 280–286.)
   This article is particularly appropriate to the testing of "culturally deprived" groups.
Bloom, B. S. *Stability and change in human characteristics*. New York: John Wiley, 1964.
   Development of intelligence and achievement is discussed. There are some interesting and perhaps surprising data as to when this development occurs.
Cronbach, L. J. *Essentials of psychological testing*. New York: Harper & Row, 1970. Chapters 7, 8, 9, 10, 11, and 12.
   Extensive discussion of the appraisal of general ability and the research and theory on which it is based will be found in these chapters. Group and individual test instruments are included as well as factor analysis and the use of ability profiles in guidance.
Davis, A. Cultural factors in remediation. *Educational Horizons*, 1965, **43**, 231–251.
   The important aspect of this article is the discussion of the IQ and its relationship to cultural differences. The author emphasizes the great variation in IQ among low socioeconomic groups as well as those more fortunate groups of

higher status. He contends that genetic factors are not unequally distributed by socioeconomic groups, and that powerful cultural influences affect problem solving of the kind required on scholastic aptitude tests.

Goslin, D. A. *Teachers and testing.* New York: Russell Sage Foundation, 1967.
The report discussed gives an excellent picture of the uses to which standardized tests are put in school, and opinions of teachers about tests and the state of their knowledge and competency in the use of tests.

Guthrie, F. A. What to look for in a review of an individual intelligence test. *Personnel and Guidance Journal,* 1964, **43,** 67–70.
Although the discussion is oriented toward a review of the individual tests, the principles discussed are pertinent to all measures of scholastic aptitude.

Hills, J. R. Use of measurement in selection and placement. In R. L. Thorndike (ed.), *Educational measurement.* (2nd ed.) Washington: American Council on Education, 1970. Chapter 19.
A sophisticated treatment of the history and problems in selection for college and placement in college. Cronbach's and Glaser's decision theory is discussed.

Levine, A. S. Aptitude versus achievement tests as predictors of achievement. *Educational and Psychological Measurement,* 1958, **18,** 517–525.
The author suggests that aptitude and achievement tests are differentiated not so much by the nature of their content as to the use to which they are put. Two different types of achievement tests are discussed.

McCollum, H. W. Relationship of anxiety to intelligence test scores of tenth-grade students. *Journal of Educational Research,* 1964, **58,** 35–37.
The hypothesis that high anxiety is related to low IQ scores was not proven. However, a tendency of this nature was noted. The predicted relationship was stronger for girls than for boys.

McNemar, Q. Lost: Our intelligence? Why? *American Psychologist,* 1964, **19,** 871–882.
The author makes a strong case for general intelligence as opposed to special abilities determined by factor analysis for predictive purposes. In addition, he severely criticizes some of the research done in creativity.

Millman, J., and M. D. Glock. Trends in the measurement of general mental ability. *Review of Educational Research,* 1965, **35,** 17–24.
The authors indicate that the environment of the young child, especially his educational experience, plays a key role in the development of intelligence. Therefore, intelligence tests are important in controlling the environment as well as in predicting future intellectual development.

National Council on Measurement in Education. *Untangling the tangled web of education.* Princeton, N.J.: Educational Testing Service, 1969.
The papers presented in a special symposium dealing with the problems of evaluating early schooling for disadvantaged children are included in this research memorandum.

National Education Association. *Ability grouping.* Washington: Research Division, National Education Association, 1968.
A summary of the research on ability grouping indicates no conclusive evidence as to its merits. Recommendations are offered.

Pinneau, S. R. *Changes in intelligence quotient, infancy to maturity.* Boston: Houghton Mifflin, 1961.
Four important topics are emphasized in the book. First, the constancy of the IQ from the early years to late adolescence is analyzed. Secondly, accurate

mental age scores and revised IQ tables for the *Stanford-Binet Intelligence Scales* have been developed. Thirdly, a table of IQ changes with age has been prepared and explanations provided. Fourthly, consideration is given to the rate of mental maturation by individuals of different levels of ability.

Tuddenham, R. D. Intelligence. In R. L. Ebel (ed.), *Encyclopedia of Educational Research*. (4th ed.) London: Macmillan, 1969. Pp. 654–667.

A thorough review of basic research concerning intelligence, including intellectual development during the life span.

Tyler, F. T. Readiness. In R. L. Ebel (ed.), *Encyclopedia of Educational Research*. (4th ed.) London: Macmillan, 1969. Pp. 1062–1069.

Readiness is of prime consideration in aptitude for learning. The author presents a thorough review of the research on all facets of this topic including readiness as it relates to maturation, Piaget's theories, learning theories, cognitive structure and style, and structure of knowledge.

Wallach, M. A. Review of Torrance Tests of Creative Thinking. *American Educational Research Journal*, 1968, **5**, 272–281.

The author raises a question as to whether these tests measure anything different than the typical scholastic aptitude test. Furthermore he raises questions on the psychometrics of the search in creativity testing.

Yates, A. (ed.) *Grouping in education*. New York: John Wiley, 1966.

According to the editor, this book will "provide for a thoughtful reappraisal of existing systems in order to arrive at a more effective and harmonious academic, mental, and emotional development of the children of all ages within a school system."

References Cited

Allen, M. M. The relation between Kuhlmann-Anderson tests and achievement in grade IV. *Journal of Educational Psychology*, 1944, **35**, 229–239.

Bayley, N. Consistency and variability in growth of intelligence from birth to 18 years. *Journal of Genetic Psychology*, 1949, **75**, 165–196.

Bayley, N. Mental growth during the first three years. A developmental study of 61 children by repeated tests. *Genetic Psychological Monographs*, 1933, **14**, 1–92.

Bayley, N. On the growth of intelligence. *American Psychologist*, 1955, **10**, 805–818.

Bennett, G. K., H. G. Seashore, and A. G. Wesman. *Differential Aptitude Tests, Forms L and M, Manual*. (4th ed.) New York: Psychological Corporation, 1966.

Bereiter, C. The future of individual differences. *Harvard Educational Review*, 1969, **39**, 310–318.

Bradway, K. P., and N. M. Robinson. Significant IQ changes in twenty-five years: A follow-up. *Journal of Educational Psychology*, 1961, **52**, 74–79.

Bradway, K. P., and C. W. Thompson. Intelligence at adulthood: A twenty-five year follow-up. *Journal of Educational Psychology*, 1962, **53**, 1–14.

Cleary, T. A. Test bias: Validity of the Scholastic Aptitude Test for negro and white students in integrated colleges. *Educational Testing Service Research Bulletin*, 1966, RB-66-31.

Cohen, J. The factorial structure of the WAIS between early adulthood and old age. *Journal of Consulting Psychology*, 1957, **21**, 283–290.

College Entrance Examination Board. *A description of the College Board Scholastic Aptitude Test*. Princeton, N.J.: College Entrance Examination Board, 1965.

College Entrance Examination Board. *Effects of coaching on Scholastic Aptitude Test scores*. Princeton, N.J.: College Entrance Examination Board, 1968.

Cooley, W. W. Techniques for considering multiple measurement. In R. L. Thorndike (ed.), *Educational measurement*. (2nd ed.) Washington: American Council on Education, 1970. Chapter 16.

Cronbach, L. J. Heredity, environment, and educational policy. *Harvard Educational Review*, 1969, **39**, 338–347.

Cronbach, L. J. *Essentials of psychological testing*. (3rd ed.) New York: Harper & Row, 1970.

Crow, J. F. Genetic theories and influences: Comments on the value of diversity. *Harvard Educational Review*, 1969, **39**, 301–309.

Davis, F. B. *Educational measurements and their interpretation*. Belmont, Calif.: Wadsworth, 1964.

Dearborn, W. F., and J. W. M. Rothney. *Predicting the child's development*. (2nd ed.) Cambridge: Sci-Art Publishers, 1963.

Elkind, D. Piagetian and psychometric conceptions of intelligence. *Harvard Educational Review*, 1969, **39**, 338–347.

Ewing, T. N., and W. M. Gilbert. Controlled study of the effects of counseling on the scholastic achievements of students of superior ability. *Journal of Counseling Psychology*, 1967, **14**, 235–239.

Fishman, J. A., and others. Guidelines for testing minority group children. *Journal of Social Issues* (Supplement), 1964, **20**, 129–145.

Fogan, J., and others. Comparison of the Binet and WPPSI with lower-class five-year-olds. *Journal of Consulting and Clinical Psychology*, 1969, **33**, 607–609.

Freeman, F. N., and C. D. Flory. Growth in intellectual ability as measured by repeated tests. *Monographs of the Society for Research in Child Development*, 1937, **2**, No. 2.

Gaier, E. L., and W. F. White. Trends in the measurement of personality. *Review of Educational Research*, 1965, **35**, 63–81.

Glaser, R., and A. J. Nitko. Measurement in learning and instruction. In R. L. Thorndike (ed.), *Educational measurement*. (2nd ed.) Washington: American Council on Education, 1970. Chapter 17.

Goslin, D. A. *Teachers and testing*. New York: Russell Sage Foundation, 1967.

Guilford, J. P. Three faces of intellect. *American Psychologist*, 1959, **14**, 409–479.

Guilford, J. P. Intelligence: 1965 model. *American Psychologist*, 1965, **21**, 20–26.

Harris, A. J. *How to increase reading ability*. (5th ed.) New York: David McKay, 1970.

Hills, J. R. Prediction of college grades for all public colleges of a state. *Journal of Educational Measurement*, 1964, **1**, 155–159.

Hills, J. R. Use of measurement in selection and placement. In R. L. Thorndike (ed.), *Educational measurement*. (2nd ed.) Washington: American Council on Education, 1970. Chapter 19.

Hunt, J. M. Has compensatory education failed? Has it been attempted? *Harvard Educational Review*, 1969, 39, 278–300.

Jensen, A. R. How much can we boost IQ and scholastic achievement? *Harvard Educational Review*, 1969a, 39, 1–123.

Jensen, A. R. Reducing the heredity-environment uncertainty: A reply. *Harvard Educational Review*, 1969b, 39, 449–483.

Kagan, J. S. Inadequate evidence and illogical conclusions. *Harvard Educational Review*, 1969, 39, 274–277.

Kuhlmann, F., and R. G. Anderson. *Kuhlmann-Anderson Intelligence Tests, handbook.* (7th ed.) Princeton, N.J.: Personnel Press, 1963.

McGowan, R. J. The effect of brief contact interviews with low ability, low achieving students. *School Counselor*, 1968, 15, 386–389.

MacKinnon, D. W. Personality and the realization of creative potential. *American Psychologist*, 1965, 20, 273–281.

McNemar, Q. *The revision of the Stanford-Binet scale.* Boston: Houghton Mifflin, 1942.

Pinneau, S. R. *Changes in intelligence quotient, infancy to maturity.* Boston: Houghton Mifflin, 1961.

Pintner, R. *Pintner General Ability Tests: Non-language series.* New York: Harcourt, Brace & World, 1945.

Stanley, J. C. On the adequacy of standardized tests administered to extreme norm groups. *Peabody Journal of Education*, 1951, 29, 145–153.

Stanley, J. C. Identification of superior learners in grades ten through fourteen. *Educational Monographs*, 1954, 81.

Stroud, J. B. The intelligence test in school use: Some persistent issues. *Journal of Educational Psychology*, 1957, 48, 77–85.

Super, D. E., and J. O. Crites. *Appraising vocational fitness by means of psychological tests.* (Rev. ed.) New York: Harper & Row, 1962.

Taylor, C. W. (ed.) *Creativity: Progress and potential.* New York: McGraw-Hill, 1964.

Terman, L. M., and M. A. Merrill. *The Stanford-Binet Intelligence Scale: Manual for the third revision.* Boston: Houghton Mifflin, 1960.

Thorndike, R. L. The measurement of creativity. *Teachers College Record*, 1963, 64, 423.

Torrance, E. P. Current research on the nature of creative talent. *Journal of Counseling Psychology*, 1959, 6, 309–316.

Torrance, E. P. *Guiding creative talent.* Englewood Cliffs, N.J.: Prentice-Hall, 1962.

Wechsler, D. *Wechsler Intelligence Scale for Children.* New York: Psychological Corporation, 1949.

Werner, M. Organization of mental abilities from ages 14 to 54. *Educational and Psychological Measurement*, 1964, 24, 573–587.

Wolfle, D., and T. Oxtoby. Distributions of ability of students specializing in different fields. *Science*, 1952, 116, 311–314.

CHAPTER 13

Evaluating Personal-Social Adjustment

The Greek myth of Daedalus and his son Icarus tells how Icarus met his death because he could not adjust to a new situation. When Daedalus, who had been held captive, made his escape from prison, he found no other way to flee the heavily guarded island but by air. Rarest of craftsmen, he set to work making great feathered wings for himself and for his son, binding the large feathers with thread, the small with wax. When all was ready for flight he gravely cautioned the boy Icarus always to fly close to him in a moderate course between sky and sea, warning that if they flew too low the weight of sea spray in their feathers would drag them down, and if too high, the heat of the sun would melt the wax that bound them.

All went well until Icarus, lacking his father's realistic caution and giddy with the joy of flight, soared away into the heavens. The blazing sun melted the wax bonds of the wings and feathers and as they fell away, nothing was left to hold the boy in the air but his flailing arms. Suddenly missing his beloved son, Daedalus cried out to him but was answered only by the terrible sight of scattering feathers swirling in the sea beneath.

Icarus' behavior seems to defy explanation. What foolhardiness caused him to behave so? Men have always concerned themselves with human behavior. It was once believed that patterns of adjustment were entirely inherited, and personality traits passed on to children in the same way as blue eyes and red hair. Even today we hear people say of nonconforming children: "Well, he comes by it honestly; he's a chip off the old block," assuming, however unconsciously, a hereditary basis for atypical behavior.

Modern psychology has shown that personal-social development depends on the interplay of many factors, not only on learned patterns of adjustment, but on such elements as the chemical function and physical structure of the body, and the general level of intelligence. The small boy may become aggressive to compensate for his size, or withdraw from physical con-

413

tact and compensate through intellectual prowess or fantasy. The dull girl with high standards may resort to atypical actions in an attempt to adjust to an impossible situation, but her reaction is learned, not inherited.

The maladjusted individual is no longer assumed to be immoral or suffering over his sins. Neither is he accused of deliberate nonconformist behavior. The clinician accepts the individual and approaches his problem with sympathy, but objectifies the situation and tries to determine its antecedents. Instead of focusing on symptoms, he seeks causes.

Yet some parents and teachers still subject "different" children to sarcasm, and believe that if these children would only "try," they would improve. The shy child is urged to show more spunk; daydreamers are asked to wake up. Too often this approach convinces the child that he is right in his estimation of himself, that he is indeed inadequate, and, too often, he accepts the situation as hopeless. Thus, his behavior may actually be reinforced by exhortations to reform. Admonishing or ridiculing are not effective ways to initiate a positive change in behavior.

The process of adjustment is the individual's attempt to create a more congruous relationship between himself and his environment. The process may consist of an attempt to change the environment or his behavior, or to modify both. The teacher should play a very important role in helping the child manage the adjustment. Certainly, he cannot assume that the burden to adjust rests entirely on the individual alone. Yet, if he is careless of his responsibility, he may establish a social climate in which it is impossible for his pupils to meet even their basic personality needs. A teacher who stipulates equal requirements for all is frustrating many pupils by denying them any opportunity for success. Equally, when able children are forced to repeat much that they have already experienced and learned, the teacher is denying them the challenge that comes through new experience and that stimulates new learning and growth. The authoritarian taskmaster who expects everyone in his classroom to conform is stifling creativity and the satisfaction that comes through self-expression.

TEACHERS' CONCEPTS OF ADJUSTMENT

One of the most difficult problems in evaluating the personal-social adjustment of pupils lies in the teacher's understanding of adjustment. Just because certain kinds of behavior disrupt the well-oiled machinery of a carefully controlled classroom is no defensible reason to label them maladjustment. Yet a number of studies indicates that teachers fail to differentiate between behavior that disturbs the activities of the classroom and behavior which may lead to serious emotional difficulty (Wickman, 1928; Dale, 1941).

In one study (Sparks, 1952), teachers were asked to rank fifty-five problems, those most serious for the pupil and those most troublesome to the teacher. Table 20 shows clearly that the participating teacher did not have an accurate concept of what constitutes evidence of serious adjustment problems. Apparently they considered traits that violate society's social and moral code as most likely to produce adjustment problems in the individual. They listed as most "serious," traits that proved troublesome to them as teachers, not symptoms related to the emotional conflicts of children. They tended to make no differentiation between academic success and emotional health. In general they considered pupils who did satisfactory academic work to be well-adjusted individuals, while if a pupil's achievement was low, they were inclined to think of him as a behavior deviant or just stupid.

TABLE 20.   Traits Ranked Most Troublesome to the Teacher and Most Serious to the Pupil.

	Traits	
Rank	*Most troublesome to teacher*	*Most serious to pupil*
1	Interrupting	Stealing
2	Carelessness to work	Untruthfulness
3	Inattention	Unreliableness
4	Restlessness	Cruelty and bullying
5	Silliness, smartness	Cheating
6	Whispering and note writing	Heterosexual activity
7	Tattling	Impertinence
8	Thoughtlessness	Imprudence
9	Disorderliness	Selfishness
10	Inquisitiveness	Laziness

One of the classic studies (Wickman, 1928) trenchantly exhibits the differences between teachers' and mental hygienists' concepts of problem behavior. In 1928, when members of each group were asked to rank behavior problems according to their importance, they sharply disagreed. Stouffer (1952) repeated this study after a period of twenty-five years. Although some change is noticeable, there are still numerous points of wide disagreement. A comparison of these rankings is shown in Table 21. Note the high teacher-ranking given in 1952 to problems that might tend to disturb class routine or defy society's code of right and wrong, such as stealing, truancy, untruthfulness, unreliability, cheating, and impertinence. Failure to understand children's emotional conflicts is evident in the low ranking given such problems as suspiciousness, shyness, enuresis, and dreaminess.

Another investigation (Tolor, Scarpetti, and Lane, 1967) further ex-

TABLE 21. Comparison of Behavior Problem Rankings by Mental Hygienists and Teachers in 1928 and 1952.

Behavior problem	Ranking by mental hygienists	Ranking by teachers 1928	Ranking by teachers 1952
Unsocial, withdrawing	1	40	6
Unhappy, depressed	2	22	3
Fearfulness	3	36	23
Suspiciousness	4	37	35
Cruelty, bullying	5	8	4
Shyness	6	50	34
Enuresis	7	19	30
Resentfulness	8	29	11
Stealing	9	2	2
Sensitiveness	10	48	24
Dreaminess	11	41	40
Nervousness	12	20	18
Suggestible	13	28	13
Over critical of others	14	45	27
Easily discouraged	15	23	10
Temper tantrums	16	13	16
Domineering	17	33	15
Truancy	18	6	7
Physical coward	19	31	33
Untruthfulness	20	5	5
Unreliableness	21	12	1
Destroying school material	22	10	12
Sullenness	23	35	32
Lack of interest in work	24	14	22
Cheating	25	9	9
Selfishness	26	24	17
Quarrelsomeness	27	27	28
Heterosexual activity	28	1	14
Restlessness	29	49	45
Inattention	30	26	36
Slovenly in personal appearance	31	34	31
Tattling	32	46	47
Impertinence, defiance	33	7	8
Obscene notes, talk	34	4	29
Laziness	35	17	20
Stubbornness	36	32	37
Attracting attention	37	39	43
Thoughtlessness	38	38	41

TABLE 21.   (Continued).

Behavior problem	Ranking by mental hygienists	Ranking by teachers	
		1928	1952
Imaginative lying	39	42	46
Disobedience	40	11	19
Carelessness in work	41	25	25
Masturbation	42	3	26
Imprudence, rudeness	43	16	21
Inquisitiveness	44	44	44
Disorderliness in class	45	21	39
Tardiness	46	30	38
Interrupting	47	43	48
Profanity	48	15	42
Smoking	49	18	49
Whispering	50	47	50

From Wickman, 1928; Stouffer, 1952; adapted by permission of the Commonwealth Fund.

plored this problem by focusing on patterns of functioning. The objective was to identify the types of behavioral patterns that teachers and psychologists perceive most differently. Furthermore, the effect of teacher experience was to be studied. Teachers were drawn from kindergarten through grade 7. The psychologists were functioning in clinical settings and were from the same state as the teachers. The measuring device was the *Staten Island Behavior Scale*. Items were classified into psychosomatic and physical disturbance, phobias, aggressiveness, affect expression, communication disturbance, regressive behavior, inefficiency indicators, and fantasy involvement or withdrawal. Respondents were to indicate whether an item indicated either normal or abnormal behavior for children within the age range of 1 to 16 inclusive.

Again it was found that teachers and psychologists differed significantly. In Table 22 note that the greatest percent of disagreement was in regressive, aggressive, and affective behavior. When ratings by experienced teachers and inexperienced teachers were compared with those by psychologists, the experienced teachers did not differ nearly as much from psychologists in ascribing abnormality as the less experienced teachers did. The following items regarded as normal by the experienced teachers and abnormal by the inexperienced teachers are illustrative:

Cries or whimpers
Plays with or fingers his mouth
Headache

At the slightest upset, coordination becomes poor
Is frightened in crowds
Is afraid of being alone in a wide open space
Child's thoughts are hard to understand
Lying

TABLE 22.   Types of Behavioral Patterns That Teachers and Pscyhologists Perceive Differently.

Category	Items in Scale	Percentage of Items Disagreed Upon
Physical-psychosomatic	71	10
Phobic	18	6
Aggressive	56	38
Affect	58	33
Communication	21	14
Regressive	15	40
Inefficiency	25	12
Fantasy-withdrawal	31	19

From Tolor, Scarpetti, and Lane, 1967; reproduced by permission of the American Psychological Association.

Problems

1.   Can you see any important trends emerging as you analyze the data presented in Table 21? What might account for this?

2.   Choose five behavior problems from the list in Table 21 and illustrate concretely how you would attempt to deal with each in class. Compare the data in Table 21 with those in Table 22.

3.   On the basis of your own classroom experience, list those teacher characteristics that seem to promote a high degree of personal-social adjustment among pupils.

METHODS OF EVALUATING PERSONAL-SOCIAL ADJUSTMENT

The discussion in this chapter is confined to personal-social adjustment rather than personality. The latter is much broader in meaning, as Shaffer and Shoben (1956, p. 310) emphasize:

Personality does not depend on one or a few characteristics only, but on the interplay of practically all of an individual's qualities. Physical structure, chemical functioning, learned motives, and habits of adjustment all contribute to personality, and not as separate entities but as interacting aspects of an organized system.

Of course, the individual must adjust to his physiological needs; he eats when he is hungry, he seeks warmth if he is cold. But much broader dimensions of adjustment are assumed than this simple adaptive behavior. We must consider the pupil's relationship to his social environment as well as his behavior in relation to his own psychological needs. (Shaffer and Shoben, 1956, p. 4).

In the lives of most civilized people, social adjustments are more significant than responses to physiological wants. Human beings are social persons as well as biological organisms. Social interactions among people and between groups of people are required to fulfill even some of our most elementary needs. On the other hand, people often work in competition or at cross purposes so as to thwart one another's satisfactions. When a child feels insecure and unwanted by his family, when a student feels isolated from his fellows, or when a man is unsuccessful in his work, adjustments are required to mediate between the socially defined needs and the socially determined frustrations.

Behavior patterns such as these are partial reflections of the degree to which some important educational objectives have been achieved in the pupil, and it is necessary, therefore, to attempt to evaluate them.

A variety of instruments for evaluating personal-social adjustment is available to the teacher. Some of these are based on formal observations, some are paper-and-pencil inventories to be administered to a group of pupils, others are individual instruments designed primarily for use by clinicians. The following outline is indicative of the variety of useful instruments and techniques in this area of evaluation.

Evaluation methods based on observation
   Anecdotal records
   Rating scales
   Check lists
   Interviewing
Projective techniques
   Inkblot and picture presentation
   Use of graphic and art materials
   Doll play
   Presentation of verbal stimuli
Sociometric and related techniques
   Sociograms
   Social distance scales
   "Guess who" questionnaires
Self-report inventories
   Biographical data blank
   Personal inventories
   Interest inventories
   Attitude scales and questionnaires

A selected group of standardized instruments for measuring aspects of personal-social adjustment is given in Appendix E. Neither these methods nor less formal ones are as reliable or valid as the better standardized achievement and scholastic aptitude tests. As there are extremists who harbor an indefensible degree of enthusiasm for the measurement possibilities of these tests, there are many prophets of gloom who mistrust them altogether and advocate a "hands off" policy. It seems reasonable to adopt a middle-of-the-road position. The following discussion emphasizes the limitations of various methods and techniques included in the outline above, but goes on to suggest some practical approaches to this area of evaluation.

Evaluation Methods Based on Observation

What a teacher can learn from observation of students in natural situations is generally useful to him, and is, for many reasons, a valuable addition to the study of personal-social development.

First, the results of such observation supplement information gathered elsewhere. A pupil may do well on a mechanical aptitude test, but be awkward and uninterested in the shop. Another may give the desired answers on an adjustment inventory, but be unable to work cooperatively with any of his peers.

Second, they provide the teacher with information unobtainable in other ways. He has an opportunity to notice numerous significant incidents and attitudes in the daily activities of the pupil, an opportunity which may be lacking in artificial situations. When a pupil answers "yes" to the question "Is it fun to do nice things for other boys and girls?" his behavior may not be indicative of his adjustment to a peer group; the teacher may observe that the child is really self centered.

Third, they afford an opportunity to sample the student's actual behavior. Under informal observation, a pupil is not asked to conform to what he might feel in an artificial situation, as in answering a questionnaire, and is not requested to report on his own behavior. Direct observation will, therefore, be more valid in certain instances.

Finally, the results of such observation benefit the observer. It is important that the teacher develop proper relationships with the pupils. When he observes pupils objectively, bias can be lessened and understandings deepened. Too often teachers judge their pupils in terms of their own feelings and prejudices and therefore find it impossible to help them. It should be said, however, that the teacher may need help in developing the skill of accurate reporting. A serious limitation of observation may lie within the observer himself, for what a person sees or hears depends in part on what he is predisposed to see or hear (Froehlich and Darley, 1952, pp. 84–87).

What the Teacher Observes. What should the teacher observe in the behavior of children in a natural situation? An important place to observe is in class. Does the pupil volunteer or offer to share experiences, or does he withdraw and fail to participate? What kind of questions does he ask? Does the nature of his questioning indicate that he has a genuine interest in learning, or is he more interested in his marks? What does he like to talk about? Does he ever mention his interests, problems or family? How does the group react to contributions by individual members? The teacher will find that the group will support certain individuals, contradict some, and ignore others.

The teacher should also observe the group and its interactions. Which pupils are aggressive, withdrawn, or hostile? Which lead and which follow? Does group behavior within the freedom of the playground differ from that in the classroom? The pupil who appears listless and uninterested in the classroom may come alive in a ball game. Are some pupils more aggressive when freed from the teacher's control? Do they exhibit leadership characteristics in the rough-and-tumble of sports while they are withdrawn in the classroom?

Finally, a great deal is revealed about a pupil's personal-social development through observation of his creative activity, which enables him to translate his feelings into action. Does he prefer working with abstract symbols or concrete objects, enjoy participating in dramatics and role playing? Is he overly anxious when he appears before others? What emotions does he tend to express in his drawings and paintings?

Problems

4. Describe the major personality traits of those teachers who might experience the most difficulty with the observational method. Might training in this technique serve as a therapeutic aid in improving a teacher's own personal-social adjustment?
5. How can "creative" activity be observed through your particular subject matter field?

Danger of Bias. Bias in observation is common. Take, for example, the commonly accepted fallacy that "only" children are spoiled. Teachers often interpret negative behavior in pupils without siblings as being a direct result of having their own way at home. This may or may not be the cause underlying the behavior. Mere knowledge that a pupil is an only child, without further examination of his actual relationship with his parents, is not grounds for assuming that his "onliness" will result in a handicap. Although recent research disproves the assumption that only children are universally spoiled, and disliked by peers and adults alike, "onliness" is still labeled the cause for many classroom problems.

Bias may also result when an observer does not admit his own feelings and weaknesses to himself. Failing to do so, he may attribute his inadequacies to others, and a pupil's behavior will be interpreted as similar to his own inhibited desires (Jersild, and others, 1953, pp. 6–7).

> In everyday life we often see illustrations of judgments passed on others that reflect as much of the personality of the one who judges as the one who is judged. For example, a person with pronounced authoritarian tendencies, who has a strong urge to show respect for his superiors, and to demand respect from his subordinates may see a student's frankness as a form of being "fresh"; he may regard a student who has opinions of his own as impudent, or one who voices disagreement as disobedient. The teacher who is insecure may interpret calculated flattery as genuine appreciation and regard those who make a policy of agreeing with him as true scholars. A person who is unsure of himself may take offense, and assume that an offense was intended, when someone offers a bit of well-meant criticism. A person who is defensive about his opinions may interpret an innocent question as a form of attack. A teacher who suffers from intense feelings of guilt because of his sexual impulses may interpret a little exchange of whispers or notes between two people as evidence that they have "filthy minds"; and if a student actually is guilty of behavior that is indiscreet or in poor taste, the teacher may magnify the indiscretion into a heinous crime.

This same projective type of weakness in reporting may also be reflected in a "Pollyanna" attitude toward all pupils. While it is commendable to look for strengths in children, their total behavior must be evaluated objectively, and that is not easy. Many people well-versed in factual knowledge of human behavior have never learned to apply this information to themselves or to others. An astute observer is able to analyze his feelings toward others as they relate to his own behavior, and attempts to discover their causes through an objective approach. Why does he dislike certain pupils and champion others? What makes him unhappy with the behavior of some students? Observation alone cannot yield valid answers. Lack of objectivity makes it impossible to report behavior truthfully.

Objectivity in reporting may be improved by separating description from judgment. "Johnny is undependable," and "Mary will assume no responsibility" are judgments that do not specify what happened and how, nor do they specify the responsibilities Mary failed to assume. As they stand, there is no way to check their validity; possibly they express only the teacher's dislike for a child. The following illustrates a more useful description of behavior.

> I said, "Eddie, you haven't done the work assigned you this period. Don't you understand it?" Eddie answered by saying, "I don't know." When I checked to see if he understood, he knew the answers to all of my questions relating to the assignment. Eddie seldom completes more than one assignment per week during the allotted time.
>   On the playground I overheard Susie say, "Don't choose Eddie, because he won't try hard if he doesn't like the game." Janie said, "But some one has to choose him."

Note that the above is a report; it injects no judgment. This is what the teacher said, how Eddie answered, and what was done as a result. In the same manner, the playground incident consists simply of the children's conversation.

Sampling. Adequate sampling is also important for valid observation. The teacher who concerns himself only with classroom behavior may have a very biased picture of pupils' total personal-social adjustment. The same boy who is hostile and aggressive in English class may be a cooperative and respected leader in the chemistry club, or have a helpful attitude toward his mathematics classmates.

To improve sampling, one must make observations in varied situations. However, care should also be given to timing. A pupil under observation may have a toothache on the day you have chosen to make mental notes about his actions, or perhaps difficulties have arisen in his home, and what you see or hear may not be at all typical of his behavior. Naturally, the more you observe him in a variety of situations, the more likely you are to synthesize an accurate picture of his problems of adjustment, and the more reliable your observation will become.

The teacher must plan for reliability and economy of effort. It is not practicable for him to use the technique, valuable in certain researches, of planning a schedule of short observations in advance where, by *randomizing* the schedule, numerous pupils are seen in more or less comparable situations. Nevertheless, the teacher can schedule, and, through a conscious effort, somewhat avoid the bias resulting from observation of a nonrepresentative or improperly timed situation.

Problem

6. Elementary school teachers who remain with the same children all day have ample opportunity to obtain a wide variety of behavior samples. In what specific ways might junior and senior high school teachers meet the problem of less opportunity to sample behavior?

Purpose in Observation. The teacher always seeks information that will help him promote learning; this is a very general objective, however. It is more helpful to look for something specific. Why does one pupil seem to have difficulty in getting along with other boys? Why does another refuse to make reports or enter class discussion? An intelligent search for the answers will be guided by what we already know. It may be necessary to arrange some special occasions in which there is an opportunity to test guesses and hypotheses about the source of difficulty. Some simple structuring can elicit reactions to social stimuli that are encountered in the normal course of events—perhaps assigning certain pupils specific responsibilities, formulating key questions, or organizing games that present some individual and social problems.

Anecdotal Records.   Observation techniques function most effectively when the information is written. One way of recording such information is in anecdotal records, systematic and significant records of the pupil's behavior, which generally form part of the permanent record passed on with him from grade to grade. In studying a behavior problem, it is important to look for signs of its development, because change can be evaluated only through knowledge of previous happenings.

ANECDOTAL RECORD FORM

Date: 1/23/70   Pupil's Name: Sue Collings

Observer: Dorothy Larson

Description of incident:
   Sue had won our first essay contest. When she was offered a prize for her second success, she gave it to Marlene, who was runner-up. Marlene accepted it without any expression of appreciation.

Comment:

   Sue seems to be a very well-adjusted child and quite sensitive to the needs of the other children. It was a particularly noble gesture for her to give Marlene the prize since Marlene is very selfish and uncooperative with her peers.

FIGURE 31.   Sample Anecdotal Record.

A sample anecdotal record is shown in Figure 31. Notice that the description of the incident is separated from the teacher's comments about it. In both instances, more details can be added if necessary. Incidentally, a copy of this anecdote could be placed in the files of both girls mentioned.

   The following running report on an eighth-grade boy was made over a period of several weeks. It is a condensation of a series of anecdotal records.

September 30. Bill was late to class and was sent to the principal's office for a pass. He did not return.
   Upon checking up, I found that Bill had gone to the school nurse with a complaint of illness.
   Interpretation: This may have been a deliberate attempt to avoid class.
October 7. Bill responded to my question on the assignment with "I didn't read it. It doesn't seem very important to me."
   Interpretation: Bill seems to be hunting for ways of justifying his behavior.
October 10. Bill continued to whisper, make various remarks about the class discussion, shuffle papers, and drop pencils or books. When I reprimanded him, he got up and left the room.
   Interpretation: Bill seemed to be intent on disrupting the class.

October 13. In looking at the data in Bill's cumulative file, I found a history of reading difficulty. His *Stanford-Binet* IQ was 120.

    Interpretation: Bill's inability to read might be the source of his behavior problems.

October 14. I asked Bill if he would help me build a cage for some snakes that I wanted to exhibit in the science room. He said that he would be happy to come in after school. It was 5 o'clock before we had finished.

    Then he leafed through some books and materials on snakes that I had on the shelf. He chose a booklet with low reading difficulty and asked if he could take it home with him.

    Interpretation: I believe that I am establishing a good relationship with Bill and have found a way to help him.

October 15. The interest of the class was centered around Bill. He had some information to share on the booklet he had read. He stopped after class to return the booklet and ask for another.

    Interpretation: Bill expressed satisfaction with this new role. He seemed genuinely pleased with his ability to make a contribution to the group.

October 17. Bill stopped in after school and asked if there was any way in which he could improve his reading.

Bill was a particular problem for this teacher. Therefore, he concentrated his attention on him. It is best to select one or two pupils to focus on at a time. In this way teachers find that they compile better records of each pupil and can separate the child's behavior from their own feelings and biases. It is an almost hopeless task to write daily or weekly records for all pupils; nevertheless, when significant incidents occur involving any pupil, they should be recorded.

The teacher described above has made an objective report of the incidents, separating interpretation from report. He is, therefore, able to make a more accurate description of Bill's behavior and to hypothesize the source of his difficulties. Notice in this case that extended observation has revealed the reading difficulty and its relationship to Bill's behavior problems. He has been trying to escape from responsibilities that involve reading, yet his need is not evident from any single anecdote; the pattern emerges as a number of situations are reported.

Deviant behavior may appear periodically among some pupils. Possibly certain taxing school events, like issuing report cards, coincides with this behavior. The amount of security that home life affords a child varies as it does in school. Therefore, adequate sampling is necessary for a valid interpretation of behavior. Extended observation also provides an opportunity to detect improvement or lack of it in an individual's behavior.

Problems

7. As you look at the anecdotal records of Bill can you see other plausible interpretations of his behavior?

8.   An important use of the anecdotal record is to serve as a reference, along with other data, when the teacher is making inferences and formulating hypotheses about behavior. What other important uses can you see in this technique?

Rating Scales.   Rating scales are also useful in the making and recording of observations. These instruments are popular in many schools because they emphasize important aspects of adjustment and provide data that can be treated statistically. They also make it possible for several judges to rate the same pupil, a procedure that usually increases the reliability of the rating.

Most of the rating instruments used in the elementary and secondary schools are graphic scales, constructed so that the rater can mark any point along a continuum. For example:

The rater may check any one of the defined points or rate the pupil between the points. In these examples, the rater has classified the pupil's degree of moodiness between the defined points of "never" and "seldom," but his acceptance of authority as "very well."

The foregoing scales (from Haggerty and others, 1930; adapted by permission of Harcourt, Brace & World, Inc.) can be greatly improved by substituting behavioral statements for the more general terms of "poorly," "well," and "very well." For example:

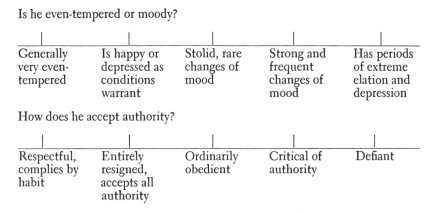

If some of these items, such as "even-tempered" and "defiant" were defined more specifically, they would provide a more common basis on which to evaluate the pupil. Specific examples of behavior, such as "refuses to hand in papers" and "talks back in a belligerent tone," will do much to offset disparity of judgment that arises because different raters employ different criteria in judging pupils according to general descriptive terms.

Another method of defining the points on a scale more clearly is by determining the approximate number of pupils that should be placed at each point. If one assumes that a trait is normally distributed for the population, and that the group of pupils in question is unselected, then the trait will approximate a normal distribution for the group.

Table 23, which is derived from tables of the area under the normal curve, can be used as a guide to determine the percentage of the group that should be placed at each point on the scale. The ratings of observers will tend to be more comparable if the number of pupils at each point is established in this manner. Of course, if your population is selected, if you teach either the best or poorest pupils, then there is no specific percentage distribution guide such as that of the normal curve. Definition of the population is important.

There are several types of error affecting the reliability and validity of ratings, namely: (1) rating all pupils either too high or too low ("personal bias" or "personal equation"); (2) rating everyone near the central point of the scale (error of central tendency); (3) inaccurate rating because of ambiguity in the scale or misunderstanding on the part of the raters; and (4) allowing one's general impression of the pupil to affect the rating ("halo effect"). The fourth type of error results if the rater is favorably impressed by a pupil and so tends to give him a higher evaluation than he deserves on

TABLE 23. Percentage Distributions for a Class of Forty Pupils for Scales Having Different Numbers of Points.

Three points	Four points	Five points	Six points	Seven points
20	11	7	5	4
60	39	24	15	10
20	39	38	30	22
	11	24	30	28
		7	15	22
			5	10
				4

From Symonds, 1931, p. 81; reproduced by permission of Appleton-Century-Crofts, Inc.

many items. Lower ratings may result for a pupil of whom the rater is not particularly fond (Wrightstone, 1960, p. 931).

The reliability of ratings can be improved by increasing the number of judges. This poses a practical problem in the elementary school where a child generally has only one teacher. In secondary school, the large pupil-teacher ratio prevents teachers from knowing all their pupils well, but because each pupil has contact with a number of teachers, there is a better opportunity to get reactions from several observers. It should be emphasized that rating pupils without sufficient evidence to make a highly reliable and valid opinion is a waste of time.

One might well be skeptical of the relative validity of ratings because of the many human errors attributable to the rater. However, some recent studies of the validity of rating scales definitely support their use. For instance, rating of aptitude for military service proved to be more highly related to ratings of performance in the field than any other information (*Technical Research Report*, 1953).

An interesting variation of the common rating scale is that involving the forced-choice technique. This, in its simplest form, requires the rater to choose between two descriptive statements, deciding which is more characteristic of the person rated. In one instance, both paired choices may represent desirable behavior, in another instance, undesirable behavior. In either case, the members of the pair appear to be equally acceptable in terms of desirability, but actually they represent different kinds of behavior. Instruments have been developed using groups of three, four and even five statements.

Below is a pair of statements concerning one aspect of a pupil's social relationships:

A. Shares his interests with the group
B. Listens attentively while others relate their experiences

Since the rater must choose between what appears to him to be equally complimentary statements, the "halo effect" is counteracted, and the judge is prevented from giving only cursory attention to the items. Actually, as determined by validity studies, the choices do not represent equal degrees of personal-social development. Choice A might reflect more maturity than choice B.

Although there is still much research to be done and many problems to be resolved, the forced-choice technique may prove to be helpful in developing more adequate instruments for evaluating personal-social adjustment in our schools. This technique is also being used successfully in self-report inventories, such as the *Gordon Personal Profile* (see Appendix E). In completing the items, the pupil himself determines which statements best describe his behavior.

Problems

9. The United States armed forces have made use of the "man-to-man" type of rating scale in evaluating officers. The individual doing the rating is first asked to

think of the best, the poorest, the average, etc., officer in his experience. Each man to be rated is then compared with these models. Could this procedure be successfully adapted to the classroom situation?

10.   Merit ratings of teachers by either the administrators or fellow teachers is a highly controversial issue in the public schools. What do you think of the practice? What problems must be met if it is to be used successfully?

Check Lists.   Check lists make it possible to record aspects of behavior rapidly. They are simply lists of personality descriptions or traits that the recorder notes as present or absent in individual pupils. Some schools construct their own, and a particularly valuable device is developed when the whole staff cooperates under a leader who is well informed about child growth and development. The experience of constructing a check list may then prove to be effective in-service training.

One of the best known standardized check lists is the *Vineland Social Maturity Scale.* The items are arranged in the order of their increasing average difficulty and represent progressive maturation in self-help, self-direction, locomotion, occupation, communication, and social relations. Below are some excerpts from the scale, ranging from those designed for very young children to those for an adult:

"Crows"; laughs
Follows simple instructions
Relates experiences
Goes to school unattended
Makes telephone calls
Performs responsible routine chores
Buys own clothing
Looks after own bath
Assumes responsibilities beyond own needs
Shares community responsibility

This scale has many possible uses. It can serve as: (1) a standard schedule of normal development to be used repeatedly for the measurement of growth or change; (2) a measure of individual differences and, consequently, of extreme deviation that may be significant in such problems as mental deficiency, juvenile delinquency, and child placement or adoption; (3) a qualitative index of development variation in abnormal subjects such as the maladjusted, the unstable, the psychopathic, the epileptic; (4) a measure of improvement following special treatment, therapy, and training; and (5) a schedule for reviewing developmental histories in the clinical study of retardation, deterioration, and rates of growth and decline.

Interviewing.   An interview with a pupil often *supplements* and *verifies* other information about his adjustment. Since the teacher is able to observe a child in only a limited variety of situations, a face-to-face encounter with no peers present provides an opportunity to observe his reactions closely and with greater attention than is possible in the classroom. Since the interview is less objective and reliable than paper-and-pencil inventories it should not supplant them. Furthermore, its lack of economy precludes its use with all pupils. At times it is most helpful with those pupils having special problems.

Several schools of thought exist concerning the interview approach. Part of the disagreement concerns the degree to which the pupil is allowed to dominate the interview, in other words, the degree of permissiveness the teacher exercises. Despite differences of opinion on this point, a number of suggestions will serve as guides for effective interviewing.

1. Be certain that you have a desirable purpose for the interview. With a purpose in mind, you can prepare for the interview by checking relative available data and formulating what you hope to accomplish.
2. Rapport must be established. Certainly a teacher cannot expect to get helpful information if he calls in a pupil after a misdemeanor and uses this as the basis for a conference. Good relationships between the pupil and the teacher can hardly be expected if the discussion revolves around an interpersonal difficulty. What the teacher says in establishing rapport is not nearly so important as how he says it and whether he is encouraging good feeling between the pupil and himself. Try to help the pupil to see that you are sincerely interested in him and his problems.
3. Guide the discussion so the pupil has an opportunity to express his feelings. If you ask questions that can be answered with a "yes" or "no" he may respond with the expected answer.
4. Avoid communicating a note of finality at the end of the interview. Suggest that there will be opportunities for other conferences if they seem desirable. The pupil should feel that the interview has been helpful and satisfying to him. If it appears that he does not, set a time for another interview.
5. After the pupil has left, make a short written summary of the salient points of the interview to place in his cumulative record. Do not trust your memory.

Interviews with parents can also yield useful information for evaluating a pupil's personal-social adjustment. As in interviewing the pupil, it is important to have a purpose in mind. Know what gaps of information you need to fill; parents can be an excellent source of missing information about behavior problems.

There are advantages in having the parents come to the school for interviewing as well as in visiting them at home. As a home visit gives the teacher a picture of a pupil's home life, a school visit lets the parent see how his child spends the day. Some parents may feel more secure in their homes because many of them recall painful childhood experiences that are, unfortunately, associated with school. Among the disadvantages to visiting the home are the shame some parents may feel about their home's physical appearance and the possibility of other family members interrupting the interview.

In learning to know the father and mother, a teacher may come away with a better understanding of the pupil in the light of parental reactions. One teacher wrote of a home visit:

The time could have been spent to no better advantage. I developed an insight into Ann's problems that I've never had before. It will be much easier for me to be sympathetic with her at school now. I'm certain that I shall conserve considerable emotional energy. Frankly, I wonder how Ann has been able to adjust so well to our classroom environment. Coming from a middle-class home, I'm afraid I didn't realize how some people live.

Problem

11.   What symptoms by the pupil might indicate the need for a home visit? What factors should the teacher keep uppermost in his mind when interviewing parents? How might you proceed with the hostile or withdrawn parent?

Projective Techniques

The general idea of projective techniques is to present the pupil with some unstructured and ambiguous situation and then to note his reaction to it. Since the individual has no clues from the examiner, he will tend to react to the situation in terms of his own personality. Whatever he does or says in such a situation will be influenced by his experiences and his state of mind at the moment.

Two very common projective tests used by highly trained specialists in clinical diagnosis are the *Rorschach Inkblot Test* and the *Thematic Apperception Test,* commonly called the *TAT.* (The *Children's Apperception Test (CAT)* is similar in type to the *TAT* and is designed for children of ages 3–10). The *Rorschach* is composed of ten inkblots that serve as unstructured and ambiguous stimuli, exciting the individual to a performance giving expression to the pattern of his personality. They are presented to the subject in a given order and he tells what he sees in each. The *TAT* consists of a series of pictures that may be interpreted in many ways. The subject is asked to tell a story about each picture, emphasizing how the scene was initiated, what is happening, how the characters feel, and what will probably result. The test is based upon the well-recognized fact that when a person interprets an ambiguous social situation, he is likely to expose his own personality as much as the phenomenon under scrutiny. Absorbed in his attempt to explain the objective occurrence, he becomes naively unconscious of himself and of the scrutiny of others and, therefore, less vigilantly defensive. To a trained ear, he is disclosing certain inner tendencies and cathexes,[1] wishes, fears, and traces of past experience (Murray and others, 1938).

Cronbach (1970, p. 651) emphasized the difference between the two kinds of test. He classifies the *Rorschach* as a stylistic-type test and the *TAT* as a thematic type. In other words, the stylistic type indicates the style with which a pupil handles a problem, while the thematic type emphasizes the content of his thoughts and fantasies. He indicates, however, that the specific strengths are not mutually exclusive and that of the two, the thematic test more nearly examines "the whole person" yielding possible information on emotions, attitudes, and cognitive processes.

There are numerous other projective procedures less well known than the above instruments. Several of these are quite similar to the *TAT*. Some present pictures as does the *TAT* while others require the examinee to draw his own pictures and interpret them. Varied approaches employ the use of finger painting, clay modeling, and doll play in unstructured situations with an opportunity for the pupil to project himself.

Another procedure in projective testing is the use of verbal materials such as word association; a list of stimulus words is read and the subject responds with another word. When he responds with unusual words or slowly, it is indicative of problem areas.

An additional example of the use of verbal materials is the sentence completion test. Partial sentences are presented such as:

My greatest difficulty is _____.
In working with other people I _____.

The completed sentences may be scored for the content as in the case of the *TAT* or the responses may be coded in terms of healthfulness of adjustment.

The classroom teacher generally is not trained to use these instruments and procedures. Their administration and interpretation require the knowledge and experience of the trained clinician; he will be familiar with the limitations of validity and reliability of these instruments and the bases for their use and interpretation. Schools fortunate enough to have psychologists on their staffs may find that they will employ projective testing for certain difficult behavioral problems. In skilled hands these procedures may provide helpful information with a comparatively small outlay of time and effort.

Problem

12.   Projective techniques such as the *Rorschach* and the *TAT* are administered only by highly trained clinicians. List the types of information that the classroom teacher should know about these tests. In what kinds of situations might you refer a child for testing of this type?

[1] Webster's Third International Dictionary defines a cathexis as an "investment of libidinal energy in a person, object, idea, or activity."

Sociometric and Related Techniques

One of the most valuable sources of information about the personal-social adjustment of pupils is their peers. Instruments that cause pupils to rate their classmates in various ways are known as sociometric techniques. Teachers will find it helpful to use these means to verify their judgment of pupils for a number of reasons. First, the teacher has an opportunity to observe boys and girls only in a limited number of situations. Second, the relationship between teachers and pupils is different from that between pupils and their peers; teachers represent authority and children respond to authority in different ways. Third, a teacher may lack objectivity in his observation.

Teachers may look on sociometric techniques as a lot of unnecessary bother, feeling that very little additional information can be obtained through their use, since, on the whole, good teachers have been quite successful in determining the degree of a pupil's adjustment to the group. There continue to be some very bad misjudgments, however. One study (Bonney, 1947) showed that the adolescent who is "smooth" and successful with his teachers is generally overrated, while those who get along well in the small group but antagonize the teacher, or respond poorly to him, are often underrated. In another report (Cunningham and others, 1951) a fourth-grade girl who was judged as most accepted by her teacher was ranked by her peers only twenty-first in a class of thirty-two on a social distance scale. The teacher had based his judgment on the observation that "some boys remarked that Pearl is pretty. Children take up for her when she is in trouble. When they hurt her feelings in a group and make her cry, they voluntarily go to apologize to her."

Teachers who use sociometric techniques are quick to admit that they have at times misjudged the relationship among pupils. Social interaction is so complex a process that many feelings are expressed in such a way that even the keenest observer cannot detect them. Pupils may admire certain traits in each other that completely overshadow behavior the teacher considers undesirable. It is also possible that the observer may, because of his own background, emphasize undesirable characteristics disproportionately.

Sociograms.   The sociometric test is a device for getting preferences among associates to determine the social structure of a group. One method of administering the test is to ask pupils to list in order of preference the three persons in the class with whom they would most like to work on a project. A sociogram is constructed by drawing a map showing, by means of names and lines, the choices of each pupil. This depicts the social structure of the group for a particular moment in a particular situation that prompted the members' choices. To obtain a complete picture of the social interaction in the group, it is necessary to give several tests involving varied situations. Pupils do not always choose the same persons for work on different assignments. The choices expressed by a pupil represent what he would like. They do not necessarily indicate what the situation is. For example, several students may indicate by their choices that they would like to be a part of the group populated by two or three leaders. If one were to observe them in the classroom, however, he would find no interaction between them and the pupils of their choice. This explains why the sociometric test can provide information that may not be available to an observer.

A natural circumstance should be selected to initiate the test, such as reseating a group, forming committees, or a similar activity. The teacher should emphasize that he will keep the pupil's preferences confidential. They must understand they may choose anyone; in some schools, where separation of boys and girls is encouraged, children may think that they must choose only from their own sex. Finally, sufficient time should be given for all pupils to make their choices.

The following is an effective way of wording the sociometric question (adapted from Jennings, 1959):

> "Our next unit is on the western movement in the United States. You have decided that you would like to take certain projects and work on them in committees. Each of you knows with whom you would like to work. Now I am going to pass out some cards. Print your name in the upper right-hand corner and then number from '1' to '3' on the left hand side of the card like this. (Illustrate on the blackboard.) Beside the '1' write the complete name of the person with whom you would like most to work in a committee. After '2' indicate your second choice and after '3' your third choice. You may choose either a boy or a girl, but of course the person must be in this class. I will arrange the committee members so that you will be with at least one of those whom you have chosen."

It is also possible to ask the children to list at the bottom of the card the name of anyone with whom they would prefer not to work. This procedure has serious limitations, however, since it is in contradiction to the social philosophy that the teacher should wish to develop in his class. When a group of eleventh graders was asked to list classmates whom they preferred not to have on their committees, a number of parents said that the pupils were disturbed by the request. Even though there were a number of cliques that operated among them, students were unhappy about having to "black-ball" someone.

The primary-grades teacher may let the children give their choices orally if they cannot write. One second-grade boy reported that he had chosen Tom because he couldn't write Marjorie, the name of his best friend. A problem also arises when children do not know each other's names. Pupils must be well acquainted before the sociometric test can be used effectively.

Figure 32 is an illustration of a sociogram of a fourth-grade class of twenty-five pupils. Only first and second choices are shown; the solid lines indicate first choices and the broken lines, second choices. The boys' names are enclosed by boxes, the girls' by circles.

Notice the sex cleavage in this class. Only one pupil, Joe, has chosen another of the opposite sex. Sue, Ann, and Jean form a clique. There are a number of mutual choices. Prominent among these are Mike and Dan, Rick and Loran, Sharon and Shirley, and Milton and Robert. There are also several isolates—pupils whom no one has chosen: Donna, Wesley, Philip, and Jack. Complete directions for constructing a sociogram such as this are given by Jennings (1959).

After the sociogram is constructed, it should be evaluated. The individual pupil should be considered first: Who are his preferences? Who has chosen him? The pupils should then be considered as a group: Who was chosen most often, very seldom, or not at all? Are there any small groups who have chosen each other and seem to stand apart from the class as a whole? Does

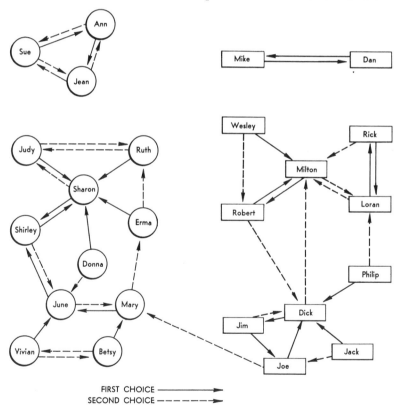

FIRST CHOICE ⟶
SECOND CHOICE ⟶

FIGURE 32.   Sociogram of a Fourth-Grade Class.

the group tend toward cleavages, boys choosing boys and girls choosing girls? Do urban children fail to choose rural children and vice versa? The answers to these questions may prove surprising when the teacher compares them with his own reactions.

The sociometric interview, a by-product of the sociometric test, is used to obtain information and explanations from children. For example, John, a high-school junior, said that he chose Bill because he wasn't as cocky as Tom. Actually, the sociogram indicated that Tom was well liked and had shown his effectiveness as a leader many times. John and Tom were rivals for high marks as well as for social position in the school, and this struggle had had its effect on John's feeling toward his rival. Tom, on the other hand, had given John his first choice for committee work. When queried about his reasons for this choice, he said simply, "John has good ideas."

Care must be taken in the interview not to place the pupil on the defensive because of his choices. The teacher should not say, "Why did you choose Bill?", but "How did you decide to choose Bill?" If the teacher finds that his duties do not leave him time to interview the whole class, he may select those few about whom he is most concerned. He might also get from all pupils written statements of the reasons for their choices. Of course, he must assure them of his intent to keep the information confidential. Written statements of this kind are seldom effective unless the teacher has excellent rapport with his class.

Both Gronlund (1959) and Jennings (1959) give specific suggestions for using the sociogram. However, a teacher will be wise not to use set formulae for dealing with group problems. Rather he should use the information as a basis for formulating hypotheses concerning procedures for helping isolates, coping with cliques, and improving the cohesiveness of a group.

Problem

13.   In a junior high school, sociograms of each seventh- and eighth-grade section were constructed by the guidance counselor on the basis of choices made in group guidance sessions during the fall semester. These data were then released to the teachers. Evaluate this procedure.

Social Distance Scales.   The sociogram is limited in the degree to which it can show the complete social structure of the group. Since each pupil typically has only three choices, we have no information on why he failed to choose other classmates. As one fourth grader said, "I didn't have enough choices to choose Sally." However, she did not choose Billy because "He is such a tattletale."

The social distance scale overcomes this particular weakness. It is possible to use this instrument to determine the degree to which the individual accepts or rejects the group as well as the degree to which the group accepts or rejects him. Table 24 shows how thirty-two elementary school pupils reacted to two classmates in terms of certain social situations. The number of checks for each item on the scale received by the most accepted child and the least accepted child are listed. Interestingly enough, this researcher found in studying many children that everyone was accepted by at least one person and even the most popular were not approved by everyone. In the above study, only four of the thirty-two children did not have their names checked on the entire range of the scale.

Nevertheless, the questions used in this technique are definitely limited. If our objective is to promote peer acceptance, we may wonder about the effect of an item like "Wish he were not in our room." Some teachers prefer not to use social distance scales because items of this kind are in opposition to their goals.

TABLE 24.   Social Acceptance of Two Pupils.

Item on scale	Checks for pupil 1 (Most accepted)	Checks for pupil 2 (Least accepted)
1. Would like to have him as one of my best friends.	20	2
2. Would like to have him in my group but not as a close friend.	7	15
3. Would like to be with him once in a while but not too often or for a long time.	3	4
4. Do not mind his being in our room but do not want to have anything to do with him.	1	3
5. Wish he were not in our room.	1	8

From Cunningham and others, 1951, p. 172; reproduced by permission of the Bureau of Publications, Teachers College, Columbia University.

"Guess Who" Questionnaires.   Another method of obtaining reports from pupils is to have them match their peers with a list of behavioral characteristics. The teacher makes a list of characteristics ranging from complimentary to unfavorable. The pupils then indicate those classmates who, in their opinion, fit each description (Hartshorne and May, 1929). Since pupils often know each other better than the teacher does, it is possible to get a great deal of information about many aspects of their adjustment. The following examples illustrate the kind of item that has proved helpful (Cunningham and others, 1951, pp. 419–422).

Here is someone who likes to talk a lot, always has something to say _____ .

Here is someone who waits for somebody else to think of something to do and always likes to follow the suggestions which others make _____ .

Here is someone who is very friendly, who has lots of friends, who is nice to everybody _____ .

Children may list themselves or as many pupils as fit the description. It is also possible that some pupils will feel that certain items apply to no one in the class. When the teacher tabulates the number of times each pupil is mentioned for each description and finds some individuals referred to by a large number of the class, it is significant information. No doubt he should disregard mention by only one or two, although possibly some children are not well known and are mentioned infrequently for this reason.

Self-Report Inventories

Since no one has an opportunity to observe an individual under as many or as varied situations as he himself, a biographical data blank elicits important factual information. The self-report test attempts to tap the wealth of information that a person has about his feelings, interests, and attitudes. If a number of standardized questions are chosen that can be relied upon to show differences among individuals, one has the basis for the so-called paper-and-pencil "personality," interest, and attitude inventories. It is obvious that the reliability and validity of these instruments depend to a great degree on how adequately the individual can or will report the facts. It is possible that some pupils with severe emotional problems cannot satisfactorily interpret their feelings and behavior to make a valid report.

Biographical Data Blank. Factual information about an individual's past history has been found helpful in predicting a pupil's future success on the job or in higher learning. Hobbies, special activities in and out of school, skills, success with past education, etc., can be used by an evaluator to make a clinical judgment about an individual. In some cases, items have been analyzed to determine the relationship of responses to future behavior of the individual. For example, it may be that in a question such as

How many things have you built out of wood?
  (a) none
  (b) several
  (c) many

the pupil answering *many* probably is more successful in shop class than one answering *none* or *several*. On the other hand, the question may have no predictive value for success in general mathematics. A *Pilot Biographical Data Blank* was useful during World War II to predict success of applicants in learning to fly. More recently, a biographic blank (Schaefer and Anastasi, 1968) was used to predict creativity in adolescents. A 165-item inventory was grouped into five sections: physical characteristics, family history, educational history, leisure-time activities, and miscellaneous. *Project Talent* also employed numerous questions of the biographical-data-blank type in the nationwide inventory of human talent. Typical of the questions used are the following:

> How many times have you been president of a class, a club, or other organization (other than athletic) in the last 3 years?
> (a) none
> (b) once
> (c) twice
> (d) three times
> (e) four times
> (f) five or more times
>
> How many books are in your home?
> (a) none, or very few (0–10)
> (b) a few books (11–25)
> (c) one bookcase full (26–100)
> (d) two bookcases full (101–250)
> (e) three or four bookcases full (251–500)
> (f) a room full—a library (501 or more)

Instruments of this type probably have predictive value because they reflect interests, personality traits, and certain abilities related to performance.

Personal Inventories. One of the typical personality inventories designed for school use is the *California Test of Personality*. This instrument was developed in five series so that it can be administered to pupils from kindergarten to adulthood. According to the authors, the primary purpose of the inventory is to reveal the extent to which the pupil is adjusting to the conditions facing him and is developing a normal, happy, and socially effective personality. Each series is divided into two sections. The first part indicates the pupil's feelings about himself (personal adjustment), and the second reflects social adjustment. Each division is further subdivided into six headings having an equal number of questions: eight in the primary series, twelve in the elementary series, and fifteen in the intermediate, secondary, and adult series. Such questions are asked of primary children as: "Do the children think you can do things well?" "Are you asked to play in other people's yards?" Older pupils are queried as follows: Do you visit with several young men and women in your neighborhood? A "yes" or "no" response is made to each question. The authors suggest that a profile be made for each pupil so that serious deviations may be determined and dealt with.

The foregoing inventory is designed to be a measure of traits or components of adjustment. Another approach to the evaluation of personal-social adjustment is through the determination of problem areas. The *Mooney Problem Check List*, which can be used with junior and senior high school pupils, is a self-report instrument whose purpose is to help individuals express their personal problems. The pupil reads through the check list and underlines the problems that concern him. After completing the first step, he is asked to go back over the items he has underlined and circle the numbers of those of greater concern to him. In the high school form there are 330 items representing common problems of adolescents that were collected from reports of pupils. Some of the items in this form are:

Getting sick too often
Awkward in meeting people
Not being attractive to the opposite sex
Being different
Too little freedom in class
Worrying about grades
Afraid of the future

The items are set up in problem areas to facilitate counseling. For the high school form there are eleven areas: health and physical development; finances; living conditions and employment; social and recreational activities; social-psychological relations; courtship, sex, and marriage; home and family; morals and religion; adjustment to school work; the future: vocational and educational; and curriculum and teaching procedures.

It would appear offhand that the pupil who has checked the most problems would be in serious need of counseling. However, an individual may check an item even though it bothers him very little. Since the number of problems checked depends on the willingness of the pupil to express himself, some individuals may not check their most serious problems. It is also possible that one problem may be more difficult for one pupil than a series of problems for another. It should be noted that what may not seem to be a problem to an adult, or at least one of little importance, may be a very real source of concern to the pupil. The first step in helping pupils to better adjustment is finding out what seem to them to be their problems. In some instances, pupils have checked problems which arise out of school or community peculiarities. Thus it is often helpful to get a group summary of the marked items. In one school a large number of pupils checked "teachers lacking interest in students." This was quite revealing information to the faculty, but happily a problem that they could rectify.

Anxiety is a component of personal-social adjustment. A common instrument used in its measurement is the self-report type (Sarason and others, 1960). Pupils rate themselves on items such as: "I often worry about the marks I receive on tests." "I am usually pretty relaxed at school." "I often feel that my classmates do not like the way I do things." However, after doing considerable research in the field, Sarason (1966) is dubious that present anxiety scales reflect the unambiguous anxiety experience that one observes in a truly anxious child. We refer to the anxiety displayed, for example, by a child who, facing his first day of school, experiences psychological pain and refuses to go. Rather, Sarason concluded, they depict a "coping" behavior to avoid the experience of anxiety. For example, dependent behavior may be a way of avoiding the painful experience of anxiety. Nevertheless, the effect on a pupil's behavior, his lack of ability to solve problems, for instance, may be identical to the situation where he is actually experiencing anxiety. Defensiveness can cause as rigid, inflexible a cognitive style as anxiety itself can. The question is not whether anxiety is an important variable to consider in educational performance; it is. The problem is to determine what anxiety scales actually measure.

Extensive investigations of the reliability and validity of the adjustment inventories, particularly of the type represented by the *California Test of Personality*, have been made. One reviewer (Ellis, 1946, p. 425) states:

> There is at best one chance in two that these tests will validly discriminate between groups of adjusted and maladjusted individuals, and there is very little indication that they can be safely used to diagnose *individual cases*, or give valid estimations of personality traits of specific respondents.

In a later survey of personality inventories, the same reviewer (Ellis, 1953, p. 48) states:

> . . . it was found that in most instances the inventories are not measuring the independent traits they are supposed to be measuring; they do not agree too well with each other nor with the results of *Rorschach* and projective tests; they are easily faked; and they usually do not give significant group discriminations when used with vocational, academic, sociometric, and disabled and ill groups. It was especially found that in none of the areas in which they are commonly employed, do personality inventories consistently show significant group discriminations.

According to Ellis, these inventories are valid if they adequately discriminate neurotics from nonneurotics, introverts from extroverts, dominants from submissives, and so forth. But the teacher administers the inventory for other purposes as well. The instruments provide an opportunity for pupils to inform school personnel of their problems. Test scores may also be used to inform pupils how they compare with their own age group. In view of this, the conclusion by Ellis must be evaluated in relation to the school's purpose.

It is suggested that pupil profiles based on subtests of the *California Test of Personality* containing as few as eight or twelve items be used to determine specific peculiarities of an individual's personality traits. Referring to the table of norms for one of these subtests, we find the pupil's score is at the twentieth percentile if he answers five questions correctly; however, if he circles the "yes" for one additional item, his score jumps to the thirty-fifth percentile. A total of seven correct answers places it at the fifty-fifth percentile. This certainly does not inspire confidence in the utility of the norms of this particular inventory. Furthermore, no systematic attempt has been made, in many instances, to validate the items in terms of the descriptive headings under which they are subsumed.

The lack of precision found in the typical personal inventory precludes their satisfactory use in the construction of diagnostic adjustment profiles. If any score is used, the total score would seem to be the wisest choice. Its reliability and validity are superior to those of the subtests.

Despite the limitations mentioned in the foregoing discussion, adjustment inventories can be helpful if they are used in conjunction with other evaluation data. The teacher must understand their weaknesses and under no circumstances use the scores from these instruments as his sole source of information about the pupil. It is possible that the pupil with a low total score may have adjustment problems; on the other hand, the teacher should not assume that a high score necessarily means good adjustment. Faking is common with this type of instrument.[1] Since the test results are much more likely to be valid if the subject wants to be truthful, rapport in the administration of this kind is very important.

One defensible use of these instruments is to screen populations for adjustment problems. Some pupils, especially those who do not interfere with the class routine, may have serious difficulties that an administration of a personal inventory may bring to the teacher's attention. On the other hand, a screening may identify pupils as maladjusted when, in effect, they have no serious problem. These cases are labeled as "false positives." In industry or in the military, the fact that large numbers of adequately adjusted individuals are referred to as maladjusted may prove troublesome. However, in the classroom where teachers are concerned with children as individuals at all stages of development, there is less harm unless the teacher fails to study the child further and to compare test results with additional data. On the other hand, the test scores may well direct the teacher's attention toward some child who was not identified as needing help. Remember, however, that screening should be done on the basis of the total score rather than through the use of subscores.

Despite this admonition, checking on the answers to individual questions of personal inventories may provide leads for further investigation of a pupil's problems. The boy or girl who never enters class discussions and who answers

[1] An attempt has been made in the *Minnesota Multiphasic Personality Inventory* to detect faking, evasion of questions, and habitually giving oneself the benefit of the doubt or vice versa. The subject is rated on these problems through another set of scores. This helps the evaluator to determine how much confidence can be placed in the answers given by the respondent.

"yes" to the question, "Do your classmates seem to think that your ideas are usually poor?" has given the teacher a basis for helping him. Likewise, the pupil who seems willing enough, but who gets discouraged easily, indicates that he needs help in developing independence when he answers affirmatively the question, "Do you need someone to give you a great deal of encouragement in order to do your work well?"

Personal inventories are only one source of information about pupils. If these data are used critically along with other knowledge, they can be of considerable help in evaluating pupil growth in terms of the educational objectives in this area. To suggest that they should not be employed in the classroom because of their limitations is to deny teachers a source of information in an area seriously lacking in effective evaluation tools and techniques.

Problem

14.   Of what specific value are personal-social adjustment inventories in the classroom? Who among the school personnel would be best fitted to interpret and utilize results gained from these inventories?

Ethical Considerations. Questions have been raised about the ethics of requiring individuals to answer very personal questions included in some personal-social adjustment inventories. These have caused some to inquire as to whether such questions constitute an invasion of privacy. Particular attention has been focused on requiring individuals who are not thought to be emotionally ill or "mentally disturbed" to answer questions about private feelings in such areas as religion, family relationships, patriotism, and so forth. Comments in the press and testimony before Congressional committees delineate some of these concerns.

Psychologists defending the use of personal-social adjustment inventories stress their present basic limitations, but emphazie their usefulness when the results yielded by them are considered along with other data. Self-regulation by the psychological profession is helpful, but a basic conflict exists. At the same time the psychologist believes firmly in the dignity and worth of the individual, he is committed to increasing man's understanding of himself and others. Hence, is the use of personal-social adjustment inventories in a given instance an invasion of privacy or a legitimate investigation of man's behavior (Messick, 1965)?

The concern for the problem of privacy in behavioral science research supported by government funds has been so acute that the President's Office of Science and Technology appointed a panel for study and recommendations. Because the use of tests has been one of the concerns of this panel, its recommendations are important to us. They are (Clark, 1967):

1. Those who are doing human research with government funds are to accept responsibility for its ethical propriety.
2. Institutions are to determine their own methodology of review relative to ethical considerations.
3. When consent of subjects and confidentiality of information cannot be met, there must be an explanation included in fund applications.
4. The onus of the burden to protect privacy falls on agencies and scientists and their institutions who receive government research monies; government agencies should not be responsible for reviewing research instruments or designs in this regard.
5. Support of education on the ethics of research is a primary responsibility of institutions and professional associations that are recipients of research money.

Interest Inventories.   The experienced teacher knows that interest plays an important part in the personal-social adjustment of children. The boy who likes sciences and has books available to him in this area will be motivated to read, thereby developing his basic reading skill and his sense of adequacy at the same time. The teacher who involves his pupils in a project that interests them will find that facility in social situations will develop much more readily than if they are made to do uninteresting or irrelevant work.

A particularly important interest for secondary school pupils is the vocation for which they wish to prepare. Two standardized inventories, Strong's *Vocational Interest Blank* (sometimes called the *VIB*) and the *Kuder Preference Record-Form C-Vocational*, have been used extensively for vocational guidance in the secondary schools. The *Kuder-Form E-General Interest Survey* is a revision and downward extension of *Form C*. It is designed for grades 6–12. Two other *Kuder* inventories, *Form D-Occupational* and *Form DD* (the *OIS*), are similar to the *VIB* in that they compare a pupil's response with those of a number of occupational groups. With *Form DD*, which uses the same items as *Form D*, there are direct item-by-item comparisons between an individual's responses and those in numerous occupational and college-major groups. Unlike *Kuder Form D* and the *VIB*, *Kuder Form DD* makes it possible to compare each individual's interest pattern with that of a given occupational group. It eliminates the general reference group of men-in-general or women-in-general. This procedure has proved to be a great improvement in scoring. Future research studies on the use of this instrument will bear watching.

One study (Wilson, 1968) reports that, in comparing the *VIB* and the *Occupational Interest Survey* (*OIS*), most of the similar scales from the two tests are measuring different factors of occupational interest; the use of both tests would result in contradictory information. Additional investigation is needed in order to substantiate these findings.

The *Kuder Preference Record-Form A-Personal* taps an individual's personal and social preferences rather than those related to vocations. It is therefore more like an adjustment inventory than the other *Kuder* forms. Its five scales reflect the following personal and social preferences: (1) preference for being in active groups; (2) preference for familiar and stable situations; (3) preference for working with ideas; (4) preference for avoiding conflict, and (5) preference for directing or influencing others. Only the *Strong Vocational Interest Blank*, the *Kuder Preference Record-Form C-Vocational*, and the *Minnesota Vocational Interest Inventory* are discussed at length in this chapter.

Strong Vocational Interest Blank.   In developing the *Strong Vocational Interest Blank*, a number of items relating to an individual's everyday living was selected. There are 399 items for men and 398 items for women, each grouped into eight parts. For the first five parts men respond by indicating whether they like, dislike, or are indifferent to a series of occupations, school subjects, amusements, activities (repairing a clock, adjusting a carburetor, etc.), and types of people (progressive, conservative, energetic). In Part VI they order a preference for activities by indicating from a series of groups those three that they like to do best and those they like to do least. They indicate a preference for items in Part VII (airline pilots versus airline ticket agents; outside work versus inside work). In Part VIII the respondent signifies whether an ability or characteristic typifies him (I win friends easily, I discuss my ideals with others). In the women's form, items relevant to feminine interests are similarly grouped.

Both men's and women's forms have four types of scales. The *Basic Interest Scales* focus on specified types of activities, such as sales, agriculture, teaching, and science. The respondent can compare his score with individuals in a relevant occupation. For example, occupations scoring high in the science scale are physicists, chemists, biologists, psychologists, etc.

In the *Occupational Scales* the respondent's score represents the degree of similarity with the scores of those in different occupations. It was found, for example, that engineers tended to express similar likes and dislikes. Persons in other fields showed the same tendency to have common interests within the occupational group and to differ from persons of other occupational groups. Thus, an individual could be questioned about his interests to determine how closely they compared to those of individuals who were successful in their chosen fields. The inventory is scored for more than fifty different occupations.

There are a number of *Non-Occupational Scales* developed by comparing responses of two contrasting groups on the *VIB*, namely *Academic Achievement* (those who do well in school versus those who don't), *Age-Related Interests* (men's profile: scores on scale increase with age), *Masculinity-Femininity* (contrast of scores of men and women working in the same occupation), *Managerial Orientation* (men's profile: good versus poor managers),

Occupational Level (men's scale: represents socioeconomic level of one's interests), and *Specialization Level* (men's profile: those who score higher have more education in the field).

The *Administrative Indices* aid in detecting problems in administering and scoring the instrument. For example, the *Total Responses* of the individual should be within two or three of the total number of items. The *Form Check* indicates whether he was using the old or the revised booklet. *Unpopular Items* may indicate that numerous unpopular responses have been selected for one reason or another. The respondent may have eccentric interests; he may be using the wrong booklet; he could have misunderstood the directions; or he may have lost his place on the answer sheet.

A great amount of research has been done with this instrument. Strong (1943) found that interests change very little from age 25 to 55, that there is a little change from 20 to 25 years of age, but that the shifts are considerable between the ages of 15 and 20. He therefore suggests that it would be wise not to use the test with boys under the age of 17 unless they are unusually mature; in any event, an allowance should be made for their youth. Interest scores may be helpful to high school juniors and seniors if the emphasis is on the general direction of a career rather than in a specific vocation. The VIB is oriented toward those occupations that college students enter. (See the *Kuder OIS* and the *Minnesota Vocational Interest Inventory* for the blue-collar vocation interests.)

The Kuder Preference Record—Vocational.   This instrument illustrates another method of construction. As in Strong's *Vocational Interest Blank,* a large number of items were collected describing everyday life. However, instead of emphasizing the interests of those in the various occupations and then attempting to determine if a person's interests were like theirs, Kuder sought to describe the interests of a subject through a logical grouping of items. If a pupil showed an interest in a certain group of items, it could be said that he had an interest in activities related to that group. Altogether there are ten areas of interest and a verification scale to identify those who answer the items carelessly or without understanding.

The *Kuder Preference Record—Vocational* has 168 items organized in groups of three. The pupil decides which of the three he likes most and which he likes least. He is forced to choose even though he likes or dislikes them equally. In the first example shown in Figure 33, the examinee has punched a hole in the left-hand circle in front of the letter *R.* In this way, he has indicated that of the three activities, *P, Q,* and *R,* he would most like to visit a museum. By punching the hole in the right-hand circle beside letter *Q,* he indicates that of the three activities he would like least to browse in a library. Similarly, in the second example, he would like most to collect autographs and would least like to collect butterflies.

DIRECTIONS:

A number of activities are listed in groups of three. Read over the activities in each group. Decide which of the three activities you like *most*. There are two circles on the same line as this activity. Punch a hole with the pin through the left-hand circle following this activity. Then decide which you like *least* and punch a hole through the right-hand circle.

P	Visit an art gallery	O	P	O
Q	Browse in a library	O	Q	⊖
R	Visit a museum	⊖	R	O
S	Collect autographs	⊖	S	O
T	Collect coins	O	T	O
U	Collect butterflies	O	U	⊖

From Kuder, 1951; reproduced by permission of Science Research Associates.

FIGURE 33.   Items from Instructional Example of the Kuder Preference Record—Vocational, Form CH.

A sample *Kuder* profile is shown in Figure 34. This profile of Jim Spencer, a high school junior, shows that he has very little interest in the computational and scientific areas. Jim's father is an engineer and holds an important executive position in his firm. Both parents are anxious that their son choose engineering as a vocation. Jim's record throughout elementary school has been satisfactory. His IQ on the *Henmon-Nelson Tests of Mental Ability* administrated at the end of the eighth grade was 136. His scores on the *Iowa Tests of Basic Skills* showed no difficulty in the basic subjects. However, in high school his final marks in algebra, plane geometry, and general science were below average. He had to repeat biology during the summer session. During his junior year he was in serious difficulty with his mathematics and science courses, though he had completed one of the best projects in social studies. He had also become a behavior problem and was absent from school quite often. Because he refused to cooperate at band practice, he was suspended from that organization.

Although the preceding data do not represent a complete case history, it seems apparent that Jim's interests are more closely related to other vocational fields than to engineering. His superior academic ability will probably be wasted if he is forced to continue his present course of study. Quite possibly a career in a social science would be appropriate for him.

The descriptive nature of the *Kuder* provides a suitable basis for counseling. Through statistical analysis, it has become possible to translate *VIB* scores into descriptions of traits as well. The form for the *Kuder* is also the same for both sexes, while the *VIB* for women is less complete than the men's form. The scoring of the *VIB* is complex and time-consuming, although it can be scored commercially for a nominal fee. On the other hand, the pupil can score his own *Kuder* record in a few minutes and the results are available immediately. It is not surprising, therefore, to find the *Kuder* used in the secondary school much more extensively than the *VIB*.

Studies indicate that the *VIB* odd-even reliability coefficient is about 0.80. The *Kuder Preference Record—Vocational* reliability coefficient is about 0.90. No adequate consideration has been given to the stability of the *Kuder*, however. One study shows a considerable shift of high school pupils' low and high interest areas when there is a difference of several years between initial and second testing (Millinson and Crumrine, 1952). Retest scores reported in the manual on the *VIB* over long periods of time, when compared with initial scores, show a relationship as high as 0.80.

A number of studies by Strong (1951; 1952a; 1952b) have shown that scores on the *VIB* have considerable criterion-related validity. In several follow-up investigations, he found a very definite relationship between the occupations in which the subjects were employed and their interest test scores. The *Kuder*, on the other hand, has not had this thorough an investigation of its criterion-related validity.

Faking is an important consideration in the test validity of interest inventories, just as it is in the personal-adjustment inventories. An examinee suitably motivated can successfully fake the *Kuder Preference Record*. Because the intent of the items is not so obvious in the *VIB*, it is less easily faked. When tests are given for employment purposes, apparent motives could promote untruthful answers, but when used with secondary school pupils, it would seem that little is gained from faking.

Despite its shortcomings, the *Kuder* has earned a place in the secondary school testing program. It is of some help to the counselor and teacher, since it focuses attention on general fields of interest rather than on the interests of successful people in various occupations, as in the case with the *Vocational Interest Blank*. However, the teacher or counselor needs to exercise caution against overinterpretation. Effective evaluation must include the use of other data gathered from varied sources as an adjunct to the interest inventory scores.

Minnesota Vocational Interest Inventory. Another instrument, the *Minnesota Vocational Interest Inventory*, should be mentioned because it is useful with non-college-bound students. It is more heavily oriented toward vocational activities than the *VIB* is. Published in 1965 and modeled after the *VIB*, it provides 21 scales for such occupations as stock clerk, milk-wagon driver, painter, and machinist. It also has nine area scales for determining an examinee's likes and dislikes for activities common to several occupations,

NAME **Spencer**   **James**   **R.**   AGE **16** SEX **M**   GROUP **Grade 11**   DATE OF TEST **1-9**
Print Last   First   Initial   M or F

First Revision, February 1951
REPRODUCTION BY ANY MEANS STRICTLY PROHIBITED

PROFILE SHEET

for the

KUDER PREFERENCE RECORD
VOCATIONAL

Forms CH, CM

MEN and WOMEN

DIRECTIONS FOR PROFILING

1. Copy the V-Score from the back page of your answer pad in the box at the right.   [40]

   If your V-Score is 37 or less, there is some reason for doubting the value of your answers, and your other scores may not be very accurate. If your V-Score is 45 or more, you may not have understood the directions, since 44 is the highest possible score. If your score is not between 38 and 44, inclusive, you should see your adviser. He will probably recommend that you read the directions again, and then that you fill out the blank a second time, being careful to follow the directions exactly and to give sincere replies.

   If your V-Score is between 38 and 44, inclusive, go ahead with the following directions.

2. Copy the scores 0 through 9 in the spaces at the top of the profile chart. Under "OUTDOOR" find the number which is the same as the score at the top. If your score is not shown, draw a line *between* the scores above and below your own. Use the numbers under M if you are a man and the numbers under F if you are a woman. Draw a line through this number from one side to the other of the entire column under OUTDOOR. Do the same thing for the scores at the top of each of the other columns. If a score is larger than any number in the column, draw a line across the top of the column; if it is smaller, draw a line across the bottom.

3. With your pencil blacken the entire space between the lines you have drawn and the bottom of the chart. The result is your profile for the *Kuder Preference Record—Vocational.*

   An interpretation of the scores will be found on the other side.

S R A   Science Research Associates, Inc.
259 East Erie Street, Chicago, Illinois 60611

A Subsidiary of IBM

From Kuder, 1951; reproduced by permission of Science Research Associates.

FIGURE 34.   Kuder Preference Record Profile Sheet.

such as mechanical work, health service, and carpentry. Tradesmen-in-general selected from a wide variety of nonprofessional occupations were used as the reference group.

This inventory does not differentiate as well among the vocations as the *VIB* does. One reason may be that, when employed at the higher work levels, an individual usually derives satisfaction from intrinsic interest in the job itself. On the other hand, at the lower levels extrinsic factors such as self-recognition, the paycheck, and the security provided tend to be more important (Darley and Hagenah, 1955).

Problems

15. The *Kuder Preference Record* is often administered during the ninth grade as an aid in the selection of high school courses and for prevocational planning for the pupil. Although counselors know that interests may shift, they find the inventory useful. Why?

16. What do you see as some of the strengths and weaknesses in the elimination of the general reference group for scoring the *Kuder Occupational Interest Survey?*

Attitude Scales and Questionnaires. The concept of attitude refers to the way individuals act and think toward and about people, objects, and situations they encounter, as a result of their previous experiences. The school is committed to the development of certain basic social attitudes in its pupils. Among the attitudes that can be learned are those toward race prejudice, bigotry, consideration, religion, democracy, and quality of man. Evaluation of attitude formation and change becomes just as important, then, as achievement in the basic skills.

The formal instruments for attitude measurement fall into two categories: opinion polling and attitude scales. Neither is very useful to the classroom teacher. Their value lies chiefly in their utility as research tools. The Gallup poll is a typical opinion survey. A person is generally approached with a single question that he is usually asked to answer with "Yes," or "No," or "Undecided." The results are typically reported in terms of the percentages of answers given in each of those categories.

Attitude scales are generally of the Thurstone (Thurstone and Chave, 1929) or Likert (1932) types. Thurstone sets up his scales so that an attitude can be measured on a continuum from unfavorable to highly favorable. A number of statements representing various degrees of favorableness give the subject an opportunity to express his feelings. For example, in measuring attitude toward the law, the excerpt in Figure 35 shows that a favorable attitude is given a higher value. Those with low numerical values suggest an unfavorable attitude. The subject identifies those statements with which he agrees and those with which he disagrees. His score is the average of the scale values of the statements toward which he is favorable.

Put a check mark (√) if you agree with the statement.
Put a cross (×) if you disagree with the statement.

			Value
( )	6.	I believe in the use of force to overthrow the law.	0.2
( )	15.	The law is made in response to the pressure of lobbies in Washington.	2.9
( )	16.	Some laws command our respect while others are mere regulations.	6.1
( )	9.	The law is more than the enactments of Congress; it is a sacred institution.	10.5

From Thurstone and Katz, 1931; reproduced by permission of the University of Chicago Press.

FIGURE 35. Excerpt from Thurstone's Scale for Measuring Attitude Toward the Law.

A subject's position on the scale of attitude toward the law is then determined by finding the average of all the scale values of statements with which he agrees. Suppose that out of the twenty items on this scale he checked statements having the following values: 10.1, 10.5, 9.1, and 6.1. He would then have the average of 35.8/4 = 8.95 or 9. The items on Thurstone scales are generally on a continuum from one to eleven. Therefore, this individual appears to have a favorable attitude toward law.

In the Likert method, statements are never neutral toward the object in question but are favorable or unfavorable in varying degrees. The subject reacts to each statement on a five-point scale, indicating that he either strongly agrees, agrees, is uncertain, disagrees, or strongly disagrees. His score is computed simply by weighting the responses from five to one for a favorable statement beginning with strong agreement. Values are assigned in reverse order for unfavorable statements.

The Likert method is illustrated by the following two items (from Likert, 1932; reproduced by permission of the Science Press) taken from a scale designed to measure attitude toward blacks on the part of white people. It will be noted that both items have the A circled, which means that the subject agreed with both statements. However, since the first item is favorable to blacks, the "Agree" has a value of four. The second item is essentially unfavorable, and so the reverse order of scoring gives it a value of two. The total score on the scale is the sum of the values of all items. The maximum possible score is five times the total number of items.

Encircle one of the symbols preceding each of the following statements: A stands for "Agree," SA for "Strongly Agree," D for "Disagree," SD for "Strongly Disagree," and "?" for "Uncertain."

SA Ⓐ ? D SD If the same preparation is required, the Negro teacher should receive the same salary as the white.

SA Ⓐ ? D SD Negro homes should be segregated from those of white people.

Reliability of the Thurstone-type scales by the split-half method yields an average coefficient of about 0.80, which is good for an instrument with so few items. The coefficients of reliability for the stability method are much lower. Likert scales have been found to have roughly equivalent reliability coefficients.

Determining the relative validity of attitude scales has been a difficult problem, chiefly because of a lack of adequate criteria by which to judge test scores. The question arises as to whether verbalized opinions actually represent attitudes. Although behavior can be checked, of course, individuals behave in different ways for different reasons. A pupil may say that he likes school and show outward signs of full cooperation. He may nonetheless dislike teachers and his classwork intensely, but find it expedient to foster good will so that he can stay on the basketball team. As is true of other self-report techniques, attitude evaluation is likely to be most valid when the pupil has no reason for falsification.

Unfortunately, standardized instruments for attitude measurements have not developed to the point where they can be practically useful to the classroom teacher, who must in large part depend on other evidences of attitude formation and change. Through observation and sociometric data, he will be able to evaluate these changes if he directs his attention toward them and systematizes his approach.

To obtain objective data, a teacher must look for attitudes in pupil behavior. Pupils may say that honesty is the best policy, but do they cheat, lie, or steal? Do they accept other pupils despite their social status? Are they responsive to the needs of others? Do they have a scientific attitude? Do they get all the facts? Do they draw logical conclusions? The teacher who has stated his educational objectives in terms of changes in pupil behavior will be able to infer attitude development and change from the modified actions of his pupils. If he then records this development in anecdotal records, if he files some of the answers to open questions, and if he summarizes these data for the group, he will make progress toward effective evaluation of attitudes.

Problem

17. There is common agreement that the degree of validity of attitude scales is generally low at best. Nevertheless, describe possible uses of these instruments in a classroom or in a group guidance session.

SUMMARY

The needs of our society emphasize the importance of adequate personal-social adjustment in schoolchildren. Fostering achievement in this area of development is as much the responsibility of our schools as the teaching of basic skills is. To provide effective learning situations leading to maturity, teachers must understand emotional problems. They must be able to differentiate between adequate adjustment and atypical behavior. It is apparent that they need to develop skill in diagnosing many less serious behavioral problems. They must determine causes and produce solutions.

Evaluation of personal-social adjustment, therefore, plays an important role in the school's instructional program. There are many approaches to this evaluation. Observing children is one of the best ways of determining how well they get along with their peers and the degree of their emotional maturity. Often this can be done in the natural situation, although care must be exercised to prevent the biases of the observer from interfering with objective reporting. To this end, it is helpful to separate reports from interpretations in anecdotal records.

Rating scales and check lists, which direct and objectify observation, can also provide quantitative data, making it possible to pool the evaluations of several observers. Many schools have constructed instruments to meet their own needs. Unfortunately, not many helpful standardized scales or check lists are available to the teacher. Still another source of information about a pupil's personal-social growth is the teacher-parent interview.

Standardized projective instruments, designed chiefly for use by clinical psychologists, are available. The present standardized instruments provide situations in which ambiguous stimuli allow an individual's personality to influence his reactions. The teacher should be informed about the utility of these instruments so he can refer pupils for testing if the need arises.

Children can report much information about each other that is not always available to teachers and parents. Such devices as the sociogram, social distance scale, and "guess-who" questionnaire can indicate how well a pupil is accepted by his peers and can reveal specific strengths and weaknesses of his personality. Follow-up interviews, in which an attempt is made to find reasons for specific choices or descriptions of children, may reveal certain adjustment problems.

Pupils should also be able to tell much about themselves since no one has so good an opportunity to observe an individual in so many different situations as he himself. Self-report tests, such as personal inventories, interest inventories, attitude scales, anxiety scales, questionnaires, and biographical data blanks, are based on self-reporting. One of the most severe drawbacks of these instruments is the faking of answers by pupils who are motivated by a desire to make themselves appear different than they really are.

Of late there has been much concern about the ethics and violation of privacy in testing individuals. Congress has investigated the situation and a study panel has been established.

A teacher should collect as much information about a pupil from as many different sources as is consistent with the need to help the child and with the appropriate ethical considerations. He must know that no one test score or single observation should be relied upon for complete evaluation. Because personal-social adjustment is such a complex process, it demands extensive and varied approaches in evaluation. In this evaluation process the teacher must exercise every precaution to be discreet with any data. There is a fine line between the dictum that a teacher should collect as much information about a pupil from as many different sources as possible, and the problem of ethics in doing so.

Suggested Readings

Amrine, M. (ed.) Testing and public policy. *American Psychologist*, 1965, **20**, 857–993; 1966, **21**, 401–478.
> These two issues of the *American Psychologist* contain testimony presented to committees of the Congress that were investigating the criticism of the use of psychological tests, particularly paper-and-pencil personality inventories. Invited comments from government officials and other individuals are also included.

Bauernfeind, R. H. What to look for in a review of an interest inventory. *Personnel and Guidance Journal*, 1964, **42**, 925–927.
> The author raises important questions in determining whether an interest inventory is appropriate for a specific group and purpose.

Bennett, C. C. What price privacy? *American Psychologist*, 1967, **22**, 371–376.
> A very stimulating discussion on the issue of "privacy." The author states that "privacy is a graceful amenity, generally to be fostered, but with discriminating restraint and with due recognition of obligations as well as privilege."

Campbell, D. P. The 1966 revision of the Strong Vocational Interest Blank. *Personnel and Guidance Journal*, 1966, **44**, 744–749.
> One of the authors of the *VIB* discusses the revised instrument. He elaborates on eight points of change, delineates some of the revision problems, and discusses the use of the instrument with pupils. Rothney is a severe critic of the instrument (see J. W. M. Rothney. Test Review: Strong Vocational Interest Blank, *Journal of Counseling Psychology*, 1967, **14**, 187–191). Campbell later answers his criticism (see D. P. Campbell. Reaction to Rothney's review. *Journal of Counseling Psychology*, 1967, **14**, 192).

Crites, J. O. Interests. In R. L. Ebel (ed.), *Encyclopedia of Educational Research*. (4th ed.) London: Macmillan, 1969. Pp. 678–686.
> The topics of dimensions of interests, development of interests, and correlates of interests should provide meaningful additional information.

Cronbach, L. J. *Essentials of psychological testing*. (3rd ed.) New York: Harper & Row, 1970. Chapters 14, 15, 16, and 17.

Extended discussions will be found on interest inventories, personality measurement, and systematic observation. The author compares, contrasts, and criticizes various procedures and instruments.

Gronlund, N. E. *Sociometry in the classroom.* New York: Harper & Row, 1959.
The three parts into which this book is divided constitute a detailed description of how to construct and administer the sociometric test in the classroom, and how to interpret its results.

Kuder, G. F. A rationale for evaluating interests. *Educational and Psychological Measurement*, 1963, **23**, 3–10.
This article is useful for those who wish to explore further the rationale and history of development of the vocational interest inventories. It emphasizes points such as the development of vocation keys and the importance of overlapping of the keys.

Kuder, G. F. The occupational interest survey. *Personnel and Guidance Journal*, 1966, **45**, 72–77.
The author of the instrument discusses its important features, problems of development, and use. The discussion will give the reader an insight into the working of this kind of instrument.

Layton, W. L. *The Strong Vocational Interest Blank, research and uses.* Minneapolis: University of Minnesota Press, 1960.
This volume includes a series of papers read at an institute concerning the *Vocational Interest Blank.* Such topics as longitudinal studies of interests, validity, correlates of interest, and maturity are presented.

Masia, B. B. What to look for in a review of personality inventory. *Personnel and Guidance Journal*, 1964, **42**, 1030–1034.
Three main functions traditionally assigned to personality measurement in the schools are discussed. Limitations of achieving these purposes are indicated. The author cites information that the user of personality inventories should know to interpret a review intelligently.

Shaw, M. E., and J. M. Wright. *Scales for the measurement of attitudes.* New York: McGraw-Hill, 1967.
The authors list the items in 176 attitude scales covering forty years of scientific work. In addition to describing the subjects, and commenting on technical data, they delineate the strengths and weaknesses of each scale. It is a good basic reference work.

Spielberger, C. D. *Anxiety and behavior.* New York: Academic Press, 1966.
This is a book of readings with discussions by recognized authorities in the field of anxiety measurement and research. It will help the reader understand anxiety and its relationship to behavior.

Weitz, H. Some practical problems in interest measurement. *Measurement and Evaluation in Guidance*, 1968, **1**, 56–62.
Examples and practical solutions are given various problems calling for the use of particular interest inventories.

References Cited

Bonney, M. E. Sociometric study of agreement between teacher judgments and student choices. *Sociometry.* 1947, **10**, 133–146.

Clark, K. E. Privacy and behavioral research: Preliminary summary of the report of the panel on privacy and behavioral research. *Science*, 1967, **155**, 535–538.

Cronbach, L. J. *Essentials of psychological testing.* (3rd ed.) New York: Harper & Row, 1970.

Cunningham, R., and others. *Understanding group behavior of boys and girls.* New York: Bureau of Publications, Teachers College, Columbia University, 1951.

Dale, G. A. A comparison of two groups of elementary school children classified for school adjustment on a basis of teacher rating. *Journal of Educational Research,* 1941, **35,** 241–250.

Darley, J. G., and T. Hagenah. *Vocational interest measurement: Theory and practice.* Minneapolis: University of Minnesota Press, 1955.

Ellis, A. The validity of personality questions. *Psychological Bulletin,* 1946, **43,** 385–440.

Ellis, A. Recent research with personality inventories. *Journal of Consulting Psychology,* 1953, **17,** 45–49.

Froehlich, C. P. and J. G. Darley. *Studying students.* Chicago: Science Research Associates, 1952.

Gronlund, N. E. *Sociometry in the classroom.* New York: Harper & Row, 1959.

Haggerty, M. E., W. C. Olson, and E. K. Wickman. *Haggerty-Olson-Wickman Behavior Rating Schedules.* New York: Harcourt, Brace & World, 1930.

Hartshorne, H., and M. A. May. *Studies in service and self-control.* London: Macmillan, 1929.

Jennings, H. H. *Sociometry in group relations.* (Rev. ed.) Washington: American Council on Education, 1959.

Jersild, A. T., and others. *Education for self understanding.* New York: Bureau of Publications, Teachers College, Columbia University, 1953.

Kuder, G. F. *Kuder Preference Record-Vocational, Form C.* Chicago: Science Research Associates, 1951.

Likert, R. A technique for the measurement of attitudes. *Archives of Psychology,* 1932, No. 140.

Messick, S. Personality measurement and the ethics of assessment. *American Psychologist,* 1965, **20,** 136–142.

Millinson, G. G., and W. M. Crumrine. An investigation of the stability of interests of high school students. *Journal of Educational Research,* 1952, **45,** 369–383.

Murray, H. A., and others. *Explorations in personality.* New York: Oxford University Press, 1938.

Sarason, I. B. The measurement of anxiety in children: Some questions and problems. In C. D. Spielberger (ed.), *Anxiety and behavior.* New York: Academic Press, 1966. Pp. 63–79.

Sarason, I. B., and others. *Anxiety in elementary school children.* New York: John Wiley, 1960.

Schaefer, C. E., and A. A. Anastasi. Biographical inventory for identifying creativity in adolescent boys. *Journal of Applied Psychology,* 1968, **52,** 42–48.

Shaffer, L. F., and E. J. Shoben, Jr. *The psychology of adjustment.* (2nd ed.) Boston: Houghton Mifflin, 1956.

Sparks, J. N. Teachers' attitudes toward the behavior problems of children. *Journal of Educational Psychology,* 1952, **43,** 283–291.

Stouffer, G. A. W., Jr. Behavior problems of children as viewed by teachers and mental hygienists. *Mental Hygiene*, 1952, **36**, 271–285.

Strong, E. K., Jr. *Vocational interests of men and women*. Palo Alto: Stanford University Press, 1943.

Strong, E. K., Jr. Interest scores while in college of occupations engaged in 20 years later. *Educational and Psychological Measurement*, 1951, **11**, 333–348.

Strong, E. K., Jr. Nineteen-year follow-up of engineer interests. *Journal of Applied Psychology*, 1952a, **36**, 65–74.

Strong, E. K., Jr. Twenty-year follow-up of medical interests. In L. L. Thurstone (ed.), *Applied psychology*. New York: Harper & Row, 1952b. Pp. 111–130.

Symonds, P. M. *Diagnosing personality and conduct*. New York: Appleton-Century-Crofts, 1931.

Technical Research Report, PRB 1077. Personnel research for the United States Military Academy, Washington: The Adjutant General's Office, 1953.

Thurstone, L. L., and E. J. Chave. *The measurement of attitude*. Chicago: University of Chicago Press, 1929.

Thurstone, L. L., and D. Katz. *The measurement of social attitude toward the law*. Chicago: University of Chicago Press, 1931.

Tolor, A., W. L. Scarpetti, and P. A. Lane. Teachers' attitudes toward children's behavior revisited. *Journal of Educational Psychology*, 1967, **58**, 175–180.

Wickman, E. K. *Children's behavior and teachers' attitude*. New York: The Commonwealth Fund, 1928.

Wilson, R. N., and H. E. Kaiser. Comparison of similar scales on the *SVIB* and the *Kuder, Form DD. Journal of Counseling Psychology*, 1968, **15**, 468–470.

Wrightstone, J. W. Observational techniques. In C. W. Harris (ed.), *Encyclopedia of educational research*. (3rd ed.) London: Macmillan, 1960. Pp. 927–933.

Using Evaluation to Improve Learning

Part Five attempts to help the reader apply his understandings of measurement and evaluation in the classroom. Chapter 14, "Diagnosis and Remediation of Problems," is devoted to outlining procedures and suggesting materials and tests to aid in diagnosing and prescribing remediation in severe learning difficulties. Practical examples are included to provide the teacher with information for the selection of tests and interpretation of test data. Specific difficulties in such subjects as reading, arithmetic, and writing are treated. The philosophy of diagnostic teaching as effective teaching directs the discussion throughout.

Chapter 15, "Determining and Reporting Growth," focuses attention on the pupil's development and how we can best use the results of measurement to aid the school and the home in helping him achieve his potential. In this context, the purposes of final marks for informing pupils, parents, and school personnel are discussed. It is suggested that specific evidence of pupil progress should be based on the school's educational objectives, among these being data on test performance, procedure and product evaluation, class participation, and projects and reports. Various methods of marking and reporting these data are given, such as the letter-number systems, check lists, written correspondence, and teacher-parent conferences. Finally, suggestions for improving marking and reporting are outlined. The chapter concludes with a discussion of promotion as it relates to final marks.

The last chapter is Chapter 16, "A Schoolwide Program of Evaluation." It stresses the importance of organizing a program of evaluation rather than one of testing alone. It also emphasizes that we must be concerned with the inputs and operations of the educational program rather than the outputs alone. The program should be developed democratically rather than imposed on the teachers by administrative officers.

CHAPTER 14

Diagnosis and Remediation

of Problems

There is more to gardening than having a "green thumb." When the expert gardener's plants do not grow well, he knows there is a reason, and he tries to determine the source of the trouble. Is an insect, a fungus, or an improper soil condition causing the damage? He searches for evidence that will help solve his problem. When he has identified the parasite or disease, he determines the treatment, which may consist of spraying fungicides or insecticides on the affected plants. The gardener knows, however, that all insecticides are not lethal to all insects, that a certain fungicide will not destroy all fungi, and that plants differ in their tolerance of various kinds of chemicals.

The gardener's approach is like that of the teacher who realizes that all members of the group of pupils he is teaching do not have the same abilities. Some of them are not growing well scholastically, and the causes must be found and remedies applied. He knows that the textbook for the class will be too difficult for some pupils, too easy for others. Some children are not able to do long-division exercises because they lack skill in multiplication, addition, and subtraction. Others are proficient in long division and can be challenged only by more advanced work in mathematics. The teacher tries to avoid the mistake of frustrating the slower pupils or boring the more able. With a range of ability and achievement from three to nine grade levels in most classes, he knows that good teaching must begin with information about the ability and achievement of each pupil.

MEANING OF DIAGNOSIS AND REMEDIATION

If a school is to reach its educational objectives, each teacher must recognize and understand the complex aspects of behavioral changes. Since a pupil's development tends to be sequential, schools must provide the most effective sequence of experiences, that is, those that will bring about behavior consonant with the abilities of the individual (Cook, 1951). Because growth patterns differ among individuals, causing various degrees of maturity at the same age, and because a developmental sequence in behavior is necessary, the teacher must determine where the individual pupil stands in this sequence, and what marks the limits of his potential.

The teacher sees each individual within the group as having different problems. In practice, of course, pupils in a class have many common difficulties and can be grouped for instruction. For example, in a class where a few advanced pupils know how to multiply common fractions, those who do not can be taught as a group. And certainly, as a gardener waters the whole garden, there are many opportunities to bring the entire class together for instruction, like listening to a poem or story, watching a demonstration, or discussing initiation of a project.

In helping the individual, the teacher must determine the stage of his development and his peculiar learning difficulties. This is educational diagnosis. Some years ago, educational diagnosis was confined for the most part to academic knowledge and skills, but its scope has kept pace with the modern concept of education, which emphasizes all aspects of development. Thus the development of the nonintellectual aspects of the pupil's personality is as much the legitimate concern of his teacher as his academic knowledge and skills. Indeed, research has shown that personal-social adjustment and personality development cannot be divorced from learning knowledge and skills.

Remediation, which is nothing more than good teaching, is possible only when the teacher understands the basis of a pupil's difficulty, and seeing his needs, teaches to meet them. Good teaching implies several things: first, that we meet the child at his own level of achievement and start from there; second, that we know something of the experiences and problems he has met in reaching that level; third, that we are aware of how present learning relates to the future sequences. The child who has suffered agonies of frustration and humiliation in arithmetic classes will present a more complex problem of remediation than his friend who simply doesn't understand long division.

DIAGNOSIS

Educational diagnosis centers on three questions. Which pupils have learning difficulties? What are the strengths and weaknesses in their achievement? What factors have caused their unsatisfactory achievement?

Identifying Pupils Having Difficulty

There are a number of ways to locate pupils with learning difficulties. One of the most effective is the survey approach. Survey achievement tests of the kind included in a school testing program are specifically designed to find pupils who need remediation. When a serious lack of achievement shows up, the teacher will need information about the pupil's scholastic aptitude to make the achievement score more meaningful. Perhaps the child is achieving as well as can be expected in terms of his potential; a pupil is not retarded simply because his score is lower than the class average. Perhaps some pupils, particularly at the secondary level, need to change their educational and vocational goals. Others may have average or above average achievement but are still below their potential. It is these brighter pupils who generally benefit most from remediation because there is a wider disparity between their achievement and their ability.

A teacher will often discover from test data that his entire class has a specific weakness. One fifth-grade teacher found that all of his pupils were below the grade norm in rate of reading, although they were above average in scholastic ability. Another uncovered a weakness in study skills; a third, difficulties with fractions; a fourth, spelling.

Many sources of information are helpful in locating the pupil who needs help. One may contact a child's former teacher, because past achievement must be evaluated. Attendance records and data on personal-social adjustment may provide clues. Information in a pupil's cumulative record, such as an anecdotal record, perhaps, may prove helpful. For example, some of the highest academic achievers are in serious need of guidance in their social relations. Case histories show that some pupils, having no friends, strive for high scholastic achievement as a means of compensating for lack of personal-social development.

Problems

1. Define retardation with regard to academic achievement. Illustrate with specific examples. The general public customarily links the term "remedial instruc-

tion" with the below-average pupil or slow learner. What subtle influence has this exerted on educational programs?

2.   A high school biology teacher who meets with 150 pupils per day along with being responsible for a tenth-grade homeroom, maintains that, under these circumstances, individual pupil diagnosis is an impossible task. What arguments would you use to refute the position he is taking?

Determining Strengths and Weaknesses

The pupil's improvement is the goal of all diagnosis and remediation, and to achieve it, a good teacher helps the pupil correct his weaknesses by building on his strengths. For example, if he has a reading disability, it is just as important to know that he is good in his word attack skills as it is to know that he is poor in his use of context clues. One of the basic principles in effective remediation is that the pupil must experience success, and building on his strengths makes this possible.

Competencies in Diagnosis.   Determining a pupil's strengths and weaknesses requires essential diagnostic skills that a teacher must develop even though he is not a trained clinician. He should first understand the principles of learning and their application. Second, he should be able to recognize behavioral symptoms that suggest the causes of specific difficulties. Third, he should be able to apply diagnostic and remedial techniques.

Before a teacher can be a successful diagnostician, he must be familiar with the psychology of learning in general, and with regard to specific subject areas. He can formulate useful hypotheses about the nature of a child's difficulties far more readily if he has a grasp of the way learning normally develops in a subject area and is aware of the difficulties most frequently encountered in it.

Take, for example, the problem of transfer of learning. If we learn how to shift gears in a Chevrolet, most of us can then shift gears in a Ford. Learning from the original task has transferred to the new. But if we are then asked to drive a Volkswagen with a four-forward-speed shift, our previous learning tends to interfere with the new task, and this psychological process is known as the negative transfer effect.

Research in transfer of learning indicates that though considerable transfer occurs from some learning tasks to others, there are cases in which there is little transfer unless we teach for it. In one such case, a teacher discussed word endings and rhyming with his class. He followed the prescribed procedures carefully; *Jane* rhymes with *rain, cane, train*. A little girl went home and announced, "We learned about rhyming today. Try me. You say *Jane*." When the parent dutifully obeyed, the child responded with a triumphant "*rain, cane, train*." Asked whether other words rhymed with *Jane*, the child said no, only the three she had just given them. Clearly her concept of rhyming was the relationship among four specific words and no useful learning transfer was gained.

We can further illustrate the importance of understanding in learning as it applies to concept formation. A teacher cannot give a pupil a concept; concepts can only be formed by the individual out of his own experiences. Research shows, for instance, that difficulties in all arithmetic processes can be traced to a failure to understand basic number concepts. Too often understanding is evaluated on the basis of the products of learning without considering learning processes. When a pupil's answers are correct, does he understand the problem? He may not. It is possible that he got the correct answer by coincidence or, having dutifully learned a method, followed it blindly down a corridor of computation to the proper reply. Can you explain why you invert and then multiply when you divide by a fraction? If you cannot, you were probably taught how to perform the operation without understanding the process. Understanding number concepts comes through many experiences in which the pupil is required to think through the reasons for performing an operation. Therefore, diagnosis in mathematics should begin with a study of the pupil's concept of a number as it relates to his particular difficulty.

A second competency in diagnosis is the ability to recognize symptoms related to the physical and psychological aspects of growth. Sometimes the underlying causes of a pupil's difficulty are so complex that the teacher will need to rely on the services of a specialist for diagnosis, but he should be familiar with symptoms of poor vision, inadequate hearing, and lack of energy. Further, the informed teacher understands the common mental mechanisms used by poorly adjusted children to reduce their tension. Pupils with severe anxieties are not ready for learning. Remediation is, after all, exceedingly demanding of the pupil, requiring both concentration and a high degree of motivation.

The psychological bases of a problem may be hard to reach. One pupil of above average intelligence was having great difficulty with arithmetic. His achievement in subjects demanding verbal facility was high, relationships with his peers appeared satisfactory, and his rapport with his teacher was excellent. The teacher tried every approach he could think of to help the pupil but made little progress. Finally, in a case history, he discovered the child's mother had always done poorly in arithmetic and persisted in talking about it. The youngster had identified with his mother, building up a self-concept of his inability that completely negated his efforts.

The third competence is the ability to use the various diagnostic and remedial techniques, devices, and materials with understanding. Among these devices are standardized and classroom tests and practice exercises. Detailed discussions of specific difficulties, particularly in arithmetic and reading, are to be found in the literature, and suggested remedial procedures are outlined in detail. The teacher can do much diagnosis and remediation without a clinical specialist. Available printed materials help him in the classroom, and this experience expands his knowledge.

Factors Causing Unsatisfactory Achievement

The teacher who knows the more common causes of unsatisfactory achievement has some basis for making intelligent hypotheses about the difficulties of his pupils. Lack of achievement may be attributed to personal and/or environmental factors reflected in scholastic aptitude, physical development, and health, with special emphasis on visual and auditory abilities, and personal-social adjustment.

Scholastic Aptitude.   If a child has low scholastic aptitude, lack of achievement cannot necessarily be interpreted as the result of faulty teaching or lack of application. He may be doing as well as he can. Many pupils who are poor in reading and mathematics have low scholastic aptitude scores, but a low score does not necessarily mean that a pupil has low innate mental ability. His score on most group tests of scholastic aptitude can be seriously affected by poor reading ability, lack of motivation, or distractions from poor test administration. Therefore, a principal diagnostic problem is to get as accurate an estimate of the pupil's ability as possible. The teacher should not conclude that a pupil has a low scholastic aptitude unless he has considered various data. If at all possible, an individual intelligence test should be administered to those pupils who have low achievement and low group scholastic aptitude scores. It is often surprising to learn that some of these pupils have higher mental ability than some of the high achievers. Too often teachers equate ability to pass tests, conformity, good grooming, and verbosity with high intelligence. Many shy, withdrawn, poorly groomed or nonconformist pupils excel intellectually.

Health.   A pupil's health influences his ability to achieve, because learning is hard work. Many things cause inadequate stamina: malnutrition, glandular difficulty, or improper rest. In one fourth-grade class a teacher discovered that forty percent of the pupils were consistently watching television until after ten o'clock on school nights. It is understandable that this group was difficult to teach. Poor health may also cause excessive absences, which are especially detrimental to achievement in such subjects as arithmetic and reading, with their requirement of cumulative sequences of skills.

There is no unequivocal evidence that visual anomalies are a primary cause of educational disability. While some pupils with good vision are poor readers, others who fail to pass vision tests read well, but the latter perform with considerable discomfort. Many cannot attend to print and can only read for short periods of time. If a pupil is nearsighted, and if his teacher uses a visual approach, the pupil may miss basic instruction.

Poor hearing is a distinct disadvantage. Pupils may successfully camouflage hearing anomalies with apparent attention and go unnoticed by the teacher. Even pupils who pass common hearing tests may have serious auditory deficiencies. If there is a high tonal frequency loss, it is difficult to differentiate among consonant sounds so that an oral approach to beginning reading distinctly handicaps such a pupil.

An alert teacher can often detect symptoms of poor hearing. Pupils so handicapped may speak without expression and with the voice pitched unnaturally. Because they cannot differentiate among sounds, they are often poor spellers, and their speech and pronunciation lack clarity and precision. When they cannot understand what is being said, their attention often wanes; they may stare out the window or disturb other students. Others may frequently request that statements or questions be repeated. Whether speech defects result from loss of hearing or some other cause, they seriously impair a pupil's achievement.

There are also organic symptoms of poor hearing, such as earache, sinus condition, and ear discharge. Because such disorder can be corrected, teachers can prevent permanent disabilities by referring these pupils for medical attention.

Motor coordination is another physical factor to which the elementary teacher in particular should be attentive, since it can have a detrimental effect on handwriting. Because handwriting is important in developing other skills, a disability may have far-reaching effects. If a student writes slowly, he may understand test items but find it impossible to complete them within the time limit. His score implies low achievement but the real deficiency lies in the handwriting.

Personal-Social Adjustment.   The emotionally disturbed pupil dissipates his energy before he can apply it. It is difficult to determine whether emotional difficulties are causing learning difficulties or vice versa. Learning difficulties can at times be cause or effect. Indeed, a pupil may become an outstanding achiever to compensate for some emotional problem. But too often the child with an emotional disturbance finds himself caught in a vicious circle, anxious over lack of achievement, and performing poorly because of the emotional disturbance.

Harris (1970) lists ten kinds of emotional problems that contribute to reading disabilities, but which can also be applied to other subjects.

1. Conscious refusal to learn.
2. Overt hostility—Because some children have built up intense feelings of resentment, they find it difficult to exercise control of their emotions. Pupil-teacher relationships are not conducive to learning.

3. Negative conditioning to reading—Reading has been associated with something the child dislikes intensely like a teacher or punishment. Therefore, he learns to dislike reading.

4. Displacement of hostility—Suppose a child dislikes or fears a parent or a teacher. The child realizes that this person enjoys reading. Since it may arouse feelings of anxiety and guilt to direct his hostility toward this individual, he expresses these hostile feelings toward reading.

5. Resistance to pressure—When an overambitious parent pressures his child to achieve, the reaction of the child may be a disinterest in reading.

6. Clinging to dependency—To avoid growing up a child may cling to a symbol of early childhood—inability to read.

7. Quick discouragement—Because some children lack a feeling of security, they become quickly discouraged. They have little confidence and respect.

8. Success is dangerous—Success may symbolize entering adult society and competing as a rival with a parent. There is an implication for the child that this competition will result in extreme retaliation.

9. Extreme distractability or restlessness—When a child has a high degree of tension, he finds it difficult to control his physical activity. This results in inattention and inability to learn.

10. Absorption in a private world—Daydreams, through which some children fulfill their wishes, result in lack of concentration and inability to learn.

The teacher should be continually aware of symptoms. If a pupil cannot solve his problems in the classroom, he may need to be referred for clinical treatment. Symptoms of aggression, withdrawal, and general problem behavior are often indicative of personal-social adjustment problems. Sometimes antisocial behavior results from a particular incident and passes quickly. Serious and deep-seated problems, however, can be identified by persistence of symptoms.

Environmental Factors. Although it is difficult to identify outside causes of a pupil's learning difficulties, the difficulties quickly show up in the pupil. A poor home environment, where the parents are separated or the child is rejected, may cause personal adjustment difficulties in the child in short order.

Some pupils are handicapped by a lack of intellectual interests in the home. Their parents provide few, if any, books or magazines for them. Lack of travel and other cultural opportunities make it difficult, if not impossible, for them to develop the concepts so readily attainable by those with broader experiences.

Poor teaching may be the cause of learning problems. The pupil may have learning disabilities that become cumulative. He may be under-equipped to learn and emotionally disturbed. Suffice it to say that in diagnosing learning difficulties, one must investigate a pupil's environment to find if the principal cause lies there.

Specific Subject Difficulties.   Learning difficulties often stem from the subject itself. The complex skills demanded by mathematics, language, spelling, and reading present learning problems. Considerable research on learning disabilities has indicated typical and specific errors and has resulted in the design of many diagnostic instruments to help locate them. But the teacher need not always administer a standardized instrument in diagnosis, because informal techniques are effective when used competently.

Buswell and John (1926) studied the common errors made by pupils in arithmetic. Table 25 shows some of their findings. Note the errors made by pupils in the third, fourth, fifth, and sixth grades when they add

TABLE 25.   Frequency of Ten Common Errors in Addition, Subtraction, Multiplication, and Division of Whole Numbers.

	Grade level				
Type of error	3	4	5	6	Total
Addition					
Errors in combinations	81	103	78	58	320
Counting	61	83	54	17	215
Added carried number last	39	45	45	26	155
Forgot to add carried number	37	38	34	17	126
Retraced work after partly done	26	34	39	22	121
Added carried number irregularly	26	30	28	18	102
Wrote number to be carried	34	25	18	12	89
Carried wrong number	28	19	26	14	87
Irregular procedure in column	16	29	23	18	86
Grouped two or more numbers	25	22	21	16	84
Total number of pupils	96	124	116	78	414
Subtraction					
Errors in combinations	62	75	69	40	246
Did not allow for having borrowed	19	50	57	36	162
Counting	43	44	39	10	136
Errors due to zero in minuend	25	39	26	15	105
Said example backward	21	38	29	12	100
Subtracted minuend from subtrahend	47	33	12	4	96
Failed to borrow, gave zero as answer	21	20	14	4	59
Added instead of subtracting	18	9	19	1	47
Error in reading	14	5	13	10	42
Used same digit in two columns	18	15	3	4	40
Total number of pupils	84	109	109	70	372

From Buswell and John, 1926, pp. 136–139; adapted by permission of The University of Chicago Press.

and subtract; similar data are also available for multiplication and division.

The interrelationships among the fundamental processes must be taken into account in any diagnosis concerning them. For example, if a child is struggling with long division because he cannot subtract or multiply, giving him more division problems to work without analyzing his difficulty is an inefficient way of helping him. Learning to subtract will make him competent in long division.

Among the common errors in language are those related to oral speech. Abney (1944, pp. 181–186) lists the following:

1. Incorrect vowel quality: Frequently heard in such words as *get, was, pretty, catch, because, creek, just.*
2. Incorrect consonant quality: Frequently heard in *length, what, luxury, immediately, walking, talking.*
3. Misplaced accent: *positively, research, museum, umbrella, discharge.*
4. Omission of requisite sounds: As in *recognize, family, really, mirror, nearer, February.*
5. Sounding silent letters: In such words as *often, toward, evening, parliament, salmon, corps.*
6. The addition of superfluous sounds: As in *athlete, mischievous, once, prairie, film, portentous, elm.*
7. The utterance of sounds in their improper order: Frequently heard in *children* (not *childern*), *hundred, larynx.*

Willing (1926) analyzed grammar errors in compositions written by secondary school pupils and developed a series of proofreading exercises that teachers may find helpful in diagnosis. Table 26 gives a number of error classifications concerning the agreement of verbs and subjects. As expected,

TABLE 26.   Frequency of Grammatical Errors—Agreement of Verbs and Subjects.

	Number Errors per 1200 Words		
Error classification	8th grade	9th grade	Both grades
Compound subject with single parts	4	1	5
Intervening expressions	5	5	10
Expletive *there* constructions	3	3	6
Don't usages	0	0	0
Subjects such as *each, everyone*	1	0	1
Attraction of predicate nouns	0	1	1
Other cases, verbs following subject	9	4	13
Miscellaneous	3	1	4

From Willing, 1926, pp. 55–63; reproduced by permission of the Bureau of Publications, Teachers College, Columbia University.

ninth-grade pupils had fewer errors than eighth-grade. Other categories reported by Willing are spelling, capitalization, punctuation, sentence structure, and word usage.

Failure to write legibly often requires attention. It is possibly the result of inadequate motor development, but considerable evidence shows that careless formation of a very few letters contributes greatly to this problem. Table 27 presents Newland's (1932, p. 256) data on illegible writing. The table lists the percentage contributions of twelve of the twenty-four common types of error to the total illegibilities recorded. Newland notes that *a, e, r,* and *t* contribute about fifty percent of the illegibilities recorded for all age groups. If legibility is to be improved, the teacher must check these letters and correct errors. It is a waste of valuable time to have intermediate grade pupils drilling on every letter of the alphabet.

TABLE 27.   Analysis of Letter Malformations.

| | Percentages Contributed | | | |
Common types of error	Ele-mentary	Second-ary	Adult	Total
Failure to close letters (*a, b, f, g, j, k, o,*				
p, q, s, y, z)	24	20	16	18
Top loops closed (*l* like *t, e* like *i*)	13	14	20	18
Looping nonlooped strokes (*i* like *e*)	12	27	12	16
Using straight up-strokes rather than				
rounded strokes (*n* like *u, c* like *i, h*				
like *li*)	11	10	15	13
End stroke difficulty (not brought up,				
not brought down, not left horizontal)	11	6	9	9
Difficulty crossing *t*	5	5	9	7
Difficulty dotting *i*	3	5	5	5
Too short (*b, d, f, h, k, l, t*)	6	7	3	5
Letters too small	4	5	4	4
Closing *c, h, r, u, v, w, y*	4	3	3	3
Part of letter omitted	4	4	3	3
Up-stroke too long	2	3	1	2

From Newland, 1932, p. 256; adapted by permission of Dembar Publications, Inc.

Spelling errors may be related to mispronunciation, speech disability, or inability to use phonic skills. A classification of typical spelling errors can reveal this relationship and give the teacher a basis for helping the pupil. Spache (1940) analyzed the errors made by poor and average spellers in the third, fourth, and fifth grades (Table 28) and showed that the average spell-

TABLE 28.   Mean Percent of Errors of Poor and Average Spellers in Third, Fourth, and Fifth Grades.

Spelling error	Poor spellers	Average spellers
Omissions		
Single letter		
Silent	12.0	13.5
Sounded	12.7	9.5
Doubled	5.7	7.4
Syllable	3.4	1.7
Total	30.7	29.9
Additions		
Single letter		
Doubling	3.0	3.3
Nondoubling: phonetic	2.1	5.5
Nondoubling: nonphonetic	9.5	9.2
Syllable	0.8	1.1
Total	14.0	18.0
Transpositions		
Phonetic	1.5	1.5
Nonphonetic	3.2	3.7
Total	4.4	4.8
Phonetic substitutions		
Vowel	17.0	19.8
Consonant	9.3	10.0
Diphthong	2.6	2.6
Syllable	3.5	6.0
Entire word	2.8	1.7
Total	33.5	37.9
Nonphonetic substitutions		
Vowel	3.2	1.6
Consonant	4.3	3.0
Diphthong	0.7	0.7
Syllable	2.0	1.4
Entire word	1.1	0.9
Total	9.5	6.2
Homonyms	1.4	1.7
Incomplete	4.5	2.1
Unrecognizable	3.8	1.8

From Spache, 1940, p. 185; adapted by permission of Dembar Publications, Inc.

ers make more phonetic substitutions than poor spellers who, in turn, are inclined to make more nonphonetic substitutions. Also, average spellers add fewer letters than poor spellers, which may be accounted for by greater use of phonics by the average spellers. Mistakes occur because English words are not always spelled as they are pronounced.

Pupils having difficulty with spelling often have difficulty with reading and vice versa; the skills are closely related. Another, and subtler, cause of reading disability is lack of background, a difficulty in all grades and areas. A first-grade pupil may not have had the visual and auditory experiences to acquire a sight vocabulary. A pupil in secondary school may lack the vocabulary to comprehend his assignments in social studies and physical science. One gifted pupil thought that a cow was about the size of a large dog. He had never seen a cow, though he could very well talk about one. Field trips provide experiences that help make classroom learning meaningful. A lesson in conservation will be much more effective if pupils have actually seen the results of erosion. A discussion of city government will be aided by a visit to the municipal buildings. Words have no intrinsic meaning; they trigger associations from the experiences of the individual. When he has no experiences to associate with the symbol, he can only memorize.

Another cause of poor reading is lack of the systematic development of the basic skills in reading, such as a sight vocabulary, techniques of word recognition, comprehension, and the work study skills. For example, if a child has not developed an adequate sight vocabulary, he may become overanalytical in his reading and break words apart without learning how to blend the syllables or use meaningful phrases and the context to help him understand. In other cases, structural analysis, syllabication, phonics, etc., have been too little emphasized, and the pupil finds himself handicapped in attacking new words. Independent reading demands a system of word attack skills.

Failure to transfer reading skills to other assignments is another difficulty. Teaching reading without applying it to assignments in, for example, biology, too often results in the pupil's inability to do everyday reading tasks. The science teacher needs to discuss main ideas of paragraphs with his students. He should show how skimming, thorough reading, and rapid reading can be applied to his assignments. He should help his pupils initiate vocabulary development programs for themselves, because skills must be applied, not allowed to remain in isolation.

Problems

3. Explain the following statement: "The emotionally disturbed pupil dissipates his energy before he can apply it to learning." Illustrate your answer.

4. A sixth-grade teacher reports that his pupils can do arithmetic computations fairly well but that they are experiencing frustration and defeat in the areas of arithmetic reasoning and problem solving. Apply the principles of diagnosis to this situation by outlining specific steps for this teacher to follow to gain a thorough understanding of the learning problem he faces.
5. Common learning difficulties in the basic skill subjects have been presented. How might teachers in the following curriculum areas approach similar analyses?
    a. Junior high school physical education
    b. Elementary art
    c. Eleventh-grade American history
    d. French I
6. Before classifying a pupil as mentally retarded, what factors must be thoroughly investigated?

REMEDIATION

Remediation would be much simpler if we could apply a trusted formula to each learning disability—a notion as sadly impossible as every other cure-all. Pupils differ, and learning disabilities are rooted in different soils. The source of one pupil's difficulty may be emotional while another suffers from faulty teaching. One pupil's handwriting is illegible because of inadequate motor development while his neighbor is simply careless.

Despite the different techniques and methods for remediation, certain guiding principles apply to all subjects and provide an operational framework.

1. Remediation should be accompanied by a strong motivational program.
2. Remediation should be individualized in terms of the psychology of learning.
3. A continuous evaluation which informs a pupil of results is vital.

Providing Motivation

No remedial technique will be successful unless the pupil can see the relationship between the purposes of the technique and his own needs. Many failing pupils have acute feelings of inadequacy and feel they are unable to succeed, that they are different. Some of them withdraw, and refuse to try; others rationalize by thinking that success is unimportant and that whatever they might learn will never be useful.

The teacher is the catalyst for changing these attitudes. Such pupils long to be understood. Many of them have been lectured, threatened, and rejected until often the first task is to help them rebuild self-confidence. Good remedial teaching has all the hallmarks of good teaching anywhere. The teacher lets the pupil know that he is liked and appreciated; above all he is optimistic and stays optimistic during the pupil's "downs" as well as his "ups." By accepting the pupil, the teacher helps him build a self-security which is vital for effective learning.

Since a pupil develops confidence when he experiences success, it is important that the teacher know his strengths as well as his weaknesses, for the teacher must build on those strengths, starting at the child's level of achievement. It helps if the pupil's first success is dramatized. Presenting progress concretely is effective, particularly for younger children. Charts, graphs, and pictures can all be used successfully, though the device must be attuned to the maturity of the pupil. A device that lets him see his improvement works well. When he competes with himself, he can better his past record and this proves highly motivating.

To sustain motivation, the teacher should stimulate interest in the remedial program and monotony should be avoided like smallpox. Different approaches prevent mental fatigue, and so do materials with high motivational value. If the pupil can help plan his program by selecting materials and procedures, his involvement will often generate a permanent interest basic to the development of his independence.

A pupil's interest may droop if he is forced into remedial activity because some pupils honestly feel that their skills are adequate in spite of painful indications to the contrary. Sometimes allowing them to take a standardized test and helping them analyze the results produces the desired effect. Ingenious teachers use many methods to help a student want to improve, and social recognition is not the least of them. Most pupils find it rewarding to demonstrate progress to their peers and parents. Above all, remedial activities should not be scheduled when they conflict with other things the pupil would like to do. To be required to work a sheaf of arithmetic exercises while a "big game" is going on is hardly motivating.

Evaluating the Program

No remedial program can be based on initial diagnosis without consistent follow-through. In the first place, the pupil's needs will change as he overcomes his learning difficulties. Just as his problems have been cumulative in nature, remedial instruction will be cumulative in its impact. The new is learned in terms of the old.

Secondly, the teacher will want to judge the success of his program. He may have to shift methods and materials to help the pupil learn; all pupils do not respond equally to the same treatment. Only a continual evaluation can determine progress and future procedure.

In the third place, evaluation is important because it lets a pupil know how he is progressing. Motivation to learn goes up when the pupil knows the results of his effort. The less mature the child, the more it is necessary to depict results graphically.

Using Clinical Personnel

Although most teachers are responsible for remedial work, special teachers are occasionally employed to help regular teachers with their problems and often to work with pupils who show severe retardation. Because reading problems are the source of much educational retardation, a number of schools employ reading specialists. Although they are most often found in the elementary schools, some secondary schools are also providing their services. In other schools a subject specialist handles problems in all basic skill or curriculum areas rather than reading alone.

Another specialist who can substantially contribute to a child's improvement is a school psychologist. Although a great share of his work will be corrective in nature, much of it will also be preventive. His task is to sensitize school personnel to the needs of pupils, and to diagnose individual problems and make the proper referrals when necessary. In this role, he serves as a coordinator for all the special services in the school as well as the community. Through him, the varying contributions of remedial teachers, mental health clinics, social agencies, and the home can be effectively utilized.

Problems

7.   Imagine that you are a foreign language teacher. Three of your pupils are having difficulties. Robert works hard but stumbles desperately in dictations and oral work. Al has a natural ear for the language but seemingly cannot understand the grammar. Donna is a rote learner who memorizes long vocabulary lists with ease, but cannot grasp the essential meaning when translating. Describe how you would provide individualized remediation for these pupils.

8.   Some teachers do not report standardized test scores to their pupils as they fear that poor results may be discouraging. Do you agree?

9.   Many regard the school psychologist as a sort of second-class psychiatrist who should solve each pupil's problem in a few brief interviews. What is your conception of the role of this specialist? What kinds of pupils would profit by referral to him?

SURVEYING CLASS ACHIEVEMENT

It is effective to identify pupils with learning difficulties by administering a survey achievement test and a scholastic aptitude test. Pupils who appear to be underachieving may then undergo thorough diagnosis and remediation. The discussion that follows is based on the results of the *Stanford Achievement Test* (Partial Battery) and the *Lorge-Thorndike Intelligence Test (Verbal)* administered in October to twenty-three pupils of a fifth-grade class who attended an elementary school in a small city. Their families varied in socioeconomic status. In analysis of the data, description is given of the use of the class record and the class analysis chart in identifying group as well as individual strengths and weaknesses. Suggestions for individual diagnosis and remediation are presented through a discussion of one pupil's difficulties.

Class Record

A class record was prepared on the basis of the test scores from both tests and is shown in Table 29. The pupil's names are listed in the order of their overall achievement as presented by their battery median grade equivalents. To find the battery median grade equivalent, the grade equivalents for the seven subtests are ranked in order of magnitude; the fourth score from the top or bottom is the battery median grade equivalent. The sex of the pupil is recorded in the first column following the name. His age is listed in the next two columns, his *Lorge-Thorndike IQ* in the fourth column, and the grade equivalent and stanines for the seven subtests of the battery in the following columns.

Class Analysis Chart

The numbers preceding the pupils' names serve as identification numbers when preparing a class analysis chart, such as that shown in Table 30. A column is available for each subtest score. Note that these scores are in terms of stanines. The distribution of stanines for each column is found by writing the identification number of each pupil in the box on the same line as his stanine score. For example, Margaret Adams (#16) has a stanine score of 5 for the *Paragraph Meaning* test. Therefore, a "16" is written in the paragraph meaning column in the box opposite the stanine score of five. The remaining twenty-two numbers are similarly recorded in this column.

For each column, the median stanine score was determined by locating the twelfth score from the top or bottom, and plotted by placing a large dot at the appropriate point in each column. The class profile is found by joining these dots with straight lines.

As you can see, the class analysis chart is a summary of the test results for the entire class. At a glance, the teacher can identify the areas in which the best and poorest work is being done. There is considerable variability in all

TABLE 29. Class Record of Stanford Achievement Test Scores for a Fifth-Grade Class.

Pupil's name	Sex	Age Yr-Mo	Lorge-Thorndike	Word mean.	Par. mean.	Spelling	Language	Arith. comp.	Arith. concepts	Arith. applic.	Batt. median
1. Mary Jones	G	10-2	132	8.8-9	9.2-9*	7.0-7	8.6-8	7.9-9	8.2-9	9.6-9	8.6
2. William Seeber	B	10-1	128	8.8-9	9.2-9	8.0-9	9.0-9	6.5-8	8.2-9	8.0-9	8.2
3. Mary Hillhouse	G	9-8	125	8.8-9	7.8-8	8.0-9	10.5-9	5.2-5	5.2-5	5.4-6	7.8
4. Ann Chitwood	G	9-10	130	8.3-9	9.2-9	6.0-6	8.6-8	5.9-7	7.6-9	7.7-8	7.7
5. Celia Graham	G	10-4	120	7.5-8	6.7-7	7.1-8	10.5-9	5.6-6	5.2-5	5.6-6	6.7
6. Carol Smith	G	10-5	125	6.7-7	6.1-6	6.3-7	6.4-6	6.8-8	6.6-8	7.1-8	6.6
7. Gloria Behrens	G	10-7	122	6.2-7	6.4-7	8.0-9	7.3-7	5.6-6	5.9-6	7.1-8	6.4
8. Sandra Black	G	10-4	123	6.7-7	7.3-8	6.3-7	10.0-9	4.6-4	5.2-5	5.6-6	6.3
9. June Nelson	G	9-10	123	6.7-7	5.1-5	6.3-7	6.4-6	4.1-3	6.1-7	7.1-8	6.3
10. Trudy Lincoln	G	10-4	115	7.1-8	6.1-6	6.3-7	7.5-7	5.1-5	5.6-5	5.4-5	6.1
11. Joe Sills	B	10-3	110	6.4-7	5.9-6	6.4-7	7.3-7	4.6-4	5.2-5	5.6-6	5.9
12. Albert Uken	B	9-11	115	5.7-6	6.1-6	6.3-7	7.7-8	4.6-4	5.6-6	5.1-5	5.7
13. John Sevaar	B	10-2	110	6.2-7	5.3-5	5.3-5	6.2-6	2.9-1	4.9-5	5.1-5	5.3
14. Cindy Bockwitz	G	10-5	104	4.4-4	2.6-1	7.1-8	4.8-5	5.1-5	4.6-4	5.4-5	4.8
15. Florence Weber	G	10-6	.98	5.7-6	4.6-4	4.8-5	4.5-4	3.8-3	3.6-3	4.0-3	4.5
16. Meg Adams	G	10-8	102	4.4-4	5.1-5	4.3-4	2.7-2	4.1-3	4.0-3	4.4-4	4.3
17. Stanley Seward	B	10-4	98	4.2-4	4.4-4	3.3-2	4.9-5	3.6-2	3.6-3	4.4-4	4.2
18. Beverly Hill	G	10-8	122	3.8-3	3.6-3	3.6-2	3.4-3	4.6-4	6.3-7	6.1-7	3.8
19. Carol Jones	G	10-6	94	3.9-3	3.2-2	4.5-4	3.6-3	2.9-1	3.1-2	4.0-3	3.6
20. Peter White	B	9-10	98	3.9-3	3.6-3	3.1-2	3.6-3	2.9-1	3.1-2	4.0-3	3.6
21. Floyd Echart	B	9-9	90	3.8-3	2.6-1	3.1-2	2.4-1	2.9-1	3.6-3	3.4-2	3.1
22. Oscar Biggs	B	10-1	88	2.7-1	2.5-1	2.8-1	2.4-1	2.9-1	2.2-1	2.9-1	2.7
23. Helen Brown	G	10-7	85	2.5-1	2.5-1	2.8-1	2.5-1	2.6-1	2.2-1	2.9-1	2.5

a The first score is the grade equivalent; the second score is the stanine based on the standardization group.

TABLE 30.   Class Analysis Chart for a Fifth-Grade Class.

Stanine	Word mean.	Par. mean.	Spelling	Language	Arith. comp.	Arith. concepts	Arith. applic.
9	1, 2, 3, 4	1, 2, 4	2, 3, 7	2, 3, 5, 8	1	1, 2, 4	1, 2
8	5, 10	3, 8	5, 14	1, 4, 12	2, 6	6	4, 6, 7, 9
7	6, 7, 8, 9, 11, 13	5, 7	1, 6, 8, 9, 10, 11, 12	7, 10, 11	4	9, 18	18
6	12, 15	6, 10, 11, 12	4	6, 9, 13	5, 7	7, 12	3, 5, 8, 11
5		9, 13, 16	13, 15	14, 17	3, 10, 14	3, 5, 8, 10, 11, 13	10, 12, 13, 14
4	14, 16, 17	15, 17	16, 19	15	8, 11, 12, 18	14	16, 17
3	18, 19, 20, 21	18, 20		18, 19, 20	9, 15, 16	15, 16, 17, 21	15, 19, 20
2		19	17, 18, 20, 21	16	17	19, 20	21
1	22, 23	14, 21, 22, 23	22, 23	21, 22, 23	13, 19, 20, 21, 22, 23	22, 23	22, 23

areas of achievement. Few pupils have scores at the very top or bottom of the class in all subtests. Notice that the low point of this class is arithmetic computation. In Table 31, an item analysis indicates that pupils tended to miss items demanding certain computational skills. If these skills are not taught, it is unlikely pupils will develop them. The class does somewhat better in arithmetic application, because needed skill in computation is on an easy level. Typical of test items in arithmetic application are:

1. Ninety children are assigned to three classrooms. What is the average number of pupils in a class?
2. Three pencils cost 10 cents. How many could you buy for $1.00?

The highest points of achievement are in word meaning and spelling. Word meaning is related to good scholastic ability. In this connection, note that the median IQ of the group is 115, which is above average. Spelling

TABLE 31. Item Analysis of the Arithmetic Computation Subtest of the Stanford Achievement Test.

Test item	Right No.	Right %	Wrong No.	Wrong %	Test item	Right No.	Right %	Wrong No.	Wrong %
1	19	83	4	17	24	3	13	20	87
2	17	74	6	26	25	9	39	14	61
3	16	70	7	30	26	8	35	15	65
4	19	83	4	17	27	16	70	7	30
5	16	70	7	30	28	8	35	15	65
6	18	78	5	22	29	5	22	18	78
7	16	70	7	30	30	8	35	15	65
8	16	70	7	30	31	17	74	6	26
9	8	35	15	65	32	6	26	17	74
10	14	61	9	39	33	7	30	16	70
11	11	48	12	52	34	4	17	19	83
12	7	30	16	70	35	4	17	19	83
13	14	61	9	39	36	9	39	14	61
14	12	52	11	48	37	5	22	18	78
15	5	22	18	78	38	3	13	20	87
16	3	13	20	87	39	9	39	14	61
17	11	48	12	52	40	13	56	10	44
18	10	44	13	56	41	11	48	12	52
19	12	52	11	48	42	6	26	17	74
20	11	48	12	52	43	3	13	20	87
21	7	30	16	70	44	5	22	18	78
22	10	44	13	56	45	4	17	19	83
23	4	17	19	83					

ability can be attributed to the school staff's special emphasis on this subject.

As the teacher studies the class analysis chart, he becomes aware of other problems. For instance, Cindy Bockwitz (#14) has a much higher score in spelling than in other parts of the achievement test. Is this an indication that Cindy could improve in other areas? Does it mean that her parents have been drilling her in spelling and find that she excels in this skill? Spelling is not as high level a verbal skill as is reading for comprehension. Cindy's IQ supports the idea that she may be giving spelling special attention.

The teacher cannot assume that two pupils with the same battery median are alike in achievement. Margaret Adams (#16) and Stanley Seward (#17) have battery medians almost alike, yet Margaret is in the second stanine in language usage, while Stanley is in the fifth. There is also considerable difference between them in spelling.

Item Analysis

Another useful aid is an item analysis chart constructed from the right and wrong answers to each item in a subtest. Table 31 lists the responses of the fifth-grade class on the arithmetic computation subtest of the *Stanford Achievement Test*. This diagnostic device gives the teacher a more detailed picture of his pupils' achievement. For example, the content represented by items like 1, 4, and 6 is fairly well learned by the class as a whole, while several items missed by a large percentage of the group represented areas of low achievement.

Items 16, 23, 24, 26, 29, and 35 all require skill with fractions, but there was little instruction in fractions when these pupils were in the fourth grade. They had only been introduced to these skills since all pupils were taught according to a syllabus that made little allowance for individual differences. This was also true for decimals, and resulted in incorrect answers or omissions for items 25, 33, and 36. The pupils had been instructed in division, yet a large percentage missed items 15, 19, and 37. In item 19, a short division exercise ($4860 \div 8$), the problem of placing a zero in the quotient seemed to confuse many pupils, indicating lack of understanding of that particular skill. Many of them selected "67½" as their answer. By a simple check of their work, they should have discarded this possibility.

In a multiple-choice test, it is possible to determine the number of pupils choosing each of the distracters as well as the number answering correctly. When items are machine-scored, the test-scoring machine can easily run the analysis. Because a good test item included plausible distracters, a study of pupils' choices will often give the teacher insight into their difficulties. He will be in a better position to diagnose and, as a result, to prescribe effective remediation.

Problems

10.   Table 29 contains both achievement and mental ability test scores. What general statement can be made about the correlation of each of these sets of achievement test scores with the mental ability scores?

11.   Can you find specific instances of retardation in achievement in the fifth-grade class in question? Are any of the pupils overachievers? In your opinion, what is the chief problem confronting the teacher of this class? What additional information about the pupils would be highly useful to him?

12.   Which pupils in the fifth-grade class under discussion might profit by referral to a reading specialist?

INDIVIDUAL DIAGNOSIS AND REMEDIATION

At this point it is clear that group strengths, weaknesses, and range of ability can be determined from the class record and the class analysis chart. Some individual problems also become apparent. Consider the case of Beverly Hill (#18), who is significantly below the average achievement in language skills of a normal fifth-grade child in the second month of the school year. Beverly has ability that surpasses the average child. Her mental age is 13 years. Therefore her "mental grade" is 8 years (Bond, 1948). Fifth-grade pupils with normal mental ability have a "mental grade" of 5 years 2 months at this stage of the school year. Despite her superior scholastic aptitude, she is definitely below the point a pupil with average mentality should be, except in arithmetic. Even her arithmetic scores represent retardation considering her scholastic aptitude.

Inability to Read

Because there was evidence that inability to read might be the cause of Beverly's difficulties, the teacher wanted to explore several related elements, but needed more information about her specific reading difficulties. Many teachers like to use an informal oral reading test for this purpose. Beverly's teacher selected several interesting narrative passages, each about 200 words long, from material that Beverly had not read. The reading level of the first passage was of first- or second-grade difficulty, the others of increasing difficulty.

This procedure threw considerable light on Beverly's reading problems.

Typical questions asked in an informal reading test are: Does she know the sounds of the vowels and consonants? Can she break a new word into syllables? Can she blend individual sounds together so that she can recognize the word? Does she read with expression, indicating that she is using the context to help identify new words? Does she rely too much on context and fail to recognize certain words, substituting those that make sense but distorting the meaning?

TABLE 32. Scores on the Gates-McKillop Reading Diagnostic Tests, First Administration.

Subtests	Beverly's grade score	Highest possible grade score
Oral Reading	3.8	7.5
Reversals	Poor Score	
Recognizing and Blending Common Word Parts	Very Low Score	
Syllabication	Low Score	

In addition to the informal reading test, the teacher administered the *Gates-McKillop Reading Diagnostic Tests*, a standardized instrument to analyze reading difficulties. Table 32 contains some of Beverly's grade scores on these tests. Her oral score is 3.8, approximately the same as her silent reading score. The other scores indicate her serious weakness in reading fundamentals.

Beverly had developed no systematic method for attacking words. She tended to concentrate on words themselves, rather than on the relationship among them, and thereby lost the train of thought. Even her word-by-word reading was marked at times with considerable confusion. Not only did she make a considerable number of reversal errors, but she had difficulty in blending word parts. A number of letter sounds were confused, particularly *a* and *e*. Recognition of syllables and phonograms was weak and because of her undue attention to word parts and units, she made very little use of context to aid her in pronunciation or comprehension.

What are the differences between a diagnostic and a survey test? A survey test provides a general appraisal of overall achievement in some subject area such as reading. It is not designed to give a detailed picture of deficiencies; that is the province of the diagnostic test. Nor is it constructed to indicate possible causes of inadequate achievement; a good diagnostic test should provide cues for the formulation of hypotheses concerning lack of growth and possible remedial procedures.

The survey test showed Beverly Hill to be very low in achievement of

CALIFORNIA CUMULATIVE RECORD
ELEMENTARY FORM
Confidential Information for use by Professional Personnel

FILE No. (Pencil)

1. IDENTIFICATION DATA

PHOTOGRAPHS

DATES PHOTOGRAPHED (Pencil)

LAST NAME	FIRST NAME	MIDDLE NAME	NICKNAME (Pencil)	CHECK SEX
Hill	Beverly	Jane		M / F / x

BIRTH DATE	BIRTH DATE VERIFICATION	PLACE OF BIRTH CITY (OR COUNTY)	STATE (OR NATION)
2/20/60	b Certificate Birth	Suburban	New York

HOME NAME	ADDRESS	TELEPHONE	IN CASE OF EMERGENCY NOTIFY NAME	ADDRESS	TELEPHONE
Mary L. Hill	101 Olde Ave.	3218	Joe S. Brown Uncle	1805 Lotus St.	8-4532

SCHOOL DISTRICT

NAME	ADDRESS	TELEPHONE
Dr. Ralph Ogden	16 Main St.	8072

2. GROUP SCHOLASTIC CAPACITY TESTS (LABEL OTHER SUB SCORES USED, e.g., PERFORMANCE, PERCEPTION, ETC. DOUBLE SPACES PROVIDED.)

DATE TEST GIVEN	GRADE	NAME OF TEST	FORM	LEVEL	C.A.	M.A.	Total	Verbal	Non-Verbal	COMMENTS	EXAMINER
10/66	1	Otis Alpha (Verbal)	A	Alpha6-8	9-0	124					
10/70	5	Lorge-Thorndike		10-8	13	122					

3. INDIVIDUAL TESTS

DATE TEST GIVEN	GRADE	NAME OF TEST	C.A.	RESULTS AND REMARKS	EXAMINER
11/70	5	Revised S-B, L-M	130 I.Q.	Had trouble with tasks demanding reading skill.	A.J.Smith

4. GROUP ACHIEVEMENT TESTS (Including Reading Readiness) (LABEL VARIOUS SUB SCORES, e.g., VOCABULARY)

DATE TEST GIVEN	GRADE	NAME OF TEST	FORM	LEVEL	READING		ARITHMETIC		LANGUAGE		EXAMINER
11/67	2	Stanford	J	Prim	Par M Wd M 1.1 1.5		Reas Comp 3.1 1.8		Spell 1.5		
10/68	3	Stanford	W	Prim	Par M Wd M 1.8 2.3		Comp Conc 2.9 2.9		Spell 2.5		
10/69	4	Stanford	W	Int I	Par M Wd M 2.3 2.7		Appl Comp Conc 5.1 3.8 5.0		Spell Lang 3.6 3.6		
10/70	5	Stanford	W	Int II	Par M Wd M 3.6 3.8		Appl Comp Conc 6.1 4.6 6.3		Spell Lang 3.6 3.4		

5. PERSONALITY AND INTEREST INVENTORIES, APTITUDE TESTS, AND OTHER TESTS (LABEL VARIOUS SUB SCORES, e.g., EMOTIONAL, SOCIAL)

DATE TEST GIVEN	GRADE	NAME OF TEST	FORM	LEVEL	Pers Soc Adj Adj				COMMENTS		EXAMINER
11/70	5	Calif. Test of Personality	AA	Elem	Kile Kile 50 60						

Reproduced by permission of A. Carlisle and Company.

FIGURE 36. Inside Half of an Elementary School Cumulative Record.

6. INFORMATION CONCERNING INDIVIDUAL ADJUSTMENT

YEAR AND GRADE	INTEREST, ACTIVITIES, LEADERSHIP	FAMILY AND HOME RELATIONSHIPS OUT OF SCHOOL RESPONSIBILITIES	ATTITUDES AND FEELINGS ABOUT: SELF, PEERS, SCHOOL	REFERRALS TO SCHOOL SERVICES AND/OR COMMUNITY AGENCIES
YEAR 19 65-19 66 KINDERGARTEN	Quiet child. Very cooperative.	Shares family experiences. Close family ties.	Has adjusted well to school and to her peers.	
YEAR 19 66-19 67 GRADE 1	Likes to do activities with hands. Doesn't choose books in free time.	Family watches television a great deal.	Sometimes appears to be day-dreaming.	
YEAR 19 67-19 68 GRADE 2	Seems withdrawn since death of father.	Mother is now working. Does not spend as much time with Beverly.	Retarded in reading. Seems un-interested.	
YEAR 19 68-19 69 GRADE 3	Evidences of some leadership. Has several close friends.	Seems to be a close relationship with the Mother.	Has shown considerable interest in arithmetic.	
YEAR 19 69-19 70 GRADE 4	Continues to be liked and accepted by her peers.	Has done some baby sitting with neighbor children during the day hours.	Has applied herself to her school work.	
YEAR 19 70-19 71 GRADE 5				
YEAR 19 -19 GRADE				
YEAR 19 -19 GRADE				
YEAR 19 -19 GRADE				
YEAR 19 -19 GRADE				

FIGURE 36. (Continued).

FORM LM—A. Carlisle & Co., S. F., 1956

7. GROWTH AND DEVELOPMENT THROUGH SCHOOL EXPERIENCES

INDICATE MAJOR CURRICULUM UNIT, DESCRIPTION OF EXPERIENCE, AND DURATION. INITIAL EACH ENTRY. THIS SPACE MAY ALSO BE USED FOR INDICATING DEGREE OF SUCCESS IN SCHOOL EXPERIENCES AND READERS USED

YEAR 1965-'66 KINDERGARTEN	YEAR 1966-'67 GRADE 1	YEAR 1967-'68 GRADE 2	YEAR 1968-'69 GRADE 3	YEAR 1969-'70 GRADE 4
Works well with group and plays independently. Neat; follows directions. Sings in tune; knows many nursery rhymes.	Reading: S-F series. Readiness bks, 3 pre-primers, 1r. primer and primer completed. Also 3 pre-primers of supp (H-M) rdrs.	Readers: S-F series. 1^1 reader ...11/20 1^2 " (H-M)..2/2 2^1 (H-M)..4/15 L-C phonics bks, A & B Cowboy Sam, 1 & 2	Readers: S-F series. 2^1 of S-F and of H-M; workbooks. Eye & Ear Fun, 1, 2, 3 L-C Phonics, bk C	Readers: In lowest group. S-F 3^1 & 3^2 Workbooks: S-F & Readers Digest Skill Builders, 2, 3, 4 Merrill Skilltexts: Niba, Nicky, Uncle Funny Bunny
Knows the letters of the alphabet, names of the colors.	Did not start first reader, but should be ready for it in Sept. Did all bks.	(started 2^1 reader in May, but finds it difficult. Cannot concentrate. Wears glasses, but forgets them.)	Completed S-F 2^2 and began 3^1, but finds it difficult. Dislikes reading.	Math: S-B bk. 4. Neat, accurate. Understands problems but has trouble reading them.
Can write her name.	Math: Knows combinations and understands meaning of concepts	Math: Understands add. & sub., knows basic facts. S-B bk.	Social Studies: Local history, Indians	Social Studies -- Foll. Regional studies. Can't read text. Does not participate in disc.
Cooperative			Math: Average in class S-B bk 3; knows all combinations and 4 processes; accurate and neat.	Science: enjoys experiments, can't read text.
Seems ready for first grade work				
YEAR 19 -19 GRADE	YEAR 19 -19 GRADE	YEAR 19 -19 GRADE	YEAR 19 -19 GRADE	YEAR 19 -19 GRADE

YEAR 1970-'71 GRADE 5

Requirements of U. S. Constitution, American History, State and Local Government satisfactorily completed.
Date Certified _____ INITIAL

Reproduced by permission of A. Carlisle and Company.

FIGURE 37. Outside Half of an Elementary School Cumulative Record.

8. SCHOOL HISTORY

DATE ENTERED	HOME ADDRESS & TELEPHONE	CITY OR COUNTY	SCHOOL & SCHOOL DISTRICT	GRADE	TEACHER	ATTENDANCE	TRANSFERRED TO	DATE LEFT
9-65	101 Olds 3218	Suburban	Suburban Central	K	Shapiro	Perfect		
9-66	"	"	"	1	Wilson	1st week -- trip		
9-67	"	"	"	2	Eddy	1 week -- death of F.		
9-68	"	"	"	3	Wood	Periodic absences		
9-69	"	"	"	4	Banner	No absences		
9-70	"	"	"	5	Green			

9. PARENTS' EDUCATIONAL AND/OR VOCATIONAL PLANS FOR PUPIL: (Pencil)

COMPLETED GRADE 6 or 8 OR ( ) ON [Month Day Year]

	HOME ADDRESS (Pencil)	SPECIFIC OCCUPATION (Pencil)	BUSINESS ADDRESS AND TELEPHONE (Pencil)
10. FATHER'S NAME Deceased			
11. MOTHER'S NAME Mary L. Hill	101 Olds Ave.	Teacher	Elmwood School
12. OR GUARDIAN'S NAME			

CIRCLE | CIRCLE (Pencil)

Pers. Lenses W/m — Yes (No) — Lenses?
Yes (No) — Yes — Lenses?
Pers. Lenses W/m — Yes — No — Lenses?
(Yes) No — Yes No — Lenses?
Pers. Lenses W/m — Yes No — Lenses?
Yes No — Yes No

13. CHILDREN OF FAMILY

NAMES	Year or Born	RELATIONSHIP TO PUPIL	Lives at [home/other]
Beverly Hill	1960		

14. ADULTS OTHER THAN PARENTS LIVING CONTINUOUSLY IN PUPIL'S HOME (Pencil)

NAME	RELATIONSHIP TO PUPIL

15. SIGNIFICANT HEALTH FACTORS

DATE	RECOMMENDATIONS OF HEALTH ADVISER	ADVISER'S NAME
9/67	Glasses prescribed	Jones
	Audiometer reading normal	Jones

DATE	TEACHER'S COMMENTS ON PUPIL'S HEALTH CONDITIONS	TEACHER
11/67	Symptoms of extreme anxiety.	Eddy

Reproduced by permission of A. Carlisle and Company.

FIGURE 37. (Continued).

language skills, but it required a diagnostic test to emphasize weakness in syllabication, recognizing and blending common word parts, and so forth, which are the bases of low performance in the language arts. The *Gates-McKillop Reading Diagnostic Tests* were used in preference to the *Stanford Diagnostic Reading Test* because they are administered individually and sample many potential reading problems. In a number of cases, the *Stanford Test*, which is designed to be group-administered, may be too difficult and too limited in what it measures to differentiate among pupils with serious reading problems.

Determining the Cause

The teacher found from Beverly's cumulative record, Figures 36 and 37, that she had a long history of retardation. She had complained of headaches during her first year of school and, in the second grade, was required to wear glasses for close work. Also, during that year her father had been killed in an accident and her mother had been compelled to work. Beverly was anxious and insecure, and her early school experience probably accounts for the reading difficulty. She was severely handicapped because learning basic skills is cumulative and she lacked a foundation on which to build. Beverly's mother remarried, and both parents expressed concern about the child's achievement. They asked for a conference, so the teacher had an opportunity to enlist their help.

The teacher realized the importance of involving the parents in learning and giving them a positive role in the process. He understood that parental nagging, forcing children to forego normal social activities, or a lack of genuine parental interest in the child can prevent a remedial program from being a success. He also knew that he must give parents specific instructions before they can help. If possible, he must avoid telling them that there is nothing they can do, that everything will work out all right.

Of course it is sometimes difficult if not impossible to elicit parental cooperation. Some parents' own lack of personal-social adjustment prevents them from being close to their children. Some are so absorbed in their own interests and professional lives that they find it impossible to become involved in their children's problems.

During the conference with Beverly's parents, the teacher explained that their child was bright and that her difficulty stemmed from immature word recognition skills and lack of concentration on the meaning and the relationship among the words. It was decided that Beverly should have individual remedial reading instruction each day. Her parents were helped to realize the need for supporting the child emotionally and were asked to praise her liberally for any improvement. They were advised against exerting pressure either overtly or through expression of concern about her progress.

The teacher was also able to discuss television and its relation to Beverly's reading problem. He helped her parents to see that if their own chief interest was television, not reading, it would be impossible to convince the child of the importance of improving her reading, that their habits would have a marked effect on Beverly's. They were advised to discuss both television programs and their reading, drawing Beverly into the conversation, thereby signifying the importance of both in acquiring and formulating ideas.

Providing Remedial Instruction

Removing the cause of a learning difficulty is only the first step. Now Beverly had to be taught to read. In her case, stress was placed on recognition of sounds, syllables, and blending. She was given opportunity for practicing a systematic attack on unfamiliar words and helped to use context for determining meanings. Her left to right orientation was developed.

Attention was also given to improving her reading rate. Beverly was encouraged to time herself on short easy exercises and to keep a record of her progress. To keep her abreast of class work, the teacher made available easy materials on topics under study.

A pupil who has had difficulty in such a basic skill as reading is probably short on confidence. Beverly was given an opportunity to read an easy passage to the class occasionally, but first her teacher made sure that she was well prepared. Recognition of this kind provided a high degree of motivation.

TABLE 33. Scores on the Gates-McKillop Reading Diagnostic Tests, Second Administration.

Subtests	Beverly's grade score
Oral Reading	7.2
Reversals	Normal progress
Recognizing and Blending	
Common Word Parts	Normal progress
Syllabication	Normal progress

At the end of the year, several tests from the second form of the *Gates-McKillop Reading Diagnostic Tests* were administered to Beverly. The scores are listed in Table 33. Notice the vast improvement. The total score in oral reading increased from 3.8 to 7.2. All other scores are now satisfactory. Moreover, her scores on the *Gates-MacGinitie Reading Tests* are as follows:

Test	Grade level
Vocabulary	6.8
Speed and Accuracy	6.3
Comprehension	6.5

Beverly kept a record of the books she read during the year, and at the last count, she had over forty to her credit. Although some were very short and easy, she also had read a number of considerable substance.

All remedial teaching does not have to be done on an individual basis. Elementary school teachers can group pupils in various ways so that special help can be given for special difficulties. More secondary school teachers need to utilize these grouping procedures. The teacher might begin with two groups. Four or five pupils who excel in the course may be grouped for special projects while the teacher works with the majority of the class. Gradually, as the teacher's skill and confidence increase, he can increase the number of groups.

Instructional Placement Reports

Help for relating diagnostic findings in reading to remedial procedures is provided by means of a computer program used with the *Stanford Diagnostic Reading Test, Level II*. It is known as the *Instructional Placement Report* (*IPR*). The IPR provides an initial grouping for instructional purposes based on pupil needs as evidenced by the diagnostic test scores. Needs are defined in terms of scores and patterns of scores. Pupils with similar profiles are grouped and instructional suggestions are provided.

The results of administering the *Stanford Diagnostic Reading Tests* are sorted and reported to the teacher in the following manner:

Group 2

STANINE SCORES

	Reading Comprehension			Vo-cabu-lary	Syl-labica-tion	Sound Disc.	Blend-ing	Rate of Read-ing
	Lit.	Inf.	Tot.					
Christner, Anthon	2	3	3	3	3	3	2	4
Costa, Norman J.	4	2	3	5	3	3	4	3
Gordon, Lawrence	2	3	3	3	2	2	2	4
Haman, Dorothy E.	3	4	3	4	4	4	3	4
Holland, Winifred	2	2	2	2	3	2	3	1

Note that these five pupils have been classified in Group 2. For this group and all others, the teacher is provided with a general group description and instructional suggestions. In the case of Group 2, they are:

Group Description.   The reading skills of pupils in Group 2 are generally very weak. Their comprehension is low; most of them probably have a poor vocabulary; they lack decoding skills; and they read very slowly. They will need intensive, individualized instruction throughout the school year. Careful study will often show that these pupils also have extensive learning problems in other school subjects, especially spelling.

Instructional Suggestions.   These pupils should be placed in a developmental reading program at their level. Such a program should cover these facets of reading:

1. The decoding skills should be taught systematically, including grapheme-phoneme relationships, variant spellings of the phonemes, syllabication, and blending of sounds and syllables.
2. Some instructional time should be devoted to vocabulary development, especially listening vocabulary. Such instruction should include lexical meanings, word parts and derivations, slang and dialects, and idiomatic expressions.
3. These pupils should read books of high interest and low reading level, to develop comprehension skills and interest in reading. This aspect of the program should be given extra emphasis with pupils who lack motivation. The books should be primarily interesting, not challenging in difficulty. Books that are extremely easy to read help to develop reading fluency.
4. These pupils have reading problems of such magnitude as to require more time and assistance than is ordinarily possible in the normal reading program.

Eleven groupings are provided. It is expected that, in the case of most classes, several of the groups will contain three or more pupils, some groups only one or two, and others none. By the way, Group 11 is typically a very small group, containing only unclassified pupils, that is, pupils having a pattern of scores that the computer system could not classify.

Properly used, the *IPR* and similar efforts should offer important help to classroom teachers. They should improve the interpretability of diagnostic test data and strengthen remedial instruction.

Problems

13.   An analysis of Beverly's reading scores has been presented. Does the interpretation given indicate a need for a certain degree of sophistication on the part of the teacher to make maximum use of these tests? How would you explain the meaning of the *Gates* subtest scores to a parent?

14. Parental conferences can be highly important in helping a child. Conversely, if not handled correctly, such meetings may aggravate a situation. Formulate a simplified set of rules or guideposts for the inexperienced teacher.

15. Figures 36 and 37 duplicate Beverly's cumulative record. What additional information do you wish had been included?

16. What criteria would you use to judge the adequacy of a diagnostic test?

17. Compare two reading diagnostic tests using the criteria established in Problem 16. (*Stanford Diagnostic Reading Test* versus *Gates-McKillop Reading Diagnostic Tests.*)

SUMMARY

Good teaching implies that each pupil should achieve in terms of his interests, needs, and potential. There are several reasons why pupils may not be learning. Among these is the promotion of "lockstep" teaching, where every pupil is required to read the same materials, spell the same words, and work the same problems. This is bound to result in some pupils repeating what they already know while others are confronted with tasks too difficult for them because they have basic disabilities.

In the diagnosing of learning difficulties, the first step is to identify the pupil with a learning problem and then pinpoint his strengths and weaknesses. If possible, the underlying cause of the difficulty should be eliminated before remedial instruction begins. Although the teacher cannot be expected to develop the proficiency of a clinician, he must have several competencies in diagnosing and providing for remediation: (1) an understanding of the psychology of learning as it applies to specific subject areas; (2) an ability to recognize those physical and psychological aspects of human development related to learning; and (3) an understanding of the important diagnostic techniques and the remedial methods and materials in various subject areas.

Research has uncovered a number of factors affecting pupil achievement. Scholastic aptitude, health, vision, hearing, motor coordination, personal-social development, and environment either contribute toward achievement or prohibit successful school work. Difficulties peculiar to a specific subject may be responsible for learning problems, and such elements have been identified in arithmetic, language, handwriting, spelling, and reading.

Certain guiding principles should be applied in remediation, as in diagnosis: motivation, individualizing learning, and keeping pupils aware of the effects of remediation through continual evaluation. Individualizing learning does not mean the abolition of group instruction; both elementary and secondary school teachers can group pupils with common problems to help them.

A school testing program is an excellent way to initiate a sound program of diagnosis and remediation. By administration of a general survey test, it is possible to screen out pupils who may be in need of special help. Devices such as the class record, class analysis chart, and results of a test item analysis prove helpful in getting a clear picture of both the group and its individual members. Analyses supported by diagnostic tests and data from cumulative records are the basis on which to build a remedial program.

Suggested Readings

Blair, G. M. *Diagnostic and remedial teaching.* (Rev. ed.) London: Macmillan, 1956.
This book is designed for both elementary and secondary teachers. In addition to discussing the problems of diagnosis and remediation in reading, arithmetic, handwriting, spelling, and English fundamentals, the author outlines remedial programs for elementary, junior high, and high schools.

Brueckner, L. J., and G. L. Bond. *The diagnosis and treatment of learning difficulties.* New York: Appleton-Century-Crofts, 1955.
The authors direct their discussion to the typical classroom teacher. Special emphasis is given to learning problems in arithmetic, language, spelling, and handwriting.

Daly, W. C. *Test scores: Fragment of a picture.* Test Service Notebook, No. 24. New York: Harcourt, Brace & World, 1959.
The "pattern" technique in child study is recommended. The goal of this technique is to make a diagnostic formulation for prediction. A large quantity of various kinds of information about the pupil is needed.

DeBoer, D. L. (ed.) *Reading diagnosis and evaluation.* Newark, Del.: International Reading Association, 1970.
Specialists in reading present their viewpoints on diagnosis and evaluation.

Goodlad, J. K. Diagnosis and prescription in educational practice. *Education Digest,* 1966, **31**, 8–11.
The underlying thesis is that, due to the monolithic structure of the American schooling system, teachers are restricted in making decisions to provide for individual differences among pupils. The three aspects of the schooling environment explored are expectations for schooling, curriculum, and school organization.

Harris, A. J. *How to increase reading ability.* (5th ed.) New York: David McKay, 1970.
This is one of the best and most widely used references in the field of diagnosis and remediation in reading. The author bases his discussion on research and practical experience. The book is a thorough and practical source of information.

Henry, N. B. (ed.) *Individualized instruction.* Sixty-First Yearbook of the National Society for the Study of Education. Chicago: University of Chicago Press, 1962. Pp. 177–282.
Section III of the yearbook discusses school practices for individualizing instruction. It presents some of the current thinking on the problems of individual differences within the schools.

Horst, P. How much information on test results should be given to students: Views of a research psychologist. *Journal of Counseling Psychology*, 1959, 6, 218–222.

Problems of communicating test results to pupils are considered. Teachers are urged to improve this type of communication by learning more about tests and the meaning of the scores they produce.

Strang, R., C. M. McCullough, and A. E. Traxler. *The improvement of reading.* (4th ed.) New York: McGraw-Hill, 1967.

This book deals with problems of reading in the secondary school and college. Such topics as special reading groups, appraisal of reading proficiency, over-coming difficulties in word recognition and vocabulary, special problems of slow and able learners, personality, and individual treatment make this an exceptional resource.

Thorndike, R. L. *The concepts of over- and under-achievement.* New York: Bureau of Publications, Teachers College, Columbia University, 1963.

The author reviews the research studies on over- and under-achievement. He points out incidents of faulty design and suggests precautionary measures for future research.

Wayson, W. W. Needed: Diagnostic attention. *Educational Leadership,* 1967, 24, 323–326.

A diagnostic approach is needed to alleviate problems of the educationally disadvantaged. The author offers suggestions for writing new programs that insure more diagnostic attention.

References Cited

Abney, L. Speech, voice, and pronunciation. In N. B. Henry (ed.), *Teaching language in the elementary school.* Forty-Third Yearbook of the National Society for the Study of Education. Part II. Chicago: University of Chicago Press, 1944. Pp. 181–186.

Bond, G. L. Identifying the reading attainments and needs of students. In N. B. Henry (ed.), *Reading in the high school and college.* Forty-Seventh Yearbook of the National Society for the Study of Education. Part II. Chicago: University of Chicago Press, 1948. Pp. 69–90.

Buswell, G. T., and L. John. *Diagnostic studies in arithmetic.* Supplemental Educational Monographs, 1926, No. 30.

Cook, W. W. The functions of measurement in the facilitation of learning. In E. F. Lindquist (ed.), *Educational measurement.* Washington: American Council on Education, 1951. Pp. 3–46.

Harris, A. J. *How to increase reading ability.* (5th ed.) New York: David McKay, 1970.

Newland, T. E. An analytical study of the development of illegibilities in handwriting from the lower grades to adulthood. *Journal of Educational Research,* 1932, 26, 249–258.

Spache, G. Characteristic errors of good and poor spellers. *Journal of Educational Research,* 1940, 34, 182–189.

Willing, M. H. *Valid diagnosis in high school composition.* Contributions to Education, No. 230. New York: Bureau of Publications, Teachers College, Columbia University, 1926.

CHAPTER 15

Determining and Reporting Growth

Suppose you have asked your physician to give you a thorough physical examination. He runs through a complex series of clinical and laboratory examinations, evaluates them, and says "Well, I guess you're worth about a B+." You leave cheerfully enough—a B+ always sounds good when you are told achievement test results—but a bit puzzled. Perhaps it means that there are not many people as physically able as you. Perhaps there are more things right than wrong with your health. But these seem to be the only conclusive judgments you can come to. You do not know how to improve your health, because you do not know what deficiencies kept you from getting an A.

Clearly a letter grading system is inadequate for summarizing the results of a physical examination. If your physician discovers circulatory difficulties, he discusses the ailment with you. Often he must interpret extensively before you understand the meaning of the evaluation. Many bits of information are related and balanced. Furthermore, a physician relates his diagnosis to remediation, and is likely to modify your activities or diet.

Similarly, evaluating a pupil's competence requires careful reflection on many aspects of his personality and abilities. Much more is examined than his knowledge of subject matter; his teachers are concerned with his personal-social adjustment, the way he represents his school, and the quality of his response to the learning situations he experiences.

Composite evaluation of something as nebulous as human behavior must be highly complex. Not all evidence can be completely objective. Every source of data available for assessing both psychological and physical characteristics must be tapped. It is almost impossible to summarize the evaluation with a single symbol.

Teachers agree that giving and reporting marks is one of their most uncomfortable responsibilities. Some lack confidence in the marks they assign; others believe their marks are fair, but find them difficult to defend. Behind these negative attitudes lies the fact that the basis for assigning marks is often unclear. Should the intelligent pupil who loafs be given a low mark? Should the pupil who works very hard but whose mental capacities are inadequate be upgraded in spite of his below-average performance on tests and assignments? Should the pupil who adjusts well to his peers but receives failing marks be promoted? What would be the effect on this child's future development if he were held back? With so many factors to consider responsibly, it is small wonder that teachers regard giving final marks as a chore.

Marking and reporting have come a long way since the earliest report cards in American education. Generally these were colorful, artistic, and vague. They contained simple little messages like "to a very industrious little girl from her affectionate teacher," or "Studiousness and good deportment in a young man are a credit to his parents and a satisfaction to his teacher." Comments about achievement in important subjects like penmanship, spelling, and reading developed later. These evaluations, together with a report on attendance and deportment, persisted in our schools for many years. Though less common today, this type of report is still in use. It informs parents of their child's attendance and tardiness, deportment, achievement in subject matter according to grade standards, and his chances of promotion or failure (Goodykoontz, 1955).

In many modern schools, there is a definite trend toward revising methods of marking and reporting. Child psychology and a redefinition of the objectives of the school have had their influence. Attention has been centered on the whole child, emphasizing his achievement in relation to his own potential for development. The complexity of this kind of evaluation is reflected in changed methods of reporting, leading to such devices as check lists, personal letters, and teacher-parent conferences.

PURPOSES OF REPORTING

The purposes of marking and reporting can best be defined in terms of those who use them—pupils, parents, teachers, school administrators, and employers. In the final analysis, reports should serve the paramount purpose of facilitating the educational development of each pupil in relation to his ability, and their effectiveness should be judged by his criterion. Reports succeed insofar as they help each pupil realize his potential.

Informing the Pupil

Motivation.   Originally, one of the purposes of reports was to exhort pupils to greater effort in school. Fear of failure, it was argued, would produce greater achievement, while if the pupil knew he would be passed on automatically from grade to grade, he would work less. Research does not support this conclusion. One study compared seventh-grade groups in nine elementary school systems employing almost universal "social promotion" and nine school systems maintaining rigid standards of promotion. No significant differences were found in either achievement or intelligence between groups. In the school where failure was common, the range of abilities was increased, resulting in aggravated instructional problems. In fact, grade standards tended to be lowered (Cook, 1941).

It has been found that certain pupils will be challenged to work for higher marks. Although they may have little interest in the subject matter at first, it may develop through feelings of accomplishment and success. Yet there are dangers in working for marks. A pupil who conforms rigidly to a teacher's set standards for an A may sacrifice his creativity and imagination in the process. Another, lacking the mental ability to meet the standards set by his teacher, is not motivated to learn when he knows he cannot succeed despite his efforts. Yet if marks represent his improvement rather than status alone, he may have incentive to strive for them.

Guidance. One of the conditions for effective learning is that a pupil should know the results of his study. For example, a diagnostic evaluation that shows the reader his mistakes in word attack skills and commends him for effective use of context clues is important for continued growth in reading. The pupil who is constructively criticized after his talk in speech class learns from suggestions. Research emphasizes that the best time to correct an error is immediately after it is made. Learning is facilitated by the help a pupil receives from the comments of his teachers and peers in day-to-day contacts. Therefore, the teacher should inform the pupil continually of his strengths and weaknesses. These daily evaluations also make possible more effective summaries at the end of a report period. The secondary school pupil has much to gain from an overall appraisal of his abilities in specific academic fields. He needs to know his possibilities for success in further education to help him decide what course of studies he should follow. Secondary school marks are useful in predicting college marks; a number of studies show relationships represented by correlation coefficients well above 0.50 (Smith and Dobbin, 1960, pp. 783–791).

On the other hand, standardized achievement test scores have been shown to have about as high a relationship with college marks as secondary school marks (Lindquist, 1962). They also provide the individual with an opportunity to compare his performance with a regional or national norm, a comparison more likely to give him a valid estimate of his achievement.

Final marks must be interpreted in terms of the quality of instruction and the general ability of the pupils in the class. In some schools where there may be a lack of talent among the pupils, it is possible for high marks to give a distorted picture of a pupil's achievement. The lower marks of some pupils in our better schools may represent more achievement than an A in schools inadequately staffed and equipped. A final mark of C in an honors class may represent greater achievement than an A in an average class.

The interpretation of marks, then, is very important. The value of the report increases as the pupil is helped to understand what it means. This implies that the teacher is prepared to defend its accuracy and show its significance. There are teachers who make it a practice to explain the meaning of marks and other data to pupils before the reports go home. This procedure also provides an opportunity to review the school's objectives with the pupils.

Informing the Parent

Parents must understand the school's objectives to advance cooperation between home and school; otherwise there is likely to be conflict. Some parents feel that academic achievements should be the only concern of the school. Many think certain kinds of academic achievement are more important than others. Learning dates, names, and places may be more desirable in their eyes than understanding the social issues. A large vocabulary may seem more important than understanding what is read. Therefore, field trips to provide background experience for reading are frowned on as a waste of time.

Such parents are perplexed when the school is concerned with group living and personal-social adjustment, despite the fact that our greatest national health problem is mental health. They fail to understand that we cannot divorce the pupil's intellectual growth from other aspects of his development. Not until a parent can accept the educational objectives of the school is he in a position to support and supplement the educational program for his child; but he can neither accept nor support without understanding. A truly informative system of reporting is formulated in terms of these objectives and of his child's growth and progress toward them, and provides a basis for understanding and the intelligent cooperation of the parent with both teacher and child.

Informing Teachers, School Administrators, and Employers

A composite evaluation of a pupil's achievement and growth should be available for his future teachers and the administration. The cumulative record is most helpful. Periodic reports should be filed therein, since they represent evaluations of much of the data. Whether or not the pupil remains in the same school system, his teachers will have information about his progress in previous grades.

The school administrator or guidance officer often must evaluate the competence and potentiality of the school's graduates. As more pupils continue their formal education, colleges and universities must exercise increasingly stringent selection, and well-organized evaluations of college-bound pupils should be available for them. Many aspects of achievement—oral expression, laboratory skills, and creativity among them—cannot be evaluated by paper-and-pencil tests. Colleges are also interested in such facets of a pupil's school life as his personal-social adjustment, his participation in extra-class activities, and the nature of his interests and goals.

Pupils who do not go to college generally seek employment. Because the tendency to practice social promotion has changed the meaning of a high-school diploma, their prospective employers often request information about them. While competence in secretarial or machine-shop skills are important for certain types of jobs, employers also want people who can get along with others, assume responsibility, have leadership potential and an attitude of cooperation. Periodic reports over the years provide an indication of the future pattern of behavior that an employer might expect of an individual.

Problems

1. If we accept the premise that report cards and final marks exist to help each pupil develop according to his ability, how then can we justify the use of rigid standards of passing and failing?

2. If standardized test scores yield information comparable to secondary school marks, could we then abolish report cards and concentrate on thorough interpretation of the achievement test results in individual conferences with the parents and child? Explain your answer.

BASES FOR REPORTING

Objectives of the School

Effective instruction and evaluation are based on the educational objectives of the school. These should be stated in terms of desired pupil behavior, which should enable a pupil to satisfy both his immediate and adult needs. It is not possible to identify the most important educational objectives for all schools and all times, or to determine when they are to be emphasized. This must be decided in terms of the individual differences of pupils, teachers, and communities.

If evaluation is to be made in terms of all of the school's objectives, general and specific, marking and reporting become very complex. In the first place, evaluation of some parts of a pupil's behavior cannot be as adequate as we would like, yet even so may be more valuable than a paper-and-pencil test indicating only what the pupil says he will do. If one of our objectives is to develop effective citizenship, statements such as "He votes in all elections for which he is eligible," and "He assumes responsibility in group work," give some direction and basis for evaluation. Secondly, it is impractical to sample enough behavior of every pupil to obtain an adequate evaluation. This is especially true for the secondary school, where a teacher meets many pupils every day. Third, to report on each one of a great number of behavioral patterns would give the false impression that valid judgments can be made in every instance. A fourth problem would arise in presenting such a report to parents, since it would be too long and complex to be interpreted easily; certainly the evaluation could not be given in a single number or letter.

So the teacher faces something of a dilemma. On one hand, he wants to base his marking and reporting on all pertinent educational objectives, general and specific. On the other, the list of these objectives is so long, and sometimes the evidence concerning them so difficult to obtain, that he faces an almost impossible task. To make his reporting task more manageable, he compromises, however reluctantly. Rather than try to report pupil progress in terms of all educational objectives each time a report is to be made, he may select a group of objectives, perhaps reporting on a different group on the next occasion. Or he may report on each pupil on each reporting occasion in terms of a group of basic objectives of special importance to the pupil and the school. Each of these may really be a combination of related specific objectives. But typically, however, grading is done more simply. Marks are awarded on what can be easily measured, namely, subject content. Too often the subject content is factual information, and skills such as problem solving, critical thinking, application, and so forth, are not emphasized in the report. Unfortunately even these marks reflect a teacher's bias in such factors as amount of work completed, neatness, and correctness of expression.

Growth and Achievement

Reports may depict growth or achievement, or both. These are distinct concepts. Growth means change or gain. To interpret it adequately, we must consider the individual, his ability, background experience, present environmental stimulation, and so on. Achievement means the pupil's present status—what he knows or can do now. Achievement is generally judged against norms or teacher's standards, and all too often is evaluated without respect to ability and prior experiences.

Differences between the two concepts can be described by use of diagrams. Figure 38 is a record of John's and Bill's growth and achievement in

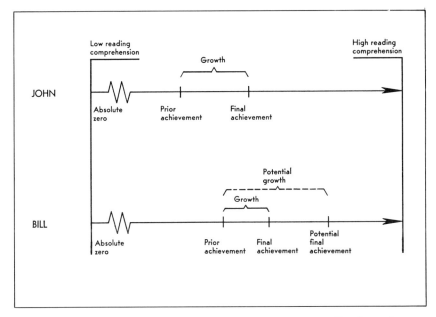

FIGURE 38.   Diagram of Growth and Achievement in Reading Comprehension of Two Fifth-Grade Pupils.

reading comprehension. The top line is a description of John's progress, the bottom line describes Bill's. Clearly there was a point in the life of each boy when his achievement in this basic skill was zero; this is represented on the far left of the two lines by the position labeled absolute zero. Proceeding to the right represents an increase in achievement. Let us assume that John and Bill have just entered the fifth grade. Each boy's achievement in reading comprehension at this particular time is represented by a point called prior achievement. Bill's prior achievement in reading comprehension exceeds John's considerably.

If we examine the boys' achievement at the end of the academic year (final achievement) we find that Bill still surpasses John. Their growth in reading comprehension is represented by the difference between prior and final achievement. Both boys have grown in this skill, but John has made a tremendous spurt. Several interpretations are possible, depending on the other information we have about these pupils. Suppose that they have equal potential in reading. We might then conclude that Bill is an overachiever who could not be expected to make tremendous growth strides, whereas John may be achieving according to his ability. It is more likely that John was retarded in the earlier grades and, through good teaching, was able to make great strides in the fifth grade. Bill, on the other hand, may or may not have shown adequate growth during the year. But suppose that Bill is a brighter boy than John. His actual growth is then inadequate; his potential growth may then be as great as that shown in Figure 38. Although his final achievement may be the highest in the class, it is still unsatisfactory in terms of what he could do.

We see from the above illustration that both growth and final achievement guide the teacher in evaluating pupil progress. However, it is questionable whether to assign marks on the basis of achievement gains rather than present status. First, gains are very unreliable because they include the errors of both the initial and final achievements. Second, if initial scores are obtained from instruments that are too easy, able pupils will have little opportunity to improve on the final assessment. Third, it is much more difficult to raise a high score even higher than to raise a low score. A gain of one-half standard deviation from a score below the mean may not be of the same substance as a gain of one-half standard deviation above the mean. The regression effect is operating (Diederich, 1956).

The problem confronting teachers is psychological. How does one prevent a pupil who receives only low marks from getting discouraged? One way, of course, is to have him compete against himself; that is, to evaluate him on the basis of his gains. However, if this is not defensible, then we can give all pupils opportunities within the school and the class to excel in some way even though it is not through overall achievement status in the subject matter. The hard facts of life dictate that all pupils must learn eventually that present status rather than growth is what counts for the most part.

In the Elementary School.   During the elementary school years, the teacher is concerned with helping each individual achieve as much and as rapidly as possible. Studies in child development inform us that children mature at different rates; every child is different and has environmental problems peculiar to him that affect his learning. Thus, it is not always possible to predict which pupils will eventually lead the group in specific areas of achievement. The elementary school teacher is in a position to manipulate the school environment so that pupils are not thwarted and stunted in their growth before they reach a degree of maturity at which they can evaluate their own strengths and weaknesses realistically. Therefore, the teacher often emphasizes self-improvement—growth, in other words. Emphasis on growth stresses the child rather than the subject matter. It can apply to all kinds of learning situations, academic and nonacademic.

Bloom (1964, p. 127) has shown how important growth in achievement is in the first three grades of elementary school. Research findings indicate that approximately 50 percent of general achievement at grade 12 (age 18) has been reached by the end of grade 3 (age 9). This means that the first few years of school as well as the preschool period contribute greatly to the development of learning patterns and general achievement.

Furthermore, Bloom's study shows the importance of the early years for the development of intelligence. He states that "in terms of intelligence measure at age 17, about 50 percent of the development takes place between conception and age 4, about 30 percent between ages 4 and 8, and about 20 percent between the ages 8 and 17."

In the Secondary School. Even in the secondary school, evaluation based on final achievement alone does not tell the whole story of the pupil's development. Achievement scores, for example, do not indicate whether he is at a particular level from lack of effort or talent. Neither does a single achievement score give an indication of whether there has been improvement or not. A teacher should consider pupil growth in evaluating his teaching. But in the secondary school, the pupil is looking forward to higher education and professional life, and it is imperative that his grades reflect achievement status. The standards that students must meet for the professions of medicine, law, and teaching, for example, exist as much to protect society as to select qualified students.

Standards and Ability to Learn

Whether to evaluate pupils in terms of standards or of achievement in relation to learning ability is a part of the growth-versus-achievement question. Standards of achievement are often thought of as the teacher's estimate of the level of achievement that a pupil must reach before he has done acceptable work. The use of such standards is sometimes defended in the following manner (Green, 1956, p. 72):

> When I pass a student in this course I am certifying to his next instructor that he has covered the material of the course, and that if he works reasonably hard he is capable of continuing with the next course in this field at least approximately at the level indicated by his letter grade. In the first place, I will not give a fraudulent certification. In the second place, it would be no kindness to your child to let him get into college or into a job only to find out that he is not prepared to do good work. Moreover, if I lower the standards, the result is a disservice to your children and your community, handicapping all future students by making colleges and universities reluctant to accept them or give them scholarships, and prospective employers mistrustful of them.

Yet when a pupil is evaluated in terms of his ability to learn, his efforts must be considered. Then all pupils, whether talented or not, will receive praiseworthy reports if they achieve as much as they possibly can under existing circumstances. This focuses on the pupil, like the method by which he was taught.

These two points of departure for evaluating pupils are not so different as one might suppose. Evaluating in terms of standards does not mean ignoring individual differences, nor does evaluating in terms of ability to learn mean abandoning standards. When standards are the criterion for evaluation, it does not follow that the talented pupils will be discouraged from progressing above the passing level nor that less able pupils will never experience success. When evaluation is based on a pupil's ability to learn, greater achievement is expected of the able pupil than his less talented classmate.

In other words, whether instructing or evaluating, the teacher cannot disregard either standards or individual differences in ability to learn. Standards are multiple; those for the superior pupil differ from those for the less able. Moreover, the level of the standards changes from one grade level to the next, from one curriculum area to another, and from teacher to teacher. Nevertheless, there is a minimum level of achievement that a pupil must reach before he receives credit for a course or can be promoted to a higher grade level. If a pupil fails to achieve at this level or one higher because of inadequate ability, he should be moved to a classroom situation that presents educational experiences better suited to his ability. Hence the selection of appropriate classroom experiences is an important factor in providing for individual differences. Special provisions may be necessary for the elementary pupil. Guidance in the selection of appropriate courses is basic for secondary school pupils.

Problems

3. If a school emphasizes self-improvement in elementary school and then suddenly shifts to group standards of achievement at the secondary level, is it creating confusion and uncertainty within adolescent children by doing so?

4. Ability grouping has been suggested as a means of accommodating to some degree individual differences on the secondary school level. Is this a satisfactory procedure? Why?

5. If there are to be multiple standards of achievement in the interests of healthful psychological development on the part of the pupil, is there a need to revise the high school diploma system as it now exists in many schools? Why?

SPECIFIC EVIDENCE OF PUPIL PROGRESS

The specific evidence needed for accurate assessment and reporting of a pupil's progress must come from the many measuring instruments and techniques discussed in detail in other chapters. Certainly data from both teacher-constructed and standardized paper-and-pencil tests, ranking and rating scales, and check lists, must be used. Data from observation of class participation and pupil success in projects and reports are helpful as well.

Test Performance

Teacher-Constructed Tests. The teacher-constructed achievement test is used extensively in common practice as a partial basis for determining final marks and making reports. As well as measuring the level of a pupil's knowledge and understanding, it can provide helpful diagnostic information. When well constructed, it is invaluable in direct learning, and can focus on topics under discussion in class. Comprehension tests in reading can give an indication of the ability to select main ideas, to summarize, and to determine meanings of unfamiliar words from context. Classroom arithmetic tests check skill in number combinations and processes, and accuracy and speed in working them out. Varied test items will analyze difficulties encountered by pupils at all levels in working word problems. Daily or weekly spelling tests reflect a pupil's progress in spelling and the legibility of his writing. Knowledge of facts. can be checked in the content areas. Understanding of various skills and of equipment use in science can be determined. Such skills as map reading and knowledge and use of various kinds of reference materials can be evaluated in social studies classes.

Classroom tests can also deal with learning difficulties that are of particular concern to the group. Of course, teachers should take care that their tests do not place a premium on verbalization and rote memorization of facts. It should also be remembered that if tests are not used correctly, they can set the learner for short-term retention; the pupil may be able to pass the quiz but fail to see the broader relationships in a unit of work.

Standardized Tests. The workmanship in the better standardized tests is generally far superior to that of the typical classroom test. Great care and extensive trial administrations result in test items that are more likely to test the pupil in the desired terms, and there are norms by which a pupil's progress can be compared with national averages. In most instances, however, it would be unwise to base reports entirely on these test scores.

Standardized tests are based on objectives generally agreed on by educational authorities. There is no consensus as to the emphasis these objectives should have or, in many instances, at what grade level they form the base for instruction and evaluation. These decisions must be made by the local school and community. Complete dependence on the use of standardized tests in marking and reporting would presuppose that the teacher has established the same objectives and emphases as the test makers. Only if this were true would the standardized test give a valid evaluation of the extent to which the class objectives had been reached.

Standardized tests can make a genuine contribution to the instructional program and effective reporting. They provide a more accurate total picture of a pupil's strengths and weaknesses in subject matter achievement than teacher-constructed tests. Available norms also make is possible to compare the pupil's achievement with that of pupils in other schools. The diagnostic tests in particular can be helpful in determining the basis of a learning difficulty. The aptitude test scores, of course, indicate a pupil's ability to achieve, and provide criteria for judging the adequacy of achievement. In addition to the achievement and aptitude test, personal-social adjustment inventories can provide helpful data if used with caution.

Procedure and Product Evaluation

Achievement of certain educational objectives cannot be evaluated effectively by paper-and-pencil instruments. Operating a microsope, writing a theme, delivering a speech, or preparing food products are kinds of behavior related to some of these and are classified as procedures and products. Ranking and rating methods, check lists, and anecdotal records are generally used in evaluating procedures. Product scales as well as ranking and rating methods are used in product evaluation. Sample products prepared by the pupil serve well as a means of explaining to him and his parents the degree of his achievement. Data yielded by procedure and product evaluation often require less explanation than some test scores.

Class Participation

Class participation here means the broad aspects of the pupil's participation in group activities rather than simple recitation. Evaluation should not be based on the number of times a pupil answers questions in class. While some students crave attention, others may be far better problem solvers and think more creatively than their more vocal peers. We can learn about pupils through the comments they make. Do they show that they have an understanding of the subject? What attitudes are reflected in their discussion? How does the class react to comments of individual pupils? Are they accepted or rejected because of the personality of the contributor rather than the essence of the remark?

Participation in class also involves getting along with others and playing one's roles as a leader and follower. Class observation is the only way in which certain personal-social aspects of the pupil's behavior can be evaluated, but objectively reporting this behavior presents a problem. Some of the subjectivity can be eliminated by evaluating in terms of educational objectives stated as observable behavior.

Projects and Reports

Some pupils prove adept at learning facts and following prescribed directions and outlined procedures. Such achievement is simple to check. But certain important educational objectives representing higher intellectual abilities are harder to evaluate with the conventional instruments. Problem solving, creative and independent thinking, and the ability to locate and select pertinent information can be evaluated through the use of projects and reports that provide occasion for the pupils to muster their inner resources apart from the artificial atmosphere of the paper-and-pencil test and to attack a problem on their own. Projects and reports often help determine pupil interest; perhaps effort lacking in teacher-dominated activities will come out with opportunities allowing greater freedom of action. Remember that achievement in terms of these objectives is not easy to assess. Reliability may be low. If we feel that such activities should be included in the determination of final marks, then we will have to cope with the problems of inadequate degrees of validity and reliability.

Problems

6.   Parents and pupils are seldom as aware of standardized achievement test scores as they are of final marks. Does this indicate a failure in communication on the part of the teachers? Would you advocate the systematic reporting of standardized achievement test results?

7.   In addition to numerical marks, a junior high school requires ratings of class participation ranging from unsatisfactory to excellent. A seventh-grade science teacher objects strongly to this procedure. He states that it is impossible for him to keep a daily record of 180 students in terms of their class participation. How would you help this teacher?

METHODS OF MARKING AND REPORTING

Typical procedures for marking and reporting are letter-number systems, check lists, correspondence with parents, and teacher-parent conferences. It is important that these methods be critically evaluated in terms of purposes, bases, and the sources of information available for reporting. Whatever system is used must be established as the best possible under existing circumstances.

Letter-Number Systems

The letter-number system has been and remains a popular method of reporting pupil progress. In essence it is an effort to summarize a variety of information about such characteristics of a pupil as his growth, final achievement, effort, ability, and general deportment. The summary is given in the form of a letter, usually A through E or F, or a number, usually *100* through *0*, reported for each subject matter area each report period.

There are two reasons why these marks are difficult to assign. First, the teacher cannot be certain whether appropriate credit is being given to growth and to final achievement for each educational objective considered. Second, since the mark represents pupil progress in terms of a combination of objectives, the teacher is uncertain whether each objective within the combination is being appropriately weighted.

Dual Marking Systems. An interesting variation of the traditional letter-number system is the use of two marks for each subject matter area. The first represents the pupil's final achievement in relation to the teacher's standards. The second is often an evaluation of effort put forth by the pupil; in other school systems it represents pupil growth in the area of achievement listed. A three-point letter system is sometimes used for recording the pupil's effort: H if the pupil exceeds what is expected of him, S if his level of work corresponds approximately to his level of ability, and U if he is capable of better work. Pupils evaluated according to this system might receive marks such as A/S or 91/S, each indicating high final achievement and normal effort. Marks such as C/H or 83/H mean that the pupil is average in terms of final achievement, and that his effort is superior.

Clearly the success of dual marking systems depends on a teacher's ability to evaluate final achievement and effort by a letter or number. Some teachers find evaluation of effort particularly troublesome since satisfactory judgment requires more accurate evaluation techniques than are available. If the second mark represents growth rather than effort, an extensive pretesting program must be set up to establish achievement levels before instruction begins and then careful consideration must be given to the problems of interpreting gains.

In actual practice, Halliwell and Robitaille (1963) found a halo effect on assigning good marks to bright students on their relative achievement as well as on subjective factors such as effort. Teachers tended to equate effort with achievement disregarding individual differences of intelligence. To correct this type of problem, no doubt teachers should have better in-service training and orientation with respect to dual reporting, and more accurate measuring techniques of pupil effort are needed.

These are central issues. If they can be resolved, dual marking systems can be expected to give a clearer picture of a pupil's progress than a single mark. However, dual reporting could still present an oversimplified picture of the teacher's evaluation. Each subject matter area encompasses many educational objectives. Theoretically, with suitable instruments, adequate teacher preparation and time, a pupil's final achievement and effort or growth could be determined and reported in terms of each one of them. Practical considerations, however, would impose some limitations.

Relative versus Absolute Standards for Marking.   Because there is no absolute zero for achievement test scores, it is impossible to assign marks on an absolute scale or standard. If a pupil responds correctly to all items on a test, it does not necessarily mean that he knows 100 percent of what is to be learned in the subject, and a mark of 50 percent does not mean that he has learned half of the subject matter. Test items are a sampling of what is learned in the subject. Furthermore, whether a pupil receives credit for having mastered a particular concept depends on how understanding of it is measured by a particular test item. Even a question about a difficult concept may be answered correctly by almost all pupils if the question requires only superficial understanding. In other words, the difficulty of an item often depends as much on how a concept is measured as what is measured.

Actually teachers who convert raw scores or percentages directly into final marks usually adjust them near the end of the year by giving bonus points, by constructing an easy or difficult test as the situation may warrant, or some such procedure, until the raw scores or percentages will convert to a distribution of final marks that was largely predetermined. This distribution involves an arbitrary decision. It may be determined by school policy, the ability and vocational plans of the pupils, gaps in the distribution of composite scores, and so forth. In a high-ability class, for example, a teacher might give 30 percent As, 40 percent Bs, 20 percent Cs and 10 percent Ds. Rarely are there as many Fs as there are As; the median final mark in many classes is often B rather than C.

Regardless of the marking system adopted, it is important that the marks present a clear message to pupils, parents, employers, and college admission officers. The meaning of marks is much clearer when school personnel agree on the criteria for choosing the percentage of pupils in a given class who will be assigned a particular mark.

To illustrate how final marks may be assigned unfairly, imagine three English classes taught by different teachers. Classes 1 and 2 are made up of college-bound pupils of comparable ability, Class 3 of pupils of lesser ability.

The teacher of Class 1 assigns 60 percent *A*s and *B*s. The teacher of Class 2, who is less liberal, gives only 40 percent *A*s and *B*s. Consequently a pupil whose English achievement is typical of college-bound pupils would probably receive a *B* if he were in Class 1, a *C* if in Class 2, and an *A* if he were a member of Class 3, in which he would probably be one of the best students.

One way of rectifying this situation is to obtain some common and relevant measure by which the three English classes could be compared. Scores from a scholastic aptitude test or from standardized or teacher-constructed English achievement tests with acceptable degrees of content validity might be used. Suppose it is decided that 15 percent of the pupils will receive *A*s. Then the cutoff score, above which only 15 percent of the pupils score on the common measure, would be determined. The number of pupils in a particular class who surpass this cutoff score provides the approximate number of *A*s to be given in that class. The same is true of the percentages of *B*s, *C*s and so on. Note that the final mark a particular student receives depends on his total performance in his class, not on his scholastic aptitude score. The scholastic aptitude tests serve here to determine percentages of letter grades assigned, not the pupils to whom they will be assigned. Some pupils will receive higher final achievement marks than their fellows who scored higher on the scholastic aptitude test.

Ebel (1965) reports a method of marking with a simplified procedure designed to promote uniformity in marking. Consideration is given to scholastic aptitude and/or prior achievement of the class to which a pupil belongs. Ebel believes that more high marks should be assigned to a class with a higher mean scholastic aptitude score or total grade-point average. The procedure is defended on the basis of the relationship between aptitude and prior achievement with future achievement.

In the procedure, a five-unit letter system is used with each letter encompassing the same interval on the score scale. This replaces percentage assignment of marks that considers only ranks and disregards score differences. It also provides an alternative that differentiates among marking levels by looking for "natural breaks" in the distribution.

The result is that each letter mark covers the same range of achievement on the scale. There will be more *C* pupils, but the *C* will encompass the same "distance" on the scale as an *A*, a *B*, or an *F*. Although for a given class there will be no fixed percent of each mark assigned, over a period of time final marks given to a number of diverse classes will tend to conform to the normal distribution.

The procedure employs one standard deviation for each letter interval. The lower limit of each letter mark is determined by adding or subtracting a determined number from the median of the scores on which the mark is to be based. This number is obtained by multiplying the standard deviation by a factor determined for each of several ability levels: exceptional, superior, good, fair, average, weak, and poor. Stanine distribution statistics have also been determined.

Michael (1960) reports another system to prevent able pupils from being penalized in terms of final marks because of ability grouping. He describes how, in a subject such as English, pupils are usually grouped into three to five categories. There may be a top section designed to prepare pupils for advanced placement. A number of classes either homogeneously or heterogeneously grouped are the designated standard college preparatory sections. Then there may be several low ability classes of pupils who in general do not intend to go to college.

In Michael's system, when a school reports letter marks, it is common to assign a certain number of points to a letter: A-5 pts; B-4 pts; C-3 pts; D-2 pts. A multiplying factor that varies according to the ability category is applied to each pupil's mark. Suppose there are three categories. The pupil in the highest group will have his A multiplied by 6; an A received in the middle group will be multiplied by 5; As in the low section are multiplied by 4. The plan has the effect of raising marks in the top section by one letter while lowering those in the bottom section by one letter.

Michael emphasizes that the point system affects only class rank. It does not appear on the report card. However, because rank is one important criterion determining college admission, pupils in the higher groups are compensated for possible lower marks than pupils receive in lower ability groups.

Weighting Data.   One of the problems the teacher encounters in giving final marks is weighting the data gathered from such various sources as informal quizzes, final examinations, and reports to obtain a valid composite score for ranking his pupils. There is no consensus on the emphasis each of these types of data should receive in the total evaluation. Some teachers maintain that a final examination should count far more than the quizzes and other tests given during the course. They point out that since the final examination measures long-term retention, and the ability to organize and deal with large units of subject matter, this score should logically be weighted more heavily than others. Other teachers are quick to retort that it is unfair to the pupil to determine such a large proportion of his final evaluation from his performance at a specified time within an interval of several hours at most. They also object to the limitations of most final examinations that preclude measurement in terms of many important educational objectives. This is a very important consideration. The weighting of various data must be determined in terms of the educational objectives of the specific grade level or class. Those data that reflect pupil progress in terms of the most important objectives must be given greater weight when computing a composite mark than those relating to less important objectives. This is equally true whether the data come from a final examination or from any other measuring instrument.

There is a precaution that must be taken in determining a composite mark no matter what weightings are chosen. Suppose we wish to base one-fifth of the final mark for a course on class reports, one-fifth on daily assignments, one-fifth on quizzes and unit tests, and two-fifths on the final examination. Inspection of the ranges and standard deviations of these measures in the following table reveals a definite lack of uniformity. If we hope to maintain the weighting scheme originally chosen, we must take into consideration these differences in variability. A failure to do this will result in inequities. To illustrate this point, let us suppose that Mary made a total of 55 points for class reports, the highest number of points for this category. However, on quizzes and unit tests her score was the lowest, 30 points. For daily assignments and the final examination she earned 61 and 91, respectively. Frank, on the other hand, did the poorest of anyone in the group on class reports; his score was 29. On the quizzes and unit tests he had a high score of 140. It happens that he also made the same scores as Mary on daily assignments and the final exam, namely 61 and 91.

Source of points	Nominal weight	Range	Standard deviation
Class reports	1	26	5.1
Daily assignments	1	46	8.6
Quizzes and units tests	1	110	20.8
Final examination	2	90	16.4

If we weight Mary's and Frank's scores for each source and add them to obtain a composite, we have the following:

Mary	Frank
$55 \times 1 = 55$	$29 \times 1 = 29$
$61 \times 1 = 61$	$61 \times 1 = 61$
$30 \times 1 = 30$	$140 \times 1 = 140$
$91 \times 2 = 182$	$91 \times 2 = 182$
Total $= 328$	Total $= 412$

Note that although class reports and quizzes and unit tests are to have the same weight, Mary is penalized because of the lesser variability of scores of class reports when compared with that of quizzes and unit tests. In other words, class-report scores with a relatively low standard deviation ($\sigma = 5.1$) have less influence than scores of quizzes and unit tests ($\sigma = 20.8$) in determining the class rankings on the composite score.

A procedure for avoiding errors like the one above would be to convert the raw scores into standard scores so that the variability of the scores for each category would be the same. When the scores for each category are converted into stanines the following formula to compute the composite is appropriate:

$$C = \frac{\Sigma \, WS}{\Sigma \, W},$$

where

C = composite average;
Σ = the sum;
W = weight for a particular category;
S = standard score for that category for each pupil.

To illustrate the use of the formula let us assume that Mary received stanine scores of 9, 5, 1, and 7 for class reports, daily assignments, quizzes and unit tests, and the final examination respectively. Frank's stanine scores were 1, 5, 9, and 7. The composite averages would be:

Mary

$$C = \frac{(1 \times 9) + (1 \times 5) + (1 \times 1) + (2 \times 7)}{1 + 1 + 1 + 2} = \frac{29}{5} = 5.8;$$

Frank

$$C = \frac{(1 \times 1) + (1 \times 5) + (1 \times 9) + (2 \times 7)}{1 + 1 + 1 + 2} = \frac{29}{5} = 5.8.$$

Although these composite averages are not stanines, they do provide means for the ranking of pupils that reflects the desired weightings of the scores for the several categories. On the basis of this distribution, the teacher may assign final marks.

Reliability and Validity.   The reliability of scores from paper-and-pencil tests is sometimes not as great as we wish it to be. Reliability of data from a teacher's observations of a pupil's procedures and his personal-social adjustment is usually even lower. Yet both are used to determine final marks. Consequently, the reliability of final marks is often less than is to be desired.

Such evidence as is available suggests that the usual reliability coefficients of semester marks may be as high as 0.70 to 0.90. This means that in many if not all cases it is difficult to defend the practice of interpreting such differences as those between an 83 and an 84 or a 91 and a 92. For that matter, the difference between a C+ and a B− may be due purely to chance. This evidence raises the question of the number of divisions that should be used in a marking system. The more categories one makes such as 90, 91, and 92, the more errors in placement of pupils is likely. The fewer the classes, such as *Satisfactory—Unsatisfactory*, the smaller the number of pupils will be given an incorrect mark, but the more serious the error. These facts must be balanced with concern for the amount of information a mark reveals; S and U reveal less than 90, 91, and 92.

Evidence of the validity of final marks is also limited. They seem to be quite valid as a measure of mastery of subject matter by the pupil, the correlation coefficient estimated to be 0.70 or possibly higher. This estimate was arrived at by summarizing the results of a number of studies concerning the correlation between the final marks in question and (1) other marks in the same subject matter area, (2) test scores from appropriate standardized tests, and (3) the pupils' estimates of the marks they deserved.

The validity of final marks has been investigated with respect to a number of different criteria, such as college entrance examination scores, college marks, economic success, and success on the job. The correlation coefficients vary a great deal. The most widely investigated use of secondary school final marks is that of predicting academic success in college. The correlation coefficients are often as high as 0.50 and seldom higher than 0.70. It has been repeatedly shown that final marks in secondary school are one of the best means of predicting college success, whether used alone or as part of a prediction battery.

Interpretation. The typical letter or number system of marking is based primarily on final achievement. Confusion results when a teacher also attempts to include an evaluation of effort and other personality traits in this single mark. Interpretation becomes almost impossible. There is no way to determine whether a low mark is the result of lack of achievement or effort. Even when a single letter mark is used to report final achievement alone, it is very difficult to make a valid interpretation. What does a *B* in general science mean? Does it show that the pupil did A work in quizzes, C work in laboratory, B work in class participation? Or more important still, does it mean that the pupil achieved at an A level with respect to one educational objective, a B level with respect to another and a C level with a third? We have no way of knowing. Therefore when letter or numerical marks are used, there must be additional data in the report that provide diagnostic information. The mark is also influenced by other factors, one of which is the nature of the pupil population. Too often pupils who have been graduated magna cum laude from their high schools find to their dismay when they face competition in a university that they do not have exceptional ability. Another factor is the peculiarity of the individual teacher who does the marking. Some teachers give consistently high marks, while others pride themselves in never being so easy as to give an A or a 95. A pupil may find it very difficult to identify a criterion by which he can judge the value of his marks.

Marks as they are now generally assigned are far from being as meaningful as people think. They are being overinterpreted; they reveal far less about the pupil than is commonly supposed, and their meaning is often ambiguous. Hence it is imperative that standardized test scores be used to supplement final marks whenever possible. It is particularly important for secondary school pupils to have this objective basis for comparing their own capacity and achievements with a broader sample of pupils, giving them a better opportunity to interpret their potentialities for future academic work.

Problems

8. On the basis of your educational experiences, can you demonstrate in a simple, clear-cut fashion the necessity of considering score variability when weighting data to obtain a composite score?
9. The importance of validity in deciding on the weighting to give various measurement data has been stressed. Should the reliability of these various data be considered? Explain.

Types of Report Cards. The report cards used to record the assigned marks can take many different forms. Commonly they provide for the recording of marks for all marking periods during the school year. Parents or guardians are requested to sign the card before it is returned at the end of each marking period.

Reports of academic achievement are often accompanied by a check list of personality traits and attitudes. The teacher may generally place a check in any one of several categories, such as "unsatisfactory," "satisfactory," or "improving." If these check lists are carefully worded, the instrument can save the teacher time and effort.

Reporting must not become a stereotype procedure. In the past, many pupils have been checked "satisfactory" in every characteristic from kindergarten through the sixth grade. The "halo effect" seems to keep some teachers from making a realistic evaluation of the pupil. This can be eliminated if the teacher bases his report on adequate data, carefully compiled and critically interpreted. Space left on the check list form for comments on pupils' problems will help individualize the method.

At the secondary level, check lists are usually used to supplement numerical or letter marks, both providing information not descernible from the mark alone, and helping to clarify the mark itself. In elementary school, check lists are often the only report given. The example shown in Figure 39 represents the type that can be used for this purpose. Observe that all main aspects of the academic program are included, and also health, music, art, and personal development. The common three-point letter system is used to represent the teacher's judgment of the pupil's success. In this case, the

---

REPORT CARD FORM

What the letters mean:

O—Outstanding for your child; commendation for special effort and achievement.

S—Satisfactory for your child; achievement consistent with ability.

N—Not Satisfactory for your child; improvement needed.

Note: Any further information in regard to the standing of your child may be secured in personal conference.

Growth in Skills	1st Report	2nd Report	3rd Report
Reading			
Understands what he reads			
Works to develop independent reading habits			
Writing			
Expresses himself well			
Uses basic writing skills			
Writes legibly			
Spells correctly			
Uses good sentence structure			
Learns to use new words			
Arithmetic			
Knows arithmetic facts			
Understands arithmetic processes (addition, subtraction, multiplication, division)			
Applies skill in solving problems			
Social studies			
History, geography, civics, government, development of American ideals			
Works to develop a knowledge and understanding of home, community, state, country, world			
Works to develop skill in the use of materials (newspapers, maps, encyclopedias, etc.)			
Science			
Works to develop keen observation			
Is growing in scientific knowledge			
Listening			
Understands what he hears and responds wisely			
Health			
Works to develop good health habits			
Helps to maintain safety			
Plays and enjoys games			
Works to develop skill in physical education			
Music			
Takes part in group singing			
Responds to rhythm			
Works to develop basic music skills			
Art			
Expresses ideas creatively			
Works to develop a variety of skills			

Personal development

Is developing a variety of interests _____ _____ _____ _____

Is courteous and considerate _____ _____ _____ _____

Respects the rights and property of others _____ _____ _____ _____

Shares outside experience, skills and materials
with others _____ _____ _____ _____

Accepts responsibility _____ _____ _____ _____

Works to the best of his ability _____ _____ _____ _____

From Heffernan and Marshall, 1955, pp. 75–76; reproduced by permission of the California State Department of Education.

FIGURE 39.   Modified Form of Check List.

letters are O for outstanding, S for satisfactory, and N for not satisfactory. Such a check list as this can give a great deal of information about the pupil's school life.

A number of schools, wishing to conserve time, are employing computers for reporting marks and organizing and analyzing data about them. In one school system (Crisler and Wogaman, 1963) each school's master class schedule and individual pupil programs are converted into punched cards. There is a deck of cards for each class with one mark-sense card for each pupil (see Figure 40). All the decks are arranged alphabetically by teacher name and each teacher's decks by period sequences.

Reproduced by permission of the Richmond (California) Schools.

FIGURE 40.   Pupil's Mark-Sense Card.

At the time of reporting, a teacher receives a deck of mark-sense cards for each of his classes. He marks these in the space representing the final mark earned by each pupil. One to four comments, such as "excellent," "satisfactory," etc., from a list of nine on each card are also marked.

The cards are then returned to the processing center where the teacher marks are printed on the report card (see Figure 41). Four copies of this report are available. The original is given to the pupil to take home and the other three copies are for office use. The reports are cumulative during a semester; that is, the pupil's previous marks also appear on successive reports. Parents do not sign these cards and pupils do not return them.

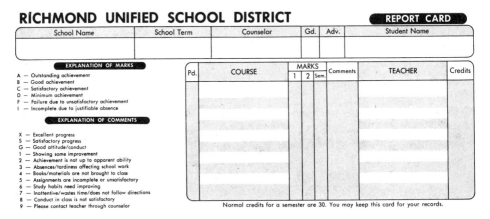

Reproduced by permission of the Richmond (California) Schools.

FIGURE 41.   Report Card.

This system of reporting provides readily available data about marks to the school staff. The number of times each pupil received each letter mark and each comment is totaled along with his average mark. Data on teachers include the number of times they made a comment such as "excellent," or "inattentive." The average mark of each teacher's class and the average for all his classes are tabulated. Marks are also available for each class grouped by subject matter area, as are the comments marked, the percentage of each mark given, and the average mark for the class.

With information showing how teachers mark, this school has the basis to set up guide lines for assigning marks and give the teacher feedback on his own marks and also those of his colleagues. There is an excellent opportunity to make marks more meaningful to pupils and their parents.

Problem

10.   What difficulties might parents face in interpreting information from a check list? How can these be minimized?

Correspondence With Parents

Communications sent to parents may range from a little notation on a report card to a long letter discussing many aspects of their child's school experiences and growth. It is possible to emphasize both pupil development and subject matter achievement. With an adequate cumulative record, the teacher has evidence to interpret patterns of development. He may discuss problems and emphasize factors pertinent to the individual pupil. If some phases of his work would profit from help at home, this can be explained to the parents. As parental comments are requested, there is provision for two-way communication. The interchange of information may lead to some fruitful conferences between teachers and parents.

One of the serious weaknesses of letters to parents is that they tend to be generalized and stereotyped, all too often appearing to have been run off an assembly line, with little variation in wording to relate to a particular pupil. For instance, the following letter is far less helpful to the parent than it might have been:

> Mary is an exceptionally likeable child. In general her progress has been quite satisfactory in all phases of her school work. She seems to be interested in all activities and is purposeful in the tasks she undertakes. Her personal-social adjustment is proceeding at a very normal rate.

What has the parent learned? Do Mary's peers accept her, or is she just liked by the teacher? Perhaps the teacher likes her because she is retiring and does not bother anyone. Certainly there must be some strength or weakness in her academic progress that could be emphasized. Does she question what she reads or is she inclined to accept it without critical evaluation? Do her reports show imagination or does she tend to string together some of the words she has read in the encyclopedia? What does the teacher mean by "purposeful?" What is "normal" personal-social adjustment?

Often the reason for inadequate reporting can be traced to vaguely stated objectives. Objectives like the following do not assure that the teacher understands the criterion behavior. There is no suggestion of how he is to determine whether an objective has been achieved (see Chapter 2).

To develop good citizenship.
To improve health habits.
To understand the scientific method.

Even with sharpened objectives, communicating with parents by letter is not easy. In one community a parent received among other comments the statement "Your child is nervous." He reacted at once with concern about the youngster's mental health, a notion the startled teacher had not meant to convey at all. Letters may annoy the parent or fail to express what the teacher means. The following note concerning a fifth-grade pupil is not helpful in cementing effective relations between home and school:

Dr. Mr. and Mrs. Knowles:
John has been a real problem in our class this year. Unlike most of the children in the group, he doesn't enjoy working with others. He is really a lone wolf. Instead of cooperating, he seems to find satisfaction in disturbing others, and he . . .

This could be changed to a much more effective report for securing parental cooperation. For example:

Dear Mr. and Mrs. Knowles:
We find that it is difficult to summarize in a single mark the things we would like to share with you about John's development this year. In addition to achievement in academic skills, there are many other aspects of growth that we feel are important.
John can be depended upon to see a task through to completion. In preparation for a recent play, he volunteered to get a number of props and he had them for us on time. When he offered to interview several city officials about our town's history, he brought back information that was exceptionally well organized and interesting. Even in activities that require considerable effort, John will finish the task. I recall a particularly long assignment in fractions with which he had some difficuly. He worked longer than he usually has to, but the paper he handed in was well done.
John seems to have no serious trouble in mastering the basic skills. He reads with understanding and he has learned how to make effective use of source materials for research reports. He is a good speller and has missed no words on our weekly spelling tests. In class discussions, he expresses himself well and reflects a background of reading and travel.
We have been trying to help John this year in associations with his classmates. He tends to prefer working by himself rather than with others. At times he is quite aggressive in a group and finds it difficult to cooperate with his classmates on a project. We feel, however, that he has made considerable progress in this respect. Of late he has commented favorably on the good ideas of his group members. He was also chosen as chairman of the entertainment committee for the last day of school.
John tells us that most of the children in his neighborhood are younger than he. It might be helpful if John had some opportunities this summer to play with children of his own age. This would enable him to enter into the "give-and-take" that is so important for his continued development.
I have enjoyed working with John this year. We anticipate that he will have a good relationship with his sixth-grade teacher and class group.
Sincerely,

Because poorly written letters may cause serious troubles, many principals supervise this type of reporting closely. Some schools have provided such suggestions as the following:

SUGGESTIONS FOR WRITING LETTERS TO PARENTS

I. Begin the letter with encouraging news.
II. Close with an attitude of optimism.
III. Solicit the parents' cooperation in solving the problems, if any exist.
IV. Speak of the child's growth—social, physical, and academic.
    A. Social (Citizenship traits)
        1. Desirable traits: attention, attitude toward school, care of property, cooperation, honesty, effort, fair play, neatness, truthfulness, obedience, promptness, reliability, self-control, self-reliance, concentration, courtesy and consideration, thrift, patience, appreciation, kindness, sympathy, orderliness, interest in associates, discrimination, politeness, respect for the rights of others.
        2. Undesirable traits: selfishness, wastefulness, untruthfulness, dishonesty, spitefulness, slow to respond, impudence, carelessness, untidiness, rudeness, noisiness, insolence, cheating, inattention, lack of self-reliance, discourtesy, tattling, snobbishness, conceit, impatience, stealing.
    B. Physical (Health conditions): posture, weight, vitality, physical handicaps, cleanliness (personal), muscular co-ordination, nervousness, emotional traits.
    C. Academic
        1. Interests: (a) in school activities; (b) in extra-school activities.
        2. Methods of work: (a) methods of attack; (b) purposing; (c) planning; (d) executing; (e) judging; (f) consistency in finishing work.
        3. Achievements; (a) growth in knowledge, appreciation, techniques; (b) list subjects in which the child is making progress and those in which he is not making progress; (c) relationship of his accepted standards to his capacities.
V. Compare the child's efforts with his own previous efforts and not with those of others.
VI. Speak of his achievements in terms of his ability to do school work.
VII. Remember it is our professional duty to know the reason why if the child is not making what, for him, is normal progress. (Some suggestive reasons for lack of progress—late entry; absence; lack of application; health defects, such as hearing, sight, undernourishment.)
VIII. Teacher's advice to parents in matters pertaining to health in which the home is a vital factor; such as diet, rest, clothing, exercise, etc.
IX. Please remember that every letter is a professional diagnosis, and as such is as sacred as any diagnosis ever made by any physician.

Reproduced by permission of the Santa Monica City (California) Schools.

Obviously it requires a great deal of time to compose a thoughtful and helpful letter and the teacher is faced with an enormous task if he must report on thirty or forty pupils. Some elementary schools have abandoned reporting by letter for just this reason. It is impractical in most secondary school situations.

The problem can be eased if reports are sent out in staggered lots rather than on all pupils at once. The number of letters for each pupil can be limited. It is better to have one good letter than three poor ones, and to use other methods for other reporting periods. Perhaps some pupils will benefit more than others by frequent letter reports, and the load can thereby be reduced.

Time spent on reporting is never lost and often produces rich dividends in parental cooperation. If the report concerns a problem child, the energy saving from better relations may be very rewarding. Too often teachers become so involved in unimportant details that they overlook more fruitful approaches.

Problem

11. What is the most serious limitation in reporting both positive and negative pupil behavior by means of a letter? If a school system requires this type of evaluative procedure, what steps can be taken to avoid poor public relations?

Teacher-Parent Conferences

The conference method of reporting is most generally used in the elementary school, although for special situations it should be more widely employed at the secondary level. It has potential for providing more information and better understanding between home and school, for misunderstanding can be eliminated far more readily when either conferee is able to raise questions than when communication is by letter. Certainly there are optimum conditions for conferences. They should not be called only when a special problem arises—rapport can hardly be at its best if this is the only basis for meeting. They should be planned periodically to serve as a regular report on the child's progress.

Sufficient time must be allowed—a minimum of thirty minutes. Attempting to rush through one interview to be prompt for the next is unfair to parent and teacher. Conferences are just as much a part of a good instructional program as teaching the multiplication table, and the teacher should be given time to prepare and hold them during his working schedule. Some schools dismiss classes for half day periods; others provide substitutes to relieve the teacher of classroom responsibilities. Because conferences involve a great deal of time, some schools arrange only one per pupil during the school year, using other methods for the remaining report periods.

Conference Preparation. Preparation is basic to an effective conference. Some school systems orient their teachers in the conference technique by distributing bulletins describing the conference purpose, policy, records to be kept, time and preparation. These typically contain numerous illustrations suggesting ideas for preparation. The following are examples:

Bobby Bates, in second grade, an only child, is 7 years, 6 months. He is sturdy and well-developed physically, energetic and active. He seems to have superior mental ability, reads very well and possesses distinct creative language ability. He loves music and the arts, expressing himself creatively and freely. He is doing very satisfactory number work. Bobby has never been able to get along in a group—he exhibits a quarrelsome and domineering attitude and a tendency to be very aggressive with his peers. He also evidences a negative and often openly resistant attitude toward adults. His parents need to give him more experience in children's groups, gradually add responsibility for certain home tasks. They have a "perfectionist" attitude, want him to excel.

Show Mrs. Bates puppet stage (point out Bobby's ideas)
Refer to room-mothers' meeting
Growth in skills
 Reading (books, reading records)
 Language arts (sample stories—dictionary—broad writing vocabulary)
 Doing two-column addition, gaining mastery of facts
 Attendance records
 Help in broadening interests
Group adjustments
 Home interests and attitudes
 Seems resistant to suggestion (examples)
 Sometimes domineering—aggressive (examples), makes group acceptance
  difficult—good ideas
 Plans for helping Bobby—home—school (boys' groups? hobbies? help to
  share his ability)
Individual work habits
 Perfectionist
 Sharing and helping others is difficult (examples—games, books, Monday
  play)
 How can we help him accept and profit by occasional failures?
 Parents' support and encouragement (suggestions)

James, age 12–8, entering junior high school, has reached sixth grade with normal physical and social growth and development. His academic achievement ranges from a year to a year and one-half beyond normal sixth grade as per the fall testing scores.
 Safety Patrol work—fine job
 Review academic progress Kgn through 6
 Indicate seventh-grade adjustment problems
 Emphasize adequate social growth for age
 Successful six years of growth
 Meeting of sixth-grade parents and junior high school guidance teachers
  on May 20.
Reproduced by permission of the Schenectady (New York) Public Schools.

Some schools have organized workshops and various kinds of training sessions for their teachers. Role playing, in which teachers assume the roles of both parent and teacher, is helpful. Writing a script of a hypothetical conference and inviting criticism from colleagues develops insight into conference skill. Often bulletins are issued outlining suggestions including "do's and don'ts." They include such helpful materials as the following (Weckler, 1955, pp. 120–121):

1. A teacher's guide sheet for each child, with appropriate headings, to be filled in prior to the conference.
2. Lists of characteristics of boys and girls at different age levels. Such lists are most helpful if these characteristics are described in terms of specific behaviors. They help teachers to identify possible problems in their early stages and to find strengths in pupils that might otherwise be overlooked.
3. An outline of the school program to help parents understand the goals of the school and the ways in which the school works to attain these goals.
4. A reminder sheet of effective and ineffective conference techniques.
5. A form to report what actually took place at the conference. Ample space is provided for the contributions made by parents. One copy of this report is often given to the parents, the other is retained in the cumulative folder.

It is helpful to foresee some of the questions parents may ask in a conference. A list of such inquiries and suggested answers is usually included in the conference bulletins for teachers. The following are typical:

Why can't my youngster sound a strange word? He's in the third grade now.

Answer: This is what he can do. He can recognize beginning consonant sounds. He is beginning to be able to sound consonant combinations. I am working with him toward . . . (an opportunity here to present a phonetic program grades one through six). It takes some children longer to reach various stages.

My older boy's first year in junior high school leads me to believe that he wasn't ready for the seventh grade. Do you send children to junior high school who aren't ready for seventh grade?

Answer: It is the policy of this school system to accept a pupil at his level of achievement in each succeeding grade level and bring him along from there. Perhaps your boy was doing arithmetic, shall we say, below seventh-grade achievement level. His seventh-grade teacher will recognize this from information sent along in the boy's folder and record and will begin his instruction where he is . . . (opportunity for interpretation of variances in the promotion policy).

I like marks. I want to know whether my youngster is an A or B student.

Answer: We have discussed the work of your child and find that he works hard and with understanding at easy material for his grade. We're satisfied with what he is doing and the effort he is putting forth. At present, he is working at a lower level of achievement than the average student in the class. If you want to think of his work in terms of marks with which you are familiar, you can apply a letter or a grade to the usual three divisions of a group such as, A, B, C, and thereby indicate to your satisfaction the mark that you are giving your child.

Reproduced by permission of the Schenectady (New York) Public Schools.

One reason why teachers do not get as much needed information from parents is that they don't ask good questions. Typical questions like the following lack the sharpness so necessary to get at specific behaviors that would be helpful for teachers to know about.

Is Jimmy generally good-natured?
Does Mary like mathematics?
Does Jack seem to be in good health?

Parents can and will provide, under adequate stimulation, information that will help the teacher determine how effective his teaching has been in transferring to pupils' behavior outside of school. Note the questions below:

Is Mary interested in graphs printed in the local newspaper?
Does she ask questions when the stock and bond quotations are broadcast?
Does Jack accept food that he has disliked or ask for a substitute to maintain a healthful diet?

Parents can also provide information to aid in remediation. Too often in answer to queries about their child's difficulties they have been told that everything is all right. They are advised not to concern themselves with instructional problems. Nothing is more frustrating to the interested and intelligent parent than this approach.

In addition to his skill, the teacher's attitude about the conference determines its success to a large degree. He has to accept the parent and look objectively at his problems and their relationship to the child's welfare. Resenting the parent for his treatment of the child is more likely to reinforce the parental attitude than to change it.

Using Specific Information.   The mother of one kindergarten child must have been perplexed to hear the teacher sum up a conference during the eighth month of school by saying, "You know, I just haven't learned to know Ann very well." This teacher violated an important rule of a good conference, namely, always have specific information available for each pupil. Anecdotes and dated illustrative examples of daily work and quizzes can mean the difference between a generally unproductive visit, however friendly, and a purposeful, helpful conference. Rather than saying "Bill is a very cooperative child," how much more informative to report "Bill is always willing to help out with class activities. He's dependable. The other day he mentioned that he could bring a book on trucks from home, and he didn't forget." Or instead of "Mary is a well-adjusted child," it is far more meaningful to the parent to hear "Children are always choosing Mary for their games and activities. She is very thoughtful of other pupils. Yesterday she helped Jim and Sally clean up their paints so they could go out to recess with the rest of the group."

Rather than comparing elementary school pupils with each other, discuss the child's progress in terms of his past achievement, and his own strengths and weaknesses. Instead of "Jack is the best reader in the room," the comment would be better phrased, "Jack reads a great many books during his free-reading period. He's always willing to discuss what he's read, and really enjoys recommending books to other children. You may be interested in this list of books that he's read since the beginning of school. Notice how varied his interests are. You may remember he wasn't nearly so interested in books last year." Try to be constructive and positive in discussing pupils. For example, rather than stating, "Sally lacks the ability to do independent reading," say "Sally is slowly becoming interested in reading books on her own. She told me you had given her a very exciting book for her birthday. It was clear that your family discussion of the hero of the story impressed her. I'm pleased to learn of your interest in this aspect of Sally's work."

A teacher can report a great deal more on children's reading if he has data to draw on. Evaluation of the child's reading rate, the adequacy of his oral reading and the grade level of the reader he comprehends present objective data for reporting. Many of the basal reading series provide tests that can give a still clearer picture of his progress. Numerous standardized tests provide information on achievement that can be meaningfully interpreted to the parent. Test norms give additional information. Areas like music and art can also be reported specifically. Can the pupil match tones, keep rhythm, and follow a tune? Does he read syllables? How effective is he in handling specific media such as crayons and watercolors? Does he show indications of creativity and originality? Can he show perspective? Does he have a grasp of the vocabulary?

Along with information about his academic work, there should be reports on a pupil's health, attendance, tardiness, and personal-social adjustment. It is important to relate these data to his scholastic achievement, for they are part of the total picture of his progress.

Limitations.   Conferences have several important limitations, one of which is the time factor. Yet as in the case of letters to parents, this time can be very important in developing learning readiness. Educating the parent may be as important as working with his child in the classroom. Teachers also find that the information gathered and the thinking they must do in preparing for the conference may be very useful in class instruction. Often they are forced by a conference to collect information they should already have.

Another limitation sometimes mentioned is that parents will not come to conferences. A great deal of the blame for this can be attributed to the school administrators, and to teachers ill-trained in the technique. The effective administrator will involve the community leaders as well as his staff in affairs of the school, and is concerned about the community's understanding of the purpose of conferences. Of course he and his staff need to exercise the greatest care that the conferences prove worthwhile and do not degenerate into sheer generalizing and passing of pleasantries. The inadequately trained teacher can do more harm than good, for the parent is often antagonized and refuses to cooperate readily in the future. In such a case, the usefulness of conference-type reporting is greatly reduced.

A third limitation is that the conference technique is difficult to use in the secondary school. It is true that most experimentation with conferences has been in the elementary school. Moreover, the consensus of many writers is that secondary school pupils do not want their parents to participate in formal teacher-parent conferences. A study of 248 junior high school pupils does not support these conclusions, however (Richardson, 1955). One hundred ten students, or 44 percent, favored teacher-parent conferences; seventy-five, or 30 percent, favored teacher-parent-pupil conferences, and only forty-five pupils, or 18 percent, wanted to exclude the parent.

No one would maintain that the child ceases to grow after he leaves the sixth grade or that parents have no place in his educational program. As the educational level of parents increases over the years, parental concern about pupil growth in the secondary school will undoubtedly be as great as for the elementary grades now. Such a trend appears to be developing. Nonetheless, a very practical problem must be solved before there can be extensive conferences at the secondary school level. The large pupil-teacher ratio will prevent conferences with the parents of all pupils during the year. The teacher's need for better home understanding and parental cooperation to help some pupils must form a basis for selection. The guidance staff will be able to alleviate the teacher's load by conferring with some of the parents. At any rate, secondary schools need to plan closer contact with the home.

Problem

12. The teacher-parent conference is often more helpful to the teacher than to the parents in terms of understanding that child. If you were allowed only one conference each year, during what month would you prefer to schedule these meetings? Support your answer.

Self-Evaluation

One aspect of the total evaluation program that is being emphasized more and more is the need for pupils to evaluate themselves. It has been pointed out that self-evaluation might well be used as a means of reporting pupil progress. After reviewing the literature, Russell (1953, p. 566) concludes:

> Children's self-evaluation of their development of habits and attitudes contained in some of the usual concepts of personality or "good citizenship" in school bears a positive but slight relationship to the other criteria of adjustment, teacher and peer ratings.

Relative to self-ratings in academic achievement he says (1953, p. 568):

> Elementary school children who have received no special instruction do not appraise their academic progress much like their teachers or peers do, although they may be fairly consistent in overestimating or underestimating their achievement.

He also finds that socioeconomic class and a pupil's level of aspiration affect achievement as well as the opinions of his teachers and peers concerning his achievement. It has been known for some time that teachers tend to approve middle-class standards of behavior because of their own backgrounds.

Though evidence is insufficient to support self-evaluation as a valid part of any marking and reporting system, teachers should guide pupils in learning to evaluate themselves. This is an important educational objective, and one helpful way of achieving it is to discuss a pupil's progress with him. He should be able to interpret his own achievement as it relates to his strengths and weaknesses and the teacher should help him to understand the various reports sent to his parents.

Problem

13. Outline a specific program in your subject matter area for implementing self-evaluation procedures. What are your underlying objectives for following this program?

BY-PRODUCTS OF MARKING AND REPORTING

Emotional Problems

Invariably a cartoonist playing on some aspect of reporting will emphasize the defensive behavior of the pupil or his fear of adult disapproval. The judgment always seems to be punitive, and the implication that life would be wonderful if report cards could somehow vanish. Certainly in many instances parents do withhold privileges or administer corporal punishment when their child brings home a bad report. Some offer prizes and rewards for an A; then the child's problems may be overlooked and the mark becomes all important. Other parents identify with their children and may blame the school for bad reports, and the necessary cooperation between the home and school is hard to come by.

In other cases, the pressures for getting high marks result in cheating, or at best, in conforming to a teacher's wishes as a ploy in working for marks. Some pupils develop feelings of inferiority and the resulting self-concept keeps them from trying to solve their difficulties. It is not uncommon for gifted children with specific difficulties in arithmetic or reading to be convinced of their general lack of intellectual prowess.

Anxieties are further aroused by threats of failure. Excessive fear does not promote effective learning; it creates tensions and disorganization. Energy is dissipated through the emotions fear creates and pupils find it difficult to learn. One seventh-grade boy wrote this when asked what he worried about:

> I worry about what my folks will say about my low marks. I hate to take home my report card. My folks get mad and scold me. I try hard, but it doesn't seem to do any good. I wish I could do better.

This is what happens with loss of perspective on the defensible use of marks. Marking and reporting need not cause these reactions. In many school systems children are eager for reporting time. The spirit is one of helpful cooperation, with the child standing to gain. Prevailing attitudes promote helpfulness rather than criticism.

Effect of Marking on Teaching

Some teachers present marks in the light of rewards or prizes, but even with this approach there will be pupils who face failure. For those able to earn high marks, it would be better for the teacher to foster interest in learning. Trying to motivate through marks seems an easy way out for the teacher, eliminating the need to provide interesting and worthwhile learning experiences. The typical textbook assignment with equal requirements for all can be followed regardless of individual differences in learning ability. Academic achievement can be emphasized while other aspects of pupil growth are ignored. It is a simple process to evaluate only in terms of test and examination averages, marks on papers, and participation in recitation, much simpler than trying to understand each pupil and evaluate his growth in terms of his own inherent characteristics and environmental problems. When marks are used for motivation, they too often degenerate into an end in themselves. They should be a tool for improvement of learning, not a crutch for ineffective teaching.

Problem

14. A high-school teacher felt that Johnny was lazy, and was concerned about his sloppy work in algebra. He reasoned that this boy needed a good jolt. Knowing

that Johnny's father held rigid, high standards for his son, the teacher assigned his pupil a particularly low mark. Evaluate this decision by the teacher.

IMPROVING MARKING AND REPORTING

The following seven steps include various suggestions advanced by schools that have studied their marking and reporting systems seriously and initiated programs of effective improvement (Strang, 1955, pp. 15–17).

Have teachers, parents, and pupils study the problem cooperatively. Involving representatives of all groups who will be concerned with marks and reports is the best way to insure understanding and cooperative effort for continued critical analysis and improvement of the system. This means calling on teachers from a range of grade levels and subjects and also a variety of specialists among school personnel, such as administrators and guidance staff. There should be representatives from the parent-teacher association and other interested organizations. It is important to provide a hearing for a cross section of the pupils, and for parents from several socioeconomic backgrounds, as their goals for their children will differ.

Begin by studying the present reporting system. The experience of all representatives with the existing marking practices of the school will generate interest, should produce profitable discussion, and do much to involve all members of the group. They should determine the effectiveness of communication under the current reporting system and the usefulness of the information that reports give to pupils and parents. Teachers can comment on how easy and effective they feel their communication to be. Certainly the group will be concerned with how well the marking and reporting evaluate in terms of the educational objectives of the school. This provides an excellent opportunity to interpret the school program to parents and pupils. Teachers will need to rethink their teaching in relation to the objectives.

Determine what marking and reporting should accomplish. The answer to this problem will evolve from the previous discussion. The group must decide what it believes important to know about the pupil, and whether it is feasible to report it. Furthermore, they should decide on suitable measurement tools and procedures. There must be exploration of such issues as the use of universal standards in marking and marking achievement in terms of the pupil's ability. The breadth of achievement and growth must be determined. If only final achievement is to be assessed, the group's problem is comparatively simple; if there is a desire for some of the reporting to be based on pupil growth, then serious consideration must be given to the problems involved.

Explore the marking and reporting systems of other schools. The group can often glean helpful ideas from the experiences and reports of other schools. Though no two school systems have identical problems, there is enough similarity to make it helpful to examine effective methods, difficulties that have been met, and suggestions made for improvement elsewhere.

Prepare a tentative form. The starting point for a reporting system is always the objectives of the school. The group must select those objectives on which they wish reports made, examine the feasibility of various methods of reporting in terms of those objectives. It is important to consider such factors as time available to the teacher. Possibly there should be time released from teaching to prepare and make the reports. If a printed form of some kind is to be used, specific suggestions should be made for its construction.

Present the tentative form to pupils, teachers, and the general public. A considerable amount of study may be necessary if a basic change in reporting is involved. Questions that may not have been considered in the representatives' group will surely be raised on general presentation. Another meeting of the group may be necessary to resolve some of them. Possibly teachers will find it helpful to meet in special session to study means of administering the system effectively. Understanding and agreement should be reached. If there is a change to teacher-parent conferences or the writing of letters, in-service training conferences will undoubtedly be needed. Possibly some basic curriculum changes will be recommended if educational objectives are reformulated. A new look at school and community relationships may be in order, and some aspects of the school program may have to be revised, such as promotional policies, guidance services, and curriculum offerings.

Give the tentative form a trial. When the basic groundwork has been completed, the new system is ready for its trial run. Plan on several semesters to appraise its strengths and weaknesses. Set up machinery to collect all possible suggestions and criticisms from pupils, parents, teachers, and the general public. Emphasize the growth of the pupil as the criterion for judgment. Has his attitude toward learning been improved? Has his personal-social adjustment matured? Is there a better relationship among pupils, teachers, parents?

We should not stop here. The new system must always be subject to revision. Parents and pupils should be involved continuously in a study of the educational program of the schools. This includes evaluation of the extent to which the program achieves the educational objectives. It also means that evaluation must keep pace when objectives are changed.

Schools and communities that follow the seven steps above to the best of their ability will not necessarily arrive at the same system of marking and reporting, for there is no single system that is the best for schools of all types or for all grade levels within these schools. Because of differences, however slight, in educational objectives, pupil talent, and points of view about the function of reports, the reporting systems selected vary from place to place and time to time. Furthermore, it is common to find variations within a school system. Different combinations of several of the reporting techniques may be used.

Regardless of which reporting system or combination of systems is chosen, it is most important that the result should receive widespread approval and that its purposes should be clearly understood by all concerned. If understanding and approval exist, cooperation among teachers, pupils, parents, and school administrators will come more easily, and the likelihood of misinterpretation (usually in the form of overinterpretations) of the reports themselves will be greatly lessened.

Problems

15. A suggested program of improving marks and reporting has been outlined. Choose one of the seven steps, and assume that you are to head a committee that is to carry out this phase of the program. Describe in detail the procedures you and your committee would follow.
16. The role of the parents and community in the development of the marking and reporting system is very often overlooked. What advantages are to be gained from enlisting this cooperation? What disadvantages may exist?

PROMOTION AND FINAL MARKS

Problems and Principles

If the philosophy of the school is concerned with the most effective development of the whole pupil, policies for promotion must be consistent with the criterion of "what is best for the pupil." Widely different practices are currently in effect in an effort to meet this criterion. Pupils in some schools must meet or exceed a "passing level" of achievement before they are promoted. Other schools have the policy of "social promotion," or one hundred percent promotion. Both of these approaches have serious limitations.

Requiring all pupils, without respect to their talents and goals, to reach a "passing level" before promotion creates a threat of failure, that can in some cases, do great harm to the pupil. To a pupil of modest ability, it becomes a perpetual threat of failure that can undermine his confidence in himself, creating feelings of inadequacy and insecurity that can do irreparable damage to his personality. Moreover, failing him not only leaves the cause of his difficulty unchanged, but aggravates the situation by his feelings of inadequacy. Some pupils are doomed to repeat failure because they do not have the intellectual capacity to meet certain standards necessary for promotion. The bad effect on their mental health is obvious.

The very nature of today's school population greatly complicates the mental health problem. The schools are committed to accept all children with few exceptions and to give them twelve or thirteen years of free education. State laws force the children to stay in school for most of these years. Great heterogeneity results. Unfortunately the curriculum of many schools has not been expanded to meet the different needs of their pupils. Consequently those placed in classes in which they may have no interest and for which they are ill prepared, are faced with failure. The result may be boredom, apathy, anxiety, belligerence, or hostility. The teacher is confronted with a complex teaching situation.

Thus the use of a "passing level" is not the source of the problem. A much more basic cause is the limited nature of the curriculum in many schools. Until they are placed in classes better suited to their needs and talents, some pupils will experience a series of failures. To assume that every pupil should receive the same dosage of subject matter in a particular grade level is to ignore the fact that, at any grade level, there are pupils at all levels of achievement with a wide range of learning capacities. There must be appropriate levels of instruction with appropriate standards.

Yet "social promotion" is not the answer. In the first place, there are some pupils who profit by repeating a course or grade level. A pupil who is generally immature might find considerable satisfaction in being with a younger group of children and a teacher who instructs accordingly. A second and more important factor is that pupils do not become a homogeneous group by some magic after they are promoted. The fact that they are all now fourth graders or sophomores in high school does not suddenly emulsify heterogeneity. Pupils must still be taught on the basis of their experience backgrounds and learning capacities. Data show that there are from three to nine grades of achievement levels in any one grade level. Indeed, effective teaching tends to make a group more heterogeneous relative to achievement. Therefore, if we are to promote pupils regardless of achievement, considerable attention must be given to the individual pupil and the problems peculiar to him.

Trying to establish the best promotion policy is about as difficult as trying to find the best marking and reporting system. In fact, there are many problems common to the two issues. In both cases, differences among schools in terms of educational objectives, pupil populations, and the opinions of all parties concerned can be reasons for differences in policies.

Six basic principles that can be used as the basis for a policy for promotion are the following (National Education Association, 1931, pp. 18–22):

1. Promotion should be decided on the basis of the individual pupil.
2. Promotion should be on the basis of many factors. The final decision as to whether a particular pupil should be promoted should rest not merely on academic accomplishment, but on what will result in the greatest good to the all-around development of the individual.
3. In order that promotion procedures may be more or less uniform throughout a particular school system, a definite set of factors should be agreed upon, which each teacher will take into consideration in forming his judgment as to whether or not a particular pupil should be promoted.
4. Criteria for promotion must take into consideration the curriculum offerings of the next higher grade or unit and the flexibility of its organization, its courses of study, and its methods.
5. It is the duty of the next higher grade or unit to accept pupils who are properly promoted to it from the lower grade or unit and to adapt its work to fit the needs of these pupils.
6. Promotion procedures demand continuous analysis and study of cumulative case history records in order that refinement of procedure may result, and guesswork and conjecture be reduced to a minimum.

The principles above were stated a number of years ago, and then only as a basis for discussion. However they are sound and applicable in today's classrooms. Notice that they stress the individual child as the central factor. In many instances, uniform promotion is the answer, yet to make this a blanket policy would work against the needs and interests of some pupils. There can be no substitute for the careful study of the individual. Decisions must be made on the basis of what is best for him.

Problem

17.   Nancy has failed four seventh-grade subjects. She is of average mental ability and has a stable home background. She is physically immature, has low vitality, and has grown very little in the past few years. This year she has been absent a great deal due to illness. The seventh-grade teachers have made the decision that she should repeat the seventh grade. What other information would you like to have before you could evaluate their action?

The Ungraded School

Goodlad and Anderson (1963) criticize present patterns of school organization that foster common expectations for all pupils, both in content of what is to be learned and in the time given to learn it. They label nonpromotion as an adjustment mechanism to counteract problems resulting from specified graded content, graded materials, and limited provision for individual differences. They propose nongrading; that is, the removal of grade levels, as a device for breaking this lockstep. Nongrading is in tune with the realities of individual differences; it provides for both the slow-moving pupil and the high achiever. It facilitates pupil progress, in terms of his readiness, by using sequentially organized subject matter with closely related instructional materials and evaluation based on individual progress rather than comparison with others. Pupils can be placed, not simply because they pass or fail, but on the basis of whether they "fit" into the group.

In one ungraded high school (Brown, 1963) pupils are placed in temporary learning situations that they can leave at any time depending on their ability to move into the next higher "phase." These "phases" are designed to group students in terms of their skill level, namely, low, minimal, medium, high, superior.

The challenge of the ungraded system is for the teacher to take advantage of a school organization that focuses on meeting individual needs. An opportunity is provided for him to break the lockstep that too often persists in the graded school.

SUMMARY

Determining and reporting pupil growth is one of the greatest concerns of teachers, parents, and pupils. Although teachers dislike it, probably no other activity has greater potential for interpreting the school program, for securing cooperation between home and school, and for promoting pupil development.

Reporting exists to inform pupils, parents and the administration on the degree to which teachers judge the pupil to be achieving certain educational objectives. The most important aspect of this judgment deals with the growth of the pupil in terms of his own capacity. The chief sources of information used for evaluating the pupil are classroom and standardized tests, procedures and product evaluation, class participation, and projects and reports.

Common methods of marking and reporting are the letter and number system, check lists, correspondence to parents, and teacher-parent conferences. The letter and number system has the very definite weakness of telling only part of the story. Correspondence with the parent and teacher-parent conferences are as broad in their evaluation of all aspects of the pupil's growth as the teacher cares to make them. Their limitations lie in the difficulty of effective communication and in the time required.

Probably the best plan of reporting is a combination of the different methods. There should be a regular program of teacher-pupil conferences and, insofar as possible, teacher-parent conferences. Parents can be active participants in the evaluation process. They have opportunity to observe many phases of their children's development that the teacher does not see. Cooperative participation is the key concept in any program for improving marking and reporting. Parents, teachers, and pupils must first study the school's educational objectives and then determine the most effective way to communicate the results of pupil progress in those terms. Only after thorough study, trials of tentative suggestions, critical reactions, and revisions can a school hope to effect a defensible system of marking and reporting.

Promotion policies should be based on what is best for the pupil. Since learning at school takes place in a group situation, the pupil should be placed in circumstances that result in the greatest interaction between himself and the other pupils. In general, interaction increases in homogeneous age groups. Therefore a definite trend has developed toward adapting "social promotion." But promoting all pupils does not solve all the problems of organizing effective learning experiences. Since typical promotional policies cannot eliminate differences among pupils, individual differences must be considered in every grade level.

A suggested solution to the problems of failure and promotion is nongrading. A pupil progresses in terms of a curriculum arranged sequentially based on important principles and concepts rather than on expectations for a particular grade.

Suggested Readings

Anderson, R. H., and C. Ritsher. Pupil progress. In R. L. Ebel (ed.), *Encyclopedia of Educational Research.* (4th ed.) London: Macmillan, 1969. Pp. 1050–1060.
  Related research on promotional policies for children is discussed. Reporting on pupil progress is included as part of the discussion.

Bailard, V., and R. Strang. *Parent-teacher conferences.* New York: McGraw-Hill, 1964.
  The setting and conditions necessary for successful parent-teacher conferences from kindergarten through high school are considered. Illustrative interviews from elementary, junior, and senior high schools are reproduced and evaluated.

Brown, B. F. *The non-graded high school.* Englewood Cliffs, N.J.: Prentice-Hall, 1963.
  The nongraded high school at Melbourne, Florida, is described. Some of the topics discussed are breaking the grade lockstep, a concept-centered curriculum, and marking and reporting in the nongraded school.

Chansky, N. M. Report cards and teacher personality. *Journal of Educational Research,* 1964, **57,** 492–494.
  A relation between certain teacher personality characteristics and preference for type of report card was found. For example, personality characteristics like empathy, aggression, confidence, anxiety, were correlated with a preference for one of seven types of report cards.

Cunningham, W. How to explain test scores to parents. *School Management,* 1968, 12, 86–87.

The emphasis is on the conversion of raw scores to standard scores and the use of profile charts. The benefits of the profile chart to be used with parents, teachers, and guidance counselors are described.

Ebel, R. L. *Measuring educational achievement.* Englewood Cliffs, N.J.: Prentice-Hall, 1965. Chapter 13.

Ebel argues strongly that poor marking procedures are the cause of many problems. He provides a number of sound suggestions to improve these procedures, and describes a method of marking that increases the interpretability of letter-number systems.

Goodlad, J. I., and R. H. Anderson. *The non-graded elementary school.* (Rev. ed.) New York: Harcourt, Brace & World, 1963.

Problems of promotion are considered in Chapter 2. In Chapter 6 the reporting of pupil progress in the nongraded school is explained.

Gronlund, N. E. *Stating behavioral objectives for classroom instruction.* London: Macmillan, 1970. Pp. 45–50.

The last chapter of the volume gives suggestions on how to use instructional objectives in marking and reporting. Goal report cards are illustrated.

Halliwell, J. W., and J. P. Robitaille. The relationship between theory and practice in a dual reporting program. *Journal of Educational Research,* 1963, 57, 137–141.

The history of marking and reporting is reviewed. A bibliography on various related studies is provided, and a research study describing some of the problems in a dual reporting program is presented.

Milton, O. "What it is . . . I measure I do not know." *Educational Record,* 1968, 49, 160–165.

A very critical discussion of marking and reporting, particularly the uses to which final marks are put.

Philbrick, J. L., and P. I. O'Donnell. Precision in grading practices: Panacea or problem? *Journal of Educational Research,* 1968, 62, 173–176.

The article addresses itself to the question: "Does greater precision in grading-recording have any effect upon the retention of those students eligible for academic disqualification?"

Thorndike, R. L. Marks and marking systems. In R. L. Ebel (ed.), *Encyclopedia of Educational Research.* (4th ed.) London: Macmillan, 1969. Pp. 759–766.

A thorough review of marking and reporting. Such topics as objections to marks, substitutes for marks, what a mark should represent, and proportion awarded each symbol are included.

Trow, W. C. Grades and objectives in higher education. *Educational Record,* 1968, 49, 85–91.

Four chief functions of marking are discussed—selection, motivation, guidance, and instruction. A system of more adequate marking is recommended.

Westbrook, B. W. Effect of test reporting on self-estimates of scholastic ability and on level of occupational aspiration. *Journal of Educational Research,* 1967, 60, 387–390.

The study sought to determine whether test reporting information is used by pupils wisely in making appropriate occupational choices. Findings indicate that information about scholastic ability is not sufficient to bring about changes in occupational aspiration level.

References Cited

Bloom, B. S. *Stability and change in human characteristics.* New York: John Wiley, 1964.

Brown, B. F. *The non-graded high school.* Englewood Cliffs, N.J.: Prentice-Hall, 1963.

Cook, W. W. *Grouping and promotion in the elementary school.* Series on Individualization of Instruction, No. 2. Minneapolis: University of Minnesota Press, 1941.

Crisler, R. D., and T. D. Wogaman. Educational data processing at Richmond. *Journal of Secondary Education,* 1963, **38**, 71–76.

Diederich, P. B. Pitfalls in the measurement of achievement gains. *School Review,* 1956, **64**, 59–63.

Ebel, R. L. *Measuring educational achievement.* Englewood Cliffs, N.J.: Prentice-Hall, 1965.

Goodlad, J. I., and R. H. Anderson. *The non-graded elementary school.* New York: Harcourt, Brace & World, 1963.

Goodykoontz, B. *Helping children get along in school.* Chicago: Science Research Associates, 1955.

Green, C. D. What shall we do with the dullards? *Atlantic Monthly,* 1956, **197**, 72–74.

Halliwell, J. W., and J. P. Robitaille. The relationship between theory and practice in a dual reporting program. *Journal of Educational Research,* 1963, **57**, 137–141.

Heffernan, H., and L. E. Marshall. Reporting pupil progress in California cities. *California Journal of Elementary Education,* 1955, **24**, 67–77.

Lindquist, E. F., and L. S. Feldt. *Manual, Iowa Tests of Educational Development.* Chicago: Science Research Associates, 1962.

Michael, K. E. What are some of the new trends in reporting student growth and achievement to parents? *National Association of Secondary School Principals Bulletin,* 1960, **44**, 146–149.

National Education Association. Pupil promotion problems. *Five Unifying Factors on American Education,* Ninth Yearbook. Washington: Author, 1931.

Richardson, S. How do children feel about reports to parents? *California Journal of Elementary Education,* 1955, **24**, 98–111.

Russell, D. H. What does research say about self-evaluation? *Journal of Educational Research,* 1953, **46**, 561–573.

Smith, A. Z., and J. E. Dobbin. Marks and marking systems. In C. W. Harris (ed.), *Encyclopedia of educational research.* (3rd ed.) London: Macmillan, 1960. Pp. 783–791.

Strang, R. *How to report pupil progress.* Chicago: Science Research Associates, 1955.

Weckler, N. Problems in organizing parent-teacher conferences. *California Journal of Elementary Education,* 1955, **24**, 117–126.

CHAPTER 16

A Schoolwide Program of Evaluation

The football coach has one overall objective—to win as many games as possible. To have a successful season, he must accomplish numerous other objectives centering around individual performance and team play. Blocking, running, tackling, and passing should develop as closely as possible to each player's potentialities. Then these skills have to be orchestrated to form a smooth-functioning team.

The coach will measure progress in various ways. This is important to him. He wants to note continuous improvement. Evaluation of the success of his program is based on data collected in various ways at various times. Speed can be timed. Effects of blocking can be visually judged. Distance and accuracy of passing can be measured. But data are not so easily obtained for other important performance objectives. On what basis does the coach measure motivation and eagerness? How can he judge player morale? How will he estimate sensitivity to and ability to profit from suggestion? How may he determine the team's confidence in the quarterback? He relies on reports, observations, a sensitivity to certain cues, and comparative mental images of past performance. From this information he evaluates progress. These evaluations continue throughout the season and into the following year.

PURPOSE OF AN EVALUATION PROGRAM

Stake and Denny (1969) define evaluation as the discovery of the nature and worth of something. They point out that in education we can evaluate pupils, teachers, curricula, administrations, systems, and programs. Evaluation, they emphasize, attempts to describe something and to determine its strengths and weaknesses. It must contribute to understanding substance, function, and worth.

The ultimate goal in an educational evaluation program is to inform the school how to enable each pupil to develop his potential. To accomplish this, the school must know the pupils' capacities, interests, and achievement. Furthermore, it must have instructional objectives that lend themselves to the evaluation process. Stated objectives like "To develop good citizenship" are of limited value if good citizenship is not defined and delineated so that the degree of the pupil's development can be determined. It is much less bewildering to assess progress toward the following objective, representing one facet of good citizenship: "The pupil does not destroy, or mutilate in any way, property that does not belong to him."

Educational objectives should reflect the needs of pupils in a particular school. Although the objectives of various schools are more similar than different, important differences inevitably exist. Some schools have a large percentage of college-bound pupils, while most students in a neighboring school will remain in the community. Out-of-school activities and their impact on the educational program will differ among communities. Many children of higher-socioeconomic-status families have access to a variety of books and magazines and may attend concerts, plays, and art exhibits at least on occasion, but pupils in certain rural areas may do little reading, and have few cultural opportunities. Community resources and the vocational goals of children must influence a school's objectives.

A schoolwide program of evaluation is based on the set of educational objectives held by that school. The task is exceedingly complex. Too often testing is confused with evaluation, and the school initiates a testing program per se. Though an important part of the evaluation program, testing is still only one part. Many kinds of evidence are needed, and from various sources. Because we do not have effective tests to measure all aspects of behavior, many other approaches including observation, rating scales, questionnaires, and interviews must be used. Evaluation that considers a variety of data can also focus on the process of learning rather than on the product alone. Data collected can then be the basis for evaluating individuals in terms of their abilities and needs.

But there should be more to a schoolwide program of evaluation than determining the status of the individual pupil in terms of his potential. If we are to attain this objective we should evaluate the instructional program. What programs are effective for learning? What procedures can be used to overcome specific weaknesses? We need information to aid in selecting among various competing instructional approaches. Glaser and Nitko (1970) discuss the many problems we face in assessing both learning and instruction. They suggest four activities that will lead to their solution, namely, subject matter analysis, determining learner characteristics, designing instruction, and evaluation of goals attained.

Astin and Panos (1970) list three components in any educational program: *outputs*, *inputs*, and *operations*. They emphasize that evaluation to be most effective for decision making must include all of these components including their interrelationships. *Outputs* refers to goals; *inputs* includes pupil characteristics and the environment in which they live; *operations* comprises all those environmental variables that characterize an educational program.

Unfortunately, we are more able to predict from test scores the possible success or failure of a pupil than we are able to suggest instructional procedures to prevent failure and assure success. We are much more sophisticated in using measurement techniques that determine a pupil's rank in a particular norm group than we are in describing what he can and cannot do (see techniques used in the National Assessment Program, pages 6–8). We need instruments and methodology that will aid us in identifying barriers to learning, barriers related to specific instructional techniques. A beginning is being made at the Research and Development Center at Pittsburgh (Cox, 1967). We also need to devise new kinds of test items for measurement (Lindquist, 1969) to determine the adequacy of the achievement of our objectives.

Problems

1. The board of education of a small community hired a team of educational specialists from a nearby university to evaluate the testing program of the school system and to make specific recommendations for improvement. The team prepared a comprehensive report, which was then presented to the faculty. Although this report was complimentary for the most part, there was a general feeling of dissatisfaction among both faculty and administration. Criticize the procedure followed by the board of education. Suggest a better approach.

2. Prepare a list of educational objectives for a secondary school program in a slum area in a large city, and another list for a secondary school program in a small rural community. In what respects are your lists similar? Are the differences sufficiently large to cause the schoolwide evaluation program at one school to be greatly different from that of the other school?

INITIATING THE PROGRAM

Since a program of evaluation cannot be separated from the total educational program, school personnel in administration, guidance, and instruction must participate in its inception, organization, and promotion. It should be a truly cooperative venture. The authoritarian principal who dictates a program may compel his staff to comply mechanically. They may administer, score, and record the results of tests, but it is doubtful that they will be motivated to understand pupil behavior and motivation. Such understanding only comes through in-service education and democratic participation of a staff; it is the basis of a good evaluation program.

In a small school, the general staff meeting should involve all teachers and specialists; everyone should have a chance to ask questions and discuss procedures. The administrator should probably assume leadership to stimulate interest, perhaps by posing such a problem as "Why do our pupils always do better on the mathematical parts of standardized achievement test batteries than on the verbal parts?" Perhaps community criticism of achievement may prompt the staff to evaluate its educational program. It is also possible to interest the staff by showing them the results of the administration of a standardized achievement test, like a reading survey test; from this they can determine the strengths and weaknesses of the pupils. When properly directed, this approach will stimulate thinking about the total evaluation problem in the school.

In the large city system it is impractical, if not impossible, to involve the entire staff in the initial evaluation discussions, so a representative committee should work out preliminary details. However, as in smaller schools, one person should be responsible for coordinating the program. He should be adept in working with people and sophisticated in measurement and statistics; it is important that he be given time to do the assignment effectively. Nevertheless, before any final action is taken in test selection or evaluation procedures, the entire staff should discuss and evaluate the proprosals, a necessity if the evaluation is to be integrated with the total educational program.

In the initial discussions, teachers should understand that evaluation is a comprehensive process requiring continuous administrative and guidance functions in addition to the more obvious instructional ones. Suggestions of the kinds of evidence needed for evaluating in terms of a group of related objectives, and where that evidence can be sought, can be made meaningful if presented in chart form, as illustrated in Table 34. This will help prevent the limited approach of paper-and-pencil testing alone.

The objectives concerning communication shown in Table 34 are adapted from Kearney (1953). Although it is desirable to refine the wording of some of the objectives in this table in terms of the discussion in Chapter 2 concerning the guidelines for stating specific objectives (Mager, 1962), note that these are not vaguely phrased. Rather than a vague statement "to develop comprehension," the objective listed is "he reads third-grade material with a comprehension of 80 percent." Rather than "to read rapidly," the objective is stated "he can read from 95 to 120 words silently each minute." The last objective could be improved by adding "and is able to answer correctly 80 percent of the comprehension questions sampling the passage." The criterion of acceptable performance is now definite. A few other objectives could be more crisply stated in behavioral terms. In "he can read orally in a meaningful way," the term "meaningful" should be clarified.

In Table 34, the statement of objectives is followed by a suggested means for gathering information to be used as a basis for evaluation. Although teacher-constructed and standardized tests are often very helpful, there are some areas of achievement where they are inapplicable. For example, no test can determine whether a pupil does his assigned reading independently. Certainly improved skill will be reflected in test results, but the teacher can only observe him in the classroom for effective evaluation of this achievement.

TABLE 34.   Educational Objectives in Communication for the Primary Period and Means of Evaluation.

Educational objective	*Means of evaluation*
Knowledge and Understanding	
He can recognize basic reading sight-vocabulary.	Standardized oral reading tests Informal word recognition tests Standardized word lists
He can define common words that he uses orally.	Standardized word meaning tests Observation: teacher listens to his use of words Informal tests: Pupil writes definitions of words
He can read orally in a meaningful way.	Standardized oral reading tests Informal tests Check lists: smooth reading, good phrasing, correct interpretation of punctuation marks.
He has developed an acquaintance with children's literature.	Check lists: books checked out of library, brought to school. Observation: talks about books
He understands that many words "pair off" as opposites, e.g., yes-no, little-big.	Informal and standardized tests Workbook exercises Informal questioning during group instruction
He can distinguish between the names of persons and things and action words.	Informal tests Observation: ability to act out directions, to make up directions for others to follow Classification lists

TABLE 34.   (Continued).

Educational objective	Means of evaluation
Skill and Competence	
He does assigned reading independently.	Informal questioning during group instruction
	Observation: independent reading
	Written work
He can recall the sequence of a story or the facts read in a story.	Standardized reading tests
	Informal reading tests: recalls and writes facts
	Observation: answers well-phrased questions during group discussion, illustrates sequence in pictures, acts out sequence
He reads simple informational material with comprehension.	Informal reading tests
	Written work: brief written reports
	Observation: discusses material read
He reads third-grade material with a comprehension of 80 per cent.	Standardized reading tests
	Informal tests
He can read seven out of ten paragraphs of third-grade material and recognize many of the main ideas.	Standardized reading tests
	Informal tests
	Working with him independently and questioning him
He can read from 95 to 120 words silently each minute.	Standardized reading tests
	Informal tests (timed)
Attitude and Interest	
He enjoys reading for recreation or information.	Observation: talks or writes about his reading, anxious to read new books, brings in objects about what he has read
He likes to recite poems and retell favorite stories.	Observation: reflects interests by what he says and does
He is interested in the sounds of words in word-families, in rhymes, and in secret languages and codes.	Observation: ability to act out direc-indicate this interest, knows how to determine word-families

Educational objectives adapted from Kearney, 1953, pp. 102–110; by permission of the Russell Sage Foundation.

Incidentally, not all pupils will be limited to the specific objectives stated in Table 34, which are only general guides for primary teachers. A number of pupils should be able to read more difficult material than those at third grade level, just as some will read faster than 120 words per minute.

Problems

3.   Table 34 presents in chart form a suggested manner of listing educational objectives in reading and a. means of evaluation for each objective. Prepare a similar table for your subject matter area but improve your statements of objectives by following the suggestions in Chapter 2.

4.   Choose one or more of the educational objectives that you have stated for your subject matter and devise reasonably reliable and valid methods by means of which you might systematically and objectively evaluate each pupil in a class.

USE OF STANDARDIZED TESTS

Although standardized tests represent only one means of obtaining data for evaluation, they are very important tools in measurement. Therefore their selection, administration, scoring, and interpretation are significant aspects of educational evaluation. A great deal of research has gone into test construction. Selection of the wrong test, its improper administration or scoring, or inadequate interpretation of the results can waste time and money, and harm pupils.

Scope of the Program

Infant and Preschool Tests.   There has been a resurgence of interest in infant and preschool tests largely because of concern for retarded children and the funding of compensatory school programs for culturally disadvantaged boys and girls. These tests are either performance or oral tests and must be individually administered. Generally, infant tests are designed for children up to 18 months of age and preschool tests are considered applicable to the 18-to-60-month period.

Some of these instruments are rating scales rather than tests to aid in the observation of children (Gesell and Amatruda, 1947). Others are downward extensions of the *Binet* scales such as the *Cattell Infant Intelligence Scale*. At the lower end of these scales the required responses are largely perceptual, such as following a moving object or focusing on sounds. There may be some motor tasks requiring movement of parts of the body or changing an object from one hand to another. Of course, as one proceeds up the scale the tasks become more complex. Some verbal responses are required and manipulative tasks require added skill.

A well-known instrument at the preschool level is the *Merrill Palmer*

Scale of Mental Tests. It tends to require performance responses and is often used along with the highly verbal *Stanford-Binet.*

Regarding use of infant and preschool tests, we must conclude that infant tests have no validity in predicting future intelligence test performance. Beginning with the age of 12 months, however, there is a constant increase in predictive power so that the preschool tests have a moderate correlation with subsequent intelligence test scores. One may conclude that the value of infant tests is to aid in the diagnosis of children who may later be judged mentally defective. There is some evidence that there is a higher correlation between scores on a developmental scale and scores on the *Stanford-Binet* at six and ten years of age with this type of child (Knobloch and Passamanick, 1967).

Elementary and Junior High School.   A minimum testing program for the elementary and junior high school consists of periodic measurement of scholastic aptitude and yearly achievement testing. Although authorities differ about the best grade level for administering scholastic aptitude tests, they generally agree that four or five administrations should occur between the time the child enters school and his completion of high school. A suggested sequence is at the beginning of the first, fourth, seventh, and tenth grades. Some schools add two more administrations in the second and eighth or ninth years. These are transitional points in the pupil's educational life, representing the beginning of formal study and of the intermediate, junior high, and senior high periods. In addition to the administrations suggested above, the pupil should be tested again whenever results are at variance with the teacher's judgment.

Another argument for frequent administrations of scholastic aptitude tests is the variation in the test results that typically occurs. IQs commonly vary as much as ten or more points when two or more tests are given. A pupil may therefore be penalized unless previous test results are continually checked.

Achievement batteries should be administered yearly. The minimal program should emphasize tests of basic skills. The basic responsibilities of the school at this level are proficiency of work-study skills, language arts, and arithmetic. These are of greater importance than content areas.

An optimum program for the elementary and junior high school would include access to all available tests that would help the pupil. In addition to survey tests of achievement, diagnostic tests would be administered whenever necessary. Special reading tests, such as readiness tests, could be added to the first-grade battery. An optimum program would also include personal-social adjustment and interest inventories. Although these instruments are inadequate in several important respects, they can be used as screening devices to identify problem children.

Senior High School.   The minimum program in the senior high school should include a test of scholastic aptitude or a differential aptitude test and measures of achievement in various subjects. It is particularly important that college-bound pupils know their adequacy in such areas as mathematics, social, biological, and physical sciences, and the language arts. Every program should also include a recheck of the basic skills. It is especially important to administer a reading test. Whether or not a pupil is college-bound, reading is important. The optimum program for the secondary school would employ personal-social adjustment inventories, problem check lists, and interest inventories. These can be used for screening purposes or educational and vocational guidance. In this regard, the limitations of adjustment inventories should be carefully considered.

Guidelines for Testing the Disadvantaged.   Attention has been given to the problem of obtaining valid scores for disadvantaged pupils in aptitude testing (see p. 382). In addition, test scores from achievement and personal-social adjustment instruments may need special interpretation for the disadvantaged. Fishman and others (1964) elaborate on three critical issues in testing the disadvantaged: (1) unreliability of differentiation within their range of scores, (2) the possible difference in predictive validity between disadvantaged groups and standardization groups, (3) the importance of understanding the group's social and cultural background. They believe that it is important to compare the disadvantaged child's test performance with his previous test performance. Such a child's progress can best be judged by using himself as his own control and employing the norms as "bench marks."

However, numerous attempts to discuss the special problems of testing the disadvantaged have led to nothing that seems particularly helpful. Perhaps the designated category is somewhat analogous to "testing males" or "testing adolescents." There undoubtedly are certain considerations important for testing those children from lower economic groups, but we do not know very much about them. Nevertheless, they are probably not nearly so important as those factors that we do know a lot about for adequate testing in general: clarity of instructions, appropriate test selection in terms of use, validity, reliability, and so on. The informed test user is sensitive to the various characteristics of a given test, the testee, and the interpretation of test scores. If he is knowledgeable about general test use, he is not likely to make gross errors with any specific individual or group.

An Illustrative School Testing Program.   School testing programs often vary considerably in terms of the tests used. In Table 35 are shown the various types of tests included in a well developed program. For each type some of the tests commonly used are listed. These lists are by no means complete.

TABLE 35. An Illustrative School Testing Program.

Testing Area	Age or Grade Level of the Instrument[a]	K	I	II	III	IV	V	VI	VII	VIII	IX	X	XI	XII
ACHIEVEMENT														
Reading Achievement:														
Gates-MacGinitie Reading Tests	I–VII		X	X	X	X	X	X						
Davis Reading Test	VIII–XI										X			
Basic Skills Battery:														
California Achievement Tests	I–XIV			X	X	X	X	X						
Comprehensive Tests of Basic Skills	II–XII					X	X							
Iowa Tests of Basic Skills	III–IX					X	X							
Content Achievement:														
Cooperative Tests	I–College							X						
Metropolitan Achievement Tests	I–IX													
Sequential Tests of Educational Progress	IV–XIV										X			
Diagnostic Tests:					(As needed)									
Gates-McKillop Reading Diagnostic Test	II–VI													
Stanford Diagnostic Arithmetic Test	II–VIII													
Stanford Diagnostic Reading Test	III–VIII													
APTITUDE														
Group Mental Ability Tests:		X				X			X			X		
California Test of Mental Maturity	I–Adult													
Lorge-Thorndike Intelligence Tests	K–XII													

TABLE 35. (Continued).

Testing Area	Age or Grade Level of the Instrument[a]	K	I	II	III	IV	V	VI	VII	VIII	IX	X	XI	XII
Otis-Lennon Mental Ability Test	K–XII													
School and College Ability Test	IV–XIV													
Differential Aptitude Test:														
Differential Aptitude Test	VIII–XII									X				
General Aptitude Test Battery	IX–XII													
College Admissions Tests:														
CEEB Scholastic Aptitude Test	XI–XII													X
American College Testing Program	XI–XII													
Individual Intelligence Tests:		(As needed)												
Stanford-Binet Intelligence Scale	2–Adult													
Wechsler Preschool and Primary Scale of Intelligence	4–6													
Wechsler Intelligence Scale for Children	5–15													
Wechsler Adult Intelligence Scale	10–Adult													
PERSONAL-SOCIAL ADJUSTMENT														
Interest:														
Kuder Preference Record—Occupational	IX–Adult													
Minnesota Vocational Interest Survey	IX–Adult										X			
Strong Vocational Interest Blank	17 and over	(As needed)												
General:														
California Test of Personality	K–Adult													
Mooney Problem Check List	VII–Adult													

[a] Age levels are given in Arabic numbers, grade levels in Roman numbers.

In Appendices C, D, and E further information is given for these and other suitable tests.

Note that many of the tests are only used for special purposes with a few pupils. For instance, individual intelligence tests would be given only when group mental ability tests produce questionable results. Diagnostic tests would be administered when there is need to study basic problems of learning experienced by certain pupils.

Also, some tests are designed for special groups only. Examples are the *General Aptitude Test Battery* and the *Minnesota Vocational Interest Survey*, which are designed for non–college-bound youth.

Problems

5. At what levels would you administer reading tests in the elementary and junior high school program? When might an aptitude battery such as the *DAT* be most useful?
6. Many colleges and universities are now asking that college-bound high-school pupils provide scholastic aptitude test scores obtained either during the junior or senior year of high school. Some school personnel feel this is unnecessary. Do you agree?

Selecting the Test

Tests should be selected on the basis of their contribution to evaluation in terms of the school's educational objectives. Therefore, a test must be studied carefully to determine both its content and its relationship to other tests and information available. The best way to do this is to take the test oneself. This indicates the processes required for correct responses, makes clear the obvious content, and enables the teacher to anticipate difficulties in administration.

In selecting tests, the teacher should consult Buros' *Mental Measurements Yearbooks*. These references are revised continually and provide quantities of information about all types of tests. At least one specialist discusses the strengths and weaknesses of most of the popular tests. Often individual items are criticized, and sometimes problems in administration and scoring are discussed. As well as being helpful in selection, these volumes provide a great deal of general learning about tests.

It is important to keep the continuity of a testing program in mind for all the grades from kindergarten through high school. The cumulative record (see page 560) is more meaningful if related tests are used at the different grade levels. If the *Stanford Achievement Tests* are selected, for example, the norms from level to level would be based on similar populations, and the relative emphasis on various types of content in the tests would tend to be similar, thereby making it easier to assess achievement. Likewise, the scores from a given scholastic aptitude test would be more comparable from level to level than comparisons made between tests having different authors.

After tests have been selected, administered, and proved functional for a school, they should not be replaced unless it appears that other instruments will be more effective, since it is necessary to compare results from year to year if the cumulative record is to be meaningful. A more recent copyright date on another test doesn't necessarily guarantee a better test. At times, because of the development of new instruments, it is wise to make a change. Then study of the results of groups of pupils will be helpful in making comparisons with previous test data.

Validity.   Validity is defined as the extent to which a measuring instrument serves the purpose for which it is intended. There are three kinds of validity: content, criterion-related, and construct. Each test in the evaluation program must possess a satisfactory degree of one or more of these types to justify its use. Hence, thoughtful attention must be given to certain questions concerning the validity of a test before it is selected. Among those of importance are the following:

Questions of general interest:
1. Are the kinds of validity reported those required by the role to be played by the test in the testing program?
2. Is evidence available that supports the validity of each of the interpretations of each of the test scores as suggested by the authors?
3. Is the basis on which the particular scope of the test was determined a sound one?
4. Do the test items seem to be well constructed and suitable in all important respects for the pupils to be tested?
5. Does the validity of this test compare favorably with that of similar tests?
6. What opinions do reviewers, critics, and research workers have about the validity of the test?

Questions concerning standardized achievement tests:
1. Are the sources from which the test items are drawn satisfactory ones?
2. Is the method of sampling the content a defensible one?
3. Is a table of specifications or the equivalent provided for each test or subtest, and are the relationships between the test items and these tables identified?
4. Are these tables very similar to those based on the educational objectives of the class that is to be given the test?
5. If a degree of criterion-related validity is claimed, is the validation sample representative and are the independent criteria adequate and meaningful?

Questions concerning standardized aptitude tests:
1. Are the correlation coefficients resulting from validity determinations so high that the likelihood of misclassifying a pupil on the basis of the test scores is slight?

2. Are variability measures of the test scores reported with each correlation co-efficient and, as far as can be determined, are they similar to those for the pupils to be tested?
3. Are suitable expectancy tables available?
4. Is the author's definition of the aptitude to be measured clearly stated and is it appropriate in terms of needs of the testing program?
5. Is there adequate evidence to show how the individual test items represent a part of this definition?
6. Is the independent criterion measure described accurately and with sufficient detail?
7. Were criterion scores determined independently from the scores of the testing being validated?
8. Is the validation sample representative of the pupils with whom the test is to be used?

Questions concerning standardized instruments for evaluating personal-social development are much like those for standardized aptitude tests in that construct and criterion-related validity are particularly important.

Reliability.   If a test does not give consistent results, it has low reliability. Caution should be exercised in interpreting scores from tests of questionable reliability. This is especially true when test results are used in the diagnosis of an individual pupil's difficulties. If test results are used with groups of individuals, reliability coefficients can be lower and the data still be helpful in indicating trends, weaknesses and strengths. In studying the reliability of a standardized instrument, questions such as the following should be posed:

1. What types of reliability determinations have been made, and have they been described in sufficient detail?
2. Is evidence presented that enables one to determine whether the test and all of its subparts, if any, are sufficiently reliable for their recommended uses?
3. Is the standard error of measurement small enough to justify the uses of test scores that are planned?
4. Is the reliability of the difference between test scores reported when the con-struction of a profile is suggested and is it relatively low?
5. Is the sample used in the reliability determination comparable to the pupils with whom the test is to be used?
6. Are measures of variability reported with each reliability coefficient and, as far as it can be determined, are they similar to those for the pupils to be tested?
7. Do the reliability coefficients of this test compare favorably with those of similar tests?
8. What opinions do reviewers, critics, and research workers have about the reli-ability of the test?

Norms.   An important feature of the standardized test is the availability of norms, which reflect relative performance. In a determination of their ade-quacy, questions such as the following should prove helpful:

1. Are various types of norms reported or easily obtained from test data presented?
2. Is there an adequate description of the distribution of the raw scores on which the norms are based?
3. Is the standardization group described clearly?
   (a) Is the method of sampling a defensible one?
   (b) Is the group described in detail with respect to talent, training, age, sex?
   (c) Is the size of the standardization group sufficiently large?
4. Are separate sets of norms available for all important subgroups of the standardization group that are known to differ in terms of the test?
5. Do the norms for this test compare favorably with those of similar tests?
6. What opinions do reviewers, critics, and research workers have about the norms of the test?
7. Are norms available for groups with which you want to compare your class members?

Ease of Administration. The information concerning validity, reliability, and norms is meaningful only if the test is administered in the same way that it was administered to the standardization group. Because untrained personnel often administer tests, the simplicity and readability of test instructions are of prime importance. Tests with complicated timing procedures often give invalid results. Tests with inadequate instructions to the examinees, inadequate sample exercises, or poor typographic makeup stimulate excessive questions.

The time required for test administration is also important. Because some tests can be administered in parts, they can be scheduled during the regular school periods; others require a reorganization of the daily schedule. Before a test is selected, its length must not hamper local conditions. The arrangement of the test booklet is an important factor in the administration of a test. In some tests pupils must turn the booklet around or fold under pages. The examinee who often finds it difficult to follow instructions may lose his place and invalidate results.

Ease of Scoring. A test may be well administered, but the results are of little value if scoring is inaccurate. When scoring is completely objective, fewer problems arise, and, of course, instructions for scoring should be clearly worded. However, when some subjectivity is involved, the scoring becomes more complex, and machine scoring is no longer possible.

The mechanics of scoring the test should be checked, and a simple scoring key provided for efficient checking. Some arrangements are awkward, time-consuming, and inaccurate. The calculations for scoring should be simple and brief.

Economy. The old adage "penny wise and pound foolish" is certainly applicable to the selection of tests. The price of a test book is a very minor part of the total cost of an evaluation program. Administration, scoring, and interpretation represent teacher and pupil man-hours of considerable magnitude. Scoring alone is very expensive for certain tests. Primarily, of course, tests should be selected for their ability to measure the achievement of school objectives. Basing choice on any other reason is false economy.

Miscellaneous.   Equivalent forms should be available to allow the testing of different classes at different times, or multiple testing of one class. Also, aids should be provided for interpretation of test results. Class charts and profile blanks ease and clarify recording and interpreting test results. Even a survey test will serve some diagnostic purposes if results can be adequately interpreted, and some manuals give suggestions for such remediation. Suggestions are correlated with the various subtests.

Problems

7.   A junior high school is using a new battery of achievement tests this year. A faculty committee has been appointed to evaluate the usefulness of the new tests and to recommend either retaining or discontinuing them. Outline a procedure for the committee to follow.

8.   Teachers tend to be confused by statistical reports of validation studies in test manuals and therefore skip over them. List four basic questions that can serve as guides in reviewing this material.

Administering the Test

If test results are to be successfully interpreted, they must be carefully administered according to the specific instructions. Results from various classes cannot be compared unless administration is standardized, nor can norms be of any value. This applies not only to reading printed instructions carefully, but to motivating the pupils to do their best on a test. Time limits must be followed rigidly. Proper administration requires very careful planning from ordering tests on time to their distribution to the classrooms.

The Test Administrator.   Who should administer the tests? Some individual tests will be given by the school psychologist. In large school systems, a testing specialist may be employed to administer group tests. In most instances, however, the teacher gives tests, and to some advantage. Not only does it identify the teacher with the testing program, since he must familiarize himself with the tests, but because he knows his pupils, he can motivate them more effectively, interpret their reactions, and establish the necessary rapport.

Those who criticize teacher administration usually focus their arguments on inaccurate timing or improper instructions. Teachers should be given instruction in the administration of the tests. The first step is to familiarize them with standardized test construction, for they must understand the importance of standardized procedure. Group instruction is advised when provision can be made for a question period. Instruction had best be given by a specialist in testing, whether from the local school or from a college or university.

If the instructions are particularly complex, teachers should be encouraged to give the test to each other. Many a test has been spoiled because instructions were not completely understood.

Special emphasis should be given to proper timing. Instructions generally appear quite simple, but when an ordinary watch is used as the timing instrument, it is easy for the examiner to err in finding the termination point. When possible, the teacher should use a stopwatch that he has operated with checks on his readings before he administers the test. When a regular watch is used, the starting time should be recorded in minutes and seconds. Then the testing time should be added to record the exact moment to stop the test. Memory should never be trusted in timing any more than in memorizing instructions. Record the time and read the instructions.

Giving the Test.   Scheduling is one of the biggest problems in a testing program. On the surface it may appear simple, but when test booklets are being reused for economy, when IBM answer sheets are used on which all the answers for several sittings are recorded, or when test length does not coincide with the length of the class periods, some complicated situations can arise. For example, since the test booklets must be checked for marks after each administration, the same booklets cannot be used in consecutive periods. Getting pupils started at the right place when their answer sheets are collected at the close of one sitting is another problem. When testing time is longer than class periods or a combination of them, it is probably wise to set up a testing timetable.

Proper physical conditions for testing will allow pupils to work with freedom without crowding, poor lighting, or interruptions. A sign should be placed on the door indicating that a test is in progress. All testing equipment must be in the room and readily available, along with extra pencils and erasers, and carefully spaced functional chairs. Cheating should not be tolerated, but dealt with firmly without emotional outbursts to disturb the other pupils.

An additional factor requiring planning is the allowance of the proper amount of time for passing out test booklets, answer sheets, and pencils; they must also be collected. Too often the time requirement for these procedures is underestimated.

Even though details are carefully provided for, directions carefully followed, timing accurately completed, and interruptions eliminated, test results may not be highly valid if the pupil is not motivated to do his best. The pupil must be confident that testing is for his own welfare and not for determining promotion or for assigning final marks. He must understand the purpose of the test and the demands it will make on him. Unless testing is of value to him, he may not do his best work.

On the other hand, overstimulation produces anxiety, which interferes with good performance. It is particularly aggravated among those pupils who have the greatest need to earn high marks (Sarason, 1960). The test administrator provides the best testing atmosphere for dealing with anxiety when he establishes a relaxed, businesslike atmosphere with a touch of humor. He encourages the pupil to do his best, but does not threaten.[1]

Furthermore, pupils need to have a certain amount of sophistication or testwiseness to give evidence of their best performance. Teachers should exhort pupils to listen carefully to instructions, mark their papers neatly and accurately, plan wise use of their time, leave enough time to recheck their answers, and understand when to omit or answer a question.

Time of Year for Test Administration.   An important decision in any evaluation program is the time for test administration. Should standardized tests be administered in the spring or fall? Fall administration has a number of advantages:

1. With today's itinerant population, fall administration assures the teacher a record for each pupil. Transfer pupils may not bring adequate records with them from other schools. If tests are administered in the spring the teacher is more likely to have inadequate data for some pupils throughout the year, a deficit which prevents him from focusing his attention on pupil needs rather than on what is supposed to be taught in a certain class. If pupils have specific weaknesses and the teacher knows about them, he can plan remedial work. If they rank high in achievement, he won't make the serious mistake of having them repeat what they already know just because it appears in the syllabus. The information enables him to meet the needs of individuals through grouping or through any other practical approach.

2. Fall testing provides a more realistic measure of pupils' achievement. During the summer vacation, certain skills may improve; others may deteriorate. If the child does know arithmetic, he may not be as proficient in September as he was in June. On the other hand, he may have done considerable reading during the summer, thereby improving his skill in this area.

3. Testing can be helpful to pupils in self-evaluation. If the results are used wisely, they can provide aid in formulating goals. The objective data from standardized tests can give the pupil direction and purpose for the new school year.

---

[1] A self-inventory for those who administer tests has been prepared by Thompson, in which many of the important details of test administration are listed. See Anton Thompson, *Test-Giver's Self-Inventory.* Test Service Bulletin No. 85. New York: Harcourt, Brace & World, Inc. Also, Anton Thompson, "Test-Giver's Self-Inventory," *California Journal of Educational Research* (1956, pp. 67–71).

4. Too often it appears that tests are administered to determine the effectiveness of the teacher rather than the status of the pupils. This may result in coaching the pupils for tests or in invalid administration such as lengthening time limits. Fall testing lessens this possibility.
5. Testing in the spring is generally done under pressure of time. As the school year draws to a close, teachers are busy filling out reports and completing final details. Testing may tend to be more of a chore than an aid to good teaching.

Although fall testing is generally recommended, certain conditions may require spring testing. This is particularly true when ability grouping requires that data be available for determining programs of the pupils for the following year.

Problems

9.   Imagine that you are in charge of a schoolwide achievement testing program in which classroom teachers will administer the tests. What steps would you take to insure standard testing procedures? What difficulties would have to be anticipated?
10.   Many school systems do not tell pupils in advance when standardized tests are to be administered, in the hope that undue anxiety and absenteeism will thereby be avoided. Evaluate this practice.

Scoring the Test

Although essay and objective tests of the supply type are generally scored by hand, many standardized and classroom objective tests can be machine-scored. Central agencies providing this scoring service at a nominal fee offer some definite advantages:

1. Accuracy is greater; machine-scoring results in fewer errors.
2. It saves time for the busy teacher, who can spend his time more profitably than doing clerical work. For some tests a pressure-sensitive label, containing each pupil's scores, is available to attach to the cumulative record. Scores are easily recorded without retyping.
3. Item-analysis data can be quickly prepared when needed.

Hand-scoring by the teacher also results in certain benefits:

1. Results are generally more quickly available.
2. It is possible that by scoring some tests the teacher will gain better insight into a pupil's strengths and weaknesses. However, this is not as likely to occur in the case of the objective test as it is in the case of the essay test.

The advantages and disadvantages of hand-scoring notwithstanding, the fact remains that many test papers are scored in this manner, so the scorer must avoid injustice due to inaccuracy. This is so important a matter that school officials must exert considerable effort and care in training teachers and checking scoring accuracy.

Two types of errors are frequently made: compensating and biased. In the first category are those errors made by carelessness in checking, adding, or using formulas; they score too high in one instance and too low in another. The other type of error is a misinterpretation of a scoring formula, which slants scores all in one direction, high or low. There is no opportunity for them to be cancelled out.

How should these errors be prevented? Teachers must be taught how to score, and carry out the scoring instructions to show they have understood them. A discussion of procedures is not enough. The papers first scored should be rescored. When high accuracy is maintained, only a sampling of papers need be checked. One out of five or ten papers may be selected for this purpose. Because biased errors prove to be so serious, the second scoring should be done by a different person. In some schools all papers are scored twice with different colored pencils. One helpful idea is to have one or more teachers responsible for each subtest. They can then become thoroughly proficient in their task; scoring becomes much more efficient and accurate.

Another check is to see if any extreme scores show up in a pupil's profile. It is possible that they are valid, but if such scores occur, these subtests should be scored again. Also, if scores seem unrealistic in terms of a pupil's past achievement, the corresponding parts or the entire test should be rescored.

Problem

11. Some argue that, if each teacher scores the tests of those pupils whom he meets every day, test results become meaningful to the teacher; in the process of scoring the teacher will become conscious of specific areas of subject matter difficulty. Evaluate this position.

Interpreting and Using the Testing Results

Regardless of the care with which the tests have been selected, administered, and scored, little value will accrue from them unless the results are used in the evaluation program. This means that they must be available to teachers, counselors, and school administrators. In Chapter 14, summarization and interpretation of group and individual test scores provide information for improving diagnostic and remedial programs. In Chapter 15, suggestions are given for the use of test scores in reporting to pupils and their parents.

It is sometimes advantageous to use test scores in interpreting the school program for the public or special community groups; presenting information comparing pupil achievement with national norms of those having comparable ability is one procedure. It may focus attention on a school's educational objectives to portray achievement in various subjects, and at different grade levels. Such a summary may, on the other hand, reveal specific weaknesses that should be remedied through increased financial support by the community.

Test data should be presented in the most meaningful ways. The use of numerical or graphic charts is clearer than a narrative. Figure 42 shows the distribution of ability scores of a senior high school class compared with national norms. Information about achievement in various subject areas would be helpful. Insight could also be gained from comparing achievement in various subject areas for specific groups through several grades. Groups could vary in terms of racial and socioeconomic characteristics. It is possible that comparisons of groups exposed to different curricula would also be timely. In Figure 42 it would also have been possible to graph the achievement of the group to provide a comparison with their ability. Note that stanines are employed (see page 262).

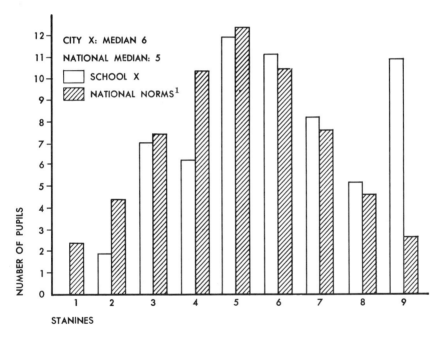

1 Expected frequencies of a representative sample; the same number of pupils were selected from the standardization group.

FIGURE 42.   Distribution of the School and College Ability Test, Total Score, for a Twelfth-Grade Class.

The group of pupils from School X tends to be above the national norms. No pupils have a stanine score of 1, and fewer have stanine scores of 2, 3, 4, and 5 than is true of those from the national norm group; there is a larger proportion of pupils from School X having stanine scores of 6, 7, 8, and 9.

Problem

12.   Suggest possible data relationships that would be useful in evaluating the results of a school's program. Construct graphs and tables to depict these relationships.

THE CUMULATIVE RECORD

The cumulative record is a device for recording and filing all pertinent data that will lead to a better understanding of the pupil for educational and vocational guidance purposes. Various kinds of data from many sources are more helpful than data obtained from a single source. A systematic, long-range accumulation of data clearly produces more intelligent interpretation than data collected at one time.

Cumulative records take various forms, the most common of which are the card, the folder, or a combination of them. The folder is printed for recording data, and any pertinent materials such as anecdotal records may be placed inside. A typical cumulative record of the folder type for the elementary grades is shown in Chapter 14 (pages 485–488). Notice the information required, the recording method, and the insert for recording additional health data. A surprisingly large amount of information can be permanently recorded on such a form.

Traxler (1953, pp. 74–75) suggests that the school staff should plan the record form cooperatively, and lists the following guiding principles for its construction:

1. It should agree with the educational objectives of the local school.
2. It should be the result of the group thinking of the faculty members.
3. It should either provide for a continuous record of the development of the pupil from the first grade to the end of the junior college or be one of a series of forms which make provision for such a record.
4. It should be organized by time sequence; that is, it should be set up by yearly divisions which run throughout the form.
5. It should contain ample and carefully planned space for a record of the results of all types of tests and for an explanation of the norms in terms of which the results were interpreted.

6. It should provide for the annual recording of personality ratings of behavior descriptions, which represent the consensus of the pupils' counselors and teachers.
7. While it should be as comprehensive as possible it must be simple enough to avoid overwhelming the clerical resources of the school.
8. It should be accessible to the teachers as well as to the counselors and principal. Highly confidential information that the counselor may possess should be filed elsewhere.
9. The record form should be reevaluated periodically and revised as needed to take account of educational change and progress.

A number of Traxler's suggestions are followed in many cumulative record forms on the market.

Information Needed

One of the best ways to select data to include in the cumulative record is to determine the usefulness of each in understanding the pupil. In general, the following information is thought helpful.

1. *Identifying data.* These include items such as name, address, age, and date of birth.
2. *Scholastic achievement and mental development.* This would include not only information about the pupil's achievement in various areas but data concerning his general and special aptitudes. Some of this information can be recorded in anecdotal form. Other data can be tabulated as the results of classroom and standardized tests and as school marks.
3. *School attendance record.* Many factors, such as the suitability of the curriculum, home conditions, and the pupil's health, are related to a poor attendance record. These should be reported as well as the source of this information.
4. *Home and family background.* The educational and cultural backgrounds of the parents should be noted. It is also important to know the father's occupation, whether parents are living together, and any other information about home conditions that may be reflected in the pupil's behavior.
5. *Personal-social development.* Such factors as a pupil's degree of self-confidence, emotional stability, predominant moods, relationship to peers and authority figures, and his general mental health should be recorded.
6. *Health.* Under this category, items such as a history of medical and dental care, disabilities, and special information on vision and hearing are included. If a pupil has a disability, it is also wise to record his attitude toward it.
7. *Special activities and interests.* Discovering how a pupil uses his free time in and outside school often provides answers to important questions about his behavior. Any skills in athletics, music, or art, and any other special talents, and also any work experience that he had, should be reported.
8. *Educational and vocational plans.* For the pupil in secondary school, this item becomes a prime factor in his selection of subjects and in his decision for the future. As his plans develop they should be noted, even though the pupil may be somewhat vague about them.

Interpretation and Use of the Cumulative Record

The cumulative record will be useful to all school personnel concerned with educational and vocational guidance. The three key persons involved are the teacher, the counselor, and the school administrator.

The Teacher.   The teacher facilitates learning through improved instruction. Though he must consider the individual differences in his class, the practical demand is that he instruct the group. The discussion of the class record and class analysis chart in Chapter 14 shows how an orderly presentation of data enables the teacher to analyze the needs of his class and know the strengths and weaknesses of the group as a whole. For example, a large percentage of the class may be having trouble with decimals, finding the main idea in a paragraph, or problem solving in science. Knowing this, the teacher can use group instruction effectively. Those pupils who do not need help can explore new material.

But the teacher must go further than release pupils from areas they have already mastered. He must help them select projects and materials. The direction the students need should be readily available in the cumulative record from achievement and aptitude scores, samples of their work, and indications of their interests.

The cumulative record can also find a pupil's weaknesses. For example, a pupil often appears to succeed, but only in comparison with his lackluster classmates. A mediocre performance often looks good if the competition is weak. Because the pupil seems to be doing all right, the teacher attends to those whose difficulties are more obvious and who are generally the less able. But when the teacher matches achievement with ability, and notices from the record of the able pupil that he does poorly in areas hitherto unnoticed, instructional problems are seen that would otherwise have gone overlooked.

After the teacher has located learning difficulties, he must prescribe remediation and try to prevent such difficulties in the future. Chapter 14 includes a discussion of the process of identifying group and individual difficulties, and suggests remedial help. Again in the attacking of remedial problems, the importance of data from the cumulative record is emphasized.

The cumulative record also plays an important role in marking and reporting a pupil's progress. Obviously a teacher cannot prepare a progress report without adequate information. To make marking and reporting meaningful to parents, he must have such data as objective test scores, illustrative work samples, and reports of critical behavioral incidents.

The Counselor. Darley and Anderson (1951, pp. 74–75) list seven significant measurements needed in the counseling process:

1. General scholastic ability
2. Differential measures of achievement
3. Evidence of special aptitudes or disabilities
4. Interests
5. Personality structure and dynamics, including attitudes and beliefs
6. Socioeconomic and cultural derivation and relations
7. Health and physical attributes

They also give four types of questions with regard to counseling pupils that may be answered by data obtained from the above measurements.

1. Questions regarding vocational planning
2. Questions regarding underachievement
3. Questions regarding personal development and adjustment
4. Questions regarding motivation and interest

The choice of a vocation should depend on the pupil's ability, often with emphasis on scholastic aptitude. In certain cases, vocational choice must be made on the basis of past achievement, health, physical attributes, or the ability to adjust to people. Jobs are classified into families; if the pupil is interested in a particular area, he may select a vocation appropriate to his talents. The low-IQ pupil who is interested in medicine can, after all, be a hospital orderly.

Although the pupil may have excellent academic potential, and be a well-adjusted individual, his lack of interest can result in underachievement. For a determination of the causes, it is helpful to turn to interest inventory scores, notations of hobbies, leisure-time activities, and anecdotal records. Possibly a pupil's parents may be insisting on a particular course of study because they think it is prestigious or, thwarted in their own lives, are trying to live through their children. Parents may exhort their children so violently to greater effort that the child refuses to try at all.

To be most effective, counselors and teachers must cooperate. Evaluation is improved as additional data are added to the record available to both. Teachers, through observation of pupil behavior, can give important information to the counselor, just as the counselor can share interpretations of test scores and other information found in the pupil's cumulative record.

An important objective for the counselor is to develop in the pupil a capacity for self-evaluation. Society is competitive and each pupil must have an understanding of his behavior to cope effectively with it. It is encouraging that more and more tools and information are becoming available so that counselors can advise all pupils no matter what their level of occupational interest (see Berdie, 1969, pp. 51–80). The pupil should see test scores and other discreetly selected portions of information in the cumulative record to help him understand his strengths and weaknesses; decisions must be based on adequate data.

These suggestions represent advice to the practitioner under the conditions of our present research findings. However, we need a greater variety of inquiry in terms of design and content (Thoresen, 1969, p. 265) in counseling. Thoresen emphasizes that counseling has never had a disciplined research tradition. He points out that guidance people have been too busy counseling to investigate in a serious manner the consequences of their endeavor. He concludes that "like kissing, counseling is so intrinsically interesting and satisfying that few bother to critically examine it."

An answer to the void in the conducting of serious inquiry may be the systems research approach (Cooley and Hummel, 1969). The model of a system must have clearly delineated objectives, specified procedures, identified and relevant variables, delineated activities of the participants, and evaluational procedures in terms of the stated objectives. Cooley and Hummel point out that the systems approach goes farther than traditional research, for it extends into the domain of development.

The School Administrator.   Data from cumulative records prove helpful to the school administrator in organizing class groups, and in providing information to colleges, prospective employers and schools to which pupils may transfer. Some of the data can be used in a public relations program, particularly such elements as recorded results of standardized achievement and aptitude tests.

As our population increases, even small schools must have more than one class at each grade level. Combination grades, such as a fifth and sixth, may be formed. At other times, particularly at the secondary level, pupils may be grouped into more or less homogeneous groups on the basis of their educational and vocational aims, or of scores from standardized scholastic aptitude tests. Achievement is related to these variables, though not perfectly correlated. In other cases some pupils may be grouped because of such things as their lack of basic skills in English.

As applications for higher education increase, college officials must have data on which to base selection, and one source is systematic records of standardized tests. Because final marks given in small schools are often not comparable to those assigned in larger ones, and because the quality of instruction varies from school to school, standardized test data provide a basis for comparison of candidates across the country. Though many colleges use college entrance examinations, the data from a school testing program present a child far more completely than the single test administration.

Many pupils work after high school. As recently as fifty years ago, graduation from secondary school was a measure of achievement, but when most children receive high school diplomas and variability of achievement becomes the rule, the wise employer must contact the high school administration about a prospective employee. As requests of this kind increase, the administrator must have a well-kept cumulative record.

But this is not the whole of the administrator's informational obligation. He must also interpret the school program for the general public, a task that may involve brochures, speechmaking, and public discussion. Since most standardized achievement tests measure those fundamentals that the public considers important, criticism can be very effectively dealt with if students are achieving in terms of their ability. It is particularly important to have this information available when some curriculum innovation is introduced. The cry, "Let's teach the basic skills," may well be raised. Adequate achievement scores are a satisfactory answer to this demand. If test scores show achievement comparable to ability in arithmetic and the language arts, the school will not be on the defensive.

The school administrator should not evaluate the effectiveness of the school's program only by standardized achievement tests. He should also consider the pupils, keeping in mind that achievement tests are not designed to measure attainment of all the school's educational objectives. For example, none of the instruments in common use measures critical thinking.

Nevertheless, test results help keep him alert to development. In the teaching of the basic skills of reading and arithmetic, continuous and systematic attention must be focused on their development. Some skills are prerequisite to learning others. A pupil cannot do long division unless he can subtract and multiply. The pupil who does not know his basic word attack skills will have trouble reading difficult materials. Standardized test results help keep the busy administrator abreast of the effectiveness of various educational programs.

Problems

13. Traxler (1953 pp. 74–75) recommends that the cumulative record should provide for the annual recording of personality ratings of behavior descriptions. Do you agree? Explain your answer.

14. The cumulative record folder accompanies the pupil as he moves from elementary to junior high school and also when he enters senior high school. At the transfer points, many counselors go through the folders and discard materials that, in their opinion, are no longer useful or which might jeopardize the child in a new setting. What kinds of material might they prefer to discard? Is this a wise practice?

15. Darley and Anderson (1951, pp. 74–75) present a rather comprehensive list of measurements to be used by counselors. Other schools of counseling theory,

such as the Rogerian school, reject this approach; they point to serious dangers, which, in their opinion, are inherent in counseling based on measurement results. With which counseling theory are you more in agreement? Why?

SUMMARY

A sound evaluation program is based on the measurable educational objectives of the school. Unfortunately all too often what is measured may be only a trivial and inconsequential part of the total educational outcome. The input of the student's characteristics and his environment along with the variables of the educational program should be a part of total evaluation. Progress in measuring these components has been slow.

For a successful evaluation program it is mandatory that all school personnel, teachers, counselors, and school administrators, be involved from its initiation throughout its integration with the other educational activities of the school. In many schools this means providing in-service education programs to prepare staff members for their roles in the evaluation.

Tests, whether teacher-constructed or standardized, are an integral part of any evaluation program. A minimal testing program includes tests of scholastic aptitude and achievement. The optimum program adds interest and personality inventories. While standardized achievement tests are most helpful when administered yearly, scholastic aptitude tests can be scheduled at the beginning of the first, fourth, seventh, and tenth grades.

Considerable interest has developed of late in infant and preschool testing. Large federal programs designed to aid the disadvantaged have given impetus to this early testing. It should be emphasized that guidelines to testing disadvantaged children have been reported in the literature.

In selecting a test, the first consideration should be its usefulness to the evaluation program as a whole. Attention should be given to its validity, reliability, and norms, and to the complexity of its administration and scoring. One of the most helpful reference works, including much data on tests, is Buros' *Mental Measurements Yearbooks*, which will provide effective guidance in test selection. Consideration should be given to ease of interpretation by selecting one test series for all grade levels if possible.

Valid test results depend on effective administration and scoring. Teachers must be carefully instructed in both. It is not only necessary to review all instructions, but advisable to give a mock test, as well as to practice scoring and then recheck the papers initially scored. Time and place are also important considerations in test administration. The fall of the year is preferred to the spring. In many cases, tests are administered in the pupil's own classrooms, but there must be ample lighting, space to work, and freedom from interruptions. Of course, adequate physical facilities must always be supplemented by a good testing atmosphere for the pupil to be motivated to do his best work.

Test scores can be used to help interpret the school's program to the public. Charts and diagrams are helpful in such a public relations program.

Test data are but one kind of information helpful in the evaluation program. Personal-social adjustment, anxiety, and interest inventories provide information on the effective outcomes of learning as well as help in the diagnosis of learning difficulties in the school. Rating scales aid in observation, an effective technique for collecting certain kinds of information. Recording such information as anecdotal records systematizes the data.

Methods of recording evaluation data and their availability to school personnel largely determine their contribution to the program. There can be no substitute for a cumulative record in which many kinds of data are filed. Both counselors and teachers use cumulative records in helping pupils attack their problems in vocational planning, underachievement, personal development and adjustment, and motivation and interest. Both have their own means, unavailable to the other, of securing data about pupils, so it is in sharing and working cooperatively that they can be most helpful to pupils.

A greater quantity and variety of tools are becoming available to counselors so that they can advise pupils who have many different levels of vocational goals. There is a pressing need, however, for disciplined research in guidance. Unfortunately little effort has gone into an investigation of the consequences of counseling.

The school administrator is vitally concerned with the evaluation program. He needs information for organizing class groups and for supplying to colleges, prospective employers, and schools to which his pupils transfer. Evaluation data are the basis for keeping him and the public informed about the educational progress of the school.

Suggested Readings

Austin, M. C., C. L. Bush, and M. H. Huebner. *Reading evaluation: Appraisal techniques for school and classroom.* New York: Ronald Press, 1961.
    A practical guide for the evaluation of reading progress in classroom and school. Suggestions are given for the proper use of numerous tests and techniques.

Belanger, L. L. Policy statement on the use of standardized tests in California schools. *California Education,* 1964, 2, 8–10.
    Official representatives of various educational organizations in California have developed a statement on test usage that classroom teachers will find useful.

Berdie, R. F. The uses of evaluation in guidance. In R. W. Tyler (ed.), *Educational evaluation: New roles, new means.* Sixty-Eighth Yearbook of the National

Society for the Study of Education. Part II. Chicago: University of Chicago Press, 1969. Pp. 51–80.

An excellent discussion on evaluation and its use in terms of a counselor's philosophy. The chapter includes references on recent research dealing with predictive data.

Buros, O. K. (ed.) *Tests in print.* Highland Park, N.J.: Gryphon Press, 1961.

As a companion to the *Mental Measurements Yearbooks*, this volume provides (a) useful information concerning more than 2000 currently available tests, (b) cross references to additional information about these tests, (c) short descriptions of more than 800 tests now out of print, and (d) index-directories of test publishers. Also of value are two other volumes edited by Buros, namely, *Reading Tests and Reviews* (1968) and *Personality Tests and Reviews* (1969).

Denton, D. E. Cumulative records: Invalid and unethical. *Educational Forum,* 1968, **33,** 55–58.

The author criticizes the cumulative record on three counts: metaphysical, statistical, and civil libertarian. Cumulative records can be helpful, but unfortunately they are sometimes misused.

Ebel, R. L. External testing: Response to challenge. *Teachers College Record,* 1962, **64,** 190–198.

The author replies to six concerns that the school administrators have expressed about external testing.

Ebel, R. L. Prospects for evaluation of learning. *National Association of Secondary School Principals Bulletin,* 1968, **52,** 32–42.

Common criticisms of evaluation programs are discussed. The author concludes that testing will be used more widely and constructively in the future.

Findley, W. G. (ed.) *The impact and improvement of school testing programs.* Sixty-Second Yearbook of the National Society for the Study of Education. Chicago: University of Chicago Press, 1963.

Highly useful information is contained in this volume. Individual chapters have been prepared by a number of well-known testing specialists. Particularly pertinent are Chapter 10, which deals with the selection and use of tests, and Chapter 12, which contains recommendations concerning the interpretation of test scores.

Goslin, D. A. Social impact of testing. *Personnel and Guidance Journal,* 1967, **45,** 676–682.

The author discusses counselor uses of test scores, reporting of test scores, social effects of test use, and the reporting of scores.

Gronlund, N. E. *Stating behavioral objectives for classroom instruction.* London: Macmillan, 1970.

The author describes how to obtain a broad spectrum of objectives, how to state general and specific objectives, and how to relate them to classroom instruction and use them in the preparation of tests. It would be well to read this short volume in conjunction with the organization of school evaluation program.

Linn, R. L., D. A. Rock, and T. A. Cleary. Development and evaluation of several programmed testing methods. *Educational and Psychological Measurement,* 1969, **29,** 129–146.

Schools must anticipate new directions in testing like programmed testing. A programmed test is one in which the presentation of test items is contingent on the previous responses of the examinee.

State Committee on Cumulative Records. *Handbook on California cumulative records.* Sacramento: California State Department of Education, 1956.

The purpose of this handbook is to serve as a guide to school personnel who wish to develop adequate cumulative records. Not only does it give thorough instructions on how to initiate and keep these records up to date, but it also has illustrations of completed records.

Stone, S. C., and B. Shertzer (eds.) *Guidance monograph series, Set III: Testing.* Boston: Houghton Mifflin, 1968.

There are nine paperbacks in this series concerning testing. Although these volumes are a part of a guidance series, they are appropriate for all school personnel concerned with tests and testing. (For a complete list of titles, see Appendix F, page 603.)

Womer, F. B., and N. K. Wahi. Test use. In R. L. Ebel (ed.), *Encyclopedia of educational research.* (4th ed.) London: Macmillan, 1969. Pp. 1461–1469.

A good review of the research and writings on the development of testing programs, test administration, scoring and interpretation, and test norms.

References Cited

Astin, A. W., and R. J. Panos. The evaluation of educational programs. In R. L. Thorndike (ed.), *Educational measurement.* (2nd ed.) Washington: American Council on Education, 1970. Chapter 20.

Berdie, R. F. The uses of evaluation in guidance. In R. W. Tyler (ed.), *Educational evaluation: New roles, new means.* Sixty-Eighth Yearbook of the National Society for the Study of Education. Part II. Chicago: University of Chicago Press, 1969. Pp. 51–80.

Cooley, W. W., and R. C. Hummel. Systems approaches in guidance. *Review of Educational Research,* 1969, 39, 251–262.

Cox, R. C. Achievement testing in a program of individualized instruction: Some considerations. *Learning Research and Development Center Newsletter,* Vol. IV, No. 3, 1967.

Darley, J. G., and G. W. Anderson. The functions of measurement in counseling. In E. F. Lindquist (ed.), *Educational measurement.* Washington: American Council on Education, 1951.

Fishman, J. A., and others. Guidelines for testing minority group children. *Journal of Social Issues* (Supplement), 1964, 20, 129–145.

Gesell, A., and C. S. Amatruda. *Developmental diagnosis.* (2nd ed.) New York: Harper & Row, 1947.

Glaser, R., and A. J. Nitko. Measurement in learning and instruction. In R. L. Thorndike (ed.), *Educational measurement.* (2nd ed.) Washington: American Council on Education, 1970. Chapter 17.

Kearney, N. C. *Elementary school objectives.* New York: Russell Sage Foundation, 1953.

Knobloch, H., and B. Passamanick. Prediction from the assessment of neuromotor and intellectual status in infancy. In J. Zubin and G. A. Jervis (eds.), *Psychopathology of mental development.* New York: Greene & Stratton, 1967.

Lindquist, E. F. The impact of machines on educational measurement. In R. W. Tyler (ed.), *Educational evaluation: New roles, new means.* Sixty-Eighth Yearbook of the National Society for the Study of Education. Part II. Chicago: University of Chicago Press, 1969. Pp. 351–369.

Mager, R. F. *Preparing instructional objectives.* Palo Alto, Calif.: Fearon Publishers, 1962.

Sarason, I. G. Empirical findings and theoretical problems in the use of anxiety scales. *Psychological Bulletin,* 1960, 403–415.

Stake, R. E., and T. Denny. Needed concepts and techniques for utilizing more fully the potential of evaluation. In R. W. Tyler (ed.), *Educational evaluation: New roles, new means.* Sixty-Eighth Yearbook of the National Society for the Study of Education. Part II. Chicago: University of Chicago Press, 1969. Pp. 370–390.

Thoresen, C. E. Relevance and research in counseling. *Review of Educational Research,* 1969, **39**, 263–281.

Traxler, A. E., and others. *Introduction to testing and the use of test results in public schools.* New York: Harper & Row, 1953.

Appendices

APPENDIX A: STATISTICAL METHODS[1]

Part One

Measure of central tendency: the arithmetic mean. The arithmetic mean is a measure of central tendency. In other words, it is a value that attempts to represent the clustering that is so commonly found in test-score distributions. In the cases in which the test scores are for all practical purposes normally distributed, the arithmetic mean corresponds closely to two other measures of central tendency, the mode (the most common score) and the median (the point below which 50 percent of the test scores fall).

The arithmetic mean is the sum of all test scores in a distribution divided by the number of test scores. Many people call it "the average." This definition can be translated into the following equation:

$$M = \frac{\Sigma X}{N},$$

where

M = arithmetic mean;
Σ = the sum;
X = any test score;
N = number of test scores.

This formula can be applied to any set of ungrouped data to determine the arithmetic mean, for example, the following mental ability scores of twenty fifth-grade pupils.

107	123	112	97	100
93	88	83	109	91
101	96	98	114	106
115	105	85	118	111

The sum of the twenty values (ΣX) is 2052. The arithmetic mean is 2052 divided by 20, or 102.6. The substitution in the formula is as follows:

$$M = \frac{2052}{20} = 102.6.$$

Test scores are not always available in the ungrouped fashion illustrated in the foregoing table. Occasionally they are grouped in a frequency distribu-

---

[1] For those who wish to engage in independent study of statistical concepts useful in tests and measurements, a programmed textbook is available entitled *Statistics and Measurement: A Programmed Introduction*, 2nd ed., by L. A. Schoer, Allyn and Bacon, Inc., 1971.

tion, as in the case of the 360 vocabulary scores shown in Table 4 (Chapter 8). In a frequency distribution the exact test score for any particular pupil is unknown, and the formula for the arithmetic mean as presented above cannot be applied.

One method of computing the arithmetic mean of test scores included in a frequency distribution is to guess the arithmetic mean and then correct the guess. The only requirement for a guessed mean is that it be the midpoint of one of the intervals of the frequency distribution. The guessed mean is corrected by a simple coding operation.

The first steps of the computation of the arithmetic mean of the 360 vocabulary scores included in the frequency distribution cited are shown in the following table.

Raw-score interval	Frequency (f)	Deviation (d)	fd
90–94	4	7	28
85–89	6	6	36
80–84	12	5	60
75–79	20	4	80
70–74	28	3	84
65–69	36	2	72
60–64	40	1	40
55–59	46	0	0
50–54	43	−1	−43
45–49	39	−2	−78
40–44	32	−3	−96
35–39	24	−4	−96
30–34	13	−5	−65
25–29	9	−6	−54
20–24	5	−7	−35
15–19	3	−8	−24
Total	360		−91

The guessed mean is 57, the midpoint of the 55–59 interval. The values in the deviation column are found by counting, in terms of the number of intervals, how far each interval deviates from the interval containing the guessed mean. Thus, the d value of the 60–64 interval is $+1$ because it is one interval above the 55–59 interval; the d value of the 50–54 interval is -1 because it is one interval below the 55–59 interval. The fd values are determined by multiplying each frequency by the corresponding d value.

The complete formula for finding the arithmetic mean of a frequency distribution is as follows:

$$M = \text{G.M.} + (h)\left[\frac{\Sigma fd}{N}\right],$$

where

M = arithmetic mean;
G.M. = guessed mean;
h = size of the intervals of the frequency distribution;
Σfd = algebraic sum of the entries in the fd column;
N = number of test scores.

The expression following the plus sign corrects the guessed mean by increasing it if it is too small or reducing it if it is too large.

The appropriate values can be readily taken from the table and substituted in the equation as follows:

$$M = 57 + (5)\left[\frac{-91}{360}\right] = 55.7.$$

The fact that the guessed mean is slightly higher than the actual arithmetic mean causes the sign of the Σfd to be negative.

The formula for computing the arithmetic mean of test scores arranged in a frequency distribution is nothing more than a convenient substitute for the definition formula for the arithmetic mean that is applied to ungrouped data. The frequency distribution formula is none too satisfactory at times. It often yields inaccurate answers when the number of cases in the frequency distribution is small.

The formula for computing the median of test scores included in a frequency distribution is shown in Part Four of Appendix A. For the frequency distribution of 360 vocabulary test scores the median is 55.8. Since the distribution of test scores is approximately normal, it is very close to the arithmetic mean.

Part Two

Measure of variability: the standard deviation. The standard deviation, like the range, is a measure of variability, or dispersion, as it is sometimes called. It is a distance expressed in test-score units rather than a point such as the arithmetic mean. If the test scores of a distribution are widely scattered above and below the arithmetic mean of the scores, the standard deviation is large; the distribution has considerable variability. If the test scores of a distribution cluster closely around the arithmetic mean, the standard deviation is small; the distribution has little variability.

Like the arithmetic mean, the standard deviation can be computed for ungrouped data or test scores arranged in a frequency distribution. The formula for computing the standard deviation of ungrouped data can serve as a definition of the standard deviation. The formula for computing the standard deviation of test scores arranged in a frequency distribution is a somewhat imperfect substitute for the first formula.

To compute the standard deviation of ungrouped test scores, the following formula is used:

$$\sigma = \sqrt{\frac{\Sigma X^2 - [(\Sigma X)^2/N]}{N}}$$

where

σ = standard deviation;
Σ = the sum;
X = any test score;
N = number of test scores.

This formula was used to determine the standard deviation of the 200 American history achievement test scores cited in Chapter 10. In the following chart are a few of the 200 test scores, and opposite each is its square.

Pupil	Test score (X)	X²
1	80	6,400
2	21	441
3	62	3,844
4	76	5,776
5	32	1,024
6	47	2,209
•	•	•
•	•	•
•	•	•
200	75	5,625
Total	10,620	585,979

Summing the two columns yields the two values needed for the numerator of the standard deviation equation. Substitution of all values gives the following equation:

$$\sigma = \sqrt{\frac{585,979 - [(10,620)^2/200]}{200}} = 10.5.$$

Finding the standard deviation of test scores arranged in a frequency distribution is a simple extension of the process used to compute the arithmetic mean of those test scores. A convenient interval is selected, the deviations of the remaining intervals from the selected interval are identified, and a systematic series of multiplications follow.

The frequency distribution of vocabulary test scores shown in Table 4 (Chapter 8) is reproduced in the following table.

Raw-score interval	Frequency (f)	Deviation (d)	fd	fd²
90–94	4	7	28	196
85–89	6	6	36	216
80–84	12	5	60	300
75–79	20	4	80	320
70–74	28	3	84	252
65–69	36	2	72	144
60–64	40	1	40	40
55–59	46	0	0	0
50–54	43	−1	−43	43
45–49	39	−2	−78	156
40–44	32	−3	−96	288
35–39	24	−4	−96	384
30–34	13	−5	−65	325
25–29	9	−6	−54	324
20–24	5	−7	−35	245
15–19	3	−8	−24	192
Total	360		−91	3,425

The 55–59 interval is chosen as the starting point and all other intervals are identified in the deviation column according to the number of intervals they happen to be above or below the selected interval. The entries in the fd column are found by multiplying each frequency by the corresponding d value. The entries in the fd² column are determined by multiplying each fd value by the corresponding d value.

The sums of the fd column and fd² columns are needed if the standard deviation is to be found. The complete formula for the standard deviation is as follows:

$$\sigma = (h) \sqrt{\frac{\Sigma fd^2}{N} - \left(\frac{\Sigma fd}{N}\right)^2},$$

where

$$\sigma = \text{standard deviation};$$
$$h = \text{size of the intervals of the frequency distribution};$$
$$\Sigma fd^2 = \text{sum of the entries in the } fd^2 \text{ column};$$
$$\Sigma fd = \text{algebraic sum of the entries in the } fd \text{ column};$$
$$N = \text{number of test scores}.$$

Substitution of the values computed in the table yields the following:

$$\sigma = (5) \sqrt{\frac{3425}{360} - \left(\frac{-91}{360}\right)^2} = 15.3.$$

A simpler method of determining the size of a standard deviation is available provided that the distribution of the test scores is approximately normal. All that is necessary is to (a) sum the scores for the top sixth of the group of pupils, (b) sum the scores for the bottom sixth, (c) find the difference between these two values, and (d) divide the difference by half of the number of pupils in the total group. The formula is as follows:

$$\sigma = \frac{\Sigma X_t - \Sigma X_b}{N/2},$$

where

$$\sigma = \text{standard deviation};$$
$$\Sigma X_t = \text{sum of scores for top sixth};$$
$$\Sigma X_b = \text{sum of scores for bottom sixth};$$
$$N/2 = \text{half of the number of pupils in the total group}.$$

Values yielded by this formula are often quite satisfactory for the needs of a classroom teacher.

Part Three

Measure of relationships: the product-moment coefficient of correlation. The Pearson product-moment coefficient of correlation represents the degree of straight-line relationship between two sets of measurements, such as those of two characteristics of each of a group of pupils. The correlation coefficient reflects the tendency of these pupils to have, in some systematic manner, similar relative positions or dissimilar relative positions in the two distributions. If pupils who are high in one distribution tend to be high in the second, and if pupils who are low in one distribution tend to be low in the other, the correlation coefficient is positive: a direct relationship exists between the two characteristics. If pupils who are high in one distribution tend to be low in the other, and if pupils who are low in one distribution tend to be high in the other, the correlation coefficient is negative: an inverse relationship exists between the two characteristics.

The amount of straight-line relationship between two characteristics is indicated by the size of the correlation coefficient. If the correlation coefficient is +1.00 or −1.00, the straight-line relationship is perfect, that is, plotting one measurement against the other will yield a series of points that can be joined by a single straight line. If the correlation coefficient were 0.00, there would be absolutely no straight-line relationship between the two characteristics. Thus, correlation coefficients can vary in size from +1.00 to −1.00, the sign reflecting the direction of the relationship and the size reflecting the amount of the relationship. The fact that two characteristics are correlated does not necessarily mean that one is the immediate cause of the other.

A correlation coefficient is useful in situations such as that described in Chapter 9 in connection with the discussion of criterion-related validity. Table 10 (Chapter 9) shows the test scores of the scholastic aptitude and social studies achievement of each of twenty pupils.

The following formula is used to compute the coefficient of correlation:

$$r = \frac{\Sigma XY - [(\Sigma X)(\Sigma Y)/N]}{\sqrt{\left[\Sigma X^2 - \frac{(\Sigma X)^2}{N}\right]\left[\Sigma Y^2 - \frac{(\Sigma Y)^2}{N}\right]}},$$

where

r = product-moment coefficient of correlation;

Σ = the sum;

X = any test score of one characteristic (i.e., any scholastic aptitude test score);

Y = any test score of the other characteristic (i.e., any social studies test score);

N = number of pupils.

Solution of the formula can be simplified by preparing a worksheet. The following table, based upon Table 10, is such a worksheet.

The new entries in the worksheet are products, either the square of a test score or the cross product of two test scores for a pupil. The sums of these products as they are listed in the last row of the table are the values necessary to solve the r formula. The following needed values can be taken from the table:

ΣX	=	2,142	ΣY =	1,256
ΣX^2	=	232,750	ΣY^2 =	84,188
ΣXY	=	137,085	N =	20

Pupil	Scholastic Aptitude Test (X)	Social Studies Test (Y)	XY	X²	Y²
Jim	135	66	8,910	18,225	4,356
Sam	130	90	11,700	16,900	8,100
Ruth	120	68	8,160	14,400	4,624
Mary	117	85	9,945	13,689	7,225
John	116	81	9,396	13,456	6,561
Louise	114	47	5,358	12,996	2,209
Ralph	113	69	7,797	12,769	4,761
Mae	112	77	8,624	12,544	5,929
Quinton	111	65	7,215	12,321	4,225
Sandra	109	56	6,104	11,881	3,136
Larry	107	89	9,523	11,449	7,921
Norma	106	49	5,194	11,236	2,401
Frank	101	57	5,757	10,201	3,249
Milton	100	58	5,800	10,000	3,364
Dave	97	71	6,887	9,409	5,041
Joe	95	60	5,700	9,025	3,600
Bill	94	38	3,572	8,836	1,444
Sally	90	31	2,790	8,100	961
Margaret	88	40	3,520	7,744	1,600
Sue	87	59	5,133	7,569	3,481
Total	2,142	1,256	137,085	232,750	84,188

Substitution of these values into the formula for the correlation coefficient yields the following:

$$r = \frac{137,085 - [(2142)(1256)/20]}{\sqrt{\left[232,750 - \frac{(2142)^2}{20}\right]\left[84,188 - \frac{(1256)^2}{20}\right]}} = 0.61.$$

As in the case of arithmetic means and standard deviations, coefficients of correlations can be computed by use of measurements arranged in frequency distributions as well as of ungrouped data. The formula must be altered somewhat to do this. A complete description of the computation of a correlation coefficient from a two-way frequency distribution can be found in most introductory textbooks of statistical methodology.

A simple means of obtaining a somewhat accurate estimate of the size of the product-moment coefficient of correlation is to compute a Spearman rank-difference coefficient of correlation, known as rho (ρ). It represents the tendency of the pupils to have similar or dissimilar ranks in terms of two variables. Rho values are computed by means of the following formula:

$$\rho = 1 - \frac{6\,\Sigma D^2}{N\,(N^2 - 1)},$$

where

ρ = rank-difference coefficient of correlation;
Σ = the sum;
D = difference between a pair of ranks;
N = number of pupils.

In Table 10 (Chapter 9) are shown the ranks of each of the twenty pupils for both a scholastic aptitude test and a social studies achievement test. When the differences between these pairs of ranks are squared and added, a sum of 526 is found. Hence,

$$\rho = \frac{(6)\,(526)}{20\,(400 - 1)} = 0.60.$$

Another quick way of obtaining an estimate of the degree of relationship that exists between two variables is to compute a tetrachoric correlation coefficient. Such coefficients can be determined by finding the percentage of pupils who are in the top half of the class in terms of both sets of test scores being correlated, and then looking up the correlation coefficient corresponding to this percentage in a table published by the Educational Testing Service. The table is as follows:

%	r	%	r	%	r	%	r	%	r
45	0.95	37	0.69	29	0.25	21	−0.25	13	−0.69
44	.93	36	.65	28	.19	20	− .31	12	− .73
43	.91	35	.60	27	.13	19	− .37	11	− .77
42	.88	34	.55	26	.07	18	− .43	10	− .81
41	.85	33	.49	25	.00	17	− .49	9	− .85
40	.81	32	.43	24	− .07	16	− .55	8	− .88
39	.77	31	.37	23	− .13	15	− .60	7	− .91
38	.73	30	.31	22	− .19	14	− .65	6	− .93

Unfortunately, the tetrachoric correlations yielded by this table are not precise. At best they can be thought of as a rough approximation of the size of the product-moment coefficient of correlation for the data in question.

Part Four

Measure of relative performance: the quartile, decile, and percentile. Quartiles, deciles, and percentiles are points in a distribution of test scores. The first quartile, often identified as Q_1, is the point in the distribution below which 25 percent of the test scores fall; the first decile (D_1) is the point below which 10 percent of the test scores fall; the first percentile (P_1) is the point below which 1 percent of the test scores fall. Other quartiles, deciles, and percentiles are similarly defined and symbolically identified.

Quartiles divide the test-score distribution into four equal parts in terms of the number of test scores. Deciles divide such a distribution into ten equal parts, and percentiles divide it into one hundred equal parts.

A computation of any quartile, decile, or percentile can be based on a frequency distribution of test scores such as that shown in Table 4 (Chapter 8). This frequency distribution contains vocabulary test scores obtained by testing 360 pupils. It is reproduced in the following table.

Raw-score intervals	Frequency (f_w)	Cumulative frequency (f_c)
90–94	4	360
85–89	6	356
80–84	12	350
75–79	20	338
70–74	28	318
65–69	36	290
60–64	40	254
55–59	46	214
50–54	43	168
45–49	39	125
40–44	32	86
35–39	24	54
30–34	13	30
25–29	9	17
20–24	5	8
15–19	3	3
Total	360	

The formula for determining any quartile, decile, or percentile is as follows:

$$Q, D, \text{ or } P = 1 + (h) \left[\frac{(F)(N) - f_c}{f_w} \right],$$

where

$1 =$ theoretical lower limit of the interval containing the quartile, decile, or percentile desired;

$h =$ size of the intervals in the frequency distribution;

$F =$ a fraction that varies according to which quartile, decile, or percentile is desired;

$N =$ number of test scores;

$f_c =$ cumulative frequency below the interval containing the quartile, decile, or percentile desired;

$f_w =$ number of test scores within the interval containing the quartile, decile, or percentile desired.

Two of the values used in the formula, 1 and F, deserve further explanation. That 1 is a theoretical lower limit of an interval and not a reported lower limit simply recognizes the fact that all measurements are limited in accuracy. Although test scores are reported to the nearest whole number, theoretically each score represents the interval that extends from 0.5 below the test score in question to 0.5 above it. A reported score of 50 represents an interval from 49.5 to 50.5 in a test-score distribution. Whenever test scores are reported to the nearest whole number, the value of 1 is 0.5 less than the reported value of the lower limit of the frequency distribution interval containing the quartile, decile, or percentile to be computed.

The value of F is defined as the size of a fraction associated with the quartile, decile, or percentile. For the median, the point below which 50 percent of the scores fall, the fraction is 50/100, or 1/2. For the third decile (D_3), the point below which 30 percent of the scores fall, the fraction is 30/100 or 3/10. For the sixty-third percentile (P_{63}), the fraction is 63/100. All other fractions can be found in a similar manner.

Suppose that P_{32} is to be computed. The first step is to find the interval containing P_{32}. The most rapid way of doing this is to determine F, which is 32/100, and multiply it by N, which is 360. The answer, 115.2, is entered in the cumulative frequency column of the table. Observe that 86 pupils have test scores of 44 or less, whereas 125 pupils have test scores of 49 or less. Therefore, P_{32}, which corresponds to 115.2, falls somewhere within the 45–49 interval.

Now that the interval is identified, three of the required values can be quickly identified. The number of test scores within the interval (f_w) is 39; the cumulative frequency below the interval (f_c) is 86; the theoretical lower limit of the interval (1) is 44.5. Substitution of these and other needed values yields the following equation:

$$P_{32} = 44.5 + 5 \left[\frac{32/100(360) - 86}{39} \right] = 48.2.$$

The determination of a decile or quartile is equally simple. The steps needed to compute D_6 are as follows:

1. $F = 60/100$, or $6/10$
2. $(F)(N) = 6/10 (360) = 216$
3. Therefore, the interval containing D_6 is the 60–64 interval.
4. $f_w = 40$
5. $f_c = 214$
6. $l = 59.5$

Therefore

$$D_6 = 59.5 + 5 \left[\frac{6/10 (360) - 214}{40} \right] = 59.8.$$

A quartile, such as Q_3, is computed as follows:

1. $F = 75/100$, or $3/4$
2. $(F)(N) = (3/4)(360) = 270$
3. Therefore, the interval containing Q_3 is the 65–69 interval.
4. $f_w = 36$
5. $f_c = 254$
6. $l = 64.5$

Therefore

$$Q_3 = 64.5 + 5 \left[\frac{3/4 (360) - 254}{36} \right] = 66.7.$$

Quartile, decile, and percentile ranks can be determined by inspecting the appropriate quartiles, deciles, and percentiles; inspecting an appropriate ogive curve; or computing from ungrouped test scores arranged according to size from low to high. These techniques are described in many introductory textbooks of statistical methodology.

APPENDIX B: PUBLISHERS AND DISTRIBUTORS OF STANDARDIZED EVALUATION INSTRUMENTS[1]

Name	Address
1. American Guidance Service, Inc.	720 Washington Avenue, S. E., Minneapolis, Minnesota 55414
2. Bureau of Educational Research and Service	Extension Division, State University of Iowa Iowa City, Iowa 52240
3. Bureau of Publications	Teachers College, Columbia University, 525 W. 120th Street, New York, New York 10027
4. California Test Bureau	Del Monte Research Park, Monterey, California 93940
5. Committee on Diagnostic Reading Tests, Inc.	Mountain Home, North Carolina 28758
6. Consulting Psychologists Press	577 College Avenue, Palo Alto, California 94306
7. Cooperative Test Division, Educational Testing Service	Princeton, New Jersey 08540
8. Harcourt, Brace & World, Inc.	757 Third Avenue, New York, New York 10017
9. Houghton Mifflin Company	2 Park Street, Boston, Massachusetts 02107
10. Institute for Personality and Ability Testing	1602 Coronado Drive, Champaign, Illinois 61822
11. Personnel Press, Inc.	20 Nassau Street, Princeton, New Jersey 08540
12. The Psychological Corporation	304 East 45th Street, New York, New York 10017
13. Science Research Associates, Inc.	259 E. Erie Street, Chicago, Illinois 60611
14. Sheridan Supply Company	P.O. Box 837, Beverly Hills, California 90213
15. C. H. Stoelting Company	424 N. Homan Avenue, Chicago, Illinois 60624

[1] Other publishers are listed in Buros' *Mental Measurements Yearbooks*.

APPENDIX C: SELECTED LIST OF STANDARDIZED ACHIEVEMENT TESTS

Name of test	Publisher[a]	Age or grade level[b]	Time	Recent review in Buros' M.M.Y.[c]
Anderson-Fisk Chemistry Test	8	X–XIII	40	TIP-1604
Biology: BSCS Comprehensive Final Examination	12	X	45	None
Biology: BSCS Tests for Patterns and Processes	12	IX–XII	45	None
Blyth Second Year Algebra Test, Revised Edition	8	X–XII	40	TIP-986
Boehm Test of Basic Concepts	12	Preschool	30–40	None
Brown-Carlsen Listening Comprehension Test	8	IX–Adult	45–50	6–739
California Achievement Tests	4	IV–XIV	114–153	6–3
California Arithmetic Test	4	I–XIV	39–72	6–616
Comprehensive Tests of Basic Skills	4	II–XII	170–195	None
Contemporary Mathematics Test	4	III–XII	35–45	None
Cooperative English Tests	7			
Reading Comprehension		IX–XII, College	40	6–256
English Expression		IX–XII, College	40	

586

APPENDIX C (Continued)

Name of test	Publisher[a]	Age or grade level[b]	Time	Recent review in Buros' M.M.Y.[c]
Usage, Spelling, Vocabulary Test		IX–XII, College	70	
Cooperative Foreign Language Tests (MLA)	7	H.S., College		None
		Skills tested are:		
French Tests		Listening	25	
German Tests		Reading	35	
Italian Tests		Speaking	10	
Russian Tests		Writing	35	
Spanish Tests				
Cooperative French Listening Comprehension Test	7	X–XV	30	TIP–635
Cooperative Latin Test	7	H.S., College	40	TIP–668
Cooperative Mathematics Tests	7			
Arithmetic		VII–IX	40	6–607
Structure of the Number System		VII, VIII	40	6–655
Algebra I		VIII, IX	40	6–594
Algebra II		H.S.	40	6–594

587

APPENDIX C (Continued)

Name of test	Publisher[a]	Age or grade level[b]	Time	Recent review in Buros' M.M.Y.[c]
Algebra III		H.S., College	40	6-594
Geometry		H.S.	80	6-645
Analytic Geometry		H.S., College	40	6-643
Trigonometry		H.S., College	40	6-657
Calculus		H.S., College	80	6-654
Cooperative Primary Tests	7	I–III	210	None
Cooperative Science Tests	7			
General Science		VII–IX	40	6-872a
Advanced General Science		VIII–IX	80	6-876a
Biology		X–XII	80	6-887a
Chemistry		X–XII	80	6-909a
Physics		X–XII	80	6-931a
Tests of PSSC		H.S.		None
Cooperative Sequential Tests of Educational Progress (STEP I) (STEP II available in 1971)	7	IV–XIV	70 each 35 essay	6-25

Name of test	Publisher[a]	Age or grade level[b]	Time	Recent review in Buros' M.M.Y.[c]
Cooperative Social Studies Tests	7			
American History		VII, VIII	40	None
Civics		VIII–IX	40	None
American History		X–XII	40	TIP-1763
Modern European History		X–XII	40	TIP-1765
World History		X–XII	40	TIP-1766
American Government		X–XII	40	TIP-1801
Problems of Democracy		X–XII	40	None
Crary American History Test, Revised Edition	8	X–XIII	40	TIP-1768
Cummings World History Test, Revised Edition	8	IX–XIII	40	TIP-1769
Davis Reading Test	12	VIII–XI	40	6–786
Diagnostic Reading Tests	5	II–XIII	40–60	6–823
Diagnostic Tests and Self-Helps in Arithmetic	4	III–XII	Unspecified	TIP-1054

APPENDIX C (Continued)

Name of test	Publisher[a]	Age or grade level[b]	Time	Recent review in Buros' M.M.Y.[c]
Dunning-Abeles Physics Test	8	X–XIII	40	None
Durrell-Sullivan Reading Capacity and and Achievement Tests	8	II–VI	30–65	TIP–1468
Engle Psychology Test, Revised Edition	8	XI–XIII	40	TIP–1295
Essentials of English Tests	1	VII–XII	45	6–266
Gates-MacGinitie Reading Tests	3	I–XII	30–60	None
Gates-McKillop Reading Diagnostic Test	3	II–VI	60	6–824
Iowa Tests of Basic Skills	9	III–IX	329–459	6–13
Iowa Tests of Educational Development	13	IX–XII	198–360	6–14
Kepner Mid-Year Algebra Achievement Test	2	IX	50	None
Lankton First-Year Algebra, Revised Edition	8	VIII–XII	40	TIP–1005
Metropolitan Achievement Tests	8	I–IX	90–270	None

590

APPENDIX C (Continued)

Name of test	Publisher[a]	Age or grade level[b]	Time	Recent review in Buros' M.M.Y.[c]
Nelson Biology Test	8	IX–XIII	40	TIP-1592
Nelson-Denny Reading Test	9	IX–Adult	30	6–800
Nelson Silent Reading Test	9	III–IX	30	6–802
New Purdue Placement Test in English	9	XI–College	65	6–276
Pimsleur Modern Foreign Language Proficiency Tests	8	IX–X	25–45	None
Read General Science Test, Revised Edition	8	VII–IX	40	TIP-1570
SRA Achievement Series	13	I–IX	360–480	6–21
Stanford Achievement Test	8	I–IX	160–300	6–26
Stanford Achievement Test: High School Battery	8	IX–XII	320	None
Modern Mathematics Concepts Test	8	V–IX	58	None
Stanford Diagnostic Arithmetic Test	8	II–VIII	205–250	None
Stanford Diagnostic Reading Test	8	III–VIII	110–160	None

APPENDIX C (Continued)

Name of test	Publisher[a]	Age or grade level[b]	Time	Recent review in Buros' M.M.Y.[c]
Stanford Early School Achievement Test: Level 1	8	K–1	90	None
Templin-Darley Tests of Articulation	2	No grade	No time limit	None
Verbal Language Development Scale	1	1 mo.–15	Untimed	6–316

[a] The number designating the publisher refers to Appendix B.
[b] Age levels are given in Arabic numbers, grade levels in Roman numbers.
[c] The number before the dash indicates the Yearbook; TIP refers to Buros' Tests in Print; the number after the dash indicates the instrument entry.

APPENDIX D: SELECTED LIST OF STANDARDIZED APTITUDE TESTS

Name of test	Publisher[a]	Age or grade level[b]	Time	Recent review in Buros' M.M.Y.[c]
SCHOLASTIC APTITUDE TESTS				
Academic Ability Test	7	XII	40	None
Academic Promise Tests	12	VI–IX	90	6–766
California Short-Form Test of Mental Maturity	4	K–Adult	34–43	6–443
California Test of Mental Maturity	4	K–Adult	48–83	6–444
College Qualification Tests	12	XI–XIII	80	6–450
First Grade Screening Test	1	K–I	30–40	None
Henmon-Nelson Tests of Mental Ability, Revised Edition	9	III–XII, College	30	6–462
IPAT Culture-Fair Intelligence Tests	10	4–Adult	30	6–453a
Kuhlmann-Anderson Tests, Measure of Academic Potential, Seventh Edition	11	K–XII	40–60	6–466

APPENDIX D (Continued)

Name of test	Publisher[a]	Age or grade level[b]	Time	Recent review in Buros' M.M.Y.[c]
Kuhlmann-Finch Intelligence Tests	1	I–XII	30	TIP–785
Lorge-Thorndike Intelligence Tests	9			6–467
Multi-level		3–13	62	
Separate Level Edition		K–XII	20–61	
Ohio State University Psychological Test	13	IX–XIII	90	TIP–808
Otis-Lennon Mental Ability Test	8	K–XII	30–40	None
Pintner-Cunningham Primary Test	8	K–II	25	TIP–827a
Quick Word Test	8	4–Adult	15	None
School and College Ability Test (Series II)	7	IV–XIV	45–50	None
SRA Pictorial Reasoning Tests	13	IX–Adult	20	None
SRA Primary Mental Abilities Test	13	K–Adult	35–60	6–780
Terman-McNemar Test of Mental Ability	8	VII–XIII	40	TIP–860

APPENDIX D (Continued)

Name of test	Publisher[a]	Age or grade level[b]	Time	Recent review in Buros' M.M.Y.[c]
TESTS FOR OTHER APTITUDES				
Differential Aptitude Tests (DAT)	12	VIII–XII, Adult	181	6-767
Engineering and Physical Science Aptitude Test	12	Cand. for Tech. School	80–90	TIP-2001
Flanagan Aptitude Classification Tests (FACT)	13	IX–Adult	258	6-770
General Aptitude Test Battery	USES	IX–XII, Adult	120–150	6-771
Graves Design Judgment Test	12	VII–XVI, Adult	20–30	TIP-588
Horn Art Aptitude Inventory	15	XII–XVI, Adult	50	TIP-589
Lee-Clark Reading Readiness Test	4	K–1	20	6-846
Lee-Clark Reading Test	4	I–II	15–25	6-795

APPENDIX D (Continued)

Name of test	Publisher[a]	Age or grade level[b]	Time	Recent review in Buros' M.M.Y.[c]
MacQuarrie Test for Mechanical Ability	4	VII–Adult	20	TIP-1922
Meier Art Test: I, Art Judgment	2	VII–Adult	45–60	6–346
Meier Art Test: II, Aesthetic Perception	2	IX–Adult	45–60	6–346
Metropolitan Readiness Tests	8	K–I	60	TIP-1500
Minnesota Clerical Test	12	VIII–XII, Adult	15	6–1040
Minnesota Mechanical Assembly Test	15	II & over	17–21	TIP-1928
Modern Language Aptitude Test	12	IX–Adult	30–60	6–357
Revised Minnesota Paper Form Board Test	12	IX–Adult	20	6–1092
Seashore Measures of Musical Talents, Revised Edition	12	IV–Adult	60	6–353
SRA Tests of Educational Ability	13	IV–XII	26–42	6–495
Test of Mechanical Comprehension (Bennett)	12			
Form AA: Men		IX & over	25–45	TIP-1946
Form W-I: Women		IX & over	25–45	
Forms S and T		XI–Adult	30	

596

APPENDIX D (Continued)

Name of test	Publisher[a]	Age or grade level[b]	Time	Recent review in Buros' M.M.Y.[c]
Tests in Fundamental Abilities of Visual Art	4	III–Adult	85	TIP–594

[a] The number designating the publisher refers to Appendix B.
[b] Age levels are given in Arabic numbers, grade levels in Roman numbers.
[c] The number before the dash indicates the Yearbook; TIP refers to Buros' Tests in Print; the number after the dash indicates the instrument entry.

Name of test	Publisher[a]	Age or grade level[b]	Time	Recent review in Buros' M.M.Y.[c]
Bell Adjustment Inventory, Revised Student Form	6	VIII–XVI	35	6-59
Bonney-Fessenden Sociograph	4	K–Adult	Indefinite	TIP-119
California Psychological Inventory	6	13 & over	45–60	6-71
California Test of Personality	4	K–Adult	40–50	6-73
Early School Personality Questionnaire (ESPQ)	10	6–8	60–100	None
Edwards Personal Preference Schedule	12	College–Adult	45	6-87
Gordon Personal Inventory	8	IX–XVI, Adult	15	6-102
Gordon Personal Profile	8	IX–XVI, Adult	15	6-103
Guilford-Zimmerman Temperament Study	14	IX–XVI, Adult	50	6-110
IPAT Children's Personality Questionnaire (CPQ)	10	8–12	100	None
IPAT High School Personality Questionnaire (HSPQ)	10	12–18	40–50	None

APPENDIX E (Continued)

Name of test	Publisher[a]	Age or grade level[b]	Time	Recent review in Buros' M.M.Y.[c]
Kuder Preference Record—Personal (Form A)	13	IX–Adult	30–40	6–132
Kuder Preference Record—Vocational (Form C)	13	IX–XII	30–40	6–1063b
Kuder Preference Record—Occupational (Form D)	13	IX–XII, Adult	30–40	6–1062
Kuder Preference Record—General Interest (Form E)	13	7–12	30–40	6–1061a
Kuder Preference Record—Occupational (Form DD)	13	XI–Adult	40	None
Minnesota Counseling Inventory	12	IX–XII	50	6–142
Minnesota Multiphasic Personality Inventory, Form R	12	16–Adult	Indefinite	6–143
Minnesota Vocational Interest Inventory	12	9–Adult	45	None
Mooney Problem Check Lists	12	VII–Adult	30	6–145

599

Name of test	Publisher[a]	Age or grade level[b]	Time	Recent review in Buros' M.M.Y.[c]
Occupational Interest Inventory (Lee-Thorpe)	4	VII–Adult	30–40	6–1064
Omnibus Personality Inventory	12	College	45–60	6–150
The Personality Inventory (Bernreuter)	6	IX–Adult	25	6–157
School Interest Inventory	9	VII–XII	20–30	None
Sixteen Personality Factor Questionnaire (16 PFQ)	10	17–Adult	45–60	None
Study of Values, Third Edition	9	X–Adult	20	6–182
Survey of Study Habits and Attitudes (Forms C and H)	12	7–14	20–35	TIP–1539
Thorndike Dimensions of Temperament	12	11–16, Adult	35–45	None
Thurstone Interest Schedule	12	IX–Adult	10	TIP–1889
Vineland Social Maturity Scale	1	Birth–Maturity	20–30	6–194
Vocational Interest Blank–Men (Strong)	12	17 & over	30–45	6–1070

APPENDIX E (Continued)

Name of test	Publisher[a]	Age or grade level[b]	Time	Recent review in Buros' M.M.Y.[c]
Vocational Interest Blank—Women (Strong)	12	17 & over	30–45	6–1071

[a] The number designating the publisher refers to Appendix B.
[b] Age levels are given in Arabic numbers, grade levels in Roman numbers.
[c] The number before the dash indicates the Yearbook; TIP refers to Buros' Tests in Print; the number after the dash indicates the instrument entry.

601

APPENDIX F: FREE AND INEXPENSIVE MATERIALS ON MEASUREMENT AND EVALUATION

I. Test Bulletins Published at Irregular Intervals

Normline, Harcourt, Brace & World, Inc.
Test Data Reports, Harcourt, Brace & World, Inc.
Test Service Bulletins, Harcourt, Brace & World, Inc.
Test Service Bulletins, The Psychological Corporation
Test Service Notebook, Harcourt, Brace & World, Inc.
Testing Today, Houghton Mifflin Company

II. Newsletters Concerning Measurement

The ACT Newsletter, American College Testing Program
Education Recaps, Educational Testing Service
ETS Developments, Educational Testing Service
Items, Cooperative Test Division, Educational Testing Service
Measurement in Education, National Council on Measurement in Education
NAEP Newsletter, National Assessment of Educational Progress
Test Collection Bulletin, Educational Testing Service

III. Educational and Psychological Journals

American Educational Research Journal
Education and Psychological Measurement
Journal of Educational Measurement
Journal of Educational Psychology
Measurement and Evaluation in Guidance
Psychological Abstracts: "Methodology and Research Technology: Testing" and "Educational Psychology: Testing"
Review of Educational Research

IV. Annual Reports and Proceedings

Annual Reports, College Entrance Examination Board
Annual Reports, Educational Testing Service

Proceedings, Annual Invitational Conference on Testing Problems, Educational Testing Service

Proceedings, Annual Western Regional Conference on Testing Problems, Educational Testing Service

V. Miscellaneous Paperback Books and Bulletins

Evaluation and Advisory Series, Educational Testing Service

ETS Builds A Test, 1965.

Locating Information on Educational Measurement: Sources and References, 1969.

Making the Classroom Test: A Guide for Teachers, Second Edition, 1961.

Multiple-Choice Questions: A Close Look, 1963.

Selecting an Achievement Test: Principles and Procedures, Second Edition, 1961.

Short-Cut Statistics for Teacher-Made Tests, Second Edition, 1964.

Guidance Monograph Series, Set III: *Testing,* Houghton Mifflin Company, 1968.

Modern Mental Measurement: A Historical Perspective

Basic Concepts in Testing

Types of Test Scores

School Testing Programs

Intelligence, Aptitude, and Achievement Testing

Interest and Personality Inventories

Tests on Trial

Automated Data Processing in Testing

Controversial Issues in Testing

Engelhart, M. D. *Improving Classroom Testing.* Washington: National Education Association, 1964.

French, J. W., and W. B. Michael. *Standards for Educational and Psychological Tests and Manuals.* Washington: American Psychological Association, 1966.

McLaughlin, K. F. *Interpretation of Test Results.* Washington: U.S. Government Printing Office, 1964.

Index of Names

Index of Subjects